THE OXFORD HANDBOOK OF

NEW AUDIOVISUAL AESTHETICS

THE OXFORD HANDBOOK OF

NEW AUDIOVISUAL AESTHETICS

Edited by
JOHN RICHARDSON
CLAUDIA GORBMAN
CAROL VERNALLIS

OXFORD
UNIVERSITY PRESS

OXFORD
UNIVERSITY PRESS

Oxford University Press is a department of the University of Oxford.
It furthers the University's objective of excellence in research, scholarship,
and education by publishing worldwide.

Oxford New York
Auckland Cape Town Dar es Salaam Hong Kong Karachi
Kuala Lumpur Madrid Melbourne Mexico City Nairobi
New Delhi Shanghai Taipei Toronto

With offices in
Argentina Austria Brazil Chile Czech Republic France Greece
Guatemala Hungary Italy Japan Poland Portugal Singapore
South Korea Switzerland Thailand Turkey Ukraine Vietnam

Oxford is a registered trade mark of Oxford University Press
in the UK and certain other countries.

Published in the United States of America by
Oxford University Press
198 Madison Avenue, New York, NY 10016

First issued as an Oxford University Press paperback, 2015.

Library of Congress Cataloging-in-Publication Data

The Oxford handbook of new audiovisual aesthetics / John Richardson,
Claudia Gorbman, and Carol Vernallis.
pages cm
Includes bibliographical references and index.
ISBN 978-0-19-973386-6 (hardcover : alk. paper); 978-0-19-024459-0 (paperback : alk. paper)
1. Mass media—Aesthetics. 2. Digital media—Technological innovations.
I. Richardson, John, 1964—editor of compilation. II. Gorbman, Claudia, editor of
compilation. III. Vernallis, Carol.
P93.4.O94 2013
302.23—dc23
2013000220

CONTENTS

PART IV EXPANDED SOUNDTRACKS

PART V EMERGING AUDIOVISUAL FORMS

MUSIC VIDEO AND BEYOND

VIDEO, FILM, AND INSTALLATION ART

GAMING

PART VI AUDIOVISUALITY IN PERFORMANCE AND DAILY LIFE

LIST OF CONTRIBUTORS

Philip Auslander, Georgia Institute of Technology

Rob Bridgett, Sound Designer and Mixer at Arkhivesound

Philip Brophy, Independent Artist and Writer

Michael Bull, University of Sussex

Carter Burwell, Independent Artist

Michael Chanan, Roehampton University

Michel Chion, University of Paris III

Karen Collins, University of Waterloo

Steven Connor, University of Cambridge

Nicholas Cook, University of Cambridge

Annette Davison, University of Edinburgh

Tia DeNora, University of Exeter

K.J. Donnelly, University of Southampton

Caryl Flinn, University of Michigan

Daniel Goldmark, Case Western Reserve University

Claudia Gorbman, University of Washington Tacoma

Janet K. Halfyard, Birmingham Conservatoire

Mariko Hara, University of Exeter

Stan Hawkins, University of Oslo

Paula Hearsum, University of Brighton

Ian Inglis, Northumbria University

Helmi Järviluoma, University of Eastern Finland

Anahid Kassabian, University of Liverpool

Mark Kerins, Southern Methodist University

Mathias Bonde Korsgaard, Aarhus University

Lawrence Kramer, Fordham University

Charles Kronengold, Stanford University

Meri Kytö, University of Eastern Finland

Joseph Lanza, Independent Writer

Lisa Perrott, University of Waikato

John Richardson, University of Turku

Holly Rogers, University of Liverpool

Jeff Smith, University of Wisconsin - Madison

Robynn J. Stilwell, Georgetown University

Randy Thom, Independent Artist

Maureen Turim, University of Florida

Susanna Välimäki, University of Turku

Carol Vernallis, Stanford University

Noora Vikman, University of Eastern Finland

Michael Walsh, University of Hartford

Ying Xiao, University of Florida

ABOUT THE COMPANION WEBSITE

www.oup.com/us/ohnaa

Oxford has created a password-protected Web site to accompany *The Oxford Handbook of New Audiovisual Aesthetics*, and the reader is encouraged to take full advantage of it.

Examples available online are referred to throughout the book and are signaled with the symbol ⊛. Additional online content includes video examples for Chapters 7, 17, and 34, and an extensive list of hyperlinks to online sources for chapter 28. Please visit the Web site to enhance your experience of these chapters.

You may access the site using the username Music5 and password Book1745.

PART I

CHAPTER 1

INTRODUCTION

JOHN RICHARDSON AND CLAUDIA GORBMAN*

THIS book calls for a reassessment of both the center and boundaries of the audiovisual. It responds to debates that have been flourishing for several decades by asking how the field has changed and in which directions it might expand. Research on audiovisuality is now a firmly established and theoretically advanced field of study whose composite nature means that it sits equally well in several scholarly disciplines. It is principally found in university programs teaching media, film, and music, but a quick glance at the profiles of our contributors shows that it is by no means restricted to these academic contexts. The field of audiovisual studies listens to and, increasingly, trains practitioners. This connection says something about the relevance of our work—that we have a feedback loop between media producers and those engaged in critical inquiry about these forms. We consider it unhelpful to erect fences between academic and practice-based forms of knowledge; in fact, not only is it arrogant to assume that practitioners are somehow unaware of principles, effects, and implications of what they do, but soundmen, composers, and many filmmakers (at least as far back as Eisler and Adorno's *Composing for the Films* [1947], not to mention Eisenstein in the 1920s and 1930s—and we need look no further for evidence than the contributions to this volume from Carter Burwell, Randy Thom, and Rob Bridgett) have proven an unusually articulate group, with much to tell scholars about the interactions between sounds and images.

How does the work in this collection differ from what has come before? It is difficult to generalize, especially because we aimed to be inclusive and represent a considerable range of approaches. Writing on film music, in particular, has undoubtedly dominated the landscape of audiovisual studies. Important lessons have been learned over the years about the nature of what Michel Chion has called the "audiovisual contract" by concentrating on cinema, which seemed at the time to be the most obvious

* We would like to thank our coeditor Carol Vernallis for her valuable input on this introduction. This handbook is part of a two-volume project in which the volumes are perceived as broadly complementary. The other handbook, edited by Carol Vernallis, Amy Herzog, and John Richardson, *The Oxford Handbook of Sound and Image in Digital Media*, focuses more on digital aesthetics and involves a greater number of scholars from media studies to illuminate the sound–image nexus.

example of audiovisual practices. Studies authored by several of our contributors set the tone for research on film music, including Claudia Gorbman's *Unheard Melodies*, Chion's *Audio-Vision*, Caryl Flinn's *Strains of Utopia* and Anahid Kassabian's *Hearing Film*, while others have advanced our understanding of the cinematic by attending to more particular theories or practices in monographs and edited collections.[1] Jeff Smith's *The Sounds of Commerce*, Annette Davison's *Hollywood Theory: Non-Hollywood Practice*, Kevin Donnelly's *Film Music: Critical Approaches*, Phil Powrie and Robynn Stilwell's *Changing Tunes*, James Buhler, Caryl Flinn, and David Neumeyer's *Music and Cinema*, and Daniel Goldmark, Lawrence Kramer, and Richard Leppert's *Beyond the Soundtrack* are a handful of the most influential publications.[2] Yet almost all our authors, oriented in film music studies or otherwise, responded to the editors' call to address boundary issues either by attending to non- or extracinematic forms—everything from television to Twitter and flash mobs—or by considering how the soundtracks of movies are changing with the times and simultaneously changing the times.

The layout of this book reflects these points of departure. We begin with a section whose purpose is to identify theoretical pressure points that respond to evolving priorities in the field. The section on narrative, genre, and meaning charts how genres and expressive means have changed across the board in response to the current atmosphere of media convergence, digital technologies, and global communication. The section on emerging audiovisual forms continues on a similar tack by addressing practices commonly regarded as new or that strive to renew or shake up expectations about the nature of audiovisual experience: music videos, video art, and gaming. In the section on cinema, contributors reflect on a turn toward a cinema of the senses, in which affective intensity and an emphasis on sound design over traditional underscoring figure prominently. The final section asks questions about the very boundaries of the audiovisual. Isn't daily life itself an audiovisual experience, or does the term *audiovisual*, at least in its current usage, imply reproduction, representation, technology? With media proliferating and dominating our lives at one end of the scale, and daily life recorded in greater detail on digital media at the other, the most urgent questions for audiovisual analysis

[1] Michel Chion, *Audio-Vision: Sound on Screen*, trans. Claudia Gorbman (New York: Columbia University Press, 1994); Caryl Flinn, *Strains of Utopia: Gender, Nostalgia, and Hollywood Film Music* (Princeton, N.J.: Princeton University Press, 1992); Claudia Gorbman, *Unheard Melodies: Narrative Film Music* (Bloomington: Indiana University Press, 1987); Anahid Kassabian, *Hearing Film: Tracking Identifications in Contemporary Hollywood Film Music* (London: Routledge, 2001). An important additional early source is Kathryn Kalinak, *Settling the Score: Music and the Classical Hollywood Film* (Madison: University of Wisconsin Press, 1992).

[2] James Buhler, Caryl Flinn, and David Neumeyer, eds., *Music and Cinema* (Hanover, N.H.: Wesleyan University Press, 2000); Annette Davison, *Hollywood Theory, Non-Hollywood Practice: Cinema Soundtracks in the 1980s and 1990s* (Aldershot, UK: Ashgate, 2004); Kevin Donnelly, ed., *Film Music: Critical Approaches* (New York: Continuum, 2001); Daniel Goldmark, Lawrence Kramer, and Richard Leppert, eds., *Beyond the Soundtrack: Representing Music in Cinema* (Berkeley: University of California Press, 2007); Phil Powrie and Robynn Stilwell, eds., *Changing Tunes: The Use of Pre-Existing Music in Film* (Aldershot, UK: Ashgate, 2006); Jeff Smith, *The Sounds of Commerce: Marketing Popular Film Music* (New York: Columbia University Press, 1998).

today would seem to be located at these limits: how the audiovisual interfaces with our daily lives. The inventor of soundscape studies, R. Murray Shafer, famously called for the "tuning of the world," intending to foster sensitivity toward the ways in which our auditory environment is encoded and nurtured.[3] If such an awareness is carried over to experiences of cinema and other audiovisual domains, even those that are generally not recognized as such, then a new set of questions arises, perhaps leading to answers that can enrich our understanding of both art and life—which are ultimately, as any self-respecting avant-gardist knows, one and the same thing.

Just how is the audiovisual landscape changing? So much centers on audiovisual media these days. Smart phones ensure that we are seldom out of reach of the digital matrix, even when we make concerted efforts to get away. In the workplace and at home, many of us spend as much time welded to computer screens as we do conversing with family and friends. Social media allow us instantly to connect with family, friends, and like-minded people as well as total strangers, no matter where we are physically. Multiple screens beam down on us at stadium concerts and political and sporting events, to magnify and mediatize what we witness with our own eyes and ears; meanwhile, we might capture what we perceive on wireless phones and relay it back to the Internet, where it becomes the subject of net-based exchanges. Films increasingly look and sound like games, and games like films. Music videos merge with new media such as computer tablet apps and in so doing become more interactive. Theatrical performances incorporate films, and gallery installations are taken to the street. A climate of rapid and far-reaching technological and social change informs new audiovisual culture, whose implications for modern life we are only beginning to grasp.

Yet amid all this change, cinema somehow retains a special aura and is central in many of our authors' accounts for this reason. Whether this appeal is as strong today as it was in the past is open to debate, and some of our authors, like Anahid Kassabian, pointedly challenge this assumption. Gaming, the Internet, and social media are certainly impinging on popular consciousness to an unprecedented degree, and their ubiquity in the lives of younger generations of consumers may portend the end of a cinema- and narrative-based aesthetic. However, a strong case for the continued salience of cinema, albeit in regurgitated forms, can nevertheless be made. The ideal for television (or smart television) viewing at home these days is cinematic: immense high-definition, flat-screen televisions linked up to surround sound hi-fi systems equipped with subwoofers and connected to cloud-based Web servers are increasingly becoming the norm for households in the West, almost regardless of income level or social class. Beyond cinematic "cut scenes" (montage scenes found in games that resemble film narrative more closely than they do gaming action), the aesthetic ideal of hyperrealism in gaming increasingly draws on cinematic models, as the chapters dealing with gaming by Rob Bridgett (Chapter 31), Karen Collins (Chapter 32), and Mark Kerins (Chapter 33), all powerfully affirm. To play a game increasingly resembles adopting the role of star actor in a film.

[3] R. Murray Schafer, *The Tuning of the World* (New York: Knopf, 1977).

Gaming and social media might well create expectations for interactivity that are unique, but it is film that holds the greatest promise for experiences that are sufficiently rich in detail and sensory impact to transport us to other worlds.[4] The waves of film theory that grew out of semiotics and psychoanalysis, with all their emphasis on suture and identificatory mechanisms, got that much right: we are inexorably drawn in by audiovisual media, in much the same way certain movie scenes show audio-viewers being physically dragged into television screens—Hooper's *Poltergeist* (1982), Cronenberg's *Videodrome* (1984), and Lynch's *Inland Empire* (2006) among them. We see this tension between the cinematic model and other ways of conceiving the audiovisual as a productive tension and have given it free rein in this volume.

To be glued to the box (even if it isn't even a box these days, but a flat screen) has special resonance in an age of cable broadband, twenty-four-hour news coverage, and smart phone video apps. Immersion and interactivity are ideals in several "new" media forms; the notion of immersion presupposes a cinematic sensibility, just as gaming is closely associated with interactivity (see Karen Collins's work in Chapter 32). Sound contributes in no small way to making our experiences of media feel more immersive, because hearing is frequently held to be the most immersive sense.[5] Sound projects itself from the borders of the screen three-dimensionally to make images feel more real—all the more so given the heavy emphasis on low-register sounds in recent soundtracks, which invite embodied responses.[6] Yet Steven Connor argues in his chapter "Sounding Out Film" (Chapter 6) that this is true even of visual perception when understood in the light of phenomenological theory. In his view, "visual perception is proleptic, because, as Merleau-Ponty and others have shown, it is closely bound up with the active throwing forward or reaching out of ourselves and our projects into the world." We always meet films, or any audiovisual event, halfway as we respond internally with embodied actions and built-in empathetic mechanisms to the sounds and images we encounter. Cinema considered from this perspective involves audiences in more profound ways than we have been accustomed to thinking. Regardless of the level of tangible (or directly tactile) interactivity, cinema confronts us with audiovisual situations that are familiar to us from life, entertainment, and the arts ("structures of feeling") in ways that unavoidably involve both physiological and emotional responses and therefore entail some level of participation.[7] Recent movies do this even more directly through their heightened

[4] The question of identification with gaming characters, what it is like to *be* the character, to some extent transcends the ongoing debates about ludic versus narratively entangled experiences of game play. Regardless of whether the player is embroiled in a coherent, sequentially structured story, she is able to identify with or even become the character, and this experience is intensified by the cinematic elements of game play.

[5] Frances Dyson, *Sounding New Media: Immersion and Embodiment in the Arts and Culture* (Berkeley: University of California Press, 2009), 124.

[6] For a spectatorship theory perspective on the spatially engulfing qualities of film sound, see Mary Ann Doane, "The Voice in Cinema: The Articulation of Body and Space," in *Film Sound: Theory and Practice*, ed. Elisabeth Weis and John Belton (New York: Columbia University Press, 1985), 162–176.

[7] For a neurophysiological perspective on the integrative relationship among perception, sensory, and emotional responses, see Antonia Damasio, *The Feeling of What Happens* (London: Vintage, 1999), 55.

emphasis on the sensory (see Michel Chion's work in Chapter 19 and Charles Kronengold's in Chapter 24).

We also see this new participatory and immersive sensibility in performances of experimental theater, which can leave audiences feeling as though they are actors in a surreal film.[8] Much of our experience of so-called virtual reality involves a kind of cinematic immersion, just as this sensibility is finding its way into installation art, multimedia theater, live action role-playing games (LARP) and environmental sound art. We are increasingly made to feel as though we are part of the work or performance (for more on this, see the chapters by Maureen Turim and Michael Walsh [Chapter 30], Holly Rogers [Chapter 29] and Lisa Perrott [Chapter 14]). Users of portable music players also experience such heightened immersion. Michael Bull's chapter (Chapter 36) explores the ways in which we project a cinematic understanding of reality onto our surroundings, and in so doing aestheticize the world and ourselves, when we use portable music players.

Cinema is not what it used to be. It is becoming increasingly "larger than life." On the one hand, filmmakers strive to involve audiences more viscerally, and on the other, the cinema is ever more connected with audio-viewers' daily lives, beyond the boundaries of the movie theater, through bonds with other consumption activities. Digital techniques make stories on screen feel "up close," while marketing synergy reinforces brands and creates stronger emotive ties to product lines from games and smart phone apps to T-shirts and movie character dolls. Everything seems geared toward creating more powerful and discursively connected experiences—and at the same time toward making more money. The new, expanded cinema is a place of booming, rumbling, soaring, and whooshing surround-sound technologies, 3D graphics that jump off the screen, and CGI renderings of ever more spectacular visual landscapes. In this volume, Michel Chion (Chapter 19) sees all these developments as evidence of a new sensory cinema. Along similar lines, chapters by Jeff Smith (Chapter 20), Carol Vernallis (Chapter 25), and Stan Hawkins (Chapter 26) explore how formal means like new filming techniques in feature films and music videos use shorter average shot duration and more dynamic use of cameras to complement these technological developments. The resulting intensification and sensory magnification of the audiovisual brings life and entertainment into ever more intimate interplay. While some bemoan the loss of narrative clarity that the new, more visceral approach to audiovisuality entails, others celebrate the new cinema's capacity to *move* audiences more effectively. We are living, it seems, in an age of Eisenstein's cinema of attractions, regardless of genre or media form.[9]

8 The Finnish director Kristian Smeds's music theater performance *12Karamazovs—Karamazov Workshop*, performed in Turku in 2011, conveys such a sensibility. Combining classical theater, cabaret, stand-up comedy, and live musical performance, perhaps the most accurate description of these events is something akin to life inside a David Lynch film. In the sister volume of this book, *The Oxford Handbook of Sound and Image in Digital Media*, Amy Herzog makes similar observations about Punchdrunk's *Sleep No More*, immersive performances that draw on audiovisual imagery from films by Stanley Kubrick and Alfred Hitchcock.

9 See Sergei Eisenstein's "The Montage of Attractions: An Essay," in *The Film Sense* (London: Faber and Faber, 1943), 166–168. See also Tom Gunning, "The Cinema of Attraction: Early Film, Its Spectator, and the Avant-Garde," in *Film and Theory: An Anthology*, ed. Robert Stam and Toby Miller (London: Blackwell, 2000), 229–235.

One consequence of the new sensuality, which media scholars have warned us about for several decades, is the peril of getting lost in sounds and images—assuming for a moment that this is something to be avoided. The popular media commonly report on children becoming addicted to continuously running online games, like *World of Warcraft*, and suffering neurological symptoms or even death as a result;[10] relationships being destroyed because of addiction to online porn; overreliance on social media at the expense of more meaningful interpersonal relationships; and young men going on shooting rampages after training themselves with first-person shooter games or pathologically identifying with fictional film characters. New media undoubtedly do introduce a new array of social problems, and the new immersive and interactive media seem to have provoked more influence-of-the-media debate than ever before. Media violence, it seems impossible now to deny, bears some sort of relation to violence in society, but what is needed is balanced debate and research to temper knee-jerk reactions, and for that matter, uncritical acceptance of hyperviolent media on the part of many film and media scholars.[11]

In a related vein, the familiar media skepticism of the Frankfurt School scholars and their descendants holds that the media give us by design the dreams we consume: to keep us chained to bad consumption habits and distract us from the higher goal of critical citizenship while upholding the economic-political status quo. There are many sides to this particular line of critical thinking, advocated most notably by Marxist theorists like Theodor Adorno and Raymond Williams, some of which resonate with current media life. We would do well to ask to what extent the participation that mediatized life offers us is *actual* (with an impact on our lives beyond solipsistic self-involvement) and subjectively rewarding. Do mediatized dreams shield us from the real conditions of labor and disconnect us from our fellow beings (other than in the shallowest possible terms)? Is "connecting people," to borrow a marketing slogan from Nokia, electronically

[10] Godfrey Reggio makes a similar case apropos of television in his short film *Evidence* (1995), which documents children's facial responses to television viewing. The documentary shows its subjects in a state of near hypnosis. This sort of media skepticism was a part of the critical paradigms brought to the field by researchers like Raymond Williams and Friedrich Kittler. Williams's classic study of media flow addresses how television viewers are drawn into following a relentless stream of unfolding images (Raymond Williams, *Television: Technology and Cultural Form* [London & New York: Routledge, 1974], 77–120); while Kittler's work advances the provocative view that our reliance on recording technologies, from the typewriter to the computer chip, deprives us of our capacity to remember. Friedrich Kittler, *Gramophone, Film, Typewriter* (Stanford, Calif.: Stanford University Press, 1999). The French Marxist situationalist scholar Guy Debord's *Society of the Spectacle* arguably represents the most comprehensive vision of the alienating effects of new media and has resonated with some of the more recent theory. Guy Debord, *Society of the Spectacle* (London: Rebel Press, 2004 [1967]).

[11] An important exception is Jeffrey Goldstein, ed., *Why We Watch: The Attractions of Violent Entertainment* (New York & London: Oxford University Press, 1998). The editor's introduction and final chapter offer a balanced overview of perspectives on the subject, including considerations of both the salutary and damaging effects of violent entertainment.

disconnecting us in more meaningful ways?[12] What we know about the entertainment industries does nothing to allay our fears. High-level production lies in the hands of a shrinking number of transnational conglomerates, and even those media that promise participatory pleasures are designed primarily to advance the financial interests of a small number of industry players. We see evidence of this involvement in the endless streams of lawsuits and counter-lawsuits over patents among Apple, Samsung, and other big players. Entertainment and media industries jockey over who controls what data, who reaps royalties from which chart-topping record or blockbuster film, and who holds patents for the latest techie gadgets. Apple's parting of ways with Google's mapping service in iOS6 illustrates better than anything what is at stake in such negotiations: the desire to map, and in so doing, to shape the world. Ever more tangibly, the dystopic visions of thinkers like Jorge Luis Borges, Marshall McLuhan, and Jean Baudrillard are taking on a special resonance.

The concept of participatory media nevertheless has positive meanings for many users. Bands and filmmakers get to exhibit their wares online without having to bow to the demands of the music and film industry gatekeepers, and some will make their breakthroughs by reaching large audiences in this way. Others will not care about extending their influence or seeking financial gain beyond more modest contexts. In some respects we live in an age of hobbyists, when creative play can be its own reward, and not all artists seek financial security by making it big in "the industry." In the digital age, anonymity is the preferred modus operandi for many,[13] or performatively constructed ("fictional") and hybrid identity. In such circumstances the word "amateur" might be losing some of the stigma it accrued in the modern era, when labor took precedence over leisure, and the etymology of the word (from the Latin *amator,* meaning lover) comes into sharper focus.[14] This changing attitude might even be reflected in the activities of recognized performers, who increasingly release their own music online—sometimes for free—or look to live concerts, more than royalties earned from recordings, as their principal source of revenue. At the other end of the spectrum, software (like Apple's Logic Audio and Final Cut) for advanced audio and visual production and high-performance computer processors is becoming affordable to greater numbers than ever before. This new access has largely been responsible for the rise of digital aesthetics and might well justify all the talk of democratization. Feedback works more effortlessly in the digital age than in the past and can be instantaneous. Our modes of interaction with media are, moreover, more active and flexible, catering to different

[12] See, for example, Charlie Gere, *Community without Community in Digital Culture* (Basingstoke, UK, and New York: Palgrave MacMillan, 2012). Manuel Castells raises some similar concerns in his classic study of the information age, *The Rise of the Network Society: The Information Age: Economy, Society and Culture*, vol. 1 (Oxford: Blackwell, 1996).

[13] On the ideological implications of anonymity in dance cultures, see Jason Toynbee, *Making Popular Music: Musicians, Creativity and Institutions* (London: Arnold, 2000).

[14] Roland Barthes was a champion of the skilled amateur throughout his career. In particular, he appreciated the amateur's "antiheroic" attitude, which allows for an engagement with the material level of *practices* that has little to do with mastery or competition. See Roland Barthes, *Roland Barthes* (London and Basingstoke: Macmillan, 1977), 52.

demands and minority or alternative taste cultures. Artistic forms have emerged that are characterized by an anarchic and DIY attitude; a culture of remix and interactivity has in many contexts replaced Romantic ideas about creativity and genius. This is reflected in film aesthetics too: *vérité*-like approaches are encroaching on the more traditional, polished cinematography and sound design, resulting in films that look and sound as though they might have been produced by their audiences, possibly uploaded to the net, and which therefore foster closer identifications among audiences (see, e.g., Ying Xiao's writing on Chinese rock 'n' roll films in Chapter 16).[15]

The democratizing impact of digital networking technologies has been widely celebrated. Mobile phones precipitated the "Arab Spring"; Skype and other video chat platforms allow us to communicate globally in sound and vision. We can follow stars' and politicians' thoughts from moment to moment on Twitter (an ostensibly positive development, even though the impression of intimacy these communications promise can be deceptive). Scholars of new media have generally been more trusting of the salutary effects of digital technologies than the public; with a few exceptions, techno-optimism appears to be the prevalent discourse when it comes to the digital. Scholars have good reasons for this. It's all too easy to blame the technologies themselves (in a species of technological determinism) or to target a degenerate generation Z and its flaky libertarian guardians for the collapse of moral fiber in modern society. It requires more effort to investigate public policy and politics or to critically examine the role of transnational corporations in disseminating values that leave our youth feeling disempowered and alienated. The catch-22 is that the same technologies that offer the greatest potential for emancipation are those that are most closely controlled by corporate interests, which do not hesitate to assert themselves if something subversive seems to be happening. We see this in the co-optation of YouTube and the removal of materials Google regards as infringing copyright—including some of the most challenging forms of remix and mashup culture. Similarly, what happens to the data we post on Facebook, Spotify, YouTube, and even private messages sent via Gmail is a cause for concern; advertisers and other industry players access these communications in order to profile users and target marketing. Privacy, it would seem, is a thing of the past as surveillance culture infiltrates the technologies we increasingly depend on in our daily lives.[16]

If the new digital media are more participatory, as several of our contributors claim (see, e.g., chapters by Mathias Bonde Korsgaard [Chapter 28], Paula Hearsum and Ian Inglis [Chapter 27], and Caryl Flinn [Chapter 15] on YouTube), this comes at the cost of considerable constraints imposed from above. Moreover, participation does not guarantee *access*, although it can offer the illusion of access to things (and people) we

[15] For different perspectives on the culture of sampling, remix, and mashup, see, for example, Mark Katz, *Capturing Sound: How Technology Has Changed Music* (Berkeley: University of California Press, 2004); Paul D. Miller, aka DJ Spooky, *Sound Unbound: Sampling Digital Music and Culture* (Cambridge, Mass.: MIT Press, 2008); and Simon Reynolds, *Retromania: Pop Culture's Addiction to Its Own Past* (London: Faber & Faber, 2011).

[16] See David Lyon, *Surveillance Studies: An Overview* (Cambridge, UK: Polity, 2007).

desire—stars, for example. Audiovisual media give an impression of heightened "presence" and loss of distance; yet paradoxically, in many of our quotidian interactions, we spend much of our day communicating with others who are removed from us in both place and time. Walter Benjamin was among the first to address this sense of presence, and the loss of "aura," in the age of mechanical reproduction; others have updated his arguments with reference to digital material culture.[17] Audiovisual media certainly have their own material reality, but they shield other realities and create barriers between the worlds they channel and the world at large. Manuel Castells's "spaces of flows" of the digital communication era have replaced traditional "spaces of places," creating a vibrant, accelerated, globally connected, and more interactive basis for interpersonal communications, which, however, keeps players at a physical distance from one another.[18]

Discussions of new media forms commonly invoke the idea of virtual reality. Sometimes a contentious metaphysics accompanies the term, however, when people assume that technologically mediated realities are somehow less ontologically "real" than pretechnological ones. The realities encountered in new media might not always be as rich or subjectively rewarding as those that came before, but they are every bit as real even if they represent a *different* ontology. Thus theorists like Katherine Hayles, Lev Manovich, and Castells prefer terms like "real virtuality," "fake reality," and "embodied virtuality" over the traditional virtual reality.[19] All share the idea that there is certainly substance to our experiences of new media, but the pleasures or displeasures they offer us come packaged with the recognition that interpersonal distance and technological mediation are difficult to escape. Of course it is possible to use these very means to highlight the mediatized nature of our existence, and in so doing, to ask critical questions about the current media landscape. Gabriella Giannachi observes: "The virtual has become the main theatre of the real—the place from where the real can be viewed, a space for critique, art and politics."[20] She claims, provocatively, that those media forms that "expand, augment or enlarge" what we ordinarily regard as "the real," rather than those that replace it entirely with an alternate reality, hold the greatest potential for conveying exhilarating and challenging content. Thus, "virtual forms" from VR itself to oneiric films have the potential to reflect critically on society. But such forms can also be understood purely as affectively stimulating environments with their own internal rules and contingencies, independent of everyday reality: in a very real sense "game play." A third (troubling) alternative is that these parallel digital realities can become confused

[17] See Walter Benjamin, "The Work of Art in the Age of Mechanical Reproduction," in *Illuminations: Essays and Reflections*, ed. Hannah Arendt and trans. Harry Zohn (New York: Schocken, 1968), 217–251; see also Dyson, *Sounding New Media*.

[18] See Castells, *Rise of the Network Society*.

[19] Castells's term is "real virtuality" (403). "Fake realities" belongs to Lev Manovich, *The Language of New Media* (Cambridge, Mass.: MIT Press, 2001), 3; "Embodied virtuality" was coined by N. Katherine Hayles, *How We Became Posthuman: Virtual Bodies in Cybernetics, Literature, and Informatics* (Chicago: University of Chicago Press, 1999), 15.

[20] Gabriella Giannachi, *Virtual Theatres: An Introduction* (London and New York: Routledge, 2004), 124.

with ordinarily life: they offer modes of interaction that have no place in our daily lives and can create false expectations through the feelings of omnipotence and invulnerability they foster in some people. Digital media have conditioned us to desire sensations that are ever more vivid; or have they simply responded to preexisting desires, which stem from the very alienated nature of current mediatized society? Either way, when even these increasingly vivid experiences fail to live up to expectations, when they tantalize but do not deliver, we are wont to transpose them into an arena beyond fantasy, in which actions really count. It seems like the logical next step: Artaud's theater of cruelty transposed onto a larger stage. This is one of the sicknesses of our age and at the same time, one of its greatest opportunities.

An Audiovisual Olympics for the Digital Age

These issues come into sharper focus with the help of an example. As we write this introduction, we are bombarded with media images from the London 2012 Olympic games. From the standpoint of the audiovisual, it is noteworthy that a movie director was picked to design the opening ceremony rather than a media or theater impresario. And not just any movie director: Danny Boyle is best known for his contribution to independent cinema in *Shallow Grave* (1994) and *Trainspotting* (1996), films known for their provocative, sometimes surreal, gritty, and visceral style. Only after directing *Slumdog Millionaire* (2008) did Boyle become a household name, however, and it is most likely *Slumdog*'s success, its élan and British multiculturalism, that put him in the running for the Olympics job. Boyle had worked in the theater before moving to cinema, and several of his films include settings that could be understood as broadly theatrical. The value of choosing a film director for the task was immediately apparent in the montage sequence that preceded the opening ceremony, a digitally rendered and accelerated airborne journey from the source of the Thames in the Cotswolds to the Olympic venue near the river's mouth in the East End of London. The journey incorporated numerous surrealistic diversions across popular culture and history, much of the action taking place within a digitally altered time frame and with throbbing electronic dance music mixed up with progressive rock (Pink Floyd's "Time"), punk (the Sex Pistols' "God Save the Queen"; the Clash's "London Calling"), and fragments of television music (Andrew Lloyd Weber's *South Bank Show* theme when the roving camera passes the South Bank area; the *Eastenders* title music and accompanying aerial shot of London's East End) to engender a sense of excitement and youthful energy (for more on the working of television themes, see Annette Davison's work in Chapter 8).[21]

[21] See also Philip Tagg and Bob Clarida, *Ten Little Title Tunes: Toward a Musicology of Mass Media* (New York, Montreal: The Mass Media Musicologists' Press, 2003).

Audiences might recognize such techniques from the montage sequences in *Slumdog Millionaire*. A short film extra accompanying the DVD on the Olympic ceremonies, called "Isles of Wonder Deconstruction," shows the extent to which CGI technologies were employed in the opening sequence. Far from being a natural representation of London, it was largely fictional and shaped according to the pace, moods, and narrative agendas of the accompanying music.[22] Two additional music video–style montages interrupted the ceremony, preceding the arrival of the Queen and the Olympic flame, taking a more youth- and popular-culture-oriented approach than the usual pomp and circumstance of such events.

As Julie Brown writes, opening ceremonies become a means for a nation to dream about itself by reflecting on its past, but also by offering a vision for the present and the future.[23] The London ceremony was an emphatic case in point, and it challenged traditional representations by offering a fresh interpretation of nationhood and history. Boyle's design for theatrical parts of the ceremony featured a constantly evolving set that depicted a Google Maps–style representation of London and its agrarian surroundings, embedded in a stadium within the city itself—a *mise-en-abyme* on a grand scale.[24] This was a suitably miniaturized version of "the green and pleasant land" of previous generations, and a reworking of poet William Blake and composer Hubert Parry's rousing hymn "Jerusalem," with all of its lightly veiled colonialist sentiments about relocating Jerusalem on English soil.[25] Blake's hymn took on a distinctly Olympian flavor because of its phrase "chariots of fire," recalling that Olympic movie. Electronic composer Vangelis's airy theme music for *Chariots of Fire* (dir. Hugh Hudson, 1981) sets an epic tone, in a movie that depicts how the educated classes of a nation that believed in its divine right to rule over others sought to dominate in sports as well. In the ceremony this music was given a welcome ironic twist, when "Mr. Bean," actor Rowan Atkinson, joined

22 *London 2012 Olympic Games: The Opening Ceremony and Sporting Highlights*, DVD package (BBC Worldwide Ltd., 2012). BBCDVD3745.

23 Julie Brown, "Australian Dreaming" (unpublished manuscript on the opening ceremony of Sydney 2000 Olympic Games). The Australian Olympic Games were widely compared with the British opening ceremony, not least because of the emphasis in both on popular culture and multiculturalism. They are further linked through an element of Anglophilia in the Australian ceremony, including the use of the hymn "Jerusalem" and Elgar-esque classical music. Danny Boyle specifically used the small and personal scale of the Australian games as a model rather than the larger and more impersonal scale of the Beijing Olympics.

24 The Google Maps style was even more in evidence in the closing ceremony, where the Olympic stadium's running track became a scaled-down representation of the M25 ring-road populated by articulated trucks and taxis, and the center space featured model village renditions of London landmarks that doubled as performance spaces.

25 The aspiration of the authors of "Jerusalem" was undoubtedly to give voice to a form of universal humanism and ecumenicism. However, the religious content of the lyrics leave little doubt that this vision prioritizes Christianity and British colonial interests as the fulcrum for a new moral code. This genealogy is complicated, however, by the prominent role the song has played in the English labor and women's suffrage movements. Danny Boyle appears to have been thinking of the latter discursive context when he commented in the Opening Ceremony Program that the "idea of Jerusalem" was to express "the world of real freedom and true equality," a "Jerusalem for everybody."

an orchestra conducted by Simon Rattle to playfully deconstruct the film's nationalism. The irony created in the opening ceremony was missing when the same music was heard before victory ceremonies for each Olympic event.

These lines are not the only parts of "Jerusalem" that Boyle dramatized. His background as an independent filmmaker surfaced in his critical treatment of the phrase "dark satanic mills," which in Blake's poem describes how the Industrial Revolution sullied the emotive and ecological landscapes of its era. The Olympic ceremony went on to depict the positive legacy of the trade union movement in improving working conditions. The Dickensian, grim rise of industry in Britain was depicted in the ceremony in the elevation of full-scale chimney stacks, synchronized to pounding music and the mechanically choreographed actions of actors. The Industrial Revolution sequence ended with the forging of five Olympic rings, in a moment of Wagnerian grandeur. The percussionist Evelyn Glennie, together with the fittingly named Pandemonium Drummers—throngs of them filling the stadium walkways wielding plastic buckets—and the electronic duo Underworld (including the musical director of the ceremony, Rick Smith, who had worked with Boyle on *Trainspotting*), provided the music for this section.[26] Almost entirely deaf, Dame Glennie feels and sees the rhythms of her music more than she hears sounds, and the stadium and television audiences were encouraged to do the same. The Bolero-like buildup of the track "And I Will Kiss," its cumulative musical structures incorporating "bell ringing" figures reminiscent of Arvo Pärt's "tintinnabuli" style, electronic sounds, plaintive whistling, and energetic chanting, provided narrative continuity and sonic power to supercharge the spectacle that unfolded in the stadium. Above all, the spectacular vista and baby-booming sounds were cinematic.

A cinematic sensibility permeated the conception of the opening ceremony in a more indirect manner. The main inspiration for the opening section came from a book written by the documentary filmmaker, social scientist, and author Humphrey Jennings. *Pandaemonium 1660–1886: The Coming of the Machine as Seen by Contemporary Observers* is a collage of texts strung together to form a loose narrative about the impact of technology on those who lived through the Industrial Revolution.[27] Jennings was one of the founders of the mass-observation movement of social research in the 1930s, which sought to document the everyday experiences of people around Britain, using diaries, questionnaires, and ethnographic methods including films, and he was a close associate of the international surrealist movement. The style of *Pandaemonium* is in keeping with the tenets of 1930s mass-observation and with the collagelike approach to writing

[26] Rick Smith describes in an interview how his mandate from Danny Boyle was "to frighten people" in the Pandemonium section. Robin Turner, "Underworld's Brief to 'Frighten People' at the London 2012 Opening Ceremony," *The Guardian*, August 2, 2012, at http://www.guardian.co.uk/music/2012/aug/02/underworld-london-2012-opening-ceremony (accessed November 3, 2012).

[27] The influence of Humphreys can be attributed to Boyle's collaborator on the opening ceremony, the writer Frank Cottrell Boyce. See Frank Cottrell Boyce, foreword to *Pandaemonium 1660–1886: The Coming of the Machine as Seen by Contemporary Observers*, by Humphrey Jennings (London: Icon, 2012), vii–xii. Thanks to Kari Kallioniemi for drawing our attention to this connection.

and the documentation of everyday life that was undertaken by surrealist writers like Breton and Aragon.[28] Jennings adapted his filmmaking approach to written texts when working on the book, which he thought of as a series of loosely interrelated "images" intended to be musical and, above all, cinematic in tone.[29] Danny Boyle aimed for a similar musical-cinematic character as he designed the ceremony. From Jennings he borrowed the idea of surrealist collage, a panoramic perspective encompassing both the sense of wonder at technological changes and the social problems they brought in their wake, as well as an interest in charting the mood and changing identity of the nation.

Following the Pandaemonium section of the ceremony, Boyle celebrated the British National Health Service. With hundreds of real nurses and doctors, and children dancing on real hospital beds, the spectacle sent a potent critical message in the form of a tribute to public health care in an age of increasing privatization and outsourcing of public services. The role of these public servants was mythologized in the euphoric and grandiose tones of Mike Oldfield's progressive rock classic "Tubular Bells"—continuing the theme of bells that began with the chiming of a specially forged giant bell at the beginning of the ceremony. Oldfield and his band offered lighter fare when performing a folky jig ("In Dulci Jubilo") on the flute and solo electric guitar while the hospital kids bounced up and down in their beds. The atmosphere of these scenes felt like a Busby Berkeley musical: the illuminated beds were pushed into different graphic and textual configurations, one of these being the distinctly English Britishism GOSH—also an acronym for the Great Ormand Street (children's) Hospital. During these segments the musical soundtrack shifted to raucous swing jazz, a genre-appropriate choice that set a comical tone.

Ultimately, through music and dramatic action, Boyle depicted a nation in the ceremony that comes closer to Paul Gilroy's "convivial culture" than a nation suffering from collective "postcolonial melancholy," driven by the cultural plurality of its urban centers more than by the desire to retain a position of global dominance. The opening ceremony showed "cool Britannia" over "rule Britannia." This projection of the UK found confirmation in other aspects of the games, such as the naming of the British team "Team GB" and Stella McCartney's design of the UK athlete's kit: a Union Jack fragmented into abstract geometric patterns and rendered only in cool blue tones rather than the more traditional tricolors.[30] Boyle's representation of Britain as ethnically diverse and unapologetically *post*colonial seems especially fitting for the Olympics, whose British athletes (as well those of many other nations) come from all sectors and ethnic groupings of British society. In the opening ceremony this multiculturalism appeared most directly through the inclusion of the ship (the *Empire Windrush*) that brought hundreds

[28] On the relationship between surrealism and mass-observation, see Ben Highmore, "Mass-Observation," in *Everyday Life and Cultural Theory. An Introduction* (London: Routledge, 2002), 75–112.

[29] In fact, one strategy offered to readers for how to approach the book is "as a continuous narrative or *film* on the Industrial Revolution." See introduction to Jennings, *Pandaemonium*, xxviii.

[30] See Maysa Rawi, "Oh no, they've turned the Union flag blue! Team GB models new Olympics 2012 kit designed by Stella McCartney for Adidas," *Mail Online*, May 26, 2013, at http://www.dailymail.co.uk/femail/article-2118709/London-2012-Team-GB-models-Olympics-kit-designed-Stella-McCartney-Adidas.html (accessed September 27, 2012).

of Caribbean migrants to Britain in 1948 and by the choices of music, ranging from urban artists like Dizzee Rascal and Tinie Tempah to more established vintage stars like Elton John and Paul McCartney. Sound figured prominently in the design of Boyle's spectacle, taking a cue from a line from Shakespeare's *Tempest* spoken by Kenneth Branagh: "Be not afeard; the isle is full of noises." A cinematic sensibility permeated the ceremony, including a short section on the big screen that included excerpts from classic British cinema and a sequence on the big screen that showed 007 hero Daniel Craig meeting up with the Queen to fly a helicopter to the games. More fundamentally, though, the cinematic approach was conveyed in Boyle's directorial style, which came through both in the director's choice of music and in his characteristically visceral cinematography: montage sequences, handheld cameras, booming sounds, and images cut to the music.

Not all of these cinematic elements translated well to the stadium setting. Some of the close-ups of actors came across as comically misplaced in a setting that lends itself more to collective spectacle than emotional realism. Indeed, some seasoned collaborators working on the project had resisted the meticulous attention to detail that Boyle pressed for and eventually implemented, which they considered inappropriate.[31] A further area of questionable planning was the popular music of the final section (the house projection sequence), which was used for its iconic status more than its musical or audiovisual impact. The mixing together of tracks from fragments wasn't as skillfully executed as one might have expected given the talent at Boyle's disposal; the main purpose of the songs seems to have been to comment on the quantity rather than the quality of classic British popular music and to elicit nods of recognition from the audience rather than sustain an infectious musical beat. In short, Boyle didn't always take a sufficiently "musical" approach to his audiovisual uses of popular songs.

A noteworthy feature of these Olympic games is the extent to which they were conditioned by uses of social media. The final section of the opening ceremony itself was constructed as a commentary on the impact of the Internet, particularly social media. At its culmination, the British inventor of the Internet, Tim Berners-Lee, tweeted to the audience the text, "This is for everyone," optimistically implying that it is beyond the control of oppressive governments and corporate interests. Apart from this, the popular music collage section of the ceremony was built around a condensed narrative performed by two actors, whose romance unfolded through messages sent via social media. The inclusion of social media in the opening ceremony would prove to be prophetic, because in these games audiences would have more direct access to athletes than ever before, through Twitter. But it was access accompanied by unpleasant consequences for some. Two athletes were expelled because they expressed extremist views on Twitter, which naturally went global the moment they pressed send. How easily we relinquish privacy these days or dupe ourselves into believing that extreme views of peer groups online will find global acceptance.

The audiovisual and cinematic orientation of the opening ceremony carried over to the sporting events themselves. In an effort to involve audiences more directly, the organizing

[31] Danny Boyle, commentary for *London 2012 Olympic Games, The Opening Ceremony and Sporting Highlights*. DVD package. BBC Worldwide Ltd., 2012. BBCDVD3745.

committee carefully selected music to liven up the crowds at the events. Long events can lack sparkle, so music figured prominently at events like long-distance running, synchronizing the actions of the runners with electronic dance music. Music can stimulate joggers and participants in aerobics classes, but for professional athletes the addition of music might be off-putting. It temporalizes actions and conditions mood, which is the very reason the organizers used it in the first place to "warm up" audiences. But what if this imposed soundtrack interferes with an athlete's internal sense of time, race strategy, or cultural affiliation? The organizers seemed unfazed by criticism, choosing to emphasize the music's entertainment value over sporting achievements, but the matter did spark controversy in the British broadsheet press.[32] In a similar vein, the parade of athletes into the stadium was accelerated to a tempo of 120bpm, faster than in any previous ceremony. This was a decision made by drum'n'bass producer High Contrast (Lincoln Barrett) in collaboration with Boyle, whose aesthetic priority was to convey a mood of youthful speed and energy, even if this meant compelling the athletes to walk at a very brisk pace.[33] There prevailed an ethos of keeping the paying customer satisfied, a model taken from the business world rather than the world of sports (or the arts, for that matter). Controversy over uses of music at Olympic events provides some evidence of growing public feeling that limits should be set on the reach of the cinematic audiovisual so that it doesn't infringe on personal space. Questions of individual liberty about how sounds and visual perception are combined resonate with Michel Chion's notion of the *audio-divisual* and with objections raised to the audiovisual in chapters of this volume by Philip Auslander (Chapter 34), Mariko Hara and Tia DeNora (Chapter 38), Nicholas Cook (Chapter 3), Lawrence Kramer (Chapter 2), and others. An attitude of guardedness concerning the audiovisual is implicit also in the writing of our soundscape and sound studies scholars, such as Helmi Järviluoma and Noora Vikman (Chapter 37), Meri Kytö (Chapter 23), and Michael Bull (Chapter 36). These instances seem to beg the question: Are some activities tarnished by the superimposition of interactive and mood-shaping strategies borrowed from audiovisual culture? Audiovisuality is the dominant modality, or in Cook's terminology mentality, of our time, and it has brought many welcome changes, but these shouldn't be taken for granted as somehow inevitable or even fundamentally "new." Interactive or intensified audiovisual media shouldn't automatically be taken as progressive, salutary, or attuned with the zeitgeist.

Does everything in our current era need to be supercharged with audiovisual steroids? At stake is not necessarily a defense of the aesthetic autonomy of musical sounds or old-fashioned ideas about the boundaries between art and entertainment. Rather, several of our authors stress the right of listeners, users, and audiences to supply something that is missing from the audiovisual event. Simply put there seems to be a desire for a move toward an aesthetic in which less is more. Game theory makes a compelling

32 See Paul Kelso, "Stadium DJs are drowning out the golden moments of London 2012," The Telegraph, August 4, 2012, at http://blogs.telegraph.co.uk/sport/paulkelso/100025637/stadium-djs-are-drowning-out-the-golden-moments-of-london-2012/ (accessed May 26); Owen Gibson, "London 2012: loud music makes the Games even better, insist organisers," *The Observer*, August 5, 2012, at http://www.guardian.co.uk/sport/2012/aug/05/london-2012-olympics-loud-music (accessed May 26).

33 Interview with Lincoln Barrett by Dorian Lynskey, "Oblivion with Bells," *Q Magazine*, January 2013, 82–88, 86.

case that users supply the missing "content," although the "ludic" argument about the autonomy of game play undervalues the role played by style, character identification, and intertextual references in providing relatively stable inscribed content. Still, the player supplies something that is not present in the game. YouTube at least offers the potential to subtract from as well as to add to the content that is currently in circulation as well to reconfigure it into new compound forms. This propensity inherent in new media (but certainly present in early forms as well) toward masking, silencing, and interrupting is at least as important as the more celebrated additive and recombinatory tendencies that have received more coverage in critical discussions. So while it is possible to recognize a nostalgic tendency in the hankering for a world less full to the brim of audiovisual stimuli and a mode of technophobia in resistance to new mediated forms, resistance to the audiovisual can be justified in other ways as well.

In film criticism, likewise, we can note a turn toward slow and contemplative forms that are characterized more by their use of ambient sounds than a constant auditory hustle and bustle.[34] The slow movement has often been associated with other forms of slowness such as slow cooking and the "downsizing" trend in personal lifestyle. In film, this taste for paring-down stems from a fatigue with the narrative construction and pacing associated with continuity editing that has "intensified" since the early years of sound cinema (see especially Jeff Smith's chapter [Chapter 20], which elaborates on David Bordwell's concept of intensified continuity). A productive way of looking at this might be in terms of an ecological sensibility connected to an appreciation of silence, which helps us to situate performances or audiovisual events within the immediate listening environment.[35] If artists/producers are determined to make every single activity as immersive and volatile as possible, this quiet sensibility can get drowned. John Richardson has argued that so-called acoustic music allows for the emergence of what (in response to Laura Mulvey's pensive spectator) he has called the pensive listener.[36] Such a mode of listening does not deny that digital technologies might have changed subjectivity for the good, or that audiovisuality is bonded irrevocably to modern-day sensibilities, but it does address the role that silence plays in leaving gaps that serve as entry points for personal agency. Lawrence Kramer makes a similar argument (Chapter 2) in this volume in reference to orchestral classical music. We might be able to tweet along to program symphonies, but that doesn't necessarily mean that we should do this all the time, or that tweeting will enhance our experience.

[34] See, for example, Matthew Flannigan, "16:9 in English: Towards an Aesthetic of Slow in Contemporary Cinema (November 2008)," at http://www.16-9.dk/2008-11/side11_inenglish.htm (accessed October 14, 2012).

[35] On the ecological qualities of silence, see Roland Barthes, *The Neutral* (New York: Columbia University Press, 2005), 21–23. On silence in cinema and its connection to the digital, see Michel Chion, "The Silence of the Loudspeakers," in *Film, a Sound Art*, trans. Claudia Gorbman (New York: Columbia University Press, 2009).

[36] See John Richardson, *An Eye for Music: Popular Music and the Audiovisual Surreal* (New York, Oxford: Oxford University Press, 2011), 280–287; Laura Mulvey, *Death 24x a Second: Stillness and the Moving Image* (London: Reaktion Books, 2006), 81–96.

Representing the World

If Little Britain was transformed by Danny Boyle into a life-sized and convivial—but nevertheless miniaturized—model village, the emerging global superpower that is China takes its example from Vegas and Disneyland in constructing theme parks that include scaled-down imitations of landmarks from cities around the world, catering to a population that will most likely never see the originals. The conceit of miniaturizing the achievements of other cultures in virtual cities is exposed in the Chinese filmmaker Jia Zhangke's *The World* (2004). In his low-key and contemplative directorial style, he conveys how "global villages" become a backdrop for ordinary lives and dreams of mobility that the state denies to its individual citizens. Both Boyle and Jia in their own ways use official narratives (the Olympic ceremony, the real "World" theme park outside Beijing) as vehicles for telling new ones. Jia juxtaposes the glossy mediatized sounds of stage performances in the park with the sounds of the young alienated employees' everyday lives, including the sounds of the characters' mobile phones, which become symptomatic of modernity in general and their local circumstances in particular. And the most salutary music making, the moment in the film when characters appear to communicate authentically despite vast cultural differences, comes when two women characters simply sing a song together, unmediated. But again, we would be oversimplifying to conclude that Jia—a highly sophisticated filmmaker and poet of the heartbreaking contradictions of China's modernization—is thereby some sort of romantic.

In addition to their attempts to represent contemporary experience, our two examples are related in their respective takes on modern-day heroism. Heroism in Jia's narrative arises more from the characters' human qualities in the face of alienating forces much larger than themselves than from the traditional Romantic view, with its exaggerated individualism and transcendence. The same might be said of the Olympic ceremony. Consider especially the moment when the British team entered the stadium to the accompaniment of David Bowie's art pop classic "Heroes": the lyrics refer to how heroism is temporary and available to even the most downtrodden in the context of post–Cold War divided Europe. Janet K. Halfyard tracks a similar trajectory from traditional notions of heroism to heroism on a more human scale. In her chapter on audiovisual representations of the heroic in superhero movies (Chapter 10), she shows how traditional means have ceded to more subdued strategies whereby the human fallibility of characters is foregrounded and music is used more to construct complex identities than to celebrate heroic acts.

At the heart of Jia's *The World* and the Olympic opening ceremony are relationships between global and local, and between mediatized and pretechnological realities, which also undergo analysis in several of the chapters in this volume. Our two examples above testify to how prevalent the cinematic audiovisual is in contemporary consciousness. To deepen our understanding of these forms we need to draw on ideas from all sides of existing debates, vacillating between discourses of techno-optimism and pessimism, media skepticism and media advocacy, democratization and corporate control, theories that position us as passive consumers and active discerning agents, those that attend to historical consciousness and those that imply openness to the unfolding now. A new audiovisual aesthetic expresses our most heartfelt dreams and most frightening nightmares. It operates in an affective register in which both extremes are possible. It can reinforce hegemonic forces and destabilize them; provide a lens onto the conditions of modern life, or simply allow us to live it.

Mapping the Terrain of New Audiovisual Aesthetics

If these are the conditions of contemporary mediatized life, what means should we employ to approach the apparently bewildering array of phenomena they include? More important, what questions should we ask of audiovisual phenomena in an age of proliferating and converging media? Is it desirable even to lump such a hodgepodge of styles and media formats together in the hope that approaches taken when studying one style or media will be applicable to others? As editors, we consider that something is to be gained by striving for a general view of the audiovisual. The research to date in our field has highlighted the benefits of such a catholic approach. Our notion of the audiovisual derives from Michel Chion's "audio-vision": the sensory and semiotic result of sound placed with vision, an encounter greater than their sum.[37] Our approach is new in the manner stated in the opening lines of this introduction: we believe in the explanatory value of boundary phenomena.

What follows is a list of questions and areas of interest germane to almost any consideration of the audiovisual. Rather than a systematic or internally consistent theorization, these points should be thought of in more heuristic terms as delineating some of the main, often overlapping, areas of current inquiry within a constantly changing field.

1) *Audiovisual interrelations.* How do sound and vision interrelate in performances or situations that include both? What is the hierarchy of these elements in terms of "power," or do the elements retain relative autonomy? How does what happens in one channel transform perceptions of the other—in other words, how do they supply what Chion calls "added value"? Nicholas Cook has categorized audiovisual relations in terms of a continuum among conformance, complementation, and contestation.[38] More traditional divisions consider "harmony" and "counterpoint," empathy and anempathy. In this volume, Carol Vernallis (Chapter 25) provocatively proposes that the conversation between

[37] Our spelling of the term audiovisual without a hyphen reflects our recognition of the cross-modal and unavoidably mixed nature of experience.

[38] Nicholas Cook, *Analysing Musical Multimedia* (Oxford: Clarendon Press, 1998), 99.

sound and image resembles a couple's therapy session. Anyone fabricating such categories and making such assessments would do well to state clearly the basis for his or her evaluations: Are they based on a general sense of concord versus discord that derives from perceptions of mood and cultural/stylistic appropriateness, or do more formal criteria come into play, such as temporal synchronization? Is audiovisuality contained within a single medium, or is it spread across two or more, such as cinema and live performance? To what extent can audio-viewers influence the media or the relationships between media, by interacting with the audiovisual event, turning down the sound, closing the window of a computer interface, and so forth?

2) *Beyond audiovisuality.* Are senses other than sight and vision—smell, touch, taste, physical movement—directly involved in audiovisual performances or events? Or are these extra-audiovisual elements communicated through audiovisual means, for instance, by invoking sensory memories? Close-ups and uses of percussive or ambient sounds could communicate hapticity; close-ups of food might invoke both smell and taste; the dynamics of camera movement or editing in tandem with sound can even render sensations such as wetness and coolness (see Chion's chapter "Sensory Aspects of Contemporary Cinema" [Chapter 19] and Lisa Perrott's chapter [Chapter 14]).[39] Audio-viewing pornography might evoke bodily responses that fall under the category of affective resonance, something we respond to as a gut reaction, a largely involuntary response to changing levels of intensity more than through conventional identificatory mechanisms or narrative involvement.[40] Perhaps other audiovisual forms resemble pornography more than some of us might wish, insofar as they increasingly make a direct appeal to the senses. More generally, the quickening of the pulse occasioned by action/adventure or horror genres is embodied, in a broad sense, more than being simply audiovisual. In short, how is the audiovisual more than audiovisual?

3) *Narrativity, semiotics, and stylistic conventions.* One conceptual hub of audiovisual analysis since Claudia Gorbman's *Unheard Melodies,* at least in audiovisual narrative, has been the distinction between diegetic and nondiegetic. Does the sound source belong to the world of the characters, or is it unheard by them but recognized by audiences as accompanying and possibly interpreting actions onscreen? Lately the diegetic has been subject to debate, for example in the work of Robynn Stilwell and Anahid Kassabian (Chapter 5).[41] Most scholars agree

[39] For more on audiovisual haptics, see Laura Marks, *The Skin of Film: Intercultural Cinema, Embodiment and the Senses* (Durham, N.C.: Duke University Press, 2000), xi and 164. See also Thomas Elsaesser and Malte Hagener, *Film Theory: An Introduction Through the Senses* (New York, London: Routledge, 2000), 124–125.

[40] See Susanna Paasonen, *Carnal Resonance: Affect and Online Pornography* (Cambridge, Mass.: MIT Press, 2011).

[41] See also Robynn J. Stilwell, "The Fantastical Gap Between Diegetic and Nondiegetic," in *Beyond the Soundtrack: Representing Music in Cinema,* ed. Daniel Goldmark, Lawrence Kramer, and Richard Leppert (Berkeley: University of California Press, 2007), 184–202.

on making some theoretical distinction between background and so-called source functions of music and sound. New participatory forms and changing conventions of cinema are making it more difficult, however, to maintain a clear divide—the very idea of a diegesis is becoming problematic, perhaps since music videos rose to prominence in the 1980s and broadened the boundaries of filmic storytelling. Approaches that prioritize affective response (focusing on textures, aesthetics, mood, and embodied response) tend not to pay so much heed to these narratological distinctions, but often these factors will condition the prevalent mood of narratives.

Countless other issues and concepts arise in this category, one of the most useful being the notion of leitmotif, which originated in opera before finding a new home in musical accompaniments for films.[42] Leitmotifs anchor sounds to images and broader narrative ideas. In addition to Gorbman's *Unheard Melodies* and Michel Chion's *Audio-Vision*, the work of Philip Tagg is an excellent starting point for those wishing to theorize narrative and semiotic meanings in audiovisual contexts. The Finnish scholar Susanna Välimäki has also theorized the musical means of audiovisual signification in terms of topoi.[43] Recently, Lawrence Kramer's theorization of audiovisual rhetoric with reference to Derrida's notion of the "remainder" and what he calls the "imagetext" raises important questions about the boundaries of discourse. Images encourage us to ascribe meaning to musical discourse, but the process is always open ended, incomplete; a matter that Nicholas Cook also addresses through his concept of emergent meaning. The remainder is that part of audiovisual (and specifically musical) communication that evades easy categorization and often highlights the material qualities of the media as well as inciting the audio-viewer to interpret.[44] This category reminds us that perceptions of audiovisuality always involve interpretation with recourse to semiotic and cultural conventions that are unstable and open to recodings. It reminds us as well of the tenuous nature of distinctions between an artistic or entertainment event and the surrounding life from which it emerges.

4) *Intertextuality*. What is the relationship of a given audiovisual performance to other performances and texts? The concept of intertextuality can imply a continuum between fairly loose stylistic allusions to more concrete citation, allusion, remix, mashup, or adaptation. It can also refer to the cultural encoding of performances in general, encompassing all relevant discursive meanings. All kinds of films, whether art film or popular, make use of preexisting music (on a stylistic level, of course, all music is preexisting) or visual elements that recall those we have seen before. These uses might rely for their impact on the evocation

[42] On leitmotif, see section one of Buhler, Flinn and Neumeyer, *Music and Cinema*, 33–96.

[43] Susanna Välimäki, *Miten Sota Soi? Sotaelokuva, ääni ja musiikki* (Tampere, Finland: Tampere University Press, 2008).

[44] Lawrence Kramer, *Musical Meaning: Toward a Critical History* (Berkeley: University of California Press, 2002).

of cultural or collective memories, which creates a dialogue between historical objects and the present-day performance or event context. Some audiovisual events make reference to more than one genre. Auteur films do this most effectively, the inclusion of "competing" genres giving them a reflective feel. Many chapters in this book deal with intertextuality on some level—some more obviously than others. Susanna Välimäki's contribution (Chapter 22) deals with the conventional meanings of popular music genres, while Caryl Flinn (Chapter 15) examines what happens to a film musical most of us know once it has been adapted for new media contexts.[45] Daniel Goldmark (Chapter 12) considers what it means to spoof the traditional Disney formula of the animated musical, whereas Joseph Lanza (Chapter 35) reflects on the depersonalization of familiar tunes through their adaptation by Muzak, which assigns to them a background rather than a foreground function.

5) *Intermediality.* Above and beyond the consideration of intertextuality, is the mode of performance influenced by other media? Or does it incorporate elements or modes of expression distinctive to other media? If so, is there balance among the media, or does one dominate, revise, update, extend, comment on, or render another obsolete? These questions have been raised in research on intermediality, remediation, and media convergence in the fields of performance studies, theater studies, media studies, and studies of the arts. Intermediality can refer to the relationship between media within a performance or work, to intertextual relations extending beyond the work, or to the transformation of performances designed for a different medium. The last of these categories overlaps with the category of remediation, a mode of transformation that has been specifically associated with digital media, defined as "representation of one medium in another."[46] Remediation takes many forms and functions, from the unconscious at one end of the scale to the self-conscious and critical at the other. Performances that focus on the very nature of media have the potential to comment on the conditions of modern life and are distinctive to much of recent audiovisual aesthetics. Chapters by Lisa Perrott (Chapter 14), Philip Auslander (Chapter 34), Robynn Stilwell (Chapter 7), Daniel Goldmark (Chapter 12), John Richardson (Chapter 17), Caryl Flinn (Chapter 15), and all of the writers on gaming deal on some level with questions of intermediality.

6) *Technology.* How is technology employed or represented in the audiovisual event or performance? Is the technology "old" or "new"? Is a relationship implied between the technological and the pretechnological, as in uses of acoustic music

[45] For more on the concept of adaptation across the arts, see Linda Hutcheon, *A Theory of Adaptation* (New York and London: Routledge, 2006). Hutcheon lists three classes of adaptation: "an acknowledged transposition of a recognizable other work or works; a creative and an interpretive act of appropriation/salvaging; an extended intertextual engagement with the adapted work" (8).

[46] Jay David Bolter and Richard Grusin, "Remediation," *Configurations* 3 (1996): 311–358, 339. Also Philip Auslander, *Liveness: Performance in a Mediatized Culture* (London: Routledge, 2008), 6–7.

including orchestral music? Why are these technologies used *now*? What social forms, what social relations, do they encapsulate?[47] Do new technologies offer expressive possibilities that weren't available to users previously, or do they block or narrow some creative channels? What instruments or equipment are used, and how do these choices affect meaning, stylistic evolution, and genre evolution? (In this volume, Mark Kerins [Chapter 33] explores the "effects" of surround sound in these very terms.) What do practices like sampling, mashup, and remix tell us about contemporary life? How is technology used to mediate the actions of performers? Can we draw conclusions about agency on the basis of how the technology is used? Were specific uses of technologies originally intended by the producers/designers/manufacturers, or might they be considered misuses or distortions of their intentions? Which elements of performances are live and which are recorded, and what is the relationship between the two? Lively debates about technology focus on such issues as the following:

i) Technological determinism (the idea that technologies themselves motivate or constrain change) versus voluntarism (free will to invent or use technologies as one wishes).
ii) Ideas about progress and innovation often implied by the term "modernization" (CGI effects are superior because newer and more realistic; HD television is more advanced than its predecessor), as opposed to approaches that deliberately employ older technologies (uses of VHS video, vinyl, cassette tapes, Super8 film), often with a view to reflecting on consumption practices and historical position—or, for some critics, motivated by nostalgia.
iii) Authenticity and agency: Do new technologies make performers lazy by replacing their labor with easier, more mediated options? Do uses of technology imply passive acceptance of media mentality, or do they offer the potential for more active alignments?
iv) The democratization argument (technology makes advanced production means available to more people than before) versus concerns about access (Who can afford production media?).
v) Who controls the technologies. Traditionally technology has been controlled by men (boys with toys), but the situation is changing. What debates, whether essentialist or sociological and constructionist, are arising from women's access to technology? Another question of control involves the economic dominance by the wealthy West over the impoverished rest. Technology further raises ecological questions (see below), highlighted in research propagating dystopian views of the impact of modernity.

7) *Space and place*. What sense of space is conveyed in given audiovisual events, and how do visual and auditory space(s) relate? Does the sound cause us to hear the

[47] See Jonathan Sterne, *The Audible Past: Cultural Origins of Sound Production* (Durham, N.C.: Duke University Press, 2003), 337.

visual space differently, or vice versa? What is the relationship between filmed/recorded or diegetic space and audience space? How is audience space (the gallery, the auditorium, the headset, the living room) demarcated, and are its boundaries clear or indeterminate? Does anyone control uses of audience (or user) space, and how? Are attempts made to break down the fourth wall? Depicted, represented, or recorded spaces have been among the principal concerns of audiovisual analysis since its early days. Chion asks probing questions about the uses of such spaces: onscreen and offscreen figure prominently in screen discourse, and the diegetic–nondiegetic dichotomy is also fundamentally related to space; further, "point of view" and "point of audition" locate subjectivity in audiovisual space. Where is the audience positioned in relation to the represented space? How do camera work and editing interpolate the viewer in the audiovisual world? These questions extend to broader questions about spectatorship and subject position. Do music or images depict or represent a specific geographical or cultural locality? The semiotic encoding of music often suggests localities, localized or transnational geographical identities. How did Romantic classical music come to be perceived as transcendent and representative of universal subjectivity, when it originated in a specific place and time?[48] Much recent research has focused on the relationships among local, national, and transnational cultures (as well as urban versus agrarian), including several chapters in this volume, such as those of Michael Chanan (Chapter 11), Richardson (Chapter 17), and Susanna Välimäki (Chapter 22). Also in this collection Philip Brophy (Chapter 18) considers the relationship between naturalistic and imaginary spaces in music recordings used in audiovisual contexts. And several scholars address how music is used in environmental spaces, including the auditorium or gallery, in connection with the boundary issues that are central to this volume (Chion [Chapter 4], Bull [Chapter 36], Lanza [Chapter 35], and Rogers [Chapter 29]).

8) *Temporality and synchronization.* Ideas about time, as well as space, should be central in any consideration of audiovisual aesthetics. Audiovisual media are recorded and produced in specific times, and they should be understood in terms of their historicity. Some forms of experimental film, video art, and installation art have been specifically concerned with acknowledging their medium's temporal nature, as a means of registering or reflecting on the passing of time (accelerated time in modernity, slow-cooked time as a form of resistance). We ask of the audiovisual: When was the event performed, recorded, or re-presented? How does the piece handle time—accelerated, decelerated, elliptical, or interrupted, "realistic" (whatever this means) or controlled for intellectual or affective purposes? What sorts of worlds are depicted: historical, contemporary, or futuristic? How do music, dialogue, and other sound convey their temporal settings? How does the sound temporalize the imagery?[49]

[48] See Flinn, *Strains of Utopia*, 24–49; Kassabian, *Hearing Film*, 2–3.

[49] See Chion, *Audio-Vision*, 13–20.

More broadly, synchronization goes to the heart of audiovisuality and is bound to questions of "harmony" versus "counterpoint" that dominated discussions in the field from its genesis (S.M. Eisenstein, Hanns Eisler, and Theodor Adorno). Is the audiovisual entirely blended or more dissynchronous? Is looser synchronization becoming more prevalent in audiovisual forms? What, if anything, do new audiovisual relationships tell us about evolutions or revolutions in the surrounding culture?

9) *Aestheticism and affect as resistance.* It is a fallacy to assume that aestheticism ever was or is socially neutral. Adorno plumbed these critical depths with considerable rigor by arguing that aesthetic autonomy constituted a form of resistance to commodity culture and to the burden of historical consciousness that plagued previous generations of artists. Yet his thinking was an extension of Romantic idealism, as it was transmitted to him in a line going back to Schopenhauer and Kant. In Romanticism the aesthetic was associated with quasi-religious piety, the ascendance of the individual subject above his circumstances, and an attitude of disinterested contemplation that is attributable to the influence of Kant.[50] Camp aestheticism, on the other hand, celebrates stylistic artifice over content in a way that is designed to be provocative, fun, and socially marked. Yet not one of the above examples implies neutrality; or rather, even where neutrality is perceived, it is mobilized to mask discursive formations to which the writer does not wish to subscribe.[51]

Theories of affect, including the writing of philosophers like Gilles Deleuze, Brian Massumi, and Isobel Armstrong[52] are particular forms of aestheticism. Discussions of affect typically involve categories that are larger and more amorphous than ordinary semiotic categories and are conditioned by sensory and habituated physiological responses to material conditions as much as by narrative and discursive layers of experience. Phenomenological bracketing is also a means of shutting out conditioned responses (what H.-G. Gadamer called prejudices) in order to access more finely grained domains of experience and to expose historical conventions. However, affect is ultimately inseparable from discursive thinking, insofar as humans are predisposed to think symbolically: by means of association, analogy, contextualization, and narrativization. Some highly stylized, fine-grained, abstract, gritty, visceral, sensual, or "non-narrative" forms of audiovisual expression might suggest an affective more than a narrative disposition, but they take place within a historical context that supplies meanings.

Someone approaching an audiovisual event in one of these ways might ask questions like the following: Is a dominant mood or tone conveyed in sound

[50] See Lydia Goehr, *The Imaginary Museum of Musical Works: An Essay in the Philosophy of Music* (Oxford: Oxford University Press, 1994).

[51] Barthes's writing on the neutral is a prime example of this principle. Roland Barthes, *The Neutral* (New York: Columbia University Press, 2005).

[52] See, especially, Isobel Armstrong, *The Radical Aesthetic* (Oxford: Blackwell, 2000).

and images? How does that tone come about: through lighting, uses of color, cinematography, sparse or rapid use of dialogue, long takes and drones or visual and musical microrhythms, musical means such as an emphasis on tone color over melody, a rich orchestral texture, an energetic sub-bass in dance music, or uses of ambient sounds? Is the audiovisual style exhilarating or laid back, melancholic or stirring, homely or alienated, humorous and light, or serious and heavy? The dawn of the digital age and what some have called sensory cinema have led some writers to conclude that affectivity is at the heart of current aesthetics.[53] Notions of intensification, the visceral, embodied consciousness, and so forth can all be understood in this light. Are new audiovisual practices taking us away from conventional narrative means and toward an aesthetics of shifting intensities or episodic layering? Does audiovisuality these days live up to Artaudian standards in being made up of sonorous pulsations, vibrations, rhythmic beats, and the grain of media?

10) *Economic factors.* Research on economic factors in audiovisual aesthetics has constituted an important strain of recent scholarly work,[54] but is certainly not altogether new. Eisenstein, Bertolt Brecht, Eisler, Adorno, Raymond Williams, and many others all contributed to the understanding of economics in relation to audiovisuality. In an age of global recession and extreme geopolitical imbalances of power, the economic dimension continues to be an urgent area of inquiry. And of course it is linked with several of the previous categories, including technology and space and place. Does anyone own the performance or exert financial control over some aspect of it? Who is allowed to use it, distribute it, consume it? To what extent do corporate interests control formal and stylistic features? What is the relationship between producers and consumers, and what effect does that relationship have on audiovisual practices? Does the audiovisual form explicitly or implicitly support the existing economic order, or does it challenge it? The genre category "independent," which has had a marked impact on new audiovisual aesthetics, becomes increasingly problematic as big studios increasingly invest in independent production. Traditional distinctions between entertainment and art are moreover saturated with assumptions about economic hierarchies and social class.

11) *Interactivity and immersion.* We have already mentioned interactivity and immersion; like the work on affectivity described previously, these phenomena inspire some of the most vibrant inquiry about recent audiovisual expression. Questions we may ask are: Does the performance invite or suggest interactivity? Does interactivity imply democratization, or is the form in question constrained or regulated to prevent a genuine two-way flow of agency or participation? Does it matter if the user is having fun? What is the relationship between the

53 See, for example, Thomas Elsaesser, *Film Theory: An Introduction Through the Senses* (New York, London: Routledge, 2010).

54 See especially Jeff Smith's *The Sounds of Commerce.*

increasingly self-contained worlds of immersive forms and the outside world? Do they comment on this world or simply reflect its priorities? Interactivity is most explicitly addressed by the chapters in this volume that deal with "new media forms" such as gaming and social media, but it is implicit in research on daily life, and in fact reflects back on conventional forms that aren't even supposed to be interactive, like cinema. Assumptions about media that activate and pacify are perhaps in the most urgent need of revision and should not be taken for granted.

12) *The voice.* How have newer audiovisual forms and formats altered our perceptions of the human voice, and how have the new possibilities of representing the voice changed the audiovisual? The invention of the microphone early in the twentieth century forever changed the direction of song and speech (allowing for the development of such phenomena as crooning, the mass political rally, and the almost inaudibly whispered dramatic line). Has the preponderance of computer-generated and prerecorded voices dehumanized daily life? What has Auto-Tune done to notions of singing skill—is it like doping for athletes? On the other hand, what are the creative possibilities for devices such as Auto-Tune—an example being the Gregory Brothers' videos, which transform speaking subjects into hilariously inadvertent singers? The increasing ease with which audiovisual media can detach voices from bodies (and then reassign them at will) leads us to consider the voice as prosthesis.

Even the "authentic" physiological voice can be inflected in different ways to take on different social identities, or it can be surgically altered when it fails to match the subjective identity of its owner, as Susanna Välimäki discusses in her analysis of transgender identities in *Transamerica*. As discussed in the previous work of two of our authors, Philip Auslander and Stan Hawkins, the voice can be the outward manifestation of an identity we adopt and perform, modifiable according to different social and relational contexts and carrying different connotations according to class, locality, gender, and so forth.[55] From this perspective, it can be a sonic mask we wear in precisely the same way that mechanical technologies can be deployed to manipulate our sense of the "envoiced" subject. Or perhaps these are the exceptions that prove the rule: in other words, something about the voice is so inextricably bound up with character and identity that it is widely regarded as a reliable (sometimes deceptively reliable?) indicator of the person to whom it belongs: something solid to hold onto in an age of digital ephemera. We know the uncanny and disorienting effects of separating the voice from its natural sources, and so do filmmakers. (Michel Chion has written on this extensively.) These means of

[55] Philip Auslander, *Performing Glamrock: Gender and Theatricality in Popular Music* (Ann Arbor: University of Michigan Press, 2006); and Stan Hawkins, *The British Pop Dandy: Masculinity, Popular Music and Culture* (Farnham, UK: Ashgate, 2009).

defamiliarization predate cinema and contemporary audiovisual technologies,[56] but the ease with which they can be achieved and the forms that they take are distinctive in the present era.

Michael Chanan's chapter on Latin American video (Chapter 11) understands voice and speech in the broader social senses of the terms. But it should not be forgotten that this sense of the word metonymically extends physical articulations of the voice. Who speaks, and who is heard? Who is allowed to speak? A closely related question is: Which voices are silenced, and by whom? One could cite numerous films, for example, ranging from 1940s melodrama to Jane Campion's *The Piano*, in which women are mute or simply unheard.[57] These unheard voices, too, and others like them, are among the pressing subjects for research on new audiovisual media.

A further question is what happens to the voice in the contemporary contexts of audiovisual performance. Anyone watching reality TV talent competition shows must be struck by the use of audiovisual means—bigger and bigger stage sets and lighting schemes, professional dancers, and all sorts of visual business—to "amplify" the voice. Aside from her prodigious songwriting talent and heart-on-her-sleeve emotional appeal, did Adele strike success in part simply by being visually "unplugged," providing contrast to the prevalence of spectacle in popular song?

13) *Soundtrack elements*. Increasingly, intelligent scholarship has broken sound down into its constitutive parts. Take the "noise" track of recorded sound: owing to the growing emphasis on sound studies beyond audiovisual research, researchers are becoming increasingly aware of the extent to which sound effects, Foley, and environmental noises contribute to the entirety of the soundtrack, along with dialogue and music. The boundaries between music and sound are becoming increasingly blurred (although filmmakers have creatively challenged and blurred these boundaries ever since the coming of sound), and this in-betweenness of categories has become one of the most distinctive features of the current audiovisual terrain. A motivating factor behind this breaking down of traditional elements of the soundtrack has been the growing prominence of popular (or any) music in film starting in the 1960s, which gradually displaced the traditional functions of the classical film underscore. This has taken on new momentum since the 1980s and the advent of digital aesthetics, resulting in two-way interactions between interactive forms like gaming and television/cinema. The apparent disintegration of traditional narrative linearity in these new media contexts and their impact on traditional forms are among the most distinctive features of new aesthetics.

[56] See Steven Connor, *Dumbstruck: A Cultural History of Ventriloquism* (Oxford, New York: Oxford University Press, 2000).

[57] On muted voices in film melodrama, see Heather Laing, *The Gendered Score: Music in 1940s Melodrama and the Woman's Film* (Aldershot, UK: Ashgate, 2007), 25–29.

Rick Altman and his coauthors' theorization of "Hollywood's Multiplane Sound System" has opened our eyes to the complexities and functions of traditional cinema sound—that sound effects and dialogue are as salient factors as music and the music interacts with them.[58] But in new cinema the level of integration is even greater. The sounds of dialogue become a kind of music, like intertwining voices in an opera, and these are punctuated and set in relief against rumbling, hissing, ringing, and messages from the material world that impart to them an almost animistic and uncannily nonhuman or perhaps posthuman quality. Or at the other end of the scale, digital aesthetics renders an expanded sense of space that reminds us of the precariousness of life on Earth and in the cosmos; the message is existential at the same time that it is ecological (see below). Some relevant questions are: What are the interrelations between elements of the soundtrack? How has sound become more aestheticized and "musical"? How does sound involve audiences emotionally and affectively in an audiovisual experience—put differently, how does it make the experience more immersive? How does sound create or challenge realism? How is sound rendered, and how does it render (Chion) in audiovisual contexts—to what extent does sound need to be "real," or even *realistic*, to convince audiences of the reality of their experiences? Writers who endorse this holistic sense of sound in this volume include Mark Kerins (Chapter 33), Stephen Connor (Chapter 6), Meri Kytö (Chapter 23), Michel Chion, and Kevin Donnelly (Chapter 21).

14) *Audiovisual ecology*. This category concerns the nature of sound in audiovisual performances and its relationship to the surrounding world. Robynn Stilwell's chapter (Chapter 7) in particular addresses subject matter with a specifically ecocritical agenda. Elsewhere a mode of eco-consciousness can be found in the work of authors drawing from soundscape studies and sound studies more generally. This work shows characters' awareness of their physical environment, which in turn makes us as listeners increasingly aware of our own. Meri Kytö's chapter (Chapter 23) in particular illustrates how characters in Turkish films possess an almost painful hypersensitivity to the world in which they live. Michael Bull's work (Chapter 36), in contrast, shows the lengths to which we are willing to go to shut out that world when it begins to impinge threateningly on private consciousness. The dichotomy of nature versus culture is implicit in some of the work on technology, but also, digital technologies have allowed us to hear environmental noises in greater detail than ever before, and thus to attend more finely to the physical environments in which audiovisual performances take place. We can think of audiovisual ecology more broadly as sensitivity to how audiovisual materials are experienced in actual cultural settings. This sense of the term goes beyond the contextualization of experiments in the natural

[58] Rick Altman, McGraw Jones, and Sonia Tatroe, "Inventing the Cinema Soundtrack: Hollywood's Multiplane Sound System," in *Music and Cinema*, ed. James Buhler, Caryl Flinn, and David Neumeyer (Hanover, N.H.: Wesleyan University Press, 2000), 339–359.

sciences, to which the term "ecological" has often been applied. An ecological approach requires studying audiovisual performances where and when they actually occur: in cars, gyms, stadia, homes, concert venues, and movie theaters. It connects with a long line of research on daily life, extending back to ethnographic fieldwork and Benjamin's Arcade Project. It asks questions such as these: How are environmental concerns expressed in the audiovisual event? What are the boundaries between the event and the surrounding world? Does the event challenge existing assumptions about art or life? What are the "real-world" uses of audiovisual media? How is the environment recorded and represented in the audiovisual form? How are research methods ecological in the sense of attending to contextual considerations, whether these are concerned with production or composition, performance, or consumption practices? Finally, a question that resembles those asked in Geertzian anthropology is: How is the audiovisual performance part of a broader web of culture? More broadly still, ecocritical research addresses on a philosophical level vital questions about the environment, responsibility, sustainability, and technological dependency that pertain to human survival and the propagation of a planetary rather than a narrowly human-centered consciousness. Does the constant regeneration of the new in digital culture leave scars on the environment?

15) *Cultural identity, affiliation, and spectatorship*. All of this research turns attention to audiences, users, spectators, auditors, what we call audio-viewers, or in terms of traditional communication models, "receivers." Who are the cultural actors involved with audiovisual performances? What is their background and investment? (See, e.g., Kassabian's *Hearing Film*.) Do they belong to a particular group (e.g., gender, sexuality, ethnicity, nation, generation, language, locality) or foster looser cultural affiliations that are voluntary? How are such matters embedded in the audiovisual form in question? What distinctive modes of subjectivity are involved in our encounters with audiovisual events, and what do these tell us about current practices and cultural priorities? This category, like the preceding one, requires actively attending to cultural context.

Final Reflections

If the categories reviewed here represent some of the hot topics of research on new audiovisual aesthetics, a question that will remain largely unanswered in this book is: What methods are appropriate to the study of audiovisuality in all of its various forms? This is because the primary function of this book is not to answer questions about methods and means, in the manner of an undergraduate textbook. Our authors come from diverse backgrounds, bringing their expertise from disciplines like musicology, film and media studies, and philosophy, or from their practical work in audiovisual production. Nevertheless, our primary aim in this volume has been to provide a pathway through current reflection on the audiovisual that appeals to a wide range of readers and fields and will encourage readers to look beyond narrow concerns with specific genres or technological media.

Our book's authors share an interest in understanding what has been going on in the audiovisual domain over the past few decades. In this introduction we have tried to open a vista onto "the big picture" by theorizing across the various styles and approaches taken in the book. Superficially, this volume appears to be a diachronic survey of very recent practices, focusing largely on the present day and valorizing new technologies as well as innovative new practices that challenge stylistic and cultural conventions. Indeed, the use of the words "new" and "aesthetics" in our title might be taken as indicating that present-day realities, the sensory sheen of the unfolding Now, is so prominent in our view that it obscures just about everything that lies beyond, including history and context. The critical positioning of much of the work should allay any such fears. Aesthetics in our view indicates that experiences of the audiovisual *matter*—in a certain sense they are primary—but also that they are rooted in the material and cultural contingencies of their making and by their uses in the "real world." We don't fully understand film, television, games, music videos, video art, environmental sound art, multimedia theater, and so forth until we understand what people do with them. Moreover, although history might appear at first glance to be largely absent from the volume judging by its chapter topics, a large number of the contributions resound with echoes of audiovisual forms that have come before, which are adapted, transformed, parodied, incorporated, or simply drawn on as implicit cultural knowledge. Other contributions reflect on stages in our recent history that have already passed or offer the insight of historical comparison. For instance, see the writing by Korsgaard and Vernallis on music videos, Auslander on live performances, Stilwell on documentaries, Halfyard on superhero movies, Brophy on uses of popular music in film soundtracks, Rogers on video art, and Lanza on Muzak. Moreover, our net is cast so wide that we are confident that we have for the most part avoided the sort of partisanship that would pit one set of practices against another as inherently more progressive, reflective of the present cultural moment, or somehow more aesthetically advanced. We emphasize that for us, "new" does not imply better by default—although cultural relevance is a more complicated issue that can be addressed only through detailed critical discussion.

We hardly need to state the obvious: the warp-accelerating technological development in the digital era and the profusion of audiovisual forms and genres that has come with it challenge our ability to keep pace with meaning in our time. Will anything in *The Oxford Handbook of New Audiovisual Aesthetics* continue to have relevance ten years from now? We hope that our contributors' stock-taking, from microlevels—such as considering sounds of Istanbul in recent Turkish movies and opening credits in HBO TV series—to the macrolevels of theorizing—including chapters in the section "Theoretical Pressure Points" (from Cook's consideration of multimedia mentality to Kassabian's reevaluation of the concept of diegesis)—might leave its trace, be useful and relevant, for awhile. For alongside today's gargantuan universe of sounds and images that no Gulliver or Rabelais or Dante (but perhaps Borges) could ever have imagined, there remains the scholarly tradition of trying to make sense of it all, placing it in contexts and frames that the finite human intellect can hope still to master.

References

Altman, Rick, McGraw Jones, and Sonia Tatroe. "Inventing the Cinema Soundtrack: Hollywood's Multiplane Sound System." In *Music and Cinema*, edited by James Buhler, Caryl Flinn, and David Neumeyer, 339–359. Hanover, N.H.: Wesleyan University Press, 2000.

Auslander, Philip. *Performing Glamrock: Gender and Theatricality in Popular Music*. Ann Arbor: University of Michigan Press, 2006.

Auslander, Philip. *Liveness: Performance in a Mediatized Culture*. 2nd ed. London: Routledge, 2008.

Barthes, Roland. *Roland Barthes*. London, Basingstoke: Macmillan, 1977.

Barthes, Roland. *The Neutral*. New York: Columbia University Press, 2005.

Benjamin, Walter, "The Work of Art in the Age of Mechanical Reproduction." In *Illuminations: Essays and Reflections*, edited by Hannah Arendt and translated by Harry Zohn, 217–251. New York: Schocken, 1968.

Bolter, Jay David, and Richard Grusin. "Remediation." *Configurations* 3 (1996): 311–358.

Buhler, James, Caryl Flinn, and David Neumeyer, eds. *Music and Cinema*. Hanover, N.H.: Wesleyan University Press, 2000.

Castells, Manuel. *The Rise of the Network Society: The Information Age: Economy, Society and Culture*. Vol. 1. Oxford: Blackwell, 1996.

Chion, Michel. *Audio-Vision: Sound on Screen*. Translated by Claudia Gorbman. New York: Columbia University Press, 1994.

Chion, Michel. *Film, a Sound Art*. Translated by Claudia Gorbman. New York: Columbia University Press, 2009.

Connor, Steven. *Dumbstruck: A Cultural History of Ventriloquism*. Oxford, New York: Oxford University Press, 2000.

Cook, Nicholas. *Analysing Musical Multimedia*. Oxford: Clarendon Press, 1998.

Damascio, Antonio. *The Feeling of What Happens: Body, Emotion and the Making of Consciousness*. London: Vintage, 1999.

Davison, Annette, *Hollywood Theory, Non-Hollywood Practice: Cinema Soundtracks in the 1980s and 1990s*. Aldershot, UK: Ashgate, 2004.

Debord, Guy. *Society of the Spectacle*. London: Rebel Press, 2004.

Doane, Mary Anne. "The Voice in Cinema: The Articulation of Body and Space." In *Film Sound: Theory and Practice*, edited by Elisabeth Weis and John Belton, 162–176. New York: Columbia University Press, 1985.

Donnelly, Kevin, ed. *Film Music: Critical Approaches*. New York: Continuum, 2001.

Dyson, Frances. *Sounding New Media: Immersion and Embodiment in the Arts and Culture*. Berkeley: California University Press, 2009.

Eisenstein, Sergei. *The Film Sense*. London: Faber and Faber, 1943.

Elsaesser, Thomas. *Film Theory: An Introduction Through the Senses*. New York, London: Routledge, 2010.

Elsaesser, Thomas, and Malte Hagener. *Film Theory: An Introduction Through the Senses*. New York, London: Routledge, 2000.

Flannigan, Matthew. "16:9 in English: Towards an Aesthetic of Slow in Contemporary Cinema" (November 2008), at http://www.16-9.dk/2008-11/side11_inenglish.htm (accessed October 14, 2012).

Flinn, Caryl. *Strains of Utopia: Gender, Nostalgia, and Hollywood Film Music*. Princeton, N.J.: Princeton University Press, 1992.

Gere, Charlie. *Community Without Community in Digital Culture*. Basingstoke, UK, and New York: Palgrave MacMillan, 2012.

Giannachi, Gabriella. *Virtual Theatres: An Introduction*. London, New York: Routledge, 2004.

Goehr, Lydia. *The Imaginary Museum of Musical Works: An Essay in the Philosophy of Music*. Oxford: Oxford University Press, 1994.

Goldmark, Daniel, Lawrence Kramer, and Richard Leppert, eds. *Beyond the Soundtrack: Representing Music in Cinema*. Berkeley: University of California Press, 2007.

Goldstein, Jeffrey. *Why We Watch: The Attractions of Violent Entertainment*. New York, London: Oxford University Press, 1998.

Gorbman, Claudia, *Unheard Melodies: Narrative Film Music*. Bloomington: Indiana University Press, 1987.

Gunning, Tom. "The Cinema of Attraction: Early Film, Its Spectator, and the Avant-Garde." In *Film and Theory: An Anthology*, edited by Robert Stam and Toby Miller, 229–235. London: Blackwell, 2000.

Hawkins, Stan. *The British Pop Dandy: Male Identity, Music and Culture*. Aldershot, UK: Ashgate, 2009.

Hayles, N. Katherine. *How We Became Posthuman: Virtual Bodies in Cybernetics, Literature, and Informatics*. Chicago: University of Chicago Press, 1999.

Highmore, Ben. *Everyday Life and Cultural Theory: An Introduction*. London: Routledge, 2002.

Hutcheon, Linda. *A Theory of Adaptation*. New York, London: Routledge, 2006.

Jennings, Humphrey. *Pandaemoniun 1660–1886: The Coming of the Machine as Seen by Contemporary Observers*. London: Icon, 2012.

Kalinak, Kathryn. *Settling the Score: Music and the Classical Hollywood Film*. Madison: University of Wisconsin Press, 1992.

Kassabian, Anahid. *Hearing Film: Tracking Identifications in Contemporary Hollywood Film Music*. New York, London: Routledge, 2001.

Katz, Mark. *Capturing Sound: How Technology Has Changed Music*. Berkeley: University of California Press, 2004.

Kittler, Friedrich. *Gramophone, Film, Typewriter*. Stanford, Calif.: Stanford University Press, 1999.

Kramer, Lawrence, *Musical Meaning: Toward a Critical History*. Berkeley: University of California Press, 2002.

Laing, Heather. *The Gendered Score: Music in 1940s Melodrama and the Woman's Film*. Aldershot, UK: Ashgate Publishing Limited, 2007.

Lyon, David. *Surveillance Studies: An Overview*. Cambridge, UK: Polity, 2007.

Manovich, Lev. *The Language of New Media*. Cambridge, Mass.: MIT Press, 2001.

Marks, Laura. *The Skin of Film: Intercultural Cinema, Embodiment and the Senses*. Durham, N.C.: Duke University Press, 2000.

Miller, Paul D., aka DJ Spooky. *Sound Unbound: Sampling Digital Music and Culture*. Cambridge, Mass.: MIT Press, 2008.

Mulvey, Laura. *Death 24x a Second: Stillness and the Moving Image*. London: Reaktion Books, 2006.
Paasonen, Susanna. *Carnal Resonance: Affect and Online Pornography*. Cambridge, Mass.: MIT Press, 2011.
Powrie, Phil, and Robynn Stilwell, eds. *Changing Tunes: The Use of Pre-Existing Music in Film*. Aldershot, UK: Ashgate, 2006.
Reynolds, Simon, *Retromania: Pop Culture's Addiction to its Own Past*. London: Faber & Faber, 2011.
Richardson, John. *An Eye for Music: Popular Music and the Audiovisual Surreal*. New York, Oxford: Oxford University Press, 2011.
Schafer, R. Murray. *The Tuning of the World*. New York: Knopf, 1977.
Smith, Jeff. *The Sounds of Commerce: Marketing Popular Film Music*. New York: Columbia University Press, 1998.
Sterne, Jonathan. *The Audible Past: Cultural Origins of Sound Production*. Durham, N.C.: Duke University Press, 2003.
Stilwell, Robynn J. "The Fantastical Gap between Diegetic and Nondiegetic." In *Beyond the Soundtrack: Representing Music in Cinema*, edited by Daniel Goldmark, Lawrence Kramer, and Richard Leppert, 184–202. Berkeley: University of California Press, 2007.
Tagg, Philip, and Bob Clarida. *Ten Little Title Tunes: Towards a Musicology of Mass Media*. New York, Montreal: The Mass Media Musicologists' Press, 2003.
Toynbee, Jason. *Making Popular Music: Musicians, Creativity and Institutions*. London: Arnold, 2000.
Välimäki, Susanna, *Miten Sota Soi? Sotaelokuva, ääni ja musiikki*. Tampere, Finland: Tampere University Press, 2008.
Williams, Raymond. *Television: Technology and Cultural Form*. London, New York: Routledge, 1974.

PART II

THEORETICAL PRESSURE POINTS

CHAPTER 2

CLASSICAL MUSIC FOR THE POSTHUMAN CONDITION

LAWRENCE KRAMER

So let me begin with Twitter. Until quite recently, what *twittered* and *tweeted* were mostly birds. The use of these terms by the networking site that moved almost instantaneously from nowhere to everywhere makes birdsong a metaphor for human communication, perhaps reminding us—if the creators of Twitter knew it—that mechanical singing birds were the earliest form of artificial intelligence. For lovers of classical music, metaphorical birdsong is likely to recall Beethoven's *Pastoral* Symphony. But any connection between Twitter and the *Pastoral* would obviously be far-fetched.

Or would it? In July 2009 the National Symphony Orchestra in Washington, D.C., performed the symphony outdoors to the accompaniment of a Twitter feed—program notes tweeted along with the music. The *New York Times* heralded "A Different Tweet in Beethoven 'Pastoral,'" making precisely the connection between old-symphony and new-media metaphors that is apparently not so far-fetched after all. According to the *Times*, the tweets highlight "the countryside sights and sounds—rattling carriage wheels, singing birds—to which Beethoven was paying homage."[1]

This appeal to new media goes right to the core of the cultural changes now confronting classical music. Digital media project a model of mind drastically different from the model that has informed classical music for more than two centuries. The music acts through time and depth; digital media act through space and surface. As the digital model becomes the norm, classical music approaches an impasse. Either it finds a rapprochement with new-media culture, or it resigns itself to becoming outdated, a fading postcard from a fading past.

The Twitter concert points both ways. In one respect it is completely misguided. It acts as if the music were already obsolete, so that the audience needs a text-messaged guide

[1] *New York Times*, July 24, 2009, C2.

to identify sound effects that will probably still be obvious to everyone who hears them. Who, exactly, needs to be told when thunder rumbles and lightning strikes? Besides, even if the sound effects were obscure, they would be the wrong things to tweet about. Beethoven famously said that the symphony was more about the expression of feeling than painting; the birdsong and other mimicry are means, not ends. The conductor Emil de Cou, who wrote the tweeted commentary, knows this perfectly well. Yet his tweets consistently peg the expression of feeling to the depiction of country life: "There is joy in the countryside once the storm has subsided." Sprinklings of scholarly lore add to the impression of a guided tour through the mysteries of the obvious. The tweets act as if the joy had become a rare bird—the better to cage it for us.[2]

In another respect, however, this union of live performance and electronic media is just right for the *Pastoral* Symphony. Like all new-media technologies, Twitter involves a collapse of distance. Tweeting is prosthetic telepathy; it transports virtual thoughts like a kind of mental telephone. But the collapse of distance is also the collapse of nearness. In the twittersphere, "near" and "far" become meaningless terms. Tweeting along with the *Pastoral* may be superfluous, but it does invite listeners to ponder to what extent the music they are hearing in "real time" is near (the performance occupies the fleeting present; it can be heard live only once, and only in one place) or far (it belongs to an obsolescent genre, more so than other classical works; would you tweet to the Fifth? Even if you did, it would not be to gloss its rattling carriage wheels.). Do the tweets mark how near the music still is to us (hear the birdsong, read the tweet) or how far it has receded from us (Arcadia now has Internet access)? Can we even tell the difference?

Such investment in the logic of distance is especially pertinent to *this* music. One way to hear the *Pastoral* Symphony is as a reflection on the appeal of its own expressive mode. The symphony is a musical essay in distance: distance lost and won, distance enjoyed and regretted. There is the distance sought *in* nature from the troubles of urban life and moral confusion, and the distance *from* nature imposed by the artifice of representing it. There is the distance *in* history that prevents us from being too credulous about the pastoral ideal (the pastoral is dated, and always was), and the distance *from* history that gives the ideal its continued allure (the pastoral is timeless, and always will be). The force of distance in the music extends from the meandering third-relations and rising subdominants through which the development of the first movement blissfully drifts to the evolution of the song of thanksgiving from a faraway horn call in the finale. This distance is something to tweet about—and it gives the silent tweet a voice.[3]

The Twitter *Pastoral* may—just may—point to a new role for classical music in the digital age. To make sense of this possibility, we need first to consider how classical

[2] To follow the tweets that accompanied the symphony, go to twitter.com/nsoatwolftrap.

[3] For further discussion of this aspect of the *Pastoral*, see my *Why Classical Music Still Matters* (Berkeley: University of California Press, 2007), 177–184. See also Richard Will, "Time, Morality, and Humanity in Beethoven's *Pastoral Symphony*," *Journal of the American Musicological Society* 50 (1997): 271–329; and Raymond Knapp, "A Tale of Two Symphonies: Converging Narratives of Divine Reconciliation in Beethoven's Fifth and Sixth," *Journal of the American Musicological Society* 53 (2000): 291–343.

music has changed as a consequence of its still-evolving migration from analog to digital recording and from hardware to software.

The digital revolution is obviously a watershed in the history of perception, not least because digital technology has made it impossible to ignore the fact that perception *has* a history. Perception presupposes media. Perception requires technique. Perception is cultural. The default understanding of the digital turn is a second-order version of Marx's famous description of the world under capitalism: everything solid melts into air. For Marx this meant an essential state of dislocation in which the properly material character of people and things has virtually disappeared. Disappeared, that is, into virtuality, as reality gives way to a specter-haunted phantasmagoria under the rule of commodity fetishism. The digital epoch transposes the phantasmagoria from commodities to electronic media, from mystified objects to the flow of information.

For D. N. Rodowick, understanding this transposition requires a new concept, the *figural*. The figural enters the world insofar as the classical sign departs from it. "In the physics of language, semiology represents Newtonian mechanics.... Conceptually, the sign describes a thing: it must be replaced by a 'becoming'... a fractured, fracturing, or fractal space... [that] knows nothing of the concept of identity."[4] The figural replaces representation by simulation. It disengages reference from reality and, because all digital information can be manipulated at will, it disengages "truth" from any possible relationship between prior material states of affairs and texts or images—terms that themselves become moot or interchangeable. Everything solid melts, not into air, but into the data stream.

For N. Katherine Hayles, the rise of what Rodowick calls the figural corresponds to a loss of the sense of uniquely human embodiment, a condition that she, like many others, identifies as "posthuman," the union of the human with intelligent machines: "The posthuman view privileges informational pattern over material instantiation, so that embodiment in a biological substrate is seen as an accident of history.... In the posthuman, there are no essential distinctions [between] cybernetic mechanism and biological organism."[5] Everything solid melts into the data stream—until it morphs into the cyborg.

Insofar as we still experience the properly corporeal state of the human being as a material reality, the description of the figural or posthuman as a phantasmagoria remains plausible. But the posthuman phantasmagoria, unlike its Marxian model, is not necessarily a condition of alienation, unreality, or loss. To experience it negatively is to make two assumptions that the digital revolution has rendered uncertain at best.

The first assumption is that reality is measured by the pace, size, and scope of human bodies, according to the classical humanist principle that "man" is the measure of all things. This idea may now be only an expression of nostalgia, as anyone who has ever

4 D. N. Rodowick, *Reading the Figural, or, Philosophy After the New Media* (Durham, N.C.: Duke University Press, 2001), 46.

5 N. Katherine Hayles, *How We Became Posthuman: Virtual Bodies in Cybernetics, Literature, and Informatics* (Chicago: University of Chicago Press, 1999), 2–3.

had coffee in a café crowded with laptops and increasingly smart cell phones can attest. (Oh, and that last sentence was written before the release of the iPad.) Time and distance are negligible factors in present-day communication. It is even possible to be—virtually—in two (or more!) places at once. Although a sense of dematerialization and the collapse of distance have accompanied every modern communications medium since the telephone, the change brought about by computational power is an order of magnitude greater, a classic case of quantity becoming quality.

The second assumption is that the human body is distinct from its machinic appliances or prostheses, that there is such a thing as a natural human body. This assumption has never been genuinely true. One might even suggest that the human as such arises with the possibility of technological prosthesis. But in the twenty-first century the idea seems absurd except, again, as an object of nostalgia or a special circumstance. The increasing naturalization of the machine–human interface has led to an emergent reconception of the body. As Hayles puts it, "[T]he posthuman view thinks of the body as the original prosthesis we all learn to manipulate, so that extending... the body with other prostheses becomes a continuation of a process that began before we were born."[6]

Where does the posthuman condition leave us with music, especially classical music? And wherever that is, what "us" does it leave there?

The answers start with a critique of the figural. Rodowick derives the concept from the collapse of the distinction between the visible and the expressible, roughly image and word, the theorization of which he traces to the work of Foucault. Like all concepts of its kind, this one fails to give music a constitutive role. Indeed, it barely recognizes music at all. It does so because the opposition of the verbal and the visual, the meshing of their fields in an encompassing *imagetext*, has been the historical grid governing the production of all meaning in Western cultures.[7] The imagetext maintains its integrity by veiling the alliance between words and images behind the display of their differences. Digitalization erodes this systematic ambiguity. But it does more: it also breaks down the hidden but once very powerful division between the imagetext and the acoustic environment. The digital world is an echo chamber without walls. It is a space in which there are no clear boundaries between showing, telling, and riffing. Hence the need arises to theorize a new manifold, which I propose to call the *audiofigural*.

The place of classical music in the audiofigural is paradoxically both marginal and exemplary: marginal, because the music's audience is limited and always has been, and exemplary, because of the unique ontological claims historically associated with this music. For much of its history classical music has depended on two conceptual supports. The audiofigural removes both of them. One support is the status of a relatively stable whole identifiable as a "work" in a strong sense of that term. The other is a model

[6] Ibid., 3.

[7] On the imagetext, see J. W. T. Mitchell, *Picture Theory: Essays on Verbal and Visual Representation* (Chicago: University of Chicago Press, 1995), 9, 83–108, and my *Musical Meaning: Toward a Critical History* (Berkeley: University of California Press, 2001), 146–187.

of consciousness and attention that is increasingly anachronistic in the posthuman world. Most music in the Western world leads a loose and highly variable existence; it circulates as something other than a thing. The historical norm has been the production of melodies that may be re-created, transformed, and embellished or truncated at will. Such melodies are durable only because they are malleable; they maintain a tenuous identity through the family resemblances of their iterations. In a sense they belonged to the audiofigural before there was such a thing. Standard tunes replicate through new voicings and arrangements, iconic recordings through the supplement of cover versions, and of late, acoustic bits and pieces through sampling. But the classical composition, music committed to score for intact reproduction, seeks to be different. Since the early eighteenth century it has increasingly aspired to the condition of a work, a valued form with the relative immutability of a material thing, in open defiance of the transitoriness of any musical event.

Tunes are not works, except to copyright lawyers. Neither are recordings, which are products subject to repetition but not open to interpretation. The musical work, intact, integral, and interpretable, is the great exception in Western music, though one that, as part of its very concept, is compelled to identify itself as the rule. That rule has lately been questioned by scholars intent upon the incompleteness and textual variability of the score on the one hand and the priority of performance on the other. The persuasiveness of these critiques is open to question, but whatever one thinks of them, they cannot erase the historical and institutional power of the work concept or its continuing appeal to performers and composers.[8]

Nonetheless, it took a long time for the work to establish itself as a de facto "thing." Not until the twentieth century, when listening to recorded music replaced amateur performance as the chief means of access to classical compositions, did the classical work establish itself wholly as a standard rather than as an ideal or as one possibility of reception among others, including arrangement, transcription, abridgment, adaptation, and simplification. This era of the full-fledged work, the supposedly timeless masterwork, was relatively brief and is now essentially over. We know that digital recording and transmission are devising its replacement; what we don't know yet is how the aesthetic and cultural identity of classical music will change as a result.

With that question in mind, consider the posthuman a little further. The concept might be traced to Foucault's famous prophecy in *The Order of Things*: "Man is in the process of perishing as the being of language continues to shine ever brighter upon our horizon."[9] But the prophency has come true for a reason that is the very opposite of Foucault's: not the grand sunrise of language, but the linguistic *Götterdämmerung* of the

[8] For critiques of the work concept, see Lydia Goehr, *The Imaginary Museum of Musical Works: An Essay in the Philosophy of Music* (Oxford: Oxford University Press, 1994); and Nicholas Cook, "Music as Performance," in *The Cultural Study of Music: An Introduction*, ed. Martin Clayton, Richard Middleton, and Trevor Herbert (New York: Routledge, 2002); for a reconsideration, see my *Interpreting Music* (Berkeley: University of California Press, 2010).

[9] Michel Foucault, *The Order of Things: An Archaeology of the Human Sciences* (1966; New York: Routledge, 2002), 421.

audiofigural. The classical figure of "man" has perished, or rather morphed, above all because of technological change and its effects on the perceptual apparatus.

For a simplified description of this process, we can begin with the image of "man" as a thinking being unmediated by technology. This figure goes back to Plato's image of the craftsman, whose *techne* never exceeds the scope of the body; it returns in the speculative anthropology of the eighteenth century, most famously in Rousseau; and it persists in Heidegger's twentieth-century depictions of minimally equipped man in authentic contact with the Open of Being. But while Heidegger was fashioning this image to cling to, Freud was already calling "man" a "prosthetic god,"[10] and a little later Alan Turing conceived the test of artificial intelligence that now bears his name. Well before the twentieth century ended, "man" had been replaced by the cyborg, a machine–human interface well on its way to becoming naturalized. Much as culture, according to Hegel, became our "second nature" by supplanting the nature that bore us (shades of the *Pastoral* Symphony), the machine–human interface may be becoming our third nature by supplanting the culture on which we have been borne.[11]

Classical music has historically been addressed to a technologically unbound "man," yet it has always depended on technology. Musical instruments are machines, and machines whose design helps shape the kinds of music that can be made with them. Even a trained voice is a kind of machine. The traditions of musical performance have tended to conceal its mechanical foundations behind the potent combination of the music's expressivity and the musician's dexterity. But since the invention of sound recording music has been an essentially technological phenomenon. From its debut, recorded sound has been accompanied by an insistence on its naturalness and fidelity—even passing a kind of Turing test devised by the Edison Company in the 1920s.[12] Acoustic reality has constantly melted into technological fantasy. Playback devices from the Victrola to Bose iPod docks have supposedly transmuted the lead of recorded sound into acoustic gold. And classical music has long been the gold standard for this effect of what used to be called high fidelity.

The experience of this fidelity is an experience of representation without loss or remainder. As such, it involves the transmission not only of the classical work but also of the distance between music and audience on which the concept of the work depends. The work asks to be contemplated; contemplation requires distance. The concept of high-fidelity recording preserves the effect of distance by the age-old metaphysical device of measuring the quality of a reproduction against its inaccessible original. Even perfect reproduction requires a pair. One intriguing symptom of this

[10] The phrase occurs in Freud's *Civilization and Its Discontents* (1930), trans. James Strachey (New York: W. W. Norton, 2005), 76.

[11] On the cyborg, see Donna Haraway, "A Cyborg Manifesto," in *Simians, Cyborgs, and Women: The Reinvention of Nature* (New York: Routledge, 1991), 149–182. On second nature, see G. W. F. Hegel, *Elements of the Philosophy of Right*, ed. Allen W. Wood, trans. Hugh Barr Nisbet (Cambridge: Cambridge University Press, 1991), 195. Hegel refers in this passage to "custom" [Sitte], which is closer to "culture" in the sense relevant here than the German *Kultur*.

[12] See Emily Thompson, *The Soundtrack of Modernity* (Cambridge, Mass.: MIT Press, 2004), 237–239.

distance-preserving function was the marketing of playback equipment as fine furniture during the first half of the twentieth century. The distance experienced in the concert hall in both physical and social space moved into the living room as a fetishized commodity.

With the arrival of the digital interface, this system disappears more rapidly than "man" ever could. The distance of the machinic—the distance *from* the human that becomes the distance *of* the human—is now lost. In its absence the distinctions between the human and the machinic and between consciousness and the flow of information become meaningless. More, they are revealed as having always been meaningless. When classical music is presented in this framework, in the medium of the audiofigural, the music loses its audience, not in the sense that fewer people listen to it, but in the sense that the figure of the human, the fiction of "man," to which the music is addressed has become vestigial. Classical music, it turns out, is human, all too human.

There are at least five fundamental arenas in which posthuman interfaces upend the inherited form of classical music. By "inherited form" I specifically mean the music's recorded form. Even before the invention of the long-playing (LP) record made it possible to hear most longer works without interruption, recordings had replaced concerts, and listening had replaced performing as the principal means for reproducing classical music. The musical work had found a home, which was at various times the album, the record, the tape cassette, and the compact disc (CD): objects in which the work was reified and made available for fetishizing. The height of this trend was undoubtedly the LP era, with its large record jackets laden with art reproductions on the front and program notes on the back, something that CD jewel boxes could never quite emulate. That one was supposed to handle the LP only by its edges to avoid getting fingerprint oil in the analog grooves added to the sense of possessing something valuable. But there is no handling an MP3 file.

The five casualties of the audiofigural appeared in classical music as qualities calling for a certain mode of response well before they became established as the coordinates of normalized listening practices in the later nineteenth century. The first three we have already met: the music as quasi-thing; the musical work as integrated totality; and the music as an address to the body, or the listener, from a distance that creates the possibility of acoustic contemplation. The other casualties are the musical work as an enigma prompting interpretation, in the sense of both musical performance and conceptual explanation; and the music as something to be listened to in an activity of nothing but listening. None of these features vanishes completely in the audiofigural, but they exist there only in spectral form, a little more than phantasmal, a little less than virtual.

These changes are basic to the presentation of classical music in two of its primary current venues, iTunes and YouTube, each of which is a combination of recording technology and performance space. In describing these Web sites I will of course only be going over familiar facts, but I hope to shape my descriptions in revealing ways.

iTunes does not sell classical works; it sells "songs." Single-movement works and the movements of multimovement works are interchangeable; one can select and combine these "songs" at will, play them back individually or organize them into playlists, or let the computer "shuffle" them for random playback. It is as if iTunes had taken the once-marginal form of the compilation album—"Greatest Classical Hits," "100 Immortal Melodies"—and supercharged it. There is no imperative to preserve the order or number of movements in, say, a symphony or quartet; that arrangement is obviously possible, because everything is possible, but it has no special authority. Works are obtainable only as bundles of separate "songs" ready to be mixed and matched in any number of playlists or left to the shuffle. The reductio ad absurdum of this procedure comes with works consisting of a theme with variations; iTunes treats each variation as a separate song and lists the songs in no particular order in response to a search entry.

This situation is fundamentally different from the one produced by older recording technologies, with their fixed sequences of analog tracks. To skip an LP track required intervention by hand. With CDs analog playback is still the default option; programming is possible, but by digital standards it is slow and clumsy, and both programming and shuffling are limited by the fixed content of the discs, which in that respect might just as well be Edison cylinders. Digital recordings leave no tracks. The "songs" of iTunes are tiles in a mosaic subject to endless redistribution. In principle, every series of "songs" is the outcome of just another shuffle.

This fragmentation, the shattering of the classical work *even when the work is preserved*, goes further when the music is downloaded onto an iPod and listened to with earbuds. Not only is a great deal of "fidelity" lost, but the earbuds nearly abolish the contemplative distance between the music and the listener. Earbuds exceed the older headphones in this respect; with earbuds the apparatus is taken into the body cavity and thus literally incorporated. The earbuds become prosthetic eardrums in which the music itself becomes prosthetic, less a sound transmitted to a listener than a making-audible of what might otherwise be heard only in the mind's ear. Popular music, which traditionally relies on amplification and seeks to diminish rather than to traverse distance, is evidently less disrupted by this change of venue, perhaps even fulfilled by it. But I will leave that question to those better qualified to deal with it.

The situation on YouTube is even more extreme. Here the fragmentation of the classical work only begins with its division into multiple segments in multiple performances, no less subject to mixing into playlists than "songs" downloaded from iTunes. The music is also in every case accompanied by a video, so that even the "same" segment may be radically different in different versions. The distinctness of the music from its video habitat thins to the point of nonexistence; the music becomes something like a wholly new art form, and one that, unlike its parent form, is entirely subject to the whim and pleasure of its listener, who is also in a sense its performer. In some cases the impression of a "work" disappears completely. A recent search of the terms "Schubert Winterreise" produced 433 videos, each of which represents—literally—a single song. On iTunes the recorded music remains wedded to its traditional dimension of sound alone (unless, of course, one plays it via Windows Media Player and watches the abstract sound and light show generated by the program on the screen within a screen). But YouTube is a complete realization of the audiofigural.

These transmutations of the classical work represent an emergent norm in which classical music as it has been known traditionally will not continue, even if we still sound the notes and the notes do not change. To measure the extent of this transformation, it will prove useful to compare the presentation of classical music in two films made some 65 years apart. This turn to cinema is not entirely casual; as Lev Manovich has suggested, most of the features of digital culture began there, and that includes the audiofigural.[13]

The films are Billy Wilder's 1944 film noir *Double Indemnity* and the 2009 Pixar animated feature *Up*. *Double Indemnity* includes a pivotal scene centered on a turbulent passage from the slow movement of Schubert's "Unfinished" Symphony; *Up* accompanies an important early scene with the habanera from Bizet's *Carmen*. At first the two cases seem remarkably alike, yet the differences between them may be taken to mark the epochal shift to the posthuman. This is a shift that appears less in the perceptual surface of the films than in the mode of their address to the spectator.

Double Indemnity, with a screenplay by Raymond Chandler, is a cautionary tale of adultery and murder with Oedipal conflict and betrayal thrown in. The protagonist, Walter Neff, conspires with his lover, Phyllis Dietrichson, to kill her husband; eventually he kills her, too. As their relationship deteriorates, Neff forms a bond with Phyllis's stepdaughter, Lola, whose own troubled romantic life he helps to straighten out, gaining for her what he has ruined for himself. At one point the two meet in a secluded spot in the woods overlooking an outdoor concert site, the famous Hollywood Bowl. Framed by darkness, they sit across from one another in medium close-up; between them, at the center of the screen, is a circle of light framed by a band of darkness crisscrossed by scintillating points of light. From this radiant center come the sounds of Schubert's music, which continue throughout the scene.

Its presence is strange. The movie's characters otherwise show no interest in classical music, nor do Neff and Lola even acknowledge hearing the music as they talk. But the point of the music is precisely its incongruity. It seems to be emanating from another world. Even though its tone is tragic, the very tragedy is utopian, expressive of sufferings felt to be both dignified and meaningful, qualities conspicuously lacking in the corrupt world of the narrative. This utopian value belongs not just to the fragment of music we hear, but to its unheard remainder; what the music adds is not just a rival tone, but a rival narrative. That the rival is precisely the "Unfinished" Symphony is part of the point, something that would not have been lost on Franz Waxman, who did the music for the film, and whose grim underscore could not be less like Schubert. The symphony embodies wholeness without finality; the utopia is a memory or a hope, not a promise.

Up turns this utopian valuation upside-down. The elderly hero, Carl Fredrickson, is mourning the loss of his wife; during the film he will undergo a classic process of

[13] Lev Manovich, *The Language of New Media* (Cambridge, Mass.: MIT Press, 2001), 18–29.

Freudian mourning and transfer his affections to someone else, a young boy who stands in for the son or grandson the couple never had. In a scene set shortly after the death, Carl is shown in his house going grimly about his daily routine while the habanera fills the sound track. The music embodies his clinging to his grief, in ironic contrast to the—unheard—lines sung to it by Carmen in the opera, "Love is a little bird that none can tame." The association is the more ironic because in the end Carl will work through his grief by literally flying away—buoyed by colorful balloons with his house as a gondola—in search of, among other things, a giant bird.

The citation of *Carmen* is decontextualized despite the relevance of the allusion. The tune is independently famous; most moviegoers will find it familiar and vaguely "classical" even if they cannot identify its source. Its use here is more sampling than quotation. It does not act as a token of a larger whole, and its effect is not edifying but depressive. In this context the simple fact that the music is extradiegetic, unlike the symphony in *Double Indemnity*, becomes significant: this is music out of place; it has no proper place. The habanera is not even mentioned in the track list for the film score. It sounds as if it had wandered onto a playlist. The only sense in which this is not true is again an ironic one: this one-off music symbolizes, indeed embodies, that which Carl's psyche, and perhaps the movie, must expel if it is to regain its *own* wholeness. *Up* nostalgically maintains the value of psychic and social integration while depending on technological means to which the very notion of an integral whole is either fictitious or meaningless.

The sound of the habanera in *Up* is the sound of classical music today. As a result of digital media and their familiar consequences, the music is returning to the condition from which it began to emerge in the eighteenth century in order to constitute itself. No longer is it primarily an occasion for focused listening with deep attention, as it still is in *Double Indemnity* even though the characters do not seem to be listening. Instead, it is a fragmentary, surface-disseminated phenomenon, used not for the presentation of utopian meaning or aesthetic enigma but simply for its overt semiotic value. In that respect it is to be distinguished from other kinds of music only semiotically.

The rise of new media reveals that the classical norm of the work full in breadth and depth is a historical artifact, a passing episode rather than a law governing the whole history of classical music. But there remains an important exception, the one venue of the music that cannot be reproduced without being negated, the last condition of irreducible singularity. That exception is live concert performance. More exactly, it is live performance understood as the reenactment—the realization and interpretation—of the work precisely *as* an exception, an event, an occasion in the large sense, lacking both the security of a recording and the plasticity of a data file.

Classical music in the digital era may find its second life in the promise of live performance as an event. Not all performances will reach that threshold; probably few will. But what *may* happen, in its uncertainty, is no less compelling than what *does*. The musical work in this context takes on a new character that one might call enduring tenuousness—something of which the Twitter version of the *Pastoral* Symphony is exemplary. The work would be enduring because we can still retrieve it with exactitude, and more, because we can retrieve it precisely as a singular, once-only occurrence. The paradox of the retrieval of the singular is the crux of the matter. But the work is tenuous for the very same reason. We can retrieve it only on the condition that we immediately surrender it. Hovering between retrieval and surrender, the work would assume a new identity as something that cannot be recorded but only simulated, whether in fragments or as a whole does not matter. We would no longer experience listening to performances and listening to recordings as different modes of the "same" fundamental process. That sameness—not an identity or indiscernibility but a kind of kinship relation—would no longer be supported by the technology in play, as it was during the first century or so of recorded sound.

Prior to that era of mechanical reproducibility, live realization of the score was the only way, and a relatively rare one, to encounter the music in all of the fullness it postulated for itself. The progressive movement from the 78 rpm platter to the LP to the CD seemed for awhile to provide a superior, almost transcendent venue for that fullness, covertly supported by studio editing and the expectation (soon the requirement) of note-perfect rendition. But the fiction of fullness could not survive the obsolescence of its technological basis. The digitally spurred decline of what might, to abuse the term, be called the "aura" of recorded sound gives classical music little choice but to stake its future on the renewal of the performance event as a source of value. The musical work will have to trade its archival identity for a purely potential one.

To this new configuration of the work there corresponds a new configuration of the body. Most of the classical repertoire involves the direct transformation of bodily movement and energy into music. The only technological addition is the musical instrument; in any other respect the performing body might as well be naked. What we somewhat oddly call acoustic music arises where sounding bodies alone stand in for the technology that invents Freud's prosthetic god. Those bodies belong to both the players and their instruments. Taken as a unit, the human and the material-resonant bodies engaged in making music become a single charismatic figure that clothes and houses its audience with music. Taken as a couple, musician and instrument stand to each other as embodied partners in an intimate, often erotic relationship. The incorporation of electronic instruments into an acoustic ensemble does not dilute these effects but enhances them. And so does their reenactment in a world where music in its digital form is increasingly disembodied and phantasmic.

These bodily dimensions of classical music-making have traditionally been neglected in favor of an ideal conception of the music as a rare possession that transcends its bodily basis: music as surrogate spirit. As W. H. Auden memorably put it, "[Our] greatest comfort is music,/Which can be made anywhere, is invisible,/And does not smell."[14] During the long era when we apprehended the body as a natural form proper to the human, we often asked music to suspend the sense of embodiment. "Dissolve me into ecstasies," wrote John Milton, "and bring all heavn before my eyes."[15] But as we increasingly enter an era of general prosthesis, the era of posthuman bodies, we may learn to

[14] W. H. Auden, "In Praise of Limestone," ll. 81–83, in *Collected Poems*, ed. Edward Mendelssohn (New York: Random House 2007), 538.

[15] John Milton, "Il Penseroso," ll. 165–66.

ask this same music to restore the sense of embodiment we have lost. The restoration would be no simple regression. We would not be asking for a return of the human body, but for the gift of the clumsier, more equivocal pre-posthuman body. This would above all be the body exposed to the event. In concert it would be charged with making the event of music happen and making the music happen as an event, with the outcome uncertain until the last note has sounded.

Live classical performance, formerly superseded by recording as the music's primary venue, might thus be restored as the medium of the exceptional event, a museum of vanishing acts. The classical music on exhibit would be there to be heard as never before or since, no matter how often music by the same name had been heard before or since. Attended and attended to for its singularity, the live concert may restore this music to perceptual integrity and sensory vividness, even if, as it inevitably will, the concert format absorbs digital, visual elements like those *Pastoral* tweets. A positive vision of the concert as non-normative might restore to *listening* some of the value once possessed in an earlier classical music culture by *playing*.

With new media, playing music undergoes a migration. One can now "play" the music on a computer as one formerly played it on an instrument, as Roland Barthes long ago said one was to "play" the open-ended, infinitely malleable Text.[16] It is as if the computer were the heir to the nineteenth-century piano, which in this case means not only the site where the amateur reproduces music, but also the place where the music can be altered. Meanwhile the pace and shape of the alteration itself keeps altering; the development of the iPhone as a musical instrument will soon ("soon" as I write; it has probably already happened as you read) make possible a continuously mutating concert for which the instrument is a bodily appurtenance and the auditorium is every place at any time, the virtual scene of an endless tweet from each to all and back again.

In these circumstances classical music becomes part of a musical multiverse, distinguished only by, and effectively reduced to, its semiotic value—the case of the habanera from *Up*. But on the other hand, as an imaginary body of sound reanimated in concert by historical human bodies, a kind of acoustic doppelgänger, classical music may also become the occasion for the restoration of the event. Its performance would extend the concert event as an accidental singularity of date and time into a literal present-ing of the event as such, the event in its eventalness, that which cannot be encoded or foreseen.[17] The music would thus come to reoccupy and redefine the utopian space mapped out by its image in *Double Indemnity*. It would not only be "live"; it would re-mark its aliveness in a complex dialogue with the life of posthuman being.

There are good things on both sides of this equation. On the one hand, thanks to the digital instrument and the rise of the playlist, classical music is potentially ubiquitous,

[16] Roland Barthes, "From Work to Text" (1971) in *The Rustle of Language*, trans. Richard Howard (Berkeley: University of California Press, 1989), 56–71, at 62–63.

[17] On the event in this sense, see Jacques Derrida, "A Certain Impossible Possibility of Saying of the Event," trans. Gila Walker, *Critical Inquiry* 33 (2007): 441–461, and Alain Badiou, *Being and Event*, trans. Oliver Feltham (New York: Continuum, 2005), 173–90, 201–211.

dispersed through a worldwide playlist among those who listen to it casually, occasionally, even accidentally, even only to a random "song" now and again. On the other hand, the music's advocates can—should—reframe the live classical concert as a heightened here and now beyond the audiofigural, and beyond it in a sense not shared by other modes of performance. The reframing would come from acts of attendance closely attuned to enduring transience and bodily involvement. The result would potentially be the reclaiming of the classical work as something iterable and interpretable and yet not reproducible, a treasured something incapable of being stored and retrieved either mechanically or digitally. Classical music may thus offer a retreat, in the double sense of a backing away and of a time and place set apart for reflection and refreshment, from the posthuman condition that will be ours, already is ours, whether we like it or not. There could be worse fates.

One consequence will no doubt be a loss of identity for classical works, as digital recording flattens them into specialized sound effects used primarily for "relaxation"—an association, as I've suggested elsewhere, created mainly by the absence of a rhythm track in most of the repertoire.[18] The same deflation becomes audible when such classical music radio stations as still exist endlessly recycle baroque and classical pieces as bland advertisements of social privilege and its narcissistic mirror, the listener's refined taste. But another possibility is the one I have been outlining: the revival of the idea of the classical work as a disturbing, uncertain adventure in live performance, as an exceptional event, and more, as an embodiment of the event as singularity, what Derrida calls the im-possibility of the possible.[19] Such an event addresses its listeners from a distance and invites them to share a certain intimacy that crosses the distance. The distance can even envelop a digitized supplement, like the tweets added to the *Pastoral* Symphony. It may even be able to *impart* distance to high-definition (HD) broadcasts of live symphonic performances; as orchestras join opera and ballet companies in embracing HD—something under way as of this writing—the music will have to counter as well as count on the surplus intimacy and all-too-revealing detail of HD images.[20] Heard at a distance, in the pre-posthuman limits of the human ear, classical music may claim a renewed value not by invoking long-exhausted claims of transcendental expression, but by securing a space in which the infinity of the posthuman interface yields to the plenteousness of a simply human finitude.

[18] In *Musical Meaning*, 50.

[19] Jacques Derrida, "A Certain Impossible Possibility of Saying of the Event," *Critical Inquiry* 33 (2007): 454.

[20] According to David Sabel, the producer of HD broadcasts for the National Theater in London, live HD "goes back to the root of what makes live performance work.... You're experiencing it in the moment, and then it's gone" (*New York Times*, November 9, 2010, A3). But HD also disrupts the human (or pre-posthuman) scale of liveness, both by the monumentalizing effect of high-definition images on a large screen and by the ever-present possibility that the HD magnification of details will result in Brobdingnagian grotesqueness.

References

Auden, W. H. *Collected Poems.* Edited by Edward Mendelssohn. New York: Random House, 2007.

Badiou, Alain. *Being and Event.* Translated by Oliver Feltham. New York: Continuum, 2005.

Barthes, Roland. *The Rustle of Language.* Translated by Richard Howard. Berkeley: University of California Press, 1989.

Cook, Nicholas. "Music as Performance." In *The Cultural Study of Music: An Introduction*, edited by Martin Clayton, Richard Middleton, and Trevor Herbert, New York: Routledge, 2002: 204–214.

Derrida, Jacques. "A Certain Impossible Possibility of Saying of the Event." Translated by Gila Walker. *Critical Inquiry* 33 (2007): 441–461.

Foucault, Michel. *The Order of Things: an Archaeology of the Human Sciences.* New York: Routledge, [1966], 2002.

Freud, Sigmund. *Civilization and Its Discontents.* Translated by James Strachey. New York: W. W. Norton [1930], 2005.

Goehr, Lydia. *The Imaginary Museum of Musical Works: An Essay in the Philosophy of Music.* Oxford: Oxford University Press, 1994.

Haraway, Donna. *Simians, Cyborgs, and Women: The Reinvention of Nature.* New York: Routledge, 1991.

Hayles, N. Katherine. *How We Became Posthuman: Virtual Bodies in Cybernetics, Literature, and Informatics.* Chicago: University of Chicago Press, 1999.

Hegel, Georg Wilhelm Friedrich. *Elements of the Philosophy of Right.* Edited by Allen W. Wood. Translated by Hugh Barr Nisbet. Cambridge: Cambridge University Press, 1991.

Knapp, Raymond. "A Tale of Two symphonies: Converging Narratives of Divine Reconciliation in Beethoven's Fifth and Sixth." *Journal of the American Musicological Society* 53 (2000): 291–343.

Kramer, Lawrence. *Musical Meaning: Toward a Critical History.* Berkeley: University of California Press, 2001.

Kramer, Lawrence. *Why Classical Music Still Matters.* Berkeley: University of California Press, 2007.

Kramer, Lawrence. *Interpreting Music.* Berkeley: University of California Press, 2010.

Manovich, Lev. *The Language of New Media.* Cambridge, Mass.: MIT Press, 2001.

Mitchell, J. W. T. *Picture Theory: Essays on Verbal and Visual Representation.* Chicago: University of Chicago Press, 1995.

Rodowick, D. N. *Reading the Figural, or, Philosophy After the New Media.* Durham, N.C.: Duke University Press, 2001.

Thompson, Emily. *The Soundtrack of Modernity.* Cambridge, Mass.: MIT Press, 2004.

Will, Richard. "Time, Morality, and Humanity in Beethoven's Pastoral Symphony." *Journal of the American Musicological Society* 50 (1997): 271–329.

CHAPTER 3

BEYOND MUSIC: MASHUP, MULTIMEDIA MENTALITY, AND INTELLECTUAL PROPERTY

NICHOLAS COOK

MENTALITIES

LIKE others working in musical performance and multimedia, I have attacked traditional musicological approaches for treating a part of culture as if it were the whole. To analyze music as performance is to critique a musicology of writing that treats performance as essentially a supplement to a written text; to study performance as a form of multimedia is to see it as a phenomenon that involves the body and all its senses, not a depersonalized sound source. By implication, we in this field contrast our work to a truncated, narrow-minded musicology that reflects the autonomy-based aesthetic ideologies of the past, rather than the performative reality of music as a vital and unprecedentedly popular cultural practice in today's multimedia-oriented world. We may not spell it out, but our aim is an updated musicology that will do better justice to the richness of music as experienced beyond (and indeed within) the academy.

In no world, apart perhaps from the Castalia of Hermann Hesse's *The Glass Bead Game*, has music been practiced as an autonomous art of sounded writing, in the way that musicology has at times seemed to represent it (and so, in its own small way, helped to constitute it). Despite the best efforts of the autonomy technologists who designed nineteenth- and twentieth-century concert halls and of listeners schooled in autonomy aesthetics, music can never be a purely autonomous experience: from environmental sounds to wandering thoughts, contingencies of the everyday world intrude. Yet the point is the extent to which the listeners, teachers, aestheticians, and architects of that period all worked at making it an autonomous experience, construing musical sounds in terms of the notational grounding that was seen as representing composers' intentions in their most recoverable form. The development of the gramophone, making music infinitely repeatable and severing the links to its contexts of performance, brought the experience even closer to an aesthetic ideal based on the primacy of composition. One might say that within the limits of the possible, autonomy was collectively performed by the cultural practitioners of the Western "art" tradition. To that extent the autonomy of music is not so much an ideological illusion to be deconstructed as a historical fact to be understood. And from this it follows that rather than revealing experience as it really is, the updated musicology to which I refer is in danger of concealing period perceptions and conceptions behind an approach that is seen as more realistic but in fact is merely more contemporary.

It is the business of music history to identify foundational shifts in musical thought and practice and in this way to guard against anachronistic interpretation. Since the publication in 1992 of Lydia Goehr's *The Imaginary Musuem of Musical Works: An Essay in the Philosophy of Music*, and despite a certain amount of musicological carping, it has become received wisdom that one such shift took place around 1800, with the consolidation of the concept of the musical work. Musical culture came to be seen as structured around autonomous, timeless entities such as Beethoven's Fifth Symphony or the *Hammerklavier* Sonata. Goehr traced the development of this concept in both the aesthetic and the legal domains, and the idea that it might be seen as a coherent system of thought or belief—in the manner of Foucault's epistemes or the *Annales* historians' mentalities—was reinforced by the publication in 2007 of Karol Berger's *Bach's Cycle, Mozart's Arrow: An Essay on the Origins of Musical Modernity*. Berger argued that Bach's music was informed by a conception of time as cyclical, which he contrasted with the teleological conception of time that developed during the final decades of the eighteenth century and achieved definitive musical expression in the works of Mozart and Beethoven. Autonomy and teleology came together to form a distinctive ontology of music, a system of beliefs about what music is, that conditioned, and to some degree still conditions, the complete range of musical practices, from composition to performance, from listening to criticism. This is the ontology of autonomist aesthetics, which achieved its purest expression in twentieth-century modernism.

It is also the ontology of traditional musicology, and a concern of recent musicological writing has been to identify and explore the consequences of a shift from the modern to the postmodern, broadly comparable to the shift from the premodern to the modern. For the purposes of this chapter a particularly relevant model of this shift, because it shows how aesthetics, copyright law, and technology work together, comes from outside musicology: Lawrence Lessig's *Remix: Making Art and Commerce Thrive in the Hybrid Economy*. Published the year after Berger's book, the argument of Lessig's book turns on the distinction between what he calls Read/Only (RO) and Read/Write (RW) culture. Read/Only culture broadly maps onto modernist autonomy culture, in which art forms such as music are professionalized, generating commodities (works) designed for appreciation by passive, paying audiences. By contrast, RW culture is predicated on participation: music is conceived not as a collection of fixed works, but rather as a signifying practice in which materials are circulated and reworked in much the same way that ideas are in other domains of culture. Lessig's central premise is that "current copyright law supports the practices of the RO culture and opposes the practices of the RW culture,"[1] and in calling his book *Remix* he pinned RW culture firmly to the musical and audiovisual practices that since the 1980s have become a major legal battleground between the music industry and a new musical public.

According to Lessig, litigation involving remix culture displays all the symptoms of the fundamental miscommunication that happens when different systems of belief collide. This is what the *Annales* historians' concept of different mentalities (such as the "traditional" and the "modern") was designed to address. For Peter Burke, writing in the mid-1980s, different mentalities entail different assumptions, perceptions, and logics, and he comments that scholars from a number of disciplines "have found it impossible to solve their problems without invoking a concept like that of mentality, as opposed to a timeless rationality (which usually turns out to have been defined ethnocentrically)."[2] In this chapter, which is structured around a case study in video mashup, I explore the essential characteristics of what I term "autonomy" and "multimedia" mentalities, before returning in the final section to copyright. In essence, my claim is that there is on the one hand a set of interpretive assumptions and beliefs in terms of which it is natural to think of music as a form of sounded writing, and on the other hand a quite different set of assumptions in terms of which the primacy and performativity of music as multimedia are self-evident—and Lessig's book is symptomatic of a general perception that there has in recent years been a significant shift from the first to the second.

As Lessig makes clear, technology has played an essential role in this shift. The burgeoning of new forms of music production and consumption in which auditory and visual parameters are treated as effectively continuous, as evidenced by the range of screen media, video games, and other multimedia genres, has promoted different ways of experiencing music and of creating music to experience. But technology affords rather than determines social and cultural action, and the history of film demonstrates this. In technological terms, classic Hollywood cinema was the first major manifestation of multimedia. In cultural terms, however, it was in essence a continuation by other means of an existing tradition of authored narrative, just as its music was a continuation by other means of an existing European symphonic tradition. The long-dominant film theory to which it gave rise—according to which directorially authored meaning is inscribed in what William Mitchell calls the imagetext[3] and then expressed or nuanced in the music—is of value precisely insofar as it expresses this cultural framework, thereby functioning as a kind of ethnotheory. That is also why it is not an adequate basis for understanding contemporary multimedia, which has resulted partly from the convergence between audio and video technologies, but more important, from a different cultural framework for the realization of this technological potential.

[1] Lawrence Lessig, *Remix: Making Art and Commerce Thrive in the Hybrid Economy* (New York: Penguin, 2008), 97.

[2] Peter Burke, "Strengths and Weaknesses of the History of Mentalities," *History of European Ideas* 7 (1986): 440.

[3] William Mitchell, *Picture Theory: Essays on Verbal and Visual Representation* (Chicago: Chicago University Press, 1994).

The fundamental difference between autonomy and multimedia mentalities lies in the understanding of meaning. The idea of music as sounded writing went hand in hand with the idea that meaning is inherent, inscribed as writing into a cultural artifact. It was seen as deposited by the author, to be reconstructed in as authentic a manner as possible by the listener, and it is here that the effort to which I referred comes in, as theorized by ideologues of musical self-improvement from the nineteenth-century German music critic Adolph Bernhard Marx to the twentieth-century British educator Percy Scholes. By contrast, the idea of music as performative multimedia goes together with a belief that meaning is negotiated, that it emerges from both media and social interactions and is constituted in the experience of hearing and seeing. Understood this way, cultural artifacts do not "have" meaning, but rather afford constructions of meaning in response to them: meaning is relocated from production to reception. The trend throughout the twentieth century toward increasingly controlled alignment of audio and visual signals, which gave rise to the music video and MTV even before digital technology had fused audio and video into a single stream of information, went hand in hand with a shift in the focus of meaning production from author and text to recipient and multimedia. This illustrates how technologies, media practices, and beliefs about the nature and value of meaning come together to form distinct mentalities.

Mashed Up Meaning

"One of the things we're working with," says Jonny Wilson of the British-born but U.S.-based video mashup trio Eclectic Method, "is like creating a new narrative with video culture for the next generation of people who can perceive multiple channels of information at once." This is multimedia in the obvious, descriptive sense, but it is also multimedia in the deeper sense of a mentality, as expressed by another of the group's members, Ian Edgar: "You're creating a little strange postmodern meaning disintegration structure, where news is instantly disintegrated by adverts, which are equally disintegrated by music, or whatever, and it's all just coming at you."[4] Meaning is negotiated in the act of reception, in the attempt to make some kind of sense of the constant barrage of digital information, and video mashup might be seen as directly embodying such processes of negotiation. Eclectic Method distribute their videos via the online service Vimeo, but they also incorporate them into what the group's Myspace page calls "blistering, post-modern dance floor events,"[5] which exploit recently developed video jockey (VJ) technology (specifically the Pioneer SVM-1000 video mixer). In this way, like all disc jockeys (DJs), they bring the production of meaning into the real time of

[4] Both quotations from "Eclectic Method—Radar Series Documentary Short," at http://vimeo.com/7147850 (accessed May 24, 2011).

[5] http://uk.myspace.com/eclecticmethod (accessed December 7, 2012).

performance: "Like any good DJ," says the third group member, Geoff Gamlen, "we are always looking out for what is working for the audience and adapting our performance to that."[6]

There are two further ways in which video mashup is a good illustration of multimedia mentality. First, it is an excellent example of the convergence between audio and video technology. As explained in Eclectic Method's instructional videos,[7] Sony's Vegas software enables the manipulation of audio and video as in effect a single digital stream quantized and snapped to musical bars and beats. The result is a single, audiovisual compositional process, structured on musical principles, and in that sense more music for the eyes than video for the ears; in Gamlen's words, "getting the underlying music right is the most important thing, so that tends to come first."[8] (It is worth remembering in this context that Eclectic Method create audio as well as video mashups, though it is primarily the latter for which they are known.) Second, mashup—whether audio or video—is a paradigm case of different elements being deployed not in autonomy style, through the creation of discourse hierarchies structured around a primary and in essence narrative meaning, but in multimedia style, through continuous collisions or negotiations among heterogeneous elements, giving rise to meanings that are emergent, unpredictable, and frequently ineffable.

Such collage-like processes of meaning generation are perhaps most easily analyzed in terms of Eclectic Method's mashups based on filmed musical performances. Their 2009 mashup *Beyoncé VS Lynyrd Skynyrd*[9] is based on Beyoncé's award-winning music video "Single Ladies (Put a Ring on It)" from the previous year, directed by Jake Nava and shot in black and white, which features the singer with two look-alike dancers,[10] and on two filmed performances by Lynyrd Skynyrd of "Sweet Home Alabama," the first from their appearance on the *Old Grey Whistle Test* in 1975,[11] two years before the plane crash that killed three members of the band and resulted in a 10-year hiatus, and the second from 2003.[12] As with all mashups, we experience each song through the other: in what I see as a basic principle of multimedia, the commensurability in certain parameters between the songs that makes the mashup musically viable has at the same time the effect of throwing into relief the elements of acoustic, visual, and semantic friction between them.

The superimposition of the songs (coupled with a slight speeding-up of "Single Ladies") foregrounds both the almost insane hyperactivity of Beyoncé's routine, with its elaborate

6 "Video Mashup Masters Eclectic Method Amoeblog Interview," at http://www.amoeba.com/blog/2009/07/jamoeblog/video-mashup-masters-eclectic-method-amoeblog-interview.html (accessed May 24, 2011).

7 See, for example, "HOW TO Remix Video," at http://www.youtube.com/watch?v=gqmdB4Uvd8E (accessed May 24, 2011).

8 "Video Mashup Masters Interview."

9 http://www.youtube.com/watch?v=tinOCcOzLf4 (accessed May 24, 2011).

10 Issued by Sony BMG, at http://www.youtube.com/watch?v=4m1EFMoRFvY (accessed May 24, 2011).

11 See, for example, http://www.youtube.com/watch?v=IwWUOmk7wOo (accessed May 24, 2011).

12 The Vicious Cycle Tour, Nashville, at http://www.youtube.com/watch?v=XzbdY_rPtjw (accessed May 24, 2011).

look-alike choreography and manufactured hip gyrations and by contrast, the impeccably naturalistic, laid-back quality of Lynyrd Skynyrd's stage presence. The mashup begins with Lynyrd Skynyrd before the Beyoncé visuals are faded in. For a moment we might see them in terms of a single diegesis, as a ludicrously inappropriate dance routine for "Sweet Home Alabama," with the ludicrousnesss measuring the cultural gulf between the two acts. On a more moment-to-moment level, elements that might normally be heard as just part of a stylistic complex obtrude on one's consciousness, heard from unfamiliar angles as it were, defamiliarized. An example is Beyoncé's repeated pitch inflections on the "club" and "up" of "Up in the club we just broke up," the effect of which becomes grotesque, almost uncanny. There are times (such as from 0'49", where the visuals dominated by Beyoncé coincide with Billy Powell's country-style piano) when the perceptual, cognitive, and connotational dissonance between the elements stretches the blend to a breaking point. For some YouTube viewers this goes beyond the bounds of generic acceptability. The Spawn of Skynyd posts, "Owww!!! That doesn't match up." alanlaing responds, "and anyone who has ever been a DJ can tell this is not beat matched... actually hurts my ears it is so out of time ;-)" and insists that the attribution of *Beyoncé VS Lynyrd Skynyrd* to Eclectic Method must be wrong: "this is no Eclectic Method because... Eclectic Method know what they are doing... awful awful awful."[13]

As my reference to blend might suggest, one way to think of all this is in terms of Mark Turner's and Gilles Fauconnier's conceptual blending theory,[14] according to which different conceptual spaces align with one another, resulting in a cross-flow of qualities between them. Seen this way, the sharing of timing, harmonic, and other structural elements in *Beyoncé VS Lynyrd Skynyrd* results in a combined semantic space that is complex and paradoxical. A comment by whitegorilla70 reflects just such a process of cross-mapping: "love this mix. skynrd never sounded so sexy." (Beyoncé's and her co-dancers' sexuality is mapped onto Lynyrd Skynyrd, therefore being experienced contrafactually as an attribute of the band.) But I have in mind two other aspects of the connotational blend: between the aural and visual signifiers of authenticity of 1970s rock and the commercialism of 2000s girl group culture, and between a song by a white Southern rock group that still stirs historical and racial controversy[15] and one by a

[13] http://www.youtube.com/all_comments?v=tinOCcOzLf4 (accessed May 24, 2011).

[14] For an introduction in relation to music, see Lawrence Zbikowski, *Conceptualizing Music: Cognitive Structure, Theory, and Analysis* (New York: Oxford University Press, 2005).

[15] The following comments (continuing a previous exchange) were posted at http://www.youtube.com/all_comments?v=IwWUOmk7wOo during the three days before I first accessed it on April 14, 2010:

cessnawings67: If my Flag offends you then you can kiss my Rebel Ass!!!!!!

TheAlice1865: wve it with pride as you should it was abaout states rights but you were traitors and we defeated you/and we did nto fight for blacks no more then you did/we fouyght to presreve the USA AND DONT FORGET IT/!!!!

KittyAllChainedUp: THE SOUTH WAS FULL OF HEROES; NOT TRAITORS. THE YANKEES WANTED TO CHANGE THE CONSTITUTION, NOT US PROUD ORIGINAL AMERICANS./YOU WOULD BE CALLING WASHINGTON AND JEFFERSON TRAITORS IF WE HAD LOST THE REVOLUTION TO THE BRITISH.

bobdewild [replying to TheAlice1865]: you say WE but i dont think you really fought in the war did you?

massively successful black singer from Texas that has been celebrated as a symbol of female empowerment. In a YouTube posting flagged as spam, Banana Breakable writes, "how dare you put damn niggers in a video with lynyrd skynyrd! southern disgrace!"

Although mashup has unrivaled power to force connections between disparate ideas, reference to defamiliarization suggests another, in some ways more revealing, way to think about this: in terms of surrealist collage or Russian formalist montage. Autonomy-based analytical methods are based on the identification of wholes: linear-harmonic analysis, for example, represents compositions as hierarchies of unified elements, from the level of motif or phrase to an entire movement. Such approaches de-emphasize the transitions between wholes, and yet the increasingly influential concatenationist approach to listening implies that edge relations and juxtapositions are largely responsible for musical effects of meaning.[16] Like the juxtapositions that the surrealists used to release irrational psychic contents, so the layers of *Beyoncé VS Lynyrd Skynyrd* grate against one another in an almost literal version of Eisenstein's "vertical montage," releasing meaning that is palpable and yet hard to put into words.

If *Beyoncé VS Lynyrd Skynyrd* illustrates the second of my points about video mashups, the release of emergent meaning through friction or collision between media elements, then my first point—about audio and video being embraced in a single compositional process—is illustrated by Eclectic Method's film mashups, of which I discuss here just one, the *Tarantino Mixtape* (2009).[17] Quentin Tarantino may be a Hollywood product, but his work embodies many of the attributes I have ascribed to multimedia mentality. The entry for Tarantino in an electronic encyclopedia published in 2007[18] describes him as "an auteur indie filmmaker whose films used postmodern nonlinear storylines, and stylized violence interwoven with often-obscure cinematic references," and I explore each of these three attributes in turn. An example of Tarantino's nonlinear story lines is *Pulp Fiction* (1994), made up of a number of distinct narrative strands, of which one—about Pumpkin and Honey Bunny staging a holdup in a diner—appears in the prologue and the epilogue of the film; in fact we see the same scene unfolding in both of them, incorporating some of the same footage.

This forms the basis of one section of Eclectic Method's mashup, the first few seconds of which (from 5'20") are taken straight from the film. Eclectic Method's repetitive editing and patterning of the images in effect "musicalize" the film extract; the images are coordinated with the regular meter of the music (mainly taken from the credits sequence, which immediately follows this passage in the prologue). That, at its simplest, is what I mean by a single compositional process encompassing both audio and

16 For the argument about collage and montage see Nicholas Cook, "Uncanny Moments: Juxtaposition and the Collage Principle in Music," in *Approaches to Meaning in Music*, ed. Byron Almén and Edward Pearsall (Bloomington: Indiana University Press, 2006); for concatenationism see Jerrold Levinson, *Music in the Moment* (Ithaca, N.Y.: Cornell University Press, 1998).

17 http://vimeo.com/4368246 (accessed May 24, 2011).

18 *Encyclopedia of American Cinema for Smartphones and Mobile Devices* (Boston: MobileReference, 2007).

video—extending Mitchell's usage, what one might call musicimage text. In my book *Analysing Musical Multimedia*[19] I traced the progressive extension of musical principles of construction into the visual domain from early animations such as Disney's *Silly Symphonies* and *Fantasia* up to rap videos, but the work of Eclectic Method is a more extreme example of music for the eyes than anything in my book. This musicalization of film materials by composing them into the groove could be seen as extending the non-linear, or cyclical, time of Tarantino's original film into its moment-to-moment continuity: Eclectic Method extract and concentrate a key aspect of their source material. The resonance with Bach's cycle prompts the thought—to which I shall return—that there are aspects of multimedia mentality that are as much premodern as postmodern.

Eclectic Method's musicalization of film has further effects, which I discuss in relation to another section of the *Tarantino Mixtape*. This starts at 2'43" and is mainly based on *Reservoir Dogs* (1992), which is about a botched jewel robbery. One of Eclectic Method's techniques is to link clips from different films through what are in narrative terms purely incidental, meaningless connections. The mixtape begins with a series of clips in which people are talking on phones, while the section based on *Reservoir Dogs* begins with alternating clips from different films of car trunks being opened. These "horizontal" connections, running "perpendicularly" to the films' already problematized narrative hierarchies, serve to further subvert them. But the processes of musicalization, which are considerably more complex here than in the section based on *Pulp Fiction*, do the same thing in a more radical way. The clips of opening trunks are followed by a long passage built around guns, beginning with the cocking of a gun lifted out of one of the car trunks, then the cocking of a handgun; in both cases the sound of cocking is assimilated into and elaborated by the audio track. This is followed by an extended passage held together by a gunshot that fractures a car windshield on the second and fourth beats of each bar, and finally by vocal imitations of gunshots synchronized with the 4/4 groove.

All this relates to the second attribute the electronic encyclopedia ascribes to Tarantino: his use of "stylized violence." Tarantino's advocacy of film violence is notorious. When he appeared in January 2010 at the British Academy of Film and Television Artists (BAFTA), he declared, "I'm a big fan of action and violence in cinema.... That's why Thomas Edison created the motion picture camera—because violence is so good. It affects audiences in a big way. You know you're watching a movie."[20] And it is in terms of stylization that Tarantino's apologists defend him: in Xavier Morales's words, Tarantino "presents violence as a form of expressive art," in which "the violence is so physically graceful, visually dazzling and meticulously executed that our instinctual, emotional responses undermine any rational objections we may have. Tarantino is able to transform an object of moral outrage into one of aesthetic beauty."[21] The filmmaker is thus

[19] Nicholas Cook, *Analysing Musical Multimedia* (Oxford: Oxford University Press, 1998).

[20] http://www.thisislondon.co.uk/standard/article-23793981-quentin-tarantino-violence-is-what-makes-movies-good.do (accessed May 24, 2011).

[21] Xavier Morales, "Kill Bill: Beauty and Violence," *Harvard Law Record*, October 16, 2003, at http://hlrecord.org/?p=11285 (accessed December 7, 2012).

a major presence in the current debate about the role of violence in entertainment, on one side of which is the view that violent films and video games normalize or even advocate violence; on the other side is the assertion that such representations of violence are purely symbolic and understood as such by viewers and players. Jeffrey Goldstein notes in support of the latter position that violence is only entertaining if it is marked as artifice: "It must carry cues to its unreality—music, sound effects, a fantasy storyline, cartoon characters. People are highly selective in the violence they seek or tolerate."[22]

So where do Eclectic Method stand on this? A case could be constructed for placing them in either camp. On the one hand, their treatment of the Tarantino clips, pulling out the gun episodes and collecting them like some people collect pornography, might be seen as going even further than Tarantino in aestheticizing and so normalizing the psychopathology that gave rise to the Columbine and Jokela massacres. On the other hand, their musicalization of the gunplay, subjecting it to repetition and formal patterning, might be seen as not only further marking it as artifice, but also bringing out its inherent absurdity and thereby ridiculing the American gun cult in general. (Remember, they're British.) But it is one of the joys of working with Web-based multimedia that we can go beyond this kind of critical interpretation: What do the commentaries posted on Vimeo and YouTube tell us about how viewers construe Eclectic Method's stance?[23] As this chapter goes to press, there are 194 comments about the mixtape on Vimeo and 174 on YouTube. Of these, just two refer to violence. intavent writes that "the part with the shootings sums up to me about his films that dance along the line of commercial appeal and gratuitous violence. great work." And Paulina Plezia complains, "way to[o] many heads being smashed," but then adds, "Great work on editing though Eclectic Method."

If viewers of the *Tarantino Mixtape* seem generally unconcerned about the violence, what do they comment on? Whereas there is an occasional critical posting (Shawn Chapelle writes: "'cliche' addled—like shooting fish in a barrel—rhythmic editing of stuff like this is past tired!"), the vast majority of postings are unalloyed expressions of praise, sometimes specifically for the editing, but usually more generalized (a representative sample: "Woooow man is soooooooooooo cool !!!"; "I do believe this is the coolest thing I have ever seen."; "Fuck a duck!! Wow…"; "My computer just had an orgasm."; "This is probably Eclectic Method's best in terms of musicality."; " I LOVE THIS! OMG I'm officially in love with you!"). The Vimeo page records 3,994 likes, while on YouTube—where 87,415 views are recorded—there are 849 likes to only 6 dislikes.[24] But a particular focus of interest is the relationship between the mixtape and the films. Many postings, like intavent's, display knowledge of Tarantino: Peter Lo writes, "Excellent! I find that that sums up the Tarantino experience rather well," while

22 Jeffrey Goldstein, "Violent Video Games," in *Handbook of Computer Game Studies*, ed. Joost Raessens and Jeffrey Goldstein (Cambridge, Mass.: MIT Press, 2005), 353.

23 http://vimeo.com/4368246?pg=embed&sec=&hd=1, http://www.youtube.com/all_comments?v=uEIPCOwY4DE (accessed May 24, 2011); there are multiple copies of the Tarantino Mixtape on YouTube but this one has the lion's share of views, comments, and ratings.

24 Statistics correct as of December 7, 2012.

thejoempoem comments, "great mash-up—and somehow stays real true to Tarantino in the process." Indeed, CypherVirus says, "I suddenly have the urge to re-watch every Tarantino movie ever made." Just one commentator, Sharee Anne Gorman, feels that the mixtape undersells Tarantino: "I enjoy deconstructionism/reconstructionism (with a great soundtrack) as much as the next person but I feel Tarantino films are greater than the sum of their parts. You have a wonderful eye and great sense of flow but there is a point of view that is lost when context is lost."

Few viewers engage in this kind of critical commentary, but many enjoy tracking down the sources used in the mixtape. Several ask for a playlist, and queries about where specific parts of the mixtape come from attract prompt replies from other viewers. The intertextual pleasure afforded by the mixtape resonates with the third attribute ascribed to Tarantino in the electronic encyclopedia: his "often obscure cinematic references." Once again Eclectic Method intensify what Tarantino does: the *Tarantino Mixtape* piles intertext on intertext. It is made up of Tarantino clips, which themselves not only reference other films but also repurpose preexisting film music, particularly Morricone's. Eclectic Method incorporate materials from their mashups, including the *Tarantino Mixtape*, into live performances, looping or otherwise manipulating them to provide a further level of musicalization—and there is yet another twist when recordings of these performances are reconstructed as videos for their Web site. This is intertextual play at its most extravagant, and the rich layering of sounds, visual patterns, and easily assimilable connotations is such that one can become drawn into Eclectic Method's film mashups without actually knowing the films on which they are based, in that sense having no idea what the mixtape is all about.

But then, how far does it make sense to adopt traditional film-critical or hermeneutic approaches to productions like the *Tarantino Mixtape*, seeking to extract from them the kind of meaning that can be translated into words? Perhaps the simplest way to answer this question is to compare Eclectic Method with the much longer established dance music duo Coldcut, with which Jonny Wilson was at one time associated.[25] Coldcut's video *Re:volution*,[26] released during the run-up to the British general election of 2001, juxtaposes clips from speeches by Tony Blair and other politicians with newspaper headlines about corruption and sleaze, attacking the hypocrisy of the political establishment. So does *World of Evil*,[27] a collaboration between Coldcut and the Los Angeles–based video performance artist TV Sheriff timed to coincide with the American election of 2004. In both cases video mashup techniques are used to create a message that cannot be mistaken and could easily be put into words. An obvious Eclectic Method comparison might be *The New Puppy*,[28] based on Obama's acceptance speech, in which he promised his daughters a new puppy to come with them to the White House. The production of this music-free video is characteristically slick; there is a constant undercurrent of

[25] "Video Mashup Masters Interview."
[26] http://www.youtube.com/watch?v=S6KnJok_u7w (accessed May 24, 2011).
[27] http://www.youtube.com/watch?v=_2fdeNRvieU (accessed May 24, 2011).
[28] http://vimeo.com/2226477 (accessed May 24, 2011).

farce, not least as a result of Eclectic Method's editorial interventions (Obama repeatedly refers to "a government of the puppy, by the puppy, and for the puppy"). But compared to Coldcut's work the message is at most a gentle satire on the juxtaposition of political high-mindedness and highly mediatized family values. In fact, by the time it has been put into words, there is hardly a message at all.

My point is that this is not a very productive way to think about Eclectic Method. A much more characteristic and informative example of how meaning emerges from their work might be *Beat the Baby*, in which clips of a baby on a mat, in a high chair, and in the garden are subjected to the usual Eclectic Method treatment.[29] Compared to the Coldcut videos with their explicit political message, the overt content of *Beat the Baby* could not be more innocuous, and the majority of YouTube comments say how cute it is (the highest rated comment, from bellchap, reads: "this... was... the CUTEST VIDEO EVER!!").[30] But there are some dissenters: jvnorris writes, "Its creepy and cool all at the same time... kinda like that stalker back in 98," whereas for TKSRedpanda, "The music is fine but the footage of the babies are kind of creepy and weird." I too find the video disturbing. There is the same effect of the uncanny that I noted in relation to *Beyoncé VS Lynyrd Skynyrd*, of a meaning that can't quite be put into words but has something to do with the reification or commodification of innocence. It brings to light a conceptual dissonance between babies and adult culture, prompting questions about how we relate to babies, about who or what we think they are. As I said previously, it forces connections between ideas and values that we normally keep apart.

In summary, the meaning of Eclectic Method's work is less discursive than performative, not inherent but negotiated through interactions between different media on the one hand, and between musical patterning and intertextual references on the other. Or better, it is a multiple negotiation involving not only media traces, but also Eclectic Method as mediators and performers, together with viewers and interpreters with their various backgrounds, experiences, and interests. And as in all multiply interactive systems, changes in any of these elements result in a combinatorial explosion of possible outcomes; this is the theoretical reason for describing the meaning of multimedia as emergent—as unpredictable as the British weather and for essentially the same reason. It is also why, as in surrealist collage, meaning seems to emerge of its own accord, independent of anyone's expectations. In this way, whereas Coldcut express political commentary through multimedia, Eclectic Method deal in meanings that emerge in the real time of multimedia interaction and cannot be adequately translated back into verbal discourse. Only if we look for a position on issues such as violence or social attitudes toward babies, in the same way that Coldcut have a position on politics, will we conclude, with Vimeo commentator Alejandro Cock-Pelaez, that the *Tarantino Mixtape* "hasn't point of view." (But he immediately adds, "Nevertheless it has a lot of ritm, and visuals.")

29 http://www.youtube.com/watch?v=7q2MgeJTNrw (accessed May 24, 2011).

30 http://www.youtube.com/all_comments?v=7q2MgeJTNrw (accessed May 24, 2011).

Merleau-Ponty had a memorable image for this kind of meaning: "Like the weaver," he said, "the writer works on the wrong side of his material. He has to do only with language, and it is thus that he suddenly finds himself surrounded by meaning."[31] But as implied by Merleau-Ponty's reference to language—or my references to surrealism—such processes of meaning production predate multimedia technology. Might we not want to claim that Beethoven had to do only with notes and suddenly found himself surrounded by meaning? And in that case, doesn't the whole project of distinguishing autonomy and multimedia mentalities set up a reductive, binary-ridden image of music history, in which the ascription of performative, ineffable meaning to contemporary multimedia shoehorns the classical music tradition into a narrowly textualist stereotype? I concede that there is a problem here, but it does not lie in the attempt to formulate the more or less coherent and distinct conceptual systems that I term autonomy and multimedia mentality; it lies in the mapping of these mentalities onto the history of music. Lessig's use of the term "remix" to characterize RW culture has helped sell his message, but at the expense of encouraging the misperception that RW is the culture of today and RO the culture of yesterday. This is a misperception not only because many aspects of RO culture continue today, but also because Lessig specifically emphasizes the RW dimension of past culture. Indeed, he begins his book with the image of John Philip Sousa, in 1906, gloomily predicting the demise of participant musical culture as a consequence of mechanical sound reproduction. For Lessig, performance, which has always involved selection and often arrangement, is the RW dimension of traditional musical cultures, both "art" and popular. His argument is that the multimedia remixing practices afforded by digital technology are no different in principle from traditional forms of cultural participation, yet they are treated quite differently in the courts.

Just like Lessig's RO culture, the regime of the musical work as theorized by Goehr has been much too readily mapped onto historical periodization. I mentioned the musicological objections to her version of history; these include both examples of the work concept before 1800 and musical practices after 1800 that were not regulated by the work concept. Jim Samson, for example, has documented the existence of two quite distinct traditions in nineteenth-century pianism, one focused around faithful reproduction of the work and the other around virtuosity and the performance event.[32] But the point can be most forcefully made through direct evidence of participant culture in classical music during the supposed heyday of the autonomy regime. The *Hofmeister Monatsberichte*, a series of monthly catalogs initiated in 1829 by the Leipzig-based publisher Friedrich Hofmeister, represent the most comprehensive inventory of nineteenth-century sheet music.[33] The works we know today appear, of course. But they are swamped by a tsunami of arrangements and adaptations—occasionally of works we know, usually of ones

[31] Maurice Merleau-Ponty, *Signs* (Evanston, Ill.: Northwestern University Press, 1964), 45.

[32] Jim Samson, "The Practice of Early-Nineteenth-Century Pianism," in *The Musical Work: Reality or Invention?* ed. Michael Talbot (Liverpool: University of Liverpool Press, 2000).

[33] Rudolf Elvers and Cecil Hopkinson, "A Survey of the Music Catalogues of Whistling and Hofmeister," *Fontes Artis Musicae* 19 (1972): 1–7.

we don't—for such musical forces as cane flute; pedal piano; or an ensemble comprising physharmonica, harmonic flute, and accordion. Such traces of nineteenth-century remix culture evidence the coexistence of two quite distinct conceptions of what music is. Seeing nineteenth-century music solely in terms of RO culture results in a highly skewed understanding: concepts essential to that mentality—autonomy, the musical work, genius, and so forth—were indeed formulated in extreme forms during that century, but they circulated within the highly eclectic culture made visible by its architecture. Only with twentieth-century modernism did these concepts condense into a more or less closed belief system to which alternatives were not recognized, meaning that classical music became identified with RO culture, an identification cemented by the government subsidies for professional orchestras and opera houses that became widespread after 1945. (Lessig locates the high point of RO culture in the 1970s.[34])

This explains the sense that the ostensibly postmodern multimedia mentality is in some way continuous with the premodern. But here, too, the implicit periodization should be resisted. What I have called autonomy and multimedia mentalities are alternative systems for the conceptualization and practice of music, the difference between which is ultimately ontological: autonomy mentality is based on understanding music as a thing, multimedia mentality on understanding it as an experience. By giving them these labels I have associated these systems with specific historical junctures. But they might be better thought of as permanent possibilities for the construal of music, not so much mutually exclusive systems of belief as metaphorical constructions between which it is in principle possible to switch at will. One or the other, however, may be predominant in particular areas of musical culture or at particular times and places, while factors of institutionalization or ideology may constrain the possibility of switching between them: that is why I said 'in principle'. Returning to surrealism and *Lynyrd Skynyrd VS Beyoncé*, the increase during the twentieth century in the prominence of emergent modes of meaning production is symbolized by the contrast between an avant-garde movement with very limited impact outside admittedly influential critical circles on the one hand, and on the other hand the mass circulation and consumption of Internet-based multimedia. And in the final section I discuss a conspicuous example of what happens when institutionalization transforms a metaphorical construction into an ideology.

Contested Ownerships

Multimedia is also, of course, implicated in many other radical effects, which I can discuss only superficially. Typically the effect of new technologies can be categorized into two stages. The initial effect is to extend the scope of existing practices. I have already referred to film in this context; another example is the gramophone, listening to which in the early days frequently took the form of a public performance (audiences

34 Lessig, *Remix*, 263 (he links this with the abolition in 1976 of the U.S. system of opt-in copyright).

clapped). Even after the gramophone was firmly ensconced in the home, it remained a surrogate for the concert-hall experience, while listening to music on headphones in a darkened room is arguably a more complete expression of the aesthetics of autonomy than anything the modernist concert hall can offer. At the second stage, cultural practices are transformed, or new practices created. Mobile playback technologies, piloted by audio-only MP3s but now multimedia equipped, have reengineered the personal and social consumption of music: traditional work-based listening (including its rock derivative, album-based listening), for which music was primarily an expression of the personality of its creator or creators, has largely given way to playlist-based listening. Music is fragmented into individual movements or tracks or abstracted into genre categories, and the combinatorics of track and genre, together with their incorporation into everyday life, become crucial dimensions of the production of musical meaning. In Tia DeNora's phrase, these are technologies of the self, apparatuses for the construction and negotiation of individual and group identity. As an updated version of the appropriative practices described by Dick Hebdige in relation to the punks,[35] such digital bricolage is perhaps the most overt illustration of the core precept of multimedia mentality, that meaning emerges at the point of reception.

It is obvious that the Internet lies at the heart of group identity formation in the digital age, but again a distinction needs to be made between the extension of existing practices (as in the case of eBay) and the creation of new ones (as in the case of YouTube, which has fundamentally reconfigured the social use and signifying potential of video). There is also an important distinction to be made between synchronous and asynchronous Web practices. YouTube videos encapsulate moments from the past: they are shot, then uploaded. Concerts in Second Life create new, geographically dispersed communities, but they are not musically mediated: the streamed music may be live (though often it is not), but the technology does not support real-time interaction, at least not at the temporal resolution necessary for musical performance, and so the music is not made in-world.[36] By contrast, telematic performances mediated by the Web enable musicians in diverse locations to play together in real time (at least in theory, though bandwidth constraints frequently force compromises or workarounds). But for David Borgo, telematic performance is only the first stage in the more thoroughgoing realization of the potential of Web technology that he terms "transmusicking," which "can involve sound sources from artists musicking, ambient sounds or archives, all blended, transformed and transmitted over any distance, obscuring categorical distinctions between real-time and recorded or between sites of creation and sites of (re)production." In this way transmusicking "challenges conventional notions of artwork, artist, and audience: it works

[35] Dick Hebdige, *Subculture: The Meaning of Style* (London: Methuen, 1979).

[36] I have set out this argument at greater length in "Music and the Politics of Space," in *Music, Sound, and Space: Transformations of Public and Private Experience*, ed. Georgina Born (Cambridge: Cambridge University Press, 2013).

between and not simply with different media."[37] (It has often been observed that what we call multimedia might be better called intermedia.)

The fusing of Borgo's transmusicking and virtual reality technology to create multimediated virtual communities lies in the future, but some of their features are surely anticipated in the virtual communities that exist today. Such communities can be seen as collectively performing identity, rather in the way that "British" is a performed identity, and in either case identity is relational. Identities mediated by virtual communities proliferate and overlap, rendering normal an experience of plural identity that at one time was uncommon outside diasporic circles, just as to be British is to position oneself in relation not only to non-British but also to specifically British others. In the same way, playlist culture has turned "music" into a relational entity, with Western "art" music becoming a niche genre defined by its relationship to other genres, no longer an absolute, no longer *die Musik*—a concept which, in Philip Bohlman's words, "derives its contextual referentiality from German history and the hegemonic imagination necessary for the generation of nineteenth-century Romanticism,"[38] or as I would say, of autonomy mentality. And though meaning may be generated by playlist combinatoriality, it is also generated by the way relational identities grate against one another, much in the manner of the Lynyrd Skynyrd/Beyoncé mashup, as good a symbol as any of multimedia mentality.

In this way, cultural practices and technologies are again underpinned, given meaning, by the larger conceptual frameworks that I have called mentalities. Contemporary musicology has already gone some way toward accommodating multimedia mentality, most fundamentally through its shift in emphasis from composition and texts to performance and reception as key sites for the production of meaning, through its shift from a belief in naturally grounded essences to a reflexive and relational approach that invokes biological or other external constraints only when social constructionist accounts fail, and through its engagement with the cultural affordances of technology and the development of multimedia studies. Perhaps musicology's blind spot has been its readiness to see this new conception as somehow ethically superior to former musicological approaches, now regarded as not just old but discredited. As I have suggested, this can amount to a kind of colonization of the old by the new, whereas to think in terms of different mentalities may make it easier to maintain a balance between contemporary sense-making and evidence-based historicism.

But the most spectacular collision between established traditions of interpretation and multimedia mentality has taken place in a sphere that I have repeatedly but only lightly touched on, copyright. This collision has such deep roots that it is necessary to step back and ask a fundamental question: What makes it possible for music to be

[37] David Borgo, "Transmusicking in Cyberspace," in *Taking it to the Bridge: Music as Performance*, ed. Nicholas Cook and Richard Pettengill (Ann Arbor: Michigan University Press, forthcoming).

[38] Philip Bohlman, "Ontologies of Music," in *Rethinking Music*, ed. Nicholas Cook and Mark Everist (Oxford: Oxford University Press), 26.

owned, and even more important (since the primary purpose of copyright has always been to protect the interests of investors rather than creators), for its ownership to be assignable? Historically, what made music ownable and assignable was an authoritative and supposedly comprehensive representation in the form of a commodity into which meaning was understood to be inscribed, deposited by its creator. This role was fulfilled by the score, supplemented during the twentieth century by audio and later video recordings—so that once again it is not the technological medium that matters so much as the conceptual framework, the core of which lies in the idea of creative origination that forms the foundation of the entire edifice of intellectual property.

As Jason Toynbee, Lionel Bently, Keith Sawyer, and others have pointed out, copyright law has its basis in the romantic idea that originality should be an all-or-nothing property: original music should owe nothing to its predecessors, should be fully the work of its creator. But this never was or could be really the case. Even classical music of the autonomy tradition operated through the repurposing of public-domain elements, ranging from formal prototypes and referential topics to popular operatic tunes of that day. The law also makes a strong presumption that authorship is undivided, the expression of an individual, inspired vision. In the British case *Hadley v. Kemp* (1999), three members of Spandau Ballet made a claim for rights in the band's songs against the fourth, the singer/songwriter Gary Kemp, on the grounds that the songs were composed collaboratively. Justice Park rejected the claim on grounds that might have come out of an old-fashioned music appreciation text: "A composer can 'hear' the sound of his composition in his mind before he ever hears it played. Beethoven could hear his music in this sense even when he was deaf."[39] This obviously begs the issue of the applicability to a late twentieth-century band of principles drawn from Beethoven: songs' most distinctive features frequently evolve as bands work together on them, sometimes in collaboration with the producer,[40] just as many "art" composers have worked in close collaboration with performers in developing their instrumental or vocal style. It is difficult, in short, to quarrel with Rosemary Coombe's conclusion: "Perhaps no area of human creativity relies more heavily on appropriation and allusion, borrowing and imitation, sampling and intertextual commentary than music, nor any area where the mythic figure of the creative genius composing in the absence of all external influence is more absurd."[41]

[39] Quoted in Anne Barron, "Introduction: Harmony or Dissonance? Copyright Concepts and Musical Practice," *Social and Legal Studies* 15, no. 1 (2006): 29. Earlier Park J said: "We have all seen imaginative sketches of the great classical composers of the past sitting at their desks in what one imagines might be an attic, quill pens in hand and sheafs of musical papers before them, writing out their compositions by hand"; apart from the proverbial attic, this is an exact description of Batt's (Oswald Barrett's) drawing *Beethoven Nears the End*, plate 14 in *The Oxford Companion to Music*, ed. Percy Scholes (London: Oxford University Press, 1938).

[40] For detailed examples see Mike Howlett, *The Record Producer: A Nexus of Technology and Creative Inspiration* (PhD diss., University of Glamorgan, 2009).

[41] In her foreword ("Making Music in the Soundscapes of the Law") to *Steal This Music: How International Property Law Affects Musical Creativity*, by Joanna Demers (Athens: University of Georgia Press, 2006), ix.

But in terms of the practical operation of the law, the crunch issue is the way in which originality is conceived as an attribute of musical works, with the musical work frequently being identified in the most literal manner with its notational expression. Copyright law recognizes the contribution of both performers and producers of recordings through performing, broadcast, and mechanical rights, but these subsidiary rights have nothing to do with originality and are much less valuable than rights in the work; that was the point of *Hadley*. The distinction between rights in the work and in the recording also lies behind the American case *Newton v. Diamonte et al.* (aka The Beastie Boys), which took place in 2002 and has attracted studies by Jason Toynbee and Eric Lewis.[42] This case involved the use in a Beastie Boys song ("Pass the Mic") of a six-second sample from James Newton's "Choir" as recorded by the composer—an Afro-American musician widely regarded as the world's leading jazz flautist—on his album *Axum*. The Beastie Boys had obtained clearance for subsidiary rights, but not for rights in the work, and consequently the case focused on those respects in which Newton's work might be considered original. The judgment went against Newton, on the grounds that "[a] musical composition consists of rhythm, harmony, and melody, and it is from these elements that originality is to be determined."[43] Seen in these terms, the sample consisted merely of Newton singing the notes C-Db-C while fingering a C on the flute. Newton's claim was that, in the words of the written judgment, the Beastie Boys "also sampled the unique musical sound and characteristics created by his distinct performance technique." But the judge's identification of musical ownability and notation was so deeply embedded in her thinking that, as Lewis points out, she simply did not understand this claim, as revealed by a footnote: "Plaintiff inexplicably disputes Defendants' proposed uncontroverted fact concerning the notes they sampled."

Newton was not, of course, disputing the notes. He was claiming that originality subsisted not in the notes but in the complex of harmonics and multiphonics that resulted from his distinctive playing technique (which is why the Beastie Boys used the sample in the first place). Seen this way, originality becomes an attribute of performance. By contrast, the judge's position is a parody of Hanslickian formalism, according to which music is reduced to writing. There is an uncomfortable resonance here with the racial opposition that pervades the discourses around jazz between what Ben Sidran calls "oral" and "literate" man.[44] The identification of the musical work with writing is being presented as a self-evident expression of the "timeless rationality" to which Burke referred, but as Lewis says, "[T]his position is prejudicial to those, often from minority cultures, working in non-Western musical forms.... [A] racist and classist

[42] Jason Toynbee, "Copyright, the Work, and Phonographic Orality in Music," *Social and Legal Studies* 15 (2006): 77–99, Eric Lewis, "Ontology, Originality and the Musical Work: Copyright Law and the Status of Samples," in *Meredith Lectures 2006: Intellectual Property at the Edge: New Approaches to IP in a Transsystemic World*, ed. Faculty of Law, McGill University (Montréal: Editions Yvon Blais, 2007).

[43] Quoted by Judge Nora Manella, from Melville Nimmer and David Nimmer, *Nimmer on Copyright* (Albany, N.Y.: Matthew Bender, 1997), the definitive textbook on the subject (originally published in 1963).

[44] Ben Sidran, *Black Talk: How the Music of Black America Created a Radical Alternative to the Values of Western Literary Tradition* (New York: Holt, Rinehart and Winston, 1971).

practice and law here attempts to hide its exclusionary nature behind a metaphysics of the musical work which purports to be objective and universal, but in fact is not."[45] It is here that the ideological dimension of the mentality that underpins copyright law becomes most obvious.

In jazz improvisation—the tradition from which Newton comes—originality might be said to lie in everything *except* the printed notes, and in an appeal for support published on the *All About Jazz* Web site following the trial, Newton himself complained: "The judge consistently used European paradigms to judge my music."[46] But the interconnection of music, copyright, and race is a much broader phenomenon. It emerges explicitly in something that Paul Mac (of the Australian band The Dissociatives) told Phillip McIntyre:

> We both wrote the music from the chords and everything. But, I think those definitions are so old-fashioned. I think it was James Brown's quote, "well hang on, it's such a white way of looking at it". You can't copyright a waveline or a drum beat because it's always the melody that's deemed to be the thing of value. I think songwriting is not just melody, words and chords. It's also a headspace.[47]

According to Veit Erlmann, when South African *mbube* musicians discuss the distinguishing characteristics of their songs, they refer to such things as texture, vocal parts, dance, and dress code.[48] That is not to say that they have no conception of musical ownership (Erlmann cites a song by the King Boys in which they condemn the cowardice of another choir in stealing their songs), but it is associated with the practice of *mbube* performance, rather than with surrogate objects in which originality is thought to be inscribed.

Erlmann's discussion of a concept of musical ownership quite different from that embodied in copyright acts as a useful corrective to idealistic images of music as something that lies beyond ownership, as epitomized by Herbie Hancock's "brothers kind of thing"[49] or more

[45] Lewis, "Ontology, Originality and the Musical Work," 182.

[46] "From James Newton (Renowned Jazz Musician)," August 23, 2002, at http://www.allaboutjazz.com/php/news.php?id=1682 (accessed May 24, 2011).

[47] Phillip McIntyre, "Copyright and Creativity: Changing Paradigms and the Implications for Intellectual Property and the Music Industry," *Media International Australia Incorporating Culture and Policy* 123 (2007): 88.

[48] Veit Erlmann, "Music as Law: 'The Lion King', Counterfeit and Intellectual Property Rights" (paper delivered at the University of Cambridge, February 24, 2010). *Mbube* is the a capella choral tradition popularized by Ladysmith Black Mambazo. Erlmann's larger argument parallels Lewis's: cases like the Linda family's successful suit against the Disney Corporation for misappropriating "The Lion King" (2006), widely seen as a landmark recognition of the rights of Third World musicians, have been based on a legal framework for the definition of musical originality that only reinforces the hegemony and claimed universality of Western values.

[49] The introduction to Herbie Hancock's 1973 jazz-rock fusion remake of "Watermelon Man" was copied from a 1966 ethnomusicological recording by Simha Arom and Geneviève Taurelle of BaBanzélé pygmy music from the Central African Republic. Steven Feld asked Hancock whether he felt any moral concerns about this. Hancock said no, and explained: "[Y]ou see, you've got to understand, this is a brothers kind of thing, you know, a thing for brothers to work out.... You see, brothers, we're all making African music, that's what I'm talking about:" Steven Feld, "Pygmy Pop: A Genealogy of Schizophonic Mimesis," *Yearbook for Tradition Music* 28 (1996): 5–6.

generally by the practices of remix culture—not to mention the "entitlement philosophy"[50] through which the generation that grew up with the Internet no longer expects to pay for music. The problem is obvious enough. Autonomy mentality holds that meaning and hence originality are inscribed in musical texts that are both ownable and assignable. By contrast, multimedia mentality holds that meaning and originality are performative, emerging out of contexts of use and reuse. Toynbee attempts to reconcile this clash of mentalities through a concept of social authorship, in which "symbolic difference" arises from the incrementation of small creative acts, meaning that "creativity is manifested across series of texts rather than at the level of the individual art work."[51] Such small creative acts include the paradigmatically intertextual practice of performance; indeed, when creativity is understood this way, the distinction between composition and performance is likely to break down. But as Anne Barron has argued,[52] it is difficult to imagine how the law could handle the multiple judgments of originality this would imply, and in any case it is far from obvious that the effect on performance culture would be positive. As Philip Auslander writes: "[T]o grant a performer exclusive rights to particular performed gestures or intonations would severely limit the vocabulary available to other performers and thus 'impede rather than promote the useful arts.'"[53]

So the issue is not simply that, in Keith Sawyer's words, "These laws are based on obsolete myths about creativity."[54] A deeper problem is that they apply values drawn from one mentality to the practices of another. In effect, Lessig's claim is that a resolution of the current impasse over copyright cannot be achieved by legal means alone, but must involve fundamental changes in ways of doing business. The music business is very much a case in point. It assumed its modern form with the development of mass-circulation printed music for domestic consumption: a significant fixed cost investment up front was recouped through the low marginal costs of printing large numbers of copies, which is a roundabout way of saying that its basic commodity was intellectual property. (No wonder, then, that modern copyright law developed in the context of publishing.) This business model was adapted rather than significantly altered as the source of income generation increasingly shifted from sheet music to recordings and rights. But the fact that the music business was built on copyright is no guarantee that it always will be, and I invoke Eclectic Method to make this final point. I first encountered their work through Benjamin Franzen's and Kembrew McLeod's 2009 film *Copyright Criminals*, which in the words of the film Web site asks: "Can you own a sound?"[55] The

[50] Jason Toynbee, *Creating Problems: Social Authorship, Copyright and the Production of Culture* (Milton Keynes: Pavis Centre for Social and Cultural Research, Open University, 2001), 23, at http://www.open.ac.uk/socialsciences/__assets/b3tygo8bmj1zqfqxhw.pdf (accessed December 7, 2012).

[51] Toynbee, *Creating Problems*, 8–9.

[52] Anne Barron, "The Legal Properties of Film," *The Modern Law Review* 67, no. 2 (2004): 205.

[53] Philip Auslander, *Liveness: Performance in a Mediatized Culture*, 2nd ed. (New York: Routledge, 2007), 156, quoting from *Booth v. Colgate-Palmolive* (1973).

[54] Keith Sawyer, *Explaining Creativity: The Science of Human Innovation* (New York: Oxford University Press, 2006), 311.

[55] http://www.copyrightcriminals.com/about (accessed May 24, 2011).

film provides an answer by tracing the history and practices of sampling, remixing, and mashup through interviews with many of their exponents (Eclectic Method included). Another contributor to the film is Lessig, arguing that what he calls the remix form of expression (and what I call multimedia mentality) can be criminalized, but cannot be suppressed. Shortly after the publication of *Remix*, on January 8, 2009, Lessig made an appearance on *The Colbert Report*, the satirical late night TV show. Tongue in cheek, host Stephen Colbert explicitly forbade the making of remixes based on his discussion with Lessig, with predictable results: Eclectic Method's remix was posted the following day, and many others followed.[56]

As may be imagined, Eclectic Method's relationship to copyright law is a little complicated, but contrary to what might be expected, they have never had a cease-and-desist order served on them.[57] In an interview in 2009, the group members were asked about legal issues and replied as follows:

> IAN EDGAR: If you ask a lawyer what should happen to culture, they'd say stop and don't do anything. That's why we don't ask them. All we do is generate pay checks for them. But seriously, I guess some of the stuff we do might be considered illegal, but for example, when Motown saw our remix they hired us. We play the music because we like it and it's not meant to steal money from them.
>
> GEOFF GAMLEN: We're just DJing, really. People want their music played.
>
> JONNY WILSON: Historically, our story has been that we've tested the waters in terms of what we could get away with and it ended up that we didn't just get away with it, everyone we've "copyright infringed" has then employed us to do stuff for them. So that pattern where we've done something technically illegal then followed it up with something official. It happened with MTV, Fatboy Slim, U2 and Motown. I think we just came out at the exact right time to do what we do. People were just getting ready for this to be legit, with YouTube and things like that.[58]

Eclectic Method's own business practices bear this out. They place their videos on the Web for free download. This makes sense, not only because selling them would make them more vulnerable to litigation,[59] but also because it would be self-defeating. The perfect and effortless replicability of digital multimedia that makes Eclectic Method's work possible, coupled with the failure of the various proprietary copy protection

[56] http://vimeo.com/groups/videomusic/videos/2778282 (accessed May 24, 2011).

[57] As stated by Geoff Gamlen in the "Video Mashup Masters Interview."

[58] Beer, "Remixed Before Your Eyes: Eclectic Method," *Creativity*, June 12, 2009, at http://creativity-online.com/news/remixed-before-your-eyes-eclectic-method/137268 (accessed May 24, 2011).

[59] As Geoff Gamlen said in a 2008 interview with the online magazine *The Thing Is*: "[T]he four majors . . . can't control distribution, but attempts to make money out of copyright material are more and more the focus of litigation." http://thethingis.co.uk/2008/01/05/interview-with-geoff-gamlen-of-eclectic-method/ (accessed May 24, 2011).

systems through which the music and media industries hoped to perpetuate their existing business model, are putting an end to the artificial scarcity, resulting from the control of distribution, on which the music business was built. The advent of no-cost providers like Spotify shows that the traditional model of selling music is becoming less and less viable as the foundation of a global industry, and with the inexorable increase in bandwidth and decline in storage costs, the same is becoming the case for multimedia in general.

As John Williamson and Martin Cloonan point out,[60] the major recording companies have succeeded in persuading politicians and others that the record business *is* the music business, and this explains the widespread perception that music is in crisis. It is true that technologically and socially conditioned change is threatening musicians' traditional revenue streams (though not as dramatically as the introduction of the talkies did), but as Simon Frith observes, "[E]ven in the fifty-year era of record company dominance... the vast majority of musicians made their living from providing a service rather than from owning an asset."[61] While the major recording companies have put their efforts into lobbying to sustain a defunct business model, service industries around music have flourished. The most obvious is live concert promotion, which has become increasingly profitable since the 1990s. Williamson and Cloonan note that in 2002 the Scottish-based recording industry generated revenues of £39.5 million, whereas the live music industry generated £45.8 million.[62]

Live performance provides a significant part of Eclectic Method's income: according to their 2011 press kit, they had at that time played "350 gigs in 100 cities in 34 countries in 6 continents since 2003."[63] But the press kit also makes it clear that their business model increasingly involves other services, in particular for corporate clients, including promotional videos, viral Internet commercials, and branded video performances; the client list includes Adidas, Apple, Blackberry, Coca-Cola, and Getty Images. Again, Spotify shows how there is a new market for Internet advertising related to music (as well as for charging people to avoid it). And more generally, revenue-generating software, sometimes vertically integrated with hardware manufacture, ranges from personalized music recommendation systems to iPhone apps. Making music available to people when and how they want it makes money even if the music itself can be obtained for free, and this represents an example of the hybrid economy for which Lessig argues in *Remix*. Music no longer effectively ownable ceases to be the foundation of a copyright industry—an autonomy industry—but becomes instead the basis of innumerable new

[60] John Williamson and Martin Cloonan, "Rethinking the Music Industry," *Popular Music* 26 (2007): 305–22.

[61] Simon Frith, "Creativity as a Social Fact," in *Musical Imaginations: Multidisciplinary Perspectives on Creativity, Performance and Perception*, ed. David Hargreaves, Dorothy Miell, and Raymond MacDonald, 62–72. Oxford: Oxford University Press, 2012.

[62] Williamson and Cloonan, "Rethinking the Music Industry," 315.

[63] *Eclectic Method Video Remix 2011*, 7, formerly at http://www.eclecticmethod.net/press.pdf (accessed May 24, 2011).

service industries; as Esther Dyson wrote as long ago as 1995, with remarkable prescience, "the ancillary market is the market."[64] And it seems obvious that what is happening to music today will happen to multimedia tomorrow.

What is not so obvious is that, under such circumstances, the distinction between music and multimedia will continue to be a meaningful one, other than in a simple, descriptive sense. The center of gravity in academic studies of music continues to shift from music as ownable product to music as cultural practice—or in Christopher Small's terms, from music to musicking.[65] And although the practices of autonomy culture persist, they are beginning to take on the self-consciously retro quality characteristic of heritage-industry niche cultures: witness the Living to Music movement instigated by the British DJ Greg Wilson to rehabilitate attentive listening to classic rock albums (on vinyl of course) under carefully controlled social conditions.[66] Without the ontological grounding provided by autonomy mentality and long taken for granted by musicologists, aestheticians, and lawyers alike, music and multimedia look less like substantively distinct cultural practices and more like different aspects of a broader culture of audiovisual signifying. But that is another story.

Acknowledgment

Thanks to Geoff Gamlen for the opportunity to discuss aspects of this chapter in person.

References

Auslander, Philip. *Liveness: Performance in a Mediatized Culture.* 2nd ed. New York: Routledge, 2007.

Barron, Anne. "The Legal Properties of Film." *The Modern Law Review* 67, no. 2 (2004): 177–208.

Barron, Anne. "Introduction: Harmony or Dissonance? Copyright Concepts and Musical Practice." *Social and Legal Studies* 15, no. 1 (2006): 25–51.

Beer, Jeff. "Remixed Before Your Eyes: Eclectic Method." *Creativity*, June 12, 2009.

Berger, Karol. *Bach's Cycle, Mozart's Arrow: An Essay on the Origins of Musical Modernity.* Berkeley: University of California Press, 2007.

Bohlman, Philip. "Ontologies of Music." In *Rethinking Music*, ed. Nicholas Cook and Mark Everist, 17–34. Oxford: Oxford University Press, 1999.

[64] Quoted in Toynbee, *Creating Problems*, 24.

[65] Christopher Small, *Musicking: The Meanings of Performing and Listening* (Middletown, Conn.: Wesleyan University Press, 1998).

[66] See Greg Wilson's blog "Being a DJ," at http://www.gregwilson.co.uk/2010/06/living-to-music/ (accessed May 24, 2011). The phrase "on vinyl of course" is taken from a Guardian Music Blog feature on the associated Classic Album Sundays, at http://www.guardian.co.uk/music/musicblog/2011/jan/18/classic-album-sundays (accessed May 24, 2011).

Borgo, David. "Transmusicking in Cyberspace." In *Taking it to the Bridge: Music as Performance*, ed. Nicholas Cook and Richard Pettengill. Ann Arbor: University of Michigan Press, forthcoming.

Burke, Peter. "Strengths and Weaknesses of the History of Mentalities." *History of European Ideas* 7 (1986): 439–451.

Cook, Nicholas. *Analysing Musical Multimedia*. Oxford: Oxford University Press, 1998.

Cook, Nicholas. "Uncanny Moments: Juxtaposition and the Collage Principle in Music." In *Approaches to Meaning in Music*, ed. Byron Almén and Edward Pearsall, 107–134. Bloomington: Indiana University Press, 2006.

Cook, Nicholas. "Music and the Politics of Space." In *Music, Sound, and Space: Transformations of Public and Private Experience*, ed. Georgina Born, 224–38. Cambridge: Cambridge University Press, 2013.

Demers, Joanna. *Steal This Music: How International Property Law Affects Musical Creativity*. Athens: University of Georgia Press, 2006.

Elvers, Rudolf, and Cecil Hopkinson. "A Survey of the Music Catalogues of Whistling and Hofmeister." *Fontes Artis Musicae* 19 (1972): 1–7.

Encyclopedia of American Cinema for Smartphones and Mobile Devices. Boston: Mobile Reference, 2007.

Erlmann, Veit. "Music as Law: 'The Lion King', Counterfeit and Intellectual Property Rights." Paper delivered at the University of Cambridge, February 24, 2010.

Feld, Steven. "Pygmy Pop: A Genealogy of Schizophonic Mimesis." *Yearbook for Tradition Music* 28 (1996): 1–35.

Frith, Simon. "Creativity as a Social Fact." In *Musical Imaginations: Multidisciplinary Perspectives on Creativity, Performance and Perception*, ed. David Hargreaves, Dorothy Miell, and Raymond MacDonald, 62–72. Oxford: Oxford University Press, 2012.

Goehr, Lydia. *The Imaginary Museum of Musical Works: An Essay in the Philosophy of Music*. Oxford: Oxford University Press, 1992.

Goldstein, Jeffrey. "Violent Video Games." In *Handbook of Computer Game Studies*, ed. Joost Raessens and Jeffrey Goldstein, 341–357. Cambridge, Mass.: MIT Press, 2005.

Hebdige, Dick. *Subculture: The Meaning of Style*. London: Methuen, 1979.

Howlett, Mike. "The Record Producer: A Nexus of Technology and Creative Inspiration." PhD diss., University of Glamorgan, 2009.

Lessig, Lawrence. *Remix: Making Art and Commerce Thrive in the Hybrid Economy*. New York: Penguin, 2008.

Levinson, Jerrold. *Music in the Moment*. Ithaca, N.Y.: Cornell University Press, 1998.

Lewis, Eric. "Ontology, Originality and the Musical Work: Copyright Law and the Status of Samples." In *Meredith Lectures 2006: Intellectual Property at the Edge: New Approaches to IP in a Transsystemic World*, ed. Faculty of Law, McGill University, 169–206. Montréal: Editions Yvon Blais, 2007.

McIntyre, Phillip. "Copyright and Creativity: Changing Paradigms and the Implications for Intellectual Property and the Music Industry." *Media International Australia Incorporating Culture and Policy* 123 (2007): 82–94.

Merleau-Ponty, Maurice. *Signs*. Evanston, Ill.: Northwestern University Press, 1964.

Mitchell, William. *Picture Theory: Essays on Verbal and Visual Representation*. Chicago: Chicago University Press, 1994.

Morales, Xavier. "Kill Bill: Beauty and Violence." *The [Harvard Law] Record*, October 16, 2003.

Nimmer, Melville, and David Nimmer. *Nimmer on Copyright*. Albany, N.Y.: Matthew Bender, 1997.

Samson, Jim. "The Practice of Early-Nineteenth-Century Pianism." In *The Musical Work: Reality or Invention?* ed. Michael Talbot, 110–127. Liverpool: University of Liverpool Press, 2000.

Sawyer, Keith. *Explaining Creativity: The Science of Human Innovation*. New York: Oxford University Press, 2006.

Scholes, Percy, ed. *The Oxford Companion to Music*. London: Oxford University Press, 1938.

Sidran, Ben. *Black Talk: How the Music of Black America Created a Radical Alternative to the Values of Western Literary Tradition*. New York: Holt, Rinehart and Winston, 1971.

Small, Christopher. *Musicking: The Meanings of Performing and Listening*. Middletown, Conn.: Wesleyan University Press, 1998.

Toynbee, Jason. *Creating Problems: Social Authorship, Copyright and the Production of Culture*. Milton Keynes: Pavis Centre for Social and Cultural Research, Open University, 2001.

Toynbee, Jason. "Copyright, the Work, and Phonographic Orality in Music." *Social and Legal Studies* 15 (2006): 77–99.

Williamson, John, and Martin Cloonan. "Rethinking the Music Industry." *Popular Music* 26 (2007): 305–322.

Zbikowski, Lawrence. *Conceptualizing Music: Cognitive Structure, Theory, and Analysis*. New York: Oxford University Press, 2005.

CHAPTER 4

THE AUDIO-LOGO-VISUAL AND THE SOUND OF LANGUAGES IN RECENT FILM

MICHEL CHION

ONE thing shared by language and sound film is that both are audiovisual—sometimes, what I call "audio-divisual." Each combines something to be seen with something to be heard, in a way that is neither symmetrical nor complementary but conflictual. The visual elements I am referring to are the film "image" on the one hand and language's writing on the other, and the auditory elements are the sound track and speech, respectively.

Things become more complicated because language itself takes part in film, even if in the beginning silent film adopted language only as a foreign body and marginalized it by relegating it to intertitles (though it couldn't do without it). In language, what divides writing and speech actually has nothing to do with what differentiates sound from image. The difference between film's sounds and images does not prevent them from having certain dimensions in common, particularly the dimensions of rhythm and time. However, for language, the written word and the sound of speech, which might seem close to one another, are much more different and have chaotic relations. The often incomprehensible connections between spelling and pronunciation have complex historical causes, and logic enters very little into the picture.[1] So the presence of language again redivides what we perceive.

To illustrate the difference between language as heard and language as seen, the French often cite the example of the word "oiseau" (bird): it is pronounced *wah-zo*, and

[1] Non-English speakers know this well when they encounter the illogic of *rough*, *through*, and two pronunciations of *slough*, just to mention a few from among hundreds of examples. The sixteenth-century French word for "time" was spelled *tens*, and the final *s* was pronounced. But the *p* was reinserted officially as a reminder that the word came from Latin *tempus* and was related to words like *temporal*, although this *p* was never pronounced. The spelling *temps* has remained ever since, though the pronunciation has evolved further, dropping the final *s* to yield the current *t ã*.

almost none of the letters in it are what we hear. Nevertheless, Western writing certainly retains traces of phoneticism. And this system is not even the most extravagant system of correspondence, or rather of noncorrespondence, between speech and writing. Take the example of Japanese and its highly illogical and disparate writing system, which is partly syllabic and partly ideographic.

When I first went to Japan, I was surprised to see Western signs and logos in occidental characters (*romanji*) everywhere alongside Japanese ideograms (*kanji*). I could consequently read and pronounce the same logos that we see in the West: Sony, Toyota, Panasonic, Yamaha, JVC. I asked our guide if the Japanese brands one sees throughout the world have specific logograms in Japanese characters; she said no. Even the logos of local Japanese brands can use Western characters, which is perfectly acceptable because all Japanese learn to read *romanji* in school. This revelation, instead of disappointing my idea of "mysterious Japan," actually enchanted me. It gave me more reason to admire a culture that holds at a distance the world of brand logos and does not integrate them into its language—while Western writing, through brand-name capitalism, is increasingly undergoing a privatization of language by appropriating words from the dictionary: Apple, Amazon, Target, and so forth.[2] In France a telecommunications company adopted the word "orange" as its name, with a small *o*; that is, without even capitalizing it to signify a proper name. I imagine that in a country with three alphabetical systems, a complex and disparate system like that of Japanese, people are hyperconscious of "audio-divisuality."

Interestingly, European and American films, which represent Japan as a foreign, opaque, and mysterious country, tend to avoid showing the presence of Western writing in Japan, at least in its big cities and tourist landmarks. For example, to create the impression of a faraway land in *Lost in Translation* (a rather stupid movie redeemed by Scarlett Johansson and Bill Murray), Sofia Coppola not only has us hear Japanese, but in shots of street signs, advertising, and buildings, she minimizes any signs that might make Japan less exotic and distant, particularly avoiding any signs printed in *romanji*.[3] When hearing an unknown language, we can always at least associate it with sounds in our own language, but if it doesn't use the same alphabet, we feel entirely at sea because we cannot associate sounds, let alone meanings, with what we are looking at.

Because we can hear it, a foreign language is not that magical; it comes out of a human throat that laughs, spits, smiles, moans, and shouts just like ours. It does not command the awe and respect we feel when we see indecipherable writing.

When the synthetic computer voice was created, we were led to imagine a voice that would have the magical and abstract character of writing. Toys like Texas Instruments' Speak & Spell in the late 1970s had a synthesized voice. But pretty quickly people felt there was no longer anything mysterious about this voice; we could imagine someone uttering it, because it was a gendered voice, usually male. The fact that it was a voice at

[2] See Naomi Klein's smart analysis in *No Logo* (New York: Picador, 2002).

[3] The same goes for numbers—most are not Arabic numerals, as they appear on most real Japanese streets and as page numbers in books, but rather *kanji*.

all rendered it familiar, normal. It is as if the opacity of a culture hits us harder in the eye than through its sound.

This long preamble concerns language, and also cinema, an art at once audio-visual, audio-divisual, and audio-logo-visual. Studying sound in film, I have been haunted by the notion of division. I felt the need to emphasize this by coming up with the term audio-*logo*-visual to remind readers that language, which plays such an important part in film, can make use of both distinct "channels" of sound and image.

Some films move us by creating the poetic illusion that the dividing and divided aspects of language found both in the mismatch of languages and in the "impossible couple" of speech and writing can for once finally be transcended. Films can present this illusion of unity with varying degrees of romantic idealism. In some movies it is music that embodies this trans-linguistic language; in others it is the sign language of the deaf.

For hearing people, sign language for the deaf might represent the idea of a language that could be wholly embodied and wholly visible at the same time. I am thinking of Randa Haines's *Children of a Lesser God*, one of the most beautiful romantic movies of the 1980s. But this film poeticizes and simplifies the issue of deaf language, obscuring the fact that at the same time that they are using a gestural language, the deaf have to learn to read and write ordinary language as well. Thanks to subtitles and DVDs, deaf people can watch and understand movies and take part in society and work in general—computers, the Internet, and text messaging are a blessing for them. *Children of a Lesser God* gives the impression that sign language is privileged over other languages in not being "audio-divisual." The transition from silent film to sound entailed a great loss for many deaf people.

In its uses of language, cinema has long combined the two modalities of written and oral speech: the former of course principally in silent film, and the latter primarily in sound film. But let us not forget the significant presence of writing in sound films, in two main forms. The first is diegetic written material: letters, books, signs, inscriptions, screens, labels, and so forth. As a whole—and this crucial phenomenon has perhaps not been emphasized enough in recent years—the amount of diegetic written material increases considerably when the films' stories take place in the modern world. Examples are signs, caution warnings, advertisements, television screens stuffed with text, and obviously computer and cell phone screens and the Internet. The conventions of dubbing are increasingly inadequate to the invasion of the image by text. In American films dubbed into French, the eye sees English everywhere, while the ear hears dialogue in French. Films can no longer substitute a shot of a letter written in French for the original missive that a character is reading, as they used to do in the silent era.

The second mode of written material in the sound film is writing that is not incorporated into the film (with a few exceptions, as we shall see): subtitles. Ever since the transition to sound, which has obliged cinema to deal with language when films travel from their country of origin, people have criticized the practice of dubbing and considered subtitling the ideal solution that allows audiences to experience foreign films and cultures. Is it not preferable to show Chinese people actually speaking Chinese, Iranians speaking Farsi, and Poles speaking Polish?

This is all the more true with the proliferation of multilingual films in recent years, such as Tarantino's *Inglourious Basterds* and Steven Soderbergh's film on Che Guevara, to name just a couple. Polanski has been criticized for having resorted to the practice of having his Polish pianist hero speak English in *The Pianist* (2003), a convention today considered passé. In Bertolucci's *The Last Emperor* (1987), the Chinese are speaking English, and in the films of David Lean, Russians and Arabs speak English, too.

In 1999 John McTiernan's little-noticed *The 13th Warrior*, based on Michael Crichton's book, adopted a strategy that is not very "realistic," but is intelligent anyway. Almost the entire film, in which a literate Arab in the Middle Ages played by Antonio Banderas meets illiterate Vikings, is heard in English.[4] At first we occupy the perspective of the protagonist, whom we hear speak in English, but the solemn way he pronounces his official name allows us to hear a hint of Arabic (proper names are essentially what remains of one language when a character speaks in another). When the hero meets the Vikings for the first time, the latter speak a Nordic language that resembles modern Icelandic, and their words are not translated for us, neither by subtitles nor by a diegetic character acting as interpreter. In time Banderas learns the Viking language through observation (gestures, lip movements, etc.), and at the moment when he pronounces his first sentence in Viking, for us, he's speaking English even though we understand it's Viking in the story, because the Vikings understand him and talk with him, now in English![5] A montage sequence, consisting of brief shots of Viking mouths speaking and Banderas's face as he listens to them, has served to introduce English into the Vikings' mouths, substituting for their Nordic language.

A few seconds later, the Arabic language that we have not heard but which is the protagonist's real tongue appears in written form. A Viking asks Banderas, "Can you write sounds?" Answering that he can not only write them but read and pronounce them, too, he traces several words from the Koran into the sand, just as Christ wrote in the sand according to the Gospels, probably in Aramaic, in the episode of the adulterous woman.

The film requires a cooperative spectator who does not need literal representations. This translating of all languages into English for the film might make us smile—but come to think of it, how is subtitling any more "realistic" than dubbing?

Born in 1947 in the north of France, I recall seeing foreign films, especially American, dubbed in French in the movie theater. The "language of dubbed films" was already, and still is, a very specific language, in terms of style as well as pronunciation and accent: it contains absolutely no regional variation. Americans from Texas and Brooklyn alike speak exactly the same uniform, accentless French.

A more daring model prevailed in French dubs of 1960s Italian films: transposing the original accents into French equivalents. For example, in Vittorio de Sica's *Yesterday,*

[4] *The 13th Warrior* was thus dubbed into the principal language of each country where it was distributed.

[5] This convention predates *The 13th Warrior* in various forms: for example, James Stewart learns to speak Chiricahua Apache in *Broken Arrow* (1950), but we hear all his dialogue with the Indians in English; his voiceover explicitly explains this language setup near the beginning.

Today and Tomorrow, Marcello Mastroianni and Sophia Loren play characters of disparate social classes in Milan, Naples, and Rome. In the Neapolitan segment, Mastroianni is an unemployed worker, and Sophia Loren an ever-pregnant cigarette seller. The French dub gives them a southern French accent that conveys populism and warmth. In the segment where Loren plays the wife of a rich Milanese industrialist and Mastroianni is her lover, both take on the accent of snobbish bourgeois Parisians. Such a transposition would no longer be accepted by today's viewers. But as a convention it has one advantage: it reflects the variety of languages and accents in the original film and its society, a variety that subtitling cannot capture.

It is often said that subtitling is the ideal situation, and especially with the advent of DVDs, it is accessible to everyone. What I want to show here is the *ambiguity* of the process, because it is subject to precise technical and stylistic limitations (the amount of text must be reduced, in effect summarizing the lines uttered), and above all, that *these limitations must be forgotten*. We have to make the spectator forget that she or he is reading subtitles. A wholly novel and paradoxical form of written communication (inaugurated in the 1920s by electric news crawls on buildings), subtitling entails a bizarre paradox: it supplies written language in limited time, ephemeral text we must read in a hurry—whereas normally, writing is the way we *fix* language so that it is not subject to temporal constraints, allowing the reader to assimilate the text at a speed he or she chooses.

Because of the way it gives access to meaning, subtitling kills language. It short-circuits the issues of comprehension and translation, which it appears to do "in real time," even though it actually translates nothing but the skeleton of meaning (and this happens even with excellent subtitling). Through this short-circuiting, subtitling separates the sound of language from language itself. It *kills the signifier*, and in killing the signifier it reduces language to sound.[6]

Sounds must be distinguished from signifiers. When you use a language you hear its sounds as phonemes. An American hears English through its phonological system; she or he hears an "a" when there are all sorts of different sounds—a Boston "a" does not resemble a Detroit "a." This is certainly one of the big problems we face when we hear a completely foreign language: Which sounds are the phonemes?

What's more, subtitling irons out the different degrees of intelligibility of the text. In a French short film that is representative of French cinema in general, *Rendez-vous a Stella Plage* (*Meeting at the Stella Beach,* Shalimar Preuss, 2009), a young woman receives a phone call out of the blue from a mother who takes her for her own daughter, and she plays along. Their dialogue is in French, but we often have to strain to hear exactly what is said, not only by the voice at the other end of the phone, but also by the girl in her phone booth. Lines such as, "How's it going?" or "We're lucky it's so nice out this weekend," made indistinct by the sounds of the sea, the wind, motorcycles, and the shouting of boys, reach us periodically, but we understand that the film does this by design, and

[6] By reducing language to sound, I mean that for the audio-viewer, language becomes one sound among many. The tension between sound and sense, a tension that normally obtains as we listen to an unfamiliar language, evaporates; the ear ceases to seek out the signifiers.

that it is not a technical problem or a flaw in the players' diction. What becomes of this verbal chiaroscuro when for international distribution we have to subtitle such a film?

In another French short, *L'Aide au retour* (*Grant to Return*, Mohammed Latreche, 2010), which is about illegal immigrants in France, the characters use two languages in alternation, Serbo-Croatian and French. When the characters speak French, the French spectator has to make a bit of an effort to get it. When they speak Serbo-Croatian, brief subtitles devoid of ambiguity bluntly supply the meaning of what they are saying, in an impersonal and hyper-correct "international style": "What's the matter?" "Where were you when your brother died?"

Paradoxically, in this case the chiaroscuro-like comprehension in our own language (an effect often found in French film) when the characters are speaking French is followed by Serbo-Croatian dialogue without nuance, yielding a total clarity of meaning, a meaning that is unavoidably standardized. This is the whole problem of subtitling: it is never intended to translate the complete text (rather, it must condense what is said to avoid imposing a tidal wave of text for us to read), nor can it translate stylistic nuances in dialogue and differences in diction, nor can it render the differing levels of intelligibility that native speakers can easily perceive.

This has happened many times when I have taught courses in non-French-speaking countries and shown films in the language of the host country. Germans, for example, tell me that they cannot understand half of Fassbinder's *The Third Generation* (1979, about a group of leftists in Berlin who have fallen into terrorism), owing to the quality of sound recording or to characters' accents, acting, and sound mixing. And in Paris, Italian students have taught me that Fellini is not always intelligible in the original to Italians, because there is so much dialogue in various dialects. With films such as these, thanks to subtitles, French or American cinephiles have access, through their eyes, to a strangely uniform and comprehensive understanding of the film's text, even if it is an abridged text translated in a dry and nuance-free mode.

The Italian critic Lorenzo Codelli, irritated by *Amarcord*'s international success in 1974, wrote the following:

> In *Amarcord* Fellini uses the Sicilian actor Ciccio Ingrassia [in the role of the crazy uncle], takes away his famous accent. In addition, for the first time, all the characters were dubbed into a Rimini accent that's so particular that the movie almost has to have subtitles for Italian viewers (like the first version of Visconti's *La Terra trema).* This dialect was painstakingly reinvented; it doesn't even have the function of situating the village they're from; in fact it is "recited"—onto the soundtrack—by professional dubbers.[7]

According to Codelli, "it's the swear words in dialect that send the audience into hysterics and has made *Amarcord* such a huge box office success." Obviously this applies for Italians only, because audiences elsewhere generally cannot pick up on the dialectal flavors of the dialogue.

[7] Lorenzo Codelli, *Positif* 158 (April 1974).

In his final film, the strange and affecting *La Voce della Luna* (1990), Fellini dreamed up and constructed a village that could not be precisely situated anywhere in Italy, owing to particularities of its architecture as well as the way the characters speak. "It has absolutely no regional specificity," said the director. "It is a transnational village, so to speak. There is something neurotic, wild and chaotic about it, a quality that can now be found everywhere in the world."

From the opening scene at night in the countryside, a potpourri of accents of various regions of Italy emerges from the mouths of the characters.[8] Roberto Benigni, in the role of the Innocent Ivo Salvini, talks in his usual Tuscan accent. A group of men has banded together in the darkness to go spy on a woman who is undressing by her open window. Some of them are speaking in southern Italian accents and vocabulary; sometimes they go from a line in dialect to a line in standard Italian. The violent fellow who threatens to kill Salvini has a Neapolitan accent. The woman undressing and dancing in front of her TV has the accent of Ciocaro, a town near Rome that gave its name to a famous film with Sophia Loren (*La Ciocara*). The man named Pigafetta, who manages to recue Salvini from his predicament, has the Neapolitan accent, and he alternates sentences in dialect with others in standard Italian.

This fantastic mishmash creates for Italians the sense of an imaginary, disparate, impossible Italy (the place of the action is not a cosmopolitan city, but a remote country town at night). There is no way any of this flavor can survive in the subtitled version, or even in the dubbed version. And let's not blame the dubbers for this: they would have had to adopt some sort of system of equivalences, as was the practice during the 1960s. For the subtitled version, someone would have had to create a cumbersome code for spelling out accents.

The novel came up against the same problem a century ago. On several occasions, Balzac offered a labored and caricatured graphic transcription of a character's Alsatian accent, Baron Nucingen, and this presented problems for his translators. Edgar Allan Poe, in his short story "The Angel of the Odd," imitates the strange accent of one of his characters, and Charles Baudelaire, in his famous French translation entitled "*L'Ange du Bizarre*," transposes it, quite cleverly, from Poe's " 'I zay,' said he, 'you mos pe dronk as de pig' . . . " to " 'Che tis,' disait-elle, 'gu'y vaut que phus zoyez zou comme ein borgue,' " a Germanic-accented version of "Je dis qu'il faut que vous soyez saoul comme un porc" ("I say, said he, you must be drunk as a pig").

Tolstoy incorporated long dialogues in French into *War and Peace*, uttered by his characters of the Moscow aristocracy and by his fictional Napoleon. He didn't just impose another language on his Russian readers, but a different alphabet which they were obliged to consult footnotes in order to understand. The difference of language is dramatic, immediately visible to the eye, because of the passage from the Cyrillic alphabet to the Latin (even though they are fairly close), while it is attenuated in the French translation of *War and Peace* (even if the lines in question are in italics, signaling "this is in French in the text").

[8] I am indebted to my Neapolitan friend Silvia Angrisani for providing these observations.

In the case of foreign films, which increasingly often present not just dialects and accents but different languages, the subtitle—which I may appear to be putting on trial here, although that is not what I mean to do—often demobilizes our listening. As I have suggested, we no longer make the effort to try to hear signifiers, words and their separations, in the flow of speech of this unfamiliar language. We no longer listen to the sound of the words, and all foreign languages seem to be one.

In Amos Gitai's *Freezone* (2005), a Palestinian woman and an Israeli woman taxi driver argue over money in three languages. Sometimes it's Arabic, which the Israeli also speaks; sometimes Hebrew, which the Palestinian can understand and speak a little; and sometimes English, the language they resort to when they talk with a young American woman (Natalie Portman). This zapping from one language to another is always semiotically loaded. French and Anglophone viewers can easily note when they use English, but on the other hand, we cannot always hear the difference between Arabic and Hebrew. In part this is because reading the subtitles occupies a good part of our attention; also, there is not that big a difference between the two Semitic languages' sounds, although their different writing systems might suggest a greater gap. Conversely, the Latin alphabet is used for an incredible diversity of languages, from Vietnamese to French to Finnish, and this resemblance in reading masks the enormous differences in linguistic systems and sounds. The DVD of Gitai's *Freezone* in France includes a dubbed French version, probably because it was specified in the contract, but in translating everything into French, it necessarily omits all of the original's linguistic texturing and renders the film a bit absurd, or at least much less interesting.

There is definitely no French-language dub of Mel Gibson's *The Passion of the Christ* (2004), a film that gave us Gibson's idea of the Passion spoken in the original language of Jesus—which was not modern Hebrew but Aramaic, and also in Latin in the scenes involving the Roman occupiers. The irony is that, as few French Christians know, the Gospels—Gibson's source, which he follows closely—were written down neither in Hebrew nor in Latin, but in Greek.

In one of the best known scenes of the *Passion*, Pilate asks Jesus: "Art thou the King of the Jews?" "O basileus tôn Ioudaiôn." (Matthew 27:11). And Jesus answers, "Thou sayest" ("Su legeis"). Neither Mark, Matthew, Luke, nor John, who all wrote down the dialogue in Greek (I have transliterated the Greek into the Latin alphabet) tell us in what language the two men spoke to each other—nor who was there to hear and record their dialogue. But Gibson makes a very interesting choice. In his version, Pilate interrogates Jesus in Aramaic—a conqueror's gesture of respect for the representative of an occupied Judea—but the Son of God answers him in Latin, which remains the language they use for the rest of the scene. However, the French DVD's subtitles show the Aramaic in exactly the same format as the Latin, so only the highly trained ear could detect the difference (my classical studies help me here). I have observed that few moviegoers listen to the speech, and most do not notice this linguistic coup de théâtre, whose meaning is by no means insignificant. Though Christ is heard speaking Aramaic at the beginning, when he prays to his Father at Gethsemane to have the cup taken from him, he adapts to the language of his interlocutor, Pilate, in a universalist spirit. If Gibson's film were a literary work, the transition from Latin to Aramaic would be apparent right away.

As it happens, a considerable number of recent feature films speak in several languages. In *Babel* (Iñarritu, 2005) we hear Japanese, Arabic, Spanish, and English, and we also see a deaf girl communicating in Japanese sign language. In *Syriana* (Stephen Gaghan, 2004) we hear English, Arabic, Urdu (for the Pakistani workers in Dubai), and Farsi, which is an Indo-European language, although its writing uses Arabic characters. *Kedma* (Amos Gitai, 2002), about the first landings of Jewish immigrants in Palestine after World War II, uses Yiddish, Russian, Hebrew, and Arabic. *A Prophet* (Jacques Audiard, 2009) has French, Corsican, and Arabic dialogue, while the excellent *Band's Visit* (Eran Kolirin, 2007) has English, Egyptian Arabic, and Hebrew. To be sure, there were already some multilingual films, particularly by Fellini—Italian, French, English, German, and Latin are heard in *Casanova*, for example—and Visconti, in whose *Death in Venice* the German composer played by Dirk Bogarde speaks English, while characters around him speak Italian, Neapolitan, and Polish. But recently there seems to be a real surge, which critics tend to see as heralding a greater concern for realism and respect for other languages and cultures. However, this "linguistic authenticity" is immediately contradicted by the uniform use of subtitles, which in an effort to be neutral and standard (as if to signal that they are not part of the work and only serve to communicate to the audience), to iron out the differences, make languages uniform.

When *Inglourious Basterds* shows a deliberately caricatured, cultivated, polyglot Nazi character speaking English, French, and Italian in as pure and sophisticated a style as his German, where is the realism, which is decidedly not Tarantino's greatest concern? But if filmmakers rejoice in deploying the sounds of so many different languages, what should be done with subtitling that levels them all, translating them in the same way, into a standard, uniform English or French or whatever the language is where the film is distributed?

The Portuguese Manoel de Oliveira, in his amazing *A Talking Picture* (2002), takes pleasure in showing a long conversation around a table on a cruise ship, among Stefania Sandrelli in Italian, Irene Pappas in Greek, Catherine Deneuve in French, and John Malkovich in English (Malkovich's character also speaks French, plus a smattering of Portuguese). Here the director is at least emphasizing this motley variety in the actual content of the dialogue (subtitled in the language of the country of distribution); one of the characters, the Frenchwoman played by Deneuve, remarks how strange it is, and notes that they all understand each other anyway. Then their conversation actually raises the issue of languages, particularly the paradox that Greek, the mother language of scientific, technical, and philosophical vocabulary in much of the world, is read and spoken solely by Greeks. This is a sort of new Pentecost,[9] because it seems that to the apostles was given not the gift of languages

[9] Recall this account in Acts 2:1-6: "And when the day of Pentecost was fully come, they were all with one accord in one place. And suddenly there came a sound from heaven as of a rushing mighty wind, and it filled all the house where they were sitting. And there appeared unto them cloven tongues like as of fire, and it sat upon each of them. And they were all filled with the Holy Ghost, and began to speak with other

so much as the miracle of being understood by each in his own tongue (something cinema would certainly have enjoyed).

A Talking Picture makes no allusion to the Greek alphabet, a writing system that differs from the other European languages, even if the symbols are familiar to us from their use in the sciences and elsewhere. Not many French people notice that on the coins they have used since 2002 the word "euro" has been printed also in Greek letters.

This does not change the problem that has arisen from the otherwise useful convention of subtitles: how to translate visually the diversity of languages, but also the stylistic details of characters' speech and the degree of intelligibility of dialogue lines.

Should visual codes be developed, variations in the design of letters, to mark that the spectator is to understand the words better or worse—or the use of different fonts for different languages? This is not out of the question, in my opinion. Note also that in some English captions for the deaf that are found on DVDs for multilingual films, there is already at least a notation of the original language. The disc for *Syriana* has such a setup, for example.

The problem is obvious: the spectator is encouraged to forget that she or he is reading subtitles at all, so what would happen if we were constantly reminded of it through subtitles full of graphic variations? (The only such current practice is italics for song lyrics and for lines coming from offscreen or voice-overs.)

What should be done (you can see I am moving from one intractable problem to the next) about the fact that we also do not know to what degree people speaking different tongues onscreen are understanding each other? In *A Talking Picture*, the heroine's daughter listens to the adults conversing in English; in "waking life" we assume that a little Portuguese girl wouldn't understand a word, but in the film experience, the spectator, understanding the dialogue either through listening or reading subtitles, forgets about that. How much simpler it was when Shakespeare or Beaumarchais put his own language into the mouths of his characters, allowing us to forget that Hamlet is Danish, Romeo from Verona, and Figaro from Seville.

From time to time, just when we least expect it, a bilingual or multilingual film comes along that applies subtitles in an innovative way. This occurs in Tony Scott's otherwise mediocre thriller, *Man on Fire* (Tony Scott, 2004). Set in Mexico, it is a story about the sad phenomenon of kidnapping for ransom. Denzel Washington plays an American bodyguard seeking revenge on the abductors of the little girl he was in charge of protecting. The scenes spoken in Spanish, even in the original American release, are translated in subtitles of different size; they are placed in different locations on the screen and interact with the image in varying ways. This is one of the rare examples where subtitles are made conspicuous, in order to enter into the "audiovisual dance," so to speak.

tongues, as the Spirit gave them utterance. And there were dwelling at Jerusalem Jews, devout men, out of every nation under heaven. Now when this was noised abroad, the multitude came together, and were confounded, because that every man heard them speak in his own language." This is quite interesting, because it is not clear in the Greek text whether the apostles are speaking different languages all at once, or whether each listener understands his own language (like a hallucination, meaning that it is the listeners who have the gift of understanding languages!).

All the same, let us note that this visual effect in no way indicates specific accents, ways of talking, or character. On the other hand, it does foreground the artificiality of subtitling.

Viewers also noticed in *Avatar* (2010) that the subtitles for the Na'vi language (which the 3D causes to show up literally in front of the characters, positioning them in the theater space) appear in an unusual, elegant font, as if approximating a visual equivalent of this language that was invented for the film. At the same time, the Na'vi as conceived by Jim Cameron do not have writing, so their language reflects an idealized vision of the "natural life." Isn't the society shown on the planet Pandora (its name borrowed from Greek mythology) rather feminine, matriarchal, and without technology?

The film opposes two societies: humans on the one hand, a machistic society that uses lots of machines, erects ominous printed signs (like "CAUTION") everywhere, and knows only force; and on the other hand, a society whose language is depicted like an extension of the body, where one speaks with the body, which has no writing, no machines. We find here a fairly conventional alignment: female as body, nature, and speech; male as technology, machine, and writing.

The seemingly inevitable transition of most cinema to digital could certainly give it greater liberty to play with the size, graphics, and manner of appearance of subtitles, which could enjoy the flexibility and freedom that the sound of the voice has already developed. Will filmmakers, who already have to deal with so many problems and make so many choices, wish to take this new element, the visual presentation of subtitles, and make it part of their expressive arsenal, instead of delegating subtitles to the usual technicians? I have no idea. When one experiments with new narrative solutions, one is often accused of being a mannerist.

The question of how to "deneutralize" subtitles is a huge issue. Let us note that the same problem comes up in a third form of translating besides sync dubbing and subtitling, and is still employed in the TV systems of eastern Europe. Once in widespread use in the USSR but also in China, it consists, as we know, of addressing the ear alone: we are made to hear the original voice (at low volume) and simultaneously its translation by a neutral and inexpressive voice, whose gender might not even be that of the onscreen speaker. This nondiegetic translator's voice, which insinuates itself into the sound of film, is very disconcerting to spectators in Western Europe.

Here is another example. My Taiwanese student Chang Taoping is writing a thesis on the complex topic of languages in Taiwanese cinema. Given that a single Chinese character may have widely different pronunciations according to the region of Taiwan or mainland China—these differences being much more pronounced than in an alphabetic system—the only solution is for Taiwanese films to be subtitled in Chinese for the Taiwanese themselves.

As these examples show, there is no satisfactory solution, only compromises. Ideally, the director should oversee not only the content of the subtitles, but also graphic conventions that would allow the film to indicate, perhaps through different fonts, that the dialogue has changed to language *x* or *y*. Obviously the code would have to be explained at the beginning of the film, and as a result the spectator would lose the flattering illusion that he or she directly understands Japanese or Finnish—or for a French viewer, English. Graphic conventions could also be employed to indicate different accents in a single language, differences which, for foreign audiences, always get lost in the shuffle. Spectators would be conscious of this mode of subtitling, as in Manoel de Oliveira's film mentioned previously. That does not seem beyond the realm of possibility: movie spectators are actually increasingly aware of the role of the camera, music, and so forth, and this awareness does not seem to frighten us away. But aside from a few isolated examples such as *Avatar*, the cinema—even the European art cinema—does not yet appear ready to move in this direction.

Notes

This chapter was translated by Claudia Gorbman.

CHAPTER 5

THE END OF DIEGESIS AS WE KNOW IT?

ANAHID KASSABIAN

Let me begin diegetically, in storytelling mode. I was poking around the iPhone app store one night in 2010, not long after getting my iPhone, looking for nothing in particular, and during the course of my perusal I came across two apps that intrigued me. For £0.59, "ikamasutra" provides illustrations of all the positions for penetrative sex that are in the Kama Sutra and more, keeps track of which ones you have tried, shares your progress on Facebook and Twitter, and has a host of other features, including "soothing music." "140 Sound Effects" offers "loud and high-quality sound effects,... [the ability to] mix sounds,... delay timer," and much more, again for a mere £0.69. Its purpose was less apparent to me than ikamasutra's, but it helpfully offers some ideas:

- Thinking of making fun of your friends with funny sound effects?
- Thinking of making your conversation more interesting?
- Feeling bored?

If you answered yes to any of these questions, Sound Effects is definitely the app for you![1]

What these two relatively random apps point toward is a major shift in the uses of music and sound in audiovisual forms of art and entertainment. I suggest that the changes heralded by these quite trivial iPhone apps demand an intensive rethinking of the terminology and conceptual frameworks in our field, based as they are on a technology (i.e., film) from another age. While film music studies is not, strictly speaking, based

[1] Roland Yau, "162 Sound Effects with Ringtones—High Quality, Version 2.4," iPhone App Store, at http://itunes.apple.com/us/app/140-sound-effects-ringtones/id367826271?mt=8 (last modified June 3, 2013). It is important to mention the short life span of many apps, YouTube links, Web pages, and such. If any of the URLs used in this article have been deleted, removed for copyright infringement, or expired, it is worth searching for the items—success can often be found on alternatives to YouTube like Daily Motions, Vimeo, or Meta Café.

directly on the technology of film—we rarely, for instance, make major theoretical distinctions between film on film and film on video—the form we generally take as a starting point, the feature-length fiction film, is also an "old" form. The major audiovisual engagements in contemporary culture are with video games of all kinds on a dizzying array of platforms; the Web, which in addition to offering innumerable sites by, for, and about musicians and music making is slowly beginning to add music to certain kinds of commercial sites; viral videos, some of the main genres of which are fundamentally musical; and a whole range of other forms, such as apps, audiobooks, and much more.

This chapter inventories some significant e-genres and offers a brief description of how music functions in them. Whereas throughout most of the twentieth century we learned about audiovisual relations first through film and then through film and television together, young children are increasingly learning about them through games and other forms. The wider public, too, spends many hours playing video games and surfing the Web, so routine engagements with the relationships of audio and visual materials differ significantly from as recently as 20 years ago. This shift demands new theories and perspectives.

More specifically, however, I focus on what are perhaps the most discussed ideas in film music studies: diegetic and non- or extradiegetic music. Many scholars have weighed in on this debate, a few of whose perspectives I discuss here. Regardless of the terms we use for these distinctions, they need to be decentered. Video games, viral videos, Web sites, and other e-forms do not treat narration the same way that film and television do, and it is ultimately not productive to approach these new forms with ideas that are no longer very pertinent.

The first lines of the *Wikipedia* entry on "diegesis" quote Gerald Prince's *Dictionary of Narratology* (2003), defining diegesis as

- the (fictional) world in which the situations and events narrated occur; and
- telling, recounting, as opposed to showing, enacting.[2]

There follows a long discussion about the distinction between mimesis (which shows the action) and diegesis (which narrates the action). Since film is always framed by the camera, the article states, it is therefore a diegetic form and not a mimetic one. From the outset, the author's either/or distinction is both unwise and unhelpful. Surely all realist film forms are both diegetic and mimetic in significant proportions, and it might be more interesting to consider how, when, and why those proportions shift in one direction or another. In what genres, or auteur directors, or specific films, or even scene types or specific scenes does the diegetic modality outweigh the mimetic, or vice versa? In any case, while such questions are important, they do not help in our mutual

[2] Gerald Prince, *A Dictionary of Narratology* (Lincoln; London: University of Nebraska Press, 2003), 1964; quoted in "Diegesis," *Wikipedia*, at http://en.wikipedia.org/wiki/Diegesis (last modified August 16, 2011).

engagement with film music studies. There, the discourse of "diegesis" and "diegetic/nondiegetic" music is deeply entrenched.

Remarkably, a section in this *Wikipedia* entry entitled "Film Sound and Music" includes the term *diegesis*. I say "remarkably" because in an entry on a term from narratology, there is no reason to expect a discussion of its operations and theorizations in film or even more specifically in film music. Its appearance indicates how strongly entrenched the notions are:

> Sound in films is termed *diegetic* if it is part of the narrative sphere of the film. For instance, if a character in the film is playing a piano, or turns on a CD player, the resulting sound is "diegetic." If, on the other hand, music plays in the background but cannot be heard by the film's characters, it is termed *non-diegetic* or, more accurately, *extra-diegetic*. The score of a film is "non-diegetic" sound.[3]

This section is followed immediately by a list of sixteen examples, all of which point not to the clarity of the distinction between diegetic and non- or extradiegetic music, but in fact to the failure of these two terms to cover adequately the relationships of sound and music to a perceived narrative world.[4]

The literature in film music studies concurs. Since Claudia Gorbman posited the categories of diegetic, nondiegetic, and metadiegetic music in "Narrative Film Music" in the *Yale French Studies* special issue on cinema/sound,[5] almost all film music scholars note that the two terms are not sufficient to cover the various examples of music that cross over, through, around, and under that boundary.

My own perspective, expressed in *Hearing Film*,[6] has been that there is a logical problem in addition to the more palpable practical ones. Music and sound are among the many aspects of a film that go into producing the sense of a diegesis. They contribute to the sense of space, of character articulation, of many things that we would label part of the diegesis. From this perspective, they are on a par with all other aspects of film, such as art direction, cinematography, and costume design; each contributes to the development of a sense in the filmgoer's mind that there is a diegetic world—both implied and presented—that the film is exploring.

How, then, can the music be inside or outside of it? If it is part of the articulation of the diegesis, how can it post hoc be categorized on one side or another? One quite well-known sequence that might be fruitful to consider from the perspective of the

3 Prince, "Diegesis."

4 Although I do not explore this issue in this chapter, film music and sound scholarship are much more separate than they should be. Elsewhere I have argued that film music scholarship cannot and should not persist in segregating sound from our thinking (Anahid Kassabian, "Music, Sound and the Moving Image: The Present and a Future?" in *The Ashgate Research Companion to Popular Musicology*, ed. Derek B. Scott [Farnham, UK: Ashgate, 2009], 43–57).

5 Claudia Gorbman, "Narrative Film Music," *Yale French Studies* 60 (1980): 183–203.

6 Anahid Kassabian, *Hearing Film: Tracking Identifications in Contemporary Hollywood Film Music* (London; New York: Routledge, 2001).

visual realm is Scotty's dream sequence in Hitchcock's *Vertigo*.[7] It is an intriguing excursion from the ordinary relationship of profilmic to filmed in Hollywood cinema, and it could raise questions about the relationship of the dream to the diegesis. And yet it is never considered extra- or nondiegetic, merely within the character's mind and therefore part of the diegesis. (In this sense it may map most closely in the language of film music onto what Gorbman terms "metadiegetic" and what Elena Boschi has argued should be called "inner scoring."[8]) In one analysis of the sequence, Deborah Linderman argues that "the dream is... in part Scottie's... —it is also the *text*'s dream, its mode of organizing its own latencies. For the dream configuration is composed of mnemonic residues of the diegesis, displaced both forward and backward in the textual linearity to be condensed at this node."[9]

For Linderman, the dream is not only diegetic, but made up of its scraps while still being held within. This is a very different approach than how film music scholarship treats music being heard by characters within their heads. In *The Cell* (2001), for example, the first entry of Catherine (the psychologist played by Jennifer Lopez) into the mind of Carl Stargher (the serial killer played by Vincent D'Onofrio) is accompanied by layers of sound that become music and are tightly associated with dream images from the killer's childhood. It is unquestionable that the aural materials perceivers are hearing come from inside the serial killer's mind. On YouTube, that sequence is posted twice:[10] once with the title "First look into Carl's World" and once with the title "inside Starghers [*sic*] mind." But according to the literature in the field, we would not think of this music as diegetic in the way that Linderman thinks of Scottie's dream.

There is a good reason for this. A great deal of music, especially in the Hollywood tradition, is *not* heard by the characters within the film. We need language to describe the difference between music that characters hear and don't hear. My proposal in *Hearing Film* (which I still prefer to some extent, though see below) was to use the language of composers and composition handbooks: dramatic scoring, source scoring, and source music. Moreover, I think we need more vocabulary to develop more sensitive, more nuanced descriptions of the enormous, strange, and wonderful relationships that filmmakers—directors, composers, music supervisors, Foley artists, etc.—think up for sound and music in relation to the other aspects of a film. Although it is tempting to make a full review of all the literature on the usefulness of the terminology of diegetic and nondiegetic music, that would easily comprise a chapter or two of its own and is not my purpose here. However, I will mention two recent important articulations of the question, each with a very different but compelling and representative approach to the matter.

7 "Scottie's Nightmare Scene—Vertigo Movie (1958)—HD," MOVIECLIPS.com, June 16, 2011, at http://www.youtube.com/watch?v=4WAxDlUOw-w.

8 Elena Boschi, "Radiofreccia: A New Direction for Italian Film Music?" (Paper presented at the Sound, Music, and the Moving Image Conference, Institute of Musical Research, University of London, September 10–12, 2007); and Gorbman, "Narrative Film Music."

9 Deborah Linderman, "The Mise-en-Abyme in Hotchcock's *Vertigo*," *Cinema Journal* 30 (1991): 65.

10 Both videos were available on YouTube on July 23, 2010.

Robynn Stilwell's 2007 article "The Fantastical Gap between Diegetic and Non-Diegetic" argues compellingly that it is precisely in the productivity and complexity of the many examples that fall into the "fantastical gap" that we should recognize the importance of the terminology.[11] As she argues in her conclusion:

> Diegetic or non-diegetic may be a simple distinction, but it need not be a simplistic one. The fact that the boundary is crossed so often should not invalidate the integrity of the distinction; indeed, the manner in which the meaning in the distinction multiplies and magnifies in the crossing is indicative of its power.[12]

Stilwell argues against the twin responses she sees film music scholarship as having offered to date: on the one hand, some have made efforts to proliferate terminology so that a wider range of categories is available; on the other, some have suggested getting rid of the distinction altogether. She rejects both approaches, suggesting that the taxonomic approach faces what might be called the problem of infinite regression: there are so many ways for film music to be neither diegetic nor nondiegetic that creating a taxonomy is something of a fool's errand. Getting rid of the distinction altogether, however, would deny us terminology that actually describes an experiential distinction in the reception of film music.

As I hope is clear from my brief precis, Stilwell's essay presents a strong case for keeping the vocabulary as is. But Ben Winters, in "The Non-Diegetic Fallacy: Film, Music, and Narrative Space,"[13] makes an argument closer to what I originally had in mind in *Hearing Film*, though far more developed and refined. He argues not only that the term "nondiegetic" fails to recognize the role of music in producing the diegesis itself, but also that

> separating music as a matter of course from the events occurring in the fictional world, as the expression of a critical or narrating voice, may even be unconsciously reinforcing modernist paradigms.... Perhaps with that postmodernist shift in attitude that sees and *embraces* music as deeply implicated in our messy everyday world, so we can also regard the worlds created by filminds[14] as open to the influence of music—rather than positing underscore as something akin to a modernist

[11] Robynn J. Stilwell, "The Fantastical Gap between Diegetic and Nondiegetic," in *Beyond the Soundtrack*, ed. Daniel Goldmark, Lawrence Kramer, and Richard Leppert (Berkeley; Los Angeles: University of California Press, 2007), 200.

[12] Stilwell, "Fantastical Gap," 200.

[13] Ben Winters, "The Non-diegetic Fallacy: Film, Music, and Narrative Space," *Music and Letters* 91, no. 2 (2010): 224–244.

[14] Winters, "Non-diegetic Fallacy," 243. "Filminds" is a term Winters takes from Daniel Frampton's 2007 book, *Filmosophy*. As Winters quotes Frampton: "Filmosophy conceptualises film as an organic intelligence: a 'film being' thinking about the characters and subjects in the film.... The filmind is not an 'external' force, nor is it a mystical being or invisible other, it is 'in' the film itself, it is *the film* that is steering its own (dis)course. The filmind is 'the film itself' (7)." The idea of the filmind connects significantly to Linderman's article cited above.

> critical voice, operating above and beyond their (filmic) worlds.... We may speak of characters radiating music and thus accidentally revealing their presence, or of underscoring revealing the falsity of a character's verbal utterances, much in the way that film scholars might talk of a character's body language betraying their intentions.[15]

Winters reconceptualizes the terrain of the question in a dramatic and profoundly useful way, which helps us rethink the relationship of music to narration itself. He posits a three-termed system—extradiegetic, intradiegetic, and diegetic—that describes music's participation in the construction of "the film itself," from within the filmind, and without an overreliance on realist and modernist discourses. The extradiegetic, in his system, is "music or sound whose logic is not dictated by events within the narrative space,... [that] seems to be deliberately distanced from the here-and-now of the narrative space's everyday world."[16] His example for clarifying this category is the use of Barber's *Adagio* in Oliver Stone's *Platoon* (1986) as a kind of distanced commentary on Sgt. Elias' death.[17] The intradiegetic is most of what was formerly termed "nondiegetic," that is, music that is part of how the film's overall narration can take place on a moment-by-moment basis, but not from an externalized position; this includes a very wide range of musical instances, from Mickey-Mousing, to the articulations of a character's emotions, to themes, to temporal and geographical location. Finally, diegetic music and sound remain the same, that is, the sound and music heard by the characters within the film world.

This scheme seems to me by far the most useful, clear, and interesting system of thinking about sound and music in relation to narration and narrativity that has yet been posited. But it remains totally committed not only to the notion of diegesis itself, but also to the world of *film* sound and music. I suggest that film stopped being the primary audiovisual medium some time ago, with the advent of television, the musical and especially sound worlds of which have hardly been explored.[18] That was an imperative that was already long in place by the time film music studies came into being; we might argue that film became a generalized medium in Western Europe and North America in the 1910s, and that television gained similar prominence in the 1960s (i.e., in each case within a decade or two of its commercial introduction).

15 Winters, "Non-diegetic Fallacy,"243.

16 Winters, "Non-diegetic Fallacy," 237.

17 Winters, "Non-diegetic Fallacy," 237.

18 There was almost no writing on TV sound and music, beyond some historical work, for a long time. For work that tries to develop an approach to textual analysis, there was Michel Chion's chapter, "Television, Video Art, Music Video," in *Audio-Vision: Sound on Screen* (New York: Colombia University Press, 1994); Rick Altman's "Television Sound," in *Studies in Entertainment: Critical Approaches to Mass Culture,* ed. Tania Modleski (Bloomington: Indiana University Press, 1986); and Philip Tagg's *Kojak: 50 Seconds of Television Music. Towards the Analysis of Affect in Popular Music* (Göteborg, Sweden: Musikvetenskapliga institutionen vid Göteborgs universitet, 1979). Recently, Ron Rodman's *Tuning In: American Narrative Television Music* (Oxford; New York: Oxford University Press, 2010) has made a significant contribution, as have James Deaville's edited collection and articles by Norma Coates and Murray Forman. But there is still a long way to go in this field, and almost no work has been done on nonmusical sound. See also the "In Focus" section on sound studies, edited by Michele Hilmes, in *Cinema Journal* 48 (2008).

However, if contemporary film music studies as we know it was initiated by Claudia Gorbman's *Unheard Melodies* in 1987[19] (I do not mean to belittle the array of works that preceded it, but rather to suggest the beginning of the field as we now conceive it), then it was born at the very moment of its own undoing as a study of a dominant media form. What I mean is this: I had my first e-mail account in 1987, which makes me a relatively early adopter in the humanities. The Web as we know it was not yet in place, but it was "in the air." By the time the next important books were published—Caryl Flinn's *Strains of Utopia*, Kathryn Kalinak's *Settling the Score*, and Royal Brown's *Overtones and Undertones*—the Web was already up and running.[20] It was certainly nowhere near the entity we now know it to be; the first browsers were not widely available until 1993. But it was in place. And by the time the next important book, Jeff Smith's *The Sounds of Commerce*,[21] was published in 1998, the Web had already assumed a vivid, active, recognizable form.

This chronology matters. If we take our field of study, as this handbook does, to be sound and music in audiovisual forms, rather than film music, we are at least two forms behind. In other words, we have as yet still said rather little about television, and television stopped being the major form of audiovisual engagement sometime in the early 2000s.[22]

I argue, then, that it no longer makes sense for the vocabulary of the field to be dominated by language generated from the study of film music. My own work has focused on perception and reception as the issues of theoretical centrality, but from the perspective of production, the crossing over of composers among video game, film, and even concert music composition suggests that placing film music at the center of the scholarly worldview is no longer appropriate. A major shift is taking place under our feet, as it were, and to expect the thinking developed in relation to a determinate, linear narrative form to help us understand audiovisuality in an indeterminate, nonlinear, and substantially less narrative culture seems unlikely and unwise.

[19] Claudia Gorbman, *Unheard Melodies: Narrative Film Music* (Bloomington: Indiana University Press, 1987).

[20] Caryl Flinn, *Strains of Utopia: Gender, Nostalgia and Hollywood Film Music* (Princeton, N.J.: Princeton University Press, 1992); Kathryn Kalinak, *Settling the Score: Music and the Classical Hollywood Film* (Madison: University of Wisconsin Press, 1992); and Royal S. Brown, *Overtones and Undertones: Reading Film Music* (Berkeley; Los Angeles: University of California Press, 1994).

[21] Jeff Smith, *The Sounds of Commerce: Marketing Popular Film Music* (New York: Columbia University Press, 1998).

[22] This is a difficult concept, of course. Do we measure by average daily contact hours? By active, as opposed to background, engagement? By perceived importance? But in many ways, it is clear that video games are a force to be reckoned with. As Tom Chatfield wrote in *The Observer* in September 2009. "Last year will go down in history as the point at which the UK videogames industry pulled decisively away from cinema, recorded music and DVD sales to become the country's most valuable purchased entertainment market, with combined software and hardware sales topping the £4bn mark for the first time: more than DVD and music sales combined, and more than four times cinema box office takings" ("Videogames Now Outperform Hollywood Movies," *The Observer*, September 27, 2009).

I am interested here in three forms, each of which troubles our models in different ways. First, video games problematize everything we think we know narratologically, psychoanalytically, and musically about the engagements between players and forms. Second, the wide, wild spread of those videos we casually call "viral" includes an amazing array of forms, from documentary to parody to storytelling, from music video to animation to dance, from collage to something more like traditional film. Finally, the growing use of music on (especially commercial) Web sites seems to me in many ways the furthest away from film and potentially the most challenging to theorize.[23] I am suggesting that video games, viral videos, and Web sites upset our presumptions about audiovisual engagements in ways that might be very productive.

Of all these forms, video game music shares the most with film music, yet in many ways it differs as well. On the one hand, at least in some genres, the lush orchestral vocabulary of classical Hollywood film music provides one of several sites of identification—the music changes according to the player's character's actions, for instance, and it offers a recognizable semiotic system through which to signify heroism, danger, success, romance, and so forth. The *Final Fantasy* series exemplifies this kind of music strategy; its music has even been turned into orchestral suites and performed by major orchestras, beginning, outside of Japan, with the performance of some of Nobuo Uematsu's score for the series in the Symphonic Game Music Concert in Leipzig in 2003.[24] This use of music is fairly common in role-playing games (RPGs), and to some extent in real-time strategy (RTS) and first-person shooter (FPS) games as well. Other genres, like fighting games, are much more likely to use the equivalent of compiled scores, with a great deal of hard rock and techno/electronica. These games include *Tekken*, *Street Fighter*, and *Mortal Kombat*. There are also hack 'n' slash games, such as *Devil May Cry*, that use techno-rock and industrial scores. In these cases, the music is being used to help create a "vibe" for the game, a package of mood and look and feel meant to speak not only to players from particular subcultures (e.g., alt kids), but also to players who understand what that "vibe" is supposed to mean and what it offers in terms of gaming experience.

As in films, however, compiled scores do not offer many opportunities to match visual and aural events. It is much trickier to make a film match with preexisting musical material, unless it is a highly mediated sequence like a montage. The problem of matching in video games is far more acute, because the timing and sequence of events generally rest in the hands of the player, not the gamemaker. Video games have had to develop musical strategies to cope with the challenges of user independence—commonly called interactivity—and find ways to keep music interesting and useful in two

[23] Although I am writing here about mainstream audiovisual forms, it is worth noting that online art projects can also have sound and music. Somewhat strangely, many do not. See, for example, Damien Hirst's *Pharmacy*, an online project of the Tate, at http://www.tate.org.uk/pharmacy/, (accessed August 29, 2010). There is no sound whatsoever—it does not even have room tone.

[24] For more on this phenomenon, see for example Sophia Tong's interview of Thomas Boecker "Sound Byte: Symphonic Game Music Concerts," at http://uk.gamespot.com/news/sound-byte-symphonic-game-music-concerts-6275522 (accessed July 8, 2013).

senses. First, the music has to be meaningful and helpful to the development of the game's action and characters. Second, it cannot be so simple a loop that players will get annoyed with it if they decide, for example, to stay in one area for a while to build up health or wealth.

There are several points to summarize here. First, although there are many narrative game genres (RPG, FPS, RTS, and even massively multiplayer online role-playing [MMORPG]), non-narrative (or less narrative, or perhaps differently narrative) games like arcade and puzzle games abound. So not all video game music is defined in relation to narratives. Second, many narrative games, across the genres just mentioned, are fundamentally nonlinear, since they can have multiple endings, or in some cases no endings (especially MMORPGs), or user-created levels (like some contemporary sidescrollers). Third, there is a very high degree of indeterminacy to the audiovisual relationships in games. Although most music cues begin on a synced spot, such as entry into a particular area, the middle will consist of a loop of indeterminate length, depending on the player's actions. At the end of the "scene," cued by an event such as the player's victory in a battle, the loop leads into an end cue, which could be a cut scene.[25] Aside from the beginning and end, then, there is no matching between visual and musical events. Fourth, in video games, because of these formal distinctions and the fundamental indeterminacy of interactive forms, music tends to be additive rather than indicative, as it is in films. In films, music often precedes events such as a cut, whereas the indeterminacy of games makes that impossible, and hence the music is an addition. For example, in *Silent Hill IV*, enemy characters called nurses can be preceded by the entrance of their musical cue, but they sometimes appear at the same time as the musical cue, depending on where they are in the area the player enters. The music in the latter case is therefore not indicative of a forthcoming event, but simply adds to the experience of it.[26]

For all these reasons, video games demand a rethinking of narrativity. If the development of a character is not a foregone conclusion (since the outcomes can vary), how should a theme be written, if at all? If a game is entirely non-narrative, consisting of a series of levels of increasingly challenging activities, is it sufficient to have (as has long been the case) musical changes only at the transition from one level to the next? The reshaping of narrative, from linear to branching, and the de-emphasis of narrative with the inclusion of other kinds of entertainment activities require a vocabulary that does not presume a predetermined world with what Winters terms a "filmind." Rather, potential developments will have to include creating analytical approaches that focus on relationships of music and affect, or music and information, or music and interactivity.

Viral videos raise a different set of questions. Various types have come into focus in the recent past, and they beg for clear, focused study. There are parodies, such as

[25] Cut scenes are short, fixed minifilms that move the narrative forward in a variety of ways. They are often explications, but often, as I have suggested here, also transitions from one scene to the next. Players cannot interact with them, and they are quite brief.

[26] My thanks to Maral K. Svendsen for her comments on this section in particular, and for her development of the distinction between additive and indicative uses of music.

Web Site Story,[27] a brilliant parody of *West Side Story* that makes fun of many common Web activities such as tweeting, Internet dating, and the capacity of the net to keep us hooked to it. Another "genre" consists of misheard lyrics videos: someone listens carefully to the lyrics of a song, intentionally mishears them, and then creates a set of visuals to the original song that encourage the same mishearings. An example is "Fishmaster," a play on Nightwish's "Wishmaster."[28] Another type of misheard lyrics video crosses language barriers, such as Hindi film song clips with English misheard lyrics. Literal videos might be thought of as the obverse of misheard lyrics. In literal videos people take the visuals of the original video and rewrite the lyrics to literalize what is being seen. (See, for example, the literal video of Bonnie Tyler's "Total Eclipse of the Heart.")[29] There are Web and pop culture homages, such as the LeetStreet Boys "Yuri the Only One for Me."[30] In this song, wave upon wave of references accumulate, matched with quickly shifting images from video games and popular manga and anime series. Then there are two kinds of choreography videos. In the first, people choreograph movement to well-known songs, such as Daft Hands[31] and the dancing prisoners in the Philippines' version of Michael Jackson's "Thriller."[32] In the second, the music is placed after the performance (e.g., Dramatic Chipmunk and Arabic Michael Jackson Dance).[33] Parodies of viral videos also appear: the Numa Numa Guy, a silly little lip-synching video parody that has had more than fifty million hits on YouTube since it was posted in 2006,[34] spawned a parody of him on American Idle (a parody of *American Idol*)[35] and was part of a *South Park* episode about Internet characters.[36]

27 "Web Site Story," at http://www.collegehumor.com/video/4054209/web-site-story (last modified June 29, 2009).

28 "Wishmaster—The Misheard Lyrics," uploaded by Kewen on July 11, 2006, at http://www.youtube.com/watch?v=gg5_mlQOsUQ.

29 "Total Eclipse of the Heart: Literal Video Version," uploaded on October 18, 2010, at http://www.youtube.com/watch?v=BLPWVwNKMAc..

30 "LeetStreet Boys—Yuri The Only One," uploaded by Leet StreetBoys on March 24, 2008, at http://www.youtube.com/watch?v=189QSTKC5no.

31 "Daft Hands Justice D.A.N.C.E," uploaded by hawaiianboii7714 on August 9, 2008, at http://www.youtube.com/watch?v=iUVcZuMz01Y.

32 "Thriller (original upload)," uploaded by byronfgarcia on July 17, 2007, at http://www.youtube.com/watch?v=hMnk7lh9M30.

33 "Dramatic Chipmunk," uploaded by cregets on June 19, 2007, http://www.youtube.com/watch?v=a1Y73sPHKxw, and "MIchael Jackson clip with an arabic song," uploaded by Anmar Hamad on October 7, 2008, http://www.youtube.com/watch?v=4XQD1smxKeo.

34 Original video "Numa Numa," uploaded by xloserkidx on August 14, 2006, at http://www.youtube.com/watch?v=60og9gwKh1o. This doesn't come near to representing the total number of hits for this video, because there are multiple versions of it in circulation. Another version, with digitally remastered audio (why?), has had over nine million hits in roughly the same period of time.

35 "'American Idle'—Numa Numa," uploaded by DustoMcneato on September 28, 2006, at http://www.youtube.com/watch?v=BE3DNJHWFSo&feature=related.

36 In this YouTube clip, someone has helpfully edited in the originals, so you can get a quick tour of a number of very famous viral videos: "Internet Stars," at http://www.youtube.com/watch?v=hSKG1JRXyk4.

None of these videos is narrative in the usual sense of the word, except perhaps the *South Park* episode. All exhibit an extreme degree of self-referentiality, a very tongue-in-cheek approach composed of references to references to references that has come to be thought of as postmodern, demands a high degree of literacy and attention from its audiences, and in many cases provokes genuine discomfort with discontinuity and non-linearity. In most of these videos—and in utter opposition to video games—the art is all in the matching of visual and musical event, in getting a good sync, but there is no place for thinking about something like a diegesis. So while they share little with video game music in any practical sense, these videos share a position of critique in relation to film music studies. No theories of film music seem to help understanding of audiovisual relationships in viral videos, beyond what any other thoughtful consumer might be able to point out.

Web sites, the final category I consider here, are undergoing a period of transition. They generally do not have music (I do not mean the plethora of Web sites devoted to music, such as artists' pages, label pages, and Internet radio stations); most Internet information or commerce pages are silent, for reasons that we might be able to speculate about, such as the time and money saved by Web masters and the appeal for users of being able to surf without anyone within earshot knowing. Yet increasingly, music is beginning to appear on high-end product sites, such as race cars, fashion houses, and real estate developments.[37] High-end real estate Web sites began to use music around the year 2000 in a trend that was genuinely surprising. The *New York Times* did a piece in its real estate section on the phenomenon, noting that many high-end condo developers in New York City were using a range of music, from soft jazz to classical to world lounge, to sell their properties.[38]

Commercial Web sites are nonfictional. They take place in *this* world, ostensibly, but they also spend no time or resources on implying anything beyond themselves. They don't need to imply a whole rest of the world beyond the images on the screen; the beautiful, shiny, glorious object of consumption on offer suffices unto itself. The use of audio and video suggests both that the producer has the means to spend money on Web site production and that the potential customer is presumed to have the necessary resources, time, and sophistication to read the audiovisual presentation. Perhaps even more interestingly, these sites are not organized by a logic of identification, which is the presumption from which much scholarship on film music has proceeded, because it has focused on Euro-American mainstream fiction feature films, which take identification

[37] For example, see Lamborghini's "Blancpain Super Trofeo" page, last modified September 28, 2011, at http://www.supertrofeo.com; Chanel's Fall/Winter 2010/2011 Haute Couture show, at http://www.chanel.com/fashion/8-fall-winter-2010-11-haute-couture-chanel-fashion-show-19,0#8-fall-winter-2010-11-haute-couture-chanel-fashion-show-19,0 (accessed August 19, 2010); or the Plaza Hotel, at http://www.theplazany.com (accessed June 4, 2013).

[38] Stephanie Rosenbloom, "Selling a Concept with a Song," *New York Times*, August 5, 2007, at http://www.nytimes.com/2007/08/05/realestate/05cov.html?_r=1&oref=slogin&ref=music&pagewanted=all (accessed September 28, 2011).

as an organizing principle.[39] It is also the way much advertising works, using characters with the same identity as the target demographic or building brief ongoing narratives. The means of drawing perceivers into a relationship of desire and consumption with the product on offer is organized differently on Web sites; if there were a substantial critical literature on music in advertising, we might go to it for some help, but this is also an area in dire need of development.[40] While we could debate whether the world outside of fashion shows is implied by them, and whether they are narrative in some sense, the shows themselves do nothing to build identification or a sense of a diegetic world. Whatever the logic of such sites, they are not dependent on narration in the sense we generally mean in fiction film and literature; they allow users to move through them in the order and at a rate of their own choosing, and they do not depend on the creation of a whole fantasy world.

Movie Web sites frequently open with music, or if not, the music begins with the trailer and thereafter many of the pages will have music as well. Many recent, current, and forthcoming films maintain Web sites with not just trailers, but games, information, and more.[41] Video game sites are quite similar, and they are structured similarly. Music appears not only in the trailers, where it is predictable, but also in other parts of the sites, like games, menu pages, and so forth. There is a sense emerging of a new use of music to accompany a user's walk through the virtual spaces on the site.

Most of these kinds of sites with music have a mute button, suggesting a whole new quandary for composers and producers: How does one set about creating an audiovisual complex in which the audio is not only expendable, but expendable at the whim of the user?

[39] In fact, since the early 2000s this focus on narrative and identification has begun to change, due to disciplinary shifts. All of the works from the 1980s and 1990s mentioned here so far, as well as *Hearing Film*, come from scholars trained in the film studies tradition, which is deeply influenced by literary studies, narratology and psychoanalysis. For good or ill, this has changed, so that much scholarship is now taking place in music departments, whose institutional and intellectual traditions are quite different. The participation of musicologists in the field is a welcome change, but the absence of film studies scholars is not. It is nothing short of shocking that some film departments continue to teach entire degree programs without a single course on sound and music, and that film scholars write entire articles about "films" without ever mentioning the auditory realm.

[40] There are a few important exceptions. The most recent are Nicolai Graakjær and Christian Jantzen's *Music in Advertising: Commercial Sounds in Media Communication and Other Settings* (Aalborg, Denmark: Aalborg Universitetsforlag, 2009), which is not as available as it should be; and *As Heard on TV: Popular Music in Advertising*, by Bethany Klein (Aldershot, UK: Ashgate, 2009). Other important contributions include sections of Nicholas Cook's *Analysing Musical Multimedia* (New York: Oxford University Press, 1998); David Huron's "Music in Advertising: An Analytic Paradigm," *Musical Quarterly* 73 (1989); and the body of research in consumer behavior, marketing, and advertising journals. It is also crucial to note work on sonic branding: Devon Powers, "Strange Powers: The Branded Sensorium and the Intrigue of Musical Sound," in *Blowing Up the Brand: Critical Perspectives on Promotional Culture*, ed. Melissa Aronczyk and Devon Powers (New York: Peter Lang, 2010); Steve Goodman, *Sonic Warfare: Sound, Affect, and the Ecology of Fear* (Cambridge, Mass.: MIT Press, 2010); and others.

[41] See, for example, http://www.paranorman.com, http://thegreatgatsby.warnerbros.com/, and http://megamind.com/ (all accessed June 4, 2013). *Megamind* was released in early November 2010, and no films with later release dates were found to have music on their Web sites yet.

One must be able to turn off the music, since colleagues and employers might be able to hear that the user isn't attending to work matters, or a housemate might be annoyed by it, or it might conflict with the music to which the user is listening while browsing.

Moreover, because the sites cannot be narratively conceived, there is usually no obvious preferred order to the sections one visits, and while there is nominally a beginning—the first page you get to, usually the home page—there does not seem to be any "end" page. The theoretical world we have created as film music scholars begins to recede in the face of these Web sites.

In all of these Web uses, the music cannot presume any control over matching between music and visuals; thus, in significant ways they resemble the video game music discussed previously. While music cannot count on hitting important visual points—a crucial function of film music and viral videos—the music on these sites has to convey mood and intensity.[42] If we imagine all the people worldwide who are at any given moment playing video games, engaging with viral videos, playing Web-based games, and browsing goods and movie pages, we understand that an enormous population is thus engaged in some or all of these activities.

This is no small matter. It suggests that our expectations and presumptions about the place of music in audiovisual texts are in the process of changing radically. People in their teens and twenties have had their expectations shaped for the first time since the advent of sound on film by media environments in which closely matched audio and visual tracks that combine to form a clear diegetic world are the minority.

Moreover, as I have argued elsewhere,[43] the strength of linear narrative itself is waning. While no one would argue that linear narrativity is disappearing, it certainly has been dethroned as the primary motor of popular culture, in favor of sensory and sensual experience. Films that are profoundly narrative continue to be made, but over the past decade or more the narratives of blockbuster films have been being leached out in favor of addressing the sensorium. Films now feature 3D, surround sound, and many other technologies, styles, and effects that make them almost tactile in their address, keeping audiences engaged not through identification, but by a constant flow of sensory experience.[44] Huge, carefully placed noises and objects coming at the audience in a 3D

42 Mood and intensity are basic functions of music that Web sites share with films and video games but not viral videos. Because of their frequent visual discontinuities and their tongue-in-cheek tone, viral videos generally operate on a very conscious plane, whereas mood and intensity work subconsciously.

43 Anahid Kassabian, "The Sound of a New Film Form," in *Popular Music and Film*, ed. Ian Inglis (London; New York: Routledge, 2003); and "Rethinking Point of Audition in *The Cell*," in *Lowering the Boom*, ed. Jay Beck and Tony Grajeda (Urbana; Chicago: University of Illinois Press, 2008), 299–306.

44 John Richardson, for one, addresses the flowing, tactile and other sensory qualities of recent audiovisual experience in *An Eye for Music: Popular Music and the Audiovisual Surreal* (New York, Oxford: Oxford University Press, 2011). It is surely the case that mainstream films have yet to exploit the myriad possibilities offered by the intersection of 5.1 surround sound and current 3D visual technologies. Though both leave plenty of room for growth and for newer technologies, a film that spent the time and money to truly work the intersensory dimensional potential of 5.1 and 3D technologies would be quite impressive.

version of the same trick as the Lumieres' train[45] have often left audiences critical of poor character development or weak plots, but delighted by the wonderful, thrilling effects. One such recent film is *Avatar*, about which many critics agreed that its art lies in the visual world it creates far more than in its story. The "Consensus" on Rotten Tomatoes reads: "It might be more impressive on a technical level than as a piece of storytelling, but Avatar reaffirms James Cameron's singular gift for imaginative, absorbing filmmaking."[46] The review of *Avatar* in the *New York Times* waxed poetic about the brilliant use of technology:

> The exotic creatures in "Avatar," which include an astonishment of undulating, flying, twitching and galloping organisms, don't just crawl through the underbrush; they thunder and shriek, yip and hiss, pointy teeth gleaming....
>
> The most important of these are the Na'vi, and while their movements can bring to mind old-fashioned stop-motion animation, their faces are a triumph of tech innovation, with tremors and twitches that make them immediately appealing and empathetic.[47]

Films like *Avatar*, *The Cell*, The *Matrix* trilogy, and the *Tomb Raider* series evidence a shift from the primacy of complex narrative and character development in favor of intensity, sensuality, and physicality. In short, we are entering a period in which diegesis is receding into the background in favor of sensory experience as the primary organizing principle of audiovisual forms.

Music and its place in audiovisual forms are changing, and they will continue to morph for some time as a result of these changes. (Arguably this may be a never-ending process, since new technologies and arrangements may always develop faster than we can theorize them.) Films are becoming less focused on linear narrative and narrativity and more on intense sensory experiences. Video games and Web sites are eschewing narrative in favor of mood and intensity. Viral videos swirl in a play of postmodern pastiche and parody. As these trends continue—and there is no reason to believe they won't—our sense of the primacy of the division between story world and real world is beginning to fade.[48] Or perhaps it has been fading for quite some time.

This would suggest that the definition of textual events in relation to diegesis is becoming less crucial. While it is difficult to imagine that diegesis or linear narrativity will disappear entirely, their hegemonic status is surely severely compromised, if not mortally wounded. And so, while it is important to make the distinction between the music heard by characters

[45] "Lumière: L'Arrivée d'un train à La Ciotat (1895)," uploaded by raphaeldpm on May 27, 2006, at http://www.youtube.com/watch?v=1dgLEDdFddk&feature=related.

[46] "Avatar (2009)," at http://www.rottentomatoes.com/m/avatar/?name_order=asc (accessed August 29, 2010).

[47] Manohla Dargis, "Movie Review: Avatar (Fox) (2009): A New Eden, Both Cosmic and Cinematic," *New York Times*, December 17, 2009, http://movies.nytimes.com/2009/12/18/movies/18avatar.html (accessed August 29, 2010).

[48] Baudrillard's *Simulacra and Simulation*, trans. Sheila Faria Glaser (Ann Arbor: University of Michigan Press, 1994) is an early foray into this territory, since which there have been many, many more.

in an audiovisual text and music not heard by them—as well as to make the distinction between extradiegetic and intradiegetic sound and music, as suggested by Winters—it is also time to once and for all lay to rest the centrality of this problematic in our field.

As linear narrative forms like film are replaced with more interactive, less linear forms like Web sites, viral videos, and video games, and as synchronization becomes less commonplace in the narrative forms that remain, our theories need not just revision, but rethinking. We need to understand the relationships among players and video games, consumers and Web sites, and viral videos and their creators and audiences. Users clearly are not engaged in the same processes of identification as they are with mainstream Hollywood films (or with other kinds of films from other traditions), so the musical engagements also must be different. Video games condition remarkably intense identifications that research is just beginning to theorize;[49] central to this project will have to be an analysis of the discourse of fear surrounding gaming. We are afraid of games and the attachments of players to them, as the stories of people dying while playing point out.[50] Affect itself will also come into focus, because video games are nothing if not technologies of affect.[51] Conversely, Web sites and viral videos condition no identifications at all, operating instead according to entirely different logics.

As an example of what I am suggesting, I know of no scholarship on video game music that analyzes carefully the "middles" of cues, that is, the loops I described previously, yet they may well be the arena in which multimedia music develops most distinctively. All of these so-called new media forms are becoming, both collectively and separately, new carriers of artistic expression, with their own needs and dependencies on sound and

[49] Video game studies as a field is still creating its own theories, and the small group of game sound and music scholars is just beginning to understand some first principles. See, for important examples, Karen Collins, *Game Sound: An Introduction to the History, Theory, and Practice of Video Game Music and Sound Design* (Cambridge, Mass.; London: MIT Press, 2008); Collins, ed., *From Pac-Man to Pop Music: Interactive Music in Games and New Media* (Aldershot, UK: Ashgate, 2008); Jamie Sexton, ed., *Music, Sound and Multimedia: From the Live to the Virtual* (Edinburgh: Edinburgh University Press, 2007); Zach Whalen, "Play Along—An Approach to Videogame Music," *Game Studies* 4 (2004), at http://www.gamestudies.org/0401/whalen/ (accessed September 28, 2011); and Mark Grimshaw and Gareth Scott, "Situating Gaming as a Sonic Experience: The Acoustic Ecology of First Person Shooters," in *Situated Play (2007): Proceedings of DIGRA, Digital Games Research Association, Tokyo, Japan, September 24–28, 2007*, at http://hdl.handle.net/2436/35996 (accessed November 28, 2012).

[50] Such stories appear not infrequently in the news. For example, in 2005 the BBC reported on a 28-year-old South Korean gamer who had died after playing 50 hours straight with little sleep and no food ("S Korean Dies after Games Session," *BBC News*, August 10, 2005, at http://news.bbc.co.uk/1/hi/technology/4137782.stm [accessed November 28, 2012]). Similarly, in 2007 ZDNet's *Tech Republic* reported on a 30-year-old Chinese gamer who had died after three days of game play (Justin Fielding, "Chinese Gamer Dies from Exhaustion!" September 17, 2007, at http://blogs.techrepublic.com.com/networking/?p=340 [accessed August 29, 2010]). In both cases the men were playing in Internet cafes. Along with deaths, reports of addictions abound. There is a widespread public discourse about the intensity of gamers' identifications and relationships with the games they play and with gaming in general.

[51] Here I mean affect in the sense that Patricia Clough, Brian Massumi, and others theorize it, as a process that engages bodies, parts of bodies, technologies, and populations. See, for example, the introduction to *The Affective Turn: Theorizing the Social*, edited by Clough with Jean Halley (Durham, N.C.: Duke University Press, 2007), 1–33.

music. Because many new forms will be unable to depend on known and stable matches between audio and visual tracks, they will need new kinds of music, new compositional strategies, for what sound and music can do and how they can and should go about doing it.[52] From this perspective, the approaches of video game composers to sections of the game in which the player is just walking around may well prove to be the most significant contribution they make to the field of audiovisual studies, because many new media forms will need similar strategies.

By looking at and listening to the changes these new forms bring with them, we will open up a whole new approach not only to these forms, which as I have argued here is crucial, but also to contemporary receptions of film and television, since the sensibilities and understandings developed through these prevailing media forms cannot but affect how we engage more traditional forms as well. The audiovisual scholarly terrain is a wide open horizon, waiting to be rewritten by scholars prepared to think about video games, Web sites, viral videos, and all the multisensory phenomena that will follow them.

Notes

This article is vastly improved by the advice and insights of Leo G. Svendsen, James Barnaby, and most especially Maral K. Svendsen.

References

Altman, Rick. "Television Sound." In *Studies in Entertainment: Critical Approaches to Mass Culture*, edited by Tania Modleski, 39–54. Bloomington: Indiana University Press, 1986.

Baudrillard, Jean. *Simulacra and Simulation*. Ann Arbor: University of Michigan Press, 1994.

Boschi, Elena. "Radiofreccia: A New Direction for Italian Film Music?" Paper presented at the Sound, Music, and the Moving Image Conference, Institute of Musical Research, University of London, September 10–12, 2007.

Brown, Royal S. *Overtones and Undertones: Reading Film Music*. Berkeley; Los Angeles: University of California Press, 1994.

Chatfield, Tom. "Videogames Now Outperform Hollywood Movies." *The Observer*, September 27, 2009, at http://www.guardian.co.uk/technology/gamesblog/2009/sep/27/videogames-hollywood (accessed August 30, 2010).

Chion, Michel. "Television, Video Art, Music Video." In *Audio-Vision: Sound on Screen*, edited by Michel Chion and translated by Claudia Gorbman, 157–168. New York: Columbia University Press, 1994.

[52] This use of music in new media audiovisual forms brings it into contiguity with music composed for other uses, such as for exhibition spaces. The recent exhibit of artifacts from King Tutankhamen's tomb, for example, had different music originally composed for the exhibit in each room, and the CD was available for purchase: David Mauk, *Ambient Sounds of Ancient Egypt: The Official Music Created for Tutankhamun and The Golden Age of the Pharaohs*, B0013GBNI8 (CD) (National Geographic, 2005).

Clough, Patricia, ed., with Jean Halley. *The Affective Turn: Theorizing the Social*. Durham, N.C.: Duke University Press, 2007.

Coates, Norma. "Filling in Holes: Television Music as a Recuperation of Popular Music on Television." *Music, Sound, and the Moving Image* 1, no. 1 (2007): 21–25.

Collins, Karen, ed. *From Pac-Man to Pop Music: Interactive Music in Games and New Media*. Aldershot, UK: Ashgate, 2008.

Collins, Karen. *Game Sound: An Introduction to the History, Theory, and Practice of Video Game Music and Sound Design*. Cambridge, Mass.; London: MIT Press, 2008.

Cook, Nicholas. *Analysing Musical Multimedia*. New York: Oxford University Press, 1998.

Dargis, Mahnola. "Movie Review: Avatar (Fox) (2009): A New Eden, Both Cosmic and Cinematic." *New York Times*, December 17, 2009, at http://movies.nytimes.com/2009/12/18/movies/18avatar.html (accessed August 29, 2010).

Deaville, James, ed. *Music in Television: Channels of Listening*. New York: Routledge, 2011.

Fielding, Justin. "Chinese Gamer Dies from Exhaustion!" *Tech Republic*, September 17, 2007, at http://blogs.techrepublic.com.com/networking/?p=340 (accessed August 29, 2010).

Flinn, Caryl. *Strains of Utopia: Gender, Nostalgia and Hollywood Film Music*. Princeton, N.J.: Princeton University Press, 1992.

Forman, Murray. "Television before Television Genre: The Case of Popular Music." *Journal of Popular Film and Television* 31 (2003): 5–16.

Goodman, Steve. *Sonic Warfare: Sound, Affect, and the Ecology of Fear*. Cambridge, Mass.: MIT Press, 2010.

Gorbman, Claudia. "Narrative Film Music." *Yale French Studies* 60 (1980): 183–203.

Gorbman, Claudia. *Unheard Melodies: Narrative Film Music*. Bloomington: Indiana University Press, 1987.

Graakjær, Nicolai, and Christian Jantzen. *Music in Advertising: Commercial Sounds in Media Communication and Other Settings*. Aalborg, Denmark: Aalborg Universitetsforlag, 2009.

Grimshaw, Mark, and Gareth Scott. "Situating Gaming as a Sonic Experience: The Acoustic Ecology of First Person Shooters." In *Situated Play (2007): Proceedings of DIGRA, Digital Games Research Association, Tokyo, Japan, September 24–28, 2007*, at http://hdl.handle.net/2436/35996 (accessed November 28, 2012).

Hilmes, Michele. "Foregrounding Sound: New (and Old) Directions in Sound Studies." *Cinema Journal* 48 (2008): 116–146.

Huron, David. "Music in Advertising: An Analytic Paradigm." *Musical Quarterly* 73 (1989): 557–574.

Kalinak, Kathryn. *Settling the Score: Music and the Classical Hollywood Film*. Madison: University of Wisconsin Press, 1992.

Kassabian, Anahid. *Hearing Film: Tracking Identifications in Contemporary Hollywood Film Music*. London; New York: Routledge, 2001.

Kassabian, Anahid. "The Sound of a New Film Form." In *Popular Music and Film*, edited by Ian Inglis, 91–101. London; New York: Wallflower, 2003.

Kassabian, Anahid. "Rethinking Point of Audition in *The Cell*." In *Lowering the Boom: Critical Studies in Film Sound*, edited by Jay Beck and Tony Grajeda, 299–306. Urbana; Chicago: University of Illinois Press, 2008.

Kassabian, Anahid. "Music, Sound and the Moving Image: The Present and a Future?" In *The Ashgate Research Companion to Popular Musicology*, edited by Derek B. Scott, 43–57. Farnham, UK: Ashgate, 2009.

Klein, Bethany. *As Heard on TV: Popular Music in Advertising*. Aldershot, UK: Ashgate, 2009.

Linderman, Deborah. "The Mise-en-Abyme in Hitchcock's *Vertigo*." *Cinema Journal* 30 (1991): 51–74.

Modleski, Tania. *Studies in Entertainment: Critical Approaches to Mass Culture.* Bloomington: Indiana University Press, 1986.

Powers, Devon. "Strange Powers: The Branded Sensorium and the Intrigue of Musical Sound." In *Blowing Up the Brand: Critical Perspectives on Promotional Culture*, edited by Melissa Aronczyk and Devon Powers, 285–306. New York: Peter Lang, 2010.

Prince, Gerald. *A Dictionary of Narratology*. Lincoln; London: University of Nebraska Press, 2003. As quoted in "Diegesis." *Wikipedia*, at http://en.wikipedia.org/wiki/Diegesis (last modified August 16, 2011).

Rodman, Ron. *Tuning In: American Narrative Television Music*. Oxford; New York: Oxford University Press, 2010.

Rosenbloom, Stephanie. "Selling a Concept with a Song." *New York Times*, August 5, 2007, at http://www.nytimes.com/2007/08/05/realestate/05cov.html?_r=1&oref=slogin&ref=music&pagewanted=all (accessed September 28, 2011).

"S Korean Dies after Games Session." *BBC News*, August 10, 2005, at http://news.bbc.co.uk/1/hi/technology/4137782.stm (accessed November 28, 2012).

Sexton, Jamie, ed. *Music, Sound and Multimedia: From the Live to the Virtual.* Edinburgh: Edinburgh University Press, 2007.

Smith, Jeff. *The Sounds of Commerce: Marketing Popular Film Music*. New York: Columbia University Press, 1998.

Stilwell, Robynn. "The Fantastical Gap between Diegetic and Nondiegetic." In *Beyond the Soundtrack*, edited by Daniel Goldmark, Lawrence Kramer, and Richard Leppert, 184–204. Berkeley; Los Angeles: University of California Press, 2007.

Tagg, Philip. *Kojak: 50 Seconds of Television Music. Towards the Analysis of Affect in Popular Music*. Göteborg, Sweden: Musikvetenskapliga institutionen vid Göteborgs universitet, 1979.

Whalen, Zach. "Play Along—An Approach to Videogame Music." *Game Studies* 4 (2004), at http://www.gamestudies.org/0401/whalen/ (accessed September 28, 2011).

Winters, Ben. "The Non-diegetic Fallacy: Film, Music, and Narrative Space." *Music and Letters* 91 (2010): 224–244.

Filmography

Avatar. Directed by James Cameron. (2009). Twentieth Century Fox, 2010. DVD.

Cell, The. Directed by Tarsem Singh. (2000). New Line Cinema, 2001. DVD.

Lara Croft: Tomb Raider. Directed by Simon West. (2001). Paramount Home Entertainment, 2001. DVD.

The Matrix. Directed by Andy Wachowski and Larry Wachowski. (1999). Warner Home Video, 1999. DVD.

Platoon. Directed by Oliver Stone. (1986). Twentieth Century Fox, 2000. DVD.

CHAPTER 6

SOUNDING OUT FILM

STEVEN CONNOR

The À *Voir*

For Rick Altman, sound has no essence, no definitive shape or volume, no archaic resonances, no obvious destiny in becoming part of film's body. Sound is intrinsically mobile, taken up anew in different ways according to different kinds of hearing situations, different points of view—or "points of audition." The reason for taking sound seriously in the analysis of cinema is that there is so little to be said about film sound *as such*. Sound, according to Altman, is the reminder, through its own contingent, excrescent condition, of cinema's impurity.[1] It is held together, in Altman's account, by the question of sonorous space and its coordination with the visible space of the screen. The question of space is dominant also in those, like Kaja Silverman, who take their models from Didier Anzieu's conception of the primal "acoustic envelope."[2]

This emphasis on the spatial provenance of sound fits neatly alongside the larger preoccupation of film theorists with the ways in which the viewer is to be summoned or "sutured" into the film space. Everything falls between the alternatives of diffused or centered subjectivity. It sometimes seems as though cinema issues the single command: *pull yourself together*. The demand for the screen, and for screened sound, is of a piece with the demand for a certain kind of reproportioned body, the necessity of preventing scattering, dismemberment, hypertrophy, unnaturalness, and monstrosity.

1 Rick Altman, "The Material Heterogeneity of Recorded Sound" and "Introduction: Sound History," in *Sound Theory, Sound Practice*, ed. Rick Altman (New York; London: Routledge, 1992), 15–31, 113–125.

2 Kaja Silverman, *The Acoustic Mirror: The Female Voice in Psychoanalysis and Cinema* (Bloomington: Indiana University Press, 1988).

The idea of the stabilizing function of sound seems like the reversal of the economy of sound and vision set out in a 1980 essay of Altman's, "Moving Lips: Cinema as Ventriloquism," in which sound is said to pose a question for sight to answer. In Hollywood talkies of the 1930s onward, as explicated by Altman, it is vision that perplexes and sound that reassures.[3] Vision keeps saying, "Where?" while sound says, "Here!"

Of course sound could also suggest other spaces than that of the screen, and indeed, in the form of the voice-over, times other than those represented on the screen. Sound could signify the "off." Silent cinema could refer to the "off" only through gesture, pointing to the wings or the flies—look, over there!—or by literally cutting between scenes. Sound allowed cinema to refer to other, more indeterminate spaces, even, with Michel Chion's notion of the *acousmêtre*, to indeterminate spaces within the visible space of the screen, boxes, cupboards, coffins, and the like.[4] It took cinema a long time to be able to explore the possibilities of these other spaces—to fully incorporate radio. But all this is still a matter of space, which is still to say, the operative dream of reducing sound to spatial coordinates, to some representable space relative to the space of the screen.

One can imagine how such a conception of sound might actually be assisted by the application of Bertram Lewin's idea of the "dream screen." Lewin suggested that the screen—conceived in fantasy as the invisible support underlying, but also sustaining, all the violent action played out across it—was what held the dream together.[5] We can see the concern with synchronization and cospatialization as an enlargement of this function of the screen, assisting in the task of simultaneously multiplying the stimuli to awakening—giving shock and surprise and disgust and overload—while keeping the viewer-dreamer asleep or knitted into the dream. The envelope of sound becomes equivalent to the containing skin of the screen.

This emphasis on vision, perspective, and position may perhaps be seen as no more than an accurate reflection of the evolution of cinema itself. For as Altman has shown, audiences do not even need auditory realism. It may be true that where cinema funnels the audience's attention inward, sound lets in the street and lets cinema out onto the street—for example, in the operations of ballyhoo, the broadcasting of the soundtrack through loudspeakers to passersby. But it does not matter where the sound comes from, where the loudspeakers are placed, where one is sitting in the auditorium—all of those elements that Altman and others insist are the signs of the radical heterogeneity of sound. Altman writes as though the material fact of sonorous diffusion were phenomenologically identical with the experience of cinema sound, when the reality seems to have been the opposite: a massive attempt to keep cinema silent, to keep its audience

[3] Rick Altman, "Moving Lips: Cinema as Ventriloquism," *Yale French Studies* 60 (1980): 67–79.

[4] Michel Chion, *Audio-Vision: Sound on Screen*, trans. Claudia Gorbman (New York: Columbia University Press, 1994), 129–131.

[5] Bertram D. Lewin, "Sleep, the Mouth, and the Dream Screen," *Psychoanalytic Quarterly* 15 (1946): 419–434.

asleep and sunk in its numb, tumultuous dream. The dream screen knows that sound is a toxic shock; it protects itself against sound by swallowing it up into legibility, filtering out everything but visible meaning. So imperative was the need to swallow sound and make it safe for synchronicity that cinema for a while almost lost the capacity to see anything but pairs of lips. "The people," Alberto Cavalcanti rather snootily declared in 1929, six years before the making of his own reflection on the ventriloquist powers of cinema in *Dead of Night*, "wanted to see the people speaking in sync."[6] Cinema became, for a while, a primitive, two-sided organism, an eye locked onto a mouth. It is not vision, but visible speech that comes to represent the norm. In this sense cinema recapitulates the movement of the gramophone, which quickly narrowed down the spectrum of recorded sound to the individual singing voice.

During the 1930s everything seemed to come down to the question: How can the screen be made to talk? Everything had to be returned to the screen, everything had to be given a voice, and everything heard had to be given *as* a voice. Nothing heard could remain without a visible or locatable source. Intelligibility was all. For Rudolf Arnheim, this meant an anthropomorphization of cinema's speech:

> In the universal silence of the image, the fragments of a broken vase could "talk" exactly the way a character talked to his neighbor, and a person approaching on a road and visible on the horizon as a mere dot "talked" as someone acting in close-up. This homogeneity, which is completely foreign to the theater but familiar to painting, is destroyed by a talking film: it endows the character with speech, and since only he can have it, all other things are pushed into the background.[7]

Only humans speak, but the cinema itself has become human, has become an organ of speech. Cinema became a kind of visual speech—what Vivian Sobchack called the "address of the eye."[8]

Everything depends on the screen, on what is seen or shown. Everything becomes a matter, not just of the visible, or of the available for sight, but of the *à voir*, of the to-be-seen, and along with that, the appropriative *à avoir*, the to-be-had. We might imagine that these conditions would be much more evident in the silent film, in which only what could be seen could register at all. There, voice is translated into gesture, the body taking over from the speaking lips. But in fact, this necessity to refer everything to the screen seems to have become more rather than less remorseless in sound cinema, in which nothing will be audible that cannot be screened—filtered through the

[6] Alberto Cavalcanti, "Sound in Films," in *Film Sound: Theory and Practice*, ed. Elizabeth Weis and John Belton (New York: Columbia University Press, 1985), 102.

[7] Rudolf Arnheim, "A New Laocoön: Artistic Composites and the Talking Film," in *Film as Art* (Berkeley; Los Angeles; London: University of California Press, 1957), 227.

[8] Vivian Sobchack, *The Address of the Eye: A Phenomenology of Film Experience* (Princeton, N.J.: Princeton University Press, 1992).

requirements of the visible, which for the greater part of the cinema's history has meant visible speech.

The demand for the eye is the infant (= speechless) demand of cinema. Children demand the eye of their parents or caretakers; there is something deeply unsatisfactory for them in narrative or description. Come here; come and look; stop what you are doing and look at me. The desire to be looked at, to capture the gaze of another, is much more imperious than the desire to be a bodiless, invisible, Cartesian eye, taking possession of a world yielded up for it. The allegedly objectifying power of the male gaze in cinema, hungrily and cannibalistically consuming everything on the screen, is repeatedly overcome by the objectifying power of the screen, which demands "look at this," capturing and fixing the eye, and in the process capturing and fixing everything *in* the eye, making everything a matter of the *à voir*, of the to-be-seen. The *fascinum*, which deflects and captures the evil eye, is really an interception of cinema in the net of sight. Sound is quickly recruited to this economy.

Deaf Cinema

The central insight of Vivian Sobchack's work concerns the ways in which cinema gives us mediated perception—the embodied perceptions of another—directly, in a way that we take into our own being as we view the film. Watching a film is both a direct and mediated experience of direct experience as mediation. We both perceive a world *within* the immediate experience of an "other" and *without* it, as immediate experience mediated by an "other." Watching a film, we can see the seeing as well as the seen, hear the hearing as well as the heard, and feel the movement as well as the moved. We thus take into ourselves, appropriating it as our own, another's way of perceiving: the film's body. The kind of perception in which we engage while watching a film is signification: it is access to that primary perception-as-signification that is one of Merleau-Ponty's leading themes: "This is how I see it." Film grows its body through this capacity for double looking, for looking, via our eyes, over its own shoulder. As we look at a film, we give it the eyes to see itself and to see itself seeing. As we watch a film, film watches its own body coming into shape. When I see something on the screen, I do not see an object. I redouble an act of looking; I take into myself and reenact the camera's look. What is more, I am the film's prosthesis, the means by which it can show what it sees as a seeing; I am the otherness by which it can complete its circuit of self-seeing, can watch itself seeing, by showing itself as an act of seeing, for me to see. When I hear something on a soundtrack, I may listen with the microphone's ears, redouble its way of listening, but I do not in the same way speak with its speech, in unison.

This is to say that I do not altogether accept Michel Chion's characterization of the process of auditory identification with what he calls "the I-voice," when he claims that, in a film, "when the voice is heard in sound closeup without reverb, it is likely to be at once the voice the spectator internalizes as his or her own and the voice that takes total possession of the diegetic space. It is both completely internal and invading the entire universe."[9] Chion is here suggesting that there could be a kind of vocal point of view that is equivalent to the visual point of view offered to us by the camera. Others have connected this process of identification with voice-over narrative. I think that the reason the audio-viewer does not identify in this way lies in the question of synchronization. There is always something belated about auditory identification, partly because the nature of sound is to occupy a passage rather than an instant of time, a duration rather than a moment. To hear a sound, one must have already heard it start to decay, or come to an end; one must already have started finishing hearing it. One hears very largely analeptically, in memory, even with the most shockingly immediate of sound effects; they appear to punch a hole in auditory attention, which is then only slowly filled up with definition. Sound is always, as Rick Altman has put it, "sound hermeneutic." A question is always broached by a sound, a question that cannot be laid to rest until the sound is embodied, prescribed an origin, and returned to the source from which it can then be seen to have come. Sound must be sighted.[10] Sound comes first, so that it can be shown to have come second, to have emanated from a source. This is because sound is temporal, a matter of events rather than states. In the subordination of sound to sight, do we not see the priority of spatiality to temporality, the repeated demonstration that there are states that produce or result in events. We always seem to hear the sound of an event after the event itself. Sound is the actualization of a potential, but it has no potency, no puissance or pressure of its own.

By contrast, visual perception is proleptic, because, as Merleau-Ponty and others have shown, it is closely bound up with the active throwing forward or reaching out of ourselves and our projects into the world. I do not merely see the tennis ball coming over the net; as I see it, I am already disposing my limbs in a kind of anticipatory visualization to make contact with it, the seeing being always a kind of preparatory motion. We use our eyes not merely to fix ourselves in position, to put ourselves in the place of the camera, but also to move ourselves into the place that we wish or expect it and ourselves imminently to be. The imminence of looking is what enables one to internalize the camera's look as one's own, appearing to drive and direct its gaze with our curiosity and appetite. The cinema satisfies our longing for identification because it seems obedient to our wishes. This is what makes the physical fact of the projectedness of cinema so potent a metaphor of its workings. If we do indeed internalize voices and even sounds, by contrast, it is as a result of our compliance with them rather than theirs with us. If we identify with the "I-voice" of the unseen or *acousmêtric* narrator, it is because this voice has exceptionally gathered to it the powers to direct or produce or project what we are about to see in advance.

It may be objected that music and song are also special cases here. Does this not sometimes imply or enable a kind of identification or introjection, if only because music, unlike speech, is predictable? Those who come to know a film's soundtrack like a melody

9 Chion, *Audio-Vision*, 79–80.

10 Altman, "Moving Lips," 74.

are indeed able to lip-synch it, as in those cinemas that show *Casablanca* to its adoring audiences: when the sound fails, the audience can intone the missing dialogue. I think these are important exceptions, and they point us to the link between obliquity and memory. We can only anticipate sound as a result of the reactivation of memory; memory is much less requisite for the operations of visual projection. This perhaps points to a difference between music and raw sound: music allows the film to hear itself, allows hearing itself to rise into self-consciousness. But music does not come from cinema's mouth, from the mouth of the screen, from the speaking lips. Music, like sound, is emitted rather than spoken. It comes from somewhere else in film's body, from the underneath or backside of that body. There is nothing to correspond in the visual image to this emission.

If film's eye is the means by which it acquires a reflexive, self-seeing body and is the point in the film apparatus at which the body of the film and the body of the viewer come together—in particular in the proffering and acceptance of a "point of view"—there is no equivalent prosthetic organ for film sound. Clearly, in one sense the microphone is equivalent to the camera, in being film's ear where the camera is its eye. But we do not naturally or easily orient ourselves with respect to the microphone as we do with respect to the camera. There seem to be a number of reasons for this. The first is that the microphone is studiously kept invisible; indeed, a whole art and technology has grown up to keep the devices for registering sound themselves unregistered. The camera cannot be looked through without announcing itself as being looked through, so it is always itself visible in what it makes available to see. It is not just that microphones happen to be invisible; cameras usually are, too. It is also that, as Chion puts it, "the mike must remain excluded not only from the visual and auditory field (microphone noises, etc.), but also from the spectator's very *mental representation*."[11] This implies that we do not find it natural to identify what have been called "points of audition" in the same way that we naturally identify point of view, partly because of the magnetizing pull of the visual, which will tend to pull everything into its own visual configurations. Point of audition mixing is difficult to maintain, for this reason.

The unrepresentability of point of audition, the difficulty of forming the same kind of bond between the microphone and the ear of the viewer as is formed between the camera and the eye of the viewer, also seems to derive from another important distinction between seeing and hearing. We can cut visual material, but cannot, apart from specific and exceptional circumstances, such as lap-dissolves, sustainedly or tolerably *mix* this material, as we can mix sound. In split-screen films or in sustained passages of superimposition, the eye is forced to flick uncomfortably backward and forward between the two images thus combined, as in certain optical illusions. The reason for this is that we experience and think of seeing as an action necessarily performed from one particular perspective. Although we have two eyes, so accustomed are we to synthesizing the information they collect that there is no difficulty in identifying ourselves with the monocular mode of cinema. Experientially, none of us can see with two eyes. Perhaps this very

[11] Chion, *Audio-Vision*, 93.

built-in limitation in looking, the very fact that we cannot see something from two different points of view simultaneously—least of all, perhaps, in a cubist painting—is what makes looking apt for reflexivity, for the cognitive doubling of the eye of flesh by the eye of the mind, which can see the outward eye looking.

We do not experience hearing as material coming to a point, whether in ourselves or anywhere else. We have two ears, as well as many other channels of hearing: the bones of the skull, the fingertips, the soles of the feet. Sound is mapped across the whole body, rather than converging conelike on one organ of entry. When we hear a sound that we refer to a place high above our heads or off to one side, the effect is of a sound striking us on the appropriate portion of the body, rather than necessarily being conducted toward the ears. We feel sight come in at the eyes, which is one of the things that make visual response feel so actively forensic. The projector is an eyelike device for producing rather than collecting visual material. We feel hearing coming in almost at every portion of our bodies, which then become a variably vibrating membrane rather than a projector. This, along with the fact that it is so easy to mix together sounds gathered from different points of audition at different times or to transform them in various ways, militates against the identification with and internalization of the microphone as a single hearing point. Seeing is monoptic in the way it brings things to a point; hearing is panaural. The hearing body, if body it is, is thus in a very literal sense a body without a single identifying organ. I show later in this discussion that not having an organ seems to deprive the hearing body of film of reflexivity, of being able to intend itself as the means of intending the world, of a means of knowing its own way of knowing.

It was often said during the 1920s and 1930s that the addition of sound to the cinema meant that the cinema had learned to talk. This makes for some striking parallels between the new technology and the long history of concern about how to give speech to the deaf, a history that has been charted in Jonathan Rée's *I See a Voice*.[12] The majority of "deaf and dumb" people in history have not been mute for any organic reason, but only because they have never heard themselves. Rée shows the recurrent split between those who have believed in the power of visible speech, in the form of signing and gesture, and those who have attempted to train the deaf to speak without the normal feedback mechanism provided by self-hearing. It has seemed to many of the latter that only by being given access to a spoken language could the deaf be given a fully living, fully human body. The recurrent concern is that, unless one can hear the words one speaks, the result of teaching the deaf to speak is just the creation of a talking machine, a parrot or ventriloquist's dummy.

One may perhaps see the so-called silent cinema in these terms: not as a form of representation that cannot make itself heard, but as a deaf cinema, that cannot sufficiently speak up for itself, because it cannot hear itself through our ears as it sees itself through our eyes. Just as "deaf and dumb" people typically engage in many and varied kinds of

[12] Jonathan Rée, *I See a Voice: A Philosophical History of Language, Deafness and the Senses* (London: HarperCollins, 1999).

vocalizations, so is the silent cinema actually extravagantly full of utterance and sonorous occasion—cries, concussions, explosions, expostulations, general sound and fury. It was of course necessary to signify this sound in all kinds of different ways—by movement, posture, gesture, expression, and intertitle. It took the coming of sound to make silence possible in the cinema. Even the most deadpan and inexpressive performers, like Buster Keaton or Harold Lloyd, derive their innocence or serenity from their apparent deafness to the clamor around them. They are cut off, belonging with us in the audience, because *they can't hear either*.

Perhaps we should think of silent cinema in terms of the transmigration of faculties sometimes reported in nineteenth-century mesmerism and hysteria. In silent cinema, sound passed across into the visible signs of bodily posture, movement, and appearance. It does indeed seem to have been the case, as Alan Williams has argued, that the coming of sound resulted in a much more docile, less melodramatic body.[13] Contemporary commentators also noticed the stilling of the camera. Speech had been taken back from the body, into which, under the regime of mutism and aphonia before the talkies, it had hysterically passed, to the mouth; had been taken back from the body of the world, for the human body. Indeed, the mouth itself seems to have thinned, to have become ever more tight lipped and immaterial.

The ambition here, for cinema to complete its circuit of self-recognition in self-audition, may be mistaken. For as sound has evolved, it has been the dimension of noise, rather than dialogue or music, that has most developed, a noise that is always an unencompassable part of the voice. Cinema wants its own voice and wants to hear itself speaking, but it remains a talking head that cannot hear itself. Cinema sees for itself, sees things with its own eyes. Words—and sounds—by contrast are always being put into its mouth. Perhaps in some fundamental sense, even the talking cinema remains deaf. We see what the cinema cannot hear of itself. Much of the dialogue and speaking sound effects for films is in fact supplied for the image, rather than derived from it, in ADR (automatic dialogue replacement), Foleying, and other processes, in a process of lip-reading. Sound speaks, and the sound editor reads its lips.

This is one of the most important reasons that it does not make complete sense to speak of a sonorous body of film to correspond to, or even to compete with, its visual body. Film can never coincide with itself as sound. The body of sound is a body all right, but it is not film's own body.

Cutting and Mixing

Sight sees double. Seeing is layered and folded, one thing superimposed against, or cut out of, something else: a figure against a ground, a framed action or event. There is

[13] Alan Williams, "Historical and Theoretical Issues in the Coming of Recorded Sound to the Cinema," in *Sound Theory, Sound Practice*, ed. Rick Altman (New York; London: Routledge, 1992), 135.

near-universal agreement about the minimal unit of the visual language of film: it is the shot, that which exists between one cut and another. Shots have visible edges. We see the end of the shot and the beginning of another as an edge, just as we keep in view the edge of the frame even as we concentrate our attention on what is going on in the frame. The universal language of cutting replicates the blinking and flickering, the continuous intermittence (and concomitant power of looking away) that constitutes sight and is the basis of the kinetic illusion of cinema. Everywhere there are visible ridges, fringes, folds, edges, lines, guillotines, splits, discontinuities, and overlayerings.

The fact that cinematic vision is a matter of edges and intermittences is related to its reflexivity, its power to see itself for itself, to hold itself in view. In cinema there is an ostension: the presentation of something like a "sight-act" that corresponds to the speech act. When we acknowledge the illocutionary force of what somebody has said to us, we say, "I see what you're saying," meaning: I understand that, in saying what you have just said, you were meaning to perform this or that action, of warning, promising, congratulation, reproof, permission, pardoning, etc. Similarly, we acknowledge the act of seeing constituted at any moment in a film and perhaps also the total way of seeing constituted by an entire film, or filmic oeuvre, by saying, "Yes, I see what you're seeing; I see how you've seen that, and I see how you are presenting to my view what appeared to yours." As we watch a film, our attention is a seam, flickering between seeing the object and seeing the camera's look at the object. It is therefore no accident that the distinctiveness and power of silent film should have been understood above all in terms of collage and montage, or the laying of discrete elements adjacent to or on top of each other.

So film undoubtedly has a language, perhaps because it always already was one. Film was always capable of showing what it was by the same means that it employed to be what it was. There is a language—of forms, processes, events, actions, and concepts—that is *adequate* to the visual experience of film: not identical with it, but adequate to it. It is much harder to come up with a language that is adequate in the same way to film sound. The language of vision suffices because it replicates (refolds, isomorphically transposes) vision's power to see and grasp itself, to abstract itself, to reflect and reflect on itself. We can analyze the visual components of film in language because the gap between the language and the film is isomorphic, within the visual experience of film itself. The language of sound is not adequate to sound because it is contaminated by it; it does not represent sound, but merges with it. This is not isomorphism, which preserves two equivalent structures in their equivalence, but metamorphosis: language and its object entering into each other in mutually mutative mimicry.

So the space of visuality in film is always at least double. It is a space in which heterogeneous objects can move around. There is always a space within which what visibly happens takes place. There is always a mise-en-scène, a setting, a setup, a putting into the scene. But sound, though always recruited and commuted to this scenography, can also participate in another, more uncertain, and perhaps archaic order. Sound, as Michel Chion has emphasized, has no frame. There is nothing to *hold* it in, so there is nothing to hold it *in*. Vision has the screen, and on top of the screen the image, which can be full or empty of images, but is always there as the space within which images play. There is always an edge and an outside to the frame, even, perhaps especially, when action seems to spill beyond it. There is no "framing" of sound in the metaphorical sense, either: no way to put the hearing of sound into a frame and overhear it. Hearing is always and only exposure of the ear. There is no ear of the mind as there is an eye of the mind, just as, and perhaps just because, there are no earlids to correspond to eyelids.

Mixed Bodies

It can be agreed that sound in cinema is bodily. But it is bodiliness of a certain kind, diffuse and intermittent. It is intense, but evanescent. It has no place to reside or come to rest. The image on the screen installs us at the point of view, every seat being the monarch's seat, the best seat in the house. The sound of the screen is not primarily "on" the screen, but in the listener. The very concern about the spatiality of film sound, shared by early sound recordists, technicians, and cinema designers and contemporary film theorists alike, may be a concern not so much to establish the right place for sound and hearing, as to make them signify in a spatial register at all. For sound works—or can work—by a special kind of proximity, which ducks underneath proxemics, perspective, position. Sound depends, for example, on the apprehension of the *behind* and the *underneath*.

Sound must be understood as primarily experienced, or at least at times experiencable, not in the modality of ostension, or exhibition, but in the modality of what might be called the *mutative commixture of substances*. Sound is substantial, plastic, voluminous. In sight, things move across or come up against each other. The visual channel of film is, to borrow a Joycean word, a "collideorscape." Everywhere in the order of cinematic sight (which is not identical with the order of cinema in total, or as such) there is this combination and correlation, distinction and differentiation. What sight does not permit is commixture. When sounds come together, by contrast, they change and are changed; they enter into each other. Edges dissolve. When one hears a sound, one never hears just one thing. One hears the sound of contact, of echo, reverberation of one thing against another; any sound is always at least two. One never even hears a particular commingled sound—a footstep, a punch, a shot, a shout—alone and uncommingled; one hears the sounding of the sound in a particular environment, the sound as it has been touched and retouched in the acoustic context through which it has spread, which has imparted its own particular qualities to the sound, bleaching out certain frequencies, dampening or sharpening the attack or decay of the sound, desiccating or liquefying its timbre, and emaciating it or doubling it in reverberation. There is no pure silence to be heard in the cinema, just as there is no blank screen to be seen that does not strike us as blankness projected onto the supporting screen. Sound recordists always take care never to leave a location without recording several samples of its characteristic silence-imprint—of its room-tone, which they can stir into the dialogue during ADR. In sound, things merge and interpenetrate. Sound is the mixing and reciprocal mutation of bodies and substances. It is the realm of metamorphosis. This is why sound is so much closer to touch and even to smell than to sight; Walter Murch has spoken of the importance to him of "the smell of the sound."[14] Sight is upright; in Freud's terms, the magisterial quality of seeing in *Homo erectus* is defined mostly by the fact that it signifies the triumphant departure of the nostrils from the genitals. Sound is not only sometimes quadrophonic; it is also quadruped.

One of the ways in which cinema strives to keep its visual and sound tracks together is through postproduction. However, there is a striking difference between optical and sonorous postproduction. The processes of visual editing, though they involve a great deal more than mere sequencing of material—mixing, filtering, crosscutting—nevertheless never escape from the demands of the *à voir*. This means that something of the image always survives the process of editing. Editing is an optimization of sight, a sharpening of focus, never a fundamental transformation of the seen. The processes of sound postproduction involve much more fundamental transformations, transcodings, manglings, and inventions. Recorded sound has the quality of being much more manipulable than the image. An image can be repeated, or sustained, filtered, or faded down, but it cannot be subjected to anything like the range of variations in intensity or condition that recorded sound can. A single sound can, if necessary, be stretched out to occupy the entire soundtrack of a film. It can be contracted, sweetened, dirtied up, damaged, accelerated, or slowed. It is perhaps not surprising that these effects in the order of sound-substance or mutative commixture are to the fore in thrillers or action films involving violence. For it may be that a certain violence, a violence done to the notion of a continuous and organized and individuated body, is inseparable from sound.

Film is limited to rendering the sensory fullness of the world in terms only of sound and vision, both of which must therefore be to some degree synesthetic. But the degrees are markedly different. Sight has a close synesthetic correspondence with touch; like the cinema, it works in *takes*. But the majority of the remaining sensory apprehensions of the world—wetness, texture, weight, heat, and odor—are channeled in film through sound rather than vision. Hearing, which is anyway more intrinsically mixed than the action of seeing, seems to be more inclined to enter into synesthetic exchanges than seeing.

Although sound always adds time or temporality to the image, subjecting the visual to the idea of elapse, the plastic manipulability of sound also expresses the possibility of time being congealed into spatial form. Speed, for example, is transposed in sound into effects of intensity or definition. A soundtrack in which lots of things are happening, or in which a percussive beat is accelerating, achieves its effects largely through the intensification of alertness achieved through heightened definition and contrast. What matters is not so much the variation of speed, as the intensification of the sense of the sound as a substance, undergoing violent agitation. One could say that some of the fluidity of visual construction, the sense that the film might be shot and projected at varying speeds to correspond to the exigencies of mood and feeling, passed across into the soundtrack.

[14] Vincent LoBrutto, *Sound-on-Film: Interviews with Creators of Film Sound* (Westport, Conn.; London: Praeger, 1994), 96.

These exigencies, though the imperious demands of synchronization (which come down to the ventriloquial demand to glue the voice to the lips) do not allow it to pull away very far from the demands of synchronized here-say and see-hear, allow for the production of different kinds of intensity and definition.

However, the association of sound with synesthetic transformation and oscillating intensity is also one of the reasons that the sound of a film can never really achieve or maintain autonomy. The tendency of sound is always to cling around or lock onto visual or visualizable events, in the process transforming those events, in that process of synchresis, the "spontaneous and irresistible weld produced between a particular auditory phenomenon and visual phenomenon when they occur at the same time" identified by Michel Chion. The effect of this is to break up the continuity of the soundtrack. Indeed, I think that Chion is right when he says that there is no such thing as a sound track, nor any possibility of a real or sustained "counterpoint between image and sound."[15]

Despite ways in which the language of sound engineers and sound aestheticians mimics visual processes of cutting, layering, combining, coordinating, and correlating, and despite the attempts to mimic sound mixtures in visual terms—through cross-fading, lap-dissolves, double-exposure, and use of color to "bleed" scenes into one another—the order of correlation is fundamentally separate from the order of commixture.

Coming to Life

Vivian Sobchack's illuminating analysis of the forms of living expressiveness that cinema uniquely makes available suggests that what cinema most wants is to come to life. It is the beginning of the fulfillment of every historical art form that has similarly craved the condition of life. It is this that links cinema to literature in modernism; cinema is taken into literature as the form of its most distinctive outrunning. Modern literature becomes itself in sprinting to keep up with the cinema that is leaving it so far behind, in its fluency, lyricism, sensory inclusiveness, and immediacy. Modern literature dispenses with itself in the way that cinema dispenses with it, outruns itself in the ways that it is outrun by cinema.

Cinema has thematized this ambition in the many stories it tells of automata endowed with life: Frankenstein's monsters, robots, cyborgs, computers, puppets, ventriloquist's dummies, and animated cartoons. The stories cinema tells of life animated are about its own power to bring to life. Sobchack's analysis suggests that the very form of cinema is the embodiment of this will-to-life, film's will to form its own body. In this, her analysis draws close to that of Deleuze, who devotes the final chapter of his *Cinema 2* to the form and idea of cinema's automatism.[16]

[15] Chion, *Audio-Vision*, 63, 39–40.

[16] Gilles Deleuze, *Cinema 2: The Time-Image*, trans. High Tomlinson and Robert Galeta (London: Athlone Press, 1989), 262–270.

Sound is often the warrant and enactment of this coming to life. The cinema comes to life by coming to sound and plays anxiously with its powers to simulate life by artificially synchronizing sound in films like *Dead of Night*. Where noise becomes voice in film, here, just for a moment, voice has become inhabited by noise.

Just as cinema brought to life a different kind of literary writing, an aspiration in writing to be the more-than-itself that cinema represented, so perhaps what cinema continues to want to bring to life is an *hors-corps*, the body of a body-beyond-cinema. It is perhaps not surprising that cinema should attempt to make out this body-beyond-itself through its obsession with figuring "life but not as we know it" and with the making of other kinds of body: robots, monsters, and artificial organisms. Sound is often closely implicated in this process. Walter Murch describes how, to produce the unearthly sound of a robot in the film *THX 1138*: "We had one Nagra tape recorder with the clean voices on it. We ham-radioed them into the universe, received them back again as if they were coming from another country, fiddling with the tuning so that we would get that wonderful 'sideband' quality to the voices."[17]

Sound, which belongs to and yet never sufficiently cleaves to the body of cinema, just as the voice originates in and yet never sufficiently inheres in the individual body, may be one of the avenues to this body-beyond-cinema. Soundstuff is not simply sonic gravy, not just a kind of all-purpose, indeterminate plasma that can be applied to the film at will. It is form informed, a kind of thinking through things. Could it be that we may be discovering the archaic and counterfactual delights of the matter of sound in an auditized environment characterized by decompositions, becomings, and compoundings as much as by articulations? It is easy to represent this as simply an infantile or archaic plunge back into a kind of formlessness. But it may turn out to mark the beginnings of a new reorganization, or dispensation of the organs, which responds to the complex phase-spaces and topologies of modern physics and mathematical modelings as much as it looks back to the infantile dominion of merely blind or brutish touch. So many of the complex forms with which engineers, astrophysicists, mathematicians, systems managers, physicists, and even architects work produce challenges to the simple kinds of articulation apprehensible by the eye. Walter Murch tried to imagine the ways in which sound might belong to the new media organisms of the future:

> You tune in channel 432, one wall of your room disappears, and what you see is a live transmission of a volcano in South America, or the earth as seen from the moon. What is the sound for that? If you really could tune in the earth from the moon, live, our whole relationship to the earth would change. When there's that moon channel 432, and you see the earth right before you, instead of the fourth wall, what's the sound for *that*?[18]

Film theory has done its best to bring to life a phenomenological film-body in which everything is commuted into the narrow channel of visual perception. What part is left

[17] LoBrutto, *Sound-on-Film*, 85.

[18] LoBrutto, *Sound-on-Film*, 99.

for sound to play in the raising of this film-body, other than docile servant of the here-say and the see-hear? I have been saying here that certain kinds of sound belong, not to the order of ostension that dominates the image—in which everything is *à voir*, to be had by and made clear to the eye—but to an order of mutative commixture, characterized by the encounter and transformation of imaginary substances. It is sound, not in the civilian garb of music or voice, but as noise, that broaches the possibility that interests me of a wild phenomenology of film. There is no sense looking for a sonorous body to complete or even to compete with film's body *à voir*. Having learned to see things with its own eyes, film wants also to hear its own voice, but remains a deaf or dummy medium. The body of sound is a body all right, but not film's own. The new sound films perhaps look beyond their condition of film, look forward to or begin to sound out the more complex and turbulently convoluted worlds of matter and information, meaning and noise in the emerging sensory orders that may be coming to life. The first generation of cinema brought the human body to life in film. Whatever will succeed cinema will be trying to bring to life the body of the world. And what is the sound for that?

References

Altman, Rick. "Moving Lips: Cinema as Ventriloquism." *Yale French Studies* 60 (1980): 67–79.

Altman, Rick, ed. *Sound Theory, Sound Practice*. New York; London: Routledge, 1992.

Arnheim, Rudolf. *Film as Art*. Berkeley; Los Angeles; London: University of California Press, 1957.

Cavalcanti, Alberto. "Sound in Films." In *Film Sound: Theory and Practice*, edited by Elizabeth Weis and John Belton, 98–111. New York: Columbia University Press, 1985.

Chion, Michel. *Audio-Vision: Sound on Screen*. Translated by Claudia Gorbman. New York: Columbia University Press, 1994.

Deleuze, Gilles. *Cinema 2: The Time-Image*. Translated by High Tomlinson and Robert Galeta. London: Athlone Press, 1989.

Lewin, Bertram D. "Sleep, the Mouth, and the Dream Screen." *Psychoanalytic Quarterly* 15 (1946): 419–434.

LoBrutto, Vincent. *Sound-on-Film: Interviews with Creators of Film Sound*. Westport, Conn.; London: Praeger, 1994.

Rée, Jonathan. *I See a Voice: A Philosophical History of Language, Deafness and the Senses*. London: HarperCollins, 1999.

Silverman, Kaja. *The Acoustic Mirror: The Female Voice in Psychoanalysis and Cinema*. Bloomington: Indiana University Press, 1988.

Sobchack, Vivian. *The Address of the Eye: A Phenomenology of Film Experience*. Princeton, N.J.: Princeton University Press, 1992.

Williams, Alan. "Historical and Theoretical Issues in the Coming of Recorded Sound to the Cinema." In *Sound Theory, Sound Practice*, edited by Rick Altman, 126–137. New York; London, 1992.

PART III

NARRATIVE, GENRE, MEANING

CHANGING TIMES, CHANGING PRACTICES

CHAPTER 7

AUDIOVISUAL SPACE IN AN ERA OF TECHNOLOGICAL CONVERGENCE

ROBYNN J. STILWELL

As we hurtle asymptotically toward technological convergence, two parallel forces are likely to continue frustrating the emergence of that utopian, unitary single black box that does everything. The first is appropriately technological: the continual cycle of new formats that improves image and sound but creates the need for new equipment/software. The second is aesthetic. What is created for the big screen has a different lineage and stylistic markers than what is created for television, or a concert hall, or a video game, or the web. The different media not only have different technological features and budgets, but long histories of decisions that have created recognizably distinct configurations of audiovisual space. They are not simple nor necessarily always consistent configurations, but they have a kind of generic resemblance constrained by the technical advantages and limitations of their medium of origin.

These configurations are, for the most part, sleight-of-hand evocations of real or imagined spaces, a kind of audiovisual extension of perspective. Western theatre has had a few millennia to develop its conventions; cinema has had a bit more than a century. Certainly cinema drew on some of those theatrical conventions, but also eventually generated its own audiovisual space. The nondiegetic score started out by emulating the invisible underscore of the pit orchestra but, with increasing sophistication aesthetically and technologically, it came to wrap around the represented space like an envelope: under, behind, sometimes over, or around the image onscreen, even reaching out to embrace the audience with speakers placed in the back of the auditorium. The theatrical and cinematic experiences of music-image relationships have a different shape from each other, a different texture.

That they may also have a distinct affective power shouldn't be surprising when we think of the language we use to talk about musical texture: thick, thin, rich, glassy, *spacious*. We resort to adjectives that evoke tactile and spatial experiences, which in turn can generate affect: power (or claustrophobia), fragility, opulence, eeriness, freedom (or exposure). We don't tend to talk about this aspect as much as we might in scholarly discourse, but it often forms a significant part of the casual discussion of music — what kind of picture does this music paint? What kind of story does it tell? Once music is painting a picture or telling a story, it is only a short conceptual distance to programmatic music, incidental music for a play, or a film score.

This interplay of sound/music, image, and narrative forms a delicate synesthetic web, relying on a series of non-musical associations in addition to purely musical aspects and acoustic properties.[1] And if we extend the concept of texture outward from the purely musical properties to its physical position in a theatrical orchestra pit, its conceptual and acoustic position surrounding the diegesis in most film, we have an audiovisual configuration that is typical, if not definitive, of that medium. The closest analogy for these typical audiovisual configurations may be the storytelling configuration of genre: a set of conventional plot points and symbolism that are not so much a checklist as a wordcloud, with a dense center but hazy boundaries. A saloon is typical of a Western, but not definitive. A saloon, however, brings other affective elements to a Western—sexuality, license, and probably music.

When I discussed the ambiguity of music in the "fantastical gap" — that unmoored space between diegetic and nondiegetic in film — I framed it in terms of space, of geography (a "no-man's land") and of physics (a change of state, like an electron moving between shells in an atom, or in a superposition, where it must be observed in order to register as a particle or a wave).[2] The notion of the fantastical gap recognizes complication and change, and it made an intervention in a discussion that tended toward discrete, either-or positioning.

In essence, here, I am proposing an expansion and extension of this idea. "Diegetic" and "nondiegetic" are conceptualized as spaces within a cinematic configuration, a cinematic mode of representing audiovisual space. But if we zoom out to look across different media, we can borrow, say, a cinematic mode in a video game, or a theatrical mode in a film (the simplest would be the straight recording of a stage play, but the theatrical mode also describes many early sound films that were averse to the application of nondiegetic music).

These modes, or sets of audiovisual conventions, include not just the placement of music, but the way sound/speech are represented through sound design, camera, editing, lighting, performance, style, and so on. The very concept of diegetic and nondiegetic arises from the cinematic mode, but we can also apply it intermedially. The existence of these concepts can make us reconsider aspects of opera, for instance. Is this a diegetic

[1] See, for instance, Claudia Gorbman's discussion of musical, cultural, and cinematic codes in *Unheard Melodies: Narrative Film Music* (Bloomington, IN: Indiana University Press, 1987), 2–3.

[2] "The Fantastical Gap between Diegetic and Non-diegetic," in *Beyond the Soundtrack: Representing Music in Cinema*, ed. Daniel Goldmark, Lawrence Kramer, and Richard Leppert (Berkeley: University of California Press, 2007), 184–202.

aria? An internal monologue that only the audience can hear? The cross-media comparison makes us think in different, often productive ways.

Cinema and theatre are the most familiar modes, probably the most common in our daily experience. But we often encounter them not in their natural habitat but through an intermediary — the television (and, increasingly, our computer monitors). Television was, from its inception, an intermedium, a product of aesthetic and textual convergence. Initially, television broadcast materials primarily in the cinematic, theatrical, or sound-centered radio modes. As the content flowed, it was reshaped but also retained evolutionary traces of its original forms. When new media arise, they retain traces of contributory forms. At first they are mere transliterations; later, they may become translations or even transformations, and the influence can flow "backward" as well as outward. Many video games aspire toward a cinematic experience, but we can also discern in some action movies the audiovisual aspects of side-scrolling adventure and first-person-shooter games.

Television is a laboratory in which we can explore these aesthetic processes. While television is its own medium, we can still discern modal differences between shows that often fall along generic lines: hour-long recorded dramas tend toward the cinematic, live events toward the theatrical. Situation comedies and soap operas, which are radio genres, tend to be presented in a theatrical mode, but are heavily mediated by close-ups that emphasize the speaker and reaction to speech. News broadcasts have a long lineage that includes not only radio and newsreel, but also newspapers and magazines. However, it is also possible to "borrow" moments from another mode. A shift in the audiovisual configuration can create a theatrical moment in an otherwise cinematic show; the gesture is both audiovisually and dramaturgically "theatrical". A montage sequence in a radio/theatrical sitcom engages different editing, pacing, and sound-image relationships more usually associated with cinema. It wasn't just the narrative content of *The Wonder Years* (1988-93) that set it apart as a "dramedy". The half-hour family comedy was a staple of the situation comedy genre from its days in radio. But *The Wonder Years* was shot on film with a nostalgic, retrospective voice-over and a nondiegetic jukebox score. Essentially, it appeared in cinematic mode--a dramatic choice for a sitcom.

Documentary as a genre ranges across most audiovisual media—certainly television and film, and even some kinds of theatre pieces. It has some conventions—authoritative (usually male) narrating voice is one, its visual representation by the talking head is another—but it is generally not as conformist as other common genres. Because they are normally not as linear and story-driven overall as other genres, documentaries are usually structured by other means, including the interplay of various audiovisual modes, particularly cinematic and theatrical ones. These create a kind of textural rhythm, akin to harmonic rhythm in a musical work. Textural(/harmonic) change can create contrast at the local level, both for variety and for emphasis, but also generate rhythmic and hierarchical patterns at the larger scale. Al Gore's award-winning and politically controversial *An Inconvenient Truth* (2006) is remarkable for its steady alternation of theatrical and cinematic modes, with moments of modal inflection or "intervention." The BBC's three-part television documentary *Climate Wars* (2009) is, by contrast, deeply contrapuntal, with striking interpenetration of the predominant theatrical and cinematic modes, while it clearly relies on the contrast between them for affect, rhythm, and even narrative drive.

Bimodal and Modular: *An Inconvenient Truth*

The striking thing about the structure of *An Inconvenient Truth* is how strict it is: it alternates between "slideshow" and "movies," the theatrical and the cinematic, the lack of music and the saturation of it. Other than in its more blended opening and closing frame, the film is modular, composed of cells that each function on their own, but both by contrast and accumulation create a strong impact. The greater "continuity" is in the slideshow sections, which take place in a single, coherent, real space and seem to have been performed in a coherent sequence (although they were edited together from several different performances with occasional additional dialogue recording [ADR] for updated information).

A lecture is not normally recognized as a performance—though many of us who do them certainly understand them as performances. Al Gore—climate change activist, former vice president and as he ruefully introduces himself, once the next president of the United States—gives a lecture. The very fact that he starts off with a joke recognizing a complex political status highlights the performativity of what could seem like a dry recitation of facts.

The space is a round lecture hall fitted with a huge screen onto which the slides are projected. Gore is positioned in the center of a round floor space (the seats arrayed outward are slightly raked) (see figure 7.1a.); a podium bears his open Mac laptop, a visual motif that is one of the few—other than Gore himself—to carry across both elements of the film's construction. That small screen with his Keynote slideshow is mirrored by two more moderately sized screens on either side of the floor space. (See figures 7.1b, 7.1c, 7.1d.) The four screens together provide several lines of sight in the round space, not only optimizing visibility in the real space, but creating interesting visual rhythms when captured by the camera, which roams through the hall throughout the film. (See figures 7.2a, 7.2b.)

Already the "purity" of the theatrical mode is compromised, as it almost invariably is when a camera is present. One could certainly argue that the mobility of the camera edges toward the cinematic, as one normally has only a single line of sight in any theatrical performance. A further, and I think more interesting, erosion of theatrical purity is the relationship between Gore as lecturer and the slides themselves. In a live presentation the slides, however overpowering, are always sharing visual space with the presenter. Gore is in control of the information via the computer; the slides are an adjunct to his lecture.

One of the most famous moments relies on theatricality for its impact: Gore climbs aboard a scissor lift to follow the infamous "hockey stick graph" off the top of the enormous screen (an additional screen was added on top), a theatrical stroke that works precisely because it is in real space, demonstrating the proportion of the graph's fluctuation to the height of a (tall) man (at minute 23:00). (See video clip 7.1. ▶) But many of the interactions between Gore and the slides are more slippery.

A subtle modal shift occurs when the slides are presented full screen. The theatrical space is eliminated from the frame, and the slide becomes a screen that opens up

FIGURES 7.1A, B, C, AND D: Screens within screens create internal visual rhythms.

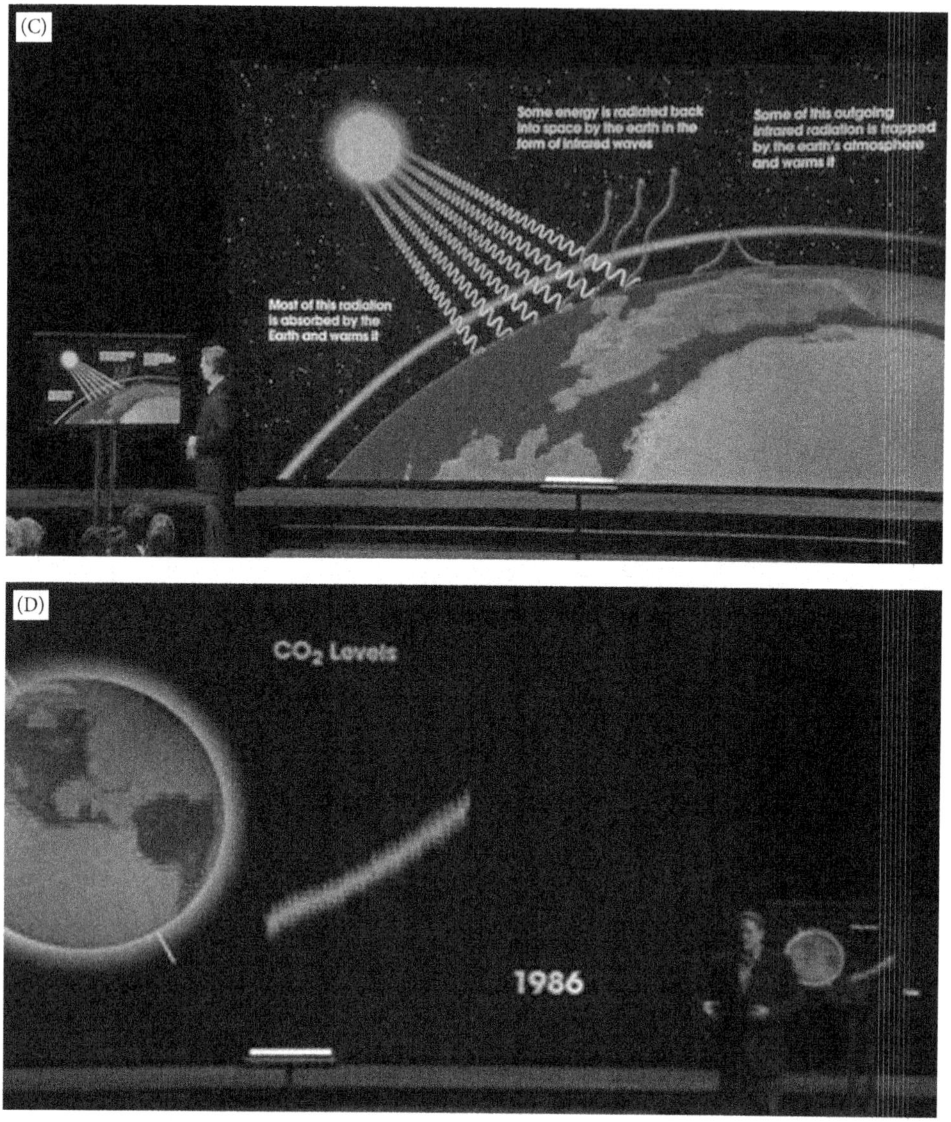

FIGURES 7.1A, B, C, AND D: (Continued)

a cinematic bubble. Suddenly Gore's voice is coming not from "off" so much as from "over," a nondiegetic space. The two extended animation sequences—the cartoon *Global Warming: Or, None Like It Hot* (10:00), which explains global warming in a spoof of 1950s and 1960s educational films,[3] and the cartoon of a frog that is placed in a slowly boiling pot until it is rescued and placed on a chaise longue with a cold drink

[3] The sequence is a clip from *Futurama* (1998–2003, 2008–), Matt Groening's futuristic cartoon television series. It is an excerpt from episode #501 "Crimes of the Hot" (2002), which has a climate change theme. Gore's daughter Kristin was a writer for *Futurama* and also worked on *An Inconvenient Truth*, and a cartoon Gore appeared in *Futurama*.

FIGURES 7.2A AND B: Screens within screens can echo and sustain key images while generating an editing rhythm in the camera angles.

(1:09:00) have sound tracks that highlight their imbedded cinematic nature. The animation of a polar bear seeking ice strong enough to support its weight is made even more immediate and urgent by the subtle sounds of the bear's labored breathing and the cracking of the ice floes as it tries to climb aboard (45:20). A gasp or laugh from the audience helps restore the theatrical space, but those subtle shifts can be effective—and affective, drawing us closer, as with the polar bear.

Even more static slides can be animated by the movement of the camera. In a sequence dealing with how the influx of freshwater from North American glaciers shut down the oceanic conveyor current at the end of the last ice age, the camera moves slightly, twice, with different effects. (See video clip 7.2. ⊛) When Gore speaks of the cooling in Europe, the camera drifts slightly to the right of the map to focus on Europe, as one's eye would naturally do. Then he pretends that that could never happen again. After all, there's no other large mass of ice to threaten the North Atlantic, is there? Meanwhile the camera moves into the graphic and slides up to center on Greenland (49:14), a rhetorical flourish that is entirely visual but carries us into the image, mimicking the movement of a person raising an eyebrow and nodding toward Greenland in answer to his query. The camera has taken control of the eye in a distinctly cinematic way, cued by an implication of dialogue between the film and the audience.

A kind of persistence of perception keeps the entire theatrical mode in place for the duration of these relatively contained cinematic "bubbles," generated by the animations. The filmed "movies" trace the influences on Gore's climate change activism and are more distinct breaks. These sequences provide historical and biographical perspective and were explicitly intended to bind the audience to Gore. Linearly, they are like illustrative digressions in a classroom lecture, but on a more expansive level, they alternate in a steady rhythm that approaches a large-scale parallel editing. That steady rhythm is rather like an oscillation of tonic and dominant key areas, articulated by different themes, rhythms, and textures.

These "movies," as the sobriquet suggests, are distinctly different from the logical, linear lecture segments. They are even shot in a different format, on film stock ranging from 8mm to 35mm, starkly contrasting with the high-definition video of the lecture sequences. They are overtly constructed as "cinema": impressionistic, heavily edited sketches with emotive voice-overs from Gore reflecting on various turning points in his life (the river on the ranch where he spent time as a child contrasting with the small city apartment in Washington, D.C., where his family lived while his father was serving in Congress; the teacher who first introduced him to the concept of global climate change; his sister Nancy's death from lung cancer caused by smoking and his family's history in farming tobacco). The black-and-white, grainy look of newsprint gives temporal distance and an "authentic" nostalgia to the sequence about his son Albert's brush with death after a car accident (even though it happened in 1989, an era with notably better photographic technology); shaky news footage gives immediacy to a segment on Hurricane Katrina.

The movies are also heavily scored. Michael Brook's unobtrusive, minimalistic score is part of what makes them "movies." Usually, music precedes the shift to a movie and may bleed subtly over into the return to the lecture space, but here music resides almost entirely within the movies. Intriguingly, this structure was suggested to Guggenheim by Martin Scorsese's famous concert film *The Last Waltz* (1978), which interpolates interview segments into The Band's live performance; this emphasizes the performative aspect of Gore's lecture, but reverses the position of music in the structure.

The clear separation between scored and unscored,[4] lecture and movie, is complicated only at the beginning and end. The film begins with a "movie," beautiful shots of the river on the ranch, with Gore speaking in quiet voice-over about how the land appeals to each of the senses. A piano—an acoustic, "analog" instrument—plays a slow, repeating chordal sequence that is harmonically ambiguous; depending on the context, the chord alternation could be perfect or plagal. The sequence finally resolves as we see him tapping on his laptop, a shift to the technological and the present. As the photograph of the earth from space, known as Earthrise, appears, music drops out, and we shift to the lecture space. This sets up the dichotomy between "movies" and "lecture," an alternation that happens a couple of times quite swiftly before the credits. Music bleeds into the lecture space before a sudden visual cut takes us to Gore giving the lecture in China, and low, suspenseful strings follow him through the backstage tunnel to the set (the camera follows him from behind in a shot reminiscent of a prizefighter or a rock musician entering an arena). The long suspensions start to lose function and just become texture as, through the mediation of the laptop we have seen tucked under his arm, we watch him rearranging his slides. Dissonance builds as we move from peaceful nature images to more distressing and disastrous ones. The first substantial musical movement, in the guise of arpeggios, begins as Gore says in voice-over, "There are good people who are in politics.... [T]he moral imperative to make real changes is inescapable." The credits come up over a shot of Gore driving, and the bass takes a vertiginous whole step down (either I to ♭VII, or V-IV), a drastic musical change. As we cut into the lecture space, music drops out, and we drop into the rhythm of the large-scale alternation. A similar, shorter muddying of the alternation occurs near the end as Gore narrates what is at stake. Piano returns in the guise of a cue from *In the Bedroom* by Thomas Newman, a temp track that Guggenheim solicited from him. Though still minimalistic, this cue has the most significant amount of movement in the score and leads to a credit sequence that lists actions the audience may take, scored by Melissa Etheridge's anthemic "I Want to Wake Up."

This interpenetration of the cinematic and theatrical modes at the beginning and end makes structural sense, both as introduction and as laying a foundation. The alternation helps clarify the differences between the theatrical and cinematic modes and focus on both how those modes operate and their affects. No filmed event will ever be purely theatrical. Even a camera locked down in the audience is going to produce something that erases the liveness and immediacy of the theatrical experience. The cinematic audiovisual mode uses other means to create that immediacy, as illustrated by the one moment when music penetrates the lecture space: right at the one-hour mark in the film, Gore is showing animated slides that illustrate what rising seas will do to the coastlines of Florida, Shanghai, and Beijing. (See video clip 7.3. ⊙) Low, almost subliminal music seeps in like the water, and the dissonance increases markedly as he shows the slide

[4] That the *None Like It Hot* cartoon is scored strengthens the sense of the animations as being cinematic bubbles within the lecture sequences.

FIGURE 7.3: Ground Zero drowned in music.

of Manhattan, with "Ground Zero," the World Trade Center, prominently labeled (see figure 7.3). Stylistically consistent with the "movies" underscore, the music has an affective resonance with the last major national trauma and what Gore projects as the next.

Multimodal and Polyphonic: *Climate Wars*

Scottish geologist Iain Stewart has made several series for the BBC in the past decade, roughly one a year since 2004. Most have been in the cinematic mode of the "charismatic teacher," not far removed from the alternation of *An Inconvenient Truth*, but the removal of the "talking head" from the lecture hall out into the field is overarchingly cinematic. Carl Sagan's *Cosmos* (1980), with its early computer graphics and virtual spaces, is perhaps the apex of this model, which is emulated and intensified in *Climate Wars* (2008). Two of Stewart's most recent series, *Earth: The Power of the Planet* (known in the United States as *Earth: The Biography*, 2008) and *How the Earth Made Us* (U.S.: *How the Earth Changed History*, 2010), have come under the umbrella of the BBC's high-definition nature extravaganzas *Blue Planet*, *Planet Earth*, and *Life*, produced by David Attenborough.[5] But whereas those series have concentrated on stately,

[5] Attenborough is a pioneer of the television documentary series; he commissioned *Civilisation*, centered around art historian Kenneth Clark, in the late 1960s to take advantage of (comparatively) high-resolution color broadcast technology and followed it in 1973 with mathematician and biologist Jacob Bronowski in *The Ascent of Man*, whose producer, Adrian Malone, worked on *Cosmos*. Attenborough has also been the voice of most of the recent high-definition nature series.

spectacular views of plant and animal life made possible by the new high-definition video technology, accompanied by grand symphonic music, in this series Stewart is a dynamic (at times even hyperactive) physical presence, giving us a focal point while he engages with the "inanimate."[6] These "on location" moments are a combination of the documentary/news broadcast staple of the talking head (itself a televisual adaptation of a radio broadcast) and audience proxy; when Stewart gasps in awe at a cave or a geological formation, he is standing in for, even modeling, the audience's reaction. Though perhaps not as articulate and evocative a writer as Sagan, Stewart (a former child actor) is enthusiastic and willing to do things like paragliding over a waterfall, cave diving, or setting fire to frozen methane in Siberian lakes to make a point about a geological process.

Climate Wars is aesthetically quite different from Stewart's grand, symphonic, and spectacular cinematic series. It contains three hour-long episodes ("The Fight Begins," dealing with the history and politics; "Fightback," about the skeptic movement; and "Fight for the Future," about the science); a sequel of sorts, "Hot Planet" aired at Christmas in 2009, surveying some of the technology that could make a difference. The content is more concentrated, detail oriented, and urgent than in the other series, and that density correlates with a distinctly different texture. Among the elements that go into the series are historical footage, time-lapse photography, documents, graphics, live debate, interviews, demonstrations, and scientific experimentation. Any one individual element can be "cinematic"—the dominant mode of most of the materials—but those elements are heavily and quickly edited and at times layered on top of each other in a dense contrapuntal texture. Cinematic segments of exposition become islands of simplicity within the flow, like the seasonal fluctuations in a temperature graph, compared to the relatively smooth curve of the "average" represented by *An Inconvenient Truth*.

Music saturates *Climate Wars*, and not just the underscoring one might expect from a nature documentary. Popular music is used in a manner not unlike how it would be in a fiction film: the Lovin' Spoonful's "Summer in the City" and Martha and the Vandellas' "Heatwave" are played for sequences about (surprise!) heat waves. Other choices are less "on the nose." For a segment on the ozone layer, historical footage intercuts with a *Top of the Pops* performance by Wham! of "Young Guns (Hey Sucka)," connecting the popular culture of the period and the reason for the hole in the ozone, the chlorofluorocarbons in aerosols like hairspray and spray paint (graffiti). Bobby Darin's version of "Don't Rain on My Parade" accompanies Stewart—tooling around Las Vegas in a red Corvette convertible—as he empathizes with the residents, who seem to be ignoring the fragility of their water supply. A segment about scientist Dave Keeling, who worked at the Scripps Institution of Oceanography in San Diego beginning in the 1950s, is delineated by the beginning of The Mamas and the Papas' "California Dreamin'." The imagery has the grainy, faded look of 1950s home movies, even a still photograph of Keeling that appears to have been "animated" into a "movie" by animating flaws in the

[6] The two most recent series (*Power of the Planet/How the Earth Made Us*) contain imbedded animations, as fossils or rock art "come to life."

image. The slightly anachronistic song functions as an aural establishing shot, but with the opening lines matched to images of the sun shining through "brown leaves" and breaking through "grey skies," it subtly shifts the meaning of the original lyrics (a wintry, probably Eastern location that makes the narrator recall sunny Southern California fondly). Similarly, a little further into the same segment the surf hit "Wipeout" accompanies a stream of images about Keeling's fieldwork, but the title could be prophetic if the subject of his study—the proportion of carbon dioxide in the atmosphere—wipes out current life-forms, including us. These little musical/visual puns are among the frequent islands of tongue-in-cheek commentary within the larger texture. Other familiar music is used, perhaps more seriously, in other segments; a black-and-white segment of open-pit coal mining, industrial outgassing, and polluted cities is scored with what is, or at least sounds very much like, a segment from Philip Glass's score to Godfrey Reggio's *Qatsi* series, which also questions human impact on the environment and the consequent effect on humanity. The same point is implied in the segment, but intensified by the choice of music, even made explicit by it if one can make the connection.

Even the standard talking head aspect is given a peculiarly cinematic spin in the series. Although Stewart still abseils into a crevasse in Greenland, braves a climate skeptics' conference, and hunts for rock on a British beach with his two unimpressed daughters, he also spends a good amount of time in a studio environment interacting with historical footage of political speeches, congressional testimony, older documentaries, and even graphics, à la Gore.[7] But these segments diagrammatically explode the two-dimensionality of the cinematic in a way that draws attention to both the relative flatness of the original material and the dynamic way we relate to the information.

Stewart's studio setting is a black box of indeterminate size, eliminating all sense of proportion and shape. A pinpoint of light projects imagery onto a "screen" that seems to hang magically in space but is also transparent (see figure 7.4). This obviously replicates the projection in a movie theater, but the screen is in the center of the space, not on one wall of it.

The camera can roam around the screen and Stewart. He can watch the "movies" or turn around and talk to the audience while the "movies" are playing, becoming in their content block quotes or footnotes in his argument, but in reception they are in essence "underscore" to the foregrounded event of his speech act. The camera often circles around the screen in three dimensions, bringing into question whether Stewart is in front of or behind it, and the "eyeline" even moves up or down over a range about the height of the screen.

The mobility of the camera can also create a figure-ground reversal. During a discussion of the discrepancy between land-based temperature readings and those attained from satellite data, a graph was superimposed on an image of radio telescopes (a reminder of how the data were gathered in a perhaps unnecessary, but aesthetically interesting,

[7] *An Inconvenient Truth* is mentioned several times in the film, including the section on the "hockey stick" graph. Instead of a huge screen, Stewart has a glazier's truck with a huge poster of the graph on its side, which he drives around London, through Trafalgar Square and past Buckingham Palace and Westminster Abbey, as he talks about the graph's iconicity. The sequence ends with him driving underneath a huge billboard for *An Inconvenient Truth*.

FIGURE 7.4: Exploding the cinematic.

redundancy—rather like an emotional score in a classical Hollywood film). (See video clip 7.4. ▶) As the satellite data graph is animated, the camera swings around "behind" (in front of?) the screen so that Stewart's reaction can be seen through the semitransparent projected surface (see figure 7.5).

This polyphonic layering of information is common throughout the series, both in the studio segments and the segments in which Stewart may be narrating in voice-over. The complexity of the audiovisual field, however, is not static. The relationships change quickly in a flow much more varied and less sharply delineated than in *An Inconvenient Truth* or

FIGURE 7.5: Radio telescopes, satellite data graphs, and a "Wow!"

even most music video. Although the risk is abstraction (and at times the streams of equations incomprehensible to most viewers may approach that[8]), the visual, verbal, and often musical information resonates in a way that seems to me musical in itself—contrapuntal voices complementing, contrasting, or doubling each other; cadences where information comes together in an emphatic statement (as in figures 7.4, 7.5); and the changes in unfolding texture.

A segment from the first episode provides an idea of how the series operates. The segment is about the 1979 JASON report on climate change, the follow-up Charney report, and the political reactions of the Thatcher and particularly Reagan administrations. Even at nearly eight minutes, the segment contains too many details to chart here, but it demonstrates several of the strategies used in the series as a whole. (See video clip 7.5 ⊛)

The segment is set off by relatively clean breaks of sound and image. These borders aren't the full fade-to-black, sound-to-zero blackouts we normally would expect, but in the context they are sharp. At the end the sound and the musical cues cut exactly together, whereas the beginning has only the slightest of sound advances of Stewart's voice before we cut to him, walking in the California foothills and explaining about a "shadowy organization known as JASON" (23:24). A sharp, metallic sound and ominous low boom, fading into a drone, accompany a cut to an image of the campus of Scripps Institution. It's a bright, sunny day, and the white building and manicured landscape are beautiful, but the building is shot from a low angle through the bars of a gate and from the shadows of a large tree (see figure 7.6; video clip 7.5a. ⊛).

FIGURE 7.6: Making San Diego "mysterious."

[8] Davis Guggenheim directed one of the seminal, style-setting early episodes of the CBS television series *Numb3rs* (2005–2010), in which a mathematician helps the FBI solve crimes; the show often features sequences in which the mathematician's expositions are animated with layers of film, graphs, and equations that resemble some of the flow in *Climate Wars*.

FIGURE 7.7: Surveillance mode.

The cheekily suspenseful tone is sustained by the low, ominous bass and high-pitched violin drones as Stewart is seen peering into offices with closed venetian blinds, the low-angle shots also catching the security cameras watching him (see figure 7.7). (A quick shot from the "security camera" is inserted.)

Stewart's definition of the JASONs ("a select group, chosen for their intellectual brilliance and their patriotism. Their mission: to provide secret advice to the American government on matters scientific.") is accompanied by shaky "home video" imagery of hands writing on a chalkboard and men in 1960s-style sports shirts (we really never see their faces) with coffee cups and pocket protectors making brief appearances. Interpolated within this digression are further, even faster packets of information and affective footage: a portentous newscaster voice talks about fallout patterns as we see black-and-white footage of a Polaris missile emerging from the ocean, followed quickly by footage of a nuclear test blast. This all occurs in a brief pause in Stewart's narration as he explains that most of what the JASONs did had to do with defense. Another interpolation of a newscaster announces tests of a Nike Zeus missile, with more missile test footage, and as Stewart resumes talking about the JASONs tackling climate change, the newscaster voice is merely faded down, not disappearing entirely until the image changes—under (or over?) the words "evidence of global warming"—to a period computer screen emitting a string of numbers, cross-fading to clouds forming and jerky 1970s satellite footage of a hurricane. (See video clip 7.5b. ▶) This entire sequence lasts only 36 seconds, but has three intense bursts of visual and aural information within the verbal exposition and against the "ground" of the "home movie" footage, itself a commentative interpolation to Stewart's narration.

Stewart comments on the prestige of the JASONs, who made enough money to rent beach houses during their summer sojourns at Scripps so that their women and children could "gambol on the beach whilst the menfolk got on with saving the world. Or destroying it, depending on the year." The low drone finally fades, bringing the tongue-in-cheek segment to an end (25:37) as another low angle at the campus finds Stewart approaching the camera, head tilted slightly to the side, declaring these summers, "Less James Bond and more like Club Med." After a pause he diffuses any remaining tension with, "The kind of science I'd like to get into." A slight coda (25:48–26:13) shows more shaky "home video" of the scientists looking at maps and chalkboards and ends with Stewart explaining that they had created their own computer models, what they called "The JASON model of the world." "They didn't lack confidence, those boys," he cracks.

The second half of the segment is more serious. Stewart sits on a rock near a "brook" at Scripps with a yellowed, dog-eared copy of the original report and reads from it, occasionally running a finger along a line underlined in green ink. As he describes what the JASONs got right in their report, details are illuminated, or perhaps underlined as if with the green ink, by more "blasts" or "bursts" of audiovisual information. For example, when Stewart says that the JASON report "got it pretty well spot on" (26:52), ominous drumming and drones underscore layered images of the title page of the report, time-lapse images of the sun rising, and storm clouds gathering, and lightning seems to be matched by musical "thunderstrikes" highlighting portions of the typescript (see figures 7.8a and 7.8b; video clip 7.5c. ▶).

At 27:58 an image of the American flag flying against a blue sky visually underscores Stewart's next bit of narration: "But then something happened that always confuses the scientific issues—politics got in the way." Actual music reenters, a series of tense, suspended drones accompanies slow-motion footage from Reagan's 1980s acceptance speech (a couple of real-time moments, with sound, like his calling the election a "humbling experience," "burst" through the texture), and America's role in acid rain and carbon emissions is explained over images of rain striking new plant shoots almost violently, falling into stormy weather and then polluted cities with belching diesel trucks and factories.

At 28:56 a shot of a jet taxiing at National Airport, with the Capitol in the background, is accompanied by the loud beginning of Creedence Clearwater Revival's bitter Vietnam-era rock classic, "Fortunate Son." With each of the opening guitar stabs, a photograph of Walter Nierenberg, Reagan's choice to head up a third climate change report,[9] moves across the screen. Imitating the upward arc of the guitar, the first two photographs move as if someone were taking each out of a folder and tossing it onto a table (a nod to the opening of the 1960s spy show *Mission: Impossible*?), whereas the third sputters and turns red as if bathed in acid, a more extreme version of the grainy flicker cast on the still image of Keeling. This adds movement to the still photographs and also welds the images firmly to the music. (See video clip 7.5d. ▶) The song itself is deeply ironic, a protest against the sort of conservative values that Nierenberg held, but also

[9] After a second, the Charney report, by actual climate researchers, came up with results similar to the JASON report's.

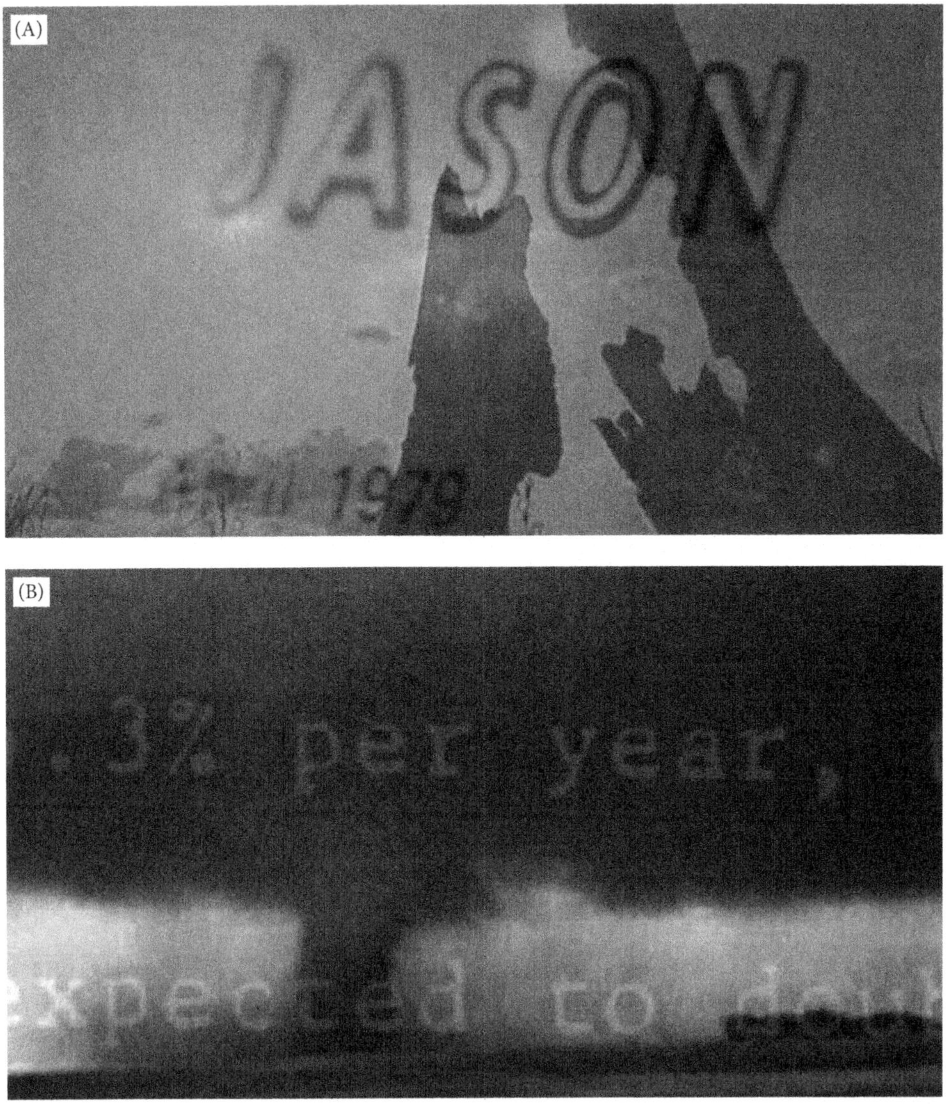

FIGURES 7.8A AND B: Informational bursts.

lends the straightlaced photographs a kind of swagger that a man of Nierenberg's power would probably have. As Stewart explains Nierenberg's connection with the Manhattan Project and nuclear testing, images of blast tests—including those with mannequins that imitate the "nuclear" family in test houses—burst across the screen. Another image of Nierenberg flickers on the screen, scratched and damaged affectively, followed by a recruiting film from Scripps featuring him, which has the sort of cheery, upbeat tone that is so easy to parody today (see figure 7.9).

At 29:40 we return to Stewart at Scripps, but now at night. Another photograph of Nierenberg is projected onto the building that bears his name (see figure 7.10), as

FIGURE 7.9: Nuclear fallout for Nierenberg.

Stewart says that Nierenberg accepted the reality of global warming, but like his boss Reagan, was a fervent believer in the free market. In antiphonal response to the theatricalization of the cinematic in the black-box studio, cinematic effect is theatricalized onto the outside of the building. (See video clip 7.5e. ▶)

The image starts to slide around the rounded corner of the building, superimposed with fragments of Nierenberg's typescript (the light beneath the overhang echoes earlier imagery of the sun) as slow-moving, mid-range strings enter (see figures 7.11a and 7.11b).

FIGURE 7.10: Theatricalizing the cinematic.

FIGURES 7.11A AND B: Dissolve from the theatricalized cinematic to superimposed layers of cinematic screens.

The strings accompany a series of sped-up images of people in a crowded, well-lit cityscape. The speed of the film accelerates, with the people growing increasingly abstracted until they are reduced to the streaming lights of cars on highways, an obvious reminder of energy consumption as we hear of Nierenberg's belief that any climate change would be gradual, so humans could adapt. The juxtaposition of the "speeding" people and the "glacially paced" music creates a musical homology to this belief. As the music crests, it comes to a stop, along with the image of a red sports car braking at a red light in the nighttime cityscape. (See video clip 7.5f ⊙) "It was," says Stewart, "just what Reagan wanted to hear" (30:48).

A sharp cut takes us to Stewart, leaning against the wall of Nierenberg Hall at night, a relaxed posture at odds with the spy-spoof tone of the beginning. He repeats an infamous, perhaps apocryphal, but telling exchange about climate change. An aide asked a climate scientist how long it would be before global warming became a serious threat. "Considered reply? 'Forty years.' The aide quipped, 'Get back to me in thirty-nine.' Global warming was duly kicked into the long grass." Stewart pushes off the wall and walks out of frame, echoing his "walk on" at the beginning and creating a beat of silence to punctuate the end of the sequence.

This one brief segment has a number of internal rhythms. Information isn't always neatly presented in logical, sequential succession, but may be layered, placed in juxtaposition, or appear in affective bursts within digressions. The shifts in editing rhythm, visual density, musical content, voice-over and on-camera narration, graphs and diagrams, photographs, words and equations, and even architecture and camera angle create a highly varied but thematically coherent texture that flows, changes tempo, and cadences like music.

Whereas in *An Inconvenient Truth* the "simple" sections in terms of audiovisual space are the theatrical lecture spaces and the complex ones are the cinematic "movies," *Climate Wars* makes the talking head/lecture space cinematic, either through the use of natural field settings or the projection of the black box, which explodes the normal "cinematic" space by putting a semitransparent screen in the middle of the space and roaming around it with the body of the narrator present. The affective, imbedded segments are in a more complex mode, something more akin to music videos but made distinct by the layering of visual information enlivened by movement of even still imagery and accompanied by bursts of music. The music weaves in and out of *Climate Wars* both as cinematic underscore (the ominous "spy" motifs as Stewart creeps around Scripps, or the ominous bass drones as sea ice breaks up) and as the harmonic rhythm holding together the images in some of the information "bursts."

Talking About Modes

Dance philosopher Francis Sparshott has proposed a succinct, yet powerful and flexible, means of describing the relationship between music and dance (which is, after all, a moving image): for him, the relationship is prepositional. One may dance to, with, for, against, around, across, or on top of music. Most of us can recognize immediately what each means, though it is only the beginning, an overall impression that must be expanded upon, explored, and untangled. Using those prepositions can be the way in: What does it mean, in real terms, for a dancer to dance "around" the music? It implies that the music is at the center, that the dancer is responding to the rhythm and perhaps melodic shape of the music, but it also implies that the relationship is looser in some way than the dancer who dances "to" or "with" the music. "I am not sure I have ever seen anyone dance '*under* the music,'" Sparshott concludes, "but I am by no means sure I haven't."[10]

My immediate thought when I first read that description was, "I think I have!" Jíří Kylián's choreography to Mahler's *Songs of a Wayfarer* seemed to me to immerse the dancers in a vast ocean of music. The music was much bigger than they were, but they moved within it, responding to its currents like fish, capable of independent motion but limited by the medium in which they were suspended. The music created a space in which the dancers moved.

This spatial dimension of sound is relatively underdeveloped as an aesthetic parameter, but can be illuminating about how we respond to audiovisual space. The simple concept of the preposition is a lens through which the welter of questions about how music, movement, and stage space come into focus. At least we now have a place to start.

In certain academic circles I am known for my *resistance* to theory. This resistance has less to do with theory itself and more to do with the way that theory can become the goal rather than a tool to aid in understanding. So I am proposing this framework of modes because I think they can be useful in getting a handle on the complex relationships of audiovisual media of all sorts. A mode, like a genre, can describe a configuration that provides a loose framework for a distinctive, individual expression that nonetheless reinforces the parameters of that configuration. Description creates the foundation for analysis. Finding ways to describe, to map out the territory, helps us know where we want to go.

References

Altman, Rick. "Toward a Theory of the History of Representational Technologies," *IRIS* 2, no. 2 (1984): 111–125.

Chion, Michel. *Audio-Vision: Sound on Screen*. Translated by Claudia Gorbman. New York: Columbia University Press, 1994.

Gorbman, Claudia. *Unheard Melodies: Narrative Film Music*. London: BFI Publications, 1987.

Jenkins, Henry. *Convergence Culture: Where Old and New Media Collide*. New York: New York University Press, 2006.

Sparshott, Francis Edward. *A Measured Pace: Toward a Philosophical Understanding of the Arts of Dance*. Toronto: University of Toronto Press, 1995.

Stilwell, Robynn. "The Fantastical Gap between Diegetic and Non-Diegetic." In *Beyond the Soundtrack: Representing Music in Cinema*, edited by Lawrence Kramer, Daniel Goldmark, and Richard Leppert, 184–202. Berkeley: University of California Press, 2007.

[10] Francis Edward Sparshott, *A Measured Pace: Toward a Philosophical Understanding of the Arts of Dance* (Toronto: University of Toronto Press, 1995), 224.

CHAPTER 8

TITLE SEQUENCES FOR CONTEMPORARY TELEVISION SERIALS

ANNETTE DAVISON

> People want, when they're in the next room, then they hear that song, they know the show is on.
>
> HBO's advice to David Chase, creator of *The Sopranos*[1]

> All you need is the opening chords, or the image of the tree and it's so evocative, people immediately know where you are or what you're talking about.
>
> Alan Poul, executive producer, *Six Feet Under*[2]

IN May 2010 a lead story in *New York* magazine focused on television: "Televisionaries: An Extraordinary TV Season, and the Rules That Shaped It."[3] Title sequences ranked among the topics covered, with the sequence for Showtime's *Dexter* as the exemplar. A brief commentary summarized how the sequence was produced, and the article presented a series of frame stills from the sequence alongside extracts of Rolfe Kent's music score in reduction (somewhat unusually for mainstream print media). The blogosphere has been

[1] "Music of the Sopranos," David Chase interview with Will Dana, at http://www.hbo.com/the-sopranos/#/the-sopranos/inside/index.html (accessed July 13, 2010). Also available on *The Sopranos*, Series 6—The Final Episodes (DVD) (HBO Home Entertainment, 2007).

[2] Alan Poul, speaking on "Under the Main Titles" (featurette on the creation of the *Six Feet Under* opening titles, directed by Joel Lipman), *Six Feet Under: The Complete First Series* (DVD) (HBO Home Entertainment, 2002).

[3] *New York*, May 24, 2010, 31–45. With thanks to Jeff Smith for drawing my attention to this.

in a state of excitement over television title sequences in recent years as well. Many sites list favorite examples of the genre and engage in detailed discussions of the music, the visuals, and their audiovisual interactions.[4] I agree with these critics. In recent years the main title sequences for high-production-value television serials, particularly those developed for broadcast on premium cable channels, have become fascinating progenitors of new audiovisual aesthetics. Such sequences have undoubtedly been influenced by developments in music video and commercials. The title sequence is today a vital tool in generating and conveying brand identity.[5]

This chapter focuses on the main title sequences of two recent serials commissioned by the influential North American premium cable channel Home Box Office (HBO): *The Sopranos* (1997–2007) and *Six Feet Under* (2001–2005). My interest lies in the relationship between the institutional context of these serials and the aesthetic character of their main title sequences. Their title sequences are utterly different in genesis and aesthetic character, but they are complementary in other ways, not least in the sense that like the signature music for any series, both must satisfy the prospective viewer while also remaining interesting to the returning viewer and fan. Both sequences ran unchanged for five seasons or more.[6]

Defining Functions and Characteristics

An opening title and/or credits sequence accomplishes several tasks simultaneously. Perhaps most tangible among these is to convey serial- and episode-specific information through text, most often including the show's title, the names of key cast members and creative personnel, and in some cases an episode title. Full credits are usually reserved for the end of a show, where interesting developments are also occurring. For example, both *The Sopranos* and, more recently, *Mad Men* (AMC, 2007–) use a different music track for their end credits each week. Do such changes increase the interpretive space for viewers?

Title sequences pitch, or make desirable, the show that follows. As a result, signifiers that suggest the show's genre are often incorporated.[7] Functioning as a trailer for

[4] Andrew Dignan's detailed analysis of *The Wire*'s fourth season title sequence for *The House Next Door*, the official blog of *Slant Magazine*, is among the best of these. Dignan, "*The Wire* and the Art of the Credit Sequence," at http://www.slantmagazine.com/house/2006/09/the-wire-and-the-art-of-the-credit-sequence/ (accessed July 30, 2010). Dignan has also produced a series of video essays on each season's sequence (with Kevin B. Lee and Matt Zoller Seltz) for New York's Museum of the Moving Image. Dignan, Lee, and Seltz, "Extra Credit, Part 1," at http://www.movingimagesource.us/articles/extra-credit-part-1-20080728 (accessed July 30, 2010).

[5] For more on this, see Bethany Klein, *As Heard on TV: Popular Music in Advertising* (Aldershot, UK: Ashgate, 2009).

[6] A shot of the twin towers was removed from *The Sopranos*' sequence after the terrorist bombings on 9/11.

[7] Not all title sequences signal genre unambiguously, a situation that has become more frequent with the blurring or hybridization of genres that has become a feature of shows that seek particular types of viewer, as mentioned below.

the coming attraction, they seek to convert the distracted potential viewer into a repeat viewer/consumer and use arresting images and notable music to achieve this.[8] Simon Frith suggests that to be televisual, "music must not only be visualised but given a sense of occasion. Television address—as a matter of both voice and setting—means inviting audiences to be part of something out there (while staying in their living rooms)."[9]

The music in title sequences acts to draw in distracted viewers, indicating that a particular show is starting. It functions as an auditory cue, a boundary in the "flow" of television's continuous programming, particularly for potential viewers who are not physically in sight of the screen.[10] Indeed, as commentators such as John Ellis, Rick Altman, and Kevin Donnelly suggest, we "listen to television sometimes more than we watch it.... [It] tends to have sound cues that we can follow when our attention is drawn elsewhere.... [We] can glance away from the television only to be brought back by sounds that appear to signal action, excitement or interest."[11] In this sense, title music acts as "curtain music," signaling the start of a show and the end of the commercials or other program trailers.

Title sequences also enable viewers to ready themselves for the move to a period of focus and engagement with a show. Given that many serials are originally broadcast in a weekly pattern (same day/time each week), such preparations may also become ritualized, born of anticipation and excitement for a planned period of escapism and/or engagement. Indeed, anecdotal evidence suggests that for many viewers a title sequence is part of this ritualized experience. It signifies the return of the familiar along with the novel, favorite characters in new situations and developing story arcs. Title music may thus encourage the regular returning viewer to undertake certain behaviors: complete chores, prepare refreshments, end conversations, and sit and watch.

Viewers may well remain distracted today, but with the advent of digitization they are offered a variety of options for content delivery; in other words, they can determine where, when, and how they view that content. Thus, although a proportion of television's audiences may still receive content via the set that plays continuously in the corner of the room, others watch differently. There has been a growth in services offered "on demand" by some channels and by cable/satellite distributors, with opportunities for the selection and downloading of content, viewable via a range of devices: television sets, computers, and handheld devices such as tablets and mobile phones. Contemporary

[8] This is particularly true of the title sequences to series pilots. The title sequence for the pilot of *Twin Peaks* was a full minute longer than the 90-second version that was used for the rest of the episodes.

[9] Simon Frith, "Look! Hear! The Uneasy Relationship of Music and Television." *Popular Music* 21, no. 3 (2002): 288.

[10] As Simon Frith states, "Music on television is less often heard for its own sake than as a device to get our visual attention." Frith, *"Look! Hear!"* 280. See also Raymond Williams, *Television: Technology and Cultural Form* (London: Routledge, 1974); and John Ellis, *Visible Fictions: Film, Television, Video* (London: Routledge, 1982).

[11] K. J. Donnelly, *The Spectre of Sound: Music in Film and Television* (London: BFI, 2005), 111. See also Ellis, *Visible Fictions*; and Rick Altman, "Television/Sound," in *Studies in Entertainment: Critical Approaches to Mass Culture*, ed. Tania Modleski (Bloomington: Indiana University Press, 1986), 39–54.

personal video recorders (PVRs) enhance the capabilities of the much earlier video cassette recorders (VCRs): viewers may set them to record an entire series at the push of a button, and some PVRs can be programmed to record what the machine *judges* viewers may wish to watch, given their previous consumer behavior. A growing number of viewers watch serials via box sets of complete seasons, previously on VHS video, now on DVD. Such modes of delivery enable (indeed, perhaps encourage) more intense viewing patterns than the original serials' weekly transmissions allow, though they also mirror the marathon ("weekender") season reruns that often precede the first broadcasting of a new season, which digital/satellite multiplexing make possible.[12] And these are just some of the legal options for viewing television content.

Television title sequences are short. The two explored here are among the longest, clocking in at 90 seconds each. In terms of other formats, they are most like audiovisual commercials or compressed music videos and are similarly promotional; they are "barkers" for the show that follows. In his study of the television soap opera *Dynasty* (ABC, 1981–1989), Jostein Gripsrud points out that the compressed character of title sequences generates the "abundance, energy, and intensity of experience" highlighted by Richard Dyer in his argument that "light entertainment presents, rather than re-presents, utopia."[13] *Dynasty*'s theme music, writes Gripsrud, provides "formal coherence, a degree of semantic clarification, and 'narrative' progress and closure to the quite disparate, 'poetic' visual montage, attempting to set or guide the overall mood of the viewing experience."[14] The same is true of contemporary title sequences, including those of *The Sopranos* and *Six Feet Under*. However, older shows' title sequences tend also to emphasize the legibility of signifiers and often display a lack of subtlety; as Gripsrud states, the *Dynasty* titles present "[a] strong, almost aggressive announcement of quite clear-cut pleasures."[15] I argue that the similarities between the sequences discussed in this chapter and the *Dynasty* sequence(s) end here. To understand the context of these differences, we need first to explore the place of these serials in the contemporary commercial television market.

Context

Rogers, Epstein, and Reeves (2002) present a history of commercial television marketing marked by three distinct phases: TV1 (ca. 1948–1975), TV2 (ca. 1975–1995), and TV3 (1995–). In the first of these, commercial television channels had as their goal to gain large numbers of viewers, any viewers, casual viewers; income from advertisers was

[12] Marc C. Rogers, Michael Epstein, and Jimmie L. Reeves, "The Sopranos as HBO Brand Equity: The Art of Commerce in the Age of Digital Representation," in *This Thing of Ours: Investigating the Sopranos*, ed. David Lavery (New York: Columbia University Press, 2002), 54.

[13] Jostein Gripsrud, *The Dynasty Years: Hollywood Television and Critical Media Studies* (London: Routledge, 1995), 193.

[14] Gripsrud, *The* Dynasty *Years*, 197.

[15] Gripsrud, *The* Dynasty *Years*, 193.

based on raw ratings statistics. In the second phase, the income received from advertisers depended on the delivery of particular types of viewers in terms of audience demographics. With this move to a desire for *quality* demographics, content innovations, such as the blurring of genre boundaries and the development of "noteworthy and notorious programming," enabled and indeed encouraged the development of a new kind of viewer experience, "avid fanship."[16] Such fanship has been described as involving "a level of quasi-religious engagement with television that may involve taping and archiving episodes, purchasing ancillary merchandise, and interacting with other fans in online discussion groups."[17] The third phase is marked by an important change in economic terms: the key revenue stream for premium cable/satellite channels, pay TV, comes from the monthly subscriptions paid by viewers. This change represents a shift from second-order to first-order commodity relations; that is, viewers pay directly for content they want to watch, rather than being delivered to advertisers, who in turn fund the channels of distribution that commission the shows. The change thus both drives content and affects consumer behavior.[18]

To provide " 'monthly audience appeal' to as broad a subscriber base as possible," premium cable services like HBO have to provide a wide range of exclusive content.[19] Home Box Office has sought to develop high-production-value, original drama serials since the combined threat of the VCR and cheap movie rentals first appeared. Since potential viewers cannot easily sample shows that are available only by means of subscription packages, however, the premium cable channels have to create a "buzz" around their products to persuade potential consumers to subscribe.

Rogers, Epstein, and Reeves argue that premium cable channels must establish a strong brand identity to set themselves apart from competition in both the ad-driven world of commercial television and their direct competitors in pay TV.[20] Indeed, as technology and the television industry in North America have changed over the last five years, brand identity may well now be the key to success in this TV3 phase.[21] Home Box Office has a distinctive brand identity, as encapsulated by a name that attempts to

[16] Rogers, Epstein, and Reeves, "The Sopranos as HBO Brand Equity," 45.

[17] Rogers, Epstein, and Reeves, "The Sopranos as HBO Brand Equity," 45. Although online activity is clearly the most recent of these behaviors, fan use of newsgroups focused on television soap operas date back to the mid- to late 1980s. By the early 1990s such activity had grown exponentially. See Nancy K. Baym, *Tune In, Log On: Soaps, Fandom, and Online Community* (London: Sage Publications, 2000), 1–34.

[18] That is, premium cable channels develop content for the viewer with the goal of gaining (and retaining) maximum subscriptions, rather than to deliver a particular demographic to an advertiser. See Rogers, Epstein, and Reeves, "The Sopranos as HBO Brand Equity," 47.

[19] Rogers, Epstein, and Reeves, "The Sopranos as HBO Brand Equity," 47.

[20] Rogers, Epstein, and Reeves, "The Sopranos as HBO Brand Equity," 47.

[21] "In the era of TV III, it is just a matter of time before channels such as HBO become a relic of the past, replaced with new technologies of distribution like on-demand program streaming. . . . By building an identity that is separate from the physicality of a conduit, HBO may survive as a brand long after it has lost its relevance as a premium channel." Michael M. Epstein, Jimmie L. Reeves, and Mark C. Rodgers, "Surviving 'The Hit': Will *The Sopranos* Still Sing for HBO?" in *Reading the Sopranos: Hit TV from HBO*, ed. David Lavery (London; New York: I. B. Tauris, 2006), 25.

synthesize the cinematic and the domestic. The cinematic in HBO's fare, and discourse about it, takes a variety of forms, including an emphasis on auteurism, more creative freedom, higher budgets than are usually the case in production for television, and the use of production team members drawn from filmmaking, such as writers, directors, cinematographers, and actors.[22] In addition, HBO provides "programming free of commercial interruption and uncontaminated by the demands of advertisers," and is "not subject to government and industry restrictions on profanity, sexuality, and violence."[23] This lack of censorship means that the channel can develop content other channels cannot. Indeed, it has become a leader in adult-oriented content on television, particularly in producing exclusive original programming.[24]

Home Box Office has been developing a brand identity built on content that exploits violence, sexuality, profanity, and the macabre since the mid-1980s, but for Rogers, Epstein, and Reeves, it was only with *The Sopranos* that the channel found a show that

22 Janet McCabe and Kim Akass, "It's Not TV, It's HBO Original Programming," in *It's Not TV: Watching HBO in the Post-Television Era*, ed. Marc Leverette, Brian L. Ott, and Cara Louise Buckley (New York; London: Routledge, 2008), 87–88. See also Avi Santo, "Para-television and Discourses of Distinction: The Culture of Production at HBO," in It's Not TV, 29, n.1, 42.

23 Rogers, Epstein and Reeves, "The Sopranos as HBO Brand Equity," 46, 51.

24 It is possible to trace this back to its earlier focus on trying to attract a demographic that broadcast channels struggled to attract: eighteen- to thirty-four-year-old males. It is also possible to understand several of HBO's flagship serials, including *The Sopranos* and *Six Feet Under*, as exhibiting the "new sensibility" that Jeffrey Sconce detects in "certain corners of North American cinema and culture over the past decade, one that manifests a predilection for irony, black humor, fatalism, relativism and, yes, even nihilisim." "Irony, Nihilism and the New American 'Smart' Film," *Screen* 43, no. 4 (Winter 2002): 350. While the films Sconce discusses under the label of new American "smart" film are varied, they share both a target audience and a "set of stylistic and thematic practices" (352). From an aesthetic point of view, they share experimentation with "tone" rather than the experimentation with film style and narrative strategies that art films of the 1960s–1970s undertook to critique codes of "'bourgeois realism' and/or 'bourgeois society'" (352). Indeed, the "'social politics' of power, institutions, representation and subjectivity so central to 1960s and 1970s art cinema" has been replaced, with new American smart film, by a concentration, "often with ironic disdain, on the 'personal politics' of power, communication, emotional dysfunction and identity in white middle-class culture" (352). Though there are clearly commonalities between the sensibility Sconce describes and some of the key HBO serials of the same period, it is important to recognize the differences, too. Critics have certainly been as critical of *The Sopranos* as they have been of new American smart films, but praise has been conferred on the show's richness of detail, complexity of storytelling and characterization, the fantastical dream sequences, its standing back and letting the audience interpret the show. Many critics and fans also write about identifying with Tony and the problems that brings. Audiences arguably seem to care more about the characters in these serials, as opposed to those presented in American smart films. But perhaps this is also a key point of difference in the mode of delivery: art/smart films are, usually, one-offs wherever they are viewed, whereas television serials require a desire for audiences to return weekly. Affiliations with and aspirations to cinema associated with these serials should also be tempered with a recognition that they also rely on, yet simultaneously are defined in opposition to, the industrial and aesthetic strategies associated with network television. Although the cinematic can be located in such serials' production teams, they are also rife with people trained and experienced almost exclusively in television; David Chase is an example. As Tony Kelso puts it, "Maybe HBO is not completely different, but it's different enough." "And Now No Word from Our Sponsor: How HBO Puts the Risk Back into Television," in *It's Not TV*, 59. See also Santo, "Para-television and Discourses of Distinction."

represented its brand identity entirely successfully.[25] *The Sopranos* takes the staples of the channel's emphases and places them in a context "where they all work together to become a unique and distinctive product."[26] In addition, the show's combination of serial and episodic elements "rewards avid fans without alienating casual viewers."[27] The show's season is shorter than many on broadcast networks, usually around thirteen episodes. More time, attention to detail, and money are devoted to individual episodes, resulting in higher production values. The show's buzz is kept alive in the hiatuses between seasons that result from these shorter seasons by ancillary content, Web content, and marathon reruns.[28]

Title sequences enable these shows—and by extension HBO—to present brand identity with intensity in a highly compressed time frame. The most successful not only tie appropriate music to a show, prompt viewers' expectations, and persuade them to buy into the serial; they also visualize the selected music in a productive manner, matching the "values" projected by the audiovisual complex to those of the serial in holistic terms. In this way they assist the generation of a strong brand identity. Earlier examples of this strategy, which I suggest were the exception and not yet the rule, include the sitcom *Taxi* (ABC and NBC, 1978–1983), with title music by Bob James, and the David Lynch and Mark Frost serial *Twin Peaks* (ABC, 1990–1991), with title music by Angelo Badalamenti.

The Audiovisual in Main Title Sequences

Scholars have attempted to analyze the interaction of sound, music, and visuals in detail in recent years. This work has focused particularly on film music and music videos, but has also resulted in more specifically music-led studies of the analysis of musical meaning and of meaning in musical multimedia. Claudia Gorbman introduced the idea of "mutual implication" between music and images, taking scholarly dialogue an essential step forward in this process.[29] As an analytical tool, the notion allows the relationship between music and visuals to be understood as dynamic and processual, rather than static or fixed, and enables a move away from the long-used terminology of parallel versus counterpoint, which inherently assumed the primacy of the image.[30] In *Analysing Musical Multimedia*, Nicholas Cook develops Gorbman's notion, essentially by further

25 Kelso, "And Now No Word from Our Sponsor," 51.

26 Kelso, "And Now No Word from Our Sponsor," 53. Or, as McCabe and Akass suggest, "the channel takes control of the illicit and encloses it within its institutional discourse of quality—implied as an original tele-literary product that places emphasis on smart writing, compelling stories told in an innovative way, high production values and a unique creative vision behind each project." "It's Not TV, It's HBO Original Programming," 89.

27 Kelso, "And Now No Word from Our Sponsor," 54.

28 Kelso, "And Now No Word from Our Sponsor," 54.

29 Claudia Gorbman, *Unheard Melodies: Narrative Film Music* (London; Bloomington: BFI and Indiana University Press, 1987), 15.

30 Gorbman, *Unheard Melodies*. See also Annette Davison, *Hollywood Theory, Non-Hollywood Practice: Cinema Soundtracks in the 1980s–1990s* (Aldershot, UK: Ashgate, 2004), 41 n.44, and chapter 3.

breaking down the term. Building on the "enabling similarity" that Lakoff and Johnson see as a precondition of metaphorical association, Cook advocates submitting music–image relationships to a two-stage test process. The first explores the character of their similarity; the second, the character of their difference. A key aim for Cook is to enable the analyst to approach multimedia works free from "unconscious *a priori* assumptions."[31] He calls on media analysis to (1) invert any medium-specific hierarchies that appear to prioritize one medium over another, (2) seek out "gaps"—the absence of closure—because such gaps may not be left in all media,[32] and (3) search for significant distributions of oppositions across media ("distributional analysis"[33]). The analyst should problematize the comparison of media and work to discover functional aspects that may involve more than one medium, such as rhythm.

A few scholars have produced analyses of television title sequences, among them musicologist Lawrence Kramer, who describes them as "the television equivalent of lyric poetry."[34] Kramer's analyses of the title sequences for *NYPD Blue* (ABC, 1993–2005) and *The X-Files* (Fox, 1993–2002) conclude a pair of book chapters concerned with musical meaning and mixed media. In analytical terms, his discussion of the generation of semantics in mixed media can usefully be read with the notion of "mutual implication" in mind:

[31] Nicholas Cook, *Analyzing Musical Multimedia* (Oxford: Oxford University Press, 1998), 133.

[32] Where a gap in one medium is filled by an element from another, Cook calls this "contextual complementation." *Analyzing Musical Multimedia*, 104.

[33] Cook, *Analyzing Musical Multimedia*, 142.

[34] Lawrence Kramer, *Musical Meaning: Towards a Critical History* (Berkeley; Los Angeles: University of California Press, 2002), 188. Television title sequences have also been discussed by Robynn Stilwell and John Richardson: Robynn Stilwell, "The Sound Is 'Out There': Score, Sound Design and Exoticism in *The X-Files*," in *Analyzing Popular Music*, ed. Allan F. Moore (Cambridge, UK: Cambridge University Press, 2003), 60–79; and John Richardson, "*Laura* and *Twin Peaks*: Postmodern Parody and the Musical Reconstruction of the Absent Femme Fatale," in *American Dreams, Nightmare Visions: The Cinema of David Lynch*, ed. Erica Sheen and Annette Davison, (London: Wallflower Press, 2004), 77–92. Philip Tagg is a key figure in the analysis of titles music and semiotics, with a book-length study of the title sequence for *Kojak* and, with Bob Clarida, a detailed study of the semiotics of *Ten Little Title Tunes*, several of which are from television. In the latter, however, the authors' focus is not on the interaction of music and visuals: Philip Tagg, *Kojak: 50 Seconds of Television Music: Towards the Analysis of Affect in Popular Music* (New York: Mass Media Music Scholars' Press, Inc., 2011/1979); Philip Tagg and Bob Clarida, *Ten Little Title Tunes* (New York: Mass Media Music Scholars' Press, Inc., 2003). Within the nascent field of television studies, the title sequence is usually discussed only in passing. Exceptions include a section on the title sequence for *Dynasty* in Gripsrud's *The* Dynasty *Years*, 189–197, and an analysis of the opening titles for the miniseries *War and Remembrance* (ABC, 1988–1989) in John Thornton Caldwell, *Televisuality: Style, Crisis, and Authority in American Television* (New Brunswick, N.J.: Rutgers University Press, 1995), 160–192. Jon Burlingame provides a history of the title theme in North American television in *TV's Biggest Hits: The Story of Television Themes from* Dragnet *to* Friends (New York: Schirmer Books, 1996). More recent studies have begun to explore television's interstitials—the bits "in between" the programs as broadcast—and other paratexts. Such approaches may well offer a productive way of thinking about main title and end credit sequences. Examples include John Ellis, "Interstitials: How the 'Bits in Between' Define the Programmes", in *Ephemeral Media: Transitory Screen Culture from Television to YouTube*, ed. Paul Grainge (London: British Film Institute), 59–69.

> musical meaning in mixed media is experienced in inverted form; it runs on a loop. The music seems to emit a meaning that it actually returns, and what it returns, it enriches and transforms.... as soon as meaning effectively runs from the imagetext to music along the semantic loop, the music seems to convey that meaning to and through the imagetext in preconceptual, prerepresentational form.
>
> ...
>
> This helps explain how and why the music-imagetext relationship may be complex, nuanced, ironic, ambiguous, and so on. It is not a simple question of matching meaning to music, like fabric swatches, but of meshing the two together and rearticulating both.[35]

Kramer highlights music's promiscuity in the way it actively seeks mixture, in contrast to text and images, which are simply "amenable" to it. Yet music's attempt to mix with everything becomes a failure to "properly mix with anything";[36] there is a "remainder."[37] The remainder comes to our attention when the "fit" between music and imagetext appears "questionable," thus pushing the notion of mixture itself to the fore.[38] In this respect, Kramer's "remainder" is related to Cook's "gap."

Turning to television title sequences, Kramer points out that the format tends toward "encapsulating the fantasies underlying the shows' narrative formulas without the need to rationalize them or bring them to closure."[39] This is true, however I suspect that if a title sequence *were* to "rationalize... or bring... to closure" a show's narrative formula, there would be little need to watch the show itself. Title sequences present a "promise" of what is to follow,[40] just enough to tantalize, inviting potential viewers to watch the show for possible answers. Indeed, with both of the title sequences he analyzes, Kramer found that "the visuals tend toward a narrative that the music tends to repudiate."[41] In this way, a door is left open for the viewer.

The Sopranos

The title sequence for *The Sopranos* was created in-house by the show's production team, who selected the music after the visuals were shot and edited together to form an impressionistic montage of a car journey. The sequence took a day and half to shoot and was filmed from the interior of a car driven by Tony Soprano, the serial's protagonist.[42] The movement and shifting focus of the camera imply subjectivity: the images approximate

35 Kramer, *Musical Meaning*, 153, 154.
36 Kramer, *Musical Meaning*, 179.
37 Kramer, *Musical Meaning*, 179.
38 Kramer, *Musical Meaning*, 181.
39 Kramer, *Musical Meaning*, 188.
40 Gripsrud, *The* Dynasty *Years*, 191.
41 Kramer, *Musical Meaning*, 191.
42 Brett Martin, *The Sopranos: The Complete Book* (London: Headline, 2007), 30–31.

the view of a person sitting alongside Tony, watching what happens. In this way the title sequence prefigures the privileged position the audience is offered in *The Sopranos*. Indeed, the show's pilot begins with Tony's first visit to his therapist, and we are privy to the therapeutic session, the most private of exchanges. This conceit underpins all of the show's six seasons, and brief shots of Tony reflected in the car's rearview mirror in the opening titles presage it, presenting a visualization of the idea of self-analysis.[43] Tony is alone in the car, however, and as the show's seasons unfold we may also understand the sequence's image of a lone driver to encapsulate Tony's loneliness.

The title sequence presents its own brief narrative: the journey, a frequent topos in recent title sequences.[44] Title sequences also operate as metaphorical journeys in themselves, of course, transporting the viewer into the world of the show. In *The Sopranos*, this "real" journey serves as our introduction to Tony and to the serial's location and themes. Rather than featuring this "alpha male" directly, the sequence gradually reveals Tony's limbs, then his face, phallic cigar, and body. The many shots of New Jersey taken from the car are intercut with these mysterious, fragmented shots of Tony, which comprise almost one in four of the sequence's sixty shots. Characterization remains enigmatic, and viewers are thus obliged to watch the show to find out more.[45]

The segment contains no static shots. The theme of driving is emphasized in the repetition of familiar signs of roads (such as white painted lines, metal barriers, and arrows) and by the massive letters painted on the side of an industrial storage tank that tell Tony to "DRIVE SAFELY." Indeed, the text of the credits behaves as an abstracted form of traffic in itself: the credits dash onscreen from the left, halt, then rush offscreen to the right. The rhythm of this "action" is synchronized with the meter of the music: against a resolute yet unhurried tempo of around 88–90 beats per minute, the credits are all held mid-screen for around three beats, while the fourth beat covers entry and exit. Similarly, a number of shots and shot-sequences create rhythmic interest via their interrelation with the sequence's music, as happens with the images of separate then converging white lines and the rhythms of occasional graphic matches and contrasts between shots during the sequence.[46]

The sequence reflects the variety of New Jersey's urban, suburban, industrial, and semirural landscapes that Tony passes through on his drive. The locations filmed are all real, with the exception of Satriale's Pork Store, though even this fictional location was created in a real-world site and retained throughout production.[47] Fans of the show have posted online lists of the possible locations featured in the sequence, inviting visitors to

43 Shots 32 and 59 feature Tony's reflected image.

44 Other examples include *Mad Men*—the journey or "fall" of the man in the suit—and the journey of the body in *Six Feet Under*.

45 It is worth noting that although title sequences from earlier periods often introduced key characters visually, in a number of contemporary title sequences there is a refusal to show *any* characters visually (e.g., *Six Feet Under*, *Weeds* [Showtime, 2005–]), or they present characters only in an abstracted or fragmented form (e.g., *Mad Men*, *The Wire* [HBO, 2002–2008]).

46 Examples of the latter include the graphic match between street lamps, shot from beneath, and a plane taking off from nearby Newark airport (shots 17–18).

47 Martin, *The Sopranos*, 31.

their sites to add to or correct this collective knowledge.[48] The identification of the music heard in each episode also became a locus of fan activity during the show's run, as the show's end credits do not include details of the music, only the name of the music editor, Kathryn Dayak.[49]

Most shots in the sequence are around a second in duration. The longest ones focus on the approach of the car to the toll lanes for the New Jersey Turnpike and Tony grabbing a ticket (at 7 and 3 seconds, respectively), then the final shots that lead up the swooping curve of the driveway to the house, where Tony parks and leaves the car (at 2, 4, and 4 seconds). It is partly through their extended duration that these moments seem to offer us insight into Tony's character—his aggressive snatch at the ticket implies impatience, for example—but he remains inscrutable. Mobile camera work during the lengthiest shot diverts attention from its duration and allows time to read the text: "NEW JERSEY TURNPIKE."

The sequence uses the song "Woke Up This Morning" by London-based band Alabama 3 (called A3 in the United States). It was originally written about a woman who took revenge on her husband after more than 20 years of abuse. David Chase, the serial's creator, had heard the track on the radio some six months earlier, but only when it was placed against the edited sequence did particular lyrics begin to resonate.[50] The mix of the song used, the Chosen One mix, has been edited to present a coherent structure in terms of the song, which in turn also forms the shape and dynamic of the visual sequence.[51]

The edited mix of the song is marked by static harmony (alternating between I and IV) established by the vocal and chords played on a Hammond organ (or a synthesizer with a Hammond organ sound); thus, the song's harmony presents little sense of momentum. The song repeats the harmonic sequence throughout, twice in each verse, once in the chorus. The instrumentation is a little more unusual. On the one hand it is organized around signifiers of gospel music and the blues, with harmonica, tambourine, the bass vocals of Larry Love, and the sampled voice of Howlin' Wolf, with a gospel chorus added in the refrains. On the other, it incorporates a more eclectic sound world, with trip-hop glitches that invoke the white noise of television sets, Latin woodblocks, a pitched drum pad, analog synth, and distorted electric guitar interjections.

48 See, for example, "Soprano Sue's Sightings," at http://www.sopranosuessightings.com/openingcredits.htm (accessed July 13, 2010). The official HBO Web site for the show also incorporates a virtual minitour that identifies some of the key locations of the sequence. "The Sopranos: Inside the Opening Credits," at http://www.hbo.com/the-sopranos/inside/behind-the-scenes/slideshow/inside-the-opening-credits.html (accessed July 13, 2010).

49 See, for example, "Soprano Sue's Sightings." Synopses for each episode on the show's official HBO Web site now also include music listings, with the opportunity to buy some tracks via a Web link to iTunes. "The Sopranos: Episodes," at http://www.hbo.com/the-sopranos/index.html#/the-sopranos/episodes/index.html (accessed July 13, 2010).

50 "Music of the Sopranos." The edited version of the song used for the credits is taken from the "Chosen One Mix," released on CD 1 of a CD Maxi: Alabama 3 and Street Angels Choir, NYC, "Woke Up This Morning" ELM 41 CDS1 (Elemental Records). Elemental Records is an autonomous label set up by London-based independent record label One Little Indian.

51 Given the structural limitations, musically speaking, involved in editing the track down to 90 seconds, it's possible that the visual edit was tweaked a little to fit.

The sound intensifies as the song progresses; gradually it accumulates more instruments, textures, and figures, creating interest at formal boundaries. Structural climaxes in the song are not marked by synchretic hit points, however. On repeated listening, the edited mix yields an effect of a strangely delicate intricacy; it sounds busy all the time, but it is also able to build to a climax despite the static harmony. *The Sopranos*' title sequence exudes a steady, controlled sense of continuity that climaxes with the final chorus and the gestures of closure in the coda, heard simultaneously with the shots of longer duration at the end of the sequence. The sequence has an ominous, brooding feel overall. The harmonically static yet accumulative character of the music is primary in this, as is the repetition of certain lyrics, particularly when Love joins the gospel choir in singing the lyrics to the final chorus ("Woke up this morning/Got yourself a gun").[52] The word "gun" is emphasized here, preempting the appearance of the gun as the letter *r* in the title card that follows, its typography an homage to the titles of the gangster movies *The Godfather* (Coppola, 1972) and *Goodfellas* (Scorsese, 1990), which are frequently referenced in the show.

More abstract resonances also contribute to a match between music and visuals in the sequence, with notions of "authenticity," for example, which also connect with the brand values of the show in more holistic terms and by extension with HBO's adult programming. Chase's conception for the title sequence was an attempt to make clear that the show's representation of the mafia would be based in New Jersey, rather than in its more familiar mythic association with New York City. Certain cast members reputedly have connections to the mafia.[53] Visually, authenticity is performed in the documentary-style filming of the title sequence and use of real-world locations. Musically, references to the blues are key to such resonances. In addition, Alabama 3/A3 has a claim on "authenticity" as a touring rock 'n' roll band. The band doesn't currently enjoy mainstream success beyond the use of this track, but it has a loyal and sizeable fan base, built from eccentric and energetic live performances.[54] The casting of guitarist Steven Van Zandt as Silvio Dante, Tony's consigliere, adds a further blues/rock inflection for some viewers; a founding member of Bruce Springsteen's E Street Band, Van Zandt is also a songwriter and producer, and he receives a text credit in the sequence.

On first viewing, however, Tony's drive out to the suburbs is incongruous with the music. Only with the serial's weekly return and the viewer's increasing familiarity with the show's characters and plot is this incongruity replaced by recognition of the sequence's resonance in relation to Tony. On the one hand, he is a powerful mob boss;

52 For example, the acquisition of a gun that morning; that he (the subject) has been chosen; that he was accursed, born "under a bad sign"; that his father didn't teach him wrong from right; that the world had "turned upside down" when he woke that morning; and that the "blues" had arrived.

53 Many of the cast are Italian American and had met on the sets of previous mob/gangster films/series such as Scorsese's *Goodfellas*. Some of the actors—such as Tony Sirico/"Paulie Walnuts"—allegedly also have a mob-related past, while others acknowledge that they have friends or relatives who are involved in the mafia.

54 The band formed in 1996, and its members describe themselves as "a pop band, a punk rock, blues and country techno situationist crypto-Marxist-Leninist electro band. We never went on X Factor or Pop Idol or Stooge Quest. We did it the old fashioned way." "About [Alabama 3]," at http://www.alabama3.co.uk/en/general_articles/about (accessed July 13, 2010).

on the other, he is lonely and depressive and suffers from panic attacks. He is so concerned with his own identity that he seeks therapy. The serial emphasizes Tony as everyman: despite his connections, he has to pay the turnpike toll just like everyone else.[55]

The title sequence for *The Sopranos* doesn't just generate a strong brand identity. Through its gapped quality, the presence of "remainders," it also encourages the engagement or interpretation of the viewer, whether new or returning. Indeed, many such recent sequences function as little mysteries that actively elicit a response, which may indeed change over the course of a viewer's relationship with the serial. Digital Kitchen's title sequence for *Six Feet Under* is just as successful at presenting the show's brand identity as that for *The Sopranos* and also offers an invitation to viewers, although this happens in an utterly different way.

Six Feet Under

Six Feet Under was the first major drama serial launched by HBO after *The Sopranos*. It was created and produced by Alan Ball, who wrote and coproduced the film *American Beauty* (1999). Like *The Sopranos*, it is a family drama that features sex, violent death, and the macabre, although these elements are contextualized rather differently; the show focuses on a family of undertakers, the Fishers, and their funeral business in Los Angeles. *Six Feet Under* deals with many of the issues one would expect of a contemporary family drama, but also involves an unusually uncompromising exploration of death and mortality. Immediately after the title sequence, each episode opens with an onscreen death, which frequently sets the tone for that episode.

Digital Kitchen designs and produces commercials, title sequences for films and television programs, and trailer campaigns to promote returning serials. Branding is key. As the company states on its Web site:

> The TV title sequence is a branding endeavor and a legitimate art form. It is the sole, consistent, and iconic moment that carries through a show's lifespan and beyond. It's what you remember most. DK is the most Emmy-nominated firm in the category. We seek assignments that tell a separate, parallel story. These are little art films really, that find their own voice, all while arming audiences with each show's unique psychology and worldview.[56]

Like the sequence for *The Sopranos*, the main title sequence for *Six Feet Under* is 90 seconds long, foregrounds motion (both camera motion and action within the frame), and

[55] On Tony's everyman appeal, see David Johansson, "Homeward Bound: Those *Sopranos* Titles Come Heavy," in *Reading the Sopranos: Hit TV from HBO*, ed. David Lavery (London: I. B. Tauris, 2006), 27–36. See also Noel Carroll, "Sympathy for the Devil," in *The Sopranos and Philosophy: I Kill Therefore I Am*, ed. Richard Greene and Peter Vernezze (Peru, Ill.: Open Court Publishing), 120–136.

[56] Digital Kitchen, "Main Titles (*Six Feet Under*)," at http://thisisdk.com/work/six-feet-under (accessed December 10, 2012).

features a journey. Just as the title sequence for *The Sopranos* was gradually enriched by viewers' ongoing relationships with the show and its protagonist, so the producers of *Six Feet Under* "wanted something that you would see week after week after week and be entertained enough to keep watching. Something that wouldn't completely reveal itself on the first viewing."[57]

Unusually for the format, the music was created prior to work on the visuals.[58] Alan Ball invited Thomas Newman to watch the pilot and compose 90 seconds of music for the as yet undevised title sequence; at that point, the producers "didn't have any idea what [they] wanted picture-wise."[59] Following discussions with the producers, Newman produced a CD of brief (30-second) extracts featuring different types of "textures, sounds, and colors."[60] The fragments that the producers felt created the right tone then formed the basis of the completed titles music. Newman's music for the sequence thus represents a more holistic response to the serial than would otherwise have been feasible.

Leading visual-effects houses were then invited to pitch their concepts for the title sequence on the basis of the show's pilot and a recording of Newman's 90-second music track. On seeing the images of the solitary tree and of hands wrenched apart devised by Digital Kitchen, Ball remembers thinking: "That's so elegant.... It's so cinematic. It's so unlike TV. I really loved that."[61] In capturing something "so unlike TV," Digital Kitchen managed also to encapsulate the serial's relationship with HBO; the channel's tagline at the time was, "It's not TV. It's HBO." But Ball acknowledges that the success of the sequence is at least partly due to the fact that the visuals were created *to* the music.[62] Indeed, the sequence's editor, Eric Anderson, recognized the potential of Newman's completed track as soon as he heard it. He remembers thinking that "it was going to be incredibly beneficial to me to edit to that piece of music because it's going to make me look like a great editor."[63]

Audiovisual Relations: Choreographing the Visuals to the Music

Newman's score is organized around two central ideas: an additive sequence, built from two-bar phrases that combine new textures and musical ideas as the track continues,

57 Poul, speaking on "Under the Main Titles."

58 Alan Ball knew Thomas Newman from his score for *American Beauty* (dir. Sam Mendes, 1999); Ball won an Academy Award for the film's script.

59 Ball, speaking on "Under the Main Titles."

60 Poul, speaking on "Under the Main Titles."

61 Ball, speaking on "Under the Main Titles."

62 Ball, speaking on "Under the Main Titles."

63 Anderson, speaking on "Under the Main Titles." Newman's theme music won an Emmy Award in 2002 for "Outstanding Main Title Theme Music" and two Grammy Awards in 2003: "Best Instrumental Composition" and "Best Instrumental Arrangement."

TABLE 8.1 Outline Form of the Sequence, as Choreographed to Newman's Music

1.	Sky (no earthly referent) Crow, then camera pans down to reveal tree, then hands separated onscreen in the foreground (the moments before death). Death and the first stage of the delivery of the body to the professional.
BREAK	(1 x 6-beat bar) Clouds in the sky with no earthly referent.
2.	(Main theme) The body begins its journey on the gurney and reaches the table of the mortuary technician.
BREAK(extd.)	(1 x 6-beat bar, plus 2 + 1 + 2 x 4/4)The body is embalmed, the body's surface cleaned, the body is displayed (lilies wilting).
3.	(Main theme) Coffin arrives at the cemetery, crow reappears in close-up.
BREAK	(1 x 6-beat bar, plus 2 + 2 x 4/4)Cloud/sky (no referent) Then panning down to solitary tree, titles appear in tree's abstracted root formation.

and disruptions *of* that accumulation. The main elements of these two-bar phrases are as follows:

1. An accented triad on the downbeat, the major third replaced by a raised fourth, the discord striking, or, as Peter Kaye describes it: "Ching!... [The chord] is bright, almost cheerful; its attack sharp, like something breaking, and yet extremely restless and harmonically, ambiguously unstable."[64]
2. An accompaniment figure on pizzicato strings that adds a more detailed sense of pulse. It is heard first in alternate bars, then extended to two bars;
3. The entry of the main theme on oboe or cor anglais.[65]

The repetition of particular elements, both musical and visual, adds symbolic weight and urges the viewer toward interpretation, perhaps in a similar way to the Magritte paintings that the opening images also invoke for some. Visually, the sequence depicts a person's journey from death through to preparation of the body, display of the body, and finally its burial. The organization of Newman's music also helps to articulate the "chunking" of the visual component of the sequence (see table 8.1). In broad terms, the bright lights, clean lines, medical equipment, and fluids of segment 2 contrast with the more earthly and celestial tones of the outer sections.

The most salient aspect of the sequence is its organization around a series of hit points that punctuate the sequence's surface, providing such a degree of satisfaction that it may

[64] Peter Kaye, "I'm Dead, Wow, Cool: The Music of *Six Feet Under*," in Kim Akass and Janet McCabe, *Reading Six Feet Under: TV to Die For* (London; New York: I. B. Tauris, 2005), 192–206. Thomas Newman states that the team discussed "starting with a kind of something, something kind of [plays chord], that evoked something celestial or heavenly, which was always for me kind of raised fourth degree." Newman, speaking on "Under the Main Titles."

[65] The main theme is minimal, emphasizing tonic and subdominant with appoggiatura figures that ornament this and add a flattened leading note and raised fourth (tritone), giving a modal inflection to the music's harmony. It describes a falling (semitone or tone) two-note figure, but one that does not always fall. Essentially it is a single-bar figure, developed to create a two-bar figure.

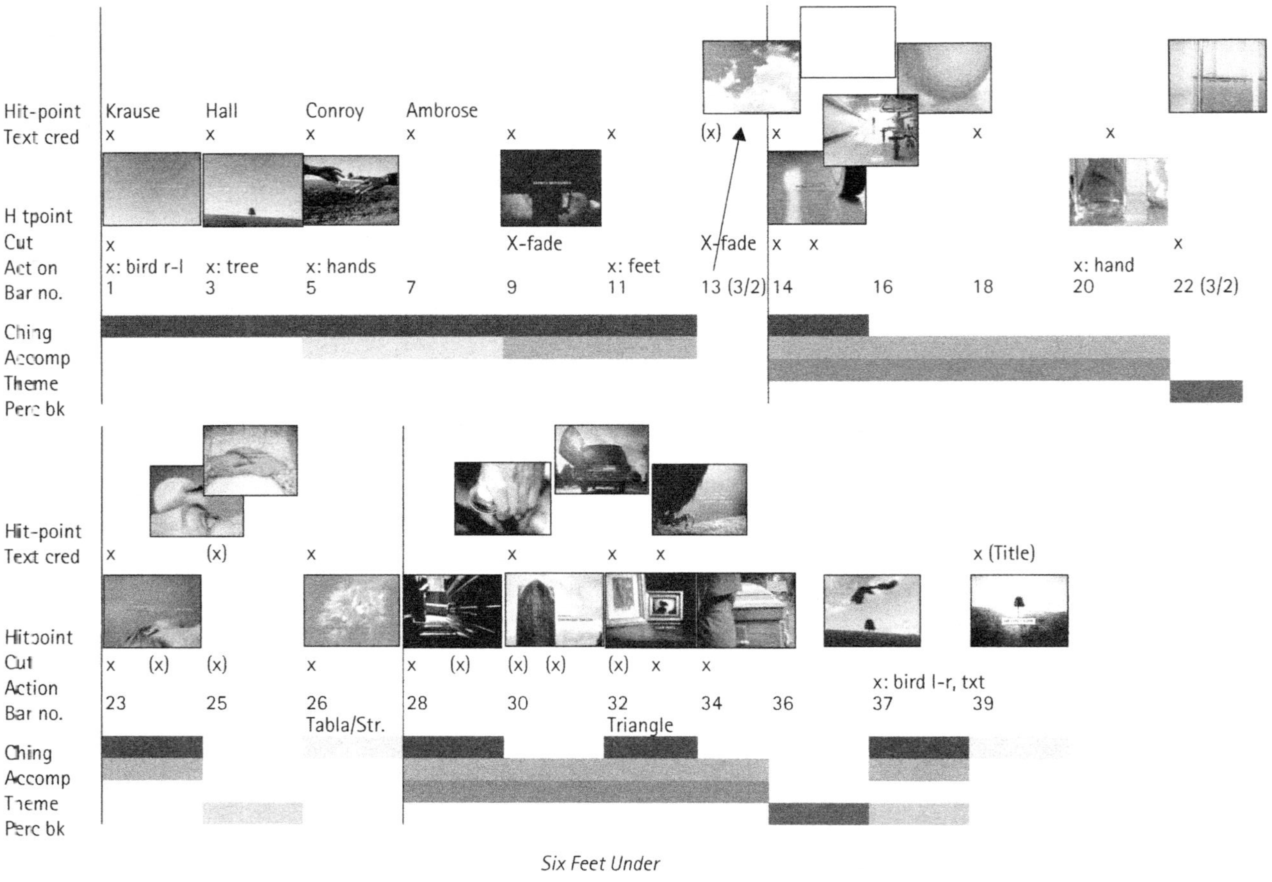

FIGURE 8.1: Musical Structure with Hit Points (Text, Cut, Action), *Six Feet Under*

even be felt bodily. As Ball puts it, "There's that moment where the wheel on the gurney turns just as the percussion track kicks in. It's such a wonderful synthesis of picture and audio that I still get chills when I watch it."[66] Such "chills" are implicit in Anderson's visceral description of his role as editor: the music understood as muscle and the visuals as a layer of skin, he sees it as *his* job to create "nerve endings."[67]

Moments of excitement and felt satisfaction occur where the two media conform in a context that is elsewhere characterized by complementarity, even contest in places (to use Cook's terminology). Both music and image are "gapped," but they complement one another contextually throughout. Within this context, the hit points, the moments of synchresis across the media, stand out, notably at the start of the sequence, where an early but short-lived pattern of predictability is initially set up. Table 2 represents this audiovisual structure.[68] The table incorporates downbeat hit points between music and text, editing, and some of the significant action within the frame (marked by "x"), but it cannot capture motion.

Overall, the sequence demonstrates a sophisticated dynamic by combining familiarity with novelty. It presents a satisfying shape, and a narrative, that incorporate moments of repose and ethereality, without compromising the sense of momentum that builds throughout. The disruptions that arrest the sense of accumulation also build anticipation, a desire for a return of the previous rhythm. As shown in the table, the regular hit points of the first segment are disrupted by the first break (the 3/2 bar at 13). After this interruption, the sequence continues to build musically, with the addition of the main theme. The second break is more complex. It begins with a hit point between the entry of jangly percussive rhythms and the first of three shots of a container of embalming fluid; the shots become progressively shorter in duration and more extreme in close-up as the fluid drains and excitement builds. Next, another hit point, and a (false) return of the two-bar phrases: a body's still, turned head is shown. Another bar of a percussive break, this time created from samples of a quirky Brazilian *quica*, as a body on display, with crossed hands, passes beneath the camera: a hit point, but a little weaker. A stronger hit point accompanies a slow-moving two-chord entry that reverses the raised-fourth/major third suspension (the latter now moving to the former), as time-lapse photography shows the wilting of lilies. With the return of the main theme in bar 28, hit points again occur more regularly, though now twice as frequently as before, building momentum, only for this to dissipate in the final shots/bars via the last interruption/coda. The editing emphasizes the downbeat only once more, with a final, lower register chord synchronized with the appearance of the serial's main title (bar 39); the music sounds both pitched and not pitched.

[66] Ball, speaking on "Under the Main Titles."

[67] "What I do is hopefully, I'm making all these nerve connections, like I have, you know, a layer of muscle and a layer of skin, and the layer of muscle is the music piece, the layer of skin is the visual, and I create these, um, nerve endings and when I feel that moment is happening, I think that's when the nerve endings between the two elements are aligned, and they're really working together." Anderson, speaking on "Under the Main Titles."

[68] That the table approximates what the sequence might look like in Logic or Final Cut Pro perhaps tells us something about the role of software in the development of the sequence.

Much more could be said about this sequence, not least how its shiny and clean, even arguably antiseptic, sound so beautifully matches the tone of the serial that follows. My aim here, however, is to highlight how the sequence differs from that of the *Sopranos*, while also drawing attention to aspects that the sequences share, particularly in terms of function. These contemporary sequences for HBO serials accomplish much the same work as earlier title sequences, but are also more consistent in their own right visually, and through their interaction with the music they present a brand identity that coheres holistically with the serial itself and, by extension, with the commissioning channel. It is in the interaction of music and image that the viewer is invited to participate in interpretation; these sequences have been devised to bear, or even encourage, repeated viewing. This may occur through a relatively high-level incongruity between music and image, as with *The Sopranos*, or in terms of the expected/unexpected patterning of exaggerated hit points across media, as with *Six Feet Under*.

Conclusion

More recent serials have offered variations on the title sequence models that *The Sopranos* and *Six Feet Under* present. The highly structured opening title sequence for HBO's *Treme* (HBO 2010–) draws on strategies used in both of these sequences, though its most noticeable feature is undoubtedly the apparent mismatch between music and images. Scenes showing the aftermath of the devastation wrought by Hurricane Katrina on the city of New Orleans are presented alongside John Boutté's contagiously effervescent performance of his rhythmically buoyant "Treme Song," a song about life in the city composed before the storm hit. In addition, however, the sequence begins with brief shots of documentary footage foregrounding the lived cultural heritage of the city as performed through the decades, thus matching the song's celebration of this heritage. There are hit points, also. Twice, eighth-beat drum fills that conclude with splash cymbal on the downbeat are synchronized with image editing: first these signal the shift from black and white to color footage of parades; second, from footage of the storm in action to footage of its consequences. After extended shots of water damage to homes, against which the text credits are placed, celebratory footage is gradually mixed with that of ruined homes, trailer parks, personal photographs that captured memories of New Orleans in happier times, and close-ups of photographs destroyed by water damage. Built into a single sequence, these strategies complicates any simple conceptions of the city and its musical culture as before/after or vibrant/tragic.

Like *The Sopranos* and *Treme*, the main title sequences for HBO's *The Wire* (HBO, 2002–2008) were created by the show's production team,[69] and although they elected to use the same song for the sequence in all five seasons, each season presented a different

[69] For an excellent analysis of these title sequences, see Andrew Dignan, "*The Wire* and the Art of the Credit Sequence."

performance or cover of the song.[70] The images used in the sequences were modulated to reflect each season's theme, with some images retained across all five seasons.[71] *The Wire*'s sequence also invites repeat viewers through an increase in the experience of "too much information," an effect achieved by presenting an extreme fluctuation in the duration of shots, rather than by presenting many more shots per se.[72]

In the case of *Weeds* (Showtime, 2005–), also produced for a premium cable channel, the main titles were created by the Thomas Cobb Group, a motion graphics design and production company. The same song—"Little Boxes" by singer-songwriter Malvina Reynolds—was used for the first three seasons. A recording of Reynolds performing the song was used for the first season, but the second and third seasons used a different performance, or cover, for each episode, culminating, at the end of season three, with Reynolds's version used with the opening titles, and a version sung by Pete Seeger (which subsequently made the song a hit in 1963) heard over the closing credits.[73]

The main title for *Dexter*, mentioned at the beginning of this chapter, features an integrated choreography of music and image that approaches more closely that used on *Six Feet Under*; indeed, Digital Kitchen's Eric S. Anderson edited both sequences. Here, however, the visuals preceded the music, although Anderson created his first cut of the sequence to music by Bernard Herrmann composed for an Alfred Hitchcock film. The decision to use music by Rolfe Kent that was much more distanced from the content of the images and the serial's content of serial killing was made by the producers, with the incongruity of Kent's "cabaret music [making] it all the more creepy."[74]

Many more of these sequences are worthy of comment than I have space here to mention, not least those for *True Blood* (HBO, 2008–) and *Mad Men* (AMC, 2007–). In relation to *Mad Men*, it is also important to note that just as nonpremium channels have sought to emulate the success of HBO's original programming[75] —AMC is a basic cable channel supported by advertising—so too have they produced opening title sequences that are equally fascinating, despite suggestions that in some commercial markets such

[70] I am grateful to Anahid Kassabian for pointing out to me that *The Cosby Show* (NBC, 1984–1992) also used a different performance of the same song for each series. At the time, this was considered highly unusual.

[71] Changing some images while retaining others is not in itself a new approach to title sequences in the case of long-running serials (or indeed soap operas). However, in the past such changes have usually been made to reflect changes to the cast, characters' hairstyles, or other alterations to appearance. The emphasis on thematic content in *The Wire*'s sequence is thus significant.

[72] This characteristic of "information overload" is taken to extremes in Digital Kitchen's sequence for *True Blood* (HBO, 2008–).

[73] Subsequent seasons rejected this approach.

[74] Eric S. Anderson, cited in Emily Nussbaum, "A Great Opening Montage Is a Bloody Good Idea," *New York*, May 24, 2010, 43. See also Catalin Brylla, "Why Do We Love Dexter Morgan in the Morning," *The Art of the Title Sequence*, at http://cdn4.artofthetitle.com/assets/WhydoweloveDexterMorganintheMorningbyCatalinBrylla.pdf (accessed December 10, 2012).

[75] A point made by a reviewer, quoted by Avi Santo, is apposite in this respect: "'For years, HBO has gone with the tagline "It's Not TV, It's HBO". But recently TV has become a lot more like HBO' (Goertz, 2002a: 63)." Santo, "Para-television and Discourses of Distinction," 39.

sequences are being squeezed out of existence.[76] Indeed, the opening title sequence for *Mad Men* is just as efficient and impressive in its audiovisual aesthetics and the branding it has generated, arguably even more so given that it is significantly shorter than those discussed in this chapter, at around 36 seconds.[77]

It is perhaps not entirely surprising that recent television title sequences function as signifiers of the commissioning channel's brand identity, but a detailed history of the aesthetics of the format has yet to be written, particularly one that explores media interaction within the sequences in detail. In many respects the format is at the cutting edge of production and digital design, something we have come to expect of the music video. It is intriguing to wonder where these intense little films/videos will go next, but it would also be productive to look back and explore the format's history. In addition, we know little about how viewers regard or use these sequences. Exploring this interaction seems even more pressing in light of recent changes to modes of content delivery. What does the loss of the "water cooler" moment mean for the future of the television title sequence?[78]

NOTES

Several people read drafts of this chapter and provided insightful and incisive comments. In particular, I would like to thank Claudia, John, and Carol (the book's editors) for their excellent suggestions, and also Simon Frith and Anahid Kassabian. I would also like to thank the organizers of, and participants at, the Audio-Visuality Conference (Aarhus, Denmark, May 2011), and Martin Parker, Sean Williams, and Jules Rawlinson, for their many perceptive comments on my initial ideas about these sequences. Nevertheless, all errors remain my own.

[76] In spring 2010 the Academy of Television Arts and Sciences sent out a ballot to members, proposing that the category "Outstanding Original Main Title Music" be replaced with "Outstanding Music Composition for a Documentary Film." According to composer Mark Watters, one of the two Television Academy Music Peer Group Governors, "the industry has abandoned this great art. Many shows have no theme what so ever. Most are less than 15 seconds. The reason for this? Easy, as shows become more expensive to produce, more time is given up to commercials thus leaving less and less time for the show itself. The main title is shortened or eliminated in order to give time to the narrative of the episode. A sad but unavoidable reality, I'm afraid." The category remains, however. Mark Watters, comment made to "Emmys Considering Dumping Main Title Theme Music Category to Create Documentary Music Category," *Film Music Magazine*, March 13, 2010, at http://www.filmmusicmag.com/?p=5152 (accessed July 30, 2010).

[77] For a more detailed discussion of this sequence, see Gary Edgerton, "Falling Man and Mad Men," the adjoining "Curator's Note" (April 2009), and the many posts and responses to Edgerton's analysis that followed, in *In Media Res: A Media Commons Project*, at http://mediacommons.futureofthebook.org/imr/2009/04/19/falling-man-and-mad-men-154 (accessed 30 July 2010).

[78] See Annette Davison, "The Show Starts Here: Viewer's Interactions with Recent Television Serials' Main Title Sequences" in *Sound Effects: An Interdisciplinary Journal of Sound and Sound Experience* 3, no. 1 + 2 (forthcoming 2013).

References

Akass, Kim, and Janet McCabe, eds. *Reading Six Feet Under: TV to Die For*. London; New York: I. B. Tauris, 2005.

Altman, Rick. "Television/Sound." In *Studies in Entertainment: Critical Approaches to Mass Culture*, edited by Tania Modleski, 39–54. Bloomington: Indiana University Press, 1986.

Baym, Nancy K. *Tune In, Log On: Soaps, Fandom, and Online Community*. London: Sage Publications, 2000.

Burlingame, Jon. *TV's Biggest Hits: The Story of Television Themes from Dragnet to Friends*. New York: Schirmer Books, 1996.

Caldwell, John Thornton. *Televisuality: Style, Crisis, and Authority in American Television*. New Brunswick, N.J.: Rutgers University Press, 1995.

Carroll, Noel. "Sympathy for the Devil." In *The Sopranos and Philosophy: I Kill Therefore I Am*, edited by Richard Greene and Peter Vernezze, 120–136. Peru, Ill.: Open Court Publishing, 2004.

Cook, Nicholas. *Analyzing Musical Multimedia*. Oxford: Oxford University Press, 1998.

Davison, Annette. "The Show Starts Here: Viewer's Interactions with Recent Television Serials' Main Title Sequences" in Sound Effects: An Interdisciplinary Journal of Sound and Sound Experience 3, no. 1 + 2 (forthcoming 2013).

Davison, Annette. *Hollywood Theory, Non-Hollywood Practice: Cinema Soundtracks in the 1980s–1990s*. Aldershot, UK: Ashgate, 2004.

Dignan, Andrew. "The Wire and the Art of the Credit Sequence." *The House Next Door* blog, at http://www.slantmagazine.com/house/2006/09/the-wire-and-the-art-of-the-credit-sequence/ (accessed February 28, 2012).

Donnelly, K. J. *The Spectre of Sound: Music in Film and Television*. London: BFI, 2005.

Ellis, John. *Visible Fictions: Film, Television, Video*. London: Routledge, 1982.

Ellis, John. "Interstitials: How the 'Bits in Between' Define the Programmes." In *Ephemeral Media: Transitory Screen Culture from Television to YouTube*, edited by Paul Grainge, 59–69. London: British Film Institute, 2011.

Epstein, Michael M., Jimmie L. Reeves, and Mark C. Rodgers. "Surviving 'The Hit': Will *The Sopranos* Still Sing for HBO?" In *Reading the Sopranos: Hit TV from HBO*, edited by David Lavery, 15–25. London; New York: I. B. Tauris, 2006.

Frith, Simon. "Look! Hear! The Uneasy Relationship of Music and Television." *Popular Music* 21, no. 3 (2002): 277–290 (Music and Television Issue).

Gorbman, Claudia. *Unheard Melodies: Narrative Film Music*. London; Bloomington: BFI and Indiana University Press, 1987.

Gripsrud, Jostein. *The* Dynasty *Years: Hollywood Television and Critical Media Studies*. London: Routledge, 1995.

Johansson, David. "Homeward Bound: Those *Sopranos* Titles Come Heavy." In *Reading the Sopranos: Hit TV from HBO*, edited by David Lavery, 27–36. London: I. B. Tauris, 2006.

Kaye, Peter. "I'm Dead, Wow, Cool: The Music of *Six Feet Under*." In *Reading Six Feet Under: TV to Die For*, edited by Kim Akass and Janet McCabe, 192–206. London; New York: I. B. Tauris, 2005.

Kelso, Tony. "And Now No Word from Our Sponsor: How HBO Puts the Risk Back into Television." In *It's Not TV: Watching HBO in the Post-Television Era*, edited by Marc Leverette, Brian L. Ott, and Cara Louise Buckley, 46–64. New York; London: Routledge.

Klein, Bethany. *As Heard on TV: Popular Music in Advertising*. Aldershot, UK: Ashgate, 2009.

Kramer, Lawrence. *Musical Meaning: Towards a Critical History*. Berkeley; Los Angeles: University of California Press, 2002.
Lavery, David. *This Thing of Ours: Investigating the Sopranos*. London; New York: Wallflower and Columbia University Press, 2002.
Lavery, David, ed. *Reading the Sopranos: Hit TV from HBO* London; New York: I. B. Tauris, 2006.
Leverette, Marc, Brian L. Ott, and Cara Louise Buckley. *It's Not TV: Watching HBO in the Post-Television Era*. New York; London: Routledge, 2008.
Martin, Brett. *The Sopranos: The Complete Book*. London: Headline, 2007.
McCabe, Janet, and Kim Akass. "It's Not TV, It's HBO Original Programming." In *It's Not TV: Watching HBO in the Post-Television Era*, edited by Marc Leverette, Brian L. Ott, and Cara Louise Buckley, 83–93. New York; London: Routledge.
Nussbaum, Emily. "A Great Opening Montage Is a Bloody Good Idea." *New York*, May 24, 2010, 43.
Richardson, John. "*Laura* and *Twin Peaks*: Postmodern Parody and the Musical Reconstruction of the Absent Femme Fatale." In *American Dreams, Nightmare Visions: The Cinema of David Lynch*, edited by Erica Sheen and Annette Davison, 77–92. London: Wallflower Press, 2004.
Rogers, Marc C., Michael Epstein, and Jimmie L. Reeves. "The Sopranos as HBO Brand Equity: The Art of Commerce in the Age of Digital Representation." In *This Thing of Ours: Investigating the Sopranos*, edited by David Lavery, 42–57. London; New York: Wallflower and Columbia University Press, 2002.
Santo, Avi. "Para-television and Discourses of Distinction: The Culture of Production at HBO." In *It's Not TV: Watching HBO in the Post-Television Era*, edited by Marc Leverette, Brian L. Ott, and Cara Louise Buckley, 19–45. New York; London: Routledge, 2008.
Sconce, Jeffrey. "Irony, Nihilism and the New American 'Smart' Film." *Screen* 43, no. 4 (Winter 2002): 349–369.
Stilwell, Robynn. "The Sound Is Out There: Score, Sound Design, and Exoticism in *The X-Files*." In *Analyzing Popular Music*, edited by Allan Moore, 60–79. Cambridge, UK: Cambridge University Press, 2003.
Tagg, Philip. *Kojak—50 Seconds of Television Music: Toward the Analysis of Affect in Popular Music*. Gothenburg, Sweden: University of Gothenburg Press, 1979.
Tagg, Philip, and Bob Clarida. *Ten Little Title Tunes: Towards a Musicology of Mass Media*. New York; Montreal: The Mass Media Musicologists' Press, 2003.
Williams, Raymond. *Television: Technology and Cultural Form*. London: Routledge, 1974.

CHAPTER 9

NO COUNTRY FOR OLD MUSIC

CARTER BURWELL

IMAGINE for a moment that the shower scene in *Psycho* had been left without music, as Hitchcock intended. It would be uncomfortable, even painful, to watch, but would it lack something? When presented with Bernard Herrmann's music, Hitchcock immediately admitted he was wrong—which he did not commonly do—and it is difficult now to disentangle the music and film.

A few years later, in *The Birds*, Hitchcock and Herrmann followed through with the project of scoring gruesome, violent images without music, using only silence and sound effects. They had come to the conclusion that music helped one film while hurting the other.

I found myself mulling over this issue while trying to write music for the film *No Country for Old Men*. Before Joel and Ethan Coen began shooting, we discussed the score, and I admit it was a puzzler. It was easier to eliminate musical ideas than contribute them. What aspect of the film should the music play? Not character; the characters in the film verge on cliché to begin with—the honest man caught up in intrigue, the crusty but affable sheriff, the unstoppable killing machine—and underscoring would only exaggerate them. It couldn't play the story, which also is a cliché: a good man stumbles on bad money and tries to get away with it. The beauty of the book and the film lies in the way it keeps drawing you away from the plot, focusing your attention on an assassin's socks, or a peanut wrapper, or a homemade silencer. How could music help?

Psycho, though it pretends to be a different film for the first 20 minutes, ultimately reveals itself to be a gothic horror story. It wears its artfulness on its sleeve right from the first shot, but nowhere more than in the shower scene, which is an exercise in montage. The filmmaker inserts himself between you and everything you see. If the scene had been shot in a less "intrusive" manner, say with the camera outside the motel window, the scene might have worked without music.

Hitchcock was famously uncomfortable with the conventions of film music, often asking, "Why is it there?" (as every filmmaker and composer should). Still, once an audience is experiencing the assault of artistry that is the shower scene, there is no reason to be coy about the artifice of score. And Bernard Herrmann was never coy.

Since the early days of film it has been assumed that when the lights go down, the music comes up. Before recorded music, it was a special treat to hear the Wurlitzer warming up, but today music suffuses our world almost without respite. Today a film without music may offer a more special experience than one with it.

The best idea I had for music in *No Country* was for it to play the landscape, a flat expanse of chalk and gravel whose indifference seems to invite violence. But that idea is not terribly helpful when you're looking at a blank score. What instrument is that? In what key?

I began with the scene in which Moss, hunting in the hills, finds a trail of blood on the ground intersecting that of the elk he has wounded. It takes him to a scene of dead and dying men in the middle of nowhere. Shakers echo the crunching caliche underfoot; sustaining tones slowly develop, blending with the wind. Eventually a guitar begins a slow repeating figure. I liked the tune, but I never figured out where the guitar should enter. Any time it played seemed too soon. I showed it to the Coens, and we tried it without guitar. Better. We tried it without shakers. Better still. All that was left was a sine wave ringing in the wind.

The last century has seen both a technological and an aesthetic convergence between "sound" and music. I won't bother to define these terms—however you define them, they have grown closer.

Before the invention of the tape recorder, music was dots on a page, melody, and rhythm, but afterward it was a length of plastic tape, indistinguishable from a length of plastic containing speech or train whistles. Composers took advantage of this to impose musical structure on unstructured sound in the art of *musique concrète*. Today that experiment is a runaway success: music, sound, and video are all manipulated with the same digital tools, and the results are common elements of both popular and art music. This aesthetic has drawn sound into the realm of music, but the opposite can be said as well. I would venture to say that the importance of melody and harmony have been reduced with increased emphasis on timbral and spatial character.

Whenever I played a traditional musical instrument against *No Country for Old Men*, the presence of music made the film less real; it relaxed the tension, diminished the experience. Eventually the music in *No Country* was reduced to steady-state tones generated with sine waves and singing bowls that had no attack whatsoever. These tones would fade in under sound effects like wind or automobile tones, then shift in pitch and volume for dramatic effect, but like a frog in a slowly warming pot, the audience's ears were unaware of what was going on. Skip Lievsay, the sound designer, collaborated with me in matching the pitch of the effects to the music.

A typical example is the gas station scene, in which Chigurh is quietly threatening the station owner, forcing him—although he does not realize it—to bet his life on a coin toss. I pitched the music in B natural, close to 60 Hz, so it would blend with the electrical hum in the station. It sneaks in very slowly, building in volume with Chigurh's threat. While the tones would be apparent to anyone who started watching the scene in the middle, because they never had an entrance, they are quite subliminal to anyone who sits through it from the start. At the moment the coin's result is revealed, the musical tone goes away, and only then do most people realize there was "music" at all.

It seems obvious that the presence of nondiegetic music—music that doesn't come from a source in the film—would diminish the naturalism of any film, but I'm not sure that this is true. I certainly doubt it's the reason traditional scoring didn't work in *No Country*. The film is not especially naturalistic or artless; quite the opposite. Our decision to do without a traditional score was entirely empirical. Whenever we tried a recognizable musical sound against the film, the tension went out of the film. In other films music is often used to induce or amplify tension; here, for some reason, it did the opposite.

In the end, the tune I wrote for that first scene was used over the end titles. But even then, I began with sound, taking the rhythm of a clock in the last scene, building up the steady-state tones used elsewhere in the film; only about a minute into the end titles does the score finally present a recognizable instrument, an acoustic guitar. When almost everyone has already left the theater.

CHAPTER 10

CUE THE BIG THEME? THE SOUND OF THE SUPERHERO

JANET K. HALFYARD

Superman and *Batman* have indisputably been the most successful and long-running comic-book superhero film franchises of modern cinema. In previous work I have noted the impact of computer-generated imagery (CGI) technology on the upsurge in comic book and superheroic films after 1999.[1] Following the relaunch of both the *Superman* and *Batman* franchises around 2005, I began to consider how digital technologies have transformed both musical representations and the narrative constructions of these two characters. In the recent digitally enabled *Batman* and *Superman* films, music and heroic action on one hand, and the iconography of the superhero on the other, have demonstrably shifted in contrast to their analog predecessors.

Superman: The Movie

John Williams is widely credited with repopularizing in the 1970s the full orchestral score and leitmotivic structure that was the standard scoring practice of Hollywood's golden age. *Superman: The Movie* (Richard Donner, 1978) was the third in a series of scores—following *Close Encounters of the Third Kind* (Steven Spielberg, 1977) and *Star Wars* (George Lucas, 1977)—that established him as the musical voice of science fiction and fantasy films. He maintained this position without facing a serious rival throughout the 1980s, until Danny Elfman composed the score for Tim Burton's *Batman* in 1989.

Drawing on the golden age scoring traditions of composers such as Erich Korngold and his "swashbuckling" scores of the 1930s, Williams established a formula for scoring his fantasy action heroes. The basic characteristics include a major-key march that gives

[1] Janet K. Halfyard, *Danny Elfman's Batman: A Film Score Guide* (Lanham, Md.: Scarecrow Press, 2004), 53.

FIGURE 10.1: Author transcription of the heroic motif from John Williams, *Superman: The Movie* (1978).

the principal melody to the brass section, with a fanfare-like introduction followed by a bold statement of the main theme from the brass, punctuated by timpani and accompanied by a rhythmic ostinato from low brass and strings.[2] What gives the formula its heroic character is largely the harmonic stability created by the use of tonic-dominant harmony and corresponding melodic intervals such as prominent open fifths, alongside the energetic character of the march rhythms. The punchy, confident, militaristic scoring of the *Star Wars* and *Superman* main titles constructs the sense of action and optimism that is central to their main characters. The upbeat mood is further enhanced by the absolute regularity of the rhythmic treatment. The use of triplets and dotted figures prevents the march rhythm from becoming too monotonous, but other than brief hemiolas between sections in *Superman*, the march rhythm is constant, and even the hemiolas do not disrupt the basic pulse. In *Superman*, the initial fanfare motif subsequently becomes the main heroic signifier in the score rather than the principal main title theme (see figure 10.1).

The film deploys this heroic motif in the narrative in a distinctive way, and all four films in the original franchise follow the same pattern. Although Williams only composed the score for the first film, the other composers used his themes—and his strategies—to create the musical sound tracks for the sequels. Given the essential similarity of the material and scoring technique in all four films, I discuss only the first film here.

Superman: The Movie starts and ends in space. It begins with a title sequence set against images of outer space, with the opening credits swooping in against a symphonic rendition of the full theme, and ends (as do all four films) with the main title theme being restated over a shot of Superman in space flying above the earth with the sun in the background. The ending conveys the reassuring and optimistic idea that he is here to guard us; the image is dominated visually by the primary red, blue, and yellow colors

[2] The musical representation of the heroic does not, of course, begin in film music: Robert Hatten's discussion of Beethoven's music identifies major keys, marches, and fanfares as elements in a musical construction of the heroic, while Philip Tagg's analyses of the *Kojak* theme and of male-identified musical characteristics similarly construct ideas of upward movement, syncopated and dotted rhythms, energetic tempi, and the martial as masculine and heroic, all observations applicable to this discussion of the music written for cinematic superheroes. See Robert Hatten, *Musical Meaning in Beethoven: Markedness, Correlation, and Interpretation* (Bloomington: Indiana University Press, 1994); Philip Tagg, "Analysing Popular Music: Theory, Method and Practice," *Popular Music* 2 (1982): 37–67; and Philip Tagg, "An Anthropology of Stereotypes in TV Music?" *Swedish Musicological Journal* (1989): 19–42, at http://tagg.org/articles/xpdfs/tvanthro.pdf (accessed July 27, 2012).

of Superman's own costume, here amplified in the image of Superman's cape, the blue earth, and the yellow sun.

The film's score reserves statements of the main title theme and heroic motif for moments of action. Even when Superman is acting as Clark Kent, or when he is only mildly engaged in action as Superman, we hear muted or brief statements of the heroic motif, as in the scene where Clark stops a mugger's bullet from hitting Lois and then pretends to faint. Likewise, in sequences that are importantly heroic but nonetheless not action packed, the motif with its distinctive dotted figure acts as a kind of musical punctuation and a general signifier of Superman's heroism; good examples can be seen/heard in the scenes in which Superman, apparently standing perpendicular to the side of a building, cheerfully apprehends a burglar who is climbing up the skyscraper, and when as Clark he jumps from an office window and transforms into Superman as he flies away.

The full opening theme from the main title occurs unambiguously only once in the body of the film. In the same way that it announced the film in the main title, it effectively announces Superman to the people of Metropolis with his first full-scale feat of public superheroism: catching first Lois Lane and then a falling helicopter above the city streets. As he seizes the plummeting helicopter with one hand, Lois safely held by the other, and flies them back up to the roof of the building from which they fell, his main title theme rings out over the cheers of the crowd below. While the music's construction encodes ideas of the heroic, its close connection to moments of action articulates the idea that Superman's heroism lies not in what he is so much as in what he *does* and the decisions he makes.

This strategy is essential to the credibility of the protagonist at a point in movie history when the height of technological sophistication consisted of front projection and blue screen. Roy Field, the film's creative supervisor for optical visual effects, claims in the documentary *The Magic Behind the Cape* that *Superman* used all the available analog effects of the time and invented several new ones to boot. The effects teams made use of models, hydraulics, and optical and matte effects; they created the flying sequences through a combination of front projection, blue screen, and manually controlled wire work. At the time, *Superman* was lauded as a landmark in this field, winning a special achievement award for visual effects at the 1979 Academy Awards. However, remarkable as the effects were for the time, the fact remains that although many are impressively convincing, others require some considerable suspension of disbelief. Notably weak sequences include the young Clark Kent running alongside a train (the actor is obviously suspended from wires, his feet not touching the ground) and the Hoover Dam sequence at the end, when Superman fails to stop a bomb hitting the San Andreas fault. The dam breach itself is reasonably convincing, but the following sequence, in which Superman shoves boulders into the water's path to prevent it from reaching a town at the end of the valley, is not (see figures 10.2a and 10.2b). The boulders Superman topples are evidently almost weightless; the valley floor and town are clearly tiny models, and Superman's improvised dam is made up of gravel-sized "rocks." Likewise, the movement in many of the flying sequences lacks naturalism. The bulk of

FIGURE 10.2: The limitations of analog effects in *Superman: The Movie*: a) Young Clark Kent running with his feet nowhere near the ground;, b) Model village saved by gravel.

these were shot using front projection: Christopher Reeve was static and horizontal on a platform, his cape apparently fluttering in the slipstream thanks to remotely controlled, umbrella-like poles underneath it. All the movement was then created by an extremely mobile front projection rig that could rotate, turn, and move horizontally and vertically in relation to Reeve. Superman's body consequently remains in the same physical position when he changes direction, going against our expectations of the relationship between movement and directionality. In sequences such as these, our potentially flagging suspension of disbelief is bolstered by the insistent heroic musical motif, which sonically reiterates Superman's superheroism, particularly in moments when it might be visually less convincing.

Batman

Burton's *Batman* marks a change in Hollywood's approach to the fantasy hero, although in terms of the contemporaneous technology, this was still very much a film of the pre-digital era. A prime feature of *Superman* was the use of special effects to allow its protagonist to act superheroically, and the musical strategy supported this idea of heroic action. The movie's tagline was "You'll believe a man can fly," and the music is integral to sustaining our belief. In contrast to Superman's active and visible heroism, Burton chooses to emphasize not what Batman does, but what he is, so the focus moves away from the action that gave Superman agency and toward Batman himself. This is primarily a function of Burton's own creative voice: his films often focus on a conflicted character who does not fit properly in the world and so needs to negotiate his role in some way, whether that is Batman, Edward Scissorhands, Ichabod Crane, or Ed Wood.

Elfman's main title for *Batman* adheres to the dramatic-military topic of Williams's formula. However, despite the superficial resemblances, Elfman's approach to scoring his superhero is altogether different from Williams's, reflecting the differences in Batman's character. His minor-key theme draws on horror-movie musical tropes as much as superheroic ones, and the score substitutes constant harmonic slippage for Superman's diatonic stability.[3] Another significant difference is how the main theme is used, resulting in an essentialist construction of the superhero that focuses primarily on his iconic status as a symbol of agency.

As in *Superman*, we first hear the theme in the main title, when Batman is not visible. The theme therefore establishes the tone of the film in the absence of the central character; with *Superman*, that tone is fundamentally optimistic, whereas with *Batman* it is musically darker and often chromatic, in Elfman's "gothic" musical style.[4] Whereas in *Superman* the main title theme does not then go on to provide the main heroic signifier for the film (this role being taken by the shorter, fanfare-like motif), the music written for Batman himself is entirely dominated by the five-note motif established in his film's main title, then subjected to thematic variation and reorchestration (see figure 10.3).

FIGURE 10.3: Author transcription of the hero theme from Danny Elfman, *Batman* (1989).

[3] For a more in-depth discussion of the music of *Batman*, see Halfyard, *Danny Elfman's* Batman.

[4] The first reviewer to use this adjective in relation to Elfman was probably Desson Howe, who in 1989 described the *Batman* score as "Gothic-rhapsodic." See Desson Howe, "*Batman*." *Washington Post*, July 23, 1989, at http://www.washingtonpost.com/wp-srv/style/longterm/movies/videos/batmanpg13howe_a0b220.htm (accessed July 20, 2011).

Batman falls into three acts. In the first act, after the main title, this principal theme is still present but oddly constrained and not directly connected to heroic action. Instead, it mostly accompanies Batman's appearances and disappearances. The second act assigns the theme more overt connections with action, but it is used most prominently in a protracted sequence of running away rather than engaging with the enemy. Batman rescues Vicki Vale from the Joker, then proceeds to escape: he is reactive and defensive rather than proactive. Superman has no equivalent sequence of running away from his enemies; in fact, he regularly seeks them out.

Batman's heroic theme appears in its most grandiose form in the cue "Descent into Mystery," which again, far from being an action sequence, involves him driving home in his car. It is one of the only instances in which the Bat-theme appears in a context of absolute harmonic stability—the cue is in an unambiguous D minor from start to finish and builds over a series of ostinato figures into ever denser and more overwhelming textures. The sheer magnitude of the music and the scale of the orchestration speak of control, coherence, and inexorable purpose, rather than the instability and unpredictability of previous cues. However, when one stops to notice what he is doing at this point—he is driving home; he is not even being pursued—it becomes clear that the music is integral to the process of constructing Batman as an intrinsically powerful figure rather than underpinning and lending credibility to the action that was the evident aspect of Superman's heroism. If we take the music away from this sequence, the car starts to look a little shaky and seems to be going at a fairly sedate speed; the music constructs the sense of speed and sleek menace. Avoiding any action that might look faked because of the limitations of the technology, Burton and Elfman instead imbue Batman with a sense of power through music.

The success of Elfman's musical construction can be measured by the fact that it is quite easy not to notice that Batman does not really do anything until the last half hour of the film, other than get in the way of the police; accidentally create the Joker; run away from the Joker; and allow his prospective girlfriend to be terrorized by the Joker, not once but three times.[5] Arguably, the music imbues Batman with an agency that the rest of the narrative does not support, given the lack of action. Jonathan Rosenbaum (not writing about music) asserts that the Joker is the primary agent, the true hero of the film: it is his actions that constantly push the narrative forward, not Batman's.[6]

If we were in any doubt that the most important thing about Batman is not what he does but what he is, that the music constructs Batman as heroic icon more than heroic

[5] The original shooting script of *Batman* contained a protracted sequence in which the Joker kidnaps Vicki from her apartment, and Bruce/ Batman—who was visiting her and conveniently had his utility belt in a bag—borrows a ski mask and launches into pursuit, using ropes and cables to fly across the city streets before commandeering a policeman's horse to continue the chase. Although the Joker ultimately gets away, Batman nonetheless rescues Vicki without her discovering his identity. In the final film, this enormously complicated and technically challenging action sequence, the only one in which Batman actively and aggressively pursues the Joker in the second act, was cut. See Sam Hamm and Walter Skaaren "Batman (1989) Movie Script [5th Draft, 1988]," *Screenplays for You*, at http://sfy.ru/?script=batman_production (accessed July 16, 2011).

[6] Jonathan, Rosenbaum, "Are We Having Fun?" *Sight and Sound* 59, no. 2 (1990): 96.

agent, the final act of the film would decisively confirm the notion. Act 3 starts by reiterating the material heard in the main title, only now even more ostentatiously, with voices added to the orchestration, in a striking affirmation of Batman's heroic identity as he prepares (at last) for action in a series of iconic framing shots. We see a locker opening to reveal the Batsuit; the fastening of the utility belt; a shot of the Bat-symbol on Batman's chest; and then the slow raising of his head to reveal the distinctive silhouette, the climax of shot and music being the point where we see his eyes (see figures 10.4a, b, and c). Once again we have an extremely strong musical construction of Batman's superheroic power in a context devoid of any action that supports that construction; here, it is quite literally a pose.

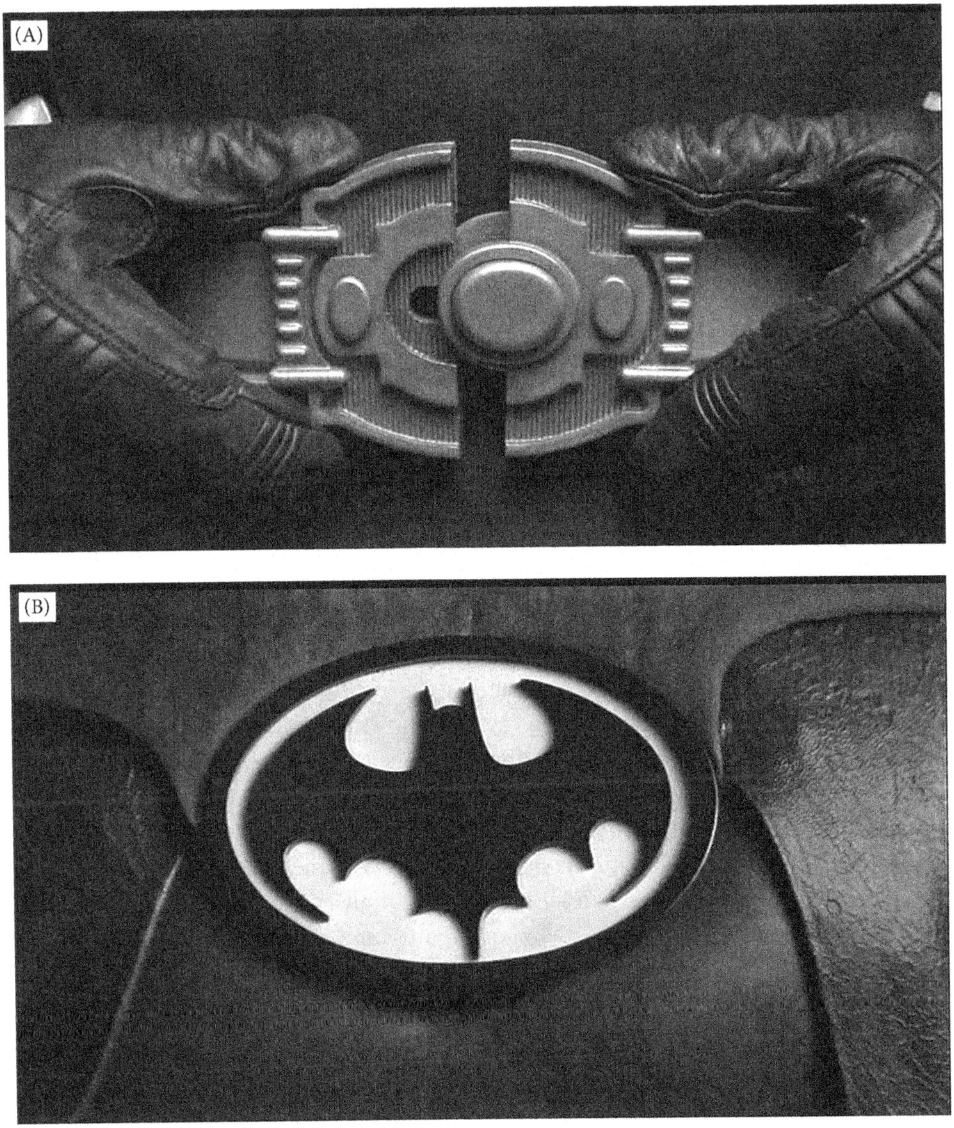

FIGURES 10.4A, B, AND C: Iconic framing shots in *Batman*.

FIGURES 10.4A, B, AND C: (Continued)

As the final section progresses, Batman acts with varying degrees of success, but he does at least act: thus far, he has been the superheroic equivalent of Hamlet, avoiding direct confrontation with his enemy. Ultimately the Joker falls to his death from Gotham Cathedral. That Batman does not capture him and hand him over to the law provides another contrast with Superman, who finishes three of his early films by successfully delivering Lex Luthor to prison. Batman is denied the final action that would bring closure, just as he is generally restrained from acting by the way his narrative has been constructed around the limitations of technology. The film then closes with yet another affirmation of his heroic status that is primarily constructed by a combination of music and static, iconographic imagery, as the Bat-signal is projected to the citizens of Gotham and the camera tilts up the side of a building to reveal Batman standing silhouetted against the night sky (see figure 10.5).

The film makes some covert allusions to *Superman* here. Each of the *Superman* movies ends with the image of Superman flying in the blackness of space, with the blue earth below him and the rising sun (a suitably Nietzschean metaphor) in the middle distance.[7] Here, Batman stands against the blue-black night, with the fake globe of his Bat-signal emblazoned on the sky, although it is the camera that does the flying rather than Batman himself. Meanwhile, whereas *Superman*'s final shot always depicts that hero smiling and then swooping off, undoubtedly to go on patrol and rescue someone from danger,

[7] In the opening of Nietzsche's epic poem, *Also Sprach Zarathustra* (1891), the prophet watches the sun rise before descending from his mountaintop to announce the coming of the Superman to the world below: this is the sequence that provides the program to the famous opening of Strauss's tone poem of the same name (1896).

FIGURE 10.5: Final shot of *Batman*: one icon regarding another.

Batman's final shot simply leaves its hero standing there, contemplating his own symbol, one icon regarding another.

Both films, however, face the same problem: how to make the superhero appear superheroic with the resources available. *Superman* solves the problem by using the most sophisticated special effects available, deploying them comprehensively throughout the film, to the point that they become a significant part of what the film is about, while incorporating music to heighten and sustain the central character's heroic nature. Burton pursues a diametrically opposed strategy, in which music effectively substitutes for action in constructing Batman's superheroism. *Batman* is rooted in the physical, in stunts, visible wires, extreme costumes and makeup, and the gadgets that have always been part of Batman's heritage and that fit with the very hands-on style of Burton's love of models and stop animation. Batman does not fly; he is human, he has no "magic" in the way that Superman does, so this directly physical strategy is in many ways appropriate.

Batman and *Superman* were both exceptionally successful, and what one expects following that kind of success is that it will produce a host of imitators. Certainly fantasy action movies did well in the early and mid-1980s: the three franchises of *Star Wars*, *Superman*, and *Indiana Jones*, all scored by Williams, continued to attract large audiences. However, no significant body of fantasy action films was made in the wake of *Batman*, other than its own three sequels and three marginally successful period pieces, *The Rocketeer* (Joe Johnston, 1991), *The Shadow* (Russell Mulcahy, 1994), and *The Phantom* (Simon Wincer, 1996), which owe as much to Indiana Jones as to the Dark Knight. Batman's true successors are to be found in the films that began to appear at the end of the 1990s, such as *The Matrix* (Andy and Lana Wachowoski, 1999) and *X-Men* (Bryan Singer, 2000). These latter films can be largely credited with starting a new era for the superhero, but their darker and more conflicted protagonists suggest that Batman is a stronger influence than the sunnily confident Superman and his effortless altruism. The most probable reason for the dearth of superheroes for much of the 1990s is the same reason that Batman himself did not engage in significant amounts of obviously superheroic action, but tended instead to pose for the camera: the fundamental problem of analog technology in creating credible superheroic action on screen.

Superman Returns

The original quartet of *Superman* films had run its course a couple of years before the first *Batman* film was released, meaning that *Superman Returns* (Bryan Singer, 2006) was Superman's first appearance on the big screen after Batman's influential recasting of superheroism. There are many points of contact between the Christopher Reeve films and Singer's 2006 film. *Superman Returns* pretends that the third and fourth films of the original franchise never happened and picks up right after *Superman II* (Richard Lester, 1980). It imagines that just five years have passed, during which time Superman has been on a personal mission to see if he can find the remnants of his home planet. It is worth recapping some of the events of *Superman II*. This was the film in which Lois Lane finally realized that Clark Kent was Superman; they confessed their love; and Superman, having consulted his Kryptonian data files, cast off his superpowers to be able to marry her. They have one night of passion together (we only see them the morning after), and then they return to the world to find it taken over by the evil Kryptonian General Zod.[8] Superman realizes he will have to somehow regain his powers to save the world, and this means he must also give up Lois; he is able to make this decision instantly. There is no real conflict, no soul searching, little evident anguish; he simply decides. He is human enough to love, but superheroic enough in the pre-Batman sense not to let human needs get in the way of action. Also, with no apparent moral qualms, he erases Lois's knowledge that Clark is Superman.

This is where *Superman Returns* begins. Superman returns from his abortive and depressing journey to find Lois in a relationship and mother to a five-year-old child (the audience realizes almost immediately that the child must be his, but Superman seems unable to do the math). The most immediate difference between Christopher Reeve's Superman and Branden Routh's is that the former's sunny optimism has gone: this Superman, emotionally devastated by finding the ruins of Krypton, has succumbed to the brooding and conflicted demeanor more associated with Batman. In many respects *Superman Returns* presents a post-9/11 hero who has seen his world destroyed and now finds he must question everything, including himself.[9] Even his costume is no longer the

[8] We saw Zod's imprisonment in the "Phantom Zone" by Jor-El, Superman's father, in the opening scene of *Superman*, and his release from the Zone early in *Superman II* was the unintended result of Superman diverting a bomb into space.

[9] My thanks to Nicholas Reyland for making the connection between 9/11 and this new incarnation of Superman.

FIGURES 10.6A, B, AND C: The changing colors of Superman's outfit: a) Superman in *Superman: The Movie*; b) Evil Superman in *Superman III*; c) Superman in *Superman Returns*.

bright scarlet and sky blue of the earlier films. Instead, he now wears the darker blue and maroon of the evil Superman from *Superman III*, in which exposure to synthetic kryptonite caused him to turn to a previously unsuspected dark side (see figures 10.6a, b, and c). In addition, although John Ottman's score reuses the main title theme, heroic motif, and love theme from Williams's scores, it significantly transforms the way these themes are used.

The heroic motif is absent at the beginning, when we first see Superman in action. He is saving a plane from crashing, in a sequence that repeatedly refers back to the helicopter sequence of *Superman: The Movie* in its dialogue but not in its music. We hear Williams's ostinato rhythm from the main title but no melodic theme, and only as Superman exits the plane and stands in full view while the crowd cheers do we hear his heroic motif. Where previously it signified action, now, as with Batman, it mainly signifies him, pointing to his power but not at the precise moments when he is exercising it. At times the motif is indeed used for action, but it is absent from two long sequences when he saves Metropolis from disaster, quite unlike the corresponding long musical cues in the original *Superman* films that accompanied action sequences. The previously solid connection between action and theme has been severed, replaced by a link between music and Superman as heroic icon. *Superman Returns* takes a page out of *Batman*'s book, but the reasons it does so are altogether different. *Batman*'s overall strategy appeared to take the view that the action could not be presented in a sufficiently convincing way and would detract from Batman's position of authority, and that music could stand in place of action to construct him as a powerful figure. This was an alternative solution to the same problem in *Superman*, where music was employed to distract from any lack of plausibility in the numerous special effects used in the action sequences.

In the era of digital technology, however, the action has become so thoroughly convincing that it does not need music to bolster its effectiveness. Heroic themes might, in fact, detract from the slick hyperrealism of a Superman who moves through the air like a swimmer through water, capable of rolling and turning, as he does when he rolls over onto his back while flying down a city street and blasts falling debris to harmless dust with heat rays from his eyes. Whereas Christopher Reeve's stationary platform was replaced with wire work for Brandon Routh's flying shots, parts of the *Superman Returns* sequences were achieved using a CGI double of the actor, created with a full-body scanning device that was able to capture the dimensions of both his body and face, allowing Routh to be seen moving through 360 degrees. Meanwhile, the Light State 2 software enabled the effects crew to capture facial characteristics in much greater detail and allowed for the realistic creation of varied skin pigmentation, light, and shadow on the face. Shots such as the one in which a bullet hits Superman's eye could therefore be created digitally without the audience realizing that it is sometimes looking at a computer-generated version of Routh's face.[10] Where the analog Superman was stationary on a platform and had to rely on the agility of the camera moving around in front of a projection to achieve the effect of flight, now CGI manipulates the entire environment around Superman as well as Superman himself. Consequently, I argue that there is no need for music to plaster over the cracks in his credibility. Despite the often continuous music, the cues for these sequences give pace to the action but do not draw attention to themselves by trumpeting the famous leitmotifs, and our attention can remain focused on the action as spectacle in its own right. There is no need for music to cast a glamor of believability over it.

[10] See Laurie Sullivan, "*Superman Returns* Captures New Visual Effects Technology," *Information Week*, June 30, 2006, at http://www.informationweek.com/news/190100011 (accessed July 16, 2011).

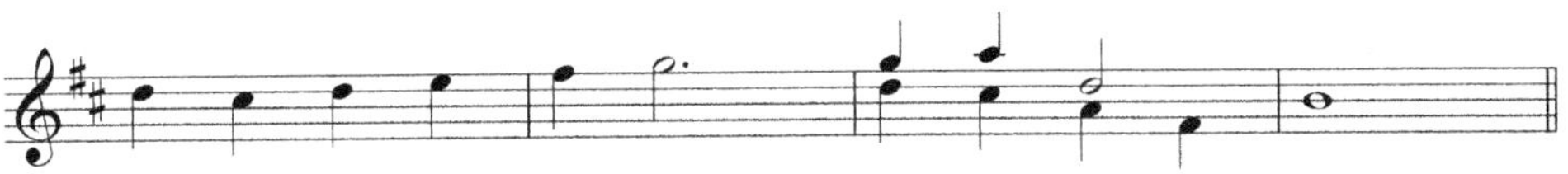

FIGURE 10.7: Author transcription of the chorale theme from John Ottman, *Superman Returns* (2006).

However, the narrative works hard to develop the emotional and psychological dimensions of Superman's character away from the action. The original films did not ignore this aspect of personality, but once Superman had dealt with his adolescent confusions about his identity and his role in the world, his journey was essentially that of a straightforward and uncomplicated character negotiating a complex situation, driven by a willing desire to do good—and thanks to his lack of psychological complexity, not having too much difficulty with this. His main moment of conflict comes at the end of *Superman*, when he tampers with time in order to save Lois. Even here, however, the actual level of conflict is minimal: he makes his decision quickly, and once he does, he seems perfectly happy and suffers no lingering guilt.

The most important new thematic idea that John Ottman contributes to the score of *Superman Returns* is what I refer to as the chorale, a theme scored for voices (see figure 10.7). We first hear the chorale early in the film. Slow, drifting music accompanies the sight of Superman flying across the city toward Lois's home at twilight. It lends his flight a reflective and somber quality quite different from the thematically heroic music that is more often associated with flying. Superman listens in on a conversation between Lois and her partner and hears her deny that she ever truly loved Superman. He ascends vertically into the night sky and looks down on the world in a scene with quite overtly messianic overtones. A voice-over from Jor-El reminds him that he is not human; Jor-El has sent him ("my only son") as the light to show humankind the way, to help us realize our capacity for good.

On one hand, the chorale creates a sense of the hero's loss, pain, and isolation—things associated with Bruce Wayne and Batman, but which an invulnerable Superman should not experience. On the other, the chorale is also a love theme, if a very different kind of love from the Superman–Lois relationship. This theme describes Superman's relationship with *us*. For the first time we see a Superman to whom heroism and altruism do not come without a cost, who suffers. This is the first of several moments that construct him as explicitly Christ-like. The chorale, then, represents his willingness to put himself at the service of humankind in general and sacrifice himself for love of us, even though he is not one of us, and the one of us he loves most has rejected him. The final world-saving action sequence therefore no longer simply depicts a moment of heroism, but represents a sacrifice, and the thematic music that plays as he lifts an entire island made of kryptonite into space is not his heroic theme but the chorale. A single statement of the heroic theme does occur at the start of the sequence, but its subsequent absence renders him vulnerable, making his success uncertain and his death possible.

The use of voices reinforces this Christ-like aspect of Superman; they evoke angelic choirs—a spiritual, religious topic rather than the military one—but the chorale also cuts away the idea of Superman's invulnerability that was so central to the earlier films. This is the post-9/11 Superman: suffering, troubled in his relationships but striving for resolution, trying to find an accommodation with the world rather than simply assuming a position of power and authority over the affairs of humans.

The decoupling of theme from action should not ultimately trouble us: there is still a "big theme," but its meaning has shifted. The narrative focuses no longer simply on the action but instead on unpacking what it is that makes a hero tick; it seeks to go beyond the superficial level of marveling at the action, instead seeing the superhero as a person rather than the invulnerable, godlike persona of the early Superman.[11] The extensive use of CGI to achieve that cinematic oxymoron—thoroughly realistic fantasy action—has contributed to this shift toward a more complexly psychological characterization of Superman. Since *The Matrix* and *X-Men*, audiences have come to expect seamlessness, credibility, and a particularly intense and revealing focus on the visual effects, such as the slow-motion machine-gun fire in the rooftop scene that immediately follows the first statement of the chorale (an idea straight out of *The Matrix*, in fact) and the bullet hitting Superman's eye in the same scene, where we see such close-up detail as the bullet's shadow crossing Superman's cheek. We have become almost complacent about CGI, forgetting how astonishingly lengthy and complex a process it is, and although many fantasy and action films do lose sight of their plot in the spectacle of their effects (e.g., *Transformers: Dark of the Moon*, Michael Bay, 2011) a high-concept franchise such as *Superman* is expected to do more, not only to impress us with the action but to engage us with its narrative as well.

Batman Begins

The expectations of a high-concept franchise are fulfilled in the reinvented Batman of *Batman Begins*, released a year before *Superman Returns*, although its approach toward digital technologies is dramatically different from the latter's. As Christopher Nolan and his collaborators said in the documentaries accompanying the DVD, he wanted to approach the action as realistically as possible. Consequently, elements of production that one might expect to have been created digitally were done in more traditional ways. According to Janek Sirrs, the visual effects supervisor, sequences were always done or at least attempted physically before resorting to digital effects.[12] Thus the "Tumbler" Batmobile is a two-and-a-half ton, custom-built, fully functioning vehicle that

[11] See Richard Reynolds, *Superheroes: A Modern Mythology* (London: Batsford, 1992), for a full discussion of Superman as Man-God.

[12] Janek Sirrs in "Saving Gotham City" in *Batman Begins*, directed by Christopher Nolan (Burbank, Calif.: Warner Home Video, 2005). DVD.

FIGURE 10.8: The Tumbler in *Batman Begins*: fully-functioning stunt vehicle.

physically performs the stunts required by the script, including jumping across spaces and driving at up to 100 miles per hour (see figure 10.8). The Gotham City scenes were shot on a set built in an airship hangar at Cardington in the United Kingdom, where city streets and the Narrows were built above a second level of set, a three-lane freeway, in a space 160 feet high and the size of approximately eight large soundstages; the Batcave was a full-size set complete with a waterfall and river, built at Shepperton Studios. However, following some issues with bat droppings, the bats themselves were eventually digitally created, as were the lengthy aerial shots of the monorail and the Wayne Enterprises building, which were created by mapping photographs and inserting other elements onto a 3D digital model. The final train crash was not created entirely digitally but employed CG enhancements of sixth-scale models filmed on a miniature version of the Gotham set in what Miniature Unit Supervisor Steve Begg believes to be one of the biggest miniature shoots ever.[13] The role of CGI was often to buff the edges of the live action and miniature shots to give them a gloss of hyperrealism that many viewers may well have mistaken for the kind of thoroughgoing CGI employed in *Superman Returns*.

As Ben Winters has observed, whereas the reuse of John Williams's themes in *Superman Returns* constitutes one of many deliberate references to the earlier *Superman* films, Nolan's *Batman Begins* (2005) and its sequels, *The Dark Knight* (2008) and *The Dark Knight Rises* (2012), "tend to act musically as if the previous [*Batman*] films did not exist."[14] Reviewers were not all happy about this arrangement. Christian Clemmenson expressed disappointment with Zimmer's score for *Batman Begins*, accusing it of "laziness," recycling too many musical ideas from the established tropes of Zimmer's previous scores, and he regretted the

[13] Steve Begg in "Saving Gotham City" in *Batman Begins*, directed by Christopher Nolan (Burbank, Calif.: Warner Home Video, 2005). DVD.

[14] Ben Winters, "*Superman* as Mythic Narrative: Music, Romanticism and the 'Oneiric Climate,'" in *The Music of Fantasy Cinema*, ed. Janet K. Halfyard (London: Equinox, 2012), 126.

FIGURE 10.9: Author transcription of the minor-third motif from Hans Zimmer and James Newton Howard, *Batman Begins* (2005).

extent to which the composers ignored the established sound of heavily thematic, "gothic" scoring that characterized both Elfman's and Goldenthal's Batman music.[15] The most prevalent musical idea in the *Batman Begins* score is a motif based on a minor third that permeates the texture of the music, used rapidly as an ostinato and slowly as a somber fanfare, the two versions often being juxtaposed (see figure 10.9).

On one level, it is difficult not to be sympathetic to Clemmenson's feeling that the score is an "enormously wasted opportunity" and that "instead of adapting himself to Batman, Zimmer tried to force Batman to adapt to his musical comfort zone."[16] However, in his desire for a score that pays tribute to the musical identity of the franchise, as Ottman's score for *Superman Returns* did a year later, Clemmenson perhaps underestimates the effectiveness of what Zimmer and his collaborator, James Newton Howard, achieve. The music Elfman wrote for the protagonist in the original *Batman* score was overwhelmingly monothematic, contrasting with the eclectic mélange of timbres and styles that he quoted and pastiched in his scoring of the Joker. Bruce Wayne is barely acknowledged, musically speaking. The Batman of *Batman Begins*, on the other hand, lacks a substantial supervillain: the main thrust of the story is Bruce Wayne's journey of self-discovery, and both the League of Shadows and the Scarecrow act as foils in this process rather than as true antagonists of equal narrative stature to the hero. Instead, we have a narrative that, like *Superman Returns*, shifts a substantial element of its focus to the psychology of the main character.

Clemmenson criticizes the persistent use of the rising minor-third motif as the principal theme because, for one thing, it means the score cannot explore the ideas of duality in the Bruce Wayne/Batman relationship that Elfman exploited. But it is actually the absence of a dualistic relationship between Bruce and his alter ego that is interesting in *Batman Begins*. Bruce, whose story we follow for the first hour of the film before Batman "begins," seems intent on obliterating his own identity. The start of the film shows the

[15] Christian Clemmenson, "*Batman Begins* (Hans Zimmer/ James Newton Howard)," *Filmtracks* (2005), at www.filmtracks.com/titles/batman_begins.html (accessed July 14, 2011). It is clear in the review that Clemmenson attributes both the sound and the structure of the score almost entirely to Zimmer, despite the co-composer credit for James Newton Howard.

[16] Clemmenson, "*Batman Begins*.". One could argue this even more strongly for *The Dark Knight*, in which Zimmer and Newton Howard recycle not just themes but complete cues from the earlier score, and where the only new thematic material is a theme for Gotham and its citizens that is arguably a reworking of Elfman's 1989 *Batman* theme. Even Harvey Dent's theme is one used in *Batman Begins* as part of Batman's heroic theme group.

multimillionaire as an anonymous prisoner in a Bhutanese jail, where he was incarcerated for apparently being involved in the theft of property from Wayne Enterprises. Evidently, revealing his identity could have secured his release, but he has refused to do this. His quest to define himself as more than the child who watched his parents die and to empower himself as a figure of justice rather than only of revenge ultimately leads him to become Batman, and Bruce Wayne's money becomes the means to Batman's ends. Two telling moments in the film point to the idea that there is no dualistic separation between Bruce and Batman, that there is only one identity. First, in a line that harkens back to the original positioning of the superhero found in the 1970s *Superman*, Batman rejects the intrinsic superheroism of Burton's Batman and instead reclaims the idea of active heroism: "[I]t is not who I am underneath, but what I do that defines me," he tells Rachel before he begins his final battle to save Gotham. His remark seems to reiterate the problem Bruce has had throughout the film with his sense of identity, but also points to its resolution through heroic action. It is not a question of dualism; instead, his problematic identity as Bruce is sublimated into his role as Batman. Second, at the end of the film Rachel looks at Bruce and tells him: "[T]his is your mask: your real face is the one the criminals now fear." This idea positions him much closer to Superman: Clark Kent is the mask that the superhero wears to disguise his true identity.

In this context, the lack of contrast between the music used for Bruce and for Batman—just as Clark Kent and Superman were not given different themes by Williams—is an entirely appropriate strategy. There is no dramatic introduction of a new hero theme halfway through the film when Batman first appears, only a continuation of the musical ideas that have characterized the score up to that point. The difference between the scores of 1978 and 2005 is that *Superman* established its heroic musical motifs in the main title and used them for the actions of Clark Kent and Superman throughout, whereas *Batman Begins* appears to lack a big theme or a clear heroic signifier used in association with action, beyond the rather muted and not automatically heroic slow, rising minor third, more a mournful cry than a call to arms. The reason for this absence of a heroic theme may be the same as that for the decoupling of action from the Superman heroic motif in *Superman Returns*: the special effects are so convincing they do not need musical support to enhance them, but can stand on their own with minimal musical padding and pacing. But we can also counter this argument when we observe that the score indeed offers a big theme—almost entirely absent from the CD sound track and therefore largely missed by both fans and reviewers.[17] In fact, Zimmer

[17] For examples of reviews that suggest there is no clearly identifiable "hero theme" in *Batman Begins*, see J. K. Moser, "Excellent Score for an Excellent Movie," *Amazon.com*, June 26, 2005, at http://www.amazon.com/batman-begins-original-picture-soundtrack/dp/b0009iw88a (accessed July 15, 2011); Paul J. Wares, "Review: The *Batman Begins* Soundtrack," *Batman on Film* (2005), at http://www.batman on film.com/opinion_pjw_reviewofbbsoundtrack.html (accessed July 16, 2011); Lunatiger, "Batman Begins Soundtrack: Taking Film Scores to the Next Level . . . ," *Eopinions. com*, June 30, 2008, at http://www.epinions.com/review/musc_mu-593543/content_439083437700 (accessed July 15, 2011); and James, "Superhero Scores," February 17, 2011, at http://atomicspud.blogspot.com/2011/02/superhero-scores.html (accessed July 15, 2011).

FIGURE 10.10: Author transcription of the hero theme and its variations from Hans Zimmer and James Newton Howard, *Batman Begins* (2005).

and Howard create a group of themes around a single harmonic base, first appearing at the moment that the young Bruce realizes his parents have died, then reappearing in relation to his actions as both Bruce and Batman (see Figure 10.10).

Different elements of the thematic group perform different functions. The rising minor third acts an adjunct to this group, frequently placed alongside elements of it, such as in the long car chase around 90 minutes into the film. It also provides an audibly recognizable Batman motif over a number of iconic shots and draws attention to itself, both because it is used so frequently (at least twenty-four times in the film, sometimes several times within a scene) and because it often occurs when there is relatively little action on screen. Theme 1a, the starting point for the theme group, represents the young Bruce's loss and grief, and 1b and 1c act as the adult Bruce's heroic themes as Batman; theme 2 is linked with the interconnected ideas of death, funerals, and Bruce's parents; theme 3 is associated with failure; and theme 4, which becomes Harvey Dent's theme in *The Dark Knight*, is another heroic signifier, starting with the same three notes as theme 3 and always very short (see table 10.1).

Table 10.1: Uses of all versions of the main theme in *Batman Begins*

Time Code[1]	Scene Description	Theme
00.13.55	Bruce's parents have just been killed. The theme, sung by a boy treble, starts as we focus on young Bruce's face as he realizes they are dead and continues into the police station scene.	1a
00.14.56	Following straight on from this, the Waynes' funeral and Bruce's return to Wayne Manor.	2
00.22.00	We see the gun in Bruce's suitcase just before Chill's parole hearing.	1a
00.23.44	Courtroom scene: Bruce listens to Chill talking about the murder of his parents.	2
00.26.50	Bruce's moment of complete failure: he has failed to kill Chill; Rachel has rejected him. He throws away the gun.	3
00.38.10	Bruce rescues Ducard from the burning building of the League of Shadows.	1b
00.38.57	Bruce struggles to save Ducard from going over the edge of the cliff.	4
00.50.48	Alfred and Bruce plan how to complete the Batsuit.	H
01.00.41	Batman corners Falcone: "I'm Batman."	1c
01.13.29	Batman scopes the room in the Narrows, tracking down Scarecrow's drugs.	1c
01.15.31	Batman, collapsing (failing), drugged by Scarecrow, hallucinates flashbacks of his father and calls to Alfred for help.	3+1a
01.19.28	Bruce runs to open the vault doors and reveals the Batsuit.	4
01.29.49	Car chase: Batman races to save Rachel.	1b
01.31.11	Car chase to save Rachel continues.	4+H
01.31.36	Car chase to save Rachel continues.	H
01.32.00	Car chase to save Rachel continues.	1b
01.32.35	Batman puts the Tumbler into stealth mode, blacking out the lights (theme cuts off after three notes as the car goes dark).	4
01.32.53	Car arrives at the Batcave and Batman races for the antidote to save Rachel.	H
01.43.25	Ducard talks about Bruce's parents and how they foiled the League's previous plan to destroy Gotham.	2
01.51.00	Batman outlines his plan to save Gotham to Gordon.	H
01.52.39	Batman rescues and then reveals his identity to Rachel on the bridge. ("It's not who I am underneath but what I do that defines me.")	H
01.53.01	Batman jumps off the bridge into the rioting Narrows.	H
01.53.34	Batman confronts Ducard.	2
01.55.00	Batman, attacked by the mob, reaches for his cable gun and shoots it to attach to the underside of the train; he is dragged along underneath it.	1b
01.57.48	Batman and Ducard fight. Gordon fires the Tumbler's weapons at the railway supports but appears to fail to bring it down. Ducard tells Batman he will fail to stop the train.	3
01.58.38	Batman tells Ducard, "I won't kill you, but I don't have to save you." He jumps from the train; Ducard closes his eyes as the train comes off the rails.	1c+3
02.05.15	Batman finishes his rooftop conversation with Gordon and jumps off the rooftop.	1c

[1] These timings are taken from the PAL version of the DVD, which runs 4% faster than the NTSC version.

The "big theme" is found in the two closely related versions of 1b and 1c. Theme 1b is the most protracted melodic theme in the group, the one that is most evidently anticipated by the use of H, the harmonic progression, as a form of ground bass detached from its melody. [18] Theme 1c is a rhythmically smoothed form (and half the length) of 1b, used to musically punctuate particular moments, while 1b underscores more protracted action in just three heroic episodes of rescue: of Ducard from a burning building in the first part of the film; of Rachel in the car chase; and of Gotham despite itself, in which Batman escapes from the mob and quite literally catches the train that Ducard intends to use to destroy the city, allowing himself to be hauled ungracefully along underneath it, dangling from a cable in a parody of flight. The harmony (H) that connects all the themes in the group is used on its own more frequently and for more extended periods than any of the individual melodies; this is probably why audiences and critics tended not to perceive any major theme: H anticipates 1b, but 1b itself is used in a very restricted manner.

This score, then, takes another approach to superhero scoring: the hero's theme is still present and directly connected to action, but no single version of the theme is used so extensively that it becomes the sole identifier of the hero, in the way that Williams's heroic motif or Elfman's Bat-theme did. The result is a score with a solidly unified musical identity in which no specific melodic theme dominates, which almost willfully avoids giving us the big theme. (Once one becomes aware of 1b, uses of the harmonic progression without it become almost frustrating, as the ear wants to hear the melody rejoined to it.) This process of disguising the theme has a direct correspondence in the way Christopher Nolan constructs his Batman. In the DVD documentary *Shaping Mind and Body*, Nolan points out that in the action sequences we often do not see Batman clearly, because of the director's desire to present things from the criminal's point of view. Batman appears and disappears with alarming speed, and we—like the criminals—often get only fleeting glimpses of him before, during, and after his assaults. Much in the same way, we get only fleeting strains of the heroic theme; the music spends much of the time anticipating it via the harmonic progression, but rarely allows us to hear it clearly.

Conclusion

These four films demonstrate that the role of technology in creating a cinematic superhero directly bears on how that superhero is constructed within the narrative, which in turn has unavoidable consequences for how he is scored. The first *Superman* film

[18] H and the minor third motif are the main thematic aspects of Batman's heroic music retained in *The Dark Knight*, which replaces the various versions of theme 1 with a little-used motif from the Bhutan scenes of *Batman Begins* as the heroic theme, alongside other motifs also established in the first film. The final film, *The Dark Knight Rises*, largely continues with this material (with a new harmonic progression) until the end of the film. As Batman appears to sacrifice himself to save the city, we hear the first three phrases of theme 1a, exactly as they first appeared in *Batman Begins*, framing the entire narrative by connecting Batman's beginnings in the wake of Bruce's parents' murder to his final act and apparent death in saving Gotham.

evidences the desire to push analog technology to its absolute limits, and its score seems designed to reinforce the idea of superheroic action and raise visual effects to epic levels, even when the technology of the day failed to create something that appeared completely realistic. *Batman*'s score also relies heavily on music to create the notion of the superheroic, sometimes in the absence of any action at all. *Batman Begins* and *Superman Returns* are both in a position to use music in a different way. Even though *Batman Begins* relies heavily on stunts, sets, and models, CGI here and in *Superman Returns* plays a major role in rendering action with photorealistic credibility. I argue that music's role consequently falls back to a potentially more traditional position of constructing character and emotion, rather than depicting the superhero as a man of action. Both later films use their scores instead to explore new aspects of their heroes.

What we see in the evolution of these superheroes and their music is in part an articulation of the increasingly problematic idea of power. Nina Auerbach, discussing vampires, has argued that "every age embraces the vampire it needs,"[19] reinventing the figure of the vampire to serve its particular needs and concerns. A corresponding argument can be made for superheroes, who, like vampires, act as ciphers through which we explore and indeed reveal our own cultural preoccupations. The original *Superman* film in the late 1970s came at a crisis point in economic history, a protracted recession affecting most of the developed world. The altruistic and uncomplicated Man of Steel was a hero who could take control and put things right, who had power and the ability to wield it, without flinching, to save us all. A decade later, figures such as Margaret Thatcher and Ronald Reagan had revitalized the economy, but in the process had created the "greed is good" culture demonized in *Wall Street* (Oliver Stone, 1987). In this climate of disillusionment with the less pleasant side of human nature when it finds itself in possession of (economic) power, a new kind of hero was called for. For the superhero to be able to work for the good of all rather than only himself, the relationship with power must not be allowed to become too comfortable or seductive; the hero must, to some extent, be unwilling to become heroic (to seize power), becoming so by accident rather than design. Burton's Batman, then, is the superhero we envisaged at this point in our history: powerful, but reluctant to exercise his power unless it is truly necessary. Batman gradually and successfully negotiated a position in relation to the law and society, rather than simply assuming the role of society's protector the way Superman did. The music for both characters reflects these positions: Superman's confident fanfare contrasts with Batman's darker and more chromatic scoring.

In the later pair of films, the position shifts again, and both *Batman Begins* and *Superman Returns* draw out narrative themes that might be traced to the cultural shock of the events of 9/11. *Batman Begins* features a non-Western terrorist organization, the League of Shadows, which seeks to destroy a city they believe to be irredeemably corrupt, with a Batman who must sometimes operate outside the law in order to protect Gotham and who sacrifices his own identity to the need to serve the city.

[19] Nina Auerbach, *Our Vampires, Ourselves* (Chicago: University of Chicago press, 1995), 145.

Superman Returns develops Christian themes to explore not dissimilar ideas of duty and sacrifice, again in the context of saving a city from destruction by an enemy who wields power without responsibility. These more recent heroes are both more emotionally complex and more willing to sacrifice themselves for us, to experience real pain and clearly life-threatening danger; these are superheroes as soldiers on the front line in wars against terror. Superman's spectacular fall from space and apparent death in *Superman Returns*, and Batman's repeated physical battering throughout *Batman Begins*, are quite unlike any of the threats and assaults their predecessors had to endure and perhaps represent another aspect of the overall desire to present the superhero realistically: even Superman bleeds. Their musical representation, significantly, plays as much to their loves, losses, and sacrifices as it does to their heroism: think of Superman's chorale and Batman's complex set of themes, which link his loss of his parents directly to his superheroism. Music therefore still plays an important role in underlining action, but modern technology means it is no longer so thoroughly essential to constructing action as heroic. In a more significant way than was possible before, music plays instead to the emotional drama of the superhero, as much as, if not more than, to the heroism of his actions.

References

Auerbach, Nina. *Our Vampires, Ourselves*. Chicago: University of Chicago Press, 1995.

Clemmenson, Christian. "*Batman Begins* (Hans Zimmer/ James Newton Howard)." *Filmtracks* (2005), at www.filmtracks.com/titles/batman_begins.html (accessed 14 July 14, 2011).

Hamm, Sam, and Warren Skaaren. "Batman (1989) Movie Script [5th Draft, 1988]." *Screenplays for You*, at http://sfy.ru/?script=batman_production (accessed July 16, 2011).

Halfyard, Janet K. *Danny Elfman's Batman: A Film Score Guide*. Lanham, MD: Scarecrow Press, 2004.

Hatten, Robert. *Musical Meaning in Beethoven: Markedness, Correlation, and Interpretation*. Bloomington: Indiana University Press, 1994.

Howe, Desson. "Batman." *Washington Post*, July 23, 1989, at http://www.washingtonpost.com/wp-srv/style/longterm/movies/videos/batmanpg13howe_a0b220.htm (accessed July 20, 2011).

Reynolds, Richard. *Superheroes: A Modern Mythology*. London: Batsford, 1992.

Rosenbaum, Jonathan. "Are We Having Fun?" *Sight and Sound* 59, no. 2 (1990): 96–97.

Sullivan, Laurie. "Superman Returns Captures New Visual Effects Technology." *Information Week*, June 30, 2006, at http://www.informationweek.com/news/190100011 (accessed July 16, 2011).

Tagg, Philip. "Analysing Popular Music: Theory, Method and Practice." *Popular Music* 2 (1982): 37–67.

Tagg, Philip. "An Anthropology of Stereotypes in TV Music?" *Swedish Musicological Journal* (1989): 19–42, at http://tagg.org/articles/xpdfs/tvanthro.pdf (accessed July 27, 2012).

Winters, Ben. "*Superman* as Mythic Narrative: Music, Romanticism and the 'Oneiric Climate.'" In *The Music of Fantasy Cinema*, ed. Janet K. Halfyard, 111–131. London: Equinox, 2012.

Filmography

Batman. Directed by Tim Burton. (1989). Burbank, Calif.: Warner Home Video, 1998. DVD.

Batman Begins. Directed by Christopher Nolan. (2005). Burbank, Calif.: Warner Home Video, 2005. DVD.

The Dark Knight. Directed by Christopher Nolan. (2008). Burbank, Calif.: Warner Home Video, 2008. DVD.

Superman: The Movie. Directed by Richard Donner. (1978). Burbank, Calif.: Warner Home Video, 2001. DVD.

Superman Returns. Directed by Bryan Singer. (2006). Burbank, Calif.: Warner Home Video, 2006. DVD.

CHAPTER 11

VIDEO SPEECH IN LATIN AMERICA

MICHAEL CHANAN

1

THERE have been two moments that directly challenged the hegemony of cinema, which since the invention of cinematography in the 1890s had been fashioned by the projector and the collective act of watching in the dark. The first was the introduction of television, the second was video—not as an adjunct of television but as a medium of audiovisual production in its own right. Neither would dethrone the big screen, which retains its prestige to this day, but the ecology of the medium was nonetheless profoundly changed by both.

First, television brought audiovisual consumption into the domestic sphere, generating new genres and aesthetics (while also incorporating cinema, which was a little like listening to a symphony on a transistor radio). Video did something similar by replacing amateur movies and enabling small-scale low-cost activity, only not of broadcast quality. It quickly came within reach of the individual with less surplus capital than it takes to buy a car, and amateurs duly abandoned Super-8 in its favor, encouraged by a cascade of technological improvements. With the passage from analog to digital in the 1990s and then convergence with the computer and the internet, the history of video entered its second phase. Well before this transition, video had already attracted a new generation of iconoclastic artists, individualists driven perhaps by oedipal rebellion and intent on exploring the frontiers of postmodernism, who invented a new kind of gallery object to become known universally as video art. This also happened in Latin America, but is not my focus here. What interests me is the social adoption of video more as a form of collective speech than individualistic artistic expression.

In its simplest sense, video speech stems from the basic technical property that video (unlike amateur moviemaking) automatically incorporates simultaneous sound recording. Press record, and both lens and microphone are activated. Press play, and you are both seeing and hearing. One thing that has altered in the passage of film/television/video has been the changing relation between image and sound, seeing and hearing, watching and listening. Silent cinema was always accompanied by music. The soundtrack began as an add-on that not only reintroduced the voice, but became a supplement, in Derrida's sense: not just an addition that makes up for a lack, but an integral part of the whole which nevertheless occupies its own space. Television was different. First, you get the contrast between the acoustics of the cinema and of domestic space, where sound is reduced in volume, dynamics and resonance. But at the same time, the image–sound relationship is reversed: television was greeted not so much as an imitation of cinema, but more like illustrated radio. Video as a medium is different again, where audio and visual are placed in a new relationship of equal simultaneity. This is not just an extension of radio-with-pictures. If radio is an aural medium, this is not say that it suffers from lack of the visual, but rather that the visual does not exist for the microphone. Video restores the connection, and does so without necessarily privileging one over the other.

The radical scope of this technical property comes from its social location. Above all, by moving outside the closed circuit of the big media producers who dominate both cinema and television, video brings new social voices into the picture, inviting us to think in different ways about the politics of speaking, hearing and listening—or in the title of a recent book, why voice matters.[1] Having a voice, for Nick Couldry, is to belong to a process that involves more than just speaking, but speaking in the expectation of being heard, of being part of a conversation, and therefore also listening. To be sure, video speech can be individualist, monological and often narcissistic. These are indeed typical characteristics of the video diary, for example in the format successfully and engagingly nurtured by the BBC at the end of the 1980s. Over several seasons, the BBC's Community Programmes unit invited amateurs to take up the video camera (under professional tutelage) to make a personal diary film, where the camera acquires a voice of its own, speaking in the first person singular. At exactly the same time in Brazil, however, in the emergence of indigenous video, video speech becomes a thoroughly collective affair, embodied in people who are socially grounded in their communities and engaging in a process of dialogue. Using video to produce their own shared narratives begets a form of audiovisual speech which is plural even when speakers are singular.

[1] Nick Couldry, *Why Voice Matters* (London: Sage, 2010).

2

There is another reason for thinking of video in relation to radio. The dissemination of video followed a pattern established not by cinema or television but by transistorized electronics in the 1960s—battery-operated radios and audio cassette players—with respect to music. Firstly, these were primarily technologies of transmission, reception and distribution, but audio cassettes could also be used for copying, from the radio, the record player, and each other, thus expanding the circulation of recorded music, both privately and by means of piracy.[2] This capacity to upset the "pure" functioning of the market is one of the key elements brought into play by all media technologies that allow copying (a capability of the original cylinder phonograph excluded by the shift to disks). It comes to play havoc with that peculiar form of capitalist property called copyright. (Now, in the internet age, intellectual property rights have become a raging battlefield worth billions of dollars, while the web has generated new forms of sharing and common rights.) In any case, if the comparison with audio is a cogent one, it means that video entered a public media space that was structured as much, if not more, by the aural as by the visual.

The second similarity with transistorized electronics was the relative speed of dissemination of the new equipment across the globe. To use the language of the time, although the take-up was slower in the second world countries of communism than in the first world countries of advanced capitalism, where it rapidly opened up huge new consumer markets, transistorized audio also displayed swift entry into the third world, the underdeveloped countries of Asia, Africa and Latin America, where it extended media space into new geographical territories by bringing radio and recorded music to zones without electricity. (The pattern would be repeated with the mobile phone, whose networks reach further than landlines, although not always with internet access—yet.) In 1972, in Bolivia, this writer attended a public debate in the *alcaldía* (town hall) in Uncía, a small town in the Altiplano, which was being broadcast live on the local radio station; the station would have had practically no audience without transistor radios. I learned that what seemed to me—coming from suburban London—like an extraordinary exercise in local democracy was the result of the marriage of local radio with a tradition of popular politics that went back to the Bolivian Revolution of 1952. Moreover, this tradition was nurtured by the ancient cultural strength of the collectivity in the indigenous communities, both Quechua and Aymara, which have remained the majority population in Bolivia. The example serves as a warning as we turn to the advent of video. New media have brought large populations into contact with the latest phase of capitalist modernization and its products, but they are not installed on a *tabula rasa*. They enter an arena already shaped and sustained by existing social, cultural and political practices, including popular political activism and the oral lore of cultural tradition.

[2] See, for example, Peter Manuel, *Cassette Culture: Popular Music and Technology in North India* (Chicago: University of Chicago Press, 1993).

Video, in its ability to get close to source, so to speak, was well placed to find an aesthetic that derives from subaltern culture, but it also drew on the tradition of film activism in Latin America that goes back to the 1950s, and the various initiatives taking place in a number of countries to make political films—at first mostly documentaries—which came together in the '60s in the movement known as *el nuevo cine latinoamericano,* the New Latin American Cinema. This movement, its ideals and practices, which created an entirely new cultural identity for Latin America on movie screens both at home and abroad, was aligned to a revolutionary Marxist politics which also took inspiration from its own Latin American sources, from the work of the Peruvian José Carlos Mariátegui in the 1920s to the ideas of Che Guevara in the '60s. A defining moment was the publication in 1969 of a manifesto by the Argentine filmmakers Fernando Solanas and Octavio Getino which introduced the concept of "third cinema," a militant cinema incompatible with the commercial values of either the Hollywood model (first cinema) or the European model of art cinema (second cinema).[3] The geography they proposed was not physical but virtual; neither was it a mapping of the political geography of the three worlds, but a metaphor. In the same way that first and second cinema could be found in other countries—in India and Argentina, for example—third cinema was not just a third world phenomenon, and they found examples among groups in the United States, Italy, France, Britain, and Japan. Just as in these latter countries, the relationship of this movement to the turn to video is not always direct, and there are significant differences. Practicing filmmakers often held back from adopting video while a new generation did so eagerly: in part because the film artistry of the former was not yet possible in video, and in part because the latter didn't think in terms of art anyway. A Brazilian video activist told an interviewer in 1992 that "The social movements appropriated the medium before the professionals."[4] In any event, in city slums and shanty towns that sustained strong traditions of solidarity and community, in rural zones where oral culture was strong and literacy remained a minority acquisition—in these milieux, video readily entered, was accepted, and quickly acquired a political function because it facilitated social speech and communication within existing social networks. But it didn't create them.

3

Video added something to the social and cultural dynamics of transistorized audio because it was more than a new domestic consumer good: it is a multifunctional

[3] Fernando Solanas and Octavio Getino, "Towards a Third Cinema," in *Twenty-five Years of the New Latin American Cinema,* ed. Michael Chanan (London: BFI and Channel 4, 1983).

[4] Alberto López, quoted in Brian Goldfarb, "Local Television and Community Politics in Brazil" in *Visible Nations, Latin American Cinema and Video, ed.* Chon Noriega (Minneapolis: University of Minnesota Press, 2000), 263–284, 278.

medium that not only facilitates copying, but also (with a little additional equipment) combines recording and editing. First-generation prototypes always have restricted capabilities, and throughout the first phase, video production did not compete in the commercial markets of cinema and television but composed a parallel sphere of circulation where the laws of the market were weak or absent. The emergent video sphere was neither uniform nor homogenous. Production was sponsored directly or indirectly by corporate publicists, government agencies, trade unions, the church, universities, international aid and development organizations, legal and illegal political groups, local communities and the grassroots—in short, right across civil society. The result was the appearance of a division in the audiovisual public sphere. The big public was supplied by television, which was highly centralized and ideologically conformist; video was small scale, decentralized, and aimed at small audiences. Writing about video culture in 1991, Sean Cubitt noted the consequence of these facts about the political economy of video in the observation that "video culture as such has no centre, and therefore no peripheries."[5] He was writing about Britain, but the same pattern can be seen abroad, for example in Latin America. Everywhere the same paradox: the distribution of the medium as commodity—the hardware of production and exhibition—is international, but the content that is made and seen—the circulating software—is predominantly local.

Take Argentina, which in the 1960s fostered both a strong oppositional political film movement and the production of anthropological shorts based on academic investigations. The first portable video system, Sony's black-and-white open reel Portapak, introduced in 1965, reached Buenos Aires in the early 70s. I learn from one of the pioneers of independent video documentary in Argentina, Guillermo De Carli, that one of the first people to use the Portapak was Fernando Solanas, who employed it in much the same way Polaroid still cameras were used, as an adjunct to research and documentation. In Chile, the documentary filmmaker Sergio Bravo acquired one in 1975, with the intention of producing newsreels for the resistance movement following the military coup two years earlier. [6] For the record, this was around the same time that in London, this writer also used a Portapak for the first (and only) time, to make a short video of an event at an inner city youth club where a friend of mine worked. (It was fun, but lack of ancillary equipment meant we had to edit in camera, or when we handed the camera over to the kids, not edit at all. It was never shown anywhere except the club, but led to producing a ten-minute promotional film for the club, which accordingly we made on 16mm.)

Videocassette machines were introduced in the early '70s. The Umatic format, comprising bulky machines and chunky, three-quarter-inch cassettes, were not exactly portable, but were soon to be found in Argentina, replacing 16mm projectors at exhibitions, congresses and trade fairs. De Carli recalls first seeing video used this way in 1974 at a

[5] Sean Cubitt, *Timeshift: On Video Culture* (London; New York: Routledge, 1991), 130.

[6] Germán Liñero Arend, *Apuntes para una historia del video en Chile* (Santiago: Ocho Libros, 2010), 14.

congress on cardiology at the Sheraton Hotel, brought from the United States to show medical and publicity films. Within a couple more years, video was being used by advertising agencies for casting purposes. When the more convenient half-inch format (VHS or Betamax) arrived at a handful of film schools at the start of the '80s, it was at first regarded with skepticism by both teachers and students, and only used to practice camera positions or to show films copied from television. Within a few years, however, video was taken up in the universities, by anthropologists for investigation and ethnographic documentation, and by medical departments for teaching—to show operations, for example—and for health and sex education. In the wider world, it was also adopted by local photographers, who now offered neighborhood customers videos as well as photos of all the usual family events.

There is nothing at all unusual in this pattern of development compared to any similar country—although cultural differences there may be—despite the fact that from 1976 to 1983 Argentina was under the rule of a military dictatorship. But then the same was true of Brazil from 1964 to 1985, and Chile from 1973 until 1990. Technocultural processes, however, are always modulated by local histories, and the case of Chile is highly instructive. Chile in the '60s was home to an important strand of new wave Latin American cinema, only to suffer the total eclipse of film production after the coup of 1973, when a whole tribe of filmmakers were forced into exile (where they produced over 150 films over the following decade out of sixteen different countries). Within Chile itself, a new generation turned to video as a matter of political necessity, working anonymously and in clandestinity to document the repression, when to do so on film would have effectively been impossible. In short, video was taken up in Chile as a means of production of alternative information—and this indeed is how Latin American video first traveled abroad.

Here the story touches on my own memory, because this was how I first encountered independent Latin American video. I was asked to produce a video for the Chile Solidarity Movement in 1984, for screening at the TUC and Labour Party conferences, on the first trade union delegation from Britain to visit Chile after the coup to investigate human rights abuses. The delegation brought back with them a tape they'd been given to be incorporated into the video which we shot of their report-back meeting. The tape carried no title or credits, but it was not merely a series of useful shots; I can recall my amazement on first viewing it to find a fully edited reportage about the repression and the fight-back taking place on the streets.

I have now been able to identify it. Judging by a recent Chilean publication on the history of video in Chile, it is either the video made by Claudio Di Girólamo of the group Ictus, with the title *Andrés de La Victoria*, or else one of the first videos of the alternative newsreel series *Teleanálisis*, a spin-off of the journal *Análisis*.[7] Both groups—and they were not the only ones—were supported by funds from nongovernmental organizations (NGOs) in Europe or North America, and exploited a loophole in the repressive laws imposed by the military junta which kept tight control on domestic media but did not

[7] Arend, *Apuntes para una historia del video en Chile*, 37–41, 59–64.

prevent production for foreign consumption. Inside the country, they were distributed to subscribers clandestinely on VHS, who would make more copies and pass them on.

Another example came up two years later at the Havana Film Festival, which by then included a section for video: a highly impressive piece of clandestine reportage called *Somos más* (*We Are More*)—the rallying cry of the demonstration portrayed in the video organized by Mujeres por la Vida (Women for Life) in Santiago on October 30, 1985, in demand of democracy and freedom. This is completely the opposite of the kind of frenzied footage of demonstrations we see nowadays taken by people's mobile phones. Instead it consists of long takes from a carefully chosen vantage point of the demonstration by a hugely observant videographer surveying the entire scene and zooming in on details: at one moment, for example, spotting a bunch of police carrying tear gas canisters, the camera zooms in and pans with them as they calmly walk into the middle of the demonstration and throw them. In short, it's a video that makes a strength of minimalism. De Carli, when I ask him about his recollections, confirms that Chile was in advance of Argentina in the political use of video, and they were influenced by its example.

4

If military repression impeded the openly political use of video, it did not halt its adoption for small-scale experiments, and hence the gathering pace of independent video production that occurred with the return to democracy in both Argentina and Brazil. The first public exhibitions and competitions in Buenos Aires took place in 1986.

Other countries experienced similar developments, and international meetings took place in the late '80s in Cuzco, Santiago, Havana, and perhaps most importantly, Montevideo in 1988. The fact that these meetings took place at all indicates that practitioners had already emerged in several countries over the preceding years. The week-long event in Montevideo was dedicated to video in popular education, and attempted to define, in general terms, the political and social practices of working with video in the countries of Central and South America.

The moment was pivotal. In the early period, if the video activists didn't think in terms of art, they still had to borrow models of audiovisual communication from either political cinema or television and transpose them into a new setting. These models were governed in various ways by a discourse of mediation that corresponded in effect to Marx's famous phrase about the French peasantry: "since they cannot represent themselves, they must be represented."[8] Politically, the video movement belonged in the tradition of third cinema, and often the most effective videos took up one of the strongest currents of third cinema, that of *cine testimonio*, the testimonial, conceived as the urgent act of

[8] Karl Marx, *The Eighteenth Brumaire of Louis Bonaparte* (Project Gutenberg, 2006), 278, at http://www.gutenberg.org/files/1346/1346-h/1346-h.htm (accessed December 13, 2011).

giving voice to those who have been kept in silence. In literary form the *testimonio* goes back a good long time, but the genre found a new paradigm as a major strand in the postwar literary "boom" in Latin America in the '60s and '70s, where it took the shape of a first-person narrative reconstructed by the author from the transcription of an oral narrative. The process is explained by John Beverley:

> Since, in many cases, the narrator is someone who is either functionally illiterate or, if literate, not a professional writer, the production of a testimonio often involves the tape recording and then the transcription and editing of an oral account by an interlocutor who is an intellectual, journalist, or writer. (To recall the Russian formalist term, testimonio is a sort of *skaz*, a literary simulacrum of oral narrative.)[9]

This procedure is easily translated into the film medium, which even intensifies the effect, since the voice that "speaks to the reader in the form of an 'I' that demands to be recognized, that wants or needs to stake a claim on our attention," acquires the force of audiovisual presence.[10] The result is comparable to the quality Gilles Deleuze found in the cinema of Pierre Perrault and Jean Rouch, where characters "begin to tell stories without ever being fictional."[11]

Beverley observes that the editorial function embedded in these texts is a hotly debated theoretical issue in the discussion of the genre, and this takes on new aspects in *cine testimonio*. He also remarks on the variety of different kinds of texts which can be fitted under the label of *testimonio*, "some of which would be considered literature, some not—," including oral history, memoir, autobiography, chronicle, confession, life history, even the novella.[12] The category, in short, is a fluid and open one, and this is also true of the subgenres of video speech. The crucial element is the presence of the voice, speaking from the position of the excluded or the marginal, refusing to be silenced or defeated, whose experience is understood, either implicitly or explicitly, as collective.

Video is not only able to take up this effect but also begins to manifest another possibility, that of handing the camera over to the subjects of the representation and thus circumventing the intellectual intermediary—leapfrogging, at least to some degree, the intervening framework of editorial mediation. In this way, the well-known formula suggested by Bill Nichols for the classic documentary, "I speak to you about them," would be transformed into "I speak to you about us," or "We speak to you about us," or even "We speak to one another about ourselves." Furthermore, this transformation would fulfill the task envisaged by the Cuban filmmaker Julio García Espinosa in another key manifesto of the time, *Por un cine imperfecto* (*For an Imperfect Cinema*), when he spoke of the need to break with "culture" as the property of social elites, and popular culture as

9 John Beverley, *Against Literature* (Minneapolis: University of Minnesota Press, 1993), 70–71.

10 Beverley, *Against Literature*, 75–76.

11 Gilles Deleuze, *Cinema 2: The Time-Image*, trans. Hugh Tomlinson and Robert Galeta (London: Athlone Press, 1989), 150.

12 Beverley, *Against Literature*.

commodities on the market, and instead to discover "the conditions which will enable spectators to transform themselves into agents—not merely more active spectators, but genuine co-authors."[13]

Ironically, these conditions would be discovered not within the Cuban Revolution as García Espinosa hoped, but in other less propitious environments. But perhaps it is not a coincidence that this development corresponded to a wider political shift in the state and its relations to civil society which came with the end of the dictatorships and the restoration of democracy, a change in which video activism moved away from the militancy of political opposition toward communication and expression as fields of political action in themselves, in a turn that favors video as speech act.

5

To recap: When consumer video came along in the 1970s, it looked at first like an added appurtenance of television—a means of "timeshifting" television programs, of watching movies at home (or replacing 16mm projectors at conventions), and of making simple home movies to show on your television set. With the addition of editing facilities, it quickly revealed a potential for alternative uses outside broadcast television and corporate publicity, and became an agent of parallel cultural production. In other words, it entered the sphere of what Jürgen Habermas has called communicative action, on the model of the speech act of the citizen entering into debate in the public sphere, or at any rate, some subsector within it. Building on the radicalization of the preceding decades, community activists of the '80s became aficionados of video (while those approaching the medium as artists created a new movement of video art).

Utopians predicted a rosy future for community and grassroots video. In practical terms, the problem was not production but replication and distribution. Early analog video could only be replicated by copying it in real time, which also resulted in loss of technical quality (degeneration) and made true mass production, on the model of the record industry, unattainable. Without organized wide-scale distribution, the work is only seen in small circles. In Britain in 1984, when 7000 copies of the *Miners' Campaign Tapes* were distributed, this was an exceptional success.[14] Alternative video production was either kept out of television altogether, or else ghettoized in community cable television channels, as happened in the United States. What emerged was a small scale, low profile, subcultural, fragmented and alternative public sphere in the margins and interstices of the big media. No individual video would ever reach the kind of large numbers recorded by box office statistics or ostensibly measured by the television ratings;

[13] Julio García Espinosa, "For an Imperfect Cinema," in *Twenty-Five Years of the New Latin American Cinema*, ed. Michael Chanan (London: BFI and Channel Four, 1983), 28–33, 30.

[14] See Sean Cubitt, *Timeshift*, 147. (The *Miners' Campaign Tapes* are now available on DVD from the BFI.)

its positions and arguments would have to insinuate themselves into public discourse through one-off screenings, lending and copying, the networks of civil society operating outside the commercial market place or on its fringes.

If this kind of activity escapes measurement, the measurable size of the audience is not the point; the impact cannot be captured in the numerical concept of the mass audience because it's not a matter of quantity but of quality—the social conversations that video helps to create among quite small groups of people (especially given the practice, taken over from third cinema, of incorporating debate into the screenings). This scenario, however, raises critical questions about the basic character of video—whether to think of it as an extension of film, or of television, or something quite other, perhaps what I've called video speech. The question arises in its most challenging form in the emergence by the end of the '80s of *video indigena*—the indigenous video movement that began in Brazil and soon spread to the Andean countries and Mexico (there were similar initiatives in native media in Australia, New Zealand, Canada and the United States) where "we speak to you about us" becomes "we talk to each other about us."

In a report on grassroots video in Latin America, Pat Aufderheide mentions a couple of precursors, a network of forty video production groups set up in Brazil in 1984 called the ABVP (Associação Brasileiro de Video no Movimiento Popular); and TV dos Trabalhadores (Workers TV) created in 1986 by the autoworkers' union headed by Lula, the future Brazilian President Luis Ignacio da Silva, which produced training tapes, documentation of meetings and events, and broadcast-quality videos.[15] Almost immediately, in the course of a general strike, TV dos Trabalhadores found itself inundated with videotapes from union members across the country, who were recording local strike events and wanted to see what was happening in other places; the group responded by editing these tapes into a video distributed through the union federation. Two years after the *Miners' Tapes* in Britain, video as an alternative form of communicative action, outside the big commercial media, had become an active force on the Brazilian scene. And then there was the phenomenon of street TV, which became a feature of urban life in poor neighborhoods in several Brazilian cities: a small team of activists would turn up in a truck, work with community members to prepare a program, and hold screenings, with debates and discussions, on a range of subjects from recipes and public health to children's items and cultural performances.[16]

The first indigenous video production can be dated to around 1987, when a project called "Video in the Villages" was set up by the Centro de Trabalho Indigenista, and they began to work with the Nambiquara of Northern Mato Grosso. The group established a pattern that would be followed with variations by other initiatives in Brazil and elsewhere, especially the Andean countries with their majority Indian populations; and other places where there were surviving pockets of indigenous peoples. In this model, an NGO sponsors the formation of a group of video activists. Videos are produced by

[15] Pat Aufderheide, *The Daily Planet: A Critic on the Capitalist Culture Beat* (Minneapolis: University of Minnesota Press, 2000), 258.

[16] Aufderheide, *Daily Planet*, 260–261.

group members, who also provide technical support to the communities to make their own; the group then exhibits the results, and circulates them around the network.

The core audience is made up of the communities directly involved and the network of NGOs and others who work with them; sometimes videos are made to address politicians, and others to address outsiders, in other countries, by way of advocacy, but this last is quite secondary. Early subjects included rituals in danger of loss, the documentation of a land campaign, the investigation of a massacre. A video of a ritual, for example, would lead to discussion and critique of its performance. As Aufderheide observes, such videos are not ethnographic, the view of an outsider documenting an event, and although often didactic in style, they have an activist and political rationale. The classifications are not easily differentiated, and *video indígena* will invent new subgenres, like the video letter that is sent between communities; nor will it shy away from fiction, which is particularly rich in the Andean countries. There is considerable diversity of audiovisual language. A video package sent out by the CAIB (Coordinadora Audiovisual Indígena de Bolivia) would typically include a selection of items, the shorter ones of about seven minutes' duration, some as long as twenty, encompassing documentary, docudrama and fiction, mostly from Bolivia but sometimes from elsewhere, like Mexico or Canada. The shorter items would feature a *video carta* (video letter) and a *video memoria* (video memory): these are usually about rituals and ceremonies, filmed with a stable camera. Short items and reports would be shot like reportage, while longer testimonials and docu-fiction enactments of oral history tend to follow the conventions of realism, and might well employ a narrator.

We must not suppose that the new indigenous communicators were not exposed to the audiovisual products of cinema and television. But this raises a crucial issue: how do they relate to the representational conventions of the big media? Do they take over or resist the codes of mainstream film and television that inscribe patriarchal and repressive ways of seeing? First impressions are that the visual language is basically the same; subject matter is not approached, as García Espinosa's imperfect cinema advocated, with a Brechtian aesthetic, or any attempt to deconstruct the codes of representation as such. On the other hand, alternative video in general and *video indígena* in particular would fulfill other criteria of imperfect cinema, above all that of addressing the viewer not as passive consumer but as interlocutor.

The primary difference is that the relations of production that emerge in the novel situation of *video indígena* alter the nature of authorship. Someone takes the position of *responsable*, the person responsible, but they speak in a kind of collaborative "third voice" (to borrow a term that Aufderheide borrows from Jay Ruby). As Freya Schiwy explains in a study of indigenous video in the Andes, "Indianizing video production... invokes traditions of shared labor" like the *mit'a* or *minga* in which the community works together in tasks like the harvest or the construction of schoolhouses or roads, so why not video?[17] Such endeavors require the collective endorsement and

[17] Freya Schiwy, *Indianizing Film, Decolonization, the Andes, & the Question of Technology* (New Brunswick, N.J.: Rutgers University Press, 2009), 72.

participation of the community, and film proposals pass through community assemblies which are geared to generating consensus. Indeed, since many videos are the product of collective discussion over the script, editing, soundtrack and so on, Schiwy suggests that this is not only about authorship but also affects the concept of the audience, since the immediate audience of indigenous video is made up of communities who have actively participated in the process of video making.[18] This puts them in a very different relationship to what they view from the attitude of passive consumption conventionally associated with the mass media, which has anyway been criticized as too crude, failing as it does to recognize the different ways people have of using its products to answer to their own predilections and construct their own identities. But this is a different relationship again, because it is rooted in two forms of immediate knowledge that do not depend on literacy. One is direct knowledge of the dialogue of collective creativity acquired through doing it. The other, more fundamental because it underpins the first, is indigenous epistemology, the forms of knowledge sustained by an oral culture that has been marginalized and deprecated.

According to one account, Quechua uses four verbs to indicate increasingly complex ways of gaining knowledge. The simplest is *rikuy*, to see. Second comes *yachay*, to know in the sense of practical knowledge, and the content of teaching. The third term is *unanchay*, to understand iconic symbols, like images of the deity, and last is *hamuttay*, to understand allusion and metaphor.[19] It is not difficult to see how video would fit in to this epistemological schema. The camera corresponds to the level of *rikuy*, seeing and hearing. To be able to operate it only needs a little *yachay*, to edit needs a little more. But editing also needs *unanchay*, to read the significations of what is seen and heard (including music, of course), and *hamuttay*, in order to tell the story, construct the narrative. If this is not too fanciful, it is clear enough that video builds a close relationship between the interaction of different modes of knowledge to be found in the culture, and that the emphasis on one level rather than another varies according to the subgenre.

If seeing, knowing, speaking and hearing are brought together here, this also means that video speech acquires another crucial quality—its polyvalence, in which the spoken word belongs to a discourse where oral, aural, and visual forms of signification are fused. Consequently, video does not displace oral communication, but extends it, directly or indirectly. In the process, it stimulates oral forms of transmitting knowledge in ways that are not possible in writing alone, within the lettered city, whose hegemony it therefore challenges. The lettered city, according to the Uruguayan literary critic Angel Rama, is not only the city whose literacy gives it access to universal culture; it also provides the intellectual apparatus of power and authority, both colonial and postcolonial, of discipline, control and coercion.[20] This apparatus is cumbersome and resistant, and has already been thrown into disarray by radio and television when

[18] Schiwy, *Indianizing Film*, 71.

[19] Regina Harrison, cited in Schiwy, *Indianizing Film*, 54.

[20] Angel Rama, *The Lettered City* (Durham, N.C.: Duke University Press, 1996).

video comes along and begins to operate beneath its radar. In this way, *video indígena* is not only a mode of representing indigenous knowledge, but becomes an instrument for the negotiation of modernity—a modernity of which video is both agent and means of entry.

The situation of *video indígena* obliges us to think about different ways of experiencing modernity, or other forms of modernity. Schiwy points out that the video activists are training indigenous communicators who are not necessarily literate, and argues against the common notion of a teleological continuum from oral culture to literacy and modernity, or from photography to film to television to video.[21] When you stop and think, this is obviously correct: teleology fails with each new generation, which discovers all existing media together alongside each other—although some are regarded for one or another reason as either archaic or unattainable. Shiwy also questions the idea that the interaction of modern technology and subjectivity marks a determinate break with the premodern forms of oral culture. Video, she thinks, bypasses literacy. She points out that indigenous fiction videos are mostly spoken in the native languages, while factual genres use Spanish as a lingua franca; that both are easily subtitled, and facilitators can read out the subtitles for the illiterate.[22] Here again, video as speech act is reinforced and its social character confirmed.

6

A short documentary about indigenous video production, *La otra mirada* (*The Other Gaze*), made by the Bolivian group CEFREC for international audiences, makes the claim that indigenous media not only invite an exchange of gazes and perspectives on diverse issues felt in the communities to be pressing for attention, but they do so in a form in which the communities are themselves the protagonists, in a world of change and transformation that obliges them to find a way of answering back. We have seen that they do this not primarily by entering the big public sphere, but rather by creating a network that places diverse communities, cultures and ethnicities in contact with each other. At the dawn of the new millennium, much the same was true of *cine piquetero* in Argentina—communities as protagonists, public issues pressing for attention, the urgent need to answer back, and the strategy of alternative circulation.

Cine piquetero is perhaps the most extraordinary manifestation of grassroots video of recent years because it appeared in the midst of the country's economic breakdown. Came the collapse of the banks in the *Argentinazo* of December 2001, when the banks shuttered, and the country defaulted on its international debt and went through five presidents in twelve days. The effect, as De Carli described it soon after,

[21] Schiwy, *Indianizing Film*, 11, 84.
[22] Schiwy, *Indianizing Film*, 56.

was that "documentary was boosted by an explosive reality." Young filmmakers, possessing their own means of production, needed no funding or commissions to go out on the streets and film. The most interesting things were happening, "from spontaneous videos which record the popular mobilizations and the *cacerolazos* [casserole-bashing]—which are then sold on the streets from stalls piled with copies—to filmmakers who are turning to documentary, and who discover a know-how, even a certain Argentinean tradition, in the way of presenting or narrating what is going on."[23] These highly militant videos were mostly filmed by groups aligned with the popular organizations that began to organize themselves in response to the crisis, and were often made "almost anonymously"—that is, without individual credits—as an immediate response to an urgent situation. The movement quickly became known as *cine piquetero* after the *piquetes*—the picketers who make their voices heard by blocking roads and bridges. The work was shown at factories, community movement assemblies, local cafés and street festivals, but not on television or in the cinemas. Screened in meetings and assemblies, in parks and on the streets, bypassing the official media entirely, it entered a parallel and alternative public sphere lying outside the channels and tributaries of parliamentary democracy, but which is rooted instead in the popular movement itself.

A few of these groups date back before the *Argentinazo*, and already earlier that year, at the Mar de Plata film festival, Solanas, the old man of Third Cinema, praised the young activists for their passion, and for showing what never gets seen on television, even calling them the heirs of third cinema. Wishful thinking? It is not as if the new videographers themselves claimed such allegiance, in part because their knowledge of the 60s and its models was limited, in part because the political conjuncture had shifted so drastically that Marxist militancy held little attraction, and in part because they were now working with digital video, which offers novel possibilities.

Nevertheless there was a certain continuity. For example, a short video dating from 2002, made by journalists at the Universidad Popular Madres de Plaza de Mayo (Popular University of the Mothers of the Plaza de Mayo), *Los policias y los guardias*, which is both characteristic and unusual.[24] It is characteristic in drawing its footage from television—intercut with still photographs and treated to a little digital tweaking and some music added—in order to critique the coverage of an incident that took place in full view of the assembled media: the police attacked a *piquete* at Puente Pueyrredon, killing two demonstrators and wounding ninety more. It is unusual in that the video takes its title from the poem that forms the soundtrack, by the Salvadorean poet Roque Dalton. As the police attack the *piquete*, the poem berates those who were "also the people, / But with the excuse of hunger and unemployment / . . . accepted a gun, / A baton and a monthly salary / To defend those who cause hunger and unemployment." Voicing the

23 Quoted in Michael Chanan, *The Politics of Documentary* (London: BFI, 2007), 17–18.

24 "Los policias y los guardias," Ágora TV, at www.revolutionvideo.org/agoratv/secciones/movimientos_sociales/los_policias.html (accessed December 13, 2011).

video with a poem is atypical, but using a poem by a revolutionary writer from Central America who died in 1975 is clearly to link the popular unrest in Argentina with the broader history of struggle across the continent; and since the television reports presented the incident exclusively from the side of the police (including a commander who was one of the walking wounded), the poem, overlaid upon and interrupted by the news clips, also serves as a powerful critique of the tendentious nature of mainstream media reportage. An example of what an earlier generation of Latin American documentarists called *cine denuncia* (cinema of denunciation), the video turns the poem into an act of collective video speech.

A year after the *Argentinazo,* as many as forty groups of video filmmakers were working alongside the local assemblies, the workers' cooperatives who took control of bankrupt firms, and the women's groups, all of which came to function with a dynamic not usually found under capitalism. The people in these videos are representing themselves (and telling their elected representatives to beat it: "¡Que se vayan todos!"—"Let them all go!") with consequent effects on the form of address: "We talk to each other about us"— exactly like the *video indígena,* but here in the urban industrial setting of the great lettered city in crisis. Sharing the dynamic of popular protest, *cine piquetero* has presented a vivid panorama of the extent and sheer inventiveness of popular action through a wide range of forms, from short reports to music videos, in a style that could be called "participant reportage": fluid handheld camera, direct sound, street interviews, the same ingredients as television reportage but differently put together: sans commentary, crosscut with found images taken from television and the press, edited with a sense of irony and deconstructive intent, and often backed by the new Argentinean rock music.[25]

In short—and this is hardly surprising in the political circumstances—the sobriety of *video indígena* gives way here to the performative spirit that characterized the dynamic of popular protest on the streets—especially the action known as the *escrache.* This is a *lunfardo* or slang word, derived from the Italian *schiacciare,* to smash or crush, for a kind of fiesta of public shaming and denunciation. The practice was begun by the organization HIJOS (Children of the Disappeared), who would suddenly turn up outside the house of a former military torturer, for example, and mount a kind of performance in the street, with several hours of drumming and slogans, music, parades, pamphlets, even street theater. Some of those being denounced, the *escrachados,* hid themselves away, others fled; some responded with bullets. After December 2001, *escraches* began to be mounted against politicians, banks, and the mass media. The extraordinary spectacle of the *escrache* can be seen in several of these videos, and its spirit pervades the whole movement, which could consequently perhaps be called *video escrache*—a style that brings to the screen the same energy and popular feeling,

[25] For information and collections of work by the leading groups, see Ágora TV, at www.revolutionvideo.org/agoratv; Contraimagen, at www.contraimagen.org.ar; Grupo de Boedo, at www.boedofilms.com.ar; Grupo de Cine Insurgente, at www.cineinsurgente.org; and Ojo Obrero, at www.ojoobrero.org (all accessed December 13, 2011).

the same mixture of elements, the symbolic gestures and imagery, the same intent for the video not just to represent but itself to constitute a communicative action, that is, an act of video speech.

Video speech is not a singular concept. It is not a simple and uniform type of utterance. It is not formulaic. It is not a genre or subgenre. It isn't even a question of style, to which, like third cinema, it remains indifferent, happy to use any style or genre that suits its needs. Different conditions of production produce other forms of video speech. On the model of both *video indígena* and *cine piquetero*, it is polyvalent, mobile, and above all dialogical—a form of audiovisual utterance answering to the socialized conditions of its production, speaking directly to its intended audience whom it addresses as its potential co-producers. The crucial element is voice. It is video speech as a plural voice that carries the greater chance of upsetting established public discourse, of challenging and undermining the hegemonic ideologies of consensus politics, and these videos don't usually make it to either television or cinema.

Meanwhile, new forms of video speech are emerging on the internet. But this only raises new questions. What happens to the politics of speaking, hearing and listening in these conditions? Can internet video generate a collective form of video speech to match its capacity for the individual? What is the difference between collective viewing and reproduction on a remote screen, perhaps with headphones? If you take away the social environment of reception within the community, do you still have the same mode of address? Can a virtual community suffice? These are all open questions, which remain for further consideration.

References

Arend, Germán Liñero. *Apuntes para una historia del video en Chile*. Santiago: Ocho Libros, 2010.

Aufderheide, Pat. *The Daily Planet: A Critic on the Capitalist Culture Beat*. Minneapolis: University of Minnesota Press, 2000.

Beverley, John. *Against Literature*. Minneapolis: University of Minnesota Press, 1993.

Chanan, Michael. *The Politics of Documentary*. London: BFI, 2007.

Couldry, Nick. *Why Voice Matters*. London: Sage, 2010.

Cubitt, Sean. *Timeshift: On Video Culture*. London; New York: Routledge, 1991.

Deleuze, Gilles. *Cinema 2: The Time-Image*. Translated by Hugh Tomlinson and Robert Galeta. London: Athlone Press, 1989.

Espinosa, Julio García. "For an Imperfect Cinema." In *Twenty-Five Years of the New Latin American Cinema*, edited by Michael Chanan, 28–33. London: BFI and Channel Four, 1983.

Goldfarb, Brian. "Local Television and Community Politics in Brazil." In *Visible Nations, Latin American Cinema and Video*, edited by Chon Noriega, 263–284. Minneapolis: University of Minnesota Press, 2000.

Manuel, Peter. *Cassette Culture: Popular Music and Technology in North India*. Chicago: University of Chicago Press, 1993.

Marx, Karl. *The Eighteenth Brumaire of Louis Bonaparte*. Project Gutenberg, 2006, at http://www.gutenberg.org/files/1346/1346-h/1346-h.htm (accessed December 13, 2011).

Rama, Angel. *The Lettered City*. Durham, N.C.: Duke University Press, 1996.

Schiwy, Freya. *Indianizing Film, Decolonization, the Andes, & the Question of Technology*. New Brunswick, N.J.: Rutgers University Press, 2009.

Solanas, Fernando, and Octavio Getino. "Towards a Third Cinema." In *Twenty-five Years of the New Latin American Cinema*, edited by Michael Chanan, 17–27. London: BFI and Channel 4, 1983.

ANIMATED SOUNDS

CHAPTER 12

PIXAR AND THE ANIMATED SOUNDTRACK

DANIEL GOLDMARK

THE climax of Pixar's feature *Ratatouille* is almost literally a Proustian moment. While tasting a steaming forkful of the film's eponymous dish, restaurant critic Anton Ego instantaneously travels back to the Arcadian days of his youth in a synesthetic time warp. Colors, sounds, (implied) smells, and music coalesce in a moment of nostalgic (and oedipal) bliss as he recalls his mother effacing a boo-boo with a bowl of ratatouille. And all is well with the world once more.

Although Disney did not take the bold step of reviving Smell-o-Vision for a film largely about food (a comeback I would have greeted with relish), the evocatively created sights, sounds, and smells (imaginary though they might have been) made *Ratatouille* more than just another animated film. What sets Pixar apart, among other things, is that this nuanced take on music and sound design is far from happenstance. The studio routinely conceptualizes each film's soundtrack from the day it goes into production. Not only does this approach go against standard Hollywood practice—which puts the soundtrack at the lowest rungs of the production hierarchy—but it also shows that animated films can be made with as much care and precision as live-action films. In this chapter I explore Pixar's approach to music and the soundtrack to show how advances in sound design, as well as an evolving approach to film scoring taken by veteran Hollywood composers, have brought a new level of complexity and even respectability to the long-maligned animated feature. Through deftly crafted stories, animation, and soundtracks, these films have a striking capacity to evoke emotional responses in many new ways.

***

Since the release of its first feature, *Snow White and the Seven Dwarfs*, the Disney studio has largely encompassed—or, better yet, enveloped—any discussion of feature animation in Hollywood. For some perspective, consider that between 1937 and 1955 twenty-five animated features were released in the United States, only seven of which were not produced by Disney.[1] The place of Disney feature animation atop the proverbial heap in the cartoon world has been challenged by several studios in the past decade, and Disney can no longer claim to be the leader in the field. Although I do not discuss in detail the growth in feature animation since the 1990s, it is worth noting just how many big-budget or big-exposure animated films have appeared of late. (The exorbitant budgets are often attributable to the hiring of Hollywood stars to provide voices.) To name just a few, *The Simpsons Movie*, *Shrek the Third*, *Ratatouille*, *Bee Movie*, and *Kung Fu Panda* all appeared in less than a year's time. This new mass of features has shown that the standard Disney production template is now only one of a variety of successful options.

The first four Disney features—*Snow White*, *Pinocchio*, *Dumbo*, and *Bambi*—established the guidelines for music in feature-length cartoons (following similar trailblazing for general cartoon scoring in the first Disney sound cartoons in 1928). All four films basically adhered to the dominant structure of the late 1930s film musical, with songs dominating the soundtrack and significantly outweighing original underscoring. The men who scored animated films during Disney's lifetime—Frank Churchill, Leigh Harline, George Bruns, and Oliver Wallace, among others—were also responsible for scoring Disney's animated shorts. Disney made no clear distinction between composing for shorts and features: both formats were animated, and that seems to have been the overriding concern. Once the studio began regularly producing live-action films and television shows, certain composers, such as Bruns or Buddy Baker, found themselves working predominantly in those media. Looking at the credited film work of composers for other animation studios—Joe de Nat, James Dietrich, Darrell Calker, Carl Stalling, and Phil Scheib—we find that very few of them ever worked in live action, and almost never on first-run features.[2] This (possibly) unintentional division of labor suggests that some in the industry felt that animation and live action could not or should not mix. From the other side of the profession, only a few film composers known for live-action scoring ever dabbled in animation, and none of the composers who constitute the ever-concretizing canon of film music (Steiner, Korngold, Herrmann, Waxman, etc.) switched formats even once. Although animated film scores have received their share of popular recognition in the form of Oscars and other awards, an underlying professional disdain or dismissiveness seems to prevail regarding scoring for cartoons.[3]

[1] Of the remaining seven, all but two were produced abroad; those two were the Fleischer studio's features *Gulliver's Travels* (Fleischer, 1939) and *Mr. Bug Goes to Town* (Fleischer, 1941). Jerry Beck, *The Animated Movie Guide* (Chicago: Chicago Review Press, 2005).

[2] Carl Stalling did score exactly one reel of the Jack Benny film *The Horn Blows at Midnight* (Walsh, 1945); Scott Bradley composed some cues for several films at MGM. See Daniel Goldmark, *Tunes for 'Toons: Music and the Hollywood Cartoon* (Berkeley: University of California Press, 2005) for more information.

[3] In *Tunes for 'Toons* (Goldmark, 2005) I discuss Scott Bradley's unsuccessful campaign to have cartoon music taken more seriously.

When a rebirth of television and theatrical animation in Hollywood occurred in the 1980s, many of the old prejudices against composing for animation appeared to resurface. This time, however, not everyone bought into the stereotype. Alan Silvestri and Bruce Broughton, both established film composers by the mid-1980s, were tapped to provide music for *Who Framed Roger Rabbit?* and *Steven Spielberg Presents Tiny Toons Adventures*. Disney went to off-Broadway composer Alan Menken to compose music for what became the next golden age of its musicals, beginning with *The Little Mermaid*. It is now commonplace to find well-known composers such as Hans Zimmer, John Debney, and James Newton Howard scoring live-action and animated features alike. Not only does it seem as if animated films have become legitimate, but the phenomenon of very current, even cutting-edge film composers writing for animated films brings the most recent techniques and sounds to a long-ghettoized segment of the film scoring world.

Crushed under the weight of its own popularity, the Disney studio ensured that it would at least have a say in the production of the most popular and critically acclaimed animated films when it bought Pixar in 2006. The irony of this situation (at least for the sake of this chapter) is that the one thing that the powers that be at Pixar always agreed upon—and apparently still do—is that they did *not* want to make a musical film in the tradition of the Disney feature. And since all but a few features produced by Disney animation have had at least one musical number in the course of the story, the rhetorical bond between Disney films and musicals has become all but unbreakable.[4]

Of the many ways in which Pixar differentiated itself from the classic animated shorts and films produced by Disney, the complete shunning of the Disney musical archetype may be the most pronounced. As Disney reestablished its hold on the animated and live-action film musical throughout the 1990s and 2000s, Pixar seemed far more intent on revisiting old narrative tropes of the animation world (and the childhoods of many an adult): robots, insects, toys come to life, and superheroes. And though Pixar could not escape the historical legacy of Disney as the source of so many modern cartoon film protocols, the people most involved in steering the studio, including John Lasseter, Brad Bird, Pete Docter, and Andrew Stanton, made a deliberate decision to avoid the formulaic Disney musical.

This is not to imply that other studios have not taken on the challenge: going all the way back to *Gulliver's Travels* (Fleischer, 1939), the Fleischers' answer to Disney's *Snow White*, studios have been trying to match Disney's success with animated musicals. And while studios large and small turned out dozens of forgettable examples, the animated musicals that have resonated with critics and fans tend to be those that pay tribute to and/or mercilessly mock the Disney formula. The *Shrek* franchise took the very fairy tale characters that populate so many Disney features, got rid of the musical numbers, and put them all in a world together, with very successful results (financially if not critically). Without a doubt, the most incisive satire/tribute to the Disney musicals was *South Park: Bigger, Longer, and*

4 That said, I would be curious to see what Pixar might do if it faced the challenge of creating an animated antimusical—that is, an animated musical film that does not fall into the conventional claptrap that was parodied quite well in the live-action Disney film *Enchanted* (Lima, 2007).

Uncut, which spoofed and skewered every Disney song formula imaginable (the "I want another life" song, the villain song, the introductory jubilee, etc.).[5]

What, then, can we expect from an animated feature when a structural element that many might consider fundamental is missing? Is there anything different about the music in an animated feature as opposed to a live-action feature? Looking at the composers writing for Pixar would suggest the answer is no: Michael Giacchino (*The Incredibles, Ratatouille, Up*), Thomas Newman (*Finding Nemo, Wall-E*), and Randy Newman (*Toy Story, A Bug's Life, Toy Story 2, Monsters, Inc., Cars, Toy Story 3*) are all seasoned Hollywood veterans, with countless feature films and television series to their combined credit. Randy Newman's six films for Pixar might indicate that he has been pigeonholed as a cartoon composer, but his dozen live-action feature scores suggest otherwise. Thomas Newman has created some of the most influential scores in recent years, including *The Shawshank Redemption, American Beauty*, and the theme to *Six Feet Under*. These latter two composers are the living legacy of the Newman family in Hollywood, a musical dynasty that dates back to the earliest days of synchronized sound.

The relative newcomer, Michael Giacchino, got his start composing for video games, moved on to television and then films, and has been straddling the last two media ever since. He became a pop culture flavor-of-the-month due to his work on *Lost*, a television series for which both critics and fans exhibited a rabid affection. As he prepared to score the sixth and final season of the series, Giacchino was also busy working on no fewer than three big-budget feature films: *Star Trek, Land of the Lost*, and Pixar's *Up*. His combined work in television and film led to tremendous popular recognition (Grammy, Golden Globe, and Academy Awards for the score to *Up*), as well as critical attention, most visibly in two articles about Giacchino's music for *Lost* by *New Yorker* music critic Alex Ross.[6]

Giacchino's first work for Pixar, and the score that brought him public recognition, was *The Incredibles*, a throwback to 1950s action-hero B-movies with a distinctly contemporary spin ("supers" with normal lives trying to assimilate into regular society). He described his concept for the score in an interview:

> When I first met with Brad [Bird], he asked me what I grew up listening to. I told him I loved the *Pink Panther* movies, *Star Wars*, "Jonny Quest," "The Flintstones," "The Jetsons," "The Twilight Zone"—all these things. And we quickly realized what he and I both had a love for those 1960s jazz orchestra scores.... Brad's point was, when he was a kid he would hear that theme to "Jonny Quest" and would want to be Jonny Quest. And that's what he wanted for *The Incredibles*. He wanted the orchestral jazz energy that they used to have in the Bond movies, *Pink Panther* movies, and

[5] Some scholarly work on music in *South Park* is beginning to show up, including Per Broman, "Aesthetic Value, Ethos, and Phil Collins: The Power of Music in *South Park*," in *South Park and Philosophy: You Know, I Learned Something Today*, ed. Robert Arp (Maldon, MA: Blackwell Publishing, 2007), 236–249; and Toni Johnson-Woods, "Token, Give Me a Sweet Bass Line: Sounds of *South Park*," in *Blame Canada!: South Park and Contemporary Culture* (New York: Continuum, 2007), 119–135.

[6] Alex Ross, "The Spooky Fill," *New Yorker*, May 17, 2010, 60–67.

everything else I mentioned—the quasi-big band stuff. That's what he wanted in the score to his film.[7]

The score for *The Incredibles* is a smooth amalgam of action-film tropes as interpreted by a jazz orchestra: dramatic stings, powerful brass fanfares, and angular melodies. Some chase scenes have traditional low brass, low percussion, and strings, while others take on a more playful sound with a drum kit playing a swinging groove underneath tightly written brass lines.

Much more than just its soundtracks, however, makes Pixar distinctive. Perhaps the studio's success comes in part from the fact that it creates movies that happen to be animated, rather than allowing past perceptions of animation as just for kids to guide its work. It seems that the filmmakers at Pixar look at animation as a gift—a way of enabling an approach to storytelling, a medium that allows for the breaking of every law of physics and logic—not as a limitation.

The studio also takes a holistic approach when conceptualizing the universe in which a film's narrative unfolds. It isn't enough simply to create the story, write it, animate it, and film it; each film's production team immerses itself in details of every type imaginable for the newly created space—physical, geographical, spiritual, musical, etc.—so that they can write, animate, and otherwise create a film from *within* the narrative world.[8] Overall, this approach provides the feeling of watching a story unfold spontaneously, as if the filmmakers had always lived in this space and were just showing the audience a naturally occurring event.

Elsewhere I have written about the construction of time and place in Sylvain Chomet's 2003 film *The Triplets of Belleville*.[9] I was intrigued by Chomet's use of two classical works and an original jazz-oriented score, in combination with carefully chosen sound effects, to fill out a soundtrack that involved practically no dialogue. Looking back, I realize how odd it was that I never examined the construction of Pixar's (or Disney's) soundtracks from the same perspective—until we consider that the creation of such a space has never been a high priority for the Disney films. Certainly each Disney film creates a sumptuously eye-popping land in which the story unfolds. Dialogue, however, and song-and-dance numbers usually take the lead over the subtler parts of the soundtrack in these films. This is not so with Pixar's more recent output. There is no *place*, of course, when one is creating the soundtrack for an animated film. Live action comes with ambient noise, street sounds, and so forth (all of which are added and/or amplified in ADR). In animation the production team creates an entire soundscape from bottom to top. So

7 Dan Goldwasser, "Incredibly Lost with Michael Giacchino," *Soundtrack.net*, at http://www.soundtrack.net/features/article/?id=132 (accessed July 18, 2010).

8 When I visited Pixar in the fall of 2008 I saw some of the conceptual/inspirational art for *Up*, much of which had to do with 1930s adventurers, travel guides, and images of South America, plastered all over one part of the studio.

9 "Sonic Nostalgia and *The Triplets of Belleville*," in *Drawn to Sound: Animation Film Music and Sonicity*, ed. Rebecca Coyle (London: Equinox Books, 2010), 141–159.

when a Pixar team creates a new world, they indeed start from nothing more than an idea. They can conceptualize what their world will look, smell, and sound like—perhaps explaining in part why sound design has become so important in their films. I return to this idea when discussing *WALL-E*.

Musically, Pixar stands out from competitors in part because of the time and thought that go into creating what I call each film's musical profile; the studio has a far more nuanced and thought-out approach to creating a sonic profile for a film than is typical in Hollywood. This musical profile is just one component of the holistic approach mentioned previously. Composer Jack Curtis Dubowsky has demonstrated the extent to which music plays a role in the *conceptual* phases of animated films at Pixar, where he worked in the music editorial department under music editor David Slusser. Although we know that music's role in the production process typically begins earlier in animation than in live-action film, Dubowsky shows that, from the very moment a story is conceived, a pre-preproduction soundtrack—a conceptual mix tape, if you will—is constructed for the production team to use as inspiration, to get them into the spirit of their story.[10] This mix tape evolves as the film itself changes and eventually becomes the musical template for the composer to begin work scoring the film.

The films' final scores sound largely as we might expect: like action-thrillers, adventure-comedies, sci-fi epics, and all the other generic sounds predominant in Hollywood today. Yet occasionally a suspiciously cartoony sound creeps out, reminding us that we are still watching a cartoon grounded in the traditions of years past, which might include the odd bit of Mickey-Mousing. We can hear echoes of the older, Carl Stalling-inspired style (along with some fairly obvious references to *The Rite of Spring*, *Firebird*, and *Carmen*) when WALL-E scoots around the trash-filled earth, or when Remy the Rat races through a Parisian kitchen.

An overwhelming sense of nostalgia pervades all of Pixar's output. As opposed to Disney's near-obsession with family ties and fairy tales, Pixar's stories dwell on the past. The *Toy Story* films, for example, highlight lost childhood. Although each of the films has a different plot, all three have an overarching theme of loss and the fear of aging (in toy terms: becoming unused or obsolete). Because so many of the featured toys come from earlier times (Woody and the rest of the *Woody's Roundup* gang, Mr. Potato Head, Etch-a-Sketch, Speak & Spell, Chatter Telephone), the characters themselves are a constant reminder of times gone by. Indeed, *Toy Story 2* is largely about Woody's past as a star on an early television show in the 1950s, and in *Toy Story 3* a college-bound Andy must come to terms with the fact that he no longer plays with toys and ends up giving them to a young girl. The other Pixar films hold parts of the past in stasis as well, from the 1950s B-action movie *The Incredibles* to *Cars*, a paean to Route 66 and life before urban sprawl.

[10] Jack Curtis Dubowsky, "The Evolving 'Temp Score' in Animation," *Music, Sound & the Moving Image* 5, no. 1 (Spring 2011): 1–24. Dubowsky quotes Slusser as saying he had worked on an inspiration reel for *Ratatouille* for six years.

The studio's ability to infuse not only the sounds of the past, but an intangible desire to relive that past, into the soundtracks of its films is only one element of what makes the Pixar soundscape almost clotted with meanings. The multiple layers of effects and music serve to embellish the new worlds that Pixar seeks to fabricate and also evokes the historical, geographic, or purely imaginative spaces that the studio draws on as inspiration for those narrative spaces.[11] Before discussing the features, however, I look briefly at Pixar's shorts, the films that attuned Hollywood to Pixar as a force in animation, following a similar path to Disney's some sixty years earlier.

Pixar had been producing shorts for years before it attempted to tackle a feature-length film, thus following the precedent set by Fleischer and Disney. Each new short demonstrated Pixar's growing abilities and creativity with computer-based animation. Its earliest shorts first appeared at festival-style screenings (mostly at SIGGRAPH, an annual computer graphics conference.)[12] In 1999, with the release of *Toy Story 2*, the studio began packaging the shorts with the features, going back to previously made short films (*Luxo Jr.*, e.g., was shown with *Toy Story 2*, even though it dated originally from 1986). Since 2003 Pixar has created two shorts per year, releasing one theatrically with a feature and assigning the other as an extra to the DVD of that same feature, using the same characters from that film.[13]

The studio's playful nature is especially evident in the music composed for these shorts. Whereas the first Pixar short, *The Adventures of André and Wally B.*, features classical music (sections from Rossini's *Barber of Seville* and *William Tell* overtures), the next several films explore a variety of genres and styles: instrumental jazz (*Luxo Jr.*, *Red's Dream*), vocal jazz (*Knick Knack*), Western swing (*For the Birds*), and French accordion swing (*Geri's Game*). Unlike the features' compositional troika (Newman, Newman, and Giacchino), the shorts include scores by film composers (Scot Stafford, J. A. C. Redford, and Giacchino) and pop musicians (Bobby McFerrin, Bud Luckey), as well as having scores based around pop songs by performers such as Riders in the Sky and Gus Viseur.

What the shorts gain from this array of composers, styles, and genres is an adventurous and stimulating musical palette.[14] Because these films operate on a limited timeline, so to speak—each is only about seven to eight minutes long—everything in the films must work very efficiently, from the plot to the music.

The shorts often contain oblique or downright obvious references to the state of being animated; they can take all the positive and negative attributes of animation and use

[11] For another take on Pixar's soundtrack and nostalgia, see Kathryn A. T. Edney and Kit Hughes, "'Hello WALL-E!': Nostalgia, Utopia, and the Science Fiction Musical," in *Sounds of the Future: Essays on Music in Science Fiction Film* (Jefferson, N.C.: McFarland & Company, 2010), 44–66.

[12] Amid Amidi, *The Art of Pixar Short Films* (San Francisco: Chronicle Books, 2009), 17, 20, 24–25.

[13] These latter films include *Jack-Jack Attack* (drawing from *The Incredibles*), *Mater and the Ghostlight* (*Cars*), *Your Friend the Rat* (*Ratatouille*), *BURN-E* (*WALL-E*), and *Dug's Special Mission* (*Up*).

[14] This musical variety is only evident when we examine the shorts as a group; most people only see them in theaters before the feature begins, just as in the earlier days of theatrical animation. And just like theatrical shorts, which can be watched in rapid succession on DVD, so can the Pixar shorts (those released prior to 2008) be seen all in a single sitting on the *Pixar Short Films Collection* DVD.

them to their advantage (or not). Certain facets of storytelling are often exaggerated or completely taken for granted without a trace of self-awareness, such as the resilience (or complete invulnerability) of living beings. It is as if the shorts are a safe space for the writers and animators to be adventurous and silly. The same is true of the soundtrack: Bobby McFerrin's entirely sung soundtrack for *Knick Knack* adds a layer of comedy that seems unimaginable through any other means; the battle between two musicians makes the story the soundtrack in *One Man Band*; and in *Presto* (the short that preceded *WALL-E*) Scot Stafford channels Carl Stalling, with instrumental nuances catching each action or reaction of a magician and his rabbit.

***

The two films that I want to focus on in the rest of this discussion—*Up* and *WALL-E*—address different senses of loss or longing, whether for a person, a location, or an ideal. In each case the music and sound design are instrumental in creating the sense of space and in turn amplifying the feeling of longing created not only in the characters, but also in the audience, which is naturally meant to empathize with the protagonists.

Although the premise for *Up* is original—a widower, Carl, uses several thousand balloons to float his home to South America to find the place of his and his (dead) wife's dreams, Paradise Falls—the narrative's driving theme of love at first sight that lasts forever is about as Hollywood as it gets. The film's action does not get under way until *after* Carl's wife has died, her passing ultimately motivating him. The filmmakers must sell the audience completely on the idea of Carl and Ellie's everlasting love in a short time in order to get to the actual story of Carl and Russell's adventure. They devised an extended montage that encapsulates Carl and Ellie's life together, from their marriage until her death many happy years later. Composer Michael Giacchino described the unusual trajectory of the narrative, and how it affected the score, in an interview:

> Pete [Docter] and I talked about the character of Ellie. She really is only technically in the first third of the movie but we wanted to do something that would keep her in the movie throughout. One of the things we talked about was, "How do we keep her alive in this movie? Okay. We need Ellie's theme! We need a theme in this film that is going to start off when they are young kids. It will be very simple and then grow with a kind of elegance as she gets older into a bold statement when Carl decides, 'I'm going to change my life. I'm going to go and live this dream.' "
>
> It was a theme that needed to start off almost as nothing and turn into something so huge and then come back to something very small again. That was our way of keeping the character of Ellie involved in the story. It's really her spirit that keeps Carl going.... It was an incredible emotional hurdle to jump because we really wanted it to work so perfectly.[15]

[15] "ScoreKeeper Chats with Composer Michael Giacchino about LAND OF THE LOST, UP, and STAR TREK!" at http://www.aintitcool.com/node/43054 (accessed November 14, 2010).

Director Pete Docter stated that since they knew the story was going to commence with an extended montage on Carl and Ellie's life together, they wanted to use music that was of the couple's time. This choice also governs the waltz theme that pervades the film, a 1920s jazz combo piece inspired by a tune by Ferde Grofé: "Alice Blue" from Grofé's suite *Three Shades of Blue* (1928).[16] This sequence is poignant not just in the way it sums up a lifelong relationship, but because it sets up the remainder of the film both dramatically and musically: Carl's desire to pursue Ellie's dream.

Before the montage of the couple's life, we see how they meet as children; they are brought together by their mutual admiration for shamed explorer Charles Muntz. At first the quiet Carl is fearful of the talkative tomboy Ellie, but quickly he becomes smitten with her—marked most clearly by the first appearance of Ellie's theme, from which the music for the montage will grow. The sequence features the instruments of a small jazz ensemble of winds, brass, piano, and occasional swells of strings for emotional punctuation. Giacchino uses muted trumpet and violin as the two main melodic instruments for the happy times and brings in the piano for the sad. By using a short, memorable theme for the montage, Giacchino ensures that viewers will tie not just the images of the sequence to the melody, but the feelings—joy, despair, fear—that those images evoke as well.

The montage tells the story of Carl and Ellie's relationship solely through music and images. The scoring here is originally composed and is thus unburdened by the structure (or lyrics) of a preexisting song or tune (assuming that no one recognizes the theme's progenitor in "Alice Blue"). The stream of images, veritable snapshots of a happy life, helps to summarize many years in just a few minutes. The pacing slows considerably when we see a doctor explaining to the couple why Ellie cannot have children; the music almost stops, implying an end to their happy story. Carl eventually reminds Ellie of her dream to visit Paradise Falls; she takes heart and sees life positively again, and the waltz begins anew. Time jumps forward in a clever sequence showing Ellie adjusting Carl's necktie, and then just close-ups of the ties themselves, each one on screen for only a second or two, shifting quickly through different widths and fabrics, ending finally with a black bow tie, at which point we once again see the happy couple, aged many years into gray-haired seniors. The waltz finally comes to a bitter close as we see Ellie in the hospital, tacitly giving Carl permission to pursue her dreams as she pushes her "My Adventure Book" to him, then transitions to Carl walking into his home, now alone.

Once Carl floats his house to South America, he and his unwilling sidekick Russell accidentally discover that they have made their way to Paradise Falls. As bittersweet as Carl's solo trip to the falls is, Ellie is also present in spirit, embodied in the house. Several times Carl speaks to the house—the home he created with his wife—as if he is speaking directly to Ellie. The score strengthens the connection, as Ellie's theme occurs every time the house reminds Carl (or the viewer) of their relationship, or whenever *her* dream of traveling to Paradise Falls comes into play in the plot. Ellie's theme ultimately represents the sound—or emotion—that Carl is trying to reacquire by living his wife's dream. By

[16] Pete Docter, interview with author, February 1, 2010.

the end, when Carl has defeated the mad Muntz and taken possession of his massive airship, we see that Carl has lived not only his wife's childhood wish, but also his own, of becoming an adventurer.

Thus Ellie's theme, introduced in the opening minutes of the movie, operates in profound ways. Viewers are set to weeping before the action really begins, because Ellie's life ends and Carl is left alone. But it is precisely because we see the couple's life narrated so eloquently and sweetly and understand something of their relationship that the rest of the plot can proceed with resonance and heightened affect. The theme, used to represent alternately a person, an object, a place, and a dream, becomes the audience's reminder of Carl's quest and Ellie's spirit.

***

WALL-E presents an anomalous case in light of Pixar's output: not only does the film eschew dialogue for its first thirty minutes (almost a third of the film), but it also may be as close as Pixar has yet come to creating a film that typifies some of the characteristics—or expectations—of the mainstream Disney musical, a point I return to presently. Also unusual for Pixar is that the primary narrative arc revolves around a love story. Love is a motivating factor in other Pixar films (Remy's love for cooking in *Ratatouille*; Sully's love for Boo in *Monsters, Inc.*; Marlin's love for his son, Nemo, in *Finding Nemo*; Carl's love for Ellie in *Up*), but this is the first typically "romantic" arc (boy finds girl, boy loses girl, boy reunites with girl) the studio has used for the driving force of the central narrative. Pixar being Pixar, however, the studio takes the expectations for a love story and shapes them with a very new mold. In this case, the twist is that the protagonists are both robots and should not (at least not in an Asimovian world) be able to feel such complex emotions as love.

The complete absence of dialogue during the first act of *WALL-E* (save the singing coming from WALL-E's VCR and a videotaped message from Buy 'n' Large, the corporation mainly responsible for humanity's abandonment of Earth) drew comparisons from many critics to the work of Buster Keaton, Charlie Chaplin, and Jacques Tati—and indeed, the writers and animators prepared for the film by watching Keaton, Chaplin, and Harold Lloyd films.[17] This "silent aesthetic" freed the soundtrack from what is typically its dominant aural component and thus allowed music and effects to drive the story completely. (This tactic was used successfully in an animated film five years earlier, *The Triplets of Belleville*.) For this reason, *WALL-E* is probably the richest example of a Pixar film's creation of place through sound: it is our world, but no longer really familiar in that way. No humans live on the planet; only machines and some forces of nature (e.g., a windstorm) fill up the otherwise bare sonic landscape. In such an empty space—empty of any organic life-form, that is—all the sounds produced take on extra resonance.

[17] For one such review, see David Edelstein, "'Wall-E' Is a Masterpiece for the Ages," *New York Magazine*, June 28, 2009, at http://nymag.com/daily/movies/2008/06/walle_pixar.html (accessed September 9, 2010). Tasha Robinson, "Interview: Andrew Stanton," *The Onion A.V. Club*, June 25, 2008, at http://www.avclub.com/articles/andrew-stanton,14263/ (accessed September 9, 2010).

Ben Burtt was brought in as sound designer and supervising sound editor. He also provided the voice of WALL-E (having developed the voice for another diminutive sci-fi creature, E.T. the Extra-Terrestrial). Burtt's work on all six *Star Wars* films would have amply sufficed to ensure his place in film history, but his credits extend far and wide in the industry. Following Pixar's holistic approach to production, Burtt created a thorough sound profile for WALL-E's world. He stated in an interview, "There were more sound files in *WALL-E* then [*sic*] any single feature film I've ever worked on, about 2500, because every character has a set of sounds and there are [*sic*] lots of movement and lots of dense activity."[18] Although Burtt is known for creating sounds himself, he is equally fond of using tried-and-true methods: "You know, it's a tradition in animation to have sound effects machines. This goes back to the earliest days of Disney cartoons—like wind machines and blowing machines and things like that. We actually built several things so we could perform WALL-E sounds that way."[19] The real challenge, Burtt noted, is that not only do robots need to sound persuasive, but they are *animated* robots, which compounds the difficulty for viewers to buy into the idea that what they are seeing is real or at least convincing.

A profoundly ironic sense of humor pervades the film. Although humans have left the planet, all their crap remains. The film dwells on the zeniths and nadirs of humankind's accomplishments, mainly through references to pop culture and consumer goods. WALL-E's home is filled to overflowing with Zippo lighters, rubber ducks, compact discs, and other detritus he has collected while working as Earth's last functioning trash compactor. While contemporary films need no excuses for using anachronistic or otherwise out-of-place songs, I read the film's three explicit musical references as simply extending the survey of popular culture into the soundtrack. While Eve begins her search on Earth for plant life, WALL-E follows her around like a lovesick puppy, trying vainly to look inconspicuous as he constantly crashes into things. Thus an entire sequence of Chaplinesque pratfalls becomes a love montage with the addition of Louis Armstrong's idiosyncratic voice singing a chorus of "La Vie en rose" (which unlike the other two songs discussed below is entirely nondiegetic and does not originate from the landscape of mass detritus).

Once we move to the Axiom, the spaceship on which humanity ekes out an existence as overfed and understimulated chair potatoes, we are treated to two references to *2001* (Kubrick, 1968). The ship's corpulent captain enters the bridge and goes through his morning routine, underscored by Strauss's "Blue Danube Waltz." At the film's climax, as the ship's autopilot (Auto) tries to prevent the deployment of "Operation Recolonize," which would send the ship back to Earth for the first time in 700 years, the captain rises unsteadily to stand, probably for the first time in decades, and then attempts to wrest control of the ship from Auto. The opening notes of Strauss's *Also Sprach Zarathustra*,

[18] "Ben Burtt Interview, Wall-E," at http://www.moviesonline.ca/movienews_14930.html (accessed November 14, 2010).

[19] "Ben Burtt Interview, Wall-E."

most famously associated with *2001*'s HAL (another disobedient computer running a spaceship), provide a not-too-subtle bit of underscoring for the captain's struggle. Not only is Auto similar to HAL in appearance (they both have a single red "eye"), but the music also refers to the sequence with primitive humanoids early in *2001*, drawing a parallel between primeval man (using rudimentary tools) and future man (barely able to stand upright).[20]

Let us return to the notion of *WALL-E* as musical. The film uses the idea of the musical as an agent for both nostalgia and love. It seems as if love is a thing of the past. We see no close relationships on the Axiom—even the babies and children are reared by robots—and it is only because of WALL-E's accidental interventions that two people stop staring at their computer screens long enough to find each other. WALL-E believes he has found that special someone (something?) in EVE and uses what he learns about interacting with others from an actual musical as his model.

Make no mistake: there are no formal musical numbers in *WALL-E*, or anything resembling them—yet the film includes two songs from the Barbra Streisand/Walter Matthau film *Hello Dolly!* (Kelly, 1969), "It Only Takes a Moment" and "Put on Your Sunday Clothes." Director Andrew Stanton described the epiphany that led him to use the musical thus:

> [W]hen I found "It Only Takes a Moment," it just became this godsend because I was always looking for ways to tell the story without the need to use conventional dialogue. This song became a great device for showing WALL-E's interest in what love is, and it gave him a way to convey his love for EVE. I happened to have read somewhere that holding hands is the most intimate public display of affection, which led to the idea of WALL-E learning that action by watching the movie.[21]

Here, then, is the motivation for the musical: it provides the robot with an idea about companionship or love that he wants to fulfill. And really, what better, what more stereotypical source than a mainstream Hollywood musical film? *WALL-E* actually *begins* with the song "Put on Your Sunday Clothes," with varying views of outer space seen as the words, "Out there, there's a world outside of Yonkers," are heard. From the first seconds of *WALL-E*, a musical is setting the stage for the immediate action as well as the larger plot.

Both songs appear a handful of times throughout *WALL-E*, most importantly when WALL-E is entertaining EVE in his "home" and is showing her all the random stuff he has collected in an effort to get her attention. She doesn't seem to understand his

[20] Of the many other pop references in the film, one in particular refers to other outer space odysseys: Sigourney Weaver, star of many sci-fi films herself (in particular the *Alien* series), provides the voice of the Axiom.

[21] I found the fact that WALL-E favors "Put on Your Sunday Clothes" especially ironic when we see that everyone on board the Axiom wears exactly the same red all-purpose unitard. Chris Willman, "'WALL-E' Meets 'Dolly!'" *Entertainment Weekly*, June 14, 2008, at http://www.ew.com/ew/article/0,,20211943,00.html# (accessed September 2010).

obsession with the musical at first and resists his attempts to hold her "hand" (an action he learned from the film). But she realizes WALL-E's devotion and goodness: her attitude eventually changes, and she becomes protective and even affectionate with him. Either the soundtrack or the video and soundtrack from the two *Hello Dolly!* songs recur at key scenes in *WALL-E*, as if to remind the robots (and the audience) what the sentiment should be at that moment. When EVE revives WALL-E at the film's finale, she is holding his hand, just as the characters in "It Only Takes a Moment" do; this is the gesture that WALL-E has been seeking to imitate throughout the film. The videotape is "coincidentally" playing that very scene just as the lovers finally come together and the film comes to a close.

Stanton keeps *Hello Dolly!* from taking over the narrative by forcing the viewer only to see the film as WALL-E sees it: played from a dilapidated videocassette, or with only the sound and no visuals whatsoever. This doubly mediated presentation emphasizes that like everything else left behind on Earth, the musical is a reminder of a time past. And because *Hello Dolly!* is a film from the 1960s about life in the 1890s, it imbues *WALL-E* with a sense of embedded nostalgia or a fabricated longing for a lost time and place (the 1890s) represented in a film re-creating (in the 1960s) that time and place. *Hello Dolly!* is itself a paean to life in fin-de-siècle America, created at a complicated time in America's history, when many looked to the past for answers and comfort. *WALL-E* thus uses the sounds and voices of another era to evoke a keen sense of nostalgia.

***

The aesthetics of the animated feature have changed considerably since the time of Walt Disney. Stories no longer convey a simplified moral universe of good versus bad; animation is accomplished by any number of technical means; and Hollywood stars lend their voices and personae to films, rather than letting the animation speak for itself. Musically we find that musicals are no longer the de facto format of choice, nor are the composers for animated features typecast as such. As composers like Giacchino and Newman continue to challenge and expand notions of what cartoon music can do both descriptively and emotionally, the possibilities for animated features can only grow. Perhaps maybe even Pixar will do a fully formed musical... someday.

References

Amidi, Amid. *The Art of Pixar Short Films*. San Francisco: Chronicle Books, 2009.

Beck, Jerry. *The Animated Movie Guide*. Chicago: Chicago Review Press, 2005.

Broman, Per. "Aesthetic Value, Ethos, and Phil Collins: The Power of Music in *South Park*." In *South Park and Philosophy: You Know, I Learned Something Today*, edited by Robert Arp, 236–249. Maldon, Mass.: Blackwell Publishing, 2007).

Dubowsky, Jack Curtis. "The Evolving 'Temp Score' in Animation." *Music, Sound and the Moving Image* 5, no. 1 (Spring 2011): 1–24.

Edelstein, David. "'Wall-E' Is a Masterpiece for the Ages." *New York Magazine*, June 28, 2009, at http://nymag.com/daily/movies/2008/06/walle_pixar.html (accessed September 9, 2010).
Edney, Kathryn A. T., and Kit Hughes. "'Hello WALL-E!': Nostalgia, Utopia, and the Science Fiction Musical." In *Sounds of the Future: Essays on Music in Science Fiction Film*, edited by Mathew J. Bartkowiak, 44–66. Jefferson, N.C.; London: McFarland & Company, Inc., 2010.
Goldmark, Daniel. *Tunes for 'Toons: Music and the Hollywood Cartoon*. Berkeley: University of California Press, 2005.
Goldmark, Daniel. "Sonic Nostalgia and *The Triplets of Belleville*." In *Drawn to Sound: Animation Film Music and Sonicity*, edited by Rebecca Coyle, 141–159. London: Equinox Books, 2010.
Goldwasser, Dan. "Incredibly Lost with Michael Giacchino." *Soundtrack.net*, at http://www.soundtrack.net/features/article/?id=132 (accessed July 18, 2010).
Johnson-Woods, Toni. "Token, Give Me a Sweet Bass Line: Sounds of *South Park*." In *Blame Canada!: South Park and Contemporary Culture*, 119–135. New York: Continuum, 2007.
Paik, Karen. *To Infinity and Beyond! The Story of Pixar Animation Studios*. San Francisco: Chronicle Books, 2007.
Robinson, Tasha. "Interview: Andrew Stanton." *The Onion A.V. Club*, June 25, 2008, at http://www.avclub.com/articles/andrew-stanton,14263/ (accessed September 9, 2010).
Ross, Alex. "The Spooky Fill." *New Yorker*, May 17, 2010, 60–67.
"ScoreKeeper Chats with Composer Michael Giacchino about LAND OF THE LOST, UP, and STAR TREK!" at http://www.aintitcool.com/node/43054 (accessed November 14, 2010).
Wells, Paul. "To Sonicity and Beyond! Gary Rydstrom and Quilting the Pixar Sound." *Animation Journal* 17 (2009): 23–35.
Willman, Chris. "'WALL-E' Meets 'Dolly!'" *Entertainment Weekly*, June 14, 2008, at http://www.ew.com/ew/article/0,,20211943,00.html# (accessed September 9, 2010).

CHAPTER 13

NOTES ON SOUND DESIGN IN CONTEMPORARY ANIMATED FILMS

RANDY THOM

Directors of contemporary animated feature films use the word "cartoon" almost exclusively as a pejorative. As a sound designer, one of the first things nearly all of them tell me these days is that they want their films to sound essentially like live-action films, specifically not "cartoony." They revere the sound and visual styles of the classic Warner Bros. shorts featuring Bugs Bunny, the Road Runner, and so forth, but they have little or no interest in emulating those styles. One reason may be duration. Sustaining that level of stylization and action for the length of a short film of a few minutes is one thing; it's quite another to try it for a feature-length production. How many frying pan hits on the head and corkscrewing body stretches can an audience take in rapid succession? (*Who Framed Roger Rabbit* is a well-known feature-length film with lots of "toony" elements, but they account for less than half of its content.) Another reason is no doubt the feeling that the slapstick boing-boing thing has been done, so why not try something new? I suspect that still another reason is the aspiration of many contemporary animation directors to do live-action films as well, or at least to bridge the gap between animation and live action to garner more respect for animation. One way to do that, they figure, is with sound.

I am often asked about the differences between doing sound for live-action and for animated films. There are fewer differences than one might assume. My process as a sound designer was essentially the same on the Robert Zemeckis live-action sci-fi film *Contact* and the Brad Bird animated sci-fi film *The Incredibles*. Because there were many, many visuals in *Contact* that were created using computer graphics techniques, creating sound effects for those sequences was very much like creating sound effects for *The Incredibles*. Even the purely live-action sequences in *Contact* also needed to be enhanced in postproduction by sound effects that could not have been gathered during principal photography, because they call for a larger-than-life aesthetic.

It is often assumed that creating the sound design for an animated film is more difficult than it is for live action. That is not necessarily true. In terms of sound effects, the number of individual sounds recorded, gathered from libraries, fabricated specifically for that film, and cut into mixable tracks tends to be about the same for a large-scale animated film and a large-scale live-action film. In big budget live-action films very little usable sound is recorded while the cameras are rolling, so most of it has to be invented in postproduction anyway.

The process for generating recordings of dialogue for animated films is where the stark contrast exists with live action. In most animated films, certainly most produced in the United States, initial dialogue recording either happens before any animation has been done or is contemporaneous with the earliest efforts at very crude animation on a project. So the typical animated film begins its life as essentially a radio play with very crude drawings, often static stick figures, some music, and a few sound effects. There is near-total reliance on dialogue to make the story clear at this early point in production. Of necessity, the dialogue is nearly nonstop; otherwise the small test audiences would be confused about what is going on. Later, as visuals, music, and sound effects become more highly developed in a sequence, an effort is made to "thin out" the dialogue a bit, but contemporary American animation still tends to be a dialogue-driven form. Anime is usually done differently. In that genre the dialogue is often not even written until animation is almost finished. Because there is no tradition of lipsynch dialogue in anime, this "reverse" approach poses no problem and is even seen as preferable by many anime directors, including Mamoru Oshii, with whom I have worked on three feature films.

Mr. Oshii's highly stylized visuals opened many doors for subjective use of sound as I worked with him on *Ghost in the Shell 2*. In one scene the character Batou is in a shoot-out with enemies in a convenience store. Most of the scene is in slow motion, which puts us in a subjective space and allowed me to create a track that was hyperfocused on individual sounds, which in turn allowed each sound to be more expressive and to carry more emotion. A more conventional visual approach to this kind of scene, featuring gunshots, glass breaking, characters screaming, and a big musical score, would have been a cacophony, just lots of incoherent noise. Instead, stylization in the visuals and the sound allows us to focus, to be more precise and dynamic emotionally, as opposed to presenting a wall of indistinguishable sounds and hoping that will translate as "exciting."

There is one area in which sound for some contemporary animation is substantially more ambitious than sound for live action: early collaboration. On an increasing number of animated films, the sound designer is being asked to create speculative sounds for characters, places, and events as a way of stimulating the imaginations of the animators. On *How to Train Your Dragon* I fabricated many sounds for dragon vocalizations and dragon fire before any animation at all had been done for those sequences. The sounds that I made suggested possible visual imagery to the animators. Then, based on the animation they created, I modified the sounds or reworked them entirely, either of which sometimes suggested still more visual possibilities. The idea of getting a film sound designer involved during preproduction is one I am proud to say I have been proselytizing about for many years, and it's very gratifying to see it gaining some traction in the industry. In the late 1990s I wrote an essay, "Designing a Movie for Sound," that discusses in some detail the nuts-and-bolts ways a filmmaker can begin to design a film for sound, beginning with the script.[1]

The dragon character called Toothless in *How to Train Your Dragon* was developed over a period of three years of experimenting with visuals and sounds. Early on the idea was that Toothless was a baby dragon, and I fabricated many, many baby dragon vocalizations using recordings of raccoons chirping, puppies yelping, and my own voice pitched up two or three octaves. This character needed to sound fierce in some moments and lovable in others. The raw animal sounds we use, like the raccoons, are usefully exotic, but they typically have little emotional range. That is why it is almost always necessary to use human vocalizations as well, often attempting to mimic some aspect of the animal accompanist as we perform them, to provide the broader range of emotions.

There is a temptation in contemporary animation to "flesh out" the sound effects and music tracks extensively during the early work on the visuals. When the visuals are still simple and crude, often only stick figures, elaborate and continuous music and sound effects are a useful storytelling crutch to make a sequence coherent and emotionally powerful. Unfortunately, once the visuals are complete and the crutch is no longer needed, it tends to stay. In my opinion this presents a problem of story focus. This legion of sounds, both concrete and musical, often tends to blunt the impact of the piece by making it less dynamic and less focused.

Coraline is a wonderful example of the virtues of using sound sparingly. Henry Selick, *Coraline*'s director, is a stickler for focused storytelling achieved by precisely presenting to the audience exactly what it needs to hear from moment to moment and nothing more. He instructed us specifically to avoid complex background sounds in most scenes because he thought, correctly in my opinion for this film, that they would be distracting. There is a controversy in Hollywood film sound circles these days about this issue of backgrounds. Some supervising sound editors and sound designers feel strongly that a film without complex and diverse ambient, atmospheric background sound effects is deficient. I couldn't disagree more. In my opinion the "background sound style" should be congruous with that of the film as a whole. The storytelling style of some films calls for richly layered and constantly shifting background ambience; the style of others does not.

On *Coraline* we could have attempted to add lots of sonic character to the house that the title character's family moves into. It is an old wooden house with many floors, so creaking and groaning would have seemed authentic and might have made the place seem creepier and more alienating to poor Coraline. Henry's choice was to have the house be mostly silent as the little girl explores its many rooms and hallways. The result may be even more mysterious and alienating than it would have been with more sound effects, and the few places where we did add a sonic flourish make more powerful statements in their isolation. The point I want to make is that each film I work on calls for its own sound design aesthetic. I try to make as few assumptions as possible at the beginning of each project, then work with the director to discover what seems to work best.

[1] Randy Thom, "Designing a Movie for Sound" (1999), at http://www.filmsound.org/articles/designing_for_sound.htm (accessed June 3, 2013).

Bob Zemeckis may be taking this "no backgrounds" aesthetic even further than Henry Selick. Zemeckis has been exclusively involved with "motion capture" (mo-cap) animated films since *The Polar Express*, which was released in 2004. The mo-cap process begins with having actors wear suits that are covered with dots. More dots are placed on their faces. A multitude of infrared cameras follow the actors as they perform scenes on a specially designed set. One potential advantage of mo-cap is that the director can choose whether the eventual look of the characters will be similar to the actors who did the mo-cap performance, or completely different. For example, Jim Carrey played both the young and old Scrooge in Zemeckis's *A Christmas Carol*. The younger Scrooge looks quite similar to Jim Carrey, but the old Scrooge, whose features have been exaggerated to mirror his change in personality, looks much less like Jim Carrey. With mo-cap, adults can play children, humans can play characters that eventually look like animals, and so forth.

In mo-cap the actors' dialogue is recorded on the set, just as it is in a live-action shoot, with a microphone on a boom. Because the actors are employing the full range of movement as they perform the scene, their voices are modulated appropriately and naturally as they move and in the end often sound more "realistic" than in a typical animated film, for which the dialogue is usually recorded with an actor standing still in front of a microphone on a floor stand that doesn't move. A notable recent exception is *The Fantastic Mr. Fox*, in which much of the dialogue was recorded outdoors on a farm, with the actors moving as if they were in a live-action film.

Zemeckis's preferred sound design approach on *The Polar Express*, *Beowulf*, and *A Christmas Carol* has been to focus strictly, sometimes exclusively, on one or two principal, foreground sound effects at any given moment. On the other hand, the focus is dynamic because it is more or less constantly shifting from sound A to sound B to sound C, often only lingering on each for a second or two. This technique gives the audience the impression that it is hearing a much broader range of sounds simultaneously than is actually the case. The ideal result is clarity of message. The sonic landscape is not muddied up with unnecessary sounds that will tend to mask and thereby emasculate one another. The sounds are chosen carefully to make each moment "realistic" enough to be believable and emotionally on point.

The term "realistic" is problematic as it applies to any film, especially an animated film. Directors often put a premium on "realistic" sounds in both live action and animation because they feel "adding realism" is one of sound's principal jobs: to provide a solid base for the fanciful visual images so that they don't float away, out of control. One example is footsteps. As Ellie traverses the metal catwalk in the giant machine, we had to make sure that her footsteps seemed "real." They had to sound metallic and to be in exact sync with each visual footfall, but also subtle enough so that they didn't call too much attention to themselves; just loud enough to be heard, but not any louder, because being too loud would make them seem artificial and could even have been unintentionally comical. Her footsteps "literally" ground her as she moves through this "incredible" visual environment. Realism is tricky indeed.

I am particularly proud of the first few minutes of *The Polar Express*. Bob Z. designed that sequence very precisely with sound in mind, and it is a playground for sound design.

I say playground not because it calls for lots of sounds, but rather because the perception and experience of sound is so profoundly worked into the story. Our narrator tells us in voice-over that as a child he would lie in bed on Christmas Eve listening for the bells on Santa's sleigh. We are therefore immediately placed in the point of view of this child as we see him waiting silently for magic to happen. Only the ticking of his bedside clock is heard. The clock stops—is this Santa's magic, or are we in the child's dream?—and suddenly we do hear the very distant sound of sleigh bells. The child rushes to the window to try to catch a glimpse of the sleigh, but sees nothing, and the sound of the bells disappears. A few moments later a deep rumble begins, and it grows louder, and louder, and louder until everything in the child's bedroom is shaking. A giant steam locomotive, the Polar Express, arrives outside his house, and the little boy goes outside in the snow to get close to it. Zemeckis wanted this train to seem almost like a living thing. I designed its expulsions of steam to be like breaths. The screeching and groaning of metal are like the old engine's bones creaking as it comes to rest. Bob told me there would be no musical score in this sequence, so I designed those metallic sounds to be especially "musical," creating many of them by bowing large pieces of sheet metal with bass violin bows. Yet there are never more than two sounds heard simultaneously.

The Incredibles and *Bolt* are animated films at the opposite end of the sonic complexity spectrum from the recent Zemeckis films. I think they are no less clear and on point than the Zemeckis films I just referred to, but the process of getting to that clarity and emotional focus is more difficult, or at least different, given that the directors of those films wanted to have a more complex and multilayered sonic landscape in each moment. I do believe that one or two sounds should predominate in each moment, but in a scene like the opening of *The Incredibles*, which is a gun battle during a car chase, it is possible to have several layers of simultaneous sound as long as there is, for lack of a better description, a "loudness hierarchy" among them. One technique for accomplishing this is to allocate parts of the sonic frequency spectrum to each category or group of sounds. For example, car engines can occupy most of the bass end of the spectrum in a given moment, while voices occupy most of the mid range of frequencies. The engine sounds therefore have to be designed to be bass intensive.

All of the sound crafts in film, except for that of the composer, have too often been categorized, misguidedly, as "technical" jobs. All sound people tend to be referred to as "engineers." Though we use technology, just as all the other film crafts do, making artistic decisions is the essential role of the sound designer in animated and live-action films. We have initial discussions with animation directors about the story and the principal characters, human and nonhuman. Then we begin to fabricate and collect sounds we think may be useful for the project. Before I am ready to play a set of those sounds in sync with picture for a director, I have made literally hundreds of artistic editorial decisions about their appropriateness relative to mood, intensity, spacing, tempo, volume dynamics, and so forth. The technology we use is directly analogous to a graphics or drafting program that a production designer would use to make early drawings of a set for the director's approval. In other words, we in the craft of sound are not simply the operators of gadgets, waiting for the director to tell us what the gadgets should do.

Though the world of animated films is rife with technology, it is all just a set of tools the artists employ.

There is no doubt that contemporary animated films are not the "cartoons" of yore. They are no less varied than live-action films in style or message, and they call for sound design styles that are just as imaginative and in some cases just as "realistic."

CHAPTER 14

ZIG ZAG: REANIMATING LEN LYE AS IMPROVISED THEATRICAL PERFORMANCE AND IMMERSIVE VISUAL MUSIC

LISA PERROTT

OUT of the darkened silence of the theater come the looped rhythmic sounds of a gently played didgeridoo.[1] Projected onto a large black screen, a thin white line emerges and gradually becomes more defined. As the music builds, the line begins to take the form of a giant pin. Filling the screen, the pin sways along with the music, moment by moment revealing itself as a responsive metallic sculpture.[2] The sculpture becomes increasingly enlivened to the ascending momentum of the music. Associations run wild; this could be a flexible shower nozzle or an upright wriggling snake. Either way, this sculpture "dances" like a person completely giving her or his body over to the music. As it moves, the line becomes abstracted, taking on the appearance of a tapeworm and then the motion of a ribbon, motivated by the wrist of a rhythmic gymnast. As the music continues to gain in intensity, the slightly abstracted creature splits off into a duplicate creature, which dances toward the audience. More duplicates split off, each becoming larger and more abstract as it moves closer to the audience. Brass instruments join in, adding to the complex mix of abstract dancing forms, indigenous instruments, eclectic jazz, and electro-acoustic sound art.

1 *Zig Zag* was a live performance that took place at the TSB Showplace, New Plymouth, New Zealand, on August 13, 2007.

2 Len Lye's kinetic sculpture, *Zebra* (1964).

The first performances of *Zig Zag*, a multimedia work inspired by the life and work of Len Lye, took place in New Zealand in August 2007[3] and delighted audiences with a radical interpretation of his oeuvre.[4] Performances of *Zig Zag* integrated traditional music, innovatively devised instruments, and audiovisual mixing software, taking the form of a live band performing alongside projected audiovisual imagery that filled the entire cyclorama at the back of the stage. Though the projected imagery and musical performers provided the primary visual stimulus, the audience was also treated to a spirited play of theatrical lighting, which danced upon the performers and enlivened the entire stage set as though it were a huge kinetic sculpture comprised of human performers, many types of instruments, and set materials. All of these elements worked together to immerse the audience in a multisensory perceptual experience.

Devised as an homage to Len Lye, *Zig Zag* could be described as a live spectacle of sound and visual imagery and as a cross-platform visual music performance. I originally set out to examine the collaborative process by which a team of artists brought together handmade art forms and digital technologies to create this multimedia performance. It became apparent that *Zig Zag* went beyond the initial intentions of its creators in functioning as a reanimation of Lye's collected body of work. The notion that a multimedia stage performance can be considered a type of animation may initially seem unusual, if we have a conventional understanding of animation (on television or on a cinema screen). My argument challenges the conventional perspective and proposes that the term "animation" can describe various situations in which the cinematic frame, screen, camera, and projector are either extraneous to, or only a part of, what actually animates the work. Both Lye's kinetic sculptures and the *Zig Zag* performance have functioned as forms of extracinematic animation that pose a challenge to audiences.

I use the term "extracinematic animation" to describe those forms that meet certain defining criteria of animation, yet do so in a way that is either extraneous or additional to cinema-specific codes and technologies.[5] While there has been debate about whether earlier generations of optical toys such as the zoetrope and praxinoscope were pre- or proto-cinematic animation,[6] various contemporary examples of extracinematic animation

[3] An edited extract of the screen show that was projected for the *Zig Zag* performance is available to view at http://www.vimeo.com/9170960 (accessed August 12, 2012).

[4] Len Lye was a filmmaker, animator, sculptor, painter, poet, and theorist. He produced a significant body of work in which he explored, among other things, motion, materiality, synesthesia, kinesthesis, the role of the unconscious in the creation and perception of art, animism, and the relationship between music and visuality. See Roger Horrocks, *Len Lye: A Biography* (Auckland, New Zealand: Auckland University Press, 2001).

[5] Bill Nichols, *Ideology and the Image: Social Representation in the Cinema and Other Media* (Bloomington: Indiana University Press, 1981), 1–8.

[6] I follow Sean Cubitt's position with regard to situating optical toys in relation to cinema. For Cubitt, optical toys "belong to a history which, as I have argued, is not strictly pre-cinematic because it is also 'pre-' many other things as well, some of which, we can hope lie ahead in the future we do not yet know." Sean Cubitt, "Observations on the History and Uses of Animation Occasioned by the Exhibition Eyes, Lies and Illusions Selected from Works in the Werner Nekes Collection," *Animation: An Interdisciplinary Journal* 3, no. 1 (2008): 55. See also Alan Cholodenko, "The Animation of Cinema," *The Semiotic Review of Books* 18, no. 2 (2008): 1–10.

have emerged owing to the development of new technologies as well as the activities of artists who wish to explore alternatives to the production and viewing contexts conventionally associated with animated media. The architectural projections of Rose Bond and Gregory Bennett are complementary examples of contemporary animations that explicitly avoid the screen in order to enliven and manipulate the architectural spaces of our lived environments and in so doing to challenge their sense of familiarity.[7] Particularly instructive and relevant to the work of Lye is Suzanne Buchan's discussion of the extracinematic animation of Gregory Barsamian's kinetic sculptures:

> By describing his work as extracinematic, I mean quite literally taking place outside of the technical and chemical means of cinema. This is in addition to the extracinematic elements his work contains according to the term's meaning in film semiotics, the extracinematic codes that are shared across media, i.e. are not unique to a medium, for instance narrative, gesture and frame (itself a cinematic term that originates from theatre).[8]

Buchan adds that the physical presence of Barsamian's "sculptures" is altogether distinct from the representation of objects in flat screen cinematic projection.[9] This is also what distinguishes the extracinematic nature of Lye's sculptures. They require audience members to engage with them via a noncinematic perceptual frame, and as such they challenge those definitions of animation that rely on the cinematic frame as a defining criterion.[10]

In the case of the *Zig Zag* performance, however, the extracinematic codes associated with theatrical performance, theater lighting, live music, and real-time audiovisual mixing operate in addition to the projected image on the flat screen. These extracinematic codes function in addition to cinematic codes such as lighting, use of the cinematic frame, and depth of field, which are utilized to create both lifelike and abstract cinematic representations of Lye's sculptures. *Zig Zag* differs from the kinetic sculptures of Barsamian and the original sculptural works of Lye in that it was exhibited in a markedly different temporal and spatial context, and as such provides an example of extracinematic animation that is characterized by the ephemeral nature of theatrical performance, digital remixing, and jazz improvisation. This integration of traditional media with digital media as immersive performance is relevant to the theory of remediation developed by Jay

[7] Rose Bond has projected her animations in small architectural spaces. See Lynda Wysong, "Animation, Architectural Articulation and the Street," Art in Public series, *ultra* (January 2010), at http://www.ultrapdx.com/zero/2011/01/04/animation-architectural-articulation-and-the-street/ (accessed August 12, 2012); and Gregory Bennett and Michael Hodgson, "Impossible Choreographies," *the big idea*, April 7, 2011, at http://www.thebigidea.co.nz/news/tbi qna/84 074-impossible-choreographies (accessed August 12, 2012). Bennett's animations were projected onto the large scale of the Smith and Caughey building in Auckland, New Zealand; see http://www.gregorybennett.org/ (accessed August 12, 2012).

[8] Suzanne Buchan, "Extracinematic Animation: Gregory Barsamian in Conversation with Suzanne Buchan," *Animation: An Interdisciplinary Journal* 3, no. 3 (2008): 292.

[9] Buchan, "Extracinematic Animation."

[10] For a discussion of the limitations of those definitions of animation that rely on the cinematic frame, see Paul Wells, *Animation: Genre and Authorship* (London: Wallflower Press, 2002), 4–7.

David Bolter and Richard Grusin, who argue that new media attain cultural distinctiveness by paying homage to and refashioning earlier media such as painting, photography, film, and theatrical stage productions.[11] The complex processes involved in this particular example of remediation are discussed later in this chapter in a close reading of specific extracts of the *Zig Zag* performance, which is supported by interviews with three of the artists involved in creating the performance.[12]

The Handmade Animation of Len Lye

The work of New Zealand–born artist Len Lye is distinctive for the way it draws together abstraction with referentiality and for linking unconscious perception with tangible experience, a combination that enables his work to be both theoretically complex and accessible. Whether creating animations, abstract films,[13] paintings, or kinetic sculptures, Lye sought to promote bodily, sensory, and imaginative engagement, while at the same time composing abstract forms from sounds and images. Lye was an animist, with an intuitive understanding of the life force embodied in living creatures, objects, and many other elements of the natural world. Drawing on his strong sense of empathy with the objects in his physical environment, he used his body to emulate the movement of things such as waves, grass, and trees. This practice enabled him to transfer the energy and specific qualities of motion into his kinetic sculptures and films.

In his animated film *Tusalava* (1927–1929), Lye utilized processes of metamorphosis and anthropomorphism, which gave life to his drawings, making their abstract form move like an Australian witchetty grub. The behavioral qualities of the abstract form in *Tusalava* have also been associated with those of a virus or macrophage gobbling up another cell.[14] This cellular interpretation of the film is in keeping with Lye's theory of "old brain memory,"[15] which explores the idea of creating art directly from the unconscious, doing so by accessing the memories stored in bodily cells and tissues.[16] This notion can be related to Deleuzian theory on embodiment, which emphasizes the role of the body and

[11] Jay David Bolter and Richard Grusin, *Remediation: Understanding New Media* (Cambridge, Mass.: MIT Press, 2000), 44–50.

[12] I conducted interviews with artist Tim Gruchy (who filmed Lye's sculptures and played the audio and video material live on stage), musician David Long, and set and lighting designer Tony Rabbit. The interviews took place on May 22 and 23, 2012.

[13] Malcolm Le Grice, *Abstract Film and Beyond* (London: Studio Vista, 1977).

[14] Horrocks, *Len Lye*, 90–95.

[15] Roger Horrocks, *Art That Moves: The Work of Len Lye* (Auckland, New Zealand: Auckland University Press, 2009), 114–118.

[16] Hanna Scott, "Len Lye's Old Brain: Primitive or Prescient?" in *Len Lye*, ed. Jean-Michel Bouhours and Roger Horrocks (Sydney, Australia: The Art Gallery of New South Wales; Govett Brewster Art Galley and Len Lye Foundation, 2001), 21–24.

sensory memory in our engagement with the moving image.[17] Drawing on these ideas, memories are understood to function more complexly than as cognitive resources in our brains, or as discursive social resources, but also as living energies, dynamically transiting, and affecting the body at a cellular level.[18] As suggested by Laura Marks, memories can be triggered by sensory stimulation within a complex system of communication between the senses. Marks applies this synesthetic system of sensory organization, which she calls the "sensorium,"[19] to the culturally informed perceptual activity involved in our experiences of media forms.[20]

Lye's theory of "old brain memory" is consistent with theoretical explorations into synesthetic and kinesthetic engagement in art and visual music.[21] However, Lye extended these ideas of bodily memory by developing his own theory about movement in art, which led to the creation of a number of kinesthetic sculptures that he called "tangible motion sculptures" or "tangibles."[22] The term "tangible" is not meant to imply that the metallic surfaces of the sculptures should actually be touched; rather, it suggests something akin to Lye's understanding of these works as corporeal perceptible entities. In his view, each tangible expressed a life force and personality through kinesthetic motion and the emanation of harmonic sound waves, in the same way that a vibrating musical instrument produces sound waves.[23] Lye treated the raw materials of his sculptures like functioning human body parts. Many of his metallic sculptures were built on the principle that metal, like a human muscle, can store and release energy, and motion can be incited through the build up and release of tension.

Although not normally understood as animation, Lye's kinetic sculptures exemplify the capacity of extracinematic animation to explore the fundamental properties of animation by engaging the audience in a perceptual timespace of real and tangible objects in motion. In keeping with several of the key concepts typically used to define animation, the sculptures are an extension of Lye's propensity to pioneer new methods of animation.

[17] Barbara M. Kennedy, *Deleuze and Cinema: The Aesthetics of Sensation* (Edinburgh: Edinburgh University Press, 2000).

[18] Nina Zimnik, "'Give Me a Body': Deleuze's Time Image and the Taxonomy of the Body in the Work of Gabriele Leidloff," *Enculturation* 2, no. 1 (1998), at http://enculturation.gmu.edu/2_1/zimnik/ (accessed August 12, 2012).

[19] Apart from its use as a general medical term, "sensorium" was used by Marshall McLuhan in his theorization about the effects of media on sensory perception. Edmund Carpenter and Marshall McLuhan, eds. *Explorations in Communication* (Boston: Beacon Press, 1960).

[20] Laura Marks, *The Skin of the Film: Intercultural Cinema, Embodiment and the Senses* (Durham, N.C.: Duke University Press, 2000), 199–201.

[21] The contributions of Wassily Kandinsky and Oskar Fischinger to theories of synesthesia are discussed in Kerry Brougher, Olivia Mattis, and Jeremy Strick, *Visual Music: Synaesthesia in Art and Music since 1900* (New York: The Museum of Contemporary Art; Los Angeles: Thames and Hudson, 2005).

[22] Horrocks, *Len Lye*, 276.

[23] Horrocks, *Len Lye*, 278.

Arguing for an extended definition of the term "animation," Sean Cubitt emphasizes a spiritual dimension: "Anima means not only spirit, but breath, and not only the breath of living animals but the breath of wind that animates the leaves."[24] Consistent with this meaning of *anima*, Lye's sculptures are composed of inanimate materials that are set in motion and brought to life. Embodying and expressing the life force of living things in the natural environment, their motion, and their behavior, is animistic and anthropomorphic.

Lye's sculpture *Grass* (1961) animates a mass of metallic upright blades that flex and jitter much like long blades of grass rustled by the wind. The metal rods of his sculpture *Fountain* (1966) behave like the spiky fronds of a New Zealand cabbage tree. These works evoke various subjective interpretations, and they are capable of triggering cultural memories of place as well as subconscious bodily memories. As Roger Horrocks describes it:

> The movement of *Fountain* is reminiscent of rippling water or merging currents in a stream. But it can also suggest other natural rhythms such as wind in tree branches. The stop start motion may remind us of human breathing. Watching the work is like listening to a quiet piece of Minimalist music—at first it seems repetitive in its slow, hypnotic rhythm, but as we pay close attention we become aware of subtle changes. Similarly, each of the "stalks" of *Grass* has a measure of independence, so their overall pattern is never perfectly symmetrical.[25]

These examples of bodily engagement with Lye's work are usefully understood in relation to the concept of kinesthesis: the sense or empathy for bodily sensations that is often triggered by watching or remembering a body in action.[26] A kinesthetic response to art can be experienced in the muscles, nerves, skin, and hair follicles, and can be evoked by audiovisual media, especially live performance, music, or dance.[27]

There are a number of consistencies between Lye's tangibles and his animated films, which have been observed by Evan Webb[28] and by the creators of *Zig Zag*. Lye made a series of films using the process of direct filmmaking, which is also known as cameraless animation. In direct filmmaking, images are scratched, painted, drawn, or otherwise applied to the emulsion, or surface of each frame of a filmstrip. A camera is not used to photograph these images. Instead, the images are animated by being projected directly from filmstrip to screen.[29] Lye's obsession with movement and passion for dance

[24] Cubitt, "Observations on the History and Uses of Animation," 54.

[25] Horrocks, *Art That Moves*, 191.

[26] Horrocks, *Art That Moves*, 102 and 117.

[27] The particular relevance of kinesthesis to dance is discussed in Marc Boucher, "Kinetic Synaesthesia: Experiencing Dance in Multimedia Scenographies," *Contemporary Aesthetics* 2 (2004), at http://www.contempaesthetics.org/newvolume/pages/article.php?articleID=235 (accessed August 12, 2012).

[28] Evan Webb, "Planting at Night" in *Len Lye*, ed. Tyler Cann and Wystan Curnow (New Plymouth: Govett-Brewster Art Gallery and Len Lye Foundation, 2009), 93–107.

[29] Tess Takahashi, "Meticulously, Recklessly Worked Upon: Direct Animation, the Auratic and the Index," in *The Sharpest Point: Animation at the End of Cinema*, ed. Chris Gehman and Steve Reinke (Toronto: YYZ Books, 2005), 166–178. See also Robert Russett and Cecile Starr, *Experimental Animation: Origins of a New Art* (New York, N.Y.: DaCapo Press, 1988), 163–177.

motivated him to utilize the process of direct filmmaking to create the graphic dance films *Colour Box* (1935), *Colour Cry* (1952), *Swinging the Lambeth Walk* (1939), and *Free Radicals* (1958). Although these films involve no actual dancers, the visual imagery moving across a sequence of frames performs an anthropomorphic dance. Particular elements of the abstract mark-making (such as lines, points, and patterns) are choreographed in rhythmic interplay with the dance sound track. Recognizing the gestural qualities and potential bodily affect of mark-making, Lye described this dance of abstract forms as "a sensory ballet."[30]

In the context of animated visual music, Lye's films are distinguished by their visual interpretation of rhythm and their embodiment of popular music, jazz, and blues. They make full use of the life-giving potential of animation by expressing the emotion and energy of the music through the anthropomorphism of abstract forms.

A number of visual music artists have explored the relationship between visual motifs and music. Wassily Kandinsky and Oskar Fischinger, for example, contributed to the development of theories of synesthetic engagement, suggesting a direct correlation between visual elements such as color and the auditory quality of particular instruments.[31] Adding a kinesthetic dimension to his persistent experimentation with synesthesia, Lye developed a basic range of motifs that he believed would visually express the specific auditory qualities of musical instruments:

> He liked to match drums with big, bouncing circles. The piano . . . was associated with a shower of coloured blobs—small circles, stars, suns or sprocket hole shapes, which suggested (and sometimes corresponded closely to) individual notes. For piano and organ there were also parallel lines like a keyboard which danced this way and that. The sax was associated with a thick, scratched vertical line that kept breaking up into a cluster of fibers. String instruments were suitably represented by lines that quivered and twanged. The violin became a thin vertical line, either painted or scratched, which swayed from side to side and sometimes split into multiple lines. The double bass received a much thicker line.[32]

This use of motifs, and the synesthetic connections among abstract visual expression, musicality, and dance, are especially apparent in *Swinging the Lambeth Walk* (1939). In this abstract film, the visual motifs observed by Horrocks appear as signifiers of the auditory qualities of particular instruments. In addition to this function of motifs, lines and shapes are personified, giving them the ability to dance along with the music, jiggle

[30] Len Lye, "Colour and the Box Office," *Life and Letters Today* (1935): 164; Ian Christie, "Colour, Music, Dance, Motion. Len Lye in England, 1927–1944," in *Len Lye*, ed. Jean-Michel Bouhours and Roger Horrocks (Paris: Éditions du Centre Pompidou, 2000), 188.

[31] Wassily Kandinsky elaborated a complex correlation between color and music, discussed in Brougher, Mattis, and Strick, *Visual Music*, 31–38.

[32] Roger Horrocks, "Swinging the Lambeth Walk: The Hand of the Filmmaker" in *Len Lye*, ed. Tyler Cann and Wystan Curnow (New Plymouth: Govett-Brewster Art Gallery and Len Lye Foundation, 2009), 28.

and jive with attitude across the screen. At times the lines behave like guitar strings, and their tension and vibration is perceptible as kinesthetic sensation, much like the way that Lye's tangibles evoke associative links between the harmonics of musical instruments and the human body. Horrocks's analysis of *Swinging the Lambeth Walk* describes this kinetic affect:

> A vertical line drawn down the length of the film was a favorite motif that Lye used for a range of instruments, and he learned to do many things with it, such as make it sway, wriggle, jump or glide. In contrast, the guitar appeared as a horizontal line, its wobble evoking the vibration of a twanged string.... [A] second line is added momentarily like an after-image, and changing colors and curving lines accent the pauses. This great example of the dynamism of direct film is followed by a double bass solo from a different jazz recording. The bass is closely matched by a thick vertical line whose movement is unusually vigorous; it twangs and stomps.[33]

Swinging the Lambeth Walk typifies the multifarious referentiality of Lye's films. The gestural quality of the mark-making itself is referential in its association with human gestural traits. Due to the direct filmmaking process, which bypasses the camera, the energy and expressive quality of the mark-making is intensified, as it is delivered "directly" to the viewer. When viewing the handmade imagery generated by the direct filmmaking process, we make a direct and explicit association with the imagery and energy of the hand that created the work.[34] This connection with the creative hand is less explicit with photographic imagery, due to the mediating presence of the camera. It is this directness of creative energy flow that Horrocks refers to when he extols "the dynamism of direct film."[35]

We might note an additional referential function in the movement of these marks. This results from a combination of Lye's kinesthetic empathy and subsequent energy transference, and from the principle of "persistence of vision" that makes still images appear to move even when the film projector moves each frame of celluloid before our eyes. The actual motion of the marks, lines, and shapes can be associated with the twanging and reverberating tension of a guitar string. Most significantly, this anthropomorphic dance of abstract imagery can trigger bodily memories, such as the movement of a dancing human body wriggling or gliding.

Lye's films are also distinctively referential due to the organic materiality of their form. In contrast to the indexical bond of realist representation that Bazin ascribed to the photographic image,[36] the painting and scratching of marks directly onto the film emulsion creates a physical presence and vitality, evoking a direct referential connection with the material qualities of film and paint and the expressive language of gesture. This notion of

[33] Horrocks, "Swinging the Lambeth Walk," 28.

[34] Len Lye's thoughts on this distinctive quality of direct animation are discussed in Takahashi, "Meticulously, Recklessly Worked Upon," 171.

[35] Horrocks, "Swinging the Lambeth Walk," 28.

[36] Steven Shaviro, "Emotion Capture: Affect in Digital Film," *Projections* 1, no. 2 (2007): 64–66.

materiality has a direct connection with sensory memory, a point articulated by Marks when she describes the skin of the film not as a screen, but "as a membrane that brings its audience into contact with the material forms of memory."[37]

This function of organic materiality is particularly relevant to the direct film *Free Radicals* (1958), in which Lye scratched abstract marks into the black emulsion of the film leader. This process draws our full attention to the material qualities of the black emulsion, to the specific ways in which the particles of this material respond to the energy of mark-making, and to the light projected through the marked celluloid. This rough-textured mark-making has a primordial quality that reminded Lye of cave art.[38] The marks' elemental quality may potentially trigger subconscious bodily memories of our earliest experiences of making marks with crayons and sticks in sand or mud. A gestural vivacity arises from the alternating texture of the scratched surface and the flashing, expressive movement of the jagged line, as it dances to the rhythm of an African drumbeat.

Organic materiality is a distinctive feature of Lye's direct films as well as his kinetic sculptures. His approach to visual music was idiosyncratically intertwined with his obsession with movement. Seemingly prescient of the integrated media possibilities of contemporary digital technologies, Lye was excited by the idea that patterns of sounds could be created by patterns of motion.[39] As the metallic sculptures move, tension accumulates within the molecular structure of the metal and is released, imparting to the resulting sound pattern a sense of dramatic tension and a characteristic timbre capable of evoking synesthetic and kinesthetic responses.

Lye was able to give life to abstract visual forms and to engage his audience through a tangible sense of bodily motion. His philosophy of "old brain memory" enabled him to tap into unconscious memory resources in the act of creating his work. In this way, Lye injected his work with memory triggers that refer us both to the internal functions of our bodies and to the external and familiar environment in which we live.

Hapticity

Hapticity is a useful concept for exploring the phenomenological significance of extra-cinematic animation, especially in relation to theatrical performance. Hapticity is particularly applicable when considering audience engagement with the explicitly handmade qualities in Lye's work, and it is fundamental to the multisensory immersive and perceptive space generated by the *Zig Zag* performance. Focusing her attention on

[37] Marks, *Skin of the Film*, 243.

[38] Horrocks, *Art That Moves*, 75.

[39] I refer here to VJ and integrated media projects that use midi software, particularly those in which motion, music, or light functions as a stimulus to trigger sound. Examples are software such as Isadora, MaxMSP, and Modul8.

cinematic codes, Marks has suggested the following formal characteristics as stimuli for haptic visuality (summarized here by Donato Totaro):

> Grainy, unclear images; sensuous imagery that evokes memory of the senses (i.e. water, nature); the depiction of characters in acute states of sensory activity (smelling, sniffing, tasting, etc.); close-to-the-body camera positions and panning across the surface of objects; changes in focus, under- and overexposure, decaying film and video imagery; optical printing; scratching on the emulsion; densely textured images, effects and formats such as Pixelvision . . . ; and alternating between film/video. The haptic image is in a sense less complete, requiring the viewer to contemplate the image as a material presence rather than an easily identifiable representational cog in a narrative wheel.[40]

Although these characteristics are applied by Marks primarily in relation to her thesis on "intercultural cinema," they also have useful application to extracinematic forms and to those forms of animated projection that bypass the camera. Aesthetic practices such as scratching on the emulsion of film leader, hand-painting, using stencils, color mats, and optical printing are trademarks of Lye's pioneering experimentation with the method of cameraless animation. A number of indices of hapticity can also be applied to both Lye's work and *Zig Zag*, such as the use of the close-ups, whether by means of the exaggerated scale of a projected visual image or through the use of "close-up" sounds; use of imagery that refers to the natural environment and thereby evokes sensory memory; and densely textured (and layered) compositions and the distinctive referential capacity to evoke a direct and tangible connection to a material presence. This tangibility is fundamental to haptic visuality (and audibility).[41] Totaro explains how Marks develops the synesthetic proposition that vision can be tactile, "as if touching a film with one's eyes":[42]

> Haptic vision is a more tactile-based, closer-to-the-body form of perception, where "the eyes themselves function like organs of touch" (162). As Marks explains, in optical visuality the eye perceives objects from a far enough distance to isolate them as forms in space. And with optical vision there is an assumed separation between the viewing body and the object. Haptic visuality is a closer form of looking, which tends to "move over the surface of its object rather than plunge into illusionist depth, not to distinguish form so much as to discern texture."[43]

Although Marks is primarily concerned here with cinematic visuality, her statement is instructive because it differentiates between perceiving an object in real space and the sensory activity involved in engaging with a cinematic representation of an object. There is a qualitative difference between perceiving a Lye sculpture in the gallery space

[40] Donato Totaro, "Deleuzean Film Analysis: The Skin of the Film," *Off Screen* 6, no. 32 (2002): 4.
[41] Totaro, "Deleuzean Film Analysis," 4.
[42] Marks, *Skin of the Film*, 162.
[43] Laura Marks, quoted in Totaro, "Deleuzean Film Analysis," 4.

and viewing a filmed representation of this object on a flat screen in a theatrical setting, as was the experience for the *Zig Zag* audience. In this context, hapticity was accentuated by the physical presence of the musicians on stage and by the multisensory and ephemeral nature of the overall performance. Hapticity was also heightened by the anthropomorphized performance of the projected forms. Consistent with the historical viewing context for Lye's direct films, the hyperbolic scale of *Zig Zag*'s digitally recorded imagery functioned like a projected close-up, engulfing the audience and insisting upon an inescapably haptic encounter with these abstract representations of the sculptures.

Zig Zag as Performance Animation

The production process for *Zig Zag* involved the collaboration of six musicians,[44] artist Tim Gruchy, and set and lighting designer Tony Rabbit. Taking direction from Rabbit's original conception for *Zig Zag*, Gruchy filmed Lye's sculptures and handed the audiovisual recordings on to the musicians, who composed the accompanying soundscape. The collaborative process became an ongoing dialogue between Gruchy and the team of musicians, with the composition of sound and visual imagery in each performance developing organically until the project formed the shape of a series of visual music acts, played together as an hour-long live performance with a structural arc made up of changes in dramatic intensity. While this structure remained in place for each of the subsequent performances, the projected imagery was not a discrete film or a set composition of visual imagery or sound. Due to the ephemeral and dialogic nature of the performance, the composition of both sound and imagery changed in each performance, much as it would during the call and response processes of jazz improvisation.

Together with the musicians and their instruments, Gruchy was an integral part of the band on stage, playing his reconfigurations of the projected imagery as another instrument within the overall improvised composition of visual music. But these were not the only instruments making up this extracinematic reanimation of Lye. Both the composition of sound and visual imagery and the stage and lighting setup were designed to express Lye's exuberance for life and penchant for playfully experimenting with motion, materials, form, and color. From either side of the stage, the theater lights were "played" in such a way that shafts of white and colored light interacted with the musicians and their instruments, acting like another performer on stage, and at times dancing to the music. As Rabbit describes it, during the performance the stage "was like a huge kinetic sculpture, with the musicians and instruments forming the moving parts of the sculpture."[45] The entire composition process was characterized by a conscious effort to ensure

[44] These six musicians from New Zealand, otherwise know as The Six Volts, include David Long, David Donaldson, Jeff Henderson, Chris O'Connor, Steve Roche, and Janet Roderick.

[45] Interview with Tony Rabbit (director, set and lighting designer for *Zig Zag*), May 23, 2012.

that, even in subtle ways, *Zig Zag* would be consistent with Lye's approach to composing motion.

It was imperative for all involved for *Zig Zag* to be created as an homage to Lye, and this objective guided the way the sounds and visual imagery were composed. However, different approaches were employed to create this work of reverence. For Rabbit and Gruchy, the kinetic sculptures were the primary focal point, driven by Rabbit's initial desire to reanimate and publicly celebrate the extensive collection of Lye's sculptures archived at the Govett Brewster Art Gallery. For the musicians, the compositional process responded initially to the digital video recordings of the kinetic sculptures in motion. They also took broader inspiration from many other facets of Lye's legacy, immersing themselves in his abstract films, sculptures, poetry, and biographical material about his approach to life and art.

Taking inspiration from Lye's sensibilities, the musicians ensured that their compositions were in keeping with Lye's love of jazz and rhythmic indigenous music. They further aimed to translate specific visual characteristics in musical terms. David Long commented that the musicians sought to emulate Lye's obsession with lines, particularly the way in which lines would interact in his abstract films.[46]

Mindful of the initial plan to use the kinetic sculptures as the primary raw material for his visual composition, Gruchy consciously avoided drawing inspiration from Lye's films. But when reflecting on how the projected imagery came together for the performance, he was pleasantly surprised by the strong visual consistencies between his compositions and Lye's abstract films.[47]

As discussed previously, a characteristic of much of Lye's work is the distinctive combination of abstract and referential imagery, which enables diverse audiences to experience these exhibits as complex and challenging, yet simultaneously tangible and accessible. *Zig Zag* also achieved a powerful experiential effect from the dynamic relationship between abstraction and tangible imagery.

Using the digital video footage of Lye's sculptures as raw material, Gruchy played this footage live with the music, sometimes manipulating several layers of footage, occasionally allowing the representations of the sculptures to become abstract to a point where the sculptural forms became barely recognizable. In the most abstract sequences, the moving sculptures appear as dancing shapes and lines, which jiggle rhythmically in a three-dimensional onscreen space. At times it seems as if the lines and forms are dancing with each other, moving close together, entwining, swinging each other around, and then pulling apart at a crucial moment in the music. The anthropomorphic motion of lines and forms is reminiscent of the scratched and painted lines in Lye's direct films, which were deeply informed by Lye's obsession with motion and his love for dance.

A sense of bodily motion is particularly evident in the projected screen show for *Zig Zag*. In one sequence Lye's sculpture *Moonbead* (1968) is partially abstract, yet still

[46] Interview with David Long (musician for *Zig Zag*), May 22, 2012.

[47] Interview with Tim Gruchy (artist for *Zig Zag*), May 23, 2012.

recognizable as an elliptical object spinning around a central rod. This digital re-creation of the sculpture in motion kinesthetically evokes the movement of a human body spinning a hula-hoop.

The kinetic sculptures' anthropomorphic qualities are further enhanced by their cinematic treatment. The lighting, which enhances the sculptures' form, wraps around them as they dance with one another like human bodies. Moving toward and away from the camera, the kinetic "dancers" fully utilize the implied depth of the illusionary onscreen space. In addition to the already imbued kinesthetic qualities of the sculptures' motion, their apparent communication with one another and their engagement with the camera augments the sense that the sculptures are performing for the audience.

In addition to the way in which the cinematography, lighting, and onscreen performance boost the anthropomorphic behavior of the sculptures, the music plays an important role in this process, enlivening and adding to the unique voice and timbre of the sculptures. The aural collage of instrumental music, voices, and digitally manipulated sounds makes the sculptures appear at times like characters on a stage, and at other times like animistic features of the natural environment. The soundscape incorporates multiple voices: extracts of Lye's voice derived from his recorded lectures, the idiosyncratic "voice" of each of the sculptures, the voices of the instruments, and the vocalists in the band. All these voices contribute differently to the sense that Lye's sculptures are characters in performance, drawing on the generic conventions of drama, romance, and comedy.

One sequence in the overall piece deviates visually, as well as musically, from the others. Lye's *Wind Wand* (1966–1999)[48] was filmed from a low angle with a static camera and natural outdoor lighting. Rather than editing or abstracting the footage, Gruchy subtly divided the image into two layers, creating the impression of two *Wind Wand* sculptures dancing with each other. This visual simplicity invites identification with the sculptures as characters, enabling the audience to become enveloped by the verisimilitude and romance of the "dance." Motivated by the breeze, the dynamic tension within the structure of the *Wind Wand* causes it to lilt and sway with the cadence and grace of a ballet dancer. The accompanying song provides associative triggers and emotional evocation, turning the motion of the *Wind Wand* into a romantic dance. The slow, lyrical folk music in this sequence comes as a pleasant contrast to the faster, rhythmic pace of the other sequences, punctuating the dramatic arc of the overall performance with a shift in pace and tone.

Just as Lye injected his work with a playful exuberance, Gruchy made use of digital technologies to reenact this playfulness in a particularly creative way. Audiovisual

[48] *Wind Wand* was designed by Len Lye and first erected in 1966 in New York. Lye was not happy with its construction at that time. Since his death in 1980, the Len Lye Foundation has followed his instructions and designs and constructed a fiberglass and carbon fiber *Wind Wand*, which was erected in New Plymouth in 1999. After breaking and being dismantled for repairs, it was resurrected in 2001. See http://www.newplymouthnz.com/OurDistrict/Attractions/PublicSculptures/LenLyeWindWand.htm (accessed August 12, 2012).

mixing software allowed him to play the digitally recorded imagery like a musical instrument, whereby he would engage in a responsive dialogue between the musicians on stage and the rhythm of his dancing imagery. Such a dialogue is entirely fitting with jazz musicians' use of their instruments to develop a live musical conversation. The digital tools at hand also assisted him in directing the representations of the sculptures as though they were performing in a play. With the aid of digital mixing tools, this integration of live theatrical performance and animation offers the potential for a playful exploration of time and space. Gruchy responded relatively spontaneously to the imagery on the screen as well as to the music being generated by his fellow musicians on stage. The musicians themselves were likewise integrally involved in this call and response dialogue, responding to the dancing and textured layering of the imagery onscreen. Each member of the *Zig Zag* creative team participated in a playful and dialogic process, best described as a visual music jazz improvisation.

Using the term "anima," I have extended the use of animation to include the act of giving life to something inanimate or reactivating objects that have lain in a dormant state. Significant for the overall meaning of the piece is how the context of theatrical performance allows extracinematic codes to breathe new life into Lye's work. The particular intersection of media involved in *Zig Zag* suggests the potential for a reconfiguration of the anticipated timespaces of immersive media, animation, and theater.[49]

Zig Zag has superseded the initial objective to use performance as a means to rejuvenate Lye's sculptures and function as an homage to his life and work. Its creators have picked up Lye's torch and carried it through time and space into a contemporary artistic terrain where digital media and mashup culture are pervasive and ubiquitous. Rather than detracting from the essence of Lye's work, this contemporary phenomenon of remediation has operated as an ideal companion to Lye's handmade aesthetic. Staying true to the referential and haptic qualities of handmade animation, the creators of *Zig Zag* have used the tool of new media to add a new layer of collaborative playfulness to Lye's work. By bequeathing his work to the Len Lye Foundation for the purposes of creative propagation, Lye made it possible for an ongoing recursive process of reanimation to be set in motion.

[49] The integration of immersive media, animation, and theatrical performance has been explored by Robert Lepage with his company, Ex Machina. Lepage's approach to theater is discussed in Aleksandar Sasa Dundjerovic, *The Theatricality of Robert Lepage* (Montreal; Kingston: McGill Queens University Press, 2007.

References

Bolter, Jay David, and Richard Grusin. *Remediation: Understanding New Media.* Cambridge, Mass.: MIT Press, 2000.

Boucher, Marc. "Kinetic Synaesthesia: Experiencing Dance in Multimedia Scenographies." *Contemporary Aesthetics* 2 (2004), at http://www.contempaesthetics.org/newvolume/pages/article.php?articleID=235 (accessed August 12, 2012).

Brougher, Kerry, Olivia Mattis, and Jeremy Strick. *Visual Music: Synaesthesia in Art and Music Since 1900.* New York: The Museum of Contemporary Art; Los Angeles: Thames and Hudson, 2005.

Buchan, Suzanne. "Extracinematic Animation: Gregory Barsamian in Conversation with Suzanne Buchan." *Animation: An Interdisciplinary Journal* 3, no. 3 (2008): 288–305.

Carpenter, Edmund, and Marshall McLuhan, eds. *Explorations in Communication.* Boston: Beacon Press, 1960.

Cholodenko, Alan. "The Animation of Cinema." *The Semiotic Review of Books* 18, no. 2 (2008): 1–10.

Christie, Ian. "Colour, Music, Dance, Motion. Len Lye in England, 1927–44." In *Len Lye,* edited by Jean-Michel Bouhours and Roger Horrocks, 177–240. Paris: Éditions du Centre Pompidou, 2000.

Cubitt, Sean. "Observations on the History and Uses of Animation Occasioned by the Exhibition Eyes, Lies and Illusions Selected from Works in the Werner Nekes Collection." *Animation: An interdisciplinary Journal* 3, no. 1 (2008): 49–65.

Dundjerovic, Aleksandar Sasa. *The Theatricality of Robert Lepage.* Montreal; Kingston: McGill Queens University Press, 2007.

Horrocks, Roger. *Len Lye: A Biography.* Auckland, New Zealand: Auckland University Press, 2001.

Horrocks, Roger. "Swinging the Lambeth Walk: The Hand of the Filmmaker." In *Len Lye,* edited by Tyler Cann and Wystan Curnow, 17–32. New Plymouth: Govett-Brewster Art Gallery and Len Lye Foundation, 2009.

Horrocks, Roger. *Art That Moves: The Work of Len Lye.* Auckland, New Zealand: Auckland University Press, 2009.

Kennedy, Barbara M. *Deleuze and Cinema: The Aesthetics of Sensation.* Edinburgh: Edinburgh University Press, 2000.

Le Grice, Malcolm. *Abstract Film and Beyond.* London: Studio Vista, 1977.

Lye, Len. "Colour and the Box Office." *Life and Letters Today* 13, (1935): 164.

Marks, Laura. *The Skin of the Film: Intercultural Cinema, Embodiment and the Senses.* Durham, N.C.: Duke University Press, 2000.

Nichols, Bill. *Ideology and the Image: Social Representation in the Cinema and Other Media.* Bloomington: Indiana University Press, 1981.

Redner, Gregg. *Deleuze and Film Music: Building a Methodological Bridge Between Film Theory and Music.* Bristol, UK: Intellect, 2011.

Russett, Robert, and Cecile Starr. *Experimental Animation: Origins of a New Art.* New York, N.Y.. DaCapo Press, 1988.

Scott, Hanna. "Len Lye's Old Brain: Primitive or Prescient?" In *Len Lye,* edited by Jean-Michel Bouhours and Roger Horrocks, 21–24. Paris: The Art Gallery of New South Wales; Govett Brewster Art Galley and Len Lye Foundation, 2000.

Shaviro, Steven. "Emotion Capture: Affect in Digital Film." *Projections* 1, no. 2 (2007): 63–82.

Takahashi, Tess. "Meticulously, Recklessly Worked Upon: Direct Animation, the Auratic and the Index." In *The Sharpest Point: Animation at the End of Cinema*, edited by Chris Gehman and Steve Reinke, 166–178. Toronto: YYZ Books, 2005.

Totaro, Donato. "Deleuzean Film Analysis: The Skin of the Film." *Off Screen* 6, no. 32 (2002), at http://www.horschamp.qc.ca/new_offscreen/skin.html (accessed November 29, 2012).

Webb, Evan. "Planting at Night." In *Len Lye*, edited by Tyler Cann and Wystan Curnow, 93–107. New Plymouth: Govett-Brewster Art Gallery and Len Lye Foundation, 2009.

Wells, Paul. *Animation: Genre and Authorship*. London: Wallflower Press, 2002.

Wood, Aylish. "Re-Animating Space." *Animation: An Interdisciplinary Journal* 1, no. 2 (2006): 133–152.

Wood, Aylish. "Recursive Space: Play and Creating Space." *Games and Culture* 7, no. 1 (2012): 87–105.

Zimnik, Nina. "'Give Me a Body': Deleuze's Time Image and the Taxonomy of the Body in the Work of Gabriele Leidloff." *Enculturation* 2, no. 1 (1998), at http://enculturation.gmu.edu/2_1/zimnik/ (accessed August 12, 2012).

Audiovisual Sources

Zig Zag. Live performance at TSB Showplace, New Plymouth, New Zealand, August 13, 2007.

Zig Zag. DVD compilation, digitally recorded excerpts from the *Zig Zag* performance at TSB Showplace, New Plymouth, New Zealand, August 13, 2007.

MUSICAL MOMENTS AND TRANSFORMATIONS

CHAPTER 15

THE MUTATING MUSICAL AND *THE SOUND OF MUSIC*

CARYL FLINN

Musical: The Resurrection of a Genre

In 2003, reports of the demise of the Hollywood film musical were struck down when *Chicago* was nominated for thirteen Academy Awards and won six. A succession of other costly screen musicals followed: *Phantom of the Opera* (2004), *Hustle and Flow* (2005), *Dream Girls* (2006), *Enchanted*, and *Sweeney Todd* (both 2007). For the first time since the 1930s (Ken Russell's work excepted), musical biopics also enjoyed popular and critical acclaim, from *I'm Not There* (2007) to *Ray* and *Walk the Line* (both 2004). Animated musicals for children and family viewing continued to enjoy bloated success, dominated as usual by Disney. New genres emerged during this time, what Jay Beck calls the "iPod musical" (*Nick and Norah's Infinite Playlist*, 2008; *High Fidelity*, 2000), in which songs reflect personal choices or the hidden hipness of nerdy white characters. Musicals, in short, seem as ubiquitous as the iPod these days, their spirit truly in the air. Although this chapter explores the trend through a largely American perspective, it is assuredly global in scope. Beyond Hollywood's lush walls, other English-language musicals include *Dancer in the Dark* (2000), *Hedwig and the Angry Inch*, and *Moulin Rouge* (both 2001), *Across the Universe* (2007), *Repo! The Genetic Opera* (2008), and *Score! A Hockey Musical* (2010).

The form has been undergoing far more than an ostensible revival since musicals are appearing in new shapes and through new media. In the process, they are also producing new utopian contexts, spaces, and feelings among a wide group of listeners. When a 2009 YouTube video shows orange-jump-suited Korean inmates performing Michael Jackson's "Thriller," we are a world away from Elvis's 1957 *Jailhouse Rock* or even Johnny Cash performing at Folsom Prison. The same goes when we watch commuters at a European train station get caught in a flash mob, with Julie Andrews's voice singing "Do Re Mi" pumped in (2009). Amateur online musicians upload show tunes, try out for musical or opera parts, or give new lyrics to familiar popular songs, some of the funniest of which appeared during the 2008 American presidential campaign, such as "Hey Sarah Palin" to Plain White T's "Hey There Delilah." There are also literal revisions that rework old music videos, such as Bonnie Tyler's "Total Eclipse of the Heart," to tremendous camp effect, and mashups that recombine songs and images from a variety of sources (any Lady Gaga music video). Some Internet musicals are created from scratch, such as Neil Patrick Harris's upscale—though robustly campy and cultish—"Dr. Horrible's Sing-a-long Blog."

In the early twenty-first century we are witnessing a highly theatrical form—traditionally limited to particular spaces and venues through its high budgets; nervous producers; the practical requirements of stage, set, and studio locations; and, not least, constraints set by musical performance—now making myriad small appearances on the Internet and nonmusical TV shows. What does it mean that musicals generate so much of the raw material for programs such as *American Idol*? Do such shows provide evidence of the musical's resurrection? And what happens when musicals go viral and get renewed life on YouTube and other Internet venues? When musical performances are less overtly or less immediately tied to profit, do they suggest different kinds of exchanges, scales, and values, economies of feeling, or utopian expressions?

The last thing I want to do is posit that the widespread, easy transmission of musicals assures any democratizing or liberatory effects. Instead, I am centrally concerned with their widened soundscape and what shifts occur with that expansion. I consider an iconic musical with a vast cultural history and trace its more recent movement through the landscape of "mutating musicals." What, in short, happens when a hyper-established musical with songs devoted to the unpretentious pleasures of nature, hills, and small Alpine flowers goes blisteringly viral?

The Sound of Music: From Loyal Adaptations to Micro-adventures and Mashups

Few films enjoy such ongoing, sustained popularity as Robert Wise's adaptation of the Rodgers and Hammerstein Tony-winning Broadway show *The Sound of Music*. A quintessentially American, white, G-rated classic, *The Sound of Music* is probably the best-established family Hollywood musical of all time. When it was released by 20th Century Fox in spring 1965, the film, which was three hours long, broke movie box office records and remained unchallenged until 1975, when *Jaws* inaugurated the unkillable trend of the summer blockbuster. Since then, *Music* has regularly aired as a special on U.S. television, increasingly around major national or religious holidays such as Thanksgiving and Christmas; it has generated special anniversary DVD editions, hefty coffee-table books, reality shows, and sing-along screenings that even provide lyrics in

Latin as the nuns sing in the convent. *The Sound of Music* has appeared onstage in commercial theater revivals and in countless school and local community productions. In cinema, it haunts international postclassical musicals such as *Moulin Rouge* and *Dancer in the Dark*.

Not only is it a classic that's loved, reviled, or at least *known* by many; *The Sound of Music* also carries substantial ideological weight for a nation constantly invoking family values and the public importance of "innocent," vulnerable children and unspoiled goodness. Its cultural status is complex, at once combining affection, nostalgia, kitsch, family ritual, and emotional intensity with almost hysterically crafted norms of heterosexuality and upper-class family life. Rodgers and Hammerstein's songs seem democratic in their utter simplicity ("Do-Re-Mi" introducing the scale) and decidedly down-market (no one would ever confuse "Lonely Goatherd" with high art). Rodgers's music is both simple and inspiring; Hammerstein's universalizing lyrics celebrate the glories of unencumbered nature: hills, mountains, flowers—the lifeblood of the good nationalism represented by the Captain, not the bad nationalism of the Nazis.

In terms of narrative problems and solutions, *The Sound of Music* could not be more exemplary of Hollywood, yet its history has always been a transnational, transmedia affair. First came Maria von Trapp's book, which was turned into two nonsinging German films; after Mary Martin and producer/husband Richard Halliday purchased the rights for a Broadway show, Rodgers and Hammerstein came on board and eventually turned it into a musical. Although Trapp was hoodwinked out of the rights to her family's filmed story in Germany, she was later able to parlay that story into entrepreneurial enterprises such as the family's ski lodge in Vermont and their ongoing singing engagements.

After close to a half century, however, the direction of that life has shifted. Now it is not the story, the adaptations, or even the new productions of *The Sound of Music* that get put into play—in other words, not wholesale revivals or new theatrical and TV screenings—so much as fragments of the show, fragments that typically center on the songs and production numbers. Scattered across media forms, these recognizable pieces make landfall across the globe. Among them include:

1. Gwen Stefani's 2007 "Wind It Up," which mashes up the yodels and instrumental fanfare of "The Lonely Goatherd." Stefani performs in a miniskirted habit with sunglasses, twirling on blocks of bright green Alpine hills ("a little more cubist," she maintained), and has chorus girls parrot the marionettes that performed the song in Wise's film. The video also references "Do Re Mi" and "My Favorite Things," with chorines mimicking the identically garbed children after Maria sewed clothes out of drapes; the villa's iron fence looms with sadomasochistic overtones.[1]
2. *Moulin Rouge*. Near the beginning of Baz Luhrmann's film, Ewan MacGregor and his fellow bohemians are searching desperately for the right lyrics for a

[1] "Wind It Up," at http://www.youtube.com/watch?v=9sY-TsLXiDo&feature=related (accessed August 2010).

show song that starts "the hills are alive...." After a few laughable false starts, MacGregor gets it right and, beaming, performs the famous line to such effect that the somnambulist strongman in the group passes out.

3. Tourist attraction. Although *The Sound of Music* hails from an era when single texts didn't spawn entire theme parks such as, say, Harry Potter has, any visitor to Salzburg, Austria, is quickly besieged by *Sound of Music* souvenirs and tchotchkes. You can go on four-hour *Sound of Music* tours that last longer than the film itself. When you spot sedate local walkers wending their way through the Mirabell Gardens, it is easy to imagine how irritated townspeople must have been when watching Julie Andrews and six American children prancing through it filming the "Do-Re-Mi" number.
4. Reality show. In summer 2008 the CBC, in preparation for a fall revival of the stage production in Toronto, went public in a search to cast Maria. To promote the series, CBC screened a free sing-along version of *The Sound of Music* downtown, complete with a master of ceremonies and several Trapp grandchildren, who sang and posed for photographs. This show and premise were based on a BBC series of the same name that had aired two years earlier in the United Kingdom to cast a Maria there.
5. *Dancer in the Dark*. Von Trier sets his English-language melodrama in small-town America in 1964, the year prior to *Music*'s release. Selma, the immigrant heroine, finds escape from oppression, drudgery, and her life of poverty in musicals and in rehearsing for the role of Maria in a community production. Yet Selma can scarcely see or sing and lacks the glamorous good looks of a tall blonde who is soon brought in as her "understudy."
6. Antwerp, Belgium train station (2009). A flash mob performance of "Do Re Mi" is at once goofy and touching, showing some commuters joining in with abandon, others looking horrified or casting looks of aspersion at the proceedings, and many simply smiling and enjoying the show. [2]
7. Other lives on YouTube. Videos show people singing songs from *The Sound of Music* drunk; songs are remixed (4th Ave Jones's "Nuckless Electro Mix" uses "Do-Re-Mi" in its mix); and there are fantasy film trailers, including one for a rather unconvincing horror film, *The Secret of the Sound of Music*. Among the more interesting of the trailers is Canadian student Jared Raab's hip-hop version. After a voice-over introduces Julie Andrews's Maria ("In a black and white world, she was grey.... A style of music 50 years too soon.") we read the title: *The Sound of Ghetto Music*. Without cruelty, the video gently and firmly exposes the almost preposterous whiteness of the original text.[3]Another YouTube mutation, part of

[2] "Do Re Mi" Flash Mob, at http://www.youtube.com/watch?v=7EYAUazLI9k (accessed August 2010).

[3] "The Sound of Ghetto Music," at http://www.youtube.com/watch?v=AHcmvHqJk3I (accessed August 2010).

a series on "movie mistakes," catches several continuity errors in the original film.[4] Other videos include screen tests, features on "the real Maria von Trapp" (she is rumored to have kissed Plummer on the cheeks when first meeting him, grateful at last for a handsome "husband"), comparisons between Maria and Mary Poppins, then-and-now photos of the cast members, and so forth.

8. Commercials. In 2010 Dove used "My Favorite Things" in a TV ad for hair conditioner. (Cultural musicologist Philip Tagg edited together "The Sound of Music" with a shampoo ad to demonstrate how the subtle connotations of one text can hawk the wares of a second.)
9. A "blue hair version" of "My Favorite Things":

> Maalox and nose drops and needles for knitting,
> Walkers and handrails and new dental fittings,
> Bundles of magazines tied up in string,
> These are a few of my favorite things.
>
> Cadillacs and cataracts, and hearing aids and glasses,
> Polident and Fixodent and false teeth in glasses,
> Pacemakers, golf carts, and porches with swings,
> These are a few of my favorite things. . . .
>
> When the pipes leak, when the bones creak,
> When the knees go bad,
> I simply remember my favorite things,
> And then I don't feel so bad. . . .[5]

These lyrics started out as a spoof on a listgroup. But when a contributor suggested, "Imagine that you are a blue-haired Julie Andrews singing it," reports quickly followed that Dame Julie actually performed it, and an urban legend was born. On October 1,

[4] "Movie Mistakes: *The Sound of Music*," at http://www.youtube.com/watch?v=xOLyX8ZLwZA&feature=related (accessed August 2010).

[5] The rest of the lyrics are:

> Hot tea and crumpets and corn pads for bunions,
> No spicy hot food or food cooked with onions,
> Bathrobes and heating pads and hot meals they bring,
> These are a few of my favorite things.
>
> Back pains, confused brains, and no need for sinnin',
> Thin bones and fractures and hair that is thinnin',
> And we won't mention our short, shrunken frames,
> When we remember our favorite things.
>
> When the joints ache,
> When the hips break,
> When the eyes grow dim,
> Then I remember the great life I've had,
> And then I don't feel so bad.

2004, on her sixty-ninth birthday, Andrews was said to have performed the updated "My Favorite Things" at an American Association of Retired Persons benefit at New York's Radio City Music Hall. In a story debunking the myth, one post not only corrects the account but steers our affective response to it, dramatically naming it "the sound of sadness," because Andrews's ability to sing had been damaged by botched vocal cord surgery in the 1990s.[6]

Camp

This last example brings *The Sound of Music* closest to camp, and it is worth exploring why the phenomenon of the mutating musical, though not uninformed by camp, is not actually coincident with it. Despite the lack of a consensus on what camp actually is, one tradition has achieved a certain influence. Articulated first by Andrew Ross, this view considers camp an effect produced by a sign, body, or system perceived as out of date, worn out, or past its prime. In this sense, camp is at once necrophilic and regenerative. It becomes a form of recycling, a necrophilic phenomenon, a "mode of cultural production [in which] the products . . . of a much earlier mode of production, which has lost its power to dominate cultural meanings, become available, in the present, for redefinition according to contemporary codes of taste."[7] Hence camp's frequent fascination with classic Hollywood glamour, old-fashioned signs and values, nuclear families, and the flesh and gender of aging bodies. Three years before *The Sound of Music*, one of camp's übertexts, *Whatever Happened to Baby Jane?*, incorporated that sense of afterlife as both narrative premise (two faded child stars of the silent era) and casting (two middle-aged icons of Hollywood's glamour days). Many of camp's other associations work within that broader understanding: that it has a "knowing wink," a bit of "superiority" or cruelty that prioritizes the present moment, generating a sense that the codes and conventions of today are somehow less ridiculous, or at least less conspicuous, than those of yesteryear.

The "blue-haired" Andrews performance is instructive in this regard. When I received the story, I noted that a previous online reader had written, "What a great sense of humor! That's our Julie! Still great after all these years!" This person, like others, *wanted* to believe the tale and unsurprisingly found it eminently believable. After all, Julie Andrews, whose voice, image, and performance style associate her almost synonymously with the film, would be ideal to lead fans on a camp expedition. With new lyrics pointing to the signs of aging, the stage is set for Dame Julie to become one of

[6] Snopes, "My Favorite Things," at http://www.snopes.com/humor/iftrue/andrews.asp (accessed June 2011).

[7] Andrew Ross, "Uses of Camp," in *No Respect: Intellectuals and Popular Culture* (New York: Routledge, 1989), 139.

those beloved camp divas whose bodies openly show the signs of long life and of wear and tear—like Judy Garland and Liza Minnelli. However, this version of "My Favorite Things" enables fans to *share* with their icon the experience of aging and have the camp be a little less vicious and externalized for it.

In truth, Andrews performs very little of campy, aging, or self-mocking divahood. In interviews, she will mention her "freak, four-octave" range, producing herself as something not quite human or mortal, an aspect of divahood explored in Wayne Koestenbaum's *The Queen's Throat*, which considers the bond between gay men and female divas partly produced by their shared status as outcasts.[8] Yet despite her "freaky" voice, Andrews herself could never be called that: she remains present, comforting, familiar, a ready tour guide into the world of *The Sound of Music* who has kept things too together to let much camp color her image. So even when these musical mutations have campy elements, it is not Andrews being camped up, or even Maria, but something else about the film. I suggest that in part, the film's strong familiarity both enables and prevents *Music* from being inordinately camped up, a point to which I will return.

Because musicals lavish attention on surface, intensely wrought emotion, style, and fantasy, they, like opera, have always been prime camp targets, and *The Sound of Music* is no exception. But again, it is not camp in the way that an Ethel Merman show is, or a Vincente Minnelli musical such as *The Pirate* (1948). True, the songs—and their lush orchestration and fanfares—intimate a Broadway long gone; compare "Climb Ev'ry Mountain" to *Avenue Q*'s "It Sucks to Be Me". But curiously, even with Rodgers and Hammerstein's old-style score, it is not the music that launches its campier send-ups so much as other aspects of the film, such as the setting (bucolic, folksy *Heimat* of Austria) or its ideological assertions (nature as refuge; evil as purely evil, and good as purely good). Indeed, the film's earnest uplift seems precious indeed and is enhanced by Andrews's acting style, which Peter Kemp has characterized for its "uncluttered sincerity and openness." Kemp says that Andrews achieves that same transparency vocally, with the "crisp clarity and precise diction" of her soprano. Moreover, and unlike other power vocalists of the time, "Andrews does not dominate or overwhelm a song to the point of egocentric appropriation.... While other performers seem to be proclaiming 'Here is *my* song' or 'This song is *me*', a Julie Andrews rendition transparently states 'Here is the *song*.'"[9] The transparency that Kemp observes here is not the same thing as naive earnestness or innocence and, as such, is more difficult to camp. Even Gwen Stefani, whose zany "Wind It Up" is punctuated by riffs of the "Goatherd" fanfare, is at pains to say how much she adores *The Sound of Music*, finding in Andrews "a great inspiration" and stating without irony, "When I actually heard the mashup I actually cried. [*sic*] I know it sounds ridiculous, but it was so good, so fresh, so amazing." Such ingenuousness—even if it is nothing

8 Wayne Koestenbaum, *The Queen's Throat: Opera, Homosexuality and the Mystery of Desire* (New York: Vintage, 1993).

9 Peter Kemp, "How Do You Solve a 'Problem' Like Maria von Poppins?" in *Musicals: Hollywood and Beyond*, ed. Bill Marshall and Robynn Stilwell (Exeter, UK: Intellect Press, 2000), 60.

more than pop PR—lies beyond the edge of camp. That is not to say that camp can't be touching, but that its affective pulls tend to work in more histrionic, less forthright ways.

For many people, *The Sound of Music*'s cultural signs were outmoded—too clean, impossible, fantastic—from the start. Critics skewered the play and then the film for being cloying and saccharine. Perhaps its camp status was there from the beginning. But significantly, its afterlife, even in campier renditions such as "Wind It Up," has not been based on the premise of demise or deterioration. Whether buying into *Music* without reflection, finding it ridiculous or offensive, or something else altogether, Americans continue to respond energetically to this family film. Interestingly, the ideals and comforts it might have offered 1960s America are scarcely different than the idealized understandings of nation, family, gender, whiteness, and sexuality at work today. In short, its camp value stems not from what is exhausted or worn out, but rather from values and codes that are still present and standing tall among us—much like the film itself. In that regard, *The Sound of Music* trades in an economy of robust familiarity.

Musical Pieces

In a 2010 study of what she calls the "musicalization of primetime," Kelly Kessler notes that beginning in the 1980s, a decade after what was arguably the Broadway musical's nadir in terms of sales, cultural influence, or prestige, musicals "hipped up." Shedding the G-rated earnestness of Rodgers and Hammerstein, musicals became self-conscious, reflexive, and ironic (consider *Spamalot*). When they tackled social problems, they did so with Big Apple irony, not tragic universalism (compare *Rent* to *West Side Story*). They relied on more than Broadway-style music and lyrics, e.g., *Def Poetry Jam* and, as Kessler concludes, regained enough cultural cachet that "musicals" could start reappearing on television. Of course in the 1950s and 1960s, shows from Broadway appeared on TV in their entirety (Mary Martin as Tinkerbell, Julie Andrews and then Lesley Ann Warren as Cinderella) or in shortened versions (Ethel Merman in *Anything Goes* and *Panama Hattie*). During the time, star vocalists performed show tunes on television variety shows like Ed Sullivan during or just before their show's run; talk shows and comedy routines were littered with references to current productions on the Big Stem.

It was not simply that Broadway's late twentieth-century output had become hip enough to make the "musical" sufficiently vernacular and popular to appear anew on television. Other factors were also at play: the 1980s ushered in music video, the 2000s gave us iTunes and iPods, and digital reproduction made songs more portable and reproducible than ever before. Music could be purchased and played by the tune, CDs selectively raided—as were the musicals themselves. As they began appearing on film and television screens for the first time in decades, musicals were no longer always presented wholesale or even as legitimate selections, like a hit song, from existing plays to tantalize potential theatergoers. In other words, musicals were coming from sources beyond Broadway and without its official imprimatur. There were one-time-only musical episodes of nonmusical shows such as *Xena: Warrior Princess*, *Buffy the Vampire Slayer*, and *How I Met Your Mother*. Moreover, instead of appearing whole, the mutated musical has typically relied on fragments, such as in the exquisite miniature music parodies of *The Simpsons*, with references to the score of *Indiana Jones* or with Sideshow Bob/Kelsey Grammer performing *H.M.S. Pinafore* to a terrorized Bart.

Other contexts also changed. No longer were musicals always considered to be potential portals to a lost golden age, a position inciting critics either to treat them as necrophilic camp artifacts or to lament the passing of Broadway's heyday. Now musicals could be stunningly up to date, glib, queer. At times the effect has been achieved by acknowledging and then skewing relationships to old-style musicals, as Trey Parker and Matt Stone did with *Cannibal! The Musical* (1993) and *South Park: Bigger, Longer and Uncut* (1999), two films that evoked the pioneer spirit, folkish patriotism, and community formation of classical Broadway musicals only to walk all over these traits. Some musical media mutations have moved away from the classic Broadway model altogether, such as *Repo! The Genetic Opera*. Even *Glee*, Fox's backstage musical TV show about a high school glee club that frequently references Broadway by mentioning icons like Barbra Streisand or focusing on gay male fandom, largely eschews Broadway music in favor of rock and pop classics. Television's mutating musical is, in many ways, as hybrid and unstable as its incarnations online.

At the time of this writing, YouTube does not yet support many two-and-a-half-hour musicals, although there are plenty of full-length musicals, operas, and plays condensed into five minutes. Even *Dr. Horrible* is a musical in miniature. These are musicals for smaller screens and shorter durations: if Frankfurt School theorist Theodor Adorno were alive, he would certainly add that they respond to diminishing attention spans and critical abilities as well. Whatever the view, it is the *fragments* of "Lonely Goatherd" in "Wind It Up," or "Do-Re-Mi" in the train station flash mob, that characterize the latest incarnation of *Music's* afterlife. More substantial than quotations, these musical iterations are also far smaller than revivals.

The process assumes but does not require audience familiarity with the original film. Even for those unfamiliar with it, *The Sound of Music* is not actually a fully unknown quantity, given its cultural prominence. For those uninitiated or uninterested viewers, these musical "pieces" might offer sites of misidentification, deflected or even restricted access. For those of us who do know *Music*, they offer familiar milestones, moments of recognition, of playing along with a comfortable friend, even if the rules of that play have been blasted open. Indeed, listener responses move in haltingly unpredictable lines, with musical mutations functioning altogether differently among constituencies with varying social, historical, and affective relationships to the film. Consider the range of what *Music* easily evokes: white bread culture, "family values," idealized family experiences, American kitsch, Europe-as-travelogue, Holocaust history blasphemed, gay romps with Julie Andrews and Eleanor Parker, or a fun escape into easily singable tunes. When the mutations foreground these things, the homage retreads very little of the film's original cultural work and meanings, and even in their robust appreciation and homage, they seldom invoke the original with seriousness or piety.

These small musical mutations show that it is not simply that the passage of time or the emergence of new production and distribution technologies that creates fresh venues and interpretive contexts, but rather that the texts *themselves* are undergoing manipulation, whether by professional singers, agents of corporate industry, and other official creative personnel, or by amateur fans, unofficial experts, and oddballs. In short, we no longer have "old texts in new contexts," but a near-constant production of an American master text whose scattered fragments do not always point to the "master text" overtly or with any ideological, aesthetic, or affective fidelity. What's more, the utopian sensibilities that accompanied these older musicals are themselves evolving and reconfiguring themselves.

Utopia

When critics have explored the relationship of film music to utopia, there has been a consistent tension between utopia's promise of change (to hint at a world more responsive to affective and material needs not met under current sociopolitical systems) and the comfort of no change at all; that is, of finding merely an exaggerated sense of peace within the familiar (consider in this regard how frequently musicals deal with finding acceptance in community). Scholars working in this area have devoted far more attention to the former—exploring how film music produces alternative worlds and experiences through contrast and opposition—than the latter, often because of their explicit political motivations.[10]

In a 1976 analysis of *The Sound of Music*, Richard Dyer cogently summarizes that perspective, writing that *Music* sets up and resolves several sets of

> human (but also specifically female) problems, and solutions to them, that by implication run counter to the interests, and hence ideology, of the dominant groups. The film attempts to recoup this through various narrative and musical procedures (not through the conscious or conspiratorial intervention of the ruling groups, but because it is always more comfortable to fit in white dominant

[10] I include my own work in this group. In *Strains of Utopia* I argued that classical Hollywood underscoring in the studio era supplemented film texts with utopian impressions of things that *weren't* provided by the films and their contexts, and that those utopian longings were frequently cast in nostalgic modes (e.g., "Tara's Theme" in *Gone with the Wind* evoked an idealized antebellum American South that provided an escape from a sense of contemporary deprivation and pain). Influenced by Marxist philosopher and music theorist Ernst Bloch and by film scholar Richard Dyer, I stressed the oppositional nature of these utopian wanderings and sensibilities, contrasting them with the realities of contemporary capital and industrial structures and of ideological imperatives more generally. In that study, however, I considered utopia to be tailored to the desires of conventional white, heterosexual masculinities and overlooked variations within and beyond that uniform, nostalgic utopian model. See Caryl Flinn, *Strains of Utopia: Nostalgia, Gender, and Hollywood Film Music* (Princeton, N.J.: Princeton University Press, 1992).

ideology—entertainment always seeks a point of comfort, whatever its point of departure).[11]

Dyer's analysis of *Music* is a compelling companion piece to his classic essay "Entertainment and Utopia" (1977), in which he asserts that film musicals establish social and ideological tensions and contradictions through representational means (narrative, dialogue) and then attempt to resolve or overpower them through nonrepresentational elements (style, color, movement, and, of course, music). Such contradictions are not confined to tensions presented in story lines and diegetic worlds, obviously. For instance, *The Gold Diggers of 1933* is a backstage musical set in the heart of the Great Depression, but it is not just its chorines who experience the period's woes; its audiences, too, were living in a world marked by scarcity. Consuming this movie gave viewers a fleeting sense of abundance, especially in Busby Berkeley's production numbers, most humorously "We're in the Money," in which Ginger Rogers and other chorines perform, literally, in costumes of outsized gold coins.

What makes *The Sound of Music* unusual for a *non*-backstage musical is the extent to which it openly and unselfconsciously celebrates music, linking it to freedom and release. The show compels music to function as the spontaneous expression of hope, endurance, folk populism, and nature. Despite the patent untruth of the premise, those musical joys emerge from their purported existence outside the tainted ideologies of race, fascism, and nationalism. Hammerstein's lyrics perform much of that labor, to be sure, but it is again music's privileged place in the film's fictional and narrative worlds that enables this ideological and utopian project to succeed. For example, it takes singing in the Trapp household to trump the Captain's emotional distance and fierce disciplinarianism, and later, singing to enable the family indirectly to trick the Nazis. That is a pretty potent utopia. Again, as Dyer states, "it is very commonly believed that music is a pure realm of feeling, beyond ideology... politics, business, advertising, the rat race—realms of manipulation, alienation, unfreedom."[12]

For members of *The Sound of Music*'s initial target audiences—North Atlantic, white, Christian, middle class, straight—its utopian refuge was readily enjoyable. Encountering the loss of their racial and gendered complacence and privilege through Civil Rights and emerging feminism, these Americans were also constrained by familial responsibilities, prescribed monogamy, and the decline of jobs over which they exerted much control. Positions in faceless corporations overtook smaller, local, even family-run

[11] Dyer's reading of *The Sound of Music* asserts that the film dramatizes the need for utopia while also showing its inability to deliver. Ultimately, Dyer maintains, the film works to encourage people to "keep on keeping on," yet falls far short in resolving any of the contradictions it reveals about heterosexual women like Maria. Obviously there is a disconnect between Dyer's savvy analysis and the satisfactions or messages other audiences might take away from *The Sound of Music*, but his piece is especially concerned with the conventions of women's melodrama operating in this 1965 family musical. See Richard Dyer, "The Sound of Music," *Movie* 23 (1976): 39–49.

[12] Dyer, "Entertainment as Utopia," 41.

jobs and the isolated, nuclear life of these Americans were a far cry from spontaneous singing atop dramatic green mountains. The collective and noble drama of fighting Nazis, moreover, seemed a far less dull way of experiencing social oppression or despair. At its many "nonrepresentational levels," then, *The Sound of Music* offered this group a utopian antidote, a pastoral white vacation into simpler, purer times, the comfort of an imagined past where these people could imagine themselves closer to the land, guardians of their own agency, able to stand up to evil and survive. Later, director Robert Wise reflected that had the film been released just two years later, it might have failed to hit a nerve;[13] its utopia horribly misplaced for a nation experiencing the "summer of love," protests against Vietnam, and demands made by other progressive and radical social movements. In 1965, *The Sound of Music* was able to squeak through its large, escapist vision and delivered it with musical fanfare and narrative simplicity. As far as utopias go, *The Sound of Music* has been a significant tutor-text for the United States, a master narrative of escapism, its nostalgia filled with naturalized, universalized freedoms, with menaces cleanly externalized. Its appeal was painted in broad strokes indeed.

It is precisely those universalizing white, middle-class utopias that the mutating musical breaks down and parses out. In so doing, even the oddest "musical pieces" challenge the fiction of unity and the privilege of the musical's earlier allure, cutting it down, piecemeal, into something ephemeral, less grandiose, and far less earnest, if no less pleasurable. For example, YouTube's "The Sound of Music in the Ghetto" points up the relentless desire for utopian resolution, and even more, the absurd improbability of black people ever locating such a thing in a white figure like Maria. The "blue-haired" version of "My Favorite Things" lets the film's older fans find relief not in defying thunderstorms, but in acknowledging their own aging bodies. Antwerp's flash mob is both critical and endearing as it juxtaposes the chipper new-world cheeriness of "Do Re Mi" against the established ritual of urban train commuting. Such utopian moments openly show a network of contradictions, conflicting intersections, and weird hybrids that do not and cannot line up into a single grand, utopian experience.

Of all the *Sound of Music*'s afterlife appearances, Lars von Trier's *Dancer in the Dark* most overtly deploys the classic, grandiose, oppositional utopian promise of the film. Yet *Dancer* brutally dramatizes the bankrupt nature of that promise, showing the extent to which the utopia of the big-budget Hollywood musical is not extended to the people who probably need it most, namely, those like its protagonist, Selma.[14] By contrast, "Wind It Up" 's references to *Sound of Music* have nothing to do with Stefani's actual song. Here, musical references function simply as stylistic embellishment, their utopian promise as politically unsure as anything "Wind It Up" might otherwise suggest. *Moulin Rouge*, on

[13] "I have often been told that if the film had been released two years earlier, or two years later, the public taste would have been different and we would not have been so successful," Robert Wise writes in his foreword to Julia Antopol Girsch, *The Sound of Music: The Making of America's Favorite Movie* (New York: McGraw Hill 1993), x.

[14] For an elaboration of the utopian function of *Sound of Music* in *Dancer in the Dark*, see Caryl Flinn, "Affect and Film Music in Wildly Uncaring Circumstances," in *Immediacy and Non-Simultaneity: Utopia of Sound*, ed. Diedrich Diederichsen and Constanze Ruhm (Vienna: Academy of Fine Arts, 2010), 89–114.

the other hand, focuses on the hyper-familiarity of *The Sound of Music*, sending it up, playing with it, enjoying it. Of course audience members know the lyrics to the eponymous song, and when MacGregor's character alights on them, they are invited to delight in his "creation" and in his comrades' twittering excitement.

That consummate familiarity of *The Sound of Music*—to Americans in particular, but also to global audiences—is crucial to explaining its robust afterlife as a musical mutating across media forms. Films like this have become touchstones, pieces easily gone back to and connected with, sources from which small pieces might be removed and made into new things. Far from turning *The Sound of Music* into a tired camp vehicle, its familiarity enables it to assume a wide range of new forms, whether as a soap ad on TV, a horror film trailer on YouTube, or a vacation tour in Salzburg. Of course the musical has always been a transmedia phenomenon, moving among stage, screen, and television technologies and industries, and that movement always connected film musicals to noncinematic musical venues such as Broadway, vaudeville, light opera, and cabaret. More recently, digital technologies, and new media at large, have stimulated the growth and movement of the film musical even further, producing and moving it through new global circulation patterns of capital and transnational boundaries.

Within this shifting circuitry, what the "mutating musical" provocatively illustrates is how much the utopian appeal, sensations, and affect that have long been affixed to music, music in film, and film musicals are themselves undergoing reconstruction. Again, I am not attributing any progressive political effect to the widening presence of musicals or to the fact that they can be produced and consumed by almost anyone with Internet access. Indeed, in some ways the more partial, ephemeral, and shortened expressions of these growing musical "pieces" suggest that our utopian energies and expressions themselves are tightly constrained, restricted to short lives slightly off the grid, and that our hopes and pleasures are likewise ephemeral, with vibrant affective intensity thriving only in short mashups and fabricated film trailers. Unlike the grand meta-utopias of old, these smaller musical expressions zoom in and out of the inboxes of bored office workers, going on- and offline without warning (copyright infringement knocked "Wind It Up" offline briefly).

The utopian impressions associated with old musicals were utopias writ large, writ universally, giving expression to the affect and hopes of dominant groups. Or so one would think. Because it was never really like that. White, middle-class Americans were not the only ones with relationships to these meta-utopias and to have "gotten" something out of the film. Countless nondominant individuals and groups have long enjoyed *The Sound of Music*, but like Lars von Trier's Selma, they were not always invited to participate in the utopias it promised. For all their global and transnational travel, then, these newer mutating musicals have the potential to be extremely intimate and localized in terms of their effects, as well as in their affect.

They also have a different relationship to temporality. The utopian energy of "Wind It Up" is arguably a mutation of *The Sound of Music*'s own celebration of music in an emphatic present tense. The song repeatedly veers back to "the beat" that Stefani announces in a call that starts the singing and dancing showbiz machine, along with the machinery of "boys" watching the "girls" throughout the video. An oversized key winding up the backs of female dancers enhances this same mechanistic theme. In the end, Stefani's repeated calls to "get it, girl!" and "keep going, girl," along with the video's coquettish chorus lines, simply have nothing in common with the more restrained, older celebrations and encouragements proffered by *The Sound of Music*. Yet if there is nothing that "Wind It Up" celebrates specifically about *Music*, the video offers nothing to lament about it either, no sense of loss or of a better life being behind us. The utopias of classical musicals, by contrast, nearly always were activated by nostalgia, a desire tethered to something lost and not regainable (e.g., *Meet Me in St. Louis*; *Brigadoon*). Unlike *Brigadoon*, however, these newer mutations possess a present-tense sparkle that doesn't have to wait a hundred years before producing an entire, coherent fantasy world all over again. Instead, the utopian microbursts of the mutating musical work and play all the time, constantly on the move and on the go.

Because many of these small musical pieces are organized around a sense of familiarity, rather than one of opposing lived experience (as *Gold Diggers* did by contrasting nonrepresentational abundance to actual material scarcity of the time), utopian expression is now, for better or worse, located within the habitual, not in movement away from it. What can we make of these pleasures of the familiar, of yearning not for what is new but for what is the same? In a way, this is just another response to pleasures not met. Worse, it could be a form of retreat or of unwitting resignation. But it might also suggest ways to refuse the promise, or premise, of hope and utopian betterment that is made and maintained by forces that do not speak to us. Perhaps familiarity enables people to cut musicals like *The Sound of Music* down to size, not out of punishment on the one hand or fetishization on the other, but to renew them and to keep them going as so many reworked pieces and revamped pleasures. After decades of existence, *The Sound of Music* continues to be raided for the overstuffed utopia it created through its songs. If that music is still performing a very old role by providing the link to utopia, at least that utopia has finally been split open. The allures and pleasures of this mutating musical are now available for many constituencies, producing all sorts of new effects and affects, even as they take origin from one master text.

References

Beck, Jay. "Another Music in a Different Kitchen, or Personal Music for Public Consumption." Paper presented at the Society for Cinema and Media Studies 2010 Conference, Los Angeles, March 19, 2010.

"Do Re Mi" Flash Mob, at http://www.youtube.com/watch?v=7EYAUazLI9k (accessed August 2010).

Dyer, Richard. "Entertainment as Utopia." In *Genre: The Musical*, edited by Rick Altman, 175–189. New York: Routledge, 1977.

Dyer, Richard. "The Sound of Music." *Movie* 23 (1976): 39–49.

Flinn, Caryl. *Strains of Utopia: Nostalgia, Gender, and Hollywood Film Music*. Princeton, N.J.: Princeton University Press, 1992.

Flinn, Caryl. "Affect and Film Music in Wildly Uncaring Circumstances." In *Immediacy and Non-Simultaneity: Utopia of Sound*, ed. Diedrich Diederichsen and Constanze Ruhm, 89–114. Vienna: Academy of Fine Arts, 2010.

Girsch, Julia Antopol. *The Sound of Music: The Making of America's Favorite Movie*. New York: McGraw-Hill, 1993.

Kemp, Peter. "How Do You Solve a 'Problem' Like Maria von Poppins?" In *Musicals: Hollywood and Beyond*, ed. Bill Marshall and Robynn Stilwell, 55–61. Exeter, UK: Intellect Press, 2000.

Kessler, Kelly. "Primetime Goes Hammerstein: The Musicalization of Primetime Fictional Television." Paper presented at the Society for Cinema and Media Studies 2010 Conference, Los Angeles, March 19, 2010.

Koestenbaum, Wayne. *The Queen's Throat: Opera, Homosexuality and the Mystery of Desire*. New York: Vintage, 1993.

"Movie Mistakes: *The Sound of Music*," at http://www.youtube.com/watch?v=xOLyX8ZLwZA&feature=related (accessed August 2010).

Ross, Andrew. "Uses of Camp." In *No Respect: Intellectuals and Popular Culture*, 135–170. New York: Routledge, 1989.

Snopes. "My Favorite Things," at http://www.snopes.com/humor/iftrue/andrews.asp (accessed June 2011).

"The Sound of Ghetto Music," at http://www.youtube.com/watch?v=AHcmvHqJk3I (accessed August 2010).

"Wind It Up," at http://www.youtube.com/watch?v=9sY-TsLXiDo&feature=related (accessed August 2010).

CHAPTER 16

CHINESE ROCK 'N' ROLL FILM AND CUI JIAN ON SCREEN

YING XIAO

Introduction: Generating a New Urban Sound, Cinema, and Culture

During the last two decades of the twentieth century, China witnessed a veritable explosion of films directed toward youth, shot through with the aesthetic and ethic of rock 'n' roll. Critics trace the origin of this phenomenon to the summer of 1986, when an angry young musician, Cui Jian, stirred up the country with "Nothing to My Name" (*Yi wu suo you*)—an innovative fusion of Western rock rhythm and "Northwest Wind"[1] melody—at the One Hundred Pop Stars concert at the Beijing Workers' Stadium.

Not only is this song acknowledged as a milestone in Chinese rock history, but it also made Cui Jian's name synonymous with Chinese rock music. Charged with a subculture sensibility, rock music (*yaogun yinyue*) was enthusiastically embraced by a large sector of Chinese youth and scholars alike, who came to valorize its unique status as politically subversive and artistically authentic. "Since its release, the wide availability of this music of anger and frustration has continued to empower opposition to the regime. *Yaogun yinyue*'s role as an objectification of anti-government feeling—as a resource for use in

[1] "Northwest Wind" is a popular music style of the mid- to late 1980s that distinctively draws from indigenous culture and folklore traditions of Northwest China.

political opposition—has intensified."[2] Brace and Friedlander's forceful characterization here invokes the ways popular culture is predicated on its political valence and social relevance. In this regard, Chinese rock is "politicized pop" par excellence.

The much celebrated "rock mythology,"[3] as Jeroen de Kloet puts it, rests on two distinct yet interdependent characteristics: although Chinese rock as a genre draws attention to its Western heritage, it also defines itself in opposition to the hegemony of the state and to the commercial mainstream. Cold War paradigms tend to dominate academic discourse on Chinese rock and a wide spectrum of cultural forms and artistic expressions, including the Sixth Generation's filmmaking. Reducing Chinese rock to a symbolic act of rebellion prioritizes narrow ideological readings and neglects nuances within the work. This chapter takes a different approach.

The Sixth Generation of Chinese filmmakers is commonly understood to be a cohort of independent vanguard artists. Their "minority" status and their defiance of mainstream cinematic institutions have earned them significant cultural capital. Mostly born in the 1960s, they were the first generation to grow up in the city; their personal narratives overlap historically with the course of socialist revolution and postsocialist reform. These film auteurs have been as marked by their youth as by their hyperbolic positioning as dissidents, their films made for and mainly circulated among a limited number of Western art house audiences. Unlike their distinguished Fifth Generation predecessors,[4] they are also the first group of filmmakers to be caught up in a maelstrom of film institutional reform. The transformation of film studios from state-monopolized entities into market-driven enterprises has pushed them to the forefront of the market with fewer attachments to (as well as protection from) the state. These artists' relative freedom from making propagandist pieces, and their newly gained economic power enabled by transnational capitalism, allow them to make films in entirely new ways. The Sixth Generation films have often been considered "political," or perhaps, "antipolitical": steering as clear as possible from the channels overseen by the state, they inherently protest state-sponsored cinema's financing, production, and distribution. The Sixth Generation has heralded a new wave of transnational cinema and independent artistic

2 Tim Brace and Paul Friedlander, "Rock and Roll on the New Long March: Popular Music, Cultural Identity, and Political Opposition in the People's Republic of China," in *Rockin' the Boat: Mass Music and Mass Movements*, ed. Reebee Garofalo (Boston: South End Press, 1992), 127.

3 Jeroen de Kloet, "Marx or Market: Chinese Rock and the Sound of Fury," in *Multiple Modernities: Cinemas and Popular Media in Transcultural East Asia*, ed. Jenny Kwok Wah Lau (Philadelphia: Temple University Press, 2003), 28–52.

4 Made up of the most prominent Chinese filmmakers, the Fifth Generation is widely understood as a group of film talents (including Zhang Yimou, Chen Kaige, Zhang Junzhao, and others) who created and defined a new wave of Chinese cinema in the 1980s. This movement is noted for its aesthetic experimentation, the innovative use of color and film technique, mesmerizing landscape shots, and legendary tales about the vast and mythical countryside of Northwest China. It is for this reason that the Fifth Generation's work is also identified as the cinematic equivalent of "Northwest Wind"—the Chinese Western—which showcases the immense, barren, and landlocked northwest of China.

practice, whose trajectory parallels the development of youth culture and popular music in the 1990s.

The new generation of urban filmmakers has fostered a direct relationship with popular music that inherited the cinematic and musical vocabularies of "Northwest Wind" and changed these traditions in the process. Popular music, rock specifically, entered into the cinematic space of everyday urbanity beginning in the late 1980s and provoked the formation of a specific film genre, Chinese rock 'n' roll. The alliances between the Sixth Generation and rock music have attracted considerable scholarly attention in recent years,[5] but many of these analyses are still limited by traditional classifications of film genres and conventional film historiography. I am not repudiating the important link between the Sixth Generation and rock culture. Driven by a group of "rock kids," the Sixth Generation films, with their youth character, subculture sensibility, and peculiar visual-vocal style, became thoroughly integrated with Chinese rock culture, as evidenced by a number of films, such as *Beijing Bastards (Beijing zazhong*, dir. Zhang Yuan, 1992), *Dirt* (*Toufa luanle*, dir. Guan Hu, 1993), *The Making of Steel* (*Gangtie shi zenyang liancheng de*, dir. Lu Xuezhang, 1995), *Age of Sensitivity* (*Ganguang shidai*, dir. Ah Nian, 1994), and *Weekend Lover* (*Zhoumo qingren*, dir. Lou Ye, 1995). Yet rock has also found its way into a vast array of works across different generations, ranging from Zhang Nuanxin's *Good Morning, Beijing* (*Beijing nizao*, 1990) and Xie Fei's *Black Snow* (*Ben Mingnian*, 1989), both with directors from the elite background of the earlier Fourth Generation; to films by the renowned Fifth Generation group, including Tian Zhuangzhuang's *Rock Kids* (*Yaogun qingnian*, 1988) and Zhang Yimou's *Keep Cool* (*Youhua haohao shuo*, 1997); to films from the more commercially oriented newcomers, such as Mi Jiashan's *The Troubleshooters* (*Wanzhu*, 1988) and Xia Gang's *Half Is Water, Half Is Flame* (*Yiban shi haisui, yiban shi huoyan*, 1989).

Deliberately crafted to assert a specific cultural identity and reflect social change in the late 1980s and early 1990s, rock became a platform upon which diverse generations of filmmakers, ideologies, styles, and artistic practices converged. The complex character and intricate intersection of rock 'n' roll and urban cinema thus call for a more nuanced deliberation, as rock in some of these films is neither merely a dissenting outcry nor a simple matter of "generation," but rather a polyphonic voice and aesthetic regime, representing a specific zeitgeist for a new period. As exemplified in films such as *Beijing Bastards* and the persona of Cui Jian, Chinese rock 'n' roll movies are not just symptomatic texts of youth rebellion or another privileged example of orchestrating sight and sound, but a lens trained on the traumatic and confounded postsocialist experience and

[5] For recent studies, see Yingjin Zhang, "Rebel Without a Cause? China's New Urban Generation and Postsocialist Filmmaking," in *The Urban Generation: Chinese Cinema and Society at the Turn of the Twenty-first Century*, ed. Zhang Zhen (Durham, N.C. and London: Duke University Press, 2007), 49–80; Jenny Kwok Wah Lau, "Globalization and Youthful Subculture: The Chinese Six-Generation Films at the Dawn of the New Century," in *Multiple Modernities: Cinemas and Popular Media in Transcultural East Asia*, ed. Jenny Kwok Wah Lau (Philadelphia: Temple University Press, 2003), 13–27; and Zhou Xuelin, *Young Rebels in Contemporary Chinese Cinema* (Hong Kong University Press, 2007).

the "lost" generation in search of identity against the backdrop of urbanization and globalization. At the core of this rock imaginary is the aesthetic of cinema vérité and postsocialist realism. In sync with the kaleidoscopic manifestation of the cityscape and long tracking shots of the protagonists roaming the metropolis, rock music, alongside the handheld mobile camera, seeks to document a reality of postmodern life and capture a feeling of postsocialist anxiety—a concern for realism also articulated through dialogue and ambient sound.

Beijing Bastards: Walking to the Beat of the City

Zhang Yuan's *Beijing Bastards* audaciously heralded the birth of the Sixth Generation. Moreover, it engaged the audiovisual confluence of Chinese rock and urban cinema, from its financing, production, and distribution to its content and style. Acclaimed as one of the first films to be made entirely outside the state studio system, this refreshing and daring film was funded in large part through the aid of investors from Hong Kong and the West (including the Hubert Bals Fund of the Film Festival Rotterdam; Shu Kei, a popular Hong Kong actress; and Christopher Doyle, the award-winning cinematographer who had worked in Hong Kong with Wong Kar-Wai on *Days of Being Wild* two years earlier). In addition, Zhang Yuan helped to finance the film with earnings from directing music videos, the style of which carries over into the film. The film was officially banned in mainland China and has never been released there. Provocatively adopting the name "Beijing Bastards" for both the film title and his production group—instead of giving credit to any of the state studios, the predominant practice on the socialist screen—Zhang Yuan poignantly parodied himself as well as his cinematic experiment as illegitimate offspring of the nation.

The film opens with a close-up of a shirtless young man playing drums. The tight framing and fetishizing lighting evoke the hypersexuality, narcissism, and mystery often associated with rock 'n' roll performance, also unveiling this once clandestine music to the gaze of ordinary viewers. The next shot shows a tableau of the band; the camera slowly tracks around it before cutting to a close-up of Cui Jian's face, singling him out as the star. This opening scene resembles the montage sequences in many music videos: like the images, the music is high-gloss, meticulously crafted, and lip-synched. But then, while providing this first striking glimpse into Chinese rock, the highly choreographed music video–style shots of the band performing begin to crosscut with a dramatic scene as the song plays underneath: in a rainy cosmopolitan city, against the noirish backdrop of traffic, a young couple stand under a highway bridge and urgently discuss what to do about the girl's pregnancy and the possibility of an abortion, until their argument is more than she can take. She runs away into the night.

Many critics observe an important link between rock music and the vérité style that underscores *Beijing Bastards* and a large number of Sixth Generation films. The integration of image and music, however, is more complex and multifaceted than the framework of "cinema vérité plus rock documentary" can account for. The two dynamics are usually closely intertwined with a high level of romanticism, in which rock has been symbolically constructed as an idealized site of authenticity and moreover a marketable commodity for alternative culture. As Geremie Barmé astutely points out, "Zhang was one of many mainland artists who over the years discovered a successful formula for the production of marketable alternative cultural material."[6] In the context of *Beijing Bastards*, a similar approach of mythmaking, or the "theatricalization" of the Chinese "bastards," as Berenice Reynaud puts it,[7] is significantly cast in many of the rock sequences and the texts of rock artists, Cui Jian in particular. In this regard, I focus more closely on the representation of Cui Jian to explore how his signature venture into the film arena taps into the discourses of authenticity, art, politics, and commerce, all central concerns of rock culture and Sixth Generation filmmaking.

Like many other rock films, *Beijing Bastards* makes extensive use of musical cues to reflect the characters' emotions and comment on dramatic situations. But what captivates the viewing public is not really how rock music serves such strictly narrative functions, but rather how it informs the film's visual style and creates affect and meaning. As a new kind of docudrama, *Beijing Bastards* defies traditional narrative structure and shifts constantly between the oppositions of onstage and offstage, fantasy and reality, fiction and documentary. Following Karzi's trajectory through the city to look for his girlfriend, the film is loosely structured around an array of incidents and visual collages that unfold in a highly stylized, MTV-like fashion.

Zhang Yuan's camera wanders like the protagonist: it pans and drifts around locations such as the streets of Beijing, construction sites, the dilapidated compound house, dark back alleys, and a boisterous marketplace to record a fast-changing urban environment as well as the marginal spaces occupied by alienated youth. It is also through this search that a network of urban drifters, social outcasts, and marginalized artists is exposed to the camera in a semidocumentary mode, a radical departure from the predominant socialist-realist tradition in Chinese cinema. Having most of these characters play themselves, sometimes talking to the camera spontaneously, Zhang Yuan reveals to us the rough reality of the underground scene that is a trademark of his work. A gang of cynical painters, writers, rock artists, and unemployed young people, who happened to be Zhang's real friends and personal acquaintances, dominates the screen. From an insider's vantage point, Zhang probes a secret life, the rarely seen underground world, endowing the film with a quality of liveliness and transparency—recalling the

[6] Geremie Barmé, *In the Red: On Contemporary Chinese Culture* (New York: Columbia University Press, 1996), 194.

[7] Berenice Reynaud, "Zhang Yuan's Imaginary Cities and the Theatricalization of the Chinese 'Bastards,'" in *The Urban Generation: Chinese Cinema and Society at the Turn of the Twenty-first Century*, ed. Zhang Zheng (Durham, N.C. and London: Duke University Press, 2007), 264–294.

Westernvaesthetic mode of rock documentary ("rockumentary"). The film's fairly loose organization and the erratic flow of the narrative are also reminiscent of the structure of rock music. Devices such as rapid zooms, and the coordination of visual editing with musical rhythm, indicate the influence of concert film and rock documentary, the two important genres with particular focus on live performances and star power. More intriguingly, ingredients of rock 'n' roll also inspire certain aspects of the film's mise-en-scene. A foggy ambience and neonish color scheme that resemble the design and lighting of onstage rock performance characterize numerous scenes of music rehearsals and performances and also penetrate the world behind the curtain, the space of postsocialist reality. It can be argued that as a whole the film seeks a kind of rock spirit—bold, furious, vernacular, and revolutionary.

Central to the film's appeal, to be sure, are the remarkable sound track and live footage of Chinese rock 'n' roll focusing on Cui Jian and several rising rock bands and stars, including Zang Tianshuo, Dou Wei, and He Yong. Cui Jian, the "Godfather" of Chinese rock 'n' roll, not only played a pivotal role in the film, but also participated extensively in the filmmaking, sharing credits with Zhang Yuan as a producer and screenwriter. This certainly was a marketing strategy to reach out to the local young audience as well as to Western festivalgoers; the film successfully capitalized on Cui Jian's cult status as a rock legend and icon of Chinese youth subculture. In the film Cui Jian's screen persona was carefully managed to enhance his public rock star persona. As mentioned previously, the first sequence places Cui Jian in a live performance and foregrounds him as a rock singer. Even when the camera shifts to the other narrative thread about the young couple, Cui Jian's singing voice remains on the sound track, serving as an authorial commentary:

> My body leans against you.
> My eyes are closed.
> My hands repeatedly touch myself.
> I want to satisfy myself and excite you as well.
> I want to tell you everything without you becoming angry.
>
> I don't love you anymore,
> But I don't hate you either.
> Although you are still you,
> I have no energy.
> And I don't think it is really necessary
> That I must fight you.
> Fuck off.
> Just fuck off.
> I curse you behind your back.
> Let's see, let's really see who can
> Stick it out right to the very end.

The song over the opening scene, "Tolerance" (*Kuanrong*), sketches out a picture of suffering youth, a sense of pain and frustration that permeates the entire film. Alienated and frenetic, the protagonist Karzi is a prototypical "Beijing bastard," lost and disoriented

FIGURE 16.1: Film poster of *Beijing Bastards* (1992).

FIGURE 16.2: Publicity still of *Beijing Bastards*.

FIGURE 16.3: Zhang Yuan.

FIGURE 16.4: Cui Jian.

FIGURE 16.5: The opening city scene in *Beijing Bastards*.

FIGURE 16.6: Cui Jian in the film.

FIGURE 16.7: Dou Wei in the film.

in postsocialist China. The film tracks his aimless wanderings on the street and shows him engaging in drinking, casual sex, and senseless brawls in a seemingly unmediated manner. It is also through his point of view that we see the city of Beijing and its underground milieus. To a great extent, Karzi is a mirror image of Cui Jian in the nonmusical world. Although these two characters are cast in the same frame in only one scene (this is also one of the very few scenes in which Cui Jian is seen talking), the film deliberately uses the theme of searching to link them together. In parallel to Karzi's search for his girlfriend, Cui Jian's band has lost its rehearsal space and is under a deadline to look for a new venue.

In many ways, *Beijing Bastards* achieves an interesting tension between stage and backstage, diegetic and nondiegetic, fiction and documentary. Its experimental innovation derives not just from such shifting boundaries, but also from a kind of musical dynamic. Rock performance occupies much of the narrative, including songs such as "Beijing Story" (*Beijing gushi*), "The Last Complaints" (*Zuihou de baoyuan*), "Like a Knife" (*Xiang yiba daozi*), "Tolerance" (*Kuanrong*), "Dreaming" (*Zuomeng*), and "Bell and Drum Towers" (*Zhonggulou*). On the other hand, the association of rock with an ideology of authenticity and cultural opposition has been assimilated into the narrative sections involving Karzi's rootless wanderings. And the symbolic, powerful presence of Cui Jian accentuates the youth subculture undertone of the film.

Rock 'n' Roll on the New Long March: Iconography of Cui Jian

For many Chinese, rock music is inseparably linked to the name of Cui Jian. Tremendously influential among Chinese adolescents and urban dwellers of the 1980s and 1990s, he became an icon for youth rebellion. He came to prominence with "Nothing to My Name" (1987), considered the first Chinese rock song, which has been widely seen as "an emotional catharsis," as well as "an allegorical jab at the dominance of the CCP."[8] His first album, *Rock 'n' Roll on the New Long March* (*Xin changzheng lu shang de yaogun*), was released in 1989; it was a commercial hit and helped to elevate rock music from its underground status to the mass public sphere. More important, his rise to fame coincided with a major historical event, the Tiananmen Square events of 1989; students played and sang his songs in the demonstrations "as a means for affective empowerment, cultural critique, and as a

[8] Andrew F Jones, *Like a Knife: Ideology and Genre in Contemporary Chinese Popular Music* (Ithaca, N.Y.: Cornell University, 1992), 137.

conduit for explicitly political protest."[9] Although he was subsequently banned from performing on television and in other public venues, Cui Jian, like many of his vanguard contemporaries, has built his career in close association with Chinese underground youth culture.

This context is key to understanding *Beijing Bastards*, for Zhang Yuan critically drew on the symbolic power of Cui Jian to formulate his version of cinematic authenticity, resistance, and criticism. The film relies on popular memory and the viewer's awareness of its intertextual references to Cui Jian's rock star persona as part of its promotional efforts. A number of his early songs, for example, "Like a Knife" from the album *Solution* (*Jiejue*), constitute a very large part of the sound track of the film, whereas newer songs such as "Beijing Story," "Tolerance," and "The Last Complaints" were successfully premiered in the film and greatly benefited from the film and music cross-promotion. In this light, it is certainly no stretch to see this independent, low-budget film as a feature-length music video, exploiting Cui Jian's cultural capital to sell a notion of "Chinese subculture" to its audiences.

In the spirit of rock documentary, *Beijing Bastards* admits us into a private, seemingly unscripted world. Improvised elements of the quotidian are exposed to the cinematic eye as much as the spectacular, onstage performance. The flip side of these raw, realistic depictions, however, is the film's rigorous control of Cui Jian's image and voice. From beginning to end, it constructs Cui Jian as a singer, in a role that closely matches his image in the popular consciousness. Even in the diegesis, he still fully lives up to his public persona: he plays music and sings in his signature growl, organizes his band and plans performances, and looks for a rehearsal space. We hear his singing voice much more than his speaking voice. He speaks only sporadically and in a constrained manner, in stark contrast to other characters' cascades of speech in heavily accented Beijing vernacular. Playing himself, Cui Jian gives the role an iconographic significance and ritual tone. In this sense Zhang Yuan reconstructs rock mythology while demystifying it at the same time.

A review of the film text and music lyrics, especially in the last scene, will illustrate my points. Karzi eventually succeeds in finding his girlfriend, but he is utterly shocked to learn that she has had the baby. The film dissolves to a close-up of his bewildered face, followed by various shots of him walking aimlessly again in the street, to the beat of Cui Jian's "Beijing Story":

> Sang for quite a while but still didn't sing completely about
> the pain of this city.
> But the more pain, the more we're able to imagine
> the happiness of tomorrow.
> I wear a smile on my face like everybody else
> still living on this earth.
> I'm prepared now to speak
> the fucking truth, lies, and nonsense.

[9] Andrew F Jones, "The Politics of Popular Culture in Post-Tiananmen China," in *Popular Protest and Political Culture in Modern China*, ed. Jeffery N. Wasserstrom and Elizabeth J. Perry (Boulder, Colo.: Westview Press, 1994), 155.

Suddenly a new movement comes along
And changes my life like a revolution.
A girl bringing love appears
Whipping my face like a storm.

On the one hand, this theme song literally rearticulates Karzi's inner world, afflicted with pain, rage, and disillusion. On the other, it leaves the film with an open, ambivalent ending and injects a metaphor of birth and growth into the story of the child's birth, an event that marks Karzi's growth out of adolescence and into adulthood.

Karzi's transition to fatherhood at the end reverse-mirrors the opening scene, in which the fatherless Karzi rejects the idea of becoming a father himself. Film scholars such as Dai Jinhua and Cui Shuqin have identified a dominant pattern of fatherlessness or the absent father in the Sixth Generation films.[10] While the motif of the denunciation of the father (and symbolic patriarchal authority) finds its greatest resonance in *Beijing Bastards*, I think the film also works to rebuild the father figure from a different angle. In contrast to the biological father who has been erased in the story of Karzi, the primacy of Cui Jian and his penetrating voice clearly serve to fill this vacuum. The film foregrounds him not only as a rock star but also as a spiritual leader and symbolic father. His deliberately constructed "ordinariness," albeit in a vérité rockumentary fashion, only reinforces Cui Jian as the Godfather of Chinese rock and the leader of the young generation.

This fatherly persona is further fleshed out in *Roots and Branches* (*Wo de xiongdi jiemei*, dir. Yu Zhong, 2001), a tearjerker in which Cui Jian plays an actual father. A cheesy reworking of Zhang Yimou's *The Road Home* (*Wode fuqin muqin*, "My Father and Mother," 1999), *Roots and Branches* (the replicated message in its Chinese title, "My Brothers and Sisters," may have been a deliberate attempt to attract a larger audience) fared well at the domestic box office but failed critically. In response to the harsh criticism leveled against it and Cui Jian's role specifically,[11] its director, Yu Zhong, explained that the association of Cui Jian with a father figure is not accidental, but rather "a look back to the past, a return to an innocent, idealist age that Cui Jian symbolizes."[12] Cui Jian played a role other than himself for the first time, but the film was nonetheless designed and scored in reference to his musical persona and iconography. He commented in

[10] See Dai Jinhua, *Wuzhong fengjing: zhongguo dianying wenhua 1978–1998* (Beijing: Beijing daxue chubanshe, 2000), 408–411; and Cui Shuqin, "Working from the Margins: Urban Cinema and Independent Directors in Contemporary China," *Post Script* 20, nos. 2–3 (Winter/Spring & Summer 2001): 77–93.

[11] The film stirred up widespread discussion in various film forums and among audiences. A good example is the film review, "*Wo de xiongdijiemei*: yige bei langfei de Cui Jian" [*Roots and Branches*: A Wasted Cui Jian], at http://www.dyddy.com/html/movie_article/1/1075.html (accessed July 11, 2011).

[12] Yu Zhong, "*Wo de xiongdijiemei* daoyan shouji" [A Manuscript from the Director for *Roots and Branches*], *Dianying yishu* [*Film Art*] 5 (2001):65–66.

self-defense, "If the role had not been specified as a music teacher, I wouldn't have participated in the project."[13] It is also through this role that the two aspects of rebellion and nostalgia—the key components of rock youth culture—are merged and intertwined.

Even though Cui Jian has a secondary role in *Roots and Branches*, it occupies a privileged space. He plays a father who only exists in flashbacks—the good old days. He is the source of enlightenment and the most intriguing figure in the film, always equipped with truth, wisdom, the highest moral standard, and above all the empowerment of song. In the climactic scene where the "father" teaches his final class and bids farewell to his students, the camera slowly pans across the entire class as they rehearse "Dream" (*Meng*, a song composed by Cui Jian specifically for the film), comes to rest on Cui Jian, and gradually zooms in until his face fills the screen. In juxtaposition to this heroic imagery, we hear his character's stentorian, philosophical remark—"wherever music is found, our soul will never feel alone"—amplified notably until a melodic and evocative music cue joins in. This aphorism about music feeding the soul immediately recalls a famous line from Cui Jian at his performance of "A Piece of Red Cloth" (*Yikuai hongbu*) during his 1990 tour: "If you feel that some things in life are not reliable, I hope you will make music your one exception. Music will never deceive you."[14] Through this statement of the song (he blindfolded himself with a piece of red cloth as he performed it), Cui Jian boldly confronts the party-state, which in his view has for decades manipulated and smothered the people's true feelings; in contrast, he celebrates the innocence, sincerity, and purity of rock. Whereas rock mythology and its aesthetic of authenticity have shaped the film, what this dreary melodrama stresses even more strongly is music's pragmatic and pedagogic function, which resonates with the traditional Confucian notion of music as a kind of safety valve, an educational tool, an instrument to soothe, and an outlet for the release of emotion and energy. Cui Jian's rebellious, rusty look and hard, rough voice were thus greatly tamed and softened to serve the dramatic and commercial interests at work in *Roots and Branches*.

Cui Jian's first above-ground appearance drew a large audience, but it also raised the eyebrows of many reviewers: "Cui Jian's stardom cannot adequately compensate for his insufficient dramatic experience."[15] Clearly aware of the gap between his musical charisma and screen persona, he commented, "I am above all a musician. I still identified myself as a musician even when I was involved in the film."[16] He recalled his performance in *Beijing Bastards*, which to him was more of a documentary experience: "I was still myself in front of the camera. I never acted intentionally and I didn't know how to

[13] "Cui Jian: Chengdu, wo ai ni" [Cui Jian: Chengdu, I Love You], at http://elite.youth.cn/zgzk/200910/t20091016_1052241.htm (accessed July 11, 2011).

[14] Zhao Jianwei, *Cui Jian zai Yiwosuoyou zhong nahan: Zhongguo yaogun beiwanglu [Cui Jian Cries Out in "Nothing to My Name": A Memorandum on Chinese Rock]* (Beijing: Beijing shifan daxue chubanshe, 1992), 74.

[15] Cui Chen, "Mishi de xuanlv: ping wode *xiongdi jiemei*" [Disconcerting Melody: A Film Review on *Roots and Branches*], *Beijing dianying xueyuan xuebiao* [*The Journal of Beijing Film Academy*] 4 (2001): 89–91.

[16] "Cui Jian: Chengdu, wo ai ni."

act at all."[17] Cui Jian's venture into cinema poses an interesting case, for he is not merely a film star, but more a rock star in a double role that both de-iconizes and re-iconizes. Moreover, his persona is predicated on the discourse of authenticity, the underlying ideology of rock music and culture he embodies. We can say that the most "authentic" moments in Cui Jian's film roles are when he is most "himself," when he gets close to his iconic stardom and engages in his signature singing.

To a certain degree, Cui Jian's singing voice is a self-sufficient entity that could flow freely as a pure, transcendental, and timeless experience. In *Beijing Bastards*, in opposition to the pervasive synchronized sound and ambient noise that characterize the sound track, the songs are the only acoustic element inserted nondiegetically. As a voice external to the events on screen, his singing connotes a position of absolute knowledge, endowed with a capacity to travel across temporal and spatial boundaries. Hence his voice acts to tie various shots and visual montages together. To put it another way, his singing functions as the "acousmêtre," the disembodied voice, which according to Michel Chion is an acoustic agency that has "the power of seeing all," "the power of omniscience," and "the gift of ubiquity."[18] Furthermore, Cui Jian's idiosyncratic voice constitutes an important signifier, a sonic manifestation of what Hebdige describes as the oppositional style of subculture.[19] At the vanguard of Chinese rock culture, Cui Jian gives voice to the political and poetic complexity of the underground scene.

The most direct, daring challenge to authority is, of course, his highly expressive and metaphorical song lyrics. Many of his songs adopt a similar narrative, in which the conflicted relationships between a man and his lover or a son and his father—and by extension, people and the party-state—are often underlined and openly interrogated. This preoccupation also characterizes the themes and concerns of the Sixth Generation films. Cui Jian's political and cultural critiques are also deeply implicated in the soundscape of his music: his style is slow and melodic, yet punctuated by a strong beat. His singing is loud, husky, low, throaty, and sometimes even unintelligible, complementing the sense of ambiguity that is often conveyed in the words. His voice is macho and powerful, but also lonely and tormented. In addition to the sounds of electric guitar and drumbeats, he deliberately incorporates traditional Chinese instruments such as the *erhu* (a Chinese two-stringed fiddle), *pipa* (a Chinese four-stringed lute), and *guzheng* (a Chinese seven-stringed zither), as well as the folk musical styles of Northwest China, so as to "Sinicize" rock and produce a hybrid, fluid, multifarious soundscape.

Cui Jian's celebrated iconoclastic pose, his singing style, and his border-crossing music have struck many other filmmakers as a new means to register the emerging ethos of youth urbanity in contemporary China. *Age of Sensitivity* (*Ganguang shidai*, dir. Ah Nian, 1994) features Cui Jian's song "Greenhouse Girl" (*Huafang guniang*) as a poignant commentary on a young photographer's painstaking, solitary struggle in a commodified

[17] Ibid.

[18] Michel Chion, *Audio-Vision. Sound on Screen*, trans. Claudia Gorbman (New York: Columbia University Press, 1994), 129–131.

[19] For the definition of youth subculture and an analysis of its various configurations, see Dick Hebdige, *Subculture: The Meaning of Style* (London and New York: Taylor and Francis, 2002).

society and his yearnings for artistic and personal freedom. In another cinematic representation of contemporary life, *Good Morning, Beijing* (*Beijing nizao*, dir. Zhang Nuanxin, 1990), Cui Jian's personality and voice are also appropriated to celebrate the birth of self-consciousness, individuality, and cosmopolitanism in the new market-driven society.

Good Morning, Beijing includes a pivotal scene in which the two protagonists, Ai Hong and Keke, visit a bar. Keke joins the band, dedicating to Ai Hong a popular song by Cui Jian, "Fake Monk" (*Jiaxingseng*):

> I want to go from south to north.
> I want to go from white to black.
> I want everybody to watch me
> But not knowing who I am.
>
> If you see me looking a little tired
> Then please pour me a bowl of water.
> If you fall in love with me
> Then please kiss me.
>
> I have these feet and legs.
> I have so many mountains and rivers.
> I want all of these—but not hatred or regret.
> If you want to love me, don't worry about regretting it,
> Because eventually I always leave everything behind.
> I never stay in one place
> And never want anyone to follow me.

The live performance, charged with youthful energy and passion, dazzles Ai Hong, who has a monotonous day job as a bus conductor. This rock song crying out for romance without restraint strikes a deep chord in her. Although she's confused upon hearing it for the first time, Ai Hong starts to use the Walkman that Keke has given her and learns the song. It is the Walkman with a rock 'n' roll tape—an emblem of modern youth culture—that enchants her and helps Keke win her heart. In contrast, her other admirer, the bus driver Zhou Yongqiang, lives with his parents in an overcrowded Beijing courtyard; his only hobby and means of self-expression, playing traditional Chinese violin and later guitar, is constantly silenced by his mother. Ai Hong's choice between the two suitors is symbolic. Her favoring the individualist, adventurous, and open-ended life over the conformist, secure, and traditional way provides a snapshot of the social change occurring in China in the 1980s and 1990s, against the backdrop of the shift from the stagnant, state-controlled life to the market-driven, "free" era.

While *Good Morning, Beijing* demonstrates a fascination with the new prospect of market reform and urban modernity, it does not express its optimism without reservation. Its ambivalence is also embodied in the song performance. At first glance Keke comes off as a positive character, energetic, romantic, and modern. His primary identity as a foreign student and his fashionable attire set him apart from the plainspoken and inhibited bus driver Zhou Yongqiang. Yet beneath Keke's charming façade lies his "truer" identity: as the film progresses, he is revealed to be a flamboyant idler, reflecting another facet of modern urban life: superficial, fabricated, fluid, and at times contradictory. The use of Cui Jian's

FIGURE 16.8: Film poster of *Roots and Branches.*

FIGURE 16.9: Film poster of *Good Morning, Beijing.*

FIGURE 16.10: DVD cover of The Making of Steel.

rock song "Fake Monk" helps establish these important features of modern life; marked by youth, romance, and sexuality, it is first of all associated with Keke's romanticism and his sunny outlook. Yet the performance, though live, is merely an act of mimicry: Keke works hard to imitate Cui Jian (who doesn't appear in the film). The imitation, which suggests Keke's shallowness and lack of creativity, contradicts the basic principle of rock culture's "authenticity." On the other hand, the young man's performance paradoxically conveys his craving for freedom and self-empowerment (two core elements of rock culture) and his wish to be transformed, synthesized, integrated into the new socioeconomic system.

Ambivalence toward rock and the postsocialist transition is further manifested in *The Making of Steel* (*Gangtie shi zenyang liancheng de*, dir. Lu Xuezhang, 1995), another striking piece about a lost generation of Chinese youth in search of "truth" in an increasingly commodified, globalized China. As in the films discussed previously, rock is incorporated into the narrative as part of everyday life. The guitar as a paramount image and the emphasis on protagonist Zhou Qing's affiliation with this specific musical instrument give the work a youth flavor. Rock figures here again as a significant marker of youth, freedom, individualism, creativity, and liberation. But this culture could lead in another direction: some of the scenes disclose the underground, in a gritty realistic style, where drug deals, miscegenation, and illegitimate activities and corrupted social mores prevail. To break away from the trap that rock unexpectedly sets for him, Zhou goes abroad. But his self-exile does not provide a satisfactory solution. The double alienation of spatial and spiritual displacement haunts him until he rediscovers a revolutionary classic, *The Making of Steel*, a Soviet novel that was translated and became tremendously popular in China during Mao's era. In addition, his old-fashioned, senior coworker becomes a kind of symbolic father, a reified hero, who comes to rescue him from the disillusionment of his rock experience. A landmark that signals the coming-of-age of the new urban generation (it has another title, *Zhangda Chengren*, which translates as "growing up"), the film is also a highly nostalgic work that, in its tortuous journey to self-discovery, pays homage to the old generation and the revolutionary past. Tian Zhuangzhuang, an eminent Fifth Generation filmmaker, was the film's producer, and he also played its mythical and imaginary father/hero.

Conclusion

The emergence of Chinese rock 'n' roll film and its development from the late 1980s to the new century can be seen as a result of widespread and multifaceted transformations in postsocialist China. Examining films ranging from the countercultural *Beijing Bastards* to the more mainstream *Good Morning, Beijing* and *The Making of Steel*, I have offered a glimpse of urban youth cinema and Chinese rock from an audiovisual perspective. "Urban youth" as a cinematic trope has been represented in contemporary Chinese filmmaking through a singular form of rock and popular music sound track. The picture given here of rock 'n' roll is not just a film genre or formal practice, but more broadly, a theoretical, analytical, and aesthetic framework that allows us to investigate how discourses of politics, youth rebellion, subculture, marginality, and authenticity—in short, the essence of rock culture—play into the formation of a new urban cinema at this particular juncture of social change.

Cui Jian's venture into film is exemplary in this light. His iconic status in Chinese rock history made him a natural to appear in rock 'n' roll movies. His screen roles have been carefully crafted in accord with his rock star identity. His intimate collaboration with the new urban filmmakers (who share a common interest in Chinese youth subculture) contributed to the burgeoning of rock 'n' roll movies, a unique brand of audio-visual synergy initiated in *Beijing Bastard*. By the time the film had garnered important awards at international film festivals in 1992, Cui Jian was at the height of his fame. His two albums, *Rock 'n' Roll on the Long March* (*Xin changzheng lu shang de yaogun*) and *Solution* (*Jiejue*), both became best sellers on the black market as well as sensational hits that topped the national music charts. Cui Jian continued to produce albums in the following years: *Balls under the Red Flag* (*Hongqi xia de dan*, 1994), *The Power of the Powerless* (*Wuneng de liliang*, 1998), and *Show Your Color* (*Gei ni yidian yanse*, 2005), none of which achieved the same success. While his prestige and Chinese rock music in general suffered a considerable decline at the turn of the new century, Cui Jian appeared in his second film during this period. His virtuous father role in *Roots and Branches* in 2001 signaled a nostalgic return to his music roots and the golden age of Chinese rock. In 2007 he played a cameo part in a surreal fantasy, *The Sun Also Rises* (*Taiyang zhaochang shengqi*, dir. Jiang Wen), as a close friend of Old Tang (played by the director). He is onscreen for only a few minutes, but the part consolidates some key aspects of his evolving star persona: spontaneous, free-willed, mysterious, and nostalgic.

Whereas these roles were by and large connected to his rock star iconography, Cui Jian's film adventure has taken another turn in recent years, as he has gradually retreated from the music stage and developed a greater interest in film. He produced and directed a seven-minute Internet film, *The Age of Repairing Virginity* (*Xiufu chunvmo shidai*), in 2007. This video on gender politics and women's liberation in contemporary China won the Best Mobile Movie of the Year award. Then, teaming up with veteran filmmakers Fruit Chan and Jin-ho Hur, he directed one of the segments of *Chengdu, I Love You* (*Chengdu, wo ai ni*), the closing film at the 2009 Venice Film Festival. His most recent project is a feature-length, eponymous drama adapted from his hit song, *Blue Bone* (*Lanse gutou*), for which he has assumed the multiple roles of screenwriter, producer, and director. While Cui Jian's rock stardom might have brought him offers of screen roles and film contracts, his latest directorial works have little to do with music, and they accordingly enrich and diversify his public image. Asked how he relates to film as a musician, Cui Jian has commented: "I believe film and music are essentially the same. It is the common desire for self-expression and showing concern that motivates me to delve into the domain of cinema. It is also the spirit and energy of rock that drive me to continue traveling the path of film and creativity."[20]

[20] "Duihua Cui Jian: Rang wo zai dianying li sadianye" [A Dialogue with Cui Jian: Let Me Play a Bit Wild in the Film], *Shidai zhoubao [Time Weekly]*, June 11, 2009, at http://culture.ifeng.com/special/shidaizhoubao001/news/200906/0611_6743_1198729.shtml (accessed August 25, 2011).

References

Baranovitch, Nimrod. *China's New Voices: Popular Music, Ethinicity, Gender, and Politics, 1978–1997*. Berkeley: University of California Press, 2003.

Barmé, Geremie. *In the Red: On Contemporary Chinese Culture*. New York: Columbia University Press, 1996.

Brace, Timothy. "Popular Music in Contemporary Beijing: Modernism and Cultural Identity." *Asian Music* 22, no. 2 (Spring/Summer 1991): 43–63.

Brace, Timothy, and Paul Friedlander. "Rock and Roll on the New Long March: Popular Music, Cultural Identity, and Political Opposition in the People's Republic of China." In *Rockin' the Boat: Mass Music and Mass Movements*, edited by Reebee Garofalo, 115–128. Boston: South End Press, 1992.

Chen, Cui. "Mishi de xuanlv: ping *wode xiongdi jiemei*" [Disconcerting Melody: A Film Review on *Roots and Branches*]. *Beijing dianying xueyuan xuebiao* [*The Journal of Beijing Film Academy*] 4, (2001).

Chion, Michel. *Audio-Vision: Sound on Screen*. Translated by Claudia Gorbman. New York: Columbia University Press, 1994.

Dai, Jinhua. *Wuzhong fengjing: zhongguo dianying wenhua 1978–1998* [*A Landscape in Mist: Chinese Film Culture 1978–1998*]. Beijing: Beijing daxue chubanshe, 2000.

Dai, Jinhua. "Sonic Sturdiness: The Globalization of 'Chinese' Rock and Pop." *Critical Studies in Media Communication* 22, no. 4 (November 2005): 321–338.

De Kloet, Jeroen. "Marx or Market: Chinese Rock and the Sound of Fury." In *Multiple Modernities: Cinemas and Popular Media in Transcultural East Asia*, edited by Jenny Kwok Wah Lau, 28–52. Philadelphia: Temple University Press, 2003.

De Kloet, Jeroen. *China with a Cut: Globalization, Urban Youth and Popular Music*. Amsterdam: Amsterdam University Press, 2010.

Fore, Steve. "From Rock Kids to Beijing Bastards: PRC Youth Subcultures on Film Before and After June 4." *Screening the Past* 18 (2005). At http://www.latrobe.edu.au/screeningthepast/firstrelease/fr_18/SFfr18a.html.

Jones, Andrew. "The Politics of Popular Culture in Post-Tiananmen China." In *Popular Protest and Political Culture in Modern China*, edited by Jeffery N. Wasserstrom and Elizabeth J. Perry, 155. Boulder, Colo.: Westview Press, 1994.

Jones, Andrew F.. *Like a Knife: Ideology and Genre in Contemporary Chinese Popular Music*. Ithaca, N.Y.: Cornell University, 1992.

Hebdige, Dick. *Subculture: The Meaning of Style*. London: Taylor and Francis, 2002.

Lau, Jenny Kwok Wah, ed. *Multiple Modernities: Cinemas and Popular Media in Transcultural East Asia*. Philadelphia: Temple University Press, 2003.

Romney, Jonathan, and Adrian Wootton, eds. *Celluloid Jukebox: Popular Music and the Movies Since the 50s*. London: British Film Institute, 1995.

Shuqin, Cui. "Working from the Margins: Urban Cinema and Independent Directors in Contemporary China." *Post Script* 20, nos. 2–3 (Winter/Spring & Summer 2001): 77–93.

Zhang, Yingjin. "Rebel Without a Cause? China's New Urban Generation and Postsocialist Filmmaking." In *The Urban Generation: Chinese Cinema and Society at the Turn of the Twenty-first Century*, edited by Zhang Zhen, 49–80. Durham, N.C. and London: Duke University Press, 2007.

Zhang, Zhen, ed. *The Urban Generation: Chinese Cinema and Society at the Turn of the Twenty-first Century*. Durham, N.C.: Duke University Press, 2007.

Zhao, Jianwei. *Cui Jian zai Yiwosuoyou zhong nahan: Zhongguo yaogun beiwanglu* [*Cui Jian Cries Out in "Nothing to My Name": A Memorandum on Chinese Rock*]. Beijing: Beijing shifan daxue chubanshe, 1992.

Zhong, Yu. "*Wo de xiongdijiemei* daoyan shouji" [A Manuscript from the Director for *Roots and Branches*]. *Dianying yishu* [*Film Art*] 5 (2001).

Zhou, Xuelin. *Young Rebels in Contemporary Chinese Cinema*. Hong Kong: Hong Kong University Press, 2007.

CHAPTER 17

THE NEOSURREALIST MUSICAL AND TSAI MING-LIANG'S *THE WAYWARD CLOUD*

JOHN RICHARDSON

THE resurgence of film musicals at the independent margins of popular culture could easily be interpreted in light of reflexive postmodernist politics. Such a view does no major disservice to the phenomena discussed below, which trade in staples of postmodernism like parody, ambiguity between high and low, and genre hybridity, but it does leave important questions unanswered about cultural significance that I attempt to address in this chapter. In my exposition of neosurrealist musicals, I approach the subject by considering the relationship between cultural memory and aesthetic experience in Tsai Ming-Liang's *The Wayward Cloud* (*Tian bian yi duo yun*, 2005). *Wayward Cloud* further exemplifies how musicals today generate meanings that transect both local and transcultural levels of experience. These two axes, historical and geopolitical, provide the dual foundations for my reading, alongside writing on surrealism and digital culture, perspectives that open up new insights into the workings and significance of contemporary art house cinema.

As a retrospective and even anachronistic genre, film musicals are unavoidably tethered to cultural memories (remembered pasts). Critical discussion of musicals therefore requires attention to genre conventions as well as cultural context. Musicals involve a specific mode of organizing narrative and spectacular events that is highly differentiated from conventional realist forms, even while they resemble other aspects of popular media culture, including an emphasis on the sensory, the spectacular, and the inclusion of commercial popular songs. New musical forms are therefore unavoidably of the past even as they stake a compelling claim for acceptance in the present. A present-day perspective emerges above all from the act of remediating historical materials, which implies a contemporary mediating agency that might be considered reflective. In other words, these musicals make use of historical sources as well as invoking a historical genre. However, the fact that contemporary agents (auteur directors) are responsible for recontextualizing outmoded materials makes the contemporary world shared by the director and audiences more relevant to critical readings than the historical one: at both ends of the communication chain one is dealing with cultural memory rather than the past itself.[1]

My choice of the term "cultural memory" rather than "historical allusion" is deliberate. Archaeologist Jan Assman uses the concept "figures of memory" to explain how cultural memory differs from other forms of historical awareness.[2] Figures of memory stand apart from everyday lived reality in that they are repeated, ritualized, or otherwise displaced from original contexts, which elevates their cultural significance. This distance from ordinary life invests cultural memories with an aura of transcendence, which causes a breach between the pastness of the repeated action and the presentness of the performative context. In my analysis of *The Wayward Cloud*, I show how musical numbers become figures of memory that simultaneously affirm presentness and pastness. Musical moments in what I will call metamusicals have what Assman, citing Aby Warburg, calls "mnemonic energy," which arises both from inherent qualities of the object (which Assman calls its potentialities), in this case the musical number, and its circulation in present-day contexts.[3] Cultural memory is reconstitutive insofar as it implies the decoding of these "immovable" figures in a contemporary frame of reference. Put differently, cultural memory implies a dialogue between the present day and something that has been taken from the past. It is also reflexive insofar as this dialogue encourages those who come in contact with figures of memory to reflect. My investigation concentrates on the way the various elements of the soundtrack in Tsai's film engage in a dialogue with the past that allows each to reflect on the other. This practice of cultural "borrowing" through recontextualization closely resembles both montage aesthetics in historical surrealism and contemporary remix culture.[4]

What are neosurrealist metamusicals? The cornucopia of practices discussed in Caryl Flinn's chapter in this book covers some of the same territory as I will cover here, although Flinn is mainly concerned with explaining how phenomena from flash mobs to reality television remediate the aesthetic codes of musicals. My focus is narrower. Implying a reflexive relationship to early musical films, metamusicals have been around almost since the birth of the genre and have interested film theorists for the past couple

[1] Jan Assman, "Collective Memory and Cultural Identity," *New German Critique* 65 (Spring–Summer), 129. See also Jan Assman, *Cultural Memory and Early Civilization: Writing, Remembrance, and Political Imagination* (Cambridge, UK: Cambridge University Press, 2011), 23–28.

[2] Jan Assman, *Cultural Memory and Early Civilization: Writing, Remembrance, and Political Imagination* (Cambridge, UK: Cambridge University Press, 2011), 23–28

[3] Ibid.

[4] I consider surrealism a productive analogy more than implying a direct line back to the historical movement. The concept offers an alternative to theories that cast recent artistic practices as implicitly decontextualized and affectively neuter. See also John Richardson, *An Eye for Music: Popular Music and the Audiovisual Surreal* (New York; Oxford: Oxford University Press, 2011); and "Plasticine Music: Surrealism in Peter Gabriel's 'Sledgehammer'," in *Games Without Frontiers: Peter Gabriel from Genesis to Growing Up*, ed. Michael Drewett, Sarah Hill, and Kimi Kärki (Farnham, UK; Burlington, Vt.: Ashgate, 2010), 195–210.

of decades. The subgenre of the backstage musical has been a prominent formula since the beginning of movie musicals, and some degree of reflexivity is an almost inherent quality of many of them: musicals are often *about* other musicals, whether produced for the stage or the silver screen.

Jane Feuer theorizes the functions and meanings of what she calls self-reflective musicals in reference to the MGM films *The Barkleys of Broadway* (1949), *Singin' in the Rain* (1952), and *The Bandwagon* (1953).[5] These films oscillate between two primary strategies: demystification and remythicization. Each unmasks the artifice of earlier musicals through attention to the mechanical aspects of staging and filmmaking. Regardless of their demystifying potential, the films function primarily as entertainment designed for mass consumption that repeats and thereby mystifies conservative and utopian attitudes about gender, consumerism, and creativity. Feuer views musicals with some skepticism as ideological products full of deception. The reflexivity of backstage musicals is therefore quite different from that found in the reflexive avant-garde films of the French *nouvelle vague*, for example, which interrogate their own narrativity in a critical or deconstructive manner.[6]

A very different lineage of film musicals, closely related to the critical premises of the art house tradition, has emerged since the 1970s. The genealogy of what I call neosurrealist metamusicals harks back to the British television writer and director Dennis Potter. Potter's genre-crossing television dramas, *Pennies from Heaven* (1978), *The Singing Detective* (1986), and *Lipstick on Your Collar* (1993), combined realistic drama with song-and-dance performances mimed to scratchy vintage recordings and garnered considerable critical acclaim. Surrealism plays a part in these stagings, as characters drift in and out of interior fantasy worlds to escape from intolerable pain or degradation in their ordinary lives. The resulting displacement of genre expectations creates a darkly humorous and highly reflexive atmosphere that dovetailed with the stylistic priorities of emerging postmodernist forms. Potter's approach in these television serials is most obviously indebted to musicals that used dream sequences as a pretext for staging elaborate and markedly surrealist song-and-dance numbers, including MGM's *An American in Paris* (1951).[7] The depiction of dream consciousness also features prominently in much of the artistic output of the surrealists, including visual artists' more populist audiovisual diversions, such as Salvador Dalí's dream sequences for Hitchcock's *Spellbound* (1945). Metamusicals produced by film auteurs in recent decades are surrealist in other ways, too, most notably in how they lay bare the tenets of their own production and the uses they make of existing popular songs.[8]

[5] Jane Feuer, "The Self-Reflective Musical and the Myth of Entertainment," in *Hollywood Musicals: The Film Reader*, ed. Steven Cohan (London; New York: Routledge, 2002), 31–40.

[6] Feuer, "The Self-Reflective Musical,", 39.

[7] For more on dream sequences in musicals, see Jane Feuer, *The Hollywood Musical* (London: Macmillan Press, 1982), 73–76.

[8] See Theodor Adorno, "Looking Back on Surrealism" (1954), in *Notes to Literature*, trans. Sherry Weber-Nicholson (New York: Columbia University Press, 1991), 1: 86–90, 87. Elsewhere I have listed assorted definitions of surrealism that have conditioned ideas about the movement since its genesis. These include (1) semiotic and linguistic definitions, (2) psychoanalytical and affective definitions, (3) stylistic definitions (or technique- and production-oriented definitions), (4) aesthetic definitions, (5) ontological/perceptual definitions, and (6) institutional definitions (Richardson, *An Eye for Music*,

Musical numbers are found in the neosurrealist films of a growing number of directors from very different backgrounds. Articulating a passionately felt distrust of Hollywood-style naturalism, filmmakers like Tsai Ming-Liang (*The Hole* [*Dong*], 1998; *Wayward Cloud*, 2005), Alain Resnais (*Same Old Song* [*On connaît la chanson*], 1997), Lars von Trier (*Dancer in the Dark*, 2000), Sally Potter (*Yes*, 2004), Baz Luhrmann (*Moulin Rouge!* 2001), Irwin Winkler (*De-Lovely*, 2004), and Neil Hardwick (*Jos Rakastat* [*If You Love*], 2010) have all worked in an idiom indebted to Dennis Potter, while nevertheless adapting their work to the particularities of local cultures, just as Potter addressed the particularities of World War II and post–World War II Britain while juxtaposing life in these periods with the escapist fantasy of musicals. Each of these examples does this differently. *Wayward Cloud* is set in a fictionally embellished version of modern Taipei while incorporating decades-older songs that were popular on the Chinese mainland. Resnais's and Hardwick's films are likewise staged in familiar localities in present-day Paris and Helsinki, while each incorporates classic or vintage songs from the local French and Finnish cultures. In *Moulin Rouge!* and *Dancer in the Dark* this organization is reversed: the settings are loosely historical and the music contemporary. Common to all of these examples are discrepancies between vivid or tawdry everyday realities and the fantastical domain of the song-and-dance musical number, to which characters are prone to escape. Underlying this primary dichotomy of reality and fantasy are secondary oppositions involving historical, geographical, and cultural distance.

The appeal of musicals to independent filmmakers might be explained in part by the obvious otherness of the audiovisual codes, which originated in the conventions of the Hollywood studio system while appearing to come from nowhere at all. It is precisely this positioning that allows musicals to critique dominant codes. Perhaps the easiest way to distinguish neosurrealist musicals from earlier forms is by attending to their stylistic hybridity, by which I mean that the codes of the film musical are represented as contingent, and therefore open to reimaginings, insofar as they appear *and sound* alongside competing codes. In *Wayward Cloud* the codes in question are chiefly those of avant-garde filmmaking, but also neighboring genres such as music video and hard-core porn.

We might theorize the reimagining of film musicals in several ways. For example, we can think of musical numbers as opportunities to stir up trouble—including gender trouble—concerning dominant cultural norms by reading each repetition of historical actions as an opportunity to introduce a critically directed performative twist.[9]

36–46). Neosurrealism implies a markedly contemporary inflection, including digital culture and global contexts of consumption.

[9] An alternative way of interpreting these performative repetitions is in terms of Gilles Deleuze's writing on repetition and difference. In this view, the structural and cultural repetitions of popular songs in metamusicals are understood as repetitions stacked atop existing repetitions. Amy Herzog pursues this line of inquiry in a persuasive reading of Tsai's *The Hole* (*Dong*). The second level of repetition implied in this understanding recontextualizes culturally conservative originals, turning them into something more radical. Amy Herzog, *Dreams of Difference, Songs of the Same* (Minneapolis: University of Minnesota Press, 2010), 2–3, 38.

Judith Butler's and Eve Kosofsky Sedgwick's writing on performativity tracks such critical appropriations. Sedgwick's view of performativity fits the present discussion well because of the value she places on the affectivity of performative actions, which serve a reparative function when viewed from the standpoint of camp aesthetics.[10] Sedgwick's idea of "reparative reading" is integral to my analytical work and requires some explanation to better understand the motivation for my reading.

Many of the theories that were developed to challenge homophobia and other forms of social oppression in the 1990s relied on what Sedgwick—drawing on Paul Ricoeur's "hermeneutics of suspicion"—has called "paranoid reading." The suspicious—or in her terminology "paranoid"—scholar modeled her work after such figureheads as Freud, Marx, and Nietzsche and took it as her duty to reveal through interpretive inquiry the hidden mechanisms of social injustice and oppression. The value of such an attitude is self-evident to anyone working in cultural studies. However, Sedgwick, who wrote the seminal *Epistemology of the Closet* in the early 1990s and was then a staunch advocate of critical theory, did an about-face in the 2000s as she was dying from cancer, calling for a complete reassessment of the priorities of cultural analysis. She contended that privileging the paranoid mindset results in an imbalance whereby our view of the world is conditioned primarily by negative affect (the suspicious scholar always expects the worst and usually finds it). A further shortcoming is the leap of faith from theory into experience that theoretically weighted models require: experience, in the form of "imaginative close reading," should direct theory, not the other way around. Hence Sedgwick advocated "weak theory," as opposed to the strong theoretical positioning of much traditional critical theory. In her view strong theory risked reproducing the same mechanisms of oppression it was invented to challenge—it ultimately became a case of the cart pulling the horse, and, what is worse, pulling the horse nowhere it wants to go.[11]

What is at stake in applications of reparative reading and "weak theory" is not a narrow aestheticism, but rather a more fulsome mode of understanding that recognizes how pleasure itself finds expression in a politicized arena; in Sedgwick's terms, how the paranoid and the reparative can productively "interdigitate." Sedgwick's retheorization of camp performativity exemplifies this turn toward sensory engagement and reparative understanding, offering perhaps the most convincing justification for her theoretical argument. Instead of viewing camp through a paranoid lens, she is determined to understand it as arising fundamentally out of the richness of experience and an appreciation of shared values and tastes among communities. In her view we underestimate the extent to which camp practices are motivated by love, good humor, empathetic identification, affective response, pleasure, the ameliorative, a desire to fix and replenish, and so forth:

[10] Judith Butler, *Gender Trouble* (London; New York: Routledge, 1990), 43–44; Eve Kosofsky Sedgwick and Andrew Parker, "Introduction: Performativity and Performance," in *Performativity and Performance* (New York: Routledge, 1995), 1–18; and Eve Kosofsky Sedgwick, *Touching Feeling: Affect, Pedagogy, Performativity* (Durham, N.C.: Duke University Press, 2003), 17.

[11] Sedgwick, *Touching Feeling*, 144–146.

> To view camp as, among other things, the communal, historically dense exploration of a variety of reparative practices is to do better justice to many of the defining elements of classic camp performance: the startling, juicy displays of excess erudition, for example; the passionate, often hilarious antiquarianism; the prodigal production of alternative historiographies; the "over"-attachment to fragmentary, marginal, waste or left over products; the rich, highly interruptive affective variety; the irrepressible fascination with ventriloquistic experimentation; the disorienting juxtapositions of present with past, and popular with high culture.[12]

Here I single out one element of this theorization and trace it back to Susan Sontag, and beyond her to Walter Benjamin and writers on surrealism, as it is particularly salient to my arguments. I am referring to the appreciation of the "old-fashioned, out-of-date, démodé" and the potential for regeneration and reparative play that inheres in such forms and practices.[13] Outmoded objects may simultaneously be mobilized to serve a critical agenda yet offer reparative pleasures that are bound up with sensory perception and a camp sense of fun. Camp aesthetic objects activate cultural memories, but it is not the act of remembering that is reparative, so much as the reflexive understanding that one is remembering.[14]

The resurrection of musicals in the present era can be interpreted both as a symptom of and a causative factor behind the turn toward a new sensory cinema, a mode of consumption that is related also to the turn toward the digital. But musicals, being an "unrealistic" and "anachronistic" cultural form, have had to adapt to the spirit of the times to satisfy moviegoers' demands for audiovisual experiences that reflect hipness and social relevance. Film musicals fell out of favor in the mainstream during the middle years of the twentieth century, even though aspects of their sensibility were retained in feature-length cartoon films, youth films, musical biopics, and music videos. At the same time as there was increasing mainstream recognition of the currency of musicals among sexual minorities,[15] a new tendency emerged. Auteur directors co-opted the subversive potential of musicals with a view to critiquing mainstream (consumerist, middle class, "straight," Western) culture.[16]

[12] Sedgwick, *Touching Feeling*, 150.

[13] Susan Sontag, "Notes on 'Camp,'" reprinted in *Camp: Queer Aesthetics and the Performing Subject. A Reader*, ed. Fabio Cleto (Edinburgh: Edinburgh University Press, 1999), 53–65, 60. For a more critical interpretation of the outmoded and camp aesthetics in reference to gender issues, see Caryl Flinn, "The Deaths of Camp," in *Camp*, ed. Fabio Cleto, 433–457.

[14] On camp aesthetics and popular music studies, see Freya Jarman-Ivens, "Notes on Musical Camp," in *The Ashgate Research Companion to Popular Musicology* (Farnham, UK: Ashgate, 2009), 189–203; Stan Hawkins, "Singing the Body Fantastic: Corporality and the Voice," in *The British Pop Dandy: Masculinity, Popular Music and Culture* (Farnham, UK: Ashgate, 2009), 121–151; and John Richardson, "Intertextuality and Pop Camp Identity Politics in Finland: The Crash's Music Video 'Still Alive,'" *Popular Musicology Online* 2 (2006), at http://www.popular musicology-online.com/issues/02/richardson-01.html (accessed December 4, 2010).

[15] See Matthew Tinkom, *Working Like a Homosexual: Camp, Capital, Cinema* (Durham, N.C.: Duke University Press, 2002); and Steven Cohan, *Incongruous Entertainment: Camp, Cultural Value, and the MGM Musical* (Durham, N.C.: Duke University Press, 2005).

[16] I wouldn't necessarily include more mainstream offerings like the film musical *Hair* (dir. Adam Shankman, 2007) and the television serial *Glee* (2009) in the category of neosurrealist metamusicals. Although camp and reflexive, they are more a continuation of fantasy youth films like *Grease* (dir. Randal

The theatrical performativity of the musical is the main reason it is able to occupy this ambivalent position: of the mainstream yet apparently able to reflect critically (on) mainstream values.

New musicals directed by art house auteurs encapsulate the surrealists' idea of the marvelous: the performativity of the musical number and its elevated (read "surreal") musical expression bring about a rupture in the continuity of dominant audiovisual discourses that has the power to kick-start the imaginative faculties. In her reading of Tsai's *The Hole*, Claudia Gorbman notes how the film articulates a "a queer surrealist sensibility."[17] The task of the remainder of this chapter is to get to the bottom of how this sensibility is expressed in the same director's later film musical, *The Wayward Cloud*, and to further elucidate the cultural work this film and others of its type accomplish, with particular reference to camp aesthetics and cultural memory.

Tsai Ming-Liang's *The Wayward Cloud*

The Wayward Cloud is a paradigmatic neosurrealist metamusical. The film brings strikingly different audiovisual genres into conversation with one another: auteur art film, documentary, musical, Chinese Mandopop, and last but not least, hard-core pornography. The film's marketing describes it as "[h]igh comedy, high-camp musical numbers and a vast amount of hardcore porn."[18] In fact, it contains little if any hard core—only what looks like (but might not be) simulated sex, and most of that serves a clear deconstructive function, because it is either too bizarre or too grotesque to titillate.[19]

The film's plot tells of a drought in Taiwan—the female protagonist spends much of her time scavenging for water containers, and watermelons become a fetishized commodity (see figures 17.01 and 17.02). The male lead, Hsiao-Kang, is an actor in a low-budget porn film being made in an apartment building in Taipei, where most of the film's action takes place. His scenes are divided between a romantic but mostly chaste relationship with Shiang-chyi, the young woman who lives downstairs and works as a

Kleiser, 1978) and backstage musical/youth film combinations like *Dirty Dancing* (dir. Emile Ardolino, 1987) and *Fame* (dir. Alan Parker, 1980; dir. Kevin Tancharoen, 2009) than they are metamusicals in the same sense as the auteur films discussed here. These examples follow existing conventions playfully more than upsetting conventions through the use of surprising juxtapositions. For the same reasons, I consider Baz Luhrmann's *Moulin Rouge!* (2001) closer to the ethos of auteurist metamusicals than this director's *Strictly Ballroom* (1992). *Evita* (dir. Alan Parker, 1996), *Chicago* (dir. Rob Marshall, 2002), and *Mamma Mia!* (Phylida Lloyd, 2008) are straightforward adaptations of stage musicals.

17 See Claudia Gorbman, "Auteur Music," in *Beyond the Soundtrack: Representing Music in Cinema*, ed. Daniel Goldmark, Lawrence Kramer, and Richard Leppert, (Berkeley: University of California Press, 2007), 151.

18 Quotation from Peter Bradshaw of *The Guardian*, "*The Wayward Cloud*," press release, November 16, 2007.

19 This assertion is based on Tsai's comments in interviews and official press releases, which fail to draw a clear line between reality and fiction when discussing the use of actors in the film.

Figure 17.1. Opening scene of *The Wayward Cloud.* The watermelon is a surrealist-absurdist yonic symbol.

Figure 17.2. Opening scene of *The Wayward Cloud.* The watermelon is a surrealist-absurdist phallic symbol.

museum tour guide, and a purely physical working relationship with the Japanese porn actress Sumomo Yozakura. (The fact that Tsai uses the actors' real names reflects the sur*realist* premises of his aesthetic, particularly how he chooses to vacillate between documentary and fictional modes of address.) From the start, an element of absurdity characterizes sex scenes in the film, as watermelons substitute for body parts both male and female. This type of semiotic slippage along a metaphorical trajectory is a classic surrealist technique, as Roland Barthes has noted in his writing on Bataille's short novel *Story of an Eye*.[20] Bataillean surrealism is otherwise present in the coarse materiality of many of the images. These depictions of sex become increasingly stark and unflattering as the film progresses, bringing to mind a number of art house films produced shortly afterward, including von Trier's *The Idiots* (1998), P. T. Anderson's *Boogie Nights* (1997), Haneke's *La Pianiste* (2001), and Chereau's *Intimacy* (2001). All of these films play on a certain deconstructive function in relation to conventional representations.

Tsai says of his intention to upset audience expectations:

> The reason for my making *The Wayward Cloud* was to show the basic nature of sex through this film. The whole process is ridiculous ... because instead of porn they were watching the shooting of porn. They'd see a porn film in it, but also the entire camera crew. And the duration is very long. They cannot control the playing speed in a cinema. You can only sit and watch. Therefore it is almost anti-pornography. Yes, it is an anti-pornography film.[21]

Things are complicated further, however: the film's deadpan drama and unglamorous sex are interrupted by five camped-up musical numbers (see table 17.1). A sixth song without an accompanying visual performance is heard over the closing credits. The first four are of local origin, but written in styles that ape imported Western songs, principally Tin Pan Alley, jazz, and blues torch. The last two are Cantonese adaptations of Western popular songs (in country-folk style), their translation having a demonstrable impact on how the songs signify in the film; notably, these songs are heard immediately before and after the final twist in the film's plot, when the characters appear at their most alienated. Two of the songs are recordings by the Chinese film actress Grace Chang; in Tsai's earlier film, *The Hole* (*Dong*, 1998), Chang's songs completely dominate and are similarly used in lip-synched musical sequences.

Structurally, the film rehearses the same upstairs–downstairs positioning one finds in many classic Hollywood musicals, including *Top Hat* (1935) with Ginger Rogers and Fred Astaire. In fact, Tsai's *The Hole* uses this spatial conceit as well. The physical distance between the two characters in *Wayward Cloud* generates an underlying tension and erotic frisson in their relationship. We see this positioning knowingly parodied in several scenes; for example, as the couple plays cat and mouse while ascending a stairwell, she remains one flight below as he ascends. But also, as the pair relaxes in her living room, he lies under a kitchen table, and she is seated on a chair above. She eventually slides down to occupy his space, causing him to slide down further into a supine position. This subtly inverts the dominant gender order of the film (in which he is on top and she is

[20] Roland Barthes, "The Metaphor of the Eye," trans. J. A. Underwood, in Georges Bataille, *Story of an Eye*, by Lord Auch [pseudonym] (London; New York: Penguin, 1982), 119–127.

[21] Interview in Tsai Ming-Liang, dir., *The Wayward Cloud* (London: Axiom Films, 2004).

below): at this moment she is on top and vertical; he is supine (see figure 17.3).[22] The action is drawn out, with no dialogue and very little else in the way of sounds to interfere with the sensory impact of what we see and hear. Only after he drifts off to sleep (implying a shift into dream consciousness) is a silence that is ubiquitous throughout the remainder of the film shattered by one of the most extravagant musical sequences. Just as the preceding love scene began with a spatially implied act of gender inversion, so Hsiao-Kang's dream depicts gender inversion through cross-dressing. The song "What a Date!" (sung and performed by Hong Chong) sounds like a Taiwanese version of "The Laughing Policeman" and is set to something resembling a Tin Pan Alley tune. (Video clip 17.1. ⊛) The male protagonist is in drag, participating in a queer adaptation of dance sequences from *Les Parapluies de Cherbourg* (*The Umbrellas of Cherbourg*, 1964). The scene departs absurdly from Demy's musical by including umbrellas themed after watermelons, and also because of the location, a spectacular riverside heritage site in Taipei. As the song progresses, Shiang-chyi appears in drag as well, transformed from her usual tomboyish demeanor into an elegantly attired male dandy. Such an option appears to be unavailable to Sumomo Yozakura, who vies with the transvestite actor for the travesti actress's amorous attentions. The film action dramatizes the lyrics, which tell of a gender-bending date on which the actors discover their true sexual identities only as they are about to part company.

Oh what fun we had that day.
The time just slipped away.
We danced and had a walk,
And sat down for a talk.
But when I see it's time to go,
Oh, what a fearful blow.
She wasn't Chen, her name was Hsiao,
And she thought I was Zhao.

The staging of this number conspicuously eschews the sleight of hand by which the classical film musical naturalizes the binary gender positioning. No traces of visual or audio dissolve are to be found here, as theorized by Rick Altman.[23] The anachronous recording fits this agenda perfectly: a corny old joke song in a major key with a bouncy tempo,

22 On the interchangeability of categories of "top" and "bottom" in queer musical experience, see Suzanne Cusick, "On a Lesbian Relationship with Music: Serious Effort Not to Think Straight," in *Queering the Pitch: the New Gay and Lesbian Musicology*, ed. Philip Brett, Elizabeth Wood, and Gary Thomas (New York: Routledge, 1994), 74–78.

23 Altman's theorization of "audio dissolve" and "video dissolve" sheds important light on how the passage from diegetic realism to supradiegetic fantasy is negotiated in the genre. Requiring a tripartite passage from the everyday realism of speech toward song and finally dance, the musical moments of the classical film musical stage a release from societal constraints that is through and through utopian. By "leaving normal day-to-day causality behind," Altman writes, "the music creates a utopian space in which all singers and dancers achieve a unity unimaginable in the now superseded world of temporal, psychological causality." Rick Altman, *The American Film Musical* (Bloomington, IN: Indiana University Press, 1987), 69.

Table 17.1 Tsai Ming-Liang's *The Wayward Cloud*: List of Musical Cues

Musical Numbers and Time Code	Information on Music and Style	Visual Dramatization
1. 00:20.50 	"Ban Ge Yue Liang" ("The Half-Moon"). Artist: Hung Chong; Writer: Jiang Yun; Composer: Xi Hua Style: 1950s-style Mandopop (Mandarin popular music) with lush film-music arrangement	While languishing in a rooftop water tank, he turns into a sequined sea monster. His androgynous appearance anticipates his musical appearance in the song "What a Date!"
2. 00:34:45 	"Ai De Kai Shi" ("Everlasting Love"). Artist: Yao Li; Writer/Composer: Wang Shu Yeh Style: 1950s-style Mandopop with film-music arrangement	She pays ironic homage to a statue of a communist leader together with a camped-up troupe of dancers. The dancers' flirtatious actions are exaggerated, and they are surrounded by oversized flowers.
3. 00:45:25 	"Tong Qin Xin" ("To Keep My Heart True"). Artist: Grace Chang; Writer: Li Jun Qing; Composer: Ryoichi Hattori Style: plaintive torch song in blues jazz style	After being subjected to the obligatory facial "money shot," the actor playing the Japanese porn actress contemplates staying true to her heart (although her soul is dead). She is pursued by a surly group of men.

(continued)

Table 17.1 Continued

Musical Numbers and Time Code	Information on Music and Style	Visual Dramatization
4. 00:57:30 	"Qi Miao De Yue Hui" ("What a Date!"). Artist: Hung Chong; Writer: Hung Chong; Composer: Nicholas Dickman Style: Tin Pan Alley style comedy song	Musical spectacular based on the gender inversion of the two stars during a date. The Japanese actress arrives, now in drag, and the two "women" vie for the travesty actress's attention.
5. 01:11:00 	"Jin Xin Deng" ("Be Patient!"; originally "Sixteen Tons"). Artist: Chang Lu; Writer: Si Tu Ming; Composer: Merle Travis Style: workingman's country-folk ballad	His musical fantasy offers advice on how best to achieve an erection, enacted with the help of J. P. Gaultier-style dancers and an anthropomorphic phallus. The lyrics of the original song are here given a perverse twist.
6. 01:46:17 	"Tian Bian Yi Duo Yun" ("The Wayward Cloud"; originally "The Wayward Wind"). Artist: Bai Guang; Writers/ Composers: Stanley R. Lebowsky & Herbert Newman Style: country ballad	The song comments on the film's denouement, in which the male porn star achieves transcendence through sexual climax. The cue reflects ironically on an earlier use of the song as a love theme. Fade to black and titles.

catchy eighth-note anacruses, and rapid-fire vocal delivery. The song is an obviously old and devalued object. It is therefore not so much the joke of the original song that amuses audiences today as the abrupt transition into a musical number, the way the characters succeed *and fail* in fitting themselves into the song, and the sheer color and frivolity—in other words, the heightened affectivity—of the audiovisual spectacle. Indeed, the song is not necessarily even funny in light of the more serious and contemplative atmosphere of the surrounding film action. Its humor is forced, designed to make us sit up in our seats and attend to what is happening in the film and how the characters dream.

Sensory Pleasures and Water Symbolism

Cooking is a privileged locus of humor and eroticism between the romantic pair. Smoking and drinking are eroticized as well, both corporeal pleasures that permit a certain amount of slippage into a sexualized zone. Water is the transformative element that characterizes their relationship, just as it is largely missing from the experiences of the Japanese porn actress. Significantly, the water supply is exhausted during the shower scene of the porn film shoot, necessitating the absurd solution of the movie crew emptying a can of murky river water onto the actors while they film. Later the woman from downstairs, upon finding the porn actress unconscious in an elevator, attempts to revive her with a bottle of water, evidently hoping it will bring about a positive transformation.

Water divides the women in architectural space. This can be seen when they walk on opposite banks of an urban canal, and Shiang-chyi falls into line behind Sumomo Yozakura as their paths converge on a concrete bridge. (Video clip 17.2. ⊛) Characteristically, the scene is drawn out over an extended period of time. Both women hold parasols, thereby encouraging comparisons between them. Shiang-chyi is scruffily dressed and moves awkwardly yet somehow endearingly; the porn actress is an apparent paragon of refined femininity, dressed in fashionable clothes and dragging a suitcase on rollers behind her—indicating mobility and some degree of affluence. Apart from these material accoutrements, however, there would seem to be little to envy in the actress's life. She fails to connect meaningfully with other characters, and her solo musical number tells of her resulting heartbreak (she lip-synchs Grace Chang's plaintive and bluesy torch song, "To Keep My Heart True").

Before this musical number, the actress takes part in a coarse enactment of her own debasement, in what is undoubtedly one of the more shocking moments in the film. Here the actress is splashed with murky river water before being subjected to the obligatory moment of transcendence in the genre: the facial "money shot." In this rendering of the popular porn trope, however, she is made to look as unattractive as possible: her makeup is smeared, her false lashes visibly peel away, and the lighting is stark. The scene thus highlights the performativity of the genre and visibly deconstructs the pleasurable tenets of porn movies. Water, such as it is, is tainted and unsuitable for human consumption, let alone spiritual replenishment.

Water or its scarcity is an omnipresent theme in Tsai's cinematic output, including his landmark films *The River* (1997) and *The Hole* (1998). The director has described his characters as plants that are short of water, and this physical thirst stands in for something equally fundamental that they crave: "Water for me is love, that's what they lack. They are never particularly well adjusted because they lack something. That something is love, which is represented by water."[24] The dream of aqueous abundance (read "abundance of love") appears in *The Wayward Cloud*'s very first musical interlude. The male protagonist is found languishing in a rooftop water tank. While sinking into musical reverie (another dream transition), he is transformed into a sequined sea monster. The transformation is less than miraculous, however, as the location loses little of its squalor even when the tank is encircled by rows of theatrical fairy lights. The music, too, is conspicuous, for two reasons. First, the presence of musical sound jolts the audio-viewer awake as a result of the relative absence of sound in preceding scenes; second, we notice it because it is so anachronistic, with its sentimental style and the crackly lo-fi vintage recording. Tsai uses this scene and the one that follows to establish the binary characteristics of the dual-focus narrative: a bubble forms in the faucet of the female protagonist's bathroom as a result of the male protagonist's rooftop bathing. This connection established through water will carry through the rest of the film, most notably in the cooking scene that precedes their most intimate encounter, culminating in the cross-dressing musical number.

Performing Pornography

Exchanges between the romantic couple stand in stark contrast to the sex scenes between Hsiao-Kang and his porn star counterpart, which are marked by either their crassness or their absurdity. These also, however, comment obliquely on the surrounding narrative action. One musical number involving the Japanese actress and Hsiao-Kang follows immediately from the latter's inability to achieve an erection during the shoot. In the musical sequence he plays an anthropomorphized phallus surrounded by a troupe of dancing girls dressed in Gaultier-style bikini tops and he is eventually draped with a giant condom. (Video clip 17.3. ⊛) The music is a Chinese adaptation of the Merle Travis song "Sixteen Tons" (made popular by Tennessee Ernie Ford), but perverted from its original function as a workingman's anthem to address the salience of concentration as an aid to male potency. Tsai clearly wishes to subvert the meanings of the Chinese translation. Sung by the silky-toned chanteuse Chang Lu, who rose to popularity as a popular Shanghai diva in the war years, the song loses a great deal in translation; the embittered lyrics, syncopated vocals, and dissonant guitar work of the American original are flattened out, and the song turns into a seductive call to follow the party line and achieve transcendence within the body politic. The verse of the original song, in

[24] Danièle Rivière, "Scouting," interview with Tsai Ming-Liang, in *Tsai Ming-Liang*, ed. Jean Pierre Rehm, Olivier Joyard, and Danièle Rivière (Paris: Editions Dis Voir, 1999), 79–118.

E minor, descends in several labored runs while the singer enumerates his grievances. Its pinnacle occurs as the singer complains that he will not qualify for admittance to heaven because he has sold his soul to the "company store." This line hits an emotive high E (e^2) on the word "owe," before descending through dark chord tones to a low B (b) for the final crushing admission of defeat. In stark contrast, the Chinese translation (transposed into B minor) turns the individual's suffering ("for happiness you need to strive") into something necessary for the greater good of the people. In this way the Chinese worker achieves a level of transcendence that was denied his North American comrade in what was originally a protest song. Resisting the ideological message of the Chinese cover version, Tsai does not have the body politic in mind when he camps up Chang Lu's version through the actions of the female dancers and an oversized male phallus, which fill the lyrics with sexual innuendo. The same goes for another musical number, "Ai De Kai Shi" ("Everlasting Love"), in which a group of women overact their devotion to the statue of a communist leader in lascivious dance moves and stagey femme-camp costumes while surrounded by oversized yonic flowers.

Another remarkable thing about the soundtrack is a pair of scenes that displace and parody the sounds of sex. In the opening sex scene, a watermelon is placed in front of the porn actress's genitals, thereby allowing the man to pleasure the fruit instead of the woman (see figure 17.1). Ludicrously, she continues to behave as if the man were stimulating her—sighing and gasping as if there were no tomorrow. Ridiculous slurping noises produced by his actions on the watermelon highlight the absurdity of sound effects in the genre and draw attention to the conventional nature of sound effects in general (the result of what Chion terms synchresis, the process by which sound effects are naturalized through synchronization).

The mirror image of this scene comes at the end of the film. The actress, now unconscious (presumably from a drug overdose, or perhaps from dehydration, an analogy for her unloved condition), is made to complete the film shoot by being physically placed by the film crew in a series of stereotyped sex positions. The male lead tries to continue as if this were business as usual—which of course it is, the woman's pleasure and agency counting for little in the sexual economy of the porn industry. Her natural failure to respond audibly to his actions undermines an important premise of the hard-core genre: performances of female pleasure, however phony and exaggerated they might be.[25]

The scene becomes more absurd still as the woman from downstairs looks on and eventually begins to lip-synch the noises of her unconscious counterpart. The scene becomes a reenactment of what happens routinely in both porn films and film musicals: unrealistic overdubbing. According to Linda Williams, the audiovisual priorities of hard-core porn are remarkably similar to those of film musicals for precisely this reason. The affective intensity of simulated intimacy in porn supersedes realism, much like the film musical, which

[25] Linda Williams has noted that the "articulate and inarticulate sounds of pleasure that dominate in aural hardcore are primarily the cries of women. Though male moans and cries are heard as well, they are never as loud or dramatic." *Hardcore: Power, Pleasure, and the "Frenzy of the Visible"* (Berkeley: University of California Press, 1989), 123.

produces utopian spaceless spaces by using unrealistic prerecorded sounds. Williams even claims that "the hard-core feature film *is* a kind of musical, with sexual number taking the place of musical number."[26] She also refers to the (surreal) effect of a great many post-dubbed sex scenes, as well as of the dialogue sequences of the more cheaply made hard-core features. When the lip movements of the performer do not match the sounds that come from those lips, the hard-won illusions of suture are rendered null and void.[27]

Surrealism is most prominent in the imagery of *Wayward Cloud* when Hsiao-Kang services his coactor in the opening scene with a watermelon placed over his head—an image worthy of Dalí or Magritte (see figure 17.2). Tsai's uses of sound, however, are every bit as surreal. Both the musical scenes and the corresponding porn scenes include a form of paradigmatic substitution, whereby audiences hear something they weren't expecting to hear: either conspicuously displaced prerecorded sounds or hyperrealistic sounds with visual sources onscreen, which are nevertheless also genre-inappropriate and involve audiovisual displacement. Performative acts of lip-synching aimed at exposing the audiovisual conventions of the genre are a common feature in metamusicals, but Tsai's juxtapositioning of this technique with similar acts of displacement and audiovisual rendering in porn is quite original. This proximity of the two genres highlights their similarities and thereby allows them mutually to deconstruct one another. Musicals in Tsai's treatment become performative enactments that comment critically on characters' escapist tendencies; porn scenes are similarly rendered with such a degree of hyperrealism that they become debased in a Bataillean way, thereby encouraging reflection on the escapist tenets of the genre.

Courtly Love and Existential Difference

If the porn actors' relationship is about crude (because loveless) physical contact, the actor and his romantic partner do not have much sexual contact at all. They engage in a form of "courtly love," which resembles what Emmanuel Levinas has in mind when he writes about interpersonal transcendence: a form of fantasy projection that is characterized by "desire without satisfaction which... understands... the remoteness, the alterity, and exteriority of the other."[28] This romantic positioning produces a certain erotic charge, which some writers have understood as implying a healthy degree of distance and respect for the other's Otherness. Looked at differently, however, this positioning engenders an autistic view of interpersonal relations in which interpersonal communication is always stilted and partial. It is a positioning that extends beyond Levinas to historical tropes of romance in the West, beyond even the dual focus narrative musicals that Tsai's film parodies, to just about every construction of romance in the Western

[26] Williams, *Hardcore*, 124.
[27] Williams, *Hardcore*, 124.
[28] Emmanuel Levinas, *Totality and Infinity* (Dordrecht, Netherlands: Kluwer Academic Publishers, 1991), 34.

imagination. Manifestations of courtly love range from Shakespeare's Romeo and Juliet to Rapunzel's castle tower, medieval troubadour ballads, and the romantic serenade—the last of which usually requires the positioning of the female object of desire on a balcony or some similar pedestal.

Žižek addresses the persistence of this cultural construction in "From Courtly Love to *The Crying Game*."[29] Drawing on Lacan's psychoanalytical theories, he notes how the exalted love object in courtly love is divested of human substance, indicating a radical Otherness that has more to do with the fantasies and projections of the perceiver than the attributes of a real person.[30] In essence the woman thus perceived becomes an empty shell, and this is precisely what we see physically enacted in the final moments of *The Wayward Cloud*. Communication with the exalted (or, equally, abjected) lady thus conceived requires an exaggerated level of courtesy and etiquette on the part of the male suitor, strategies that ensure that the object of romantic affection will remain forever out of his reach.[31] So far so harmless, and even fun in the context of performative role-play, but problems arise to the extent that the symbolic value of the woman thus perceived makes her a vehicle for male transcendence rather than a subject in her own right. The hidden agenda of courtly love is libidinal intensification, because an obstacle placed in the path of a desire is sure to strengthen the wish to attain it.[32] Obstacles are necessary in this understanding to maintain the illusion that without them the object would be "instantly accessible." The narrative trajectory therefore moves from the premise of denying another person's (phenomenal) Otherness to the consequence of constructing a sublimated Other that remains forever out of reach and thereby usurps the position of the original idealized person.[33]

In a strong critique of Levinas, the feminist philosopher Luce Irigaray has noted how Levinasian transcendence (and implicitly also courtly love) fails to attend to pleasures of the flesh (*volupté*), including everything from the loving caress to reparative carnal pleasures:

> [Levinas] knows nothing of communion in pleasure.... The distance is always maintained with the other in the experience of love. The other is "close" to him in "duality." This autistic, egological, solitary love does not correspond to the shared outpouring, to the loss of boundaries which takes place for both lovers when they cross the boundaries of the skin into the mucous membranes of the body, leaving the circle which encloses my solitude to meet in a shared space, a shared breath, abandoning the *relatively dry* and precise outlines of each body's solid exterior to enter a *fluid universe* where the perception of being two persons...becomes indistinct, and above all, acceding to another energy, neither that of the one nor that

[29] Slavoj Žižek, "From Courtly Love to *The Crying Game*," *New Left Review* 1, no. 202 (November/December 1993): 95–108.

[30] Žižek, "From Courtly Love to *The Crying Game*," 96.

[31] Žižek, "From Courtly Love to *The Crying Game*," 97.

[32] Žižek, "From Courtly Love to *The Crying Game*," 100.

[33] Žižek, "From Courtly Love to *The Crying Game*," 101.

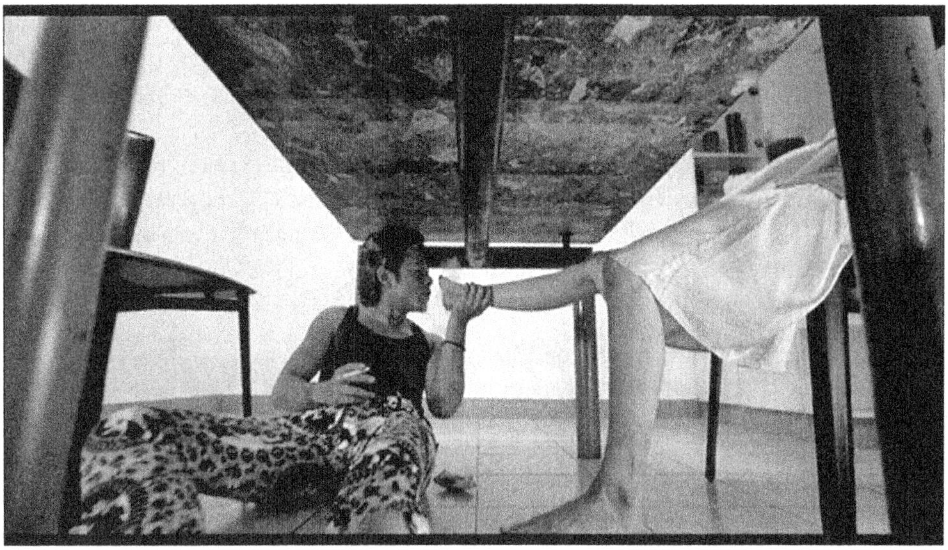

FIGURE 17.3. The spatial coding of courtly love in *The Wayward Cloud*. Here the dominant positioning of the film is inverted: Shiang-chyi's head is out of shot (dehumanizing her); Hsiao-Kang is supine (and feminized).

> of the other, but an energy produced together as a result of the irreducible difference of sex. [Emphasis added.][34]

Expressing an unwelcome desire for intimacy, the female protagonist of Tsai's film repeatedly attempts to close the Levinasian gap demarcating absolute alterity, to quench her thirst for intimacy, as it were. This happens when she follows the male protagonist up the stairwell and when she descends to his level beneath the table (see figure 17.3). However, he generally responds with countermoves toward spatial transcendence and away from intimacy. The film offers some glimpses of intimacy, which provide temporary relief from the otherwise grim direction of the narrative. One passionate encounter between the couple in a video storeroom finds her falling to her knees after a passionate embrace, only to realize immediately afterwards that her voluntary action has resulted in a loss of intimacy. This positioning only begins to break down close to the film's denouement, as the couple evidently becomes more intimate in a meaningful interpersonal sense while dancing playfully on a bridge in a tight embrace.

The fragility of this positioning is exposed in the final scene, however, when the man's move toward transcendence seems to require her debasement, as Shiang-chyi replaces the porn actress for the film's final shot. At the precise moment when Hsiao-Kang transfers his physical attention from the (now unconscious) porn actress to the leading lady in the final sex act of the film, the spell of their relationship is broken, and she is made

[34] Žižek, "From Courtly Love to *The Crying Game*," 111.

to occupy Sumomo Yozakura's impassive position, her arms flopping powerlessly while she passively performs fellatio. Significantly his head remains out of the frame, in the clouds. The scene goes on and on, as if to highlight the unevenness of this positioning, and finally segues into the final credits.

The film's last musical cue comes in at this point, a Chinese cover version of Stan Lebowsky and Herb Newman's country and western classic, "The Wayward Wind." (Video clip 17.4. ⊙) Originally a hit for Gogi Grant, in later years it was interpreted by countless country and folk artists (including Patsy Cline and Neil Young). These are the lyrics of the first verse:

> A wayward cloud, lonesome and proud,
> slipping through my hand. To a far-off land.
> My heartless love, drifting high above,
> like a wayward cloud. With no earthly bound.

Earlier in the film, Shiang-chyi was heard singing a bit of the song wordlessly in an elevator following her first amorous encounter with the man from upstairs (00:41:45). In this context its use is naïve and affecting. In the final scene, however, it is given an altogether different spin when arranged for a small group of jazz musicians and performed by a leading Chinese torch singer of the postwar period. The Mandarin cover version draws attention to the dynamic between local and global politics that has such a tangible impact on the characters' desires and aspirations—from their taste in hard-core porn (and music) to stereotyped ideas about gender identity. It does this for two reasons. First, translated songs written in imported styles highlight discrepancies between the original song and its translated copy, at least when they are recognized as such. In this case, the musical performance of a star hailing from mainland China rather than Taiwan inscribes an additional layer of defamiliarization. Second, the use of obviously antiquated country music here accentuates camp subversion at the same time that it tells audiences something has been lost in translation; these (Western) dreams of mobility, affluence, and jet-setting elegance are an uncomfortable match for the lives of the film's characters. The song represents an idealization of compliant femininity that originates in the West, but which resonates with East Asian cultural stereotypes as well. We can see this in the heavily ironic cardboard cutout image of two Air China female flight attendants (flanking the protagonists during the fellatio scene), which suggests both the ideal of jet-setting mobility and a pervasive stereotype of feminine grace. It matters that the music heard in the final denouement is of both foreign (Chinese, non-Taiwanese) and originally Western origin, and related to this, that it tells of the depicted male character's wanderlust. The porn actress represents Westernization, through her taste in clothes, her itinerant life (in one scene she drags a suitcase—is she a flight attendant in her day job?), and her career as a porn actress, many of the stylistic conventions of which originated in the United States.

Her life contrasts with the universally simple (embodied, affective, nonverbal) and markedly local pleasures enjoyed by Shiang-chyi, such as stir-fry cooking. We are reminded of the fact that Shiang-chyi steps into the porn actress's (vacuous) shoes in the denouement by the presence of the cardboard cutout flight attendants and the creaky old musical recordings from elsewhere. All of these factors signal defamiliarization, Both musical and visual cues intimate, therefore, that something is awry and reinforce the direction of the film action as Shiang-chyi drops her arms in despair while performing a blow job on her lover, whose head remains resolutely in the clouds. Here we might perceive the secret meaning of the conventional upstairs–downstairs positioning in dual focus musical narratives (and that of courtly love in general). As the song lyrics and dramatic content of the film imply, what is conveyed is above all *his* transcendence. She remains grounded in corporeal life; his very groundlessness appears to be the deciding factor in the couple's inability to connect.

Unlike "Sixteen Tons," grossly misinterpreted to become propaganda in the Chinese translation, the meaning of which is playfully perverted again in Tsai's audiovisual formula, Chinese actress Bai Guang's Mandarin interpretation of "The Wayward Wind" is close in sound and semantic meaning to Gogi Grant's original country hit. This is essentially a torch song about a male lover who is prone to wander. The original hit song (see figure 17.4) features stylistic affectations of the "Wild West" that we would expect to hear in country and western music, most audibly in the clattering wagon-wheel rhythm and Disney-style mimetic wind sounds, produced by a female choir singing wordlessly with occasional "gusts" of portamento. The Gogi Grant arrangement sounds like a big arrangement for big country, with orchestral strings, horns, harp, and jazz combo. The instrumental resources employed in the Bai Guang adaptation are more modest, comprising only a small jazz combo of accordion, lead guitar, and rhythm guitar. Although these details and the scale of the orchestration differ in the Chinese arrangement, other musical elements are quite similar in the original and the translated song. The two versions are in the same key (B major) and the same relaxed tempo. Bai's singing style is similar to Grant's; in an engaging torch style, the winsome singer pines for her itinerant lover. Bai possesses a rich low register, reaching up to more nasal tones as she pushes to the top of her range. All of this lends the music a warm and comforting quality. The singer is content to wait patiently, we are led to believe, while her lover pursues his destiny, a free spirit untroubled by worldly concerns. In this way the cover song represents an idealization not only of compliant femininity, but also of freedom and mobility associated with the West—both the Wild West and the economically advantaged modern West. The transcendence of the male protagonist, depicted in the song's lyrics and enacted spatially in the actor's position and the camera framing in the final scene, essentially turns his female coactors into nothing more than cardboard cutouts—their agency counts for little.

Such a critical reading is supported by what we know about Tsai's directorial intention and the details of the audiovisual interpretation I have offered. In the final section, however, I complicate this understanding by examining more closely the role cultural memory plays in mediating the narrative meanings communicated in the film. The formal transcendence of the musical numbers (as figures of memory) from characters' everyday lives becomes an apt vehicle for critical commentary. But more than this, Tsai's musical moments convey their own mnemonic energy, which resonates with memories

FIGURE 17.4. "The Wayward Wind" by Herb Newman and Stan Lebowsky. Extract of first verse.

of how things used to be. This energy also supersedes historical context by directing attention toward affectively elevated aesthetic experiences. These experiences are not politically neutral but rather value laden, because our ideas about pleasure connect with what people do in specific times and places and the taste cultures people are born into or choose to identify with.

Musical Moments as Figures of Memory and Vehicles for Affective Transportation

In handling existing musical material like found objects, Tsai communicates a camp, surrealist disposition that destabilizes, without eliminating altogether, those associations that ordinarily cling to these musical recordings. Found musical objects in Tsai's films are not presented to be derided, but rather should be taken as vehicles for disenchantment and re-enchantment through recontextualization. We might ask whether the songs heard in Tsai's metamusicals are anything but worthless commodities. Does such music yield only hallucinatory pleasures, having little relevance to the lives of the characters and audiences? A "paranoid" or "suspicious" interpretation, in the senses in which Eve Kosofsky Sedgwick and Paul Ricoeur have employed these terms, might support this view.[35] The twofold repurposing of the songs reveals a desire to demarcate geohistorical and ideological distances between North American originals and their Chinese Mandarin copies. Tsai brings to his encounter with this music a further critical remediation that reflects his own Taiwanese background and his positioning as an art house director addressing a niche global audience. These strategies are essentially "paranoid" and critical in the traditional sense of the word; Tsai's transnational audiovisual aesthetic conveys postcolonial and consumer-critical messages to filmgoers who understand something about their political context. *The Wayward Cloud* further strongly critiques the porn industry's conditioning of consumers' expectations in everyday sexual encounters.[36] But that is not all. Tsai's camp sensibility and the embeddedness of these songs and parodic porn stagings in the reparative continuity of the sounds and textures of daily life seem to tell a different story: that pleasure can be distilled even out of ideologically questionable and seemingly trivial base elements; that re-enchantment is possible.

In popular musicology we have long been familiar with Adorno's disparagement of popular songs composed in the Tin Pan Alley style. But rather than dismiss such songs as formulaic and worthless, we may choose to think of them as carefully crafted and willfully open ended, imbued with qualities of humane beauty, optimism, or cathartic drama, and because of their relatively depersonalized nature, as encouraging multiple points of entry for listeners and performers. This is a more reparative and "weak" theoretical way of understanding cultural borrowing than some of the dominant theories

35 See Eve Kosofsky Sedgwick, *Touching Feeling: Affect, Pedagogy, Performativity* (Durham, N.C.: Duke, 2003). See also Richardson, *An Eye for Music*, 143–145.

36 It is possible to read even the conventions of porn in a more reparative light as depending more on the preconscious identificatory mechanism of "affective resonance" than on scripting behaviors, in the straightforward manner that has commonly been assumed in critical readings. My colleague Susanna Paasonen's work is enlightening in this regard. Susanna Paasonen, *Carnal Resonance: Affect and Online Pornography* (Cambridge, Mass.: MIT Press, 2011).

in popular music studies have offered. It is akin to writing on uses of outmoded objects in surrealism, to Rose Rosengard Subotnik's eloquent defense of Tin Pan Alley songs, and to some of the theories on sampling in recent pop (such as that of Mark Katz).[37] These authors all emphasize the uses to which music has been put more than the semantic meanings encoded with the music. The argument goes that musical styles that feel depersonalized or generic or that evidence a craftsmanlike approach to musical construction (as opposed to expressing a willful desire for artistic originality) permit listeners, or "users," greater scope for adapting the music to their own individual lived circumstances—the phenomenon of popular songs becoming "our song." This shift from semantics to functionality resonates with James J. Gibson's idea of affordance and his broader ecological understanding of perception. In his view, the uses to which an object can be put determine the meanings it accrues as much as inherent properties or previous cultural encodings. These ideas again resonate with the aesthetic priorities of surrealism.

The music in *Wayward Cloud* has been put to a wide range of uses: working men's anthems, country and western torch songs, and Mandopop show tunes; songs geared to the trade union movement or belonging to the ruling party's propaganda machinery; and music that is part of normative Western commodity culture or made to comment ironically on the repercussions of cultural appropriation. In addition, these uses of music bring into play cultural memories that come heavily freighted with (lost or erased) significance, thereby signifying a Benjaminian "leap into the open air of history."[38] Adorno similarly held the ultimate surrealist music to be "use music," which he otherwise disdained. In his view, such music carried the residue of earlier encodings and was tainted by its uses by the cultural industry, but could be liberated from these functions by the mediating hand of the surrealist artist. Adorno did not explore this perspective in much depth, and this line of thinking is uncharacteristic of his writing elsewhere, but he did at least consider this subversive or against-the-grain function possible in his writing on surrealism.[39] Devalued and revalued music of this type serves a reparative function as defined by Sedgwick. Its meanings are not necessarily camp in the sense of encoded parodic critique, but more directly through the sense of exhilaration and playfulness exhibited in the space between an original and its repetition.

My reading advocates an understanding that vacillates between cultural critical and sensory/affective polarities, just as the concept of cultural memory itself is predicated

[37] Rose Rosengard Subotnik, "Shoddy Equipment for Living? Deconstructing the Tin Pan Alley Song," in *Musicological Identities: Essays in Honor of Susan McClary*, ed. Steven Baur, Raymond Knapp, and Jacqueline Warwick (Aldershot, UK: Ashgate, 2008), 205–218. Mark Katz, *Capturing Sound: How Technology Has Changed Music* (Berkeley: University of California Press, 2004), 156.

[38] Walter Benjamin, *Illuminations: Essays and Reflections*, trans. Harry Zohn (New York: Schocken, 1968), 261.

[39] On surrealist music, Adorno states that it is devalued music, "which attempts to break through alienation from within itself, even at the expense of its imminent form. This is normally identified as 'use music'. However it is precisely this typical use music—which gives evidence of such obvious dependence upon the market that it cannot enter into the present discussion." *Essays on Music*, ed. Richard Leppert, trans. Susan H. Gillespie (Berkeley: University of California Press 2002), 396–397.

on meanings that are always renegotiated with reference to contemporary codes and sensibilities. Musical numbers in *Wayward Cloud* signify transcendence, but their failure to convincingly transcend their own material circumstances becomes their ultimate success; in Sedgwickian terms their weakness is translated into their strength. Let us not overlook the cautionary message of the film, which is how the modes of consciousness we experience from mass media become templates for actions in ordinary life. However, when a director like Tsai makes everyday consciousness infiltrate cultural memories in the form of outmoded musical objects, the latter no longer condition behavior to the extent that they have done in the past, other than in terms of their residual mnemonic energies, which are easily turned to different and more radical ends.

References

Adorno, Theodor. "Looking Back on Surrealism." In *Notes to Literature*, Vol. 1, 86–90. Translated by Shierry Weber-Nicholson. New York: Columbia University Press, 1991 [1954].

Adorno, Theodor. *Essays on Music*. Edited by Richard Leppert. Translated by Susan H. Gillespie. Berkeley: University of California Press, 2002.

Altman, Rick. *The American Film Musical*. Bloomington, IN: Indiana University Press, 1987.

Assman, Jan. "Collective Memory and Cultural Identity." *New German Critique* 65 (Spring–Summer 1995): 125–133.

Assman, Jan. *Cultural Memory and Early Civilization: Writing, Remembrance, and Political Imagination*. Cambridge, UK: Cambridge University Press, 2011.

Barthes, Roland. "The Metaphor of the Eye." In *Story of an Eye*, by Lord Auch [pseudonym], 119–127. Translated by J. A. Underwood. London; New York: Penguin, 1982.

Benjamin, Walter. *Illuminations: Essays and Reflections*. Edited by Hannah Arendt. Translated by Harry Zohn. New York: Schocken, 1968.

Butler, Judith. *Gender Trouble*. London; New York: Routledge, 1990.

Cohan, Steven. *Incongruous Entertainment: Camp, Cultural Value, and the MGM Musical*. Durham, N.C.: Duke University Press, 2005.

Cusick, Suzanne, "On a Lesbian Relationship with Music: Serious Effort Not to *Think* Straight." In *Queering the Pitch: The New Gay and Lesbian Musicology*, edited by Philip Brett, Elizabeth Wood, and Gary Thomas, 67–83. New York: Routledge, 1994.

Feuer, Jane. *The Hollywood Musical*. London: Macmillan Press, 1982.

Feuer, Jane. "The Self-Reflective Musical and the Myth of Entertainment." In *Hollywood Musicals: The Film Reader*, edited by Steven Cohan, 229–235. London; New York: Routledge, 2002.

Flinn, Caryl. "The Deaths of Camp." In *Camp: Queer Aesthetics and the Performing Subject: A Reader*, edited by Fabio Cleto, 433–457. Edinburgh: Edinburgh University Press, 1999.

Gorbman, Claudia. "Auteur Music." In *Beyond the Soundtrack: Representing Music in Cinema*, edited by Daniel Goldmark, Lawrence Kramer, and Richard Leppert, 149–162. Berkeley: University of California Press, 2007.

Hawkins, Stan. *The British Pop Dandy: Male Identity, Music and Culture*. Aldershot, UK: Ashgate, 2009.

Herzog, Amy. *Dreams of Difference, Songs of the Same*. Minneapolis: University of Minnesota Press, 2010.

Jarman-Ivens, Freya. "Notes on Musical Camp." In *The Ashgate Research Companion to Popular Musicology*, edited by Derek B. Scott, 189–203. Farnham, UK: Ashgate, 2009.

Katz, Mark. *Capturing Sound: How Technology Has Changed Music*. Berkeley: University of California Press, 2004.

Levinas, Emmanuel. *Totality and Infinity*. Dordrecht, Netherlands: Kluwer Academic Publishers, 1991.

Paasonen, Susanna. *Carnal Resonance: Affect and Online Pornography*. Cambridge, Mass.: MIT Press, 2011.

Richardson, John. "Plasticine Music: Surrealism in Peter Gabriel's 'Sledgehammer.'" In *Games Without Frontiers: Peter Gabriel from Genesis to Growing Up*, edited by Michael Drewett, Sarah Hill, and Kimi Kärki, 195–210. Farnham, UK; Burlington, Vt.: Ashgate, 2010.

Richardson, John. "Intertextuality and Pop Camp Identity Politics in Finland: The Crash's Music Video 'Still Alive.'" *Popular Musicology Online* 2 (2006), at http://www.popular-musicology-online.com/issues/02/richardson-01.html (accessed December 4, 2010).

Richardson, John. *An Eye for Music: Popular Music and the Audiovisual Surreal*. New York; Oxford: Oxford University Press, 2011.

Rivière, Danièle, "Scouting" [interview with Tsai Ming-Liang]. In *Tsai Ming-Liang*, edited by Jean Pierre Rehm, Olivier Joyard, and Danièle Rivière, 79–118. Paris: Editions Dis Voir, 1999.

Sedgwick, Eve Kosofsky. *Touching Feeling: Affect, Pedagogy, Performativity*. Durham, N.C.: Duke University Press, 2003.

Sedgwick, Eve Kosofsky, and Andrew Parker, eds. *Performativity and Performance*. New York: Routledge, 1995.

Sontag, Susan. "Notes on 'Camp' [1964]." Reprinted in *Camp: Queer Aesthetics and the Performing Subject. A Reader*, edited by Fabio Cleto, 53–65. Edinburgh: Edinburgh University Press, 1999.

Subotnik, Rose Rosengard. "Shoddy Equipment for Living? Deconstructing the Tin Pan Alley Song." In *Musicological Identities: Essays in Honor of Susan McClary*, edited by Steve Baur, Raymond Knapp, and Jacqueline Warwick, 205–218. Aldershot, UK: Ashgate, 2008.

Tinkom, Matthew. *Working Like a Homosexual: Camp, Capital, Cinema*. Durham, N.C.: Duke University Press, 2002.

Williams, Linda. *Hardcore: Power, Pleasure, and the "Frenzy of the Visible"*. Berkeley: University of California Press, 1989.

Žižek, Slavoj. "From Courtly Love to *The Crying Game*." *New Left Review* 1. no. 202 (November/December 1993): 95–108.

CHAPTER 18

PARTIES IN YOUR HEAD: FROM THE ACOUSTIC TO THE PSYCHO-ACOUSTIC

PHILIP BROPHY

Scorpio Rising: Sites of Otherness

As leather-clad teens adorned with satanic trinkets prance in the voyeuristic beams of *Scorpio Rising* (dir. Kenneth Anger, 1964), a gorgeous warbling caresses their bodies in a series of echoic folds. Like radios out of reach, the reverberant voices of long-ago pop vocalists[1] seem uncannily matched to the film's cramped bedrooms, bare garages, and deserted churches. All are sites of quiet reflection, sounding all the more lonely when matched to the maudlin teen angst of said vocalists. Despite being essentially a silent film production, the necromantic eroticism of *Scorpio Rising*'s pre-gay bacchanal bikers is coded less by their overt paraphernalia than by the covert phonology of their reinterpreted songs.

The film's spirited experimental pop audiovision runs counter to the brutish shrink-wrapping of rock that sociologically embalms *Easy Rider* (dir. Dennis Hopper, 1969). The latter's brash proclamation of countercultural affectation is the polar opposite of the former's inhalation of subcultural exaltation, and one wonders if there could

[1] *Scorpio Rising*'s songs (all uncredited) were Ricky Nelson, "Fools Rush In" (1963), Peggy March, "Wind Up Doll" and "I Will Follow Him" (1963); The Angels, "My Boyfriend's Back" (1963); Bobby Vinton, "Blue Velvet" (1963); Elvis Presley, "(You're a) Devil in Disguise" (1963); Ray Charles, "Hit the Road Jack" (1961); Martha and the Vandellas, "(Love Is Like a) Heatwave" (1963); The Crystals (The Blossoms), "He's a Rebel" (1962); Claudine Clark, "The Party Lights" (1962); Kris Jensen, "Torture" (1962); Gene McDaniel, "Point of No Return" (1962); and The Surfaris, "Wipeout" (1963).

be two films so radically opposed at the nexus of sight and sound, space and stage, sex and sense. By initially contrasting the mainstream–counterculture sound track of *Easy Rider* with the amateur-subculture soundtrack of *Scorpio Rising*, I hope to clear ground for a sharper consideration of the sensory sensationalism in what is hazily defined as "rock in cinema." I then trace a trajectory from the dynamics, tonality, and aura of *Scorpio Rising*'s audiovision to discuss ways in which the acoustic sense of performed music in cinema is transformed into a psycho-acoustic sensation for both its performers and its auditors.

Perhaps film criticism's musicological deafness—attuned more to *Easy Rider*'s broadcast message than to *Scorpio Rising*'s coded signals—has not helped the situation. *Scorpio Rising*'s use of song has been footnoted at *Easy Rider*'s centrality in the rickety paradigm of rock-meets-cinema, as if the mere utterance of a rock song on the soundtrack fast-tracks one to the social imperatives of musicological discourse. *Easy Rider* seems to be treated by default as if its music and songs naturally emanate from the film, as though the film releases its music and thus signifies how music and image are indelibly fused in its audiovision. The serendipitous synchronism born of matching song to music implies that *Scorpio Rising* is the opposite: an example of how music is unnaturally laid onto film to qualify its sound track as ontologically Other. As both films have almost no location/sync-sound while their songs play (save for the occasional bike rumble), we might reverse this perspective and view *Easy Rider* as a fawning attempt to clothe itself in that which it is not, and *Scorpio Rising* as an attempt to drag that which it knows only too well that it is not.

When flatbed traveling cameras weave in front of and alongside Hollywood actors on Harleys while Steppenwolf's "Born to Be Wild" (1968) and its brittle AM-radio growl staunchly occupy the sound track, I hear the sound of advertising executives constructing aural billboards to tag and track the subjects of the film's social typing and demographic exploitation.[2] When some delinquents play out a mock initiation ceremony, tearing at the clothes of a squirming initiate while Kris Jensen's "Torture" (1962) and its tremulously murmured harmonies are gently buffeted by fairground organ and fatigued drums, I hear the sound of hidden testimonies of self-inflicted desire played out equally by Kenneth Anger and his amateur cast. Such are the material characteristics of the films' contrasting sound-worlds; such are the aural semiotics that govern their audiovisual equilibrium when one listens more carefully to the sound-world of recorded music while it becomes what we expediently term "the soundtrack." My juxtaposition of these two films proceeds from a dual purpose: (1) to demonstrate how the evocation of sensory aural space in a recorded song employed in a film mix imports an ulterior notion of how one exists in space (as a "figure in a landscape," a "man of the world," a "woman framed as a picture," etc.); and (2) to show how that aural space modulates and redefines the pictorial space counter to how it is defined according to scopic cinematic perception. For the sound of recorded music in film is, ironically, mutable: it renders image sonic.

[2] Dennis Hopper's film is often lazily aligned with countercultural perception of the era, but by 1969 most television advertising in America was employing similar symbols, tokens, effects, and gestures.

The "open road" heroics of *Easy Rider*—which are tawdry, as befits the counterculture's revolutionary stance—are matched by the dry, non-echoic, despatialized sound of late 1960s rock production. Rock microphone placement of the era tended to prioritize the clinical separation and decompartmentalized identification of sounds. This was mostly a consequence of dealing with excessive volume in the music's production. Live amplifier stacks could embolden the phenomenological presence of a band on their spectacular Mayan stage. But capturing that thrilling sense of amplification in a studio environment necessarily transformed the preceding half-century of studio microphonics dedicated to encoding acoustically reconstitutable performances. In the early rock record's sound-world, loudness was symbolically conveyed by the thickness of imposing frequencies, which warranted baffled separation in their encoding and in turn rendered the instrumentation with a notable reduction in reverberation due to the saturation of the sound. *Easy Rider*'s road-trip scenography gives a widened scopic space to the records' construction of such imaginary, voluminous spaces. And as the film boasts a "journey" narrative, its songs' driving rhythms are crucial to the heroic notions of liberated freedom and forging one's own path to self-discovery.[3]

Eschewing rock for pop, *Scorpio Rising*'s selected songs are shaped by onanistic, narcissistic, and messianic fixations on the already-discovered self. The film's "closed room" theatrics are matched by the distinctive plate reverbs and room-sends of mid-'60s-era pop songs. The soundtrack's consequent unremitting reverberation resembles sound as it would be heard by gods in their tombs, awaiting invocation and resurrection. The characters in these songs (all lamenting some sort of emotional rupture or voiding) are asocial figures, forsaking societal recognition, but desiring acknowledgment of their pitiful pantomimic status. The microphonics of pop production of the time remain embarrassingly erotic, with spatial coloring and textural incidents coalescing through open-spaced studio recording, so that all sounds infect and intonate each other. The effect is like hearing any individual instrument simultaneously near and far, creating a blur of tactile rapture and echoic confusion. This "near-but-far" simultaneity in turn honors the ultimate narcissist, who wants all to come near and gaze upon him while he dismisses their lowly attention to his sublime self and insists they stay afar. *Scorpio Rising* also perversely sublimates how Christian churches had long employed reverberant acoustics to color the human voice as a tenuous link to the voice of God. Indeed, the design of room-send reverberation follows such a ventriloquist principle: the sound of a performer is channeled by audio cable to a separate room, wherein the sound is played on a speaker that is miked to return to the mixing desk the "wet" effected sound, which

[3] Following a strong cycle of hot rod/juke joint/juvenile delinquent/teen-love B-grade movies throughout the '50s and into the '60s—most of which employed trained composers and orchestrators who sullenly attempted to replicate the sound of R & B, rock 'n' roll, and rockabilly in their scores—the rock song score came into its own with the scores produced and co-composed by pop producer Mike Curb and co-composed and performed by session guitarist Davie Allan (sometimes as Davie Allan and the Arrows). Allen's first sound track session was *Wild Angels* (dir. Roger Corman, 1966). He had been the key co-composer and/or key guitarist for eighteen biker-related movies up to 1969. *Easy Rider* did not instigate either the biker subgenre or the match of rocking hard and riding Harleys.

is blended with the originating "dry," unaffected sound. Unlike the social, worldly spaces evoked by music, which try hard to capture a performance "realistically," "naturally," and "honestly," echoic hyper-reverberant pop from the '60s encapsulates a unique phonological moment wherein ornamental headiness dressed its singers in beguiling aural attire to simultaneously alienate and entrance the listener. The sound track's imported phonological space and unworldly echoes are potent signs of *Scorpio Rising*'s "Otherness."

Vinyl: Live on Stage

A different type of "room reverb" engulfs *Vinyl* (dir. Andy Warhol, 1965), which is a very loose restaging of Anthony Burgess's novel *A Clockwork Orange* as performed by select members of Warhol's Factory clique. What is it that makes this an appalling movie? The sound of the performers' voices. What makes it an exhilarating movie? The sound of records to which they listen.[4] The rough on-set recording of *Vinyl* erodes fidelity yet heightens reality by giving one a warts-and-all portrait of the audiovisual composure of its self-centered, solipsistic performers, who care little for their vocal craft and even less for their reception. Watching the film without sound might elicit some elegiac reverence to the youthful craziness captured on celluloid, but the indifferent sound recording thrusts the film's drug-hazed circumstance into the audience's consciousness, who psycho-acoustically infer that the film is carelessly made and terminally unprofessional.

The magical charm of the bulk of Warhol's early cinema—all of it as openly amateurish as *Vinyl*—resides in its silence, within the mute pictorial energy that mobilizes its voyeuristic drive. Silence always looks good on screen. Silent cinema introduced the phenomenon of technologically mediated muteness: a literally unheard-of experience that announced the possibility of sound being removed, halted, blocked, avoided. When recorded sound was initially introduced in the medium of film via simultaneous recording of concurring audio on a nonsynchronized, parallel system, it replicated the base anthropological impulse of the moving image. It didn't simply join sound to image; it recorded the spatial ambience of the site where the visual event took place. Audio tracks would be inevitably colored with the acoustic characteristics of spaces designed for stages and lights, not performers' voices. The resulting "roomy" and "boomy" nature of on-set sound recording today still confers veracity on the eventfulness of what is being visually documented. *Vinyl* looks like 1965, but its audio is snared by a time warp that recalls how recorded sound first clumsily occurred in cinema.

While the brutish psycho-acoustics of *Vinyl*'s recording match the distracted amateur performances and their desultory staging, a deep consideration of the film's audiovision adds contradiction and complexity to the equation. Superficially, the film is

[4] *Vinyl*'s songs (all uncredited) were Martha and the Vandellas, "Nowhere to Run" (1965); The Kinks, "Tired of Waiting for You" (1965); The Rolling Stones, "The Last Time" (1965); Joey Dee and the Starlighters, "Shout" (1962); and Sir Mack Rice, "Mustang Sally" (1965).

planar: one fixed camera, one light source, one stage setting, one temporal span, one microphone perspective. Yet this is granted depth by the incorporation of (1) multiple scenographic "zones" as the onstage ensemble of performers simultaneously enact various scenes, themes, or moments from the novel; and (2) acoustic sensations of near and far, onscreen and offscreen, as audible actions move closer to or farther from the single microphone. The resulting narrative is an overload of "live" information: uninterrupted action unfolding on a stage, uncontrolled acts often occurring at the edges of the camera frame, and variably legible dialogue courtesy of unstable vocal delivery and directional relation to the microphone. The sound of such live action replicates the originating acoustic nature of cinema, one that was presumed to neutrally follow the dynamics and presence of live theater, but was slowly replaced by the positioning, rendering, and layering of sound, which complemented the camera's visual propensity to fragment time and space. Although to an extent this is ontologically evident when the technology of filmmaking is considered, what is overlooked is how advances in sound technology have psycho-acoustically transformed how we consider silence in two crucial cinematic realms: (1) physical silence on the film soundtrack when sound is absent and (2) psychological silence on the film soundtrack when music replaces location sound.

When Victor (Gerard Malanga) dances to "Nowhere to Run" by Martha and the Vandellas (1965), that is literally what we have in *Vinyl*, because the sound of the seven-inch record playing loudly on a turntable just off-camera locates the sound source as being acoustically diegetic (yet visually nondiegetic). Unlike *Scorpio Rising* and its transcendent phonological effect, *Vinyl* is "metacoustic" in its creation of a noise-scape in which dialogue (delivered and screamed) and music (blared, track-skipped, volume-ramped) collapse into each other by virtue of their shared simultaneous point of emission. Furthermore, when the song is introduced, the film's performances are transformed from embarrassing pantomime to engrossing surrender. For one need not act too much to portray the act of listening to music, and the floating, numbed senses of these Factory denizens (including infamous addicts like Edie Sedgewick and Ondine) evidence the intoxicating effect music can have on those willing to dive into its sonorum. The bad recording of the record playback only adds to the veracity of this documentary effect in the film, thereby generating a sound-world that is visibly and actually affecting the consciousness of the film's onscreen performers.

Whereas Victor's initial dance (to the song played twice in a row; once was not enough) and the records played while he is being "tortured" signpost this peculiar state of musical transcendence, the closing 15 minutes of the film indelibly demonstrate the immolating power of phonological presence on the film soundtrack. By this stage, the script or presumed scenography evaporates, as the performers have truly reached an altered pharmaceutical state. The record player is cranked up even louder, with tracks like Sir Mack Rice's "Mustang Sally" (1965) and The Rolling Stones' "The Last Time" (1965). Everyone seems to have forgotten they are making a movie. The Doctor (Tosh Carillo) occupies center screen and narcissistically gyrates while inhaling poppers. Victor lurches toward him, and the Doctor proceeds to pretend-torture the bare-chested Victor, gradually forcing him to inhale poppers, too. Victor and the Doctor start behaving more aggressively, which appears to turn on the other performers, some of whom also take the poppers. It is a wonderfully seedy scene due to the continually broken line between performers being in and out of control. Yet all the while, the played records keep them floating in a liminal performative space that they now inhabit. Here the narrative becomes a party, the stage becomes a discotheque, the actors are struck dumb, the performers become auditors, and the film sublimates its vision to the power of sound. Celluloid becomes vinyl.

Scarface: The Sensory Auditorium

If *Vinyl* becomes a performance in and of itself, using its own soundtrack to direct its performers, *Scarface* (dir. Brian DePalma, 1983) presents a soundtrack that allows the sound-world of recorded music to determine how we experience and read the textual role of recorded music in film. Deliberately replicating the name of Howard Hawks's canonical gangster genre film from 1932, DePalma's *Scarface* drags the former, salaciously declaring itself as a denial of that which it replicates. Central to this perverse operation is its decimation of the classical gangster's aural text by embracing the ground-zero hedonism of the subwoofer and pumping the soundtrack with Giorgio Moroder's glorious disco score. Parallel with *Vinyl*, *Scarface* employs music as recorded material to conduct performances, experiences, and energies whose symbolic function and textural weight are elucidated by the aural materiality of its soundtrack.

Scarface's swelling synth-strings, phased tonal pads, arpeggiated bass lines, and percolating syn-drums aurally trace the film's nightclub grotesquery while cauterizing the eardrums of those who at the time still clutched cryogenic dreams of orchestral film scores. Yet apart from the violently un-American tackiness of this determining musicological choice, Moroder's score also functions as an interpretation of Tony Montana's (played by Al Pacino) own "mega-worldly" domain of intoxicating power, lined in coke and neon and quaking to Euro-electronic disco. It's a fine line—and one largely missed by cinema history—yet it maintains this notion of musical phonology being prime matter in the audiovisuality of modern cinema. The discotheque/nightclub sound track might seem a matter of objective coverage due to this film's setting, but—as erotically implied by *Scorpio Rising* and sensationally exploited in *Vinyl*—it is a subtextual document of subjective experience, of how music is heard by its denizens. For the music of *Scarface* is the party that plays in Tony's head.

Some important pointers. Disco is the only genre of music named after the spatial environment of its occurrence, the discotheque, a space not for playing live music, but for hearing recorded music. Its consecration in the early '70s was a sign of how undeniably phonological music had inevitably become, of how the means for making music was progressively determined by an acceptance of how music could be "anacoustic" and hence unreal, unnatural, and unworldly. Having already played a key role in shaping the

European electronic school of disco in the mid-'70s,[5] Moroder's song score for *Scarface* replaced the film soundstage with the studio control room and in turn afforded the experience of hearing a public music like disco 'detourned' to reveal ulterior meaning by symbolically portraying the private experiences Tony has of his world.

By 1983 disco—already forming mutant-disco, pre-electro, and proto-club traits—had clearly defined itself as a self-centered, hedonistic, phenomenological enterprise. And as discos became "nightclubs," the ways in which club music could expand time and space within synthetic, electronic, and metronomic parameters became central to the sensory experience of its audience. Any nightclubber will know the acousmatic nature of music in such spaces. Disc jockeys might be playing vinyl—according the phonological primacy over the acoustic or the performative—but the spatialization of the music accrues its own heady sensations for the listener. One moves both within and without the music, experiencing it sometimes as lobal assault (on the floor), sometimes as spinal tapping (in toilet cubicles), and sometimes as visceral massage (moving between floors). If nightclubs have been doing this globally for the last 30 years at least, and they have been major sociosexual sites for illicit pleasure, cinema has given poor audiovisual representation of this dominant landscape where sound overwhelms vision in extending the human pleasure principle. And just as the loss of oneself in the music is fundamental to the nightclub experience, it may be no coincidence that films abstracting the human in polysexual, amoral, and existentialist guise are better attuned to the sound, space, and sense of the nightclub.

While *Scarface* corrals its musical moments into overstated scenographic and emotional zones, the unrelenting surface of its synthetic sound aligns itself with the fantasy world, which Tony believes is his and his alone. Moroder's music functions as (1) diegetic club tracks played at The Babylon and in Cadillacs; (2) associative scenographic cues (for the interned Cubans at their detainee camp, the seedy Colombians in Miami, the wealthy Bolivian drug cartel mansion, etc.); and (3) faux-moralistic, churchlike keyboard passages whenever Tony slides downward to his inevitable ruin. At least that's how one could conventionally read the score's performance in the film. But reversing this trajectory, we can audit how Tony is driven ever onward and upward to a self-immolating act of transcendence, burning all humanist and social values as combustible fuel for his projection. Indeed, Tony's self-destructive impulses are sharpened once "the world is his" and he realizes the futility of having attained his worldly dreams (in the final coked-up shoot out at his mansion). Moroder's synthetic score is then a counterpoint to the moral insinuations of the classical gangster parable: the

5 Giorgio Moroder's most famous Euro-electronic disco tracks were for Donna Summer: "Love to Love You Baby" (1975) and "I Feel Love" (1977). He also produced hit records for Sparks, Blondie, Barbara Streisand, Kiss, and Sigue Sigue Sputnik. Moroder's song scores in a similar vein include *Midnight Express* (dir. Alan Parker, 1978); *American Gigolo* (dir. Paul Schrader, 1980); *Foxes* (dir. Adrian Lyne, 1980); *Cat People* (dir. Paul Schrader, 1982); *Flashdance* (dir. Adrian Lyne, 1983); and *Electric Dreams* (dir. Steve Barron, 1984).

otherworldly, disco-derived surface of the score aurally declares that the world as it is constructed is not enough, and that the imaginary, delusional, fantastical world that both underscores and overrides social reality is the other zone that rewards posthumanist desire. Tony—intensely personified by Pacino's palpably adrenaline performance of spring-loaded muscles, vaginal-trap mouth, and laser-beam eyes—is a symbol of the hedonistic pleasure granted especially by disco's ruthless pounding of the senses. In a sense, he is as disco is heard.

Blue Velvet: Dimensional Soundstages

As willfully contemporaneous as *Scarface* is with disco, *Blue Velvet* (dir. David Lynch, 1986) is ironically nostalgic with pop music. When Dorothy (Isabella Rossellini) intones Bobby Vinton's "Blue Velvet" (1963), a resonant connection is made to *Scorpio Rising*'s use of the same song. Although the scene has become a cliché of postmodern affection in '80s cinema, it is Dorothy's reverberant voice more than the retro MTV lip-synching into a vintage microphone that contextualizes the event as an important transhistorical moment, which severs the use of song from the sociological and appends it to the psychological. Of importance is the way that in the first half-hour of the film, Angelo Badalamenti's score has been introduced first via an unseen radio and then from a lounge room television set, and in both instances carries over into scenes in a manner not dissimilar to *Scorpio Rising*'s "parallel broadcast" of song. The seeping spread of the film's narrational score outlines innocent Jeffrey's (Kyle MacLachlan) world, with which he has not yet made full contact; the moist feel of Dorothy's breath is the homing device for Jeffrey to make contact with that world through her voice.

Later in the film, Ben (Dean Stockwell) lip-synchs Roy Orbison's "In Dreams" (1963). This scene draws attention to itself in order to unresolve its existence, as Ben transforms his lair into an imaginary stage for his performance of the song played on cassette. Ben functions as an arbitrator of *Blue Velvet*'s transfigured sound track by orchestrating and conducting a corrupting audiovision, which his gang takes for granted, while Jeffrey's countenance mirrors our disjuncture from the soundtrack's nominal operation. Yes, it can be rationalized as a crazy miming of an old song, but Ben acutely characterizes how music exists reversed in the Hadean "other world" of *Blue Velvet*. Crooning into a metallic, lattice-sheathed lightbulb, he saliently perverts all we presume of audiovision's ontological fixity. A truly Lynchian denizen, he hears through makeup, mimes through light, emotes through masks, and sees through sound.

Blue Velvet's quotation of '60s pop, its association with the transsexual, and its attraction to the necrophiliac are crucial mechanisms that have determined the morphology of the modern soundtrack for the last few decades. Lynch's audiovisual agenda is to inhabit the sonorous terrain of the otherworldly aura of lost pop songs from the mid-1950s through the mid-1960s—to invoke that parallel universe of openly affected pop machinations as the stage for his dramatis personae. *Blue Velvet*'s sound track[6] audits an epoch of phonology when the voice conjured palpable angels, ghostly crooners, transgendered sirens, and erotic phonemes. Its embrace of the phonological thus defines a deeply considered take on what is otherwise loosely designated "the soundtrack."

Just as Ben is presented as a playback device channeling the voice of Bobby Vinton, *Blue Velvet*'s iconic ear is similarly a recording device: an operable unit that listens to its "other world" and channels what it hears from space to space. It has often been linked to the severed hand of *Un chien andalou* (dir. Luis Buñuel, 1929), but its role as a scopic analog of that obscure object of desire does little to position the ear as a device of acousmatic signification. In fact, the severed ear is closer to the eponymous gun of *Winchester '73* (dir. Anthony Mann, 1950) as a narrating object whose location creates its situation. Lynch's ear self-reflexively alerts us to its act of hearing with its own ear, so much so that one could reconstruct the film with this ear as its inhuman star, telling the story of an ear who dreamt he was a man. Like a tracker with his ear to the ground to gauge that which is about to occur, the severed ear audits and relays all the atmospheric soundscapes that roll into the auditorium, evidencing how sound exists in *Blue Velvet*'s realm.

Blue Velvet's "other world" is notably composed of a range of environments that privilege the transformative power of acoustics. Of the numerous darkened, tunneled, and submerged spaces, it is not by chance that the nightclub is central—a dank, smoky domain that blunts the enlivened senses into a bottomed-out saturation of sight, sound, and smell. The nightclub's musical ambience is designed and deployed aurally throughout the film's production as a method of "otherworldizing" the sonic psyche (in contrast to sound designer Walter Murch's "worldizing" radio tracks throughout *American Graffiti* [dir. George Lucas, 1972]). From Jeffrey finding a severed ear, to his own fatal attraction to the voice of Dorothy, sono-musical semes and themes are cross-patched and multitracked throughout the aural matrix of the film's soundtrack. Dorothy's sighing into a vintage microphone relays signals directly to Jeffrey's sensitized eardrum, pressing into it like a bare foot on a trousered crotch. His mind becomes receiver, recorder, and player; his erotic entrapment results from the phonological intersecting the psychological. At key moments when Jeffrey realizes his situation, he becomes one with what and how the severed ear hears.

Hindsight allows us to fantasize that embedded in director, composer, and sound designer David Lynch's head is an arsenal of vintage reverb units—even that his ears are continually severed from their surroundings so as to be attuned to all that is not visually evident. For Lynch, the "stage" with its spotlights and microphones, which rises in the clubs and bars of *Blue Velvet*, *Twin Peaks* (1990–1991), *Lost Highway* (1997), and *Mulholland Drive* (2001), symbolizes a cinesonic platform for the voicing of his recurring motifs. Always, these spaces are fixed at the borders of towns, the edge of night, the precipice of morality. Always, they exude a sonic danger through their engaging din, felt

[6] *Blue Velvet*'s sourced songs include Bobby Vinton, "Blue Velvet" (1963); Roy Orbison, "In Dreams" (1963); and Ketty Ester, "Love Letters" (1962).

as deep rumbling when heard from outside and as a lulling sensurround when heard from within. Lynch's films are thus more recording studios than production stages. Representation is governed by the sonic, sound advances image, and space prompts situations. To truly comprehend the formal, morphological, and ontological effects of this paradigmatic redress of audiovision requires nothing less than "listening to images." *Blue Velvet*'s songs—following *Scorpio Rising*'s lead—map out its fictional terrain in demonstration of how the sound of song confers ambience cinesonically. For just as reverberant recordings color a space with deeper dimensionality than a volumetric calculation of their recording environment allows, Lynch evidences how the visual screen at best can but allude to the dimensional magnitude of is its discontents, while the auditorium swells with legible depth, actualized transience, and temporal emission.

La vie nouvelle: Collapsing Sound-Worlds

Plugged into the effects units of Lynch's mental mixing desk is *La vie nouvelle* (dir. Philippe Grandrieux, 2002), a disjointed story of American transient Seymour (Zachary Knighton) fatally attracted to French ingénue Melania (Anna Mouglalis), who is interred at a Bulgarian sex club. Where *Blue Velvet* betrays an affection for the dank, erotic substructure of postwar American domesticity, *La vie nouvelle* coldly stares into the pornographic crevices of post-Glasnost/EEC Europe. This film is audiovisually matrixed within the *son-image* employed for *Blue Velvet*, quoting its near-death sirens, screaming power plays, and noisy eruptions of maddened violence, here extending their aural form and texture through sophisticated crafting.

Replicating the subjective traumas suffered by Melania as she comes to accept never knowing time or place within the club, we are rarely given any scenographic framework to follow the story. As per Lynch's mindscapes, *La vie nouvelle* is staged in an "other world," but one that is eerily banal, hiding in the breaking light of a nondescript, windowless block at the decrepit periphery of some new millennial city where housing estates meet industrial wilderness. The film violently oscillates from the pitch black inside to the blinding white outside, from corridors too sharp to too blurred, from limbs oppressively near to dispassionately far—even from positive film to negative film. Yet this is not to be misread as arty cinematography: the focal collapses of *La vie nouvelle* are "decentered stages" for sound design duo Étant Donnés' aural thickness and musical seepage, which engulfs the film's disorienting night corridors and disturbing mornings after. When image is obliterated, as it is continually throughout the story's harrowing episodes, we experience precisely what Lynch's *Blue Velvet* has nurtured: an engulfment of the sonic greater than visual discourse can impart. Strategically disorienting and reorienting sensory correlations, *La vie nouvelle*'s psycho-acoustic drive creates an existential tinnitus that rings like an obscured object of desire from some lost night. As auditors, we are more akin to club goers stumbling into the sunrise than we are to mere movie watchers.

La vie nouvelle's opening is breathtaking in this regard. For an uncomfortably long period, the film's audiovisual surface is questioned into existence—so dark in veneer and so deep in pitch that one wonders whether one is experiencing celluloid at all. A dislocated group gaze glassy-eyed into the distance at something we do not see. Barely lit, they resemble a prehistoric gathering before a black dawn, while a subterranean swell of sound rumbles their world. This primordial overture is an important means by which the film proceeds from its ground-zero audiovision. Rather than building on existing conventions, it destroys everything to start again—just as Melania is reprogrammed to be an abject vessel ideally suited to the most severe exploitations of the underground sex industry. The deep tones, then, are not ominous poetic tropes, but rather auricular probes into our consciousness, querying what if anything we might make from this humming planetary drone, which offers us no identification, no desire, no gratification.

Despite its unremitting bleakness, *La vie nouvelle* can be taken as a model for posthumanist audiovision: a realm of expression and signification predicated on the wider possibilities of how sound and image can affect us beyond our attempts to rationalize their mimetic and communicative operations. Its story of human voiding provides a suitable framework for stretching the limits of subjective experience, thereby granting us communion with borders and thresholds of cinematic language dismissed by conventional storytelling. Looking and sounding like *Amélie* (dir. Jean-Pierre Jeunet, 2001) compressed into a black, soul-destroying paste, *La vie nouvelle*'s direction is more a matter of post-dance choreography, as its night creatures—captors and captives alike—draw interconnecting *danses macabres* like exhausted automata, blurring the distinctions among sex performer, dance performer, dance patron, and sex patron. Accordingly, the film's literal drainage of the human is as central as its audiovisual imbalance is crucial to depicting the psychic space of the sex/dance/nightclub.

The exhausted self in *La vie nouvelle*'s world is one who can sublimate her aural consciousness within the noise-scape of her everyday surroundings. Consequently, the film affords a contemporaneous assessment of the meld between aural semiotics in cinema and psycho-acoustics in the outside world: of precisely how the sound of cinema reflects current shifts in the technologically mediated sounds of "everyday life." The film's erogenous tonalities (for it truly is an orchestrated sound design) constitute a poetry enlivened by acoustics, sonics, and harmonics—not by musical scripture, let alone song or cue placement. Its sound-world is acutely symptomatic of the collapse between sound and music that has proliferated in the real world, wherein all music is disinterred from its locatable source and left to nomadically rupture the last barriers that hitherto fortified the personal, the private, the domestic, the professional, the communal, the official. Listen around you. Distorted MP3s play on mobile phones in hospital emergency rooms while a detuned TV blares with distortion; cheap car window trimmings rumble with mid-range whine while club music thumps through a misaligned subwoofer in cars idling at red lights; overmedicated outpatients busk a cappella-karaoke through micro PAs while listening to R & B ballads on iPods. And all of this could be experienced within a three-minute period of transition in any urban hub. This is the actual sound-world in which we live. It's Luigi Russolo on amphetamines. John Cage on crack.

Jacques Tati on methadone. Murray Schaffer on rohypnol. It's a din neither enlightening nor expansive. But in place, it is a dimension of complex substantia and heady diffusion well beyond those sonic campaigners' collective utopian imagination. In an era in which "realism" in global cinema (of both mainstream and art house persuasion) is defined by conditional, idealistic, and moralistic paradigms of societal mimeticism, it is no wonder that noise is excluded from its domain, and that music is perceived as a cloud of beauty floating through in a cruelly staged world. *La vie nouvelle*'s noise-scape marks it as a film mercifully from an Other planet.

Irréversible: Unearthing Noise Beds

For every "visual" film that shoots slo-mo into the neon lights of a city's sleaze strip, there could have been a sonic film that bluntly shows the grotty rear entrance to a club combined with the deep thumping of brooding beats bleeding into the rear alley. This guttural noise pollution (the bane of those owning real estate in urban gentrified areas) constitutes the psycho-acoustics of crime for the contemporary urban zone: wherever we hear that dark throb, crime thrives, hiding in its volume. In a classical era of cinema, criminal presence was connoted by badly performed Hollywood swing jazz emanating from cheesy Prohibition speakeasy sets. Following the gradual abstraction of music into phonological viscera courtesy of seminal films like *Scorpio Rising*, *Scarface*, and *Blue Velvet*, the criminal element can be tagged by the pure pulse of a subwoofer: indistinct but inescapable. This is pretty much how we first gain footing in the swirling sound-world of *Irréversible* (dir. Gaspar Noé, 2002): thrown into a backward narrative, entering a reversed Hadean nightmare via back alleys and into the subterranean tunnels of a club appropriately called Club Rectum.

But before we experience the pounding waves of amphetamine-driven techno that wrack the very architecture of Club Rectum, a series of "noise beds" has been unearthed and sifted through to arrive at the score's deafening din. This is an important consequence of its narrative: while *Irréversible*'s narratological sectioning is reversed (playing each bracketed scene in forward time), the sound of the film as a whole is symbolically sequenced in forward time. Prior to the premature climax of bloody violence that occurs in Club Rectum, the film's reverse credits unroll to a drone registering almost only on the subwoofer. It sounds remarkably like the opening to *La vie nouvelle*. But whereas that film goes back to a ground hum to reprogram the aural psyche, *Irréversible* posits that same colon-quaking earth tone as the cosmological epidermis to how all sound and music manifests itself in the world of language: peel back its miasmatic drone, and we'll even hear Beethoven. Consider how we move from that meta-tone during the credit roll, to a black screen with distant high violins holding a single tri-chord while a heartbeat marks time, to the rich lower-octave rumble heard within and without the ambulances ferrying their near-dead victims while metallic fittings and equipment inside the vehicles rattle like a gaggle of chattering shamans, to the synthesizer's cycling pitch bends and drum machine rolls as the black back corridors and blood-red cubicles of Club Rectum are giddily traversed. Beethoven heard birds and wrote music. *Irréversible* hears noise and makes noise. *La vie nouvelle* textually declares through its rumble: this is where we must begin again. *Irréversible* similarly states: there is no need to begin again, because we are already here, at the primordial start of social intercourse and hence musical language.

The music heard in *Irréversible*—like *Scarface*'s folding of diegetic orchestration into psychological extrapolation—is thus logically untethered to the history of film scores' linguistic operations. In its selection of techno and house streams of club music, *Irréversible*'s applied phonology is both a key to its purpose and a guide to its world. Like most of the films already cited, *Irréversible*'s song score results from commissioning a composer who predominantly exists away from the well-lit world of film composers. In this case, Thomas Bangalter (one-half of French neo-house/retro-synth duo Daft Punk) provides a series of tracks that function like music playing in the film's locales. But Bangalter's studio mode of digital composition reflects a contemporary state of dance music technology that has been infused with the aforementioned acoustic sensations. Numerous plug-ins and effects-filters now build on the original experiments conducted in Jamaican dub studio technology from the late '60s and krautrock and post-punk adventures in noise from the late '70s, to re-create the outdoor acoustic sensations of rave music from the late '80s, where music is buffeted by wind and fractured by architecture.

This sensation of hearing music that is the procedural result of being "pre-heard" and "pre-played" accents the phonological experience peculiar to dance/club music today. Extending mainstream forms of experimentation in hyper-reverberant pop and hypersynthetic disco, which reveled in how acoustics had become psycho-acoustics, contemporary dance/club music of all sorts proceeds from the "anacoustic" world—a realm where neither instruments nor their performers seem to exist. In the resulting sound-worlds, which evoke neither a stage, a studio, nor a hall of any sort, one is locked into the music's myriad generic grooves and liberated from their location, swirling within their orchestration and mobilized by their continuity. The unending Steadicam work in *Irréversible* functions like a visualization of this otherworldly aural principle of musical production where listening is being. From the shaking house tracks during the party to the disembodied techno palpitations in Club Rectum, the music is always spatially morphing—dually, via the phase and filter effects of the songs and the shifts of the microphone recording music being played back in some of these spaces. True to the annihilating desire of the film, the music is there not to diegetically ground its scenes, but to destabilize and disorient: to place one within the headache of Marcus (Vincent Cassel), in front of the silent gape of Alex (Monica Bellucci), and among the cranial remains of Le Tenia (Jo Prestia). In such a posthuman zone, humanism must be checked at the door, and *Irréversible* presents itself imposingly like the most fearsome of nightclub bouncers.

Like *Blue Velvet*'s severed ear left on the ground to register the subsonic markings of an indifferent world, *Irréversible* moves past the ocular humanist codes that are presumed to still constitute "film language," into a shuddering penumbra where cinema is mostly blind: the sonic. The film's cosmological pondering may be embarrassingly tagged by showing us the poster to *2001: A Space Odyssey* (dir. Stanley Kubrick, 1969), but its deeper cosmology lies in its audiovision, which demonstrates how the pre-heard/subjective/psycho-acoustic character of recorded music plays a vital and energizing role in the film's narratological and semiological signification. *Irréversible*—along with *La vie nouvelle*—incontrovertibly evidences the meld between the phonological and the phenomenological. Stated another way, it is as if we have been led even deeper down the auricular canal in the severed ear held by Jeffrey. In its foreboding darkness, we do not find Plato's cave with its flickering fire accompanying sages tediously recounting ancient myths. What we do find is a party going on, maybe in our head, maybe in someone else's. It's loud, overwhelming, unstoppable. We weren't invited, and there's no exit. Here, we can listen to images, for *this* is cinema.

PART IV

EXPANDED SOUNDTRACKS

CHAPTER 19

SENSORY ASPECTS OF CONTEMPORARY CINEMA

MICHEL CHION

THIS chapter focuses not so much on digital sound's specific contribution to cinema as on certain aspects of cinema's evolution that have been made possible by digital technology and its capacity to transform and multiply data. Digital technology has aided the continued development of cinema as a sensory experience, a tendency that was already present in its early stages but has become much more pronounced.

We are all familiar with the contributions digital sound and imagery have made to cinema. I have written about it in my book *Film, a Sound Art.*[1] The sensory spectacle offered by cinema, as I argue in that book, is audio-visual, but to be more precise, it is audio-visiogenic. Although technically speaking it may be composed of sounds plus images, in reality it consists of sensations created by combinations of sounds and images, greater than the sum of the parts.

Involved here is the notion of *rendering*, which I have been writing about since the late 1980s. Here I take up the idea again, based on something I witnessed during a stay in Montreal a few years ago.

In the main atrium of the vast Desjardins shopping mall in downtown Montreal is a large circular fountain, from which very clear water shoots upward in various shapes (jets, sheets of water, bubbling). From the bench where I was sitting, I watched a woman in a motorized wheelchair move toward the fountain. She went right up to its rim and surrendered to the sensory spectacle the fountain offered. From her position she was able to capture sound, image (which almost surely filled her visual field, because she was so close to it), humidity, and coolness. From time to time she would make the whole circuit around the fountain, as if around a merry-go-round or a circus ring. Her sensory spectacle was thus both interactive and three dimensional, because she was

[1] Michel Chion, *Film, a Sound Art*, trans. Claudia Gorbman [*Le Cinema, art sonore*, 2003] (New York: Columbia University Press, 2009). Cf. especially chapters 8 and 14.

essentially performing the equivalent of the circular tracking shots seen so frequently in films of the past 20 years, which almost seem to have been helping prepare cinema to go three-dimensional.

Let us imagine that I wish to transcribe cinematically the sensations this paralyzed woman is experiencing. I am paralyzed, as is any person who sits in a movie theater, with the difference that the movie spectator has chosen to be immobile and can stop being so at will. All I have to work with is sounds and images, but through particular ways of treating and combining them, I strive to *render* wetness and coolness, the moments when droplets reach the skin. For example, a momentary increase in audio intensity or a sudden transfer of sound from one channel to another might render the rush of cool air that can be felt near moving water.

For over 20 years I have been struck by the fact that some narrative films do not try to *reproduce* sounds that would be heard in the same real situation; rather, the sounds in combination with images try to re-create an overall sensation or even an emotion, while also vaguely resembling real sounds:[2]

> [T]he film spectator recognizes sounds to be truthful, effective, and fitting not so much if they *reproduce* what would be heard in the same situation in reality, but if they *render* (convey, express) the sensations—not necessarily auditory—associated with the situation.[3]
>
> As an example of rendering (i.e., of a sound that "translates" not another sound but speed, or a force, etc.), think of the sound effects that punctuate action scenes in many movies: the whirr and clank of swords and sabers in martial arts films translate agility; the sounds of punches in fight films translate the violence the characters experience (whereas in reality the impact of bodies might make less or different noise). There are also sounds that are intended to translate impressions of materiality or immateriality, fragility or resistance, sensuality or austerity, hollowness or fullness, heaviness or lightness, something threadbare or brand new, luxurious or spartan. They are created with this in mind and not the reproduction of the real sound of the object or character in question. *A rendering is always the rendering of something.*[4]

We might wonder why cinema, relying as it does on sounds and images, is not content with representing the sounds and images of a reproduced or invented reality. As I see it, this is because any art based on imitation (what the Greeks called *mimesis*) tries sooner or later to reproduce what is sensorily unavailable to it. An art that solely addresses the eye will try to suggest sounds; some music tries to conjure up images; a text meant to be read in silence attempts to evoke the specific presence of a voice. Literature endeavors to make the characters' sensations seen and heard, starting with Balzac and especially Flaubert. (In *Madame Bovary*, for example, Flaubert gets us to smell

[2] Michel Chion, *Audio-Vision: Sound on Screen*, trans. Claudia Gorbman [*Audio-Vision*, 1990] (New York: Columbia University Press, 1994).

[3] Chion, *Audio-Vision*, 109.

[4] Chion, *Film, a Sound Art*, 488.

dust.) Purely instrumental music, lacking text and voice, tries to speak as an articulate language. The monocular painting of the quattrocento aims to translate the perspective, relief, and depth it lacks, as well as movement. Classical sculpture strains to convey motion, showing Hercules fighting lions; Rodin and Degas depict acrobats and dancers; Giacometti creates a man walking; and so forth.

Silent film took an interest in conveying music visually, but also in translating sounds through images. Monocular sound film often works to re-create a sense of three-dimensionality. Real three-dimensional cinema, as is obvious in 3D screenings of Jim Cameron's *Avatar*, tackles the tactile, suggesting richer sensations than mere three-dimensionality.

I do not believe that this pursuit of rendering complex sensations, in auteur as well as popular cinema, merely serves the film's narrative or message. Do filmmakers show and create sensations to tell the story more clearly, better illustrate an idea or a message, or create a dramatic effect? I think not: in film there is an inherent pleasure in the sensory per se. I argue that people go see certain films also to enjoy figurative pleasures: to get the feeling of the wind (whose coolness they can't feel on their skin) and the rain (whose drops don't reach them). We find this appeal in Spielberg, and also in films by Kurosawa and Tarkovsky, who, if only because of their training as painters, are great sensory filmmakers.

One could just as easily make the opposing claim (although it would be somewhat excessive): that people tell stories in film merely as a pretext for reconstituting, representing, and imitating: to induce dreaming, transport the spectator into a world of pleasure and sensuality, and give us the impression of sleeping with the characters in beautiful beds with silk sheets, but also to give us physical sensations, frissons with no danger. And also for the sole pleasure of imitating.

It is significant that one of the first successful films using computer-generated animation, *Toy Story*, affords pleasure by making us feel that the small industrial toys made of plastic, fabric, or cardboard that we see on screen, and that we know are digitally synthesized, are *real*. In other words, *Toy Story* delights through conveying the toys' texture, which in real life we don't notice or consider interesting. Pascal accused painting of "vanity" because it entices us by resembling originals that in everyday life do not interest us.

A few years ago I wrote about the way computer-generated images can emphasize textures, which were originally the weak point of animation.[5] But now I am struck by the fact that newer animated movies, such as *A Bug's Story*, *Ice Age*, *Robots*, and *Up*, rich with details, volumes, modeling, and textures (snow, earth, sand, clouds, animal furs, metals, etc.), paradoxically have not hindered the success of other films that are by contrast roughly sketched, with a very simplified texture, and make no attempt to depict volume; for example, those of the great Hayao Miyazaki. Indeed, one current in contemporary

[5] "Image, rendu, et texture"; see http://www.michelchion.com/cours/echelle_au_cinema.pdf (accessed March 3, 2012).

art aims to provide us with *fewer* sensations, fewer effects of matter and depth; in short, it aims to work on the side of what we can call *sensory fasting*.

As a composer of *musique concrète*, which is music that comes from loudspeakers, I have refused for 20 years to contribute to films or to present my work in conjunction with visual effects (laser shows, projections, choreography, etc.). My music, which is made exclusively of recorded sounds, is thereby on the side of sensory fasting. However, having only sound at my disposal has stimulated me to create rich sensations that are no longer just sound sensations but also tactile and trans-sensory. I have often observed that when there is nothing but sound, the sound becomes all the sensations and ceases to be "just" sound.

Even the films with the greatest sensory richness trigger in us a feeling of lack, of incompleteness. That is because they highlight one of the things we tend to forget: that they are based on what I call sensory *isolates*. (In chemistry, an isolate is a substance that the chemist manages to purify from another, more complex substance.)

The sensory isolate—sensation directed at just one of the senses and taken out of a multisensory context—is a phenomenon made possible by the way sound and image are recorded. In the case of sound recording, independently of the question of "fidelity" to the original, we are dealing with a sound phenomenon that is isolated from the conditions and sensations normally associated with it. For example, the noise a train makes when heard through a loudspeaker, even if recorded and reproduced in high definition and in stereo, becomes what I call an acoustic isolate, as opposed to the sensations we experience when riding in a train, where this noise is associated not only with visual sensations but also with *phoric* sensations (being carried, jostled). More simple is is the case of a familiar noise you hear but whose cause you cannot see. This audible isolate may partially awaken the original global sensations in the listener's body via a conditioned reflex.

Systematic "acousmatization," which by definition characterizes media such as radio and telephone, but also such expressive forms as *Hörspiel* and *musique concrète*, generates specific effects of the acoustic isolate. Sound is divorced from thermal, tactile, and visual sensations that would normally be most commonly associated with it.

The acoustic isolate is only a particular case of what can be called sensory isolates. I use this expression to designate the technical process through which video and sound recorders and players "artificially isolate some types of sensations (taste, sound, etc.) which would normally cluster around objects."[6] Of course this concept aims only to describe, not to judge and even less to deplore or condemn (as if we automatically preferred the natural form), a phenomenon that has become routine, mechanically generated through video and sound recording.

Cinema is by no means alone. Modern windows, which let light through while insulating us ever more efficiently from temperature and noise, are systems that create a sensory isolate. I am writing this in a café on rue Saint-Denis in Montreal, sitting next to a

[6] Michel Chion, *Le Promeneur écoutant: Essais d'acoulogie* (Paris: Plume, 1993), 178.

large picture window through which I can see the street as a visual isolate. In the winter in Canada and parts of the United States (unlike what we experience in most European dwellings), inside and outside are two separate worlds, strongly differentiated by temperature, because of the great differences between interior thermostatic control and the heat or cold outside. The soundproofing and insulating glass, protecting me at the same time from sound and cold, makes a sensory isolate out of my view of the street. It is no accident that the double-paned window was developed in the twentieth century.

Even in sensorily rich films that aim to immerse us in a world "as if we were there," we get the feeling ever more strongly that something is missing, something is "insulating" us from this world, protecting us from it, giving us the sense of visiting Niagara Falls without having to wear rain gear.

Cinema that reconstitutes or renders a reality through multisensory technical imitation creates, at the same time, an awareness of sensory isolates. With a film like *Avatar*, which gives me three dimensions, image, and sound, where it is as if I am "in reality" more than with a monocular film, I feel all the more protected from the world I am observing, insulated from temperature and tactile sensations, and of course from pain. If films in the future are made in 3D but also with thermal effects, alternating among warm, hot, cool, and cold sensations, I will certainly be immersed in this world, but then I will always be insulated from some *other* perceptions, such as smell.

Who knows whether the filmgoer we can no longer simply call the spectator seeks not so much the feeling of sensory immersion as the feeling of *protection*, particularly with respect to algesic sensations (pain), that the genuine experience brings. If digital video games sometimes seem to present simulations of the real world that are capable of leading some weak-minded individuals astray and blurring the difference between the imaginary and the real, I believe that it is because of their interactivity. Interactivity alters our perception. In a film screening, interactivity doesn't exist or at least is quite limited.

Some movies, particularly thanks to the digital synthesizing of sounds and images and the sensory multiplicity this makes possible, appear as sensory feasts, nourishment for the senses hungry for sensory variations. But other films operate in the mode of sensory fasting, mentioned previously. We can appreciate spare images and rare or nonexistent sounds in a film, whereas everyday reality, media and advertising permeated as it is, solicits us with a cacophony of sounds and a plethora of colors.

Why has it taken so long for film theory to acknowledge and consider this dimension "beyond sound and image?" Why do we continue to speak of "the cinematic image" (following Deleuze), or of "the sound track," as is still often done in France? It seems to me that this stems from a desire to keep identifying cinema with its technical basis, that is, its visual and sound recording apparatuses.

Cinematic images and sounds are produced by machines that seem to imitate human organs of perception, but the apparatuses and the organs are in fact quite different. This tendency to liken the camera to the eye, even to a pair of eyes for 3D, and the microphone to the ear, or to a pair of ears for stereophony, is misleading. Not only is the camera's sight not as acute as our eyes, and microphones and sound recording systems, no matter how perfect, do not have the acuity of our ears, but the human ear and eye are connected with the person and the body as a whole. What we perceive through our eyes quickly ceases to be just "for our eyes," because machines are ignorant of the *trans-sensory*:

> TRANS-SENSORY PERCEPTIONS: I call trans-sensory those perceptions that belong to no one particular sense but which may travel via one sensory channel or another without their content or their effect being limited to this one sense. Everything involving rhythm may serve as an example. But other cases involve spatial perceptions, as well as the verbal dimension. A word that is read or spoken belongs to the same sphere of language, even if the modes of its transmission (handwriting, vocal timbre) run in parallel sensory channels.
>
> Rhythm is the essential trans-sensory dimension, since we experience it before we are born. The fetus encounters rhythm in the form of variations in pressure on the body wall, parsed with the combined beats of the mother's heart and its own. Rhythm is everywhere. For example, at night in the days before electric lights, it was present in the subtle pulsations of candlelight, in one sensory variation that we have lost and have replaced with others.[7]

Texture and grain are another category of trans-sensory perception.

The idea of the trans-sensory (called the inter-sensory in Maurice Merleau-Ponty's phenomenology) should be marginalized no longer. Those who make cinema and who actually deploy trans-sensorial effects unwittingly may be excused for ignoring it, but those who *study* the sensory dimensions of cinema would do well to explore these phenomena further.

Notes

This chapter was translated by Claudia Gorbman.

[7] Chion, *Film, a Sound Art*, 496.

CHAPTER 20

THE SOUND OF INTENSIFIED CONTINUITY

JEFF SMITH

In a recent review of Ridley Scott's film *Robin Hood* (2010), Stuart Klawans writes,

> The ticket buyers may be content with this stuff; but I can't be content for them when I see the new-model Robin Hood going into his climactic fight armed not with a sword and not with a longbow but with a battle-ax. It's what mainstream cinema has become: a heavy object made to crash into your head.[1]

His pan of the Russell Crowe star vehicle contains a familiar plaint about contemporary Hollywood cinema, namely that it is busy and noisy and seeks to stimulate the senses rather than arouse the intellect. For Klawans, contemporary blockbusters seek to exhilarate audiences, but more often than not they only succeed in miming the outward signs of excitement, trying to create an energetic visual style, which as Klawans says we can see from "the way the camera was apparently kicked across the set, and the resulting images then spliced together by a factory of hiccupping monkeys."[2]

Klawans's review may be a hyperbolic caricature of visual style in contemporary Hollywood cinema, but the fact is that critics and scholars have charted significant changes in the look of American films from the studio era to the present day. Some have gone so far as to identify a "postclassical" style that emphasizes spectacle and sensation over narrative coherence.[3] Other critics have countered this argument by suggesting that these stylistic

[1] Stuart Klawans, "Icons and Zombies," *The Nation*, June 14, 2010, 44.

[2] Klawans, "Icons and Zombies."

[3] For a sampling of some of the most significant voices in this debate, see Thomas Elsaesser, "Specularity and Engulfment: Francis Ford Coppola and *Bram Stoker's Dracula*," in *Contemporary Hollywood Cinema*, ed. Steve Neale and Murray Smith (New York: Routledge, 1998), 191–208; Geoff King, *New Hollywood Cinema* (New York: Columbia University Press, 2002); Justin Wyatt, *High*

changes do not constitute a genuine break with the classical Hollywood tradition. As scholars like Kristin Thompson, David Bordwell, and Murray Smith point out, contemporary filmmakers may employ shiny new cinematic devices and techniques, but they are firmly committed to the principles of narrative unity, clarity, and coherence that have governed the tradition of classical cinema for nearly a century.[4]

This chapter aims to explore the contribution that the study of contemporary film soundtracks can make to this ongoing debate. David Bordwell has provided the most detailed and thoroughgoing description of contemporary Hollywood cinema's visual style. For Bordwell, this style encompasses a concatenation of devices and strategies that he has termed "intensified continuity." Using his definition as a point of departure, I sketch out the broad contours of a sonic analog to "intensified continuity." In doing so, I hope to show that the contemporary film soundtrack has undergone a parallel, albeit slightly later, series of stylistic changes. I have organized my examination of this issue into three sections: a brief review of Bordwell's concept of "intensified continuity" and the historical changes that shaped its development; an outline of six dimensions of contemporary soundtracks that make up an aural counterpart to Bordwell's model; and a comparison of the 1974 caper classic, *The Taking of Pelham 123*, to its 2009 remake. This comparison illustrates how much contemporary soundtracks have changed in the last three decades; it also demonstrates the extent to which the various dimensions of intensified continuity remain linked to strong narrative considerations.

Intensified Continuity

David Bordwell introduced the term "intensified continuity" in an essay published in *Film Quarterly* in 2002, in which he surveyed several aspects of contemporary Hollywood visual style in an effort to explicate the ways current directors deviate from the norms established in studio-era filmmaking. Bordwell then developed and refined this concept in *The Way Hollywood Tells It* (2006). As he showed there, the parameters of this new visual style do not challenge or revise the principles of classical filmmaking. Rather, they represent an *intensification* of older, established techniques: "Intensified continuity is traditional continuity amped up, raised to a higher pitch of emphasis. It

Concept: Movies and Marketing in Hollywood (Austin: University of Texas Press, 1994); and Eleftheria Thanouli, *Post-Classical Cinema: An International Poetics of Film Narration* (London: Wallflower Press, 2010).

[4] Kristin Thompson, *Storytelling in the New Hollywood: Understanding Classical Narrative Technique* (Cambridge, Mass.: Harvard University Press, 1999); David Bordwell, "Intensified Continuity: Visual Style in Contemporary Hollywood Film," *Film Quarterly* 55, no. 3 (Spring 2002): 16–28, and *The Way Hollywood Tells It: Story and Style in Modern Movies* (Berkeley: University of California Press, 2006); and Murray Smith, "Theses on the Philosophy of Hollywood History," in *Contemporary Hollywood History*, ed. Neale and Smith, 3–20.

is the dominant style of American mass-audience films today."[5] According to Bordwell, this new visual style has coalesced around four particular strategies of camerawork and editing: (1) faster cutting rates, (2) closer framings, (3) bipolar extremes of lens lengths, and (4) wide-ranging camera movements.

As Bordwell notes, "Everybody thinks that movies are being cut faster now, but how fast is fast? And faster compared to what?"[6] During the studio era, the average shot length (ASL) of a Hollywood feature was typically between 8 and 11 seconds. Obviously this average synthesizes a wide range of variants that occupy either end of a broad spectrum. Beginning in the 1960s, however, that number began to shift downward and has continued to do so ever since. In the mid-'60s, the ASL of most A-features hovered between 6 and 8 seconds; several notable titles, such as *Goldfinger* (1963) and *Head* (1967), were cut much more quickly than that.[7] The ASL of Hollywood films of the 1980s shrank slightly to between 5 and 7 seconds; by the end of the 1990s, the ASL of most Hollywood features was between 3 and 6 seconds.[8]

One reason for this faster cutting rate is that directors were increasingly relying on close shots. If the *plan américain* was often the default framing of action in the classical Hollywood period, the medium close-up is likely the default for many contemporary directors. More important, perhaps, is that whereas classical filmmakers sometimes staged conversations in roomy, static two-shots, contemporary directors have a decided preference for tighter "singles" showing only one person in the frame.[9] Such framings have helped to accelerate editing rates. In many contemporary films, long stretches of dialogue are rendered in quickly cut close-ups. Such scenes support the notion that contemporary directors have simply "amped up" established techniques, as these dialogue scenes offer more tightly framed versions of the shot/reverse shot patterns that were part of the studio-era repertoire.

Ironically, although contemporary Hollywood films display a decided emphasis on short shots, this does not always occur by bringing the cameras closer. Rather, many contemporary visual stylists, such as Michael Mann and Tony Scott, employ long lenses for their close-ups. The shallow depth of field produced through telephoto lenses sometimes adds a soft pictorialism to these close-ups as the areas of the frame surrounding the subject are rendered as blurs of abstract colors. At the same time, however, other directors such as Spike Lee and the Coen Brothers have become known for the expressive distortions that wide-angle lenses offer them. The "bulging foregrounds" evident in the work of these filmmakers offers still another visual trope that has become commonplace in contemporary Hollywood cinema as the wide-angle lens serves to exaggerate facial features or heighten the sense of distance between foreground and background planes. The end result of these bipolar extremes of lens length is that the "normal" 50mm

5 Bordwell, *The Way Hollywood Tells It*, 120.
6 Bordwell, *The Way Hollywood Tells It*, 121.
7 Bordwell, *The Way Hollywood Tells It*, 121.
8 Bordwell, *The Way Hollywood Tells It*, 122.
9 Bordwell, *The Way Hollywood Tells It*, 130.

lens—the staple of older studio-era cinematography—is the one most likely to be left behind in a cameraman's toolkit.[10]

The last of the strategies Bordwell identifies—wide-ranging camera movement—might seem to be a counter to the principle of fast cutting, because it has helped popularize extravagant tracking shots in which the camera follows a character's complex movement through space. Some of these shots, like the "Copacabana" shot in *Goodfellas* (1990) or the "Dover Beach" shot in *Atonement* (2007), may run several minutes. Yet far from undermining the emphasis on faster cutting, they often function as virtuosic moments in films that otherwise have fairly low ASLs. Furthermore, whereas a previous generation often motivated camera movement through character movement, current directors are much more likely to move the camera even when nothing else in the shot moves. Although we tend to think of this prowling camera style as associated with the global popularity of action blockbusters, it is worth noting that intensified continuity principles are found across genres. Even a somewhat stodgy costume picture like *Pride and Prejudice* (2005) displays the fast cutting rate, handheld camera, elaborate tracking shots, and long lens technique that have become hallmarks of contemporary film style.

Bordwell identifies several likely sources of influence on the development of intensified continuity. Some are aesthetic in nature, such as the telephoto lenses and flashy editing techniques displayed by European filmmakers of the '60s, the period in which most of these tendencies in American cinema first became evident.[11] Other strategies are more technologically driven. The trend toward fast cutting, for example, was aided by the development of nonlinear editing systems, like Avid and Final Cut Pro.[12] Still other strategies appeared in response to changes in distribution, particularly the emergence of lucrative ancillary markets in home video and television. Many practitioners assumed that television required faster cutting, more mobile cameras, and closer framings as means of holding the spectator's attention.[13]

Taken in toto, the four strategies go a long way toward explaining why contemporary Hollywood films look quite different from their classical counterparts. Yet as elements of Hollywood storytelling, these strategies serve some of the same narrative purposes as their studio-era forebears. Contemporary directors still aim to tell entertaining stories in a clear and coherent fashion. While certain techniques like the prowling camera are hardly unobtrusive, they nonetheless serve a style that strives for stylistic unity and provides narrative motivation for even the most unusual cinematic devices.

Bordwell's notion of intensified continuity accounts for important historical changes in the visual style of contemporary American cinema. Can we find a similar array of changes governing the development of contemporary soundtracks? Did the innovation of Dolby stereo and digital surround systems at the level of exhibition augur a parallel

[10] Bordwell, *The Way Hollywood Tells It*, 124–129.
[11] Bordwell, *The Way Hollywood Tells It*, 141–147.
[12] Bordwell, *The Way Hollywood Tells It*, 155.
[13] Bordwell, *The Way Hollywood Tells It*, 147–151.

set of strategies in sound recording and editing? Is there an aural analog to the "impact aesthetic" that is commonly associated with the bludgeoning effect of contemporary Hollywood cinema?

Intensified Continuity and the Contemporary Film Soundtrack

I argue that contemporary sound designers and mixers have developed a set of strategies for the soundtrack comparable to the changes in visual style that Bordwell identifies as central to intensified continuity. These sound strategies work in tandem with the visual strategies outlined previously, insofar as they function similarly to heighten the affective, sensory, and phenomenological dimensions of contemporary film style. If contemporary filmmaking is governed by a kind of "impact aesthetic," then it stands to reason that some of the "boom" and "woof" associated with that aesthetic comes from the sounds emanating from audio speakers, in both movie houses and home theaters.

In making the case for an intensified continuity aesthetic that extends to film soundtracks, I must first overcome some objections raised by Mark Kerins, who peremptorily rejects Bordwell's model as a way of understanding contemporary sound practices. In *Beyond Dolby (Stereo): Cinema in the Digital Sound Age*, Kerins argues that intensified continuity fails to capture some of the complexities of digital surround sound cinema. His critique of Bordwell rests on two premises: first, intensified continuity implicitly relies on a predominantly visual concept of film style; second, the vast majority of films that Bordwell used in his study were made prior to the standardization of 5.1-channel sound. Because intensified continuity emphasizes visual strategies at the expense of more recent innovations in sound editing and mixing, Kerins contends that Bordwell's account "might be more appropriately described as a 'historical description' of late twentieth century cinema than as a model for 'contemporary' cinema."[14]

Kerins's critique of Bordwell raises a number of important issues about contemporary film style, but his attempt to create an alternative model appears to provoke more questions than it answers. In sketching out the contours of a digital surround sound (DSS) style, Kerins describes the "look of 5.1" as one in which the close shot scales and fragmented editing analyzed by Bordwell are, in fact, anchored by the soundtrack, which by itself creates a stable and coherent sense of diegetic space.[15] Indeed, because DSS can accurately place all sounds of an aural environment in their proper locations, a film's visuals no longer carry the burden of explaining the spatial relationships in the diegesis. Contemporary directors and film editors are thus much more likely to reject some of the

[14] Mark Kerins, *Beyond Dolby (Stereo): Cinema in the Digital Sound Age* (Bloomington: Indiana University Press, 2010), 122.

[15] Kerins, *Beyond Dolby (Stereo)*, 91–98.

devices used to maintain spatial continuity, such as establishing shots or the 180-degree rule. Moreover, because the digital surround style allows the soundtrack to shift its orientation every time the image cuts, directors and cinematographers are much more likely to conceive of diegetic space as emanating from a single vantage point situated in the middle of an ongoing action. Thanks to the perceptual anchor provided by DSS, directors can cut between shots from virtually any angle regardless of whether they maintain consistent screen direction or match relative figure positions.[16]

While Kerins's account of a digital surround style serves as a necessary corrective to the association of intensified continuity with particular visual strategies, he also acknowledges that this type of aesthetic is not dictated by the presence of digital surround technology and further that few movies use the digital surround style through their entire length. Indeed, based on his own examples (the D-Day sequence from *Saving Private Ryan* and the lobby shootout in *The Matrix*), even the most adventurous applications of the digital surround style are confined to individual scenes. Most films use the digital surround style intermittently. Other films do not use it at all. For this reason, it is difficult to argue that the digital surround style has established itself as the *norm* for contemporary cinema. The fact that it is currently the exception rather than the rule is implicit in Kerins's admission that Bordwell's model of intensified continuity "makes a lot of sense as an overview of the way visual style works in *many* films *much* of the time."[17] Consequently, even if intensified continuity is eventually supplanted by a full-blown digital surround style, the account of sound practices associated with Bordwell's model that I propose here can establish the norms for a significant chunk of recent Hollywood history, the thirty-six years from 1973 to 2009.

It is worth noting, however, that while intensified continuity came to be associated with particular aural and visual strategies, these strategies did not develop simultaneously. As Bordwell notes, most of the visual strategies of intensified continuity have their roots in the '60s. In contrast, many of the aural strategies associated with intensified continuity did not appear until the late 1970s. This is partly an issue of technological development. Although some of these strategies were explored by an earlier generation of sound technicians working with magnetic sound or with the six-channel systems available in a 70mm format, their widespread diffusion was spurred by the introduction of Dolby stereo as an exhibition technology in 1975. The total number of movie theaters wired for Dolby stereo topped two hundred by the end of 1977, thanks largely to the success of *Star Wars*. That number rose to more than twelve hundred theaters by 1980 and soared above six thousand by the mid-1980s.[18] Although the growth of Dolby was impressive, the rapid diffusion of digital sound exhibition technologies was even more

16 Kerins, *Beyond Dolby (Stereo)*, 98–109.

17 Kerins, *Beyond Dolby (Stereo)*, 121–122. Emphasis in original.

18 David Neumeyer, James Buhler, and Rob Deemer, *Hearing the Movies: Music and Sound in Film History* (New York: Oxford University Press, 2010), 374; Alex Ben Block and Lucy Autrey Wilson, eds., *George Lucas' Blockbusting: A Decade-by-Decade Survey of Timeless Movies Including Untold Secrets of Their Financial and Cultural Success* (New York: Itbooks, 2010), 525–526.

eye-popping. Although they were not introduced until 1992, within six years more than thirty thousand screens around the globe had converted to some type of DSS system.[19] Digital theater sound provided a major impetus for various kinds of stylistic experiments, and the aural strategies that I describe were almost certainly a response to the widespread conversion of theater sound systems during the 1980s and 1990s.[20]

Scholars and historians of film sound commonly describe Dolby as an exhibition technology that altered the movie experience for viewers in significant ways. Michel Chion, for example, states:

> For musical films in multitrack (Dolby Stereo), particularly rock films where musical sound explodes throughout the space, this presence of sound only amplifies something already perceptible in older musicals: the power and definition of the musical sounds, along with their quality of overflowing the boundaries of the screen, tends to displace the "place" of the film from the screen to the movie theater itself or, more precisely, to situate the music in the large auditory space defined by the loudspeakers.[21]

William Whittington makes a similar point when describing a scene in *Star Wars*: "The use of surround sound offers a total sonic environment, which masks the real environment of the theater space to create a sonic space with no entry and no exit."[22]

Dolby's ability to enhance the visceral experience of cinema is one important component of a sonic version of intensified continuity. Yet that represents only one axis of its overall influence. Many of these historians have also analyzed and described the technology's overall enhancement of aural fidelity, frequency range, and signal-to-noise ratio for film sound. With its full frequency reproduction and elimination of distortion and ground noise, Dolby stereo, particularly in 70mm, has enabled filmmakers to "pack in" more and more auditory information.[23] Dolby's enhanced frequency range and dynamic contrast has enabled sound

[19] Paul Grainge, "Selling Spectacular Sound: Dolby and the Unheard History of Technical Trademarks," in *Lowering the Boom: Critical Studies in Film Sound*, ed. Jay Beck and Tony Grajeda (Urbana; Chicago: University of Illinois Press, 2008), 264. Grainge breaks this number down further into the competing systems. As of 1998, Dolby digital was installed in 13,073 auditoriums, DTS had 12,800, and Sony Dynamic Digital Surround was found in 5,201 theaters.

[20] I want to emphasize that I am not arguing here for a kind of technological determinism. Technological change provides a necessary condition for some types of stylistic experimentation, but it is not a sufficient one. Rather, aural strategies of intensified continuity took their particular form in response to a complex set of causal factors. As an example, consider the notion of an immersive, enveloping soundscape, something that many will recognize as an attribute of much contemporary sound design for film. The adaptation of this concept can be traced to a host of causal factors, some of which are technological (Dolby to be sure, but also Quadrophonic sound for home music consumption and also Brian Eno's experiments with ambient music); some are aesthetic (in film, the widespread use of Steadicams and handheld cameras might have encouraged a more "visceral" approach to sound design), and some are cultural (e.g., audiophile fan culture or R. Murray Schafer's "acoustic ecology" movement).

[21] Michel Chion, *Film, a Sound Art*, trans. Claudia Gorbman (New York: Columbia University Press, 2009), 416.

[22] William Whittington, *Sound Design & Science Fiction* (Austin: University of Texas Press, 2007), 122.

[23] Whittington, *Sound Design & Science Fiction*, 71.

designers to strongly differentiate sequences in terms of ambience and volume. According to Gianluca Sergi, "The way these different sequences play against each another provides possibility for contrast: some sequences might have a quiet ambience with little sound playing at a low level while others might have great density and be played at full throttle."[24]

Dimensions of Contemporary Sound

The visceral effects and technological affordances of Dolby stereo and digital surround systems sit at the heart of the "impact aesthetic" that came to be associated with intensified continuity techniques. I have identified six aural dimensions of contemporary sound production and mixing that function as counterparts to the visual strategies of intensified continuity discussed by Bordwell. These aural dimensions are closely imbricated with the technological improvements in theater sound that marked the last three decades of the twentieth century. They are

- increased volume,
- low frequency effects,
- expanded frequency range,
- the spatialization of sound,
- the "hyperdetail" of contemporary Foley work, and
- the use of nondiegetic sound effects as stylistic punctuation.

Increased Volume

Moviegoers have commented for a long time that contemporary Hollywood films seem louder and noisier than they were in the past. Indeed, the sheer loudness of many current Hollywood films is one reason they are sometimes described as bombastic or raucous.

Yet some may be surprised to learn that this same sentiment was present in the reception of several early Dolby titles in the '70s. Vincent Canby, for example, described the impact of Ken Russell's *Tommy* (1975) by observing that the film's "funhouse" imagery was "all accompanied by sound of a force to loosen one's most firmly rooted back teeth."[25] A. D. Murphy's review of *Saturday Night Fever* took note of the sheer amount of music in the film and added, "With Dolby sound and modern recording techniques, the music can be played at mercifully high noise levels." Science fiction novelist Ursula

[24] Gianluca Sergi, *The Dolby Era: Film Sound in Contemporary Hollywood* (New York: Manchester University Press, 2004), 148.

[25] Vincent Canby, "Excess and Excitement and Many Decibels," *New York Times*, March 12, 1975, 48.

K. Le Guin coined the term "decibellicosity" to capture the visceral effect of the sound in *Close Encounters of the Third Kind* (1977). Le Guin claimed that the film's soundtrack was often used to "whip up emotions, the same trick that's so easy to do with electronically amplified instruments."[26]

The increase in volume was made possible by Dolby's cutting-edge noise reduction techniques, which "companded" aural inputs during the recording process.[27] Dolby A, the company's signature technology, boosted the sound input of the frequency range above 1,000 Hz during recording. This pre-emphasis makes higher sounds sharper and more attenuated. During playback, Dolby A scales back the audio input in this frequency range comparable to its pre-emphasis measure during recording. This returns the sound to its normal balance of frequency ranges, but in a way that filters out the white noise that would be noticeable above 1,000 Hz. The effect of Dolby A was to boost the clarity and dynamics of both low and high ends.

For film sound recordists and mixers, Dolby A enabled sounds to be played back at a much higher decibel level during the final mixdown. Before Dolby, any increase in volume brought with it an increase in noise. By enhancing the signal-to-noise ratio of '70s film soundtracks, Dolby enabled sound technicians to quite literally "amp up" the sound heard in movie theaters. Like the visual strategies associated with intensified continuity, the boost in volume offered by Dolby is simply an enhancement of already existing principles of Hollywood sound design.

Low Frequency Effects

Although the overall increase in volume is one reason current Hollywood films seem noisy and bombastic, another derives from the implementation of low frequency effects (LFE) channels in DSS systems. Mark Kerins notes that the addition of low frequency capabilities enabled filmmakers to "add a sense of 'power' to creatures or objects in a way previously impossible through sound." For Kerins, the T. rex in *Jurassic Park* (1993) is a particularly effective illustration of what LFE channels can do. Because the dinosaur is introduced to the viewer through its footsteps, it is "felt" before it is actually seen.[28]

Like the increase in loudness, the implementation of LFE has its roots in the technological developments and practices of '70s cinema. "Sensurround," which was

[26] Quoted in Jay Beck, "The Sounds of 'Silence': Dolby Stereo, Sound Design, and *Silence of the Lambs*," in *Lowering the Boom*, ed. Beck and Grajeda, 70.

[27] The term "companding" is a neologism that combines compressing and expanding. In Dolby stereo, "compansion" refers to the way that a part of the frequency range of an audio signal is boosted during recording, but then reduced during playback. The signal boost "expands" the frequency range while the signal reduction "compresses" it. For more on "companding," see Jay Beck, "A Quiet Revolution: Changes in American Film Sound Practices, 1967–1979" (PhD diss., University of Iowa, 2003), 30–41.

[28] Mark Kerins, "Narration in the Cinema of Digital Sound," *The Velvet Light Trap* 58 (Fall 2006): 43.

introduced in the 1974 disaster pic *Earthquake*, was an early experiment with LFE aesthetics. It featured a control track that triggered banks of ultra-low frequency speakers. By producing sounds down to around 17 Hz, Sensurround produced subsonic acoustic vibrations that, like T. rex's footsteps, would be felt as well as heard by audiences of *Earthquake*.[29]

As Jay Beck points out, Universal created Sensurround as a gimmick intended to draw viewers away from their television sets during a period of industry recession. For this reason, the studio promoted the technology sparingly, using it only in projects where it could be motivated plausibly as an aspect of the film's spectacle. In *Earthquake*, LFE was used to create the shake and rumble that heightened viewers' experience of the seismic activity that gave the film its title. In *Midway* (1976), Sensurround heightened the experience of the film's expensive battle scenes. In *Rollercoaster* (1977), LFE created acoustic vibrations that were ostensibly caused by the amusement park rides featured in the story. As most readers know, today's intensified continuity films are often analogized to roller-coaster rides. By showcasing the possibilities of LFE in intensified continuity sound techniques, *Rollercoaster* literally displays the historical roots of these aesthetic strategies.

Expanded Frequency Range

Another benefit of Dolby A's noise reduction technology was that it allowed for the expansion of the frequency range of contemporary Hollywood soundtracks. The desire for a worldwide standard for sound production and recording had led to the adoption of the so-called Academy curve in 1938, which established industry standards for theater playback response. The Academy curve featured significant drop-off in the low and high ends of the frequency range; consequently, sound technicians during Hollywood's studio era emphasized the midrange frequencies of theater loudspeakers. According to Gianluca Sergi, the Academy curve enabled Hollywood to achieve standardization for theater playback around the globe, but at a steep price; the industry settled for sound systems whose fidelity and quality was little different from that of a telephone.[30]

Starting in the mid-'70s, Dolby's noise reduction technology minimized the distortion that tended to occur in the high and low frequency ranges of the Academy curve. By the late '70s several sound designers were experimenting with high frequency sounds as a particular affordance of Dolby stereo. On *Star Wars*, Ben Burtt created an extraordinary repertoire of high-pitched tweets and coos for R2D2, one of the two robots that provide much of the film's comic relief. Similarly, for *Days of Heaven* (1978) the low end of Dolby stereo enhanced the power of the oppressive industrial noise that appears

[29] See Beck, "Quiet Revolution," 172–187.

[30] Sergi, *Dolby Era*, 14.

in the film's first scene, while the high end showcased the piercing chirps that fill the soundtrack during *Heaven*'s famous locust attack.

The Spatialization of Sound

The widespread adoption of Dolby stereo and digital surround systems in theaters fueled experimentation with spatial sound effects as an element of contemporary sound recording and mixing. Of course this kind of sound experimentation was not unprecedented. Filmmakers had explored the use of multichannel effects as early as the 1940s. Indeed, as John Belton points out, experiments with panning effects, "swinging" dialogue, and sounds placed in the "wings" around the screen were quite common in the multichannel magnetic soundtracks used during the early widescreen era.[31] Jay Beck further notes that multichannel sound was commonly used for "road-show" presentations of big-budget musicals like *My Fair Lady* (1964) and *The Sound of Music* (1965). Set against a norm of monaural playback, these multichannel effects came to be seen as elements of artifice and spectacle, an association supported by their use in widescreen color films. More important, multichannel sound's potential to "distract" viewers meant that sound mixers grew ever more conservative in their deployment of effects. By the mid-'60s stereo effects were most prominently featured for music tracks, with dialogue confined to the center channel, which helped ensure that sound would "anchor" characters within the diegetic space depicted onscreen.

The resurgence of spatialized sound effects in the '70s was heralded in the opening sequence of *Star Wars*. As a huge spaceship enters the top of the frame, the sounds of its rumbling engine and its laser cannons appear in the surround channels, gradually moving forward along the z-axis.[32] Later, during Luke Skywalker's bombing run, the sound of Obi-Wan Kenobi's voice advising the young Jedi knight to "Use the Force" fills the surround channels of the theater, an effect that underscores this sound as part of Luke's internal consciousness.

Such types of spatialized sound, however, tend to be used sparingly in contemporary cinema. Some of the reluctance to make more thoroughgoing use of surround effects was due to the technological limitations of Dolby itself. To make multichannel sound compatible with standard 35mm optical soundtracks, Dolby relied on a Sansui Matrix converter to mix four full channels of sound into two noise-reduction-encoded optical tracks. Although this system worked extremely well with music, certain frequencies and moving sounds confused the Dolby stereo matrix, causing it to mistakenly send these

[31] John Belton, "1950s Magnetic Sound: The Frozen Revolution," in *Sound Theory/Sound Practice*, ed. Rick Altman (New York: Routledge, 1992), 154–170.

[32] The z-axis is the depth coordinate in three-dimensional geometry. In a film image, the z-axis runs from the foreground plane to the background plane. For an excellent discussion of sound effects in science fiction, see Whittington, *Sound Design & Science Fiction*, 115–126.

sounds into the surround channels.[33] To address these issues, Dolby consultants insisted that all dialogue be placed in the center channel to ensure intelligibility and avoid phasing problems. This mandate formalized a bias toward center-channel dialogue that had already appeared in the mid-'60s. Dolby consultants also monitored panning effects carefully during the mixing process to ensure that the movement of sound mirrored that of its onscreen correlate. These recommendations reinforced established industry norms for sound recording and mixing by both prioritizing dialogue intelligibility and requiring that any panning or directional sound have very clear, unambiguous narrative motivation.

Because of these attendant difficulties, some designers preferred to use the surround channels for aural ambiences. One of Dolby stereo's creators, Ioan Allen, claimed to be particularly proud of his work on films in which the surround channels were mostly used to enhance the viewer's sense of the film's aural environments. Allen recalled:

> It wasn't until probably *Days of Heaven*, Terry Malick's film, that I managed to get across this idea that every film can benefit [from using Dolby], that quiet, low-level stereo ambiences do as much to help a film as loud spatial sound effects. That's been an ongoing battle to this day. You know, people don't realize what can be done with low-level sound effects in terms of putting the audience into the environment that it sees onscreen. Some directors will say "well, there's not much value for surrounds in my movie" just because there are no flyovers, you know. Well, flyovers is the vulgar extreme, and the real meat and potatoes of surrounds I believe is ambiences, the field of waving corn is wonderful at putting you in the action.[34]

Dolby digital resolved some of the technological problems posed by Dolby stereo's matrix converter by keeping all 5.1 channels discrete. In theory, this means that any sound can be placed in any channel: left, right, center, left surround, and right surround. Yet today's sound designers remain reticent to create "true" 360-degree aural environments for their films. One reason for this is the so-called exit door effect (i.e., the potential for spot sounds in the surround channels to distract the audience's attention from the screen). The effect gets its name from concern that the sound of a door slamming offscreen might be mistaken for the real door of the theater.[35] Another reason for this reticence derives from the highly segmented and hierarchized labor force for sound production. Jay Beck notes that Dolby stereo's demand for the centrality of dialogue—both literally and figuratively—reinforced existing stratifications within the production of soundtracks.[36] Dialogue editors and mixers remain "top dog," while other sound technicians fall farther down the chain of command. Such strict divisions of labor thwarted

[33] Beck, "Sounds of 'Silence,'" 69–70.

[34] Quoted in Sergi, *Dolby Era*, 102.

[35] See Mark Kerins, "Constructing the Diegesis in a Multi-Channel World," *Offscreen* 11, nos. 8–9 (August/September 2007), 3.

[36] Beck, "Sounds of 'Silence,'" 74–75.

more experimental approaches to the soundtrack and further ensured that normative recording and mixing practices would linger long into the digital sound era. Scenes like the Normandy Beach invasion in *Saving Private Ryan* (1998), which situates the audience in an absolute cacophony of directional explosions, rifle fire, and whizzing bullets, remain the exception rather than the rule.

According to Mark Kerins, one common strategy for motivating unusual surround effects is point of view. Films that include specific shots or entire scenes that represent a character's optical perspective will sometimes accompany those shots with sounds that play with directionality and spatial orientation. In *Being John Malkovich* (1999), for example, the directional orientation of sound is prominent in scenes where the viewer is "inside" Malkovich's head. For Kerins, the film cleverly reinforces the separation between Malkovich himself and the person occupying his "portal" by employing strikingly different types of sounds for each. For the person in the portal, the voiceover is closely miked and mixed to all five main channels. In contrast, Malkovich's voice is also closely miked with some reverb, but is confined to the center channel. Other outside sounds are miked normally, but mixed directionally so that they are oriented relative to Malkovich.[37] A more recent example of this strategy is found in *Drag Me to Hell* (2009), which depicts a séance through a series of circular tracking shots around a table. Here the voices of the participants bounce from the center channel to the surrounds depending on whether or not the speaker is shown within the frame.

The spatialization of sounds in contemporary films is similar to other dimensions of intensified continuity. On one hand, the use of surround channels and directional sound effects creates an immersive aural environment for the viewer, which enhances the effect of contemporary cinema's impact aesthetic. On the other hand, the paucity of specific deployments of directional sound effects suggests that this strategy merely enhances sound recording and mixing practices already well established within the Hollywood studio system.

The "Hyperdetail" of Contemporary Foley Work

An additional feature of Dolby's noise reduction technology is that it enabled sound effects to take on a clarity and detail that they previously lacked. Vanessa Theme Ament, in a useful "behind-the-scenes" guide to contemporary Foley work, shows that Foley effects have taken on greater significance in contemporary filmmaking. According to Ament, during the studio era Foley work was mostly confined to replacing or enhancing footsteps and performing a few hand props. Today, though, Foley takes on ever more specialized functions by "sweetening" production sound recordings and playing an essential role in the layering of sound effects.[38]

37 Kerins, "Narration in the Cinema of Digital Sound," 47.

38 Vanessa Theme Ament, *The Foley Grail: The Art of Performing Sound for Film, Games, and Animation* (Boston: Focal Press, 2009), 28.

Ament further notes that most Foley effects function to support the impression of a coherent and consistent diegetic reality depicted onscreen. On the role of hand props she writes: "Whatever the actor is handling should be duplicated as closely as possible by the Foley artist. A heavy cup in the film is a heavy cup on the Foley stage. If you see fine china, the dishes should sound fine as well."[39] This desire to match the sound of props as closely as possible might be seen as an aural counterpart to the kind of "worldmaking" that David Bordwell discusses.[40] In many contemporary Hollywood films, set designers and dressers provide a richly detailed, fully furnished ambience for the film's action, often cramming sets with minutiae that escape the casual viewer's notice. As Ament points out, though, the contemporary concern with an abundantly filigreed milieu extends beyond set design. As contemporary Foley artists take on more production duties, they are able to create aural soundscapes as rich and detailed as the images and scenes they accompany.

Cloth sounds have taken on a particular saliency as an aspect of "worldmaking" via the soundtrack. Ament notes that Foley artists typically enhance the sounds of the clothes that the characters wear. In fact, most Foley artists do a dedicated "cloth pass," after other effects are recorded, that is coordinated with the film's dialogue and mixed through the center channel during the final dub. The subtle rustling of cloth as the characters move is unobtrusive, but nonetheless contributes to the sense of "hyperdetail" that characterizes the densely layered sound effects tracks of contemporary Hollywood films.

Foley artists also contribute to a film's diegetic effect by supporting its characterizations. The recording of footsteps remains a primary duty of Foley artists, and current practitioners usually have large collections of shoes so that they are able to "audition" and "cast" their footwear to match its sound to the character who wears it.[41] Ament writes: "How a character walks in different shoes varies. A woman in heels walks differently than a woman in flats. Someone in soft shoes has a more casual walk than someone in hard street shoes or dressy hard-soled shoes."[42] Ament even uses the term "Method Foley" to capture the way that, far from simply walking, contemporary Foley artists strive to walk in character.

In addition to supporting realism and characterization, Foley artists sometime heighten the expressive quality of sound effects by "sweetening" or enhancing the production track. Often they produce "married" effects that combine Foley work with library sounds. According to Ament, a typical married effect is the ever-present body fall. Often the Foley artist will be down on the ground with some cloth or padding and will thrust the trunk of his or her body onto the floor. This performance is combined with a heavy thump sound taken from an effects library. The result is a body fall with the individualized character of Foley work and the "heaviness" of the sound effects.[43]

39 Ament, *Foley Grail*, 28.

40 Bordwell, *The Way Hollywood Tells It*, 58–60.

41 Ament, *Foley Grail*, 76–79.

42 Ament, *Foley Grail*, 78.

43 Ament, *Foley Grail*, 29.

Sounds that have no counterpart in everyday reality represent an especially favorable opportunity for creative exploration on the part of the Foley artist or sound designer. Joan Rowe, for example, used a package of liver from the supermarket to capture the "liquidy and friendly" sound that Steven Spielberg desired for the title character of *E.T.: The Extra-terrestrial* (1982).[44] For the jet cars of *THX 1138*, Walter Murch herded a small group of office workers into the company's restroom and then used a portable Nagra to record them screaming. By recording the sound at a very high input level, Murch recorded the screams to the point of distortion. He then added a Doppler shift atop the distorted screaming, and the sound of the film's jet cars was born.[45] (Murch further notes that Ben Burtt created the Tie Fighter sounds for *Star Wars* in much the same way.) Gary Rydstrom used the sound of dog food sliding out of a can to create the mushy sounds that accompany the liquid metal transformations of the T1000 in *Terminator 2*.

In all these ways, contemporary Foley artists have enlarged the repertoire of sounds provided by Foley artists in the studio era. Taken together, the various functions of Foley work show very concrete and specific ways that contemporary sound design seeks to "push the premises," in David Bordwell's words, of classical-era style. Indeed, the clarity and sharp definition of current sound may help to move the narrative forward, as we see in the discussion of *Pelham* below, but it also supplements the visual strategies of "worldmaking" that serve to differentiate contemporary set design from its studio-era predecessors.

Nondiegetic Sounds as Punctuation for Visual Effects

In contemporary sound design, nondiegetic sound effects can punctuate certain kinds of visual flourishes. The most common effect is a "whooshing" sound used to underscore rapid camera movements or to highlight scene changes. In addition, some contemporary films use low-pitched, reverberant drumbeats to underline onscreen movements or moments in a scene when the narrative undergoes a shift in its dynamics.

The whoosh effect can be traced back at least to 1978, in the opening credits of Richard Donner's *Superman*. Nondiegetic whooshes accompany each of the various credits as they move outward from the screen, an effect that was further enhanced by panning the sounds from front to back in the film's multichannel mix.[46] Whooshing sounds have become much more common in recent years. Most viewers might associate them with contemporary action films and some horror films, but they appear in a number of genres, especially on television, where they can be heard in legal dramas, single-camera sitcoms, police procedurals, and even nature and wildlife documentaries.

44 Ament, *Foley Grail*, 111.

45 Whittington, *Sound Design & Science Fiction*, 72.

46 See Whittington, *Sound Design & Science Fiction*, 117.

Reverberant drumbeats are much less common than these nondiegetic whooshing sounds, but like the latter, they appear in a number of genres and dramatic contexts. In some films these drumbeats simply accent a character's gesture or movement. In *Scott Pilgrim vs. the World* (2010), for example, a drumbeat underlines Gideon's hop from an upper to a lower step on a staircase as he prepares to fight Pilgrim in the film's climactic battle. In other cases, however, a reverberant drumbeat can function to indicate a dramatic shift within a scene. In *Inception* (2010), a drumbeat highlights Mal's shifting gaze as she turns away from Cobb to look at Ariadne, who is caught eavesdropping on the couple's conversation. Here the drumbeat not only accents Mal's action, but also augurs a shift in the scene's tone as Ariadne realizes that Mal perceives her as a threat. What initially appears as a moment of marital bliss soon takes on a violent undertone as the viewer recalls earlier scenes in which Mal killed dream avatars that were close to Cobb.

As an element of the intensified continuity style, this nondiegetic punctuation differs in several crucial respects from the other dimensions outlined previously. First, because these sounds are always coordinated with visual elements, they greatly increase the number of sync points that appear throughout the film.[47] Indeed, because they accent visual effects, they reinforce the impression that sound and image work together as part of a larger audiovisual storytelling style. This approach is markedly different from the sound–image relations that adhere in "slow cinema," films made for the festival market that feature long takes, deliberate pacing, and often an elliptical style of narration. In "slow cinema," sound and image sometimes form patterns of audiovisual contrast, or at the very least, will communicate information through quite separate audio and visual channels.

Second, these nondiegetic sounds not only serve to heighten the expressive quality of particular effects by increasing their sense of speed and pace, but also increase the self-consciousness of the film's narration. By more forcefully underlining particular kinds of visual flourishes or points of dramatic tension, these nondiegetic sounds draw attention to the very means by which contemporary films tell their stories. Still, because nondiegetic sound effects are often synced to figure movement or camera movement, their operations are slightly masked by the salience of the visual elements.[48] For this reason, nondiegetic effects like whooshes do not cross the line into reflexivity, but rather,

[47] For more on synch points, see Michel Chion, *Audio-Vision: Sound on Screen*, ed. and trans. Claudia Gorbman (New York: Columbia University Press, 1994), especially 58–60 and 185–213.

[48] For more on the relationship between audiovisual media and spectatorial attention and comprehension, see Annabel Cohen, "Film Music: Perspectives from Cognitive Psychology," *Music and Cinema*, ed. James Buhler, Caryl Flinn, and David Neumeyer (Hanover, NH: Wesleyan University Press, 2000), 360–377. Writing about film music, Cohen argues that the acoustical aspect of the music is encoded by sensory memory, but fails to be transported to short-term memory. Instead, because of inferences derived from long-term memory, the acoustical aspect of music falls away, while the information about the narrative is stored. Cohen's associationist-congruence model thus explains how music in film functions as part of its narration, but often goes unnoticed by viewers. I argue that a similar process governs nondiegetic sound effects.

like some of the visual dimensions of intensified continuity, are simply a mark of greater stylization.

Finally, nondiegetic sounds also enhance the visceral effect of the intensified continuity style. By implying that the camera is capable of producing acoustic phenomena, these nondiegetic whooshes seem to endow it with a solidity and physicality that classical-era camera movements lack. Indeed, by treating the camera as an entity with force, mass, and acceleration, intensified continuity sound undermines the element of "inaudibility" that scholars like Claudia Gorbman see as a key principle of classical Hollywood narration.[49]

As I argue throughout this chapter, the aural dimensions of the intensified continuity style strengthen its association with the "impact aesthetic" that has come to define much contemporary Hollywood filmmaking. Sound functions in this way either by enhancing the immersive quality of the intensified continuity style or by heightening the visceral quality of particular storytelling devices. Yet even as intensified continuity sound serves to amplify, quite literally, the sensational qualities of contemporary Hollywood cinema, it remains firmly anchored within the principles of unity, clarity, and linearity that still govern the transmission of narrative information to viewers. No one could claim that contemporary films sound like their classical Hollywood counterparts. Yet as we see in the analysis of *Pelham* that follows, the emphasis on clear narrative motivations for particular sound techniques shows that the audio dimensions of intensified continuity do not stray far from the larger ideals of classical narration. Rather, these aural strategies reinforce Bordwell's suggestion that the "intensified continuity" style displays a higher degree of self-consciousness in its approach to storytelling.

Sound Styles, Plain and Fancy: Two Versions of *The Taking of Pelham 123*

Both the original version of *The Taking of Pelham 123* and its remake tell essentially the same story. Four men hijack a New York subway train full of passengers, and Garber, a midlevel bureaucrat in the Transit Authority, attempts to negotiate for their safe release. The hijackers demand ransom payments for the hostages—$1 million in the 1974 version, $10 million in the remake—and prove to be ruthless adversaries, willing to kill their captives in order to have their demands met. The ransom schemes unravel, however, as Garber gradually pieces together information about the identity of the hijackers and their escape plan. Both films end with the hijackers either dead or in police custody.

49 See Claudia Gorbman, *Unheard Melodies: Narrative Film Music* (Bloomington: Indiana University Press, 1987), 76–79.

Whereas the 1974 version of *Pelham* is directed with taut efficiency by Joseph Sargent, Tony Scott directs the 2009 remake by adding his usual baroque touches to the intensified continuity style that has become normative for big studio productions. Scott began as a key figure in the "high-concept" style outlined by Justin Wyatt in his book of the same name.[50] Since then, Scott has evolved into one of Hollywood's most distinctive stylists, largely because he seems never to have met a visual effect he doesn't like. In a review of *Man on Fire*, *Salon* critic Stephanie Zacharek calls attention to Scott's visual tics: "The streets jiggle, cars and people move in strange, jerky stop-motion, and everyone's faces loom alarmingly close—Mexico City must be a very rude place, where no one respects anyone else's personal space! Or wait—could it be the camerawork and editing?"[51]

Tony Scott's version of *Pelham* follows very much in the footsteps of his other work in the Naughties. As production sound mixer Tom Nelson recalled:

> He would shoot from the end of the train and he did a lot of circular tracks. You would have a track go outside the cars, around, outside. Tom Prate, the grip, was unbelievable in making this all work. You would have a camera going circular around and at the same time, he would put three or four cameras at the end, one of which would shoot with a 24mm wide angle, and then one would shoot with a 180mm of John Travolta down at the end of the train, in the cab. And it became this look of constantly moving, constantly changing frame rates.[52]

Nelson's summary of Scott's multicamera shooting style captures many of the visual dimensions of intensified continuity described by Bordwell, especially the constantly moving camera and the bipolar extremes of lens length.

More to the point, though, the sound design of each version of *Pelham* differs almost as markedly as the films' visual styles. I have organized my analysis of the sound design of the two versions of *Pelham* around three particularly prominent sound motifs: mediated communications, train sounds, and nondiegetic sound effects.

Mediated Communication

Both films involve long scenes in which the characters communicate via some type of technological interface (e.g., two-way radio, intercom, telephone, video link). Sargent and Scott both crosscut during most of these conversations to capture the facial expressions of each person talking. The sound, though, also reinforces the constant shifts in

50 See Wyatt, *High Concept*, 23–31.

51 Stephanie Zacharek, "Man on Fire," *Salon*, April 23, 2004, at www.salon.com/2004/04/23/man_on_fire/ (accessed December 18, 2012).

52 Peter Schneider, "Recording *The Taking of Pelham*—Original and Remake: Production Sound Mixers Chris Newman and Tom Nelson Talk Shop on Recording the Two *Pelhams*," *Studio Daily*, September 25, 2009, at http://www.studiodaily.com/main/casestudies/Recording-The-Taking-Of-Pelham-Original-and-Remake_11310.html (accessed June 24, 2010).

location during these dialogue exchanges. Consider, for example, the scene in the 1974 version in which the police transport the ransom money up the east side of Manhattan. Sargent ratchets up the tension of the scene by crosscutting among three lines of action: the police en route, the hijackers and hostages waiting nervously in the train car, and Garber following the money's progress from the trainmasters' workstations. Audio contrasts further highlight the spatial disjunctions of the crosscutting. With the police, we hear sirens and revving motors. The train car is marked by an eerie silence. The trainmasters' area is characterized by typical office sounds: phones ringing, typewriters, and the murmur of conversation.

The 2009 remake preserves this principle of audio contrast, but sharpens it through two audio strategies that magnify the differences in the environments even further. For example, during all of Garber's early exchanges with Ryder, production sound mixer Tom Nelson uses microphone distance, reverb, and digital surround effects to further distinguish the two spaces in which the film's action occurs. All of Garber's dialogue is closely miked with very little reflected sound. This effect is, of course, motivated by the diegesis, since Garber spends much of the early part of the film speaking directly into a radio microphone. In contrast, Ryder's dialogue is less closely miked and is given a little reverb, presumably due to the tight quarters of the motorman's cab.[53] Both of these microphone strategies are further differentiated by dialogue delivered inside the subway tunnel, which is more distantly miked and contains heavy reverb. This, too, is motivated by the diegesis, as the tunnel provides a lot of natural echo with its hollowness and hard surfaces.

The sound mix of the 2009 remake further sharpens the differences in the soundscapes of the film's settings. Much of the sound inside the subway dispatch station plays through only the center channel of the audio. Dialogue and sound effects are almost completely confined to the center channel in these scenes, while nondiegetic score plays in the left, right, and surround speakers. The scenes inside the tunnel, however, consistently use the surround channels to add ambience. This ambient sound is a kind of hollow drone that mixes low-end room tone with a little bit of white noise. The level of ambient sound in the surround speakers also varies as a kind of "point of audition"

[53] These exchanges were also recorded in a manner that was quite different from the 1974 original. As Chris Newman recalls, the dialogue between Zach Garber and Mr. Blue was recorded using playback techniques. The dialogue was recorded in advance and played back through the radio speakers that link the deskmasters to the motormen's cabs. Thus, in performing their parts of the scene, actors Walter Matthau and Robert Shaw each reacted to vocal cues that had already been recorded.

In contrast, all of the dialogue of the 2009 remake was recorded live, but with the added challenge that Denzel Washington and John Travolta agreed that they should not physically meet during production until their characters Garber and Ryder do. Here, although all the dialogue was recorded live, it was done with one of the two stars on the set and the other delivering his part from the comfort of his dressing room. This strategy posed certain challenges for the sound team, including the dialogue editor, who wanted to avoid any problems with overlap, and the production sound mixer, Tom Nelson, who had to run lengths of cable from the set to the dressing rooms and then EQ the whole intercom system that had been constructed for the film. For more about the dialogue recording on both versions of *Pelham*, see Schneider, "Recording *The Taking of Pelham*."

effect. For scenes in which we hear dialogue from inside the train car, the ambience in the surround diminishes. For scenes in which action takes place inside the subway tunnel, the volume of the ambience increases.

The audio contrasts in both films enhance the clarity of the films' narration by making it easier for the viewer to follow the constant shifts in location. Yet as a more thoroughgoing stylistic principle, the audio contrasts established by the digital surround mix in the 2009 remake have an expressive dimension as well. By confining the dialogue and sound effects to the center channel in the scenes set in the MTA's dispatch center, the sound mix serves to heighten the sense of spatial confinement. This sense of claustrophobia is further underlined by Scott's constantly roving camera. In almost every scene of Garber at his desk, the camera will continually arc around him as though his stable, unmoving presence as chief hostage negotiator exerts a kind of centripetal force on those around him. The constant use of ambient sound in the surround channels for scenes set inside the tunnel has the opposite effect. This strategy creates a wholly immersive, three-dimensional audio environment for the viewer, something that was simply not possible with the monaural optical track of the 1974 original. The hollow drones in the surrounds thus serve as a constant reminder of the underground setting in these scenes, helping to convey a sense of dreary airlessness.

Train Sounds

The interest in spatializing the sound of the 2009 remake extends to other elements of the soundtrack, especially the train effects and music. Train sounds are obviously the predominant sound effect in both versions of *Pelham*, and both films make extensive use of the myriad sounds of a New York subway train: its rumble, its squealing brake discs, the hydraulic sounds of the train doors, and the hiss the train makes when compressed air is released. Yet the 2009 version lavishes far more attention on the film's train sounds, both at the level of production sound and in postproduction mixing. Tom Nelson recalls:

> I went in and basically recorded everything in MS, an MS stereo pair and then a straight shotgun facing forward to the MS pair. We let the trains go through a sound field, panning a mono mic would give you the approach, the pass by and the recede of a train. We did it all at the highest [sample rate] setting that we could, 192K. We used extended range because the sound effects editors wanted to be able to change the speed but still have a full frequency range. We went back and recorded hours and hours, nine to ten days' worth of sound effects.[54]

[54] Schneider, "Recording *The Taking of Pelham*." The term "MS" and "MS Stereo" refers to an audio technique called "mid-side" recording. In contrast to a conventional stereo recording, which separates audio information into left and right channels, a mid-side recording places information from the center in one channel and information from the sides into the other. The advantage to mid-side recording is that it provides more options during postproduction because it allows greater control of the "spread" of a stereo mix. It is obviously well suited to multichannel sound systems that involve left, center, and right channels behind the screen. For more on mid-side recording, see http://emusician.com/mag/emusic_front_center/ (accessed November 26, 2012).

The rather intensive investment in time spent gathering train sounds paid off during postproduction; the 2009 version makes extensive use of the subway trains as LFE and as a directional or moving sound effect. For the most part, the train sounds simply enhance the verisimilitude of the film's setting. For example, when the mayor is notified of the hijacking while aboard a train, the sounds of arriving and departing trains appear in the left and right channels of the sound mix as part of the normal flow of subway traffic at a station. Later, after Garber delivers the ransom to Ryder and his crew, he uses a passing train to separate himself from the hijackers. In a loose rendering of "point of audition" sound, the passing train is panned from left to right and then into the surrounds. This is in contrast to the simultaneous gunfire directed at Garber, which is mixed so that it remains in the front part of the auditorium. In other instances, though, the train sounds serve an expressive purpose. During the scene in which Ryder coerces Garber into confessing he was bribed by threatening to shoot George, the loud sound of a passing train in the surrounds ratchets up the scene's tension as a kind of correlate to Ryder's sudden anger. We hear this sound just as Ryder exits the motorman cab and enters the train car.

Thus, even though both films make copious use of train sounds as part of their audio mix, the 2009 version heightens the impact of these effects by highlighting the visceral and spatial dimensions of these sounds. Indeed, as evidenced by past practice, train sounds are almost tailor-made to display the potential of contemporary digital surround sound systems. In June 1992 Dolby Laboratories unveiled a trailer intended to showcase its new Dolby digital format. The trailer, entitled "Train," was designed and mixed by Randy Thom and Skywalker Sound; Thom, of course, was one of the leading sound designers of the early '90s and Skywalker Sound one of the top production houses:

> The choice of a train was not incidental. In practical terms, it offered a range of illustrative audio effects. Beginning with a hollow clanking (set to a blank screen), the heavy movement of carriages (gray smoke) gives way to the compressed movement of steam and metal (train wheels), the billowing smoke of the funnel (pistons) matching the rhythmic acceleration of a heavy locomotive across a track (train moving into the near distance).[55]

Although the remake of *Pelham* doesn't replicate Thom's pioneering trailer, it certainly uses its assorted train sounds to quite similar ends. As is typical of today's intensified continuity sound style, the LFE channel used for train sounds adds to their visceral impact by adding low frequency depth to the train's rumble, while the use of train sounds as spot effects in the surround channels enhances the sense of an immersive, three-dimensional audio environment.

[55] Grainge, "Selling Spectacular Sound," 260.

Nondiegetic Sound Effects

Finally, the *Pelham* remake employs nondiegetic sounds to punctuate some of the film's visual effects in a manner similar to that of many other big-budget action films. Several of these nondiegetic sounds are used in conjunction with the film's titles. Scott and his production team have a lot of fun with the film's opening credits by moving them into and out of different parts of the frame. Sometimes the credits appear to slide into the frame from offscreen. At other times the credits move in coordination with another visual element, such as the train. The credits also receive emphasis from the soundtrack, as they are synced either to nondiegetic musical elements or to sound effects. (I should note, though, that this credit sequence, which covers the first six minutes of the film, typifies the kind of sensory overload that leads critics to see Scott's style as excessive. Besides the moving titles, a welter of other visual effects employed in the sequence ranges from changes in film speed to added motion blur to step-printing effects. The soundtrack is almost equally dense, as the mix combines myriad train sounds, nondiegetic effects, bits of Harry Gregson-Williams's score, and fragments of Jay-Z's "99 Problems.") Following is a brief list of moments in which nondiegetic sounds punctuate the appearance of individual credits:

- When the film's title appears, the numbers "1," "2," and "3" appear in rapid succession, each accompanied by the crunching beats of the guitar riff from "99 Problems."
- A nondiegetic whoosh accompanies the movement of Luis Guzman's credit over several shots as it moves from a position on the right side of Ryder to a position on the left side of Emri.
- The casting credit for Denise Chamian slides in from off right. Its afterimage re-enters the frame four separate times, with each entry synced with a disk jockey's scratching sound.
- A nondiegetic whooshing sound underlines the introduction of Tony Scott's director credit. The title appears to move into the distance after entering from the offscreen space of the auditorium (i.e., behind the camera). At the moment the title appears, the film speed also changes from normal to slow motion. The title then appears to follow the train as it disappears around the curve of the subway tunnel. Once again, a nondiegetic whoosh highlights the movement of the title as the image of the train also resumes normal film speed.

Later, as the ransom money is gathered, a nondiegetic whoosh underscores a zoom out to a satellite view of Manhattan accompanied by a title that reads "42 + Vanderbilt." The effect recurs at the tail end of this shot, which shows the geographical relationship between the site of the hostage crisis and the Brooklyn Federal Reserve. The camera appears to track and pan rapidly over lower Manhattan and the East River. A nondiegetic whoosh also punctuates the zoom in on the Federal Reserve Vault.

While most of these nondiegetic whooshing sounds are used in synchronization with credits and explanatory titles, a number of other iterations of this device act to punctuate various visual effects. In an early aerial shot of the Manhattan skyline, a nondiegetic whoosh is heard as the sun is momentarily blocked from view by a skyscraper. The sudden change from light to dark also brings the foreground plane into focus. The whooshing sound thus underscores the change in lighting and depth of field in this shot. Later, a nondiegetic whoosh accompanies a swish pan away from the sign atop the entrance of the Times Square subway station.

Although these whooshing sounds are clearly nondiegetic sound effects, other forms of nondiegetic punctuation in *Pelham* straddle the border between effects and music. Consider, for example, the stinger chord that accompanies the appearance of supertitles that mark the progress toward the deadline Ryder has given Garber. The first time it appears, the title reads "48 MINUTES TO DEADLINE" and appears over a freeze-frame of the Rail Control Center. This moment is underscored by a musical element that appears to have two parts: (1) a sudden crescendo that sounds as though it were produced using a backward reverb effect in Pro Tools, and (2) a sforzando comprised of a drumbeat and an electronic instrument playing a minor chord. This musical device recurs every time a new title and freeze-frame appears (i.e., at "37 MINUTES," "32 MINUTES," "23 MINUTES," "17 MINUTES," "11 MINUTES," and "8 MINUTES").

Unlike other intensified continuity films, *Pelham* does not use the "reverberant drum beat" technique described previously, but instead develops its own variant of this device during the scene in which Ryder shoots Wallace, the army veteran who sacrifices himself to save another hostage, the mother of a young boy. Ryder commits this act of violence as revenge for Garber's lie about the money's arrival at the 42nd Street and Vanderbilt subway entrance. The tension of this brief standoff is heightened by the use of mechanical noises that punctuate the picture editing and gestures of characters. The effect is first introduced as a kind of metallic bang on the cut to Ryder counting off the hostages as he exits the motorman's cab. This banging sound continues throughout the sequence and underscores Lt. Camonetti's turn toward Garber, a sudden zoom in on the mayor looking at the video feed, and a rapid zoom in on Ryder. As the tension builds, the metallic banging sound takes the form of a metric pulse that accompanies a series of rapidly cut tracking shots. Each of these shots is about one second long and seems to arc around the central figure or move through the hostage negotiation team as it watches the video feed of the standoff.

Conclusion

As this comparison of the 1974 and 2009 versions of *Pelham* demonstrates, contemporary sound designs employ strategies and techniques that are analogous to the visual dimensions of intensified continuity outlined by David Bordwell. More importantly, in each instance described, the 2009 remake simply "amps up" a sound element already established as an important component of the 1974 original. Both films use train sounds as a kind of aural motif, but the 2009 version avails itself of the possibilities offered by digital sound to enhance the sensation of the acoustic vibrations in the theater, to create certain "point of audition" effects, and to sharpen the audio profile of high and low frequency sounds. Put simply, the screeching brakes of the train in the 2009 remake are brighter and shriller, while the low rumbles of approaching trains are lower and louder. Both versions of *Pelham* feature car accidents during their transport scenes, but the 2009 version uses LFE and surround channels to fortify the visceral quality of the crash impact. Likewise, both films use aural contrast as a way to reinforce the constant cross-cutting to different lines of action, but the 2009 remake further refines those differences through microphone distance, reverb, and surround channel ambiences that are specific to each locale. Finally, unlike the 1974 original, the 2009 version uses nondiegetic sounds, such as whooshes, stinger chords, and mechanical noise, to accent titles and underline key moments of the drama.

As I argue throughout this chapter, the technological innovations associated with Dolby's multichannel sound systems have enabled these different audio strategies and techniques, but they have not determined them. In a pattern of innovation and diffusion evident throughout Hollywood's history, new technological affordances open up new possibilities for the film medium, but they are soon assimilated to the norms of Hollywood storytelling, particularly its emphasis on narrative clarity and coherence. Far from challenging classical principles, the new intensified continuity style simply offers an augmentation of established devices and techniques. Just as today's visuals are faster and more frenetic, contemporary soundtracks are louder, clearer, more dynamic, and more immersive.

Perhaps Stuart Klawans is right that many current filmmakers seek to bludgeon viewers into a state of helpless submission. Yet if that is the case, my analysis of the 2009 *Pelham* remake illustrates the role contemporary film sound plays in this process. Like those battle-axes in *Robin Hood*, the soundtracks of many new Hollywood films pack as much punch as a well-aimed blow to the head.

Acknowledgements

The author would like to thank David Bordwell, John Richardson, Carol Vernallis, and especially Claudia Gorbman for their helpful editorial suggestions on an earlier draft of this essay.

References

Altman, Rick. "Deep Focus Sound: *Citizen Kane* and the Radio Aesthetic." In *Perspectives on Citizen Kane*, edited by Ronald Gottesman, 94–121. New York: G.K. Hall & Co., 1996.

Ament, Vanessa Theme. *The Foley Grail: The Art of Performing Sound for Film, Games, and Animation*. Boston: Focal Press, 2009.

Beck, Jay. "A Quiet Revolution: Changes in American Film Sound Practices, 1967–1979." PhD diss., University of Iowa, 2003.

Beck, Jay. "The Sounds of 'Silence': Dolby Stereo, Sound Design, and *Silence of the Lambs*." In *Lowering the Boom: Critical Studies in Film Sound*, edited by Jay Beck and Tony Grajeda, 68–84. Urbana; Chicago: University of Illinois Press, 2008.

Belton, John. "1950s Magnetic Sound: The Frozen Revolution." In *Sound Theory/Sound Practice*, edited by Rick Altman, 154–170. New York: Routledge, 1992.

Block, Alex Ben, and Lucy Autrey Wilson, eds. *George Lucas' Blockbusting: A Decade-by-Decade Survey of Timeless Movies Including Untold Secrets of Their Financial and Cultural Success*. New York: Itbooks, 2010.

Bordwell, David. "Intensified Continuity: Visual Style in Contemporary Hollywood Film." *Film Quarterly* 55, no. 3 (Spring 2002): 16–28.

Bordwell, David. *The Way Hollywood Tells It: Story and Style in Modern Movies*. Berkeley: University of California Press, 2006.

Canby, Vincent. "Excess and Excitement and Many Decibels." *New York Times*, March 12, 1975, 48.

Chion, Michel. *Audio-Vision: Sound on Screen*. Edited and translated by Claudia Gorbman. New York: Columbia University Press, 1994.

Chion, Michel. *Film, a Sound Art*. Translated by Claudia Gorbman. New York: Columbia University Press, 2009.

Cohen, Annabel. "Film Music: Perspectives from Cognitive Psychology." In *Music and Cinema*, edited by James Buhler, Caryl Flinn, and David Neumeyer. Hanover, NH: Wesleyan University Press, 2000.

Elsaesser, Thomas. "Specularity and Engulfment: Francis Ford Coppola and *Bram Stoker's Dracula*." In *Contemporary Hollywood Cinema*, edited by Steve Neale and Murray Smith, 191–208. New York: Routledge, 1998.

Gorbman, Claudia. *Unheard Melodies: Narrative Film Music*. Bloomington: Indiana University Press, 1987.

Grainge, Paul. "Selling Spectacular Sound: Dolby and the Unheard History of Technical Trademarks." In *Lowering the Boom: Critical Studies in Film Sound*, edited by Jay Beck and Tony Grajeda, 251–268. Urbana; Chicago: University of Illinois Press, 2008.

Kerins, Mark. "Narration in the Cinema of Digital Sound." *The Velvet Light Trap* 58 (Fall 2006): 41–54.

Kerins, Mark. "Constructing the Diegesis in a Multi-Channel World." *Offscreen* 11, nos. 8–9 (August/September 2007): 1–5.

Kerins, Mark. *Beyond Dolby (Stereo): Cinema in the Digital Sound Age*. Bloomington: Indiana University Press, 2010.

King, Geoff. *New Hollywood Cinema*. New York: Columbia University Press, 2002.

Klawans, Stuart. "Icons and Zombies." *The Nation*, June 14, 2010, 44.

Neumeyer, David, James Buhler, and Rob Deemer. *Hearing the Movies: Music and Sound in Film History*. New York: Oxford University Press, 2010.

Schneider, Peter. "Recording *The Taking of Pelham*—Original and Remake: Production Sound Mixers Chris Newman and Tom Nelson Talk Shop on Recording the Two Pelhams." *Studio Daily*, September 25, 2009, at http://www.studiodaily.com/main/casestudies/Recording-The-Taking-Of-Pelham-Original-and-Remake_11310.html (accessed June 24, 2010).

Sergi, Gianluca. *The Dolby Era: Film Sound in Contemporary Hollywood*. New York: Manchester University Press, 2004.

Smith, Murray. "Theses on the Philosophy of Hollywood History." In *Contemporary Hollywood History*, edited by Steve Neale and Murray Smith, 3–20. New York: Routledge, 1998.

Thanouli, Eleftheria. *Post-Classical Cinema: An International Poetics of Film Narration*. London: Wallflower Press, 2010.

Thompson, Kristin. *Storytelling in the New Hollywood: Understanding Classical Narrative Technique*. Cambridge, Mass.: Harvard University Press, 1999.

Whittington, William. *Sound Design & Science Fiction*. Austin: University of Texas Press, 2007.

Wyatt, Justin. *High Concept: Movies and Marketing in Hollywood*. Austin: University of Texas Press, 1994.

Zacharek, Stephanie. "Man on Fire." *Salon*. April 23, 2004, at http://www.salon.com/2004/04/23/man_on_fire/ (accessed December 18, 2012).

CHAPTER 21

EXTENDING FILM AESTHETICS: AUDIO BEYOND VISUALS

K. J. DONNELLY

DIGITAL technologies and small electronic screens, rather than hastening the death of film, have transfigured it into a new format that retains fundamental continuities with its traditions.[1] Thirty years ago Noël Burch noted that classical cinema occasionally treated its sound components as musical material. He pointed to *Force of Evil*'s (1948) use of dialogue as both dramatic action and "musically organized sound."[2] In recent years such a "musical" approach to the film's music and sound as a "whole entity" is less remarkable. Film soundtracks now often evince a conceptual or aesthetic unity along the lines of musical principles, both in structure and suppositions about individual sounds. The increasing involvement within a larger sonic scheme of elements of the film soundtrack partners with the enhanced importance of offscreen sound (it is no longer necessary to painstakingly show *everything* on screen) in modern audiovisual aesthetics.[3] The crucial point is that sound *implies* visuals. This has fundamental implications for "soundtracks" outside the cinema, as well as larger ramifications for discussions of sonic culture generally. Technological developments have ensured a shared fate for film and music. Digital recording and manipulation have enabled more complexity in sound design in mainstream films as a matter of course. In the music industry it has also afforded the easy

[1] Lev Manovich notes that the now dominant principles of new digital media existed in earlier film format, and film has remained an interface and locus point for surrounding developments. *The Language of New Media* (Cambridge, Mass.: MIT Press, 2001), 50.

[2] Noel Burch, *Theory of Film Practice* (Princeton, N.J.: University of Princeton Press, 1981), 96.

[3] Michel Chion, *Audio-Vision: Sound on Screen*, ed. and trans. Claudia Gorbman (New York: Columbia University Press, 1994), 85.

construction of complex music through sampling sounds from diverse sources and precise, almost molecular manipulation. It should be no surprise that film and music have converged, and in the light of expansive notions of what constitutes music, have seemingly fused on music's terms. The film aesthetic of "musical accompaniment" or "dramatic musical scoring," has proliferated, becoming increasingly evident in media and culture beyond cinema. Indeed, little more than a permeable membrane separates "film music" (or music made for film) and music that is "absolute" or self-contained, but also combines well with images. Although film has always enjoyed a central role in "the audiovisual"—defining the term probably more than any other agent—its aesthetic traditions of assumptions, techniques, and effects have also been exported to other media. We should bear in mind that film soundtracks can constitute an aesthetic unity, with music incorporating sound effects and the whole having something of a "musical" sense to it. Rather than simply being a cog in a mechanism, soundtracks are able, to a degree, to become autonomous without explicit moving images but through the implication of accompanying visuals. [4]

Widening Superfield Theory

Both technology and aesthetics have dictated a headlong rush into establishing a unified aural field of music and other sounds in many films. Partially imposed by the overwhelming adoption of digital technologies, with their new filtering and enhancing procedures, sounds and music have increasingly become conceptualized in electronic terms (envelopes, bandpass filters, frequency spikes, pitch shifting, etc.). Although it could be argued that avant-garde films had already trodden this path before the coming of digital sound, it can be more convincingly claimed that digital technologies, adopted wholesale, have determined the "unified" approach to film sound and music. I realize that technological determinism is hardly the critical flavor of the month, but we have to accept that technological capabilities set the horizons of aesthetic capabilities, and in the vast majority of cases, users adopt the technology's path of least resistance.

Michel Chion referred to the new sonic space offered by high-definition sounds and directional multispeaker surround sound as the "superfield," which alters the perception of space and thereby the more general rules of audiovisual scene construction.[5] This superfield is not only qualitatively different from previous sonic space, but also marks an extension of offscreen space and possesses, "a kind of quasi-autonomous existence with relation to the visual field."[6] This "quasi-autonomy" frees film sound from slavishly

[4] Although there is an undoubted similarity to radio plays, the aesthetic is arguably derived more from film, and indeed, film is an unregistered influence on the trend for organic "concept albums" prevalent from the late 1960s. *Dark Side of the Moon* integrates voices and sound effects with the music, whereas *War of the Worlds* sounds like a film musical.

[5] Chion, *Audio-Vision*, 149–150.

[6] Chion, *Audio-Vision*, 150.

backing up what is seen on screen. Developments in sound have been matched by developments in image. Spatialized, multitracked sound favors passive offscreen sound (which for Chion is offscreen sound that is not narratively foregrounded). Such passive offscreen sound works to establish more close-ups and wide spaces, as well as freer movement among shots. Sound also helps prevent the audience from experiencing spatial disorientation, while contributing to a new group of aesthetics that rework the basic conceptions and practices of film. In horror films, offscreen space is regularly made threatening through sound without confirming images, and can remain a sustained "vision-less" part of the system, firing the imagination of the audience. Of course incidental music in films and music in films more generally has attained a degree of independence, and other sounds have not only drawn upon this aspect, but also followed its path to an extent.

In recent years an increasingly *aesthetic* rather than *representational* conception of sound in the cinema has emerged. Traditionally cinema sound was conceived and constructed in a basic compositional template. At its heart were clarity and intelligibility of dialogue, alongside uncluttered but functional composition of diegetic sound elements. Nondiegetic music occupied an unobtrusive position in volume and pitch, except at privileged moments. James Lastra notes that new sound pioneers such as Walter Murch, "discovered that the founding gesture of sound design, as it were, is both the complete severing of sensory experience from representation, and a compulsive linking of the two in an indissoluble unity that appeared to efface representation."[7] Sounds may almost lose their representational attributes as they serve emotional and psychological functions, the traditional domain of nondiegetic music in films. Some art films followed a long-standing tradition of imbuing sound effects with weighty emotional and symbolic significance, endowing sound with a primarily aesthetic role. Tarkovsky's *Stalker* (1979) is a case in point, during the sequence of the lengthy and memorable train journey to "the zone" where the soundtrack is dominated by the not-quite-regular diegetic clacking of the train on the track. The metallic sounds remain in the foreground, undergirded by some subtle chords, mixed from a small orchestra and synthesized nondiegetic music by Eduard Artemyev. As the journey progresses, the track noise becomes increasingly treated with electronics, so that it not so much represents the illusory world onscreen as bestows an interior sense of compulsive mental pattern and transition, an equivalent to the visuals of the film's emotional landscape. Discussing *Apocalypse Now* (1979), Jay Beck notes that "Coppola wanted a sound mix that emulated the quadraphonic musical recordings of the early 1970s, both in their multichannel location of the speakers as well as in their psychedelic sounds and style."[8] With music as inspiration, it is hardly surprising that on occasion diegetic sound

[7] James Lastra, "Film and the Wagnerian Aspiration: Thoughts on Sound Design and History of the Senses," in *Lowering the Boom: Critical Studies in Film Sound*, ed. Jay Beck and Tony Grajeda (Chicago: University of Illinois Press, 2008), 135.

[8] Jay Beck, "The Sounds of Silence," in *Lowering the Boom*, ed. Beck and Grajeda, 71.

effects adopt a function closer to that traditionally assigned to incidental music. For example, *Ju-On: The Grudge* (2003) includes extraordinary sequences in which sound could be interpreted as either music or sound effects. In both cases the ambiguity is doubtless part of the general effect of the film. *Ju-On* contains deep, ambiguous rumbles that might be construed as diegetic supernatural sounds. The status of many of the sounds remains unclear: they might be diegetic, or they might be part of the scary musical furnishings of the film. Indeed, deep sub-bass rumbles and metallic sounds with a wide frequency range have exploited the dramatic and psychological possibilities of an extended range of bass and treble tones available to 5.1 Dolby sound and Chion's multispeaker superfield.[9]

The merging of music as an art of *time* with sound effects and their way of delineating *space* produces a physical sense of time–space continuum, remarkably similar to what Albert Einstein described in "Theory of Special Relativity" (1905). Through the addition of (musical) time as the fourth dimension, nondiegetic music plus diegetic sounds establish a fully relative conception of the superfield. The superfield is no mere add-on; rather, it involves fusion at the genetic level, rendering the soundtrack as a distinct object. A point of view from Gestalt psychology would not only focus on the field as a whole, but also register that individual aspects are perhaps less important than the dynamic relationship between the elements gathered together in that field. This might be a more fruitful approach to film soundtracks than the cognitive approach dominant in film studies, which focuses on isolated cues and atomized and hierarchized elements. A Gestaltist position would engage meaning as being produced through addition rather than copresence and interrelationship of the part to the entire entity of the soundtrack (and film).[10] Furthermore, sound implies images, often suggesting a particular origin. In much the same way that Gestaltist perception diagrams prove the process of "reification," wherein we mentally "complete" objects that are only partially present, so a Gestaltist approach might suggest that we "imagine" the completion of the soundtrack's audio into a full "quasi" film, finishing the whole that is implied by significant component parts.

Audio That Implies Visuals

"Hear the pictures! See the music!" was Disney's synesthetic slogan for *Fantasia* in 1940. Filmmaker Robert Bresson claimed that sound always evokes an image, whereas

[9] Deep, almost infrasonic sounds have been exploited by horror films, such as *Lost Highway* (1997), *Dark Water* (2002), and *Paranormal Activity* (2007), which used such sounds to indicate the onset of the titular activities.

[10] See, for example, Kurt Lewin's field theory of behavior, which addresses a totality of events in a specific environment when dealing with group behavior. *Resolving Social Conflicts and Field Theory in Social Science* (Washington, D.C.: American Psychological Association, 1997).

an image never invokes a sound.[11] Indeed, the propensity for sound to suggest images has been exploited by cinema and other media.[12] The Gestalt of audio might include an absent visual component; the "audiovisual" ought also to embrace audio that *implies* visuals (and equally visuals that imply audio). Film soundtracks have influenced audiovisual culture outside the cinema—most obviously other screen culture, but also cultural forms with little or no relation to images. Examples range from Pink Floyd's *Dark Side of the Moon* (1973) and Jeff Wayne's *War of the Worlds* (1978) in the 1970s to more recent ambient music recordings.

Ambient music owes much to film music, or at least to a concept of the "cinematic"; it is premised on "atmosphere" and the construction of soundscapes, much as film composers and sound designers aim to construct.[13] Ambient music is often "image-friendly music," which can thus be used in television programs or films very easily and so has the enviable capability to be sold twice over. Brian Eno's album *Ambient 4: On Land* (released in 1982) was a harbinger of the genre of ambient music.[14] Fundamentally different from "popular music," most of this recording lacks notable melody or harmonic movement, instead focusing on slow sonic events and textures; it aims to serve as a sonic backdrop rather than as a traditionally "musical" event. As Eno himself notes on the album's cover, "cluster all disparate sounds into one aural frame: they become music."[15] Like film scores, such music aims to furnish aural impressions of locations and associated images.

"Visual music" has remained an insistent margin of music, sometimes eschewing melody and concentrating on atmospheric soundscapes and ambiences, while aiming at an extension beyond simple music. Embracing drama, film, and television culture, as well as nonmusical inspiration, certain albums appear to derive more from films than from anything else. Mount Vernon Arts Lab's album *The Séance at Hobs Lane* (2001; re-released in 2007) consists predominantly of electronics, but sometimes mixes them with conventional instruments and features guest musicians such as Coil and Portishead's Adrian Utley. An extraordinary recording, *The Séance at Hobs Lane* appears almost to be a psychogeographical investigation of subterranean London. As such it could not be farther from "popular music," yet when approached as a concept album, its concept remains obscure and occult. Tracks include titles such as "The Vauxhall

[11] Burch, *Theory of Film Practice*, 90.

[12] Of course, radio drama was an influence *on* film soundtracks, but also has arguably become influenced *by* film soundtracks.

[13] There is also often subaudible presentation. Nicholas Cook and Anthony Pople, eds., *The Cambridge History of Twentieth-Century Music* (Cambridge, UK: Cambridge University Press, 2004), 502. However, there are different kinds of "ambient music." Perhaps the most prominent use is the branch of electronic dance music that is not aimed at dancing (like Aphex Twin or Boards of Canada); there is also the "New Age ambient music," which often mixes relaxing but conventional music with environmental sounds. These are both very different from the music I am discussing here.

[14] Prendergast points to Eno's centrality, but also to later developments from electronic dance music. *The Ambient Century: From Mahler to Moby* (London: Bloomsbury, 2001), 131, 52–53.

[15] Brian Eno, cover notes to *Ambient 4: On Land*, EG 2311107 (EG Records, 1982).

Labyrinth" and "The Submariner's Song" (whose title is ironic—nothing remotely resembles a traditional "song" on the album). The sleeve notes state:

> Imagine a landscape of sets built for a never-quite-produced British science fiction film of the 1950s. Hobs End was the invented tube [London underground] station in *Quatermass and the Pit* (an MVAL [Mount Vernon Arts Lab] touchstone). *The Séance at Hobs Lane* is a late-night gathering, convened to reconnoitre this subterranean world.[16]

Quatermass and the Pit, a celebrated BBC television science fiction serial broadcast in 1958–1959, was remade into a film by Hammer Studios in 1967 (U.S. title: *Five Million Years to Earth*). In the film excavations at the Hobs End underground station in London uncover what is assumed to be a bomb, later to be revealed as a buried spaceship. Sightings of a mysterious, short, goblinlike figure occur in the vicinity. Professor Bernard Quatermass works out that the spaceship brought aliens to Earth, who then modified some humans with their genetic material. This discovery leads to an atavistic battle between those humans who are possessed by their alien DNA and those who are not. *The Séance at Hobs Lane* is shaped by isolated elements from the television serial and the film. Its second track relates directly to the shady, diminutive figures that have been sighted at Hobs Lane at various times. "Hobgoblins" sounds reminiscent of The Stranglers' "Waltz in Black," an electronic waltz with an angular "absurd" melody, whose archly comic tone has made it a popular sample for continuity music and library music on television. As it turns out, this is the nearest to a conventional piece of music on the album. "Sir Keith at Lambeth" consists of austere, continuous electronic tones (a deeper mechanical drone and more high-pitched, white-noise-based sounds). Indeed, this sounds more like a soundscape field recording from a zone of heavy industry than a piece of music. The higher tone fluctuates in intensity, at times sounding almost like a high-pressure water hose (or a distant boring machine), at others like a continuous alarm. Near the start of the track the deeper-pitched tone sounds at times close to a power line's or mains electric hum. The concluding solo note, with its slow vibrato, is less like anything heard regularly in electronic music than the sort of electronic sound effects used in science fiction films and television, most particularly for ray guns or auguring devices (such as the "tricorder" in the 1960s series *Star Trek*).

The principal member of Mount Vernon Arts Lab, Drew Mulholland,[17] plays vintage synthesizers, including an EMS VCS3 (Putney).[18] These are now much sought-after

[16] Lawrence Norfolk, sleeve notes to Mount Vernon Arts Lab, *The Séance at Hobs Lane*, GBX009 (Ghost Box, 2007).

[17] Mulholland more recently and remarkably became "composer in residence" (a Leverhulme fellow) in the Geographical and Earth Sciences Department at the University of Glasgow. Drew Mulholland, Hayden Lorimer, and Chris Philo, "Resounding: An Interview with Drew Mulholland," *Scottish Geographical Journal* 125, nos. 3–4 (September–December 2009): 379–380.

[18] VCS3 synthesizers are less contemporary electronic keyboard instruments than they are a piece of audio hardware dominated by dials and a pinhole matrix for patching between modular sections of the instrument.

early synthesizers that sell for high prices. Made by Peter Zinovieff's EMS company in the early 1970s, they featured on Pink Floyd's *Dark Side of the Moon* and were used by the BBC Radiophonic Workshop to provide sound effects and music for television science fiction programs such as *Doctor Who* (1963–1984), *Blake's Seven* (1978–1981), and *Hitchhiker's Guide to the Galaxy* (1981).[19] One of EMS's directors was the composer and electronics pioneer Tristram Cary, who provided the music, both orchestral and electronic, for the film version of *Quatermass and the Pit*. Some of the cues bear similarity to pieces on *The Séance at Hobs Lane*. For example, "Vessel" has a structure of repeated (looped) figures, one rising in pitch gradually like an engine gaining speed, one dropping lower, echo-repeated, and more percussive in character. Similarly, "Maelstrom" is based on electronic echo and sounds like a spaceship taking off or the sound effect used in films to signify extrasensory perception (consisting of a very gradual rise in pitch). Carey also provided *musique concrète* for *Doctor Who* in the early and mid-1960s, extraordinary soundscapes that are somewhere between nondiegetic music and diegetic ambience for the *Doctor Who* stories "The Daleks" (1963) and "The Daleks' Master Plan" (1965).[20] Some of this avant-garde-inspired music is remarkably similar to *The Séance at Hobs Lane*, which overall is austere and often based on repetitive drones and basic analog synthesizer sounds. Its tracks develop little, and there are no vocals for the listener to hang onto.

An extension of film, *The Séance at Hobs Lane* provides a springboard for the imagination, rather than functioning as music per se.[21] For example, the opening track, "The Fog Detonator," consists of a succession of sounds of fireworks exploding (with a slight reverb, suggesting hard reflective surfaces). Though the title may or may not refer to some obscure, imaginary fog-dispersing device particular to London, sonically the track suggests a "pre-CD event," or a particular location captured through field recording. It is doubtful that the recording could be listened to without imagery arising in the listener's head. This CD remains a long way from conventional "music." In essence, it implies an elsewhere: stories, ideas, and locations with a strong visual element. None of these is summoned through sung words, but rather, more often through sounds with an almost

[19] Louis Niebur discusses how the BBC Radiophonic Workshop "complicated the boundary between 'sound effect' and 'music.'" "The Music of Machines: 'Special Sound' as the Music of *Doctor Who*," in *Time and Relative Dissertations in Space: Critical Perspectives on* Doctor Who, ed. David Butler (Manchester, UK: Manchester University Press, 2007), 205.

[20] Cf. *Quatermass and the Pit: The Film Music of Tristram Cary, Volume One*, CNS 5009 (Cloud Nine Records, 1996). Among other things, Carey provided the electronic effects for *Casino Royale* (1966) and *musique concrète* for *Doctor Who* in the early and mid-1960s. His album *Doctor Who: Devil's Planets, The Music of Tristram Cary*, WMSF 6072-2 (BBC, 2003) showcases extraordinary electronic soundscapes, from the *Doctor Who* stories "The Daleks" (1963) and "The Daleks' Master Plan" (1965).

[21] In an interview, Mulholland discusses the film only, suggesting its sound-world is the inspiration for the album. Despite its significant reputation, the television serial was virtually impossible to see until the advent of home video. Mark Pilkington, "Mount Vernon Arts Lab: True Sound of the Underground," *Fortean Times* [2001], repr. June 2007, at http://www.forteantimes.com/features/interviews/483/mount_vernon_arts_lab.html (accessed December 13, 2010).

identifiable origin. The sonic textures remain sparse, consisting throughout of few layers of sounds and with a sense of organizational focus evident in film soundtracks. Most of this album comprises acousmatic sounds, divorced from their unapparent (visual) origins. It implies vague visuals rather than presenting "face value" sounds. *The Séance at Hobs Lane* derives less from a conventional avant-garde background (like Stockhausen) than from the edges of so-called popular music (such as Coil, who have produced film music as well as music on disc).

Films and their soundtracks can function as a cultural repository,[22] and not only in aesthetic terms. Film also functions as a repository of key ideas and abstract notions, seemingly having displaced literature as the custodian of the majority of the cultural imaginary.[23] Equally, however, it is film's place at the apex of audiovisual culture that is the aesthetic inspiration. Yet film also functions as a repository of sounds and sonic memory, alluding to an elsewhere and evoking visuals through esoteric and often elusive processes.

Technology and Intelligent Sound Design

Miguel Mera and David Burnand suggest that an aesthetic modernism in film soundtracks aspires to unify music and other sounds.[24] Although this may not be the norm across all mainstream cinema, one sees significant evidence of its taking place. As Mera and Burnand also suggest, there is not only a technological basis in unified film music and sound effects, but also an impulse from the fringes of cinematic and aural culture.

The sea change from analog to digital media occurred shortly after the turn of the millennium, completing a process that had started a couple of decades earlier in the audiovisual arts. The radical shift from analog to digital sound had a notable impact on many aspects of cinema,[25] enabling ever more precise manipulation of all its aural elements: music, sound effects, and dialogue. Although big-budget films still wanted to have the sound of real orchestras, by the late 1990s musical scores could be constructed and edited on a computer screen at home, using nonlinear editing software and musical "soft studio" technology. Digital signal processing (DSP) and integrated soft

22 Digital popular music has not only raided old musical recordings, but also exploited sound samples from films, as much as it has had recourse to images and narratives inspired by films.

23 There are many examples of music videos inspired directly by film, such as Madonna's "Material Girl" (1985), which was based on Marilyn Monroe singing "Diamonds Are a Girl's Best Friend" in *Gentlemen Prefer Blondes* (1953), and Rob Zombie's "Living Dead Girl" (1998), based on *The Cabinet of Doctor Caligari* (1920).

24 Miguel Mera and David Burnand, eds., *European Film Music* (Aldershot, UK: Ashgate, 2006), 5.

25 Gianluca Sergi, *The Dolby Era: Film Sound in Contemporary Hollywood* (Manchester, UK: Manchester University Press, 2004), 30.

studio packages were widely available by the late 1990s for home use and have followed a trajectory of increased capabilities and decreasing price. The adoption of the resulting "digital audio workstation" (DAW) has revolutionized music production, allowing easy construction of relatively high-quality music on a home computer. Versions of this product include, among others, Steinberg Cubase, Apple Logic, Ableton Live, and Propellerheads Reason. Each has its own strengths; Logic for Apple Macs and Cubase for PCs are the most popular among professional musicians. They are all based on integrated music recording and processing with dedicated software and a powerful sound card in the computer, converting sound impulses or computer instructions into a digital code that is sampled upon entry and synthesized upon exit from the terminal. One dividend of these modes of digital sound is that through their massive capabilities for signal processing, users have gained an increasingly acute awareness of aspects of sound and more developed sensitivity to precise sonic qualities. This new consciousness of sound is patent for those engaged in digital sound and music production, but also likely evident to wider populations who are consumers of more sonically sensitive material than previous generations.

This situation promotes a "sound for sound's sake" approach, wherein primary aspects of sound and its microlevel manipulation become the most attractive part of the process for practitioners. This clearly can lead to an ambiguity about what might constitute "music" and what might constitute "nonmusical sound," which at the very least has challenged the limited concepts of music and sound effects in wide circulation. Digital sound processing technology is used not only by "musical" people, but also by sound designers and editors, to manipulate sound effects in precisely the same way musicians do when they compose music. Indeed, sound designers use "musical software" and digital products designed primarily for the production of music (such as Pro Tools) for processing both dialogue and sound effects.[26] Whereas on the one hand composers are perhaps more aware of sound as a compositional element in its own right than ever before, on the other hand, film sound people approach soundtracks in a manner that might be termed "musical," or at least betrays a musical awareness of the interaction of elements and their individual sonic qualities. Consequently, music for films, and indeed film sound effects, can be produced by people with no musical or technical training. Equally, though, those with musical knowledge or sensibility can be effective sound designers for films.

The increased "musical" character of soundtracks is evident not only in the ways that sound is used and conceived, but also in its organizational imperatives. These include spatializing aspects that allow the copresence of sounds that might mask one another when mixed for mono or two-track stereo. Also, pitches can be varied and sounds rendered through musical instruments. For example, the sound effects for *Aliens* (1986)

[26] Even in the 1980s, Hollywood films sometimes processed sounds through early digital sampling musical instruments. Anonymous, "Sounds of Sci-Fi II," *Computer Music* 151 (May 2010): 64.

were processed through a Fairlight CMI digital synthesizer.[27] An example of someone with a musical background being involved in film sound effects is Alan Howarth. He is probably best known as a composer and synthesizer programmer who has worked with John Carpenter on films such as *Halloween II* (1981), *Escape from New York* (1981), and *Prince of Darkness* (1987). Yet he also created the rumbling sound for the starship at the beginning of *Star Wars* (1977) by layering recordings of white noise, air conditioning, and sounds he recorded at jet engine laboratories.[28] Howarth also produced sounds for *Star Trek: The Motion Picture* (1979) and *Poltergeist* (1982) using keyboard synthesizers as well as field recordings. For *Star Wars Episode 3: Attack of the Clones* (2002), Ben Burtt also used electronic musical instruments for sound effects.[29] George Pal's *War of the Worlds* (1953) used electric guitars for the sound of the Martian death ray, and one of the more recent remakes (2005) used pitched, musical sounds for the Martian war machines. Along similar lines, *Terminator Salvation* (2009) used pitched musical sounds for the large machines that attacked the humans, providing a degree of novelty to the cinematic convention of predictable, mechanical sounds.

The increasingly evident "musicalization" of the soundtrack might owe something to practices developed in avant-garde filmmaking and sound art. The breakdown of the partition between diegetic sound effects and nondiegetic music began once the uniqueness of their functions was questioned. The avant-garde has worked with an expanded idea of music since the early part of the twentieth century, blurring the boundary between music and not-music.[30] This novel reconceptualization of music embraced noise and environmental sound; its inclusive notion of music and composition has exerted an influence on the holistic concept of current film sound design.[31] In fact, avant-garde ideas of music are so expansive that they might conceivably include even the visuals of film itself.[32] The avant-garde impulse to expand musical vocabulary to include what habitually were classified as "nonmusical" sounds has likely had a strong but unregistered impact on film soundtracks. A notable example is *musique concrète*, which developed around composer Pierre Schaeffer in Paris after World War

[27] "Sounds of Sci-Fi II," 64.

[28] "Sounds of Sci-Fi II," 62.

[29] "Sounds of Sci-Fi II," 65.

[30] David Toop, *Ocean of Sound: Aether Talk, Ambient Sound and Imaginary Worlds* (London: Serpent's Tail, 2001), 78.

[31] As Randolph Jordan notes of Hildegard Westerkamp's avant-garde musical pieces that were used in *Elephant* (2003), "One could easily go through the entirety of the film and believe that the sounds of Westerkamp"s work were actually elements created by sound designer Leslie Shatz, or perhaps even recorded on location." "The Work of Hildegard Westerkamp in the Films of Gus Van Sant," *Offscreen* 11, nos. 8–9 (August/September 2007), 4, at www.offscreen.com/Sound_Issue/jordan_westerkamp.pdf (accessed June 22, 2010).

[32] An example of the dissolution of the border between film and music is musician DJ Spooky's 2004 "Re-Birth of a Nation," a "remix" of D. W. Griffith's *Birth of a Nation* (1915), which not only adds voice-over commentary and music but also adds graphics to the screen and recuts the film. Originally a live multi-screen event, it was later made available as a DVD.

II and processed library and field recordings into a form of abstract music. The practice was premised on manipulation of sound recordings on magnetic tape (changing speeds, running backward, and using electronic filters and effects). The music created in this manner owed less to traditions of art music than to sound assemblages that were taking place in filmmaking.

Brian Williams, a musician and sonic artist whose career has involved working across audiovisual art and mainstream media, released discs under the name Lustmord. One of his early releases, *Paradise Disowned* (1984), included field recordings and musical performances in strange spaces, such as a nuclear bunker, a slaughterhouse, and Chartres Cathedral. He worked with the experimental rock group SPK, but continued releasing his own work as well. *The Monstrous Soul* (1992) includes very prominent samples from the British horror film *The Night of the Demon* (1957) (known as *Curse of the Demon* in the United States), whereas *The Place Where the Black Stars Hang* (1994) has a first track built on the almost continuous synthetic sounds of a massive propeller swooping around, toward, and then away from the listener. The implication of not traditionally "musical" and more clearly visual aspects is unmistakable. He has tended to use first analog treatments, such as echo and reverb, and later digital sound treatment of field recordings, allied to often minimal atmospheric electronics and threatening sub-bass rumbles. Though some people have classified these recordings as "dark ambient" music, their sound-worlds owe a great deal to the kinds of ambient atmosphere evident in some horror films. Indeed, the product of the collaboration between Williams and electronic musician Robert Rich, *Stalker* (1995), was inspired directly by Tarkovsky's atmospheric and enigmatic film of the same name. Like Eno's *On Land*, this music aims to build a sense of a sonic landscape, or "soundscape." More recent albums, such as *[O T H E R]* (2008), continue to rely on large-scale electronic echo and reverb and sounds such as clanking metal bars, as well as more conventional pitched instruments. It was no surprise when Williams transported his penchant for such "atmospheres" into films, although instead of providing scores for films in the traditional sense, he has collaborated with his former colleague from SPK, Graeme Revell, and later with Paul Haslinger. Williams has been billed as a "musical sound designer" on over forty films, including *The Crow* (1994), *Streetfighter* (1994), *Strange Days* (1995), *Mighty Morphin Power Rangers* (1995), *From Dusk Till Dawn* (1996), *Spawn* (1997), *The Saint* (1997), *Bride of Chucky* (1998), *Pitch Black* (2000), *Underworld* (2003), *Touristas* (2006), and *Underworld: Rise of the Lycans* (2008).[33] He has been responsible for providing certain sounds (field recordings, treatments, samples) and ambiences that can be inserted directly into the film or manipulated by a collaborating composer as part of the score. Williams's position, despite the word "music" in his job title, is good evidence of the degree of intermixing of musical and field recording components that now prevails in many films, giving a strong sense of unified sound design.

33 Indeed, it is not uncommon to have dedicated sonic atmosphere providers, such as Mel Wesson's credit for "ambient music design" for *The Da Vinci Code* (2006).

In addition to providing sometimes quite conventional incidental music for television drama (Fox's *The Chamber* [2001] and SciFi Channel's *Proof Positive* [2004]), Williams has composed music for the video games *Master of Orion 3* (2001), *Cashflow 101* (2001), and *Cashflow 202* (2002). His career arc has stretched from sound art into films (and also into television and video games), although his early (non-audiovisual) output already resembled the music heard in horror film soundtracks. His musical career illustrates the crossover, while also indicating how far various media exploit music that incorporates a high degree of "nonmusical" sounds. Indeed, one might argue that Williams's case is far from exceptional: that horror film music and sound design have influenced the sound of video games, which in turn has fed back into horror films. Christophe Gans's film version of the video game franchise *Silent Hill*, released in 2006, appears to be a unique case, however. The film's sound is based on the existing sound-world of the game: Akira Yamaoka's highly effective and memorable video game music was used as a skeleton around which to build the film. The game's sound-world did not have to undergo many changes to make it to the film soundtrack; indeed, the lack of development between the media illustrates the extent of the sonic overlap. Video games like *World of Warcraft* (with music by Jason Hayes) and Nobuo Uematsu's music for the *Final Fantasy* series of games, for example, owe much to other music, particularly film music.[34] The dynamic sense of emotional content in orchestral film music has carried over as a desirable aspect in games, which share with film as many aural aspects as they do visual ones. As might be expected, video games that emanate from film franchises by and large contain scores that are derived from film score models.[35] Good examples are Clint Bakajanian's score for the *Star Wars Jedi Knight* series, Matt Griskey's for *Star Wars Episode 3: Revenge of the Sith* and *Harry Potter and the Goblet of Fire*, and Jamie Christopher's for *Lord of the Rings: The Battle for Middle Earth*. Established film music composers also have written for video games, such as Harry Gregson-Williams, who composed the music for the *Metal Gear Solid* series; Michael Giacchino wrote music for the *Medal of Honor* video game series before going on to write incidental music for television, such as the serial *Lost* (2004–2010, Bad Robot-ABC), and then for film, including *Star Trek* (2009) and *Let Me In* (2010). These examples demonstrate how easily music emanating from the film score aesthetic can adapt to other media, emphasizing the common core of much audiovisual culture rather than obvious differences and pointing to film aesthetics as the main unifying aspect.

Clearly, apart from technology, a central determinant has been the personnel involved and their ability to work across media. This encourages markedly similar approaches

34 Rod Munday argues that since the advent of CD-quality sound for video games there is no such thing as specific "video game music," as it is derived from other existing genres of music. "Music in Video Games," in *Music, Sound and Multimedia: From the Live to the Virtual*, ed. Jamie Sexton (Edinburgh: Edinburgh University Press, 2007), 51.

35 Karen Collins notes that it is wrong to simply evaluate video game music by film music standards and concepts, although there are points of significant connection. *Game Sound: An Introduction to the History, Theory, and Practice of Video Game Music and Sound Design* (Cambridge, Mass.: MIT Press, 2008), 5.

to different activities, illustrating the strength of certain types of music to determine something essential about character regardless of the media format.[36] In recent years the sounds and emotional functions of film have proven a most significant inspiration, underlining its position as the epicenter of audiovisual culture. Music for films and instrumental music not intended for films are becoming increasingly similar. Music that bears the influence of films and their soundtracks has been used in films and television programs. This marks a return in aesthetic terms and guarantees the directness of influence and connection. It also reveals the proximity of audiovisual media and how far the blueprint of film soundtracks has had a tangible effect on their near neighbors. Although the film and music industries have always been closely related, the proximity of film and musical aesthetics discussed here is part of a larger process leading to fading boundaries between film, music, and other culture.

Conclusion

Film soundtracks' influence outside the cinema vividly illustrates the importance that film retains as an aesthetic. Technology has engendered an expanded spatial sonic arena, wherein sonic elements (sound effects, music) have mixed into a sensual and psychological field. This development has led to varying degrees of autonomy for the soundtrack; rather than simply supporting the image track of film, it is able to imply and invoke images itself. This in turn has had a marked influence on—or engaged with—an already existing area of music that manifests audiovisual landscapes through sound only. "Soundtrack albums" of music had already extended the reach of individual films beyond their physical bounds and screen time. By the 1980s and the saturation of industrial "synergy,"[37] soundtrack albums were propagating as a parallel with their associated films, culminating in albums declaring that they were "Music Inspired by the Film," though in some cases having no discernible connection to their nominal parent. Over the years a small but insistent area of musical culture emerged, either structured or inspired by the recordings and culture of film soundtracks, with practitioners exploiting aesthetics and compositional procedures derived from film, integrating traditional musical forces with sounds not previously considered musical. In recent years the development of converging digital sound technology has allowed sound designers to use musical software to enhance sound effects in films and enabled music composers to produce their own music through the incorporation of sound effects. Such developments, in line with wider technological and aesthetic convergence and harmonizing platforms

[36] In concert hall music, "program music" usually aspires to depict or alludes to something outside the music and arguably affects a synesthetic character.

[37] R. Serge Denisoff and George Plasketes, "Synergy in 1980s Film and Music: Formula for Success or Industry Mythology?" *Film History* 4, no. 3 (1990): 257.

and industries, mean that music no longer is simply a "bolt-on" to films, but rather something more akin to a genetic integration. Technology and personnel, as well as aesthetic traditions, have instigated unified sound design. More than ever before, music makers are aware of and exploiting what traditionally were thought of as "non-musical" sounds, while film sound technicians increasingly approach soundtracks in a manner that might be termed "musical," or at least one that acknowledges the malleability of organized recorded sound rather than aspiring to notions such as fidelity to an original as a duplicate.

Chion notes that the superfield produces an extension of offscreen space, establishing a "quasi-autonomous existence" in relation to film visuals.[38] Significantly, this also marks an extension of the imagination, where sounds invoke images in relation to the film diegesis. When the images are fully absent, similar sonic and musical approaches nevertheless invoke images. While avant-garde ideas of music might be so inclusive as to embrace visuals as an integral part, this notion increasingly has become more widespread. There is a reciprocal "musical" character to sound design in many films. Here, sound effects, ambience, and even dialogue have more of an "aesthetic" character rather than only a representational value. Does this evolution signal the end of traditional film aesthetics, or a new dawn? Whatever it may be, it heralds the migration of traditional film dynamics and conception into other areas of culture. This augurs a new psychological involvement, an embodied aesthetic psychological state in films and elsewhere, enabled by the sensual aspects of sound and the emotional elevation and directness of music.

References

Anonymous. "Sounds of Sci-Fi II." *Computer Music* 151 (May 2010): 61–67.

Beck, Jay. "The Sounds of Silence." In *Lowering the Boom: Critical Studies in Film Sound*, edited by Jay Beck and Tony Grajeda, 68–83. Chicago: University of Illinois Press, 2008.

Burch, Noel. *Theory of Film Practice*. Princeton, N.J.: Princeton University Press, 1981.

Chion, Michel. *Audio-Vision: Sound on Screen*. Translated by Claudia Gorbman. New York: Columbia University Press, 1994.

Collins, Karen. *Game Sound: An Introduction to the History, Theory, and Practice of Video Game Music and Sound Design*. Cambridge, Mass.: MIT Press, 2008.

Cook, Nicholas, and Anthony Pople, eds. *The Cambridge History of Twentieth-Century Music*. Cambridge: Cambridge University Press, 2004.

Denisoff, R. Serge, and George Plasketes. "Synergy in 1980s Film and Music: Formula for Success or Industry Mythology?" *Film History* 4, no. 3 (1990): 257–276.

Eno, Brian. Cover notes to *Ambient 4: On Land*. EG 2311107. EG Records, 1982.

Jordan, Randolph. "The Work of Hildegard Westerkamp in the Films of Gus Van Sant." *Offscreen* 11, nos. 8–9 (August/September 2007): 4, at www.offscreen.com/Sound_Issue/jordan_westerkamp.pdf (accessed June 22, 2010).

[38] Chion, *Audio-Vision*, 150.

Lastra, James. "Film and the Wagnerian Aspiration: Thoughts on Sound Design and History of the Senses." In *Lowering the Boom: Critical Studies in Film Sound*, edited by Jay Beck and Tony Grajeda, 123–138. Chicago: University of Illinois Press, 2008.

Lewin, Kurt. *Resolving Social Conflicts and Field Theory in Social Science*. Washington, D.C.: American Psychological Association, 1997.

Manovich, Lev. *The Language of New Media*. Cambridge, Mass.: MIT Press, 2001.

Mera, Miguel, and David Burnand, eds. *European Film Music*. Aldershot, UK: Ashgate, 2006.

Mulholland, Drew, Hayden Lorimer, and Chris Philo. "Resounding: An Interview with Drew Mulholland." *Scottish Geographical Journal* 125, nos. 3–4 (September–December 2009): 379–400.

Munday, Rod. "Music in Video Games." In *Music, Sound and Multimedia: From the Live to the Virtual*, edited by Jamie Sexton, 51–67. Edinburgh: Edinburgh University Press, 2007.

Niebur, Louis. "The Music of Machines: 'Special Sound' as the Music of *Doctor Who*." In *Time and Relative Dissertations in Space: Critical Perspectives on* Doctor Who, edited by David Butler, 204–214. Manchester, UK: Manchester University Press, 2007.

Norfolk, Lawrence. Sleeve notes to Mount Vernon Arts Lab, *The Séance at Hobs Lane*. GBX009. Ghost Box, 2007.

Pilkington, Mark. "Mount Vernon Arts Lab: True Sounds of the Underground." *Fortean Times* [2001], repr. June 2007, at http://www.forteantimes.com/features/interviews/483/mount_vernon_arts_lab.html (accessed December 13, 2010).

Prendergast, Mark. *The Ambient Century: From Mahler to Moby*. London: Bloomsbury, 2001.

Sergi, Gianluca. *The Dolby Era: Film Sound in Contemporary Hollywood*. Manchester, UK: Manchester University Press, 2004.

Toop, David. *Ocean of Sound: Aether Talk, Ambient Sound and Imaginary Worlds*. London: Serpent's Tail, 2001.

CHAPTER 22

THE AUDIOVISUAL CONSTRUCTION OF TRANSGENDER IDENTITY IN *TRANSAMERICA*

SUSANNA VÄLIMÄKI

THE film *Transamerica* (dir. Duncan Tucker, 2005) begins with a medium close-up of a woman beginning a descending vocal slide. The voice starts out in a speech register typical of women, and the listener easily connects the voice with the woman in the scene, whose long hair, skillfully applied makeup, and sleeveless top all signify conventional femininity. But after about 10 seconds, the voice segues seamlessly into a register that is no longer easily heard as feminine, and soon it is difficult to interpret it even as the masculine voice of an extremely butch woman or that of a subcontralto. Rather, it resembles a man's baritone. The effect is transgressive when all these registers are produced by one person in the course of a single vocal articulation lasting approximately 15 seconds. The voice crosses genders in a single breath and phrase. It is a trans-voice, demonstrating how fluid voice and gender truly are. It jettisons the normative system of two genders and elegantly opens up a space for gender diversity and transgender subjectivity, which is what the film *Transamerica* is all about.

After the portamento shot the opening credits begin, and simultaneously we hear the same woman giving vocal instructions in a clear feminine voice, including the repeated phrase, "This is the voice I want to use." We are seeing and hearing a voice-training video that the film's protagonist, a male-to-female transgender woman (Felicity Huffman), watches at home while following its exercises as part of her morning routine.[1]

[1] The video is *Finding Your Female Voice* (Deep Stealth Productions, 2003–2005), made by Andrea James, who also is the voice coach seen in the video.

The search for a voice of one's own is the main theme of the film, both literally and metaphorically: the quest for a voice becomes a symbol for the transgender protagonist's journey of self-discovery, self-acceptance, and self-respect. The voice-training scene at the very beginning of the film functions as an allegory for the story that follows. At the same time, the scene emphasizes the significance of the auditory sphere to issues of identity and gender.

The production of meanings in *Transamerica*'s auditory dimension—musical, sonic, and vocal—is precisely the central focus of this chapter. In this analysis I discuss the audiovisual negotiation of gender variance in the film from the perspective of transgender studies in an effort to listen to the film in a transgender-conscious and -empathetic way.

Transgender studies take a critical view of the binary gender system, which is masked as the "natural" order of things in heteronormative culture. A transgender person,[2] solely by dint of her/his/hir existence, challenges gender normativity by exposing gender as being at odds with sex as it is traditionally defined. A form of Butlerian "gender trouble,"[3] appearances of the transgendered occasion a "split" between sex and gender (as conventionally understood), thereby revealing the crucial constructedness of all sex and gender.[4] The phenomenon of transgender demonstrates that "the sex of the body [i.e., the anatomy] does not bear any *necessary* or *deterministic* relationship to the social category in which that body lives."[5] Furthermore, there is no unambiguous way to classify people into one of two sexes or genders, for there will always be those whose bodies and identities are more complex or different and who do not fit into the rigid categories of the bigender system. The phenomenon of transgender challenges—and deconstructs—the conceptual oppositions of sex/gender, male/female, man/woman, masculine/feminine, straight/gay, and normal/abnormal. Indeed, transgender studies not only teach us about gender minorities, they also teach us about our gender norms in general.[6] Gender is historical and contingent: how many genders there are and how they are defined vary from culture to culture.[7]

Films are among the most powerful social technologies for creating, sustaining, shaping, and renegotiating conceptions of gender.[8] *Transamerica* is one of the

[2] *Transgender* is here understood as an umbrella term for individuals who are gender-variant in some way, who experience a disconnection between body, internal body image, gender identity, gender expression, or gender roles that puts them outside the normative sex/gender relations and the binary gender system. Lori B. Girshick, *Transgender Voices: Beyond Women and Men* (Hanover: University Press of New England, 2008), 2, 14–15. The term includes transsexuals, transgender/ists, cross-dressers, genderqueer, bigendered, ungendered, androgynous, and two-spirit people; butch (masculine) women; and intersex individuals, among others.

[3] Cf. Judith Butler, *Gender Trouble: Feminism and the Subversion of Identity* (New York: Routledge, 1990).

[4] Judith Halberstam, *In a Queer Time and Place: Transgender Bodies, Subcultural Lives* (New York: New York University Press, 2005), 50, 55.

[5] Susan Stryker, *Transgender History* (Berkeley, Calif.: Seal Press, 2008), 11.

[6] Susan Stryker, "(De)Subjugated Knowledges: An Introduction to Transgender Studies," in *The Transgender Studies Reader*, ed. Susan Stryker and Stephen Whittle (New York: Routledge, 2006), 3–13.

[7] Stryker, *Transgender History*, 11.

[8] Cf. Teresa de Lauretis, *Technologies of Gender: Essays on Theory, Film, and Fiction* (Bloomington: Indiana University Press, 1987).

most noteworthy of a handful of recent mainstream films in which a transgender person as the main character is portrayed in a serious and transempathetic way in a story revolving around transgender issues.[9] Because it is a critically and commercially successful film, *Transamerica* signals a shift in mainstream audiovisual representations toward more visible and realistic depictions of transgender people and thus toward more complex negotiations of gender.

Transgendering a Road Movie

Transamerica depicts a middle-aged, male-to-female[10] transsexual called Bree. Single, white, educated, and working class, her outlook and behavior are somewhat detached and conservative. Bree washes dishes in a Mexican restaurant while also working as a telemarketer. She lives alone in a small apartment in a Hispanic suburb of Los Angeles. Aside from her coworkers and therapist, she does not seem to have any close friends or family with whom to share her life.

Bree has lived as a woman for a number of years; she takes hormones and has gone through a great number of other gender-confirmation body modifications and treatments, with the single exception of genital reconstruction. She has eagerly awaited this operation, which is scheduled to take place in a week's time and will finally complete her transition.[11]

Only a week before her surgery, Bree discovers that she has a teenage son about whom she knew nothing. At first she does not want to meet the boy, because she feels that her son belongs to her former life as a man, a life she wants to leave behind, especially now that she is scheduled to have the long-awaited operation that will complete her transition. However, under pressure from her therapist (Elizabeth Peña), Bree agrees to meet the boy, and the film concerns their evolving relationship.

Bree's son, Toby (Kevin Zegers), is a 17-year-old street hustler and small-time drug user, who dreams about a career in the gay porn movie industry in Hollywood. He also

[9] Other examples are *Different for Girls* (dir. Richard Spence, 1996), *My Life in Pink* (dir. Alain Berliner, 1997), *Boys Don't Cry* (dir. Kimberly Peirce, 1999), *Another Woman* (dir. Jérôme Foulon, 2002), *Beautiful Boxer* (dir. Ekachai Uekrongtham, 2003), *Normal* (dir. Jane Anderson, 2003), *Soldier's Girl* (dir. Frank R. Pierson, 2003), *Breakfast on Pluto* (dir. Neil Jordan, 2005), and *XXY* (dir. Lucía Puenzo, 2007).

[10] *Male-to-female* (MTF, transwoman) and *female-to-male* (FTM, transman) indicate the direction of gender crossing of a transsexual or transgender individual: a woman assigned as male at birth or a man assigned as female at birth.

[11] The transsexual individual feels that she/he/ze is differently gendered from her/his/hir birth-assigned sex and usually takes steps to alter her/his/hir physical body to varying degrees (by hormones, surgery, and other medical and cosmetic procedures) as well as her/his/hir social presentation (gender role, gender expression, name, legal recognition), in order to feel greater psychological harmony. This process is called *transition*. See, for example, Girshick, *Transgender Voices*, 16, 206.

dreams of meeting his (biological) father, whom he imagines to be a rich and powerful man. Bree visits Toby in a juvenile prison in New York and bails him out. She does not reveal that she is his father (and transwoman). Instead, she pretends to be a volunteer church worker.

Together, Bree and Toby drive across America from New York to Los Angeles, from the East to West Coasts. The protagonist's travel is both literal and metaphorical, geographical and spiritual. What is exceptional about the film is that the inner journey is one of transgenderness: *Transamerica* can be interpreted as a queering—or more precisely, a *transgendering*—of the standard road movie format. Here I emphasize my concentration on non-normative *genders* (and not sexualities) by using the notion of "transgender" as an equivalent analytical term instead of or in parallel to "queer."[12]

This transgendering (queering) draws on the rhetoric of transgender inversion: the film offers viewers a traditional, tried and trusted narrative formula—the road movie—but in place of a gender normative protagonist, we are given a transgendered one. By placing the marginal in the center in this way, the transgender narrative strategy destabilizes the hegemony of gender normativity. It also allows the artificiality of gendered signs masked as "natural" in cultural mainstream practices to become visible, thereby eroding the supposed "natural difference" between "normal" and "abnormal."

Crucial to the aesthetic working of the film is how transgendering draws on the rhetoric of transgender appropriation: the classic road movie structure is adopted as the means for depicting the culmination of the protagonist's gender transition, a transgender person's "coming home" to her/his/hir true self (and new, true body). This is a powerful narrative strategy, because the journey trope—"departure, transition, and the home of reassignment"—is common in transsexual autobiographies and other discourses of transsexuality.[13] In *Transamerica* Bree has already undertaken a long journey—from being a male-bodied woman, living first a man's and then a woman's life, to being a female-bodied woman living a woman's life. In the film she is just about to end this transitional journey, which also includes accepting her parenthood and coming out to her son as his father and a transgender person.

Likewise, the film's music—most of which is archetypal "road music" mixed with travel montages in conventional ways—is appropriated to construct transgender meanings and subjectivity: an auditory version of the transsexual journey trope of traveling and border crossings.

The film is rich in both original music, composed by David Mansfield (with the exception of the title song, written by Dolly Parton), and preexisting music compiled from various sources. The assembly of music from numerous sources is used both diegetically

[12] In this sense, as a theoretical and analytical term, the notion of transgender can be used as an adjective, noun, or verb, that focuses on the demystification of (supposedly) stable sexes and genders, exposing the incoherencies and mismatches between these categories and thus demonstrating the impossibility of any "natural" sex or gender or any "natural" logic of identity politics.

[13] Jay Prosser, *Second Skins: The Body Narratives of Transsexuality* (New York: Columbia University Press, 1998), 82–83, 101, 116–117, 184.

and nondiegetically, but this distinction, as well as the distinction between the original and the assembled music, is not important from the point of view of how it works for cinematic poetics; whether diegetic or nondiegetic, the basic function of the music in this film is to communicate and construct transgender subjectivity.

In the following sections I outline and discuss in more detail these musical transgender (queer) strategies in *Transamerica*: (1) the use of American, country-based roots music to symbolize an identity in transition; (2) the use of music encoded in terms of ethnic or "racial" identity to highlight transgender people's social status and to create a potentially progressive social space of intersectionality and multiculturality; and (3) the play on the human voice.

Music of Quest, Soul-Searching, and Transition

The most important styles of music in the film for constructing transgender subjectivity are American country, bluegrass, folk, and gospel music. These indigenous styles inflect in various ways themes of travel, questing, soul-searching, and transformation, and the idea of redemption from a present burden. This music is heard during Bree's and Toby's cross-country journey. It plays on the car radio, jukeboxes, and radios in roadside bars, and it is also interwoven nondiegetically with images of driving, empty roadways, vast landscapes, and shabby roadside bars and motels. Examples are "I Am a Pilgrim" ("and a stranger / Travelin' through here…"), sung by Duncan Sheik; an old African American spiritual, "Lay My Burden Down," sung by Larry Sparks; a southern gospel song, "I Find Jesus" ("in the darkest night"), performed by the Nitty Gritty Dirt Band, and an old religious banjo song, "Take 'em Away," performed by the Old Crow Medicine Show.

In its unconventional narrative context this rootsy and spiritual "road music" becomes transgendered. The music of travel, questing, and soul-searching constructs transgenderness as subjectivity in transition, an inner journey in the process of transformation. Often the music includes Christian imagery, as in "Take 'em Away":

> Take 'em away, take 'em away, Lord.
> Take away these chains from me.
> My heart is broken cos my spirit's not free.
> Lord, take away these chains from me.[14]

This chorus fittingly applies to the transexperience, to the sense of being trapped in the wrong body, which forms a central topos in the narratives of transsexuality.[15] Heard

[14] The song was written by Christopher Day Fuqua.

[15] Prosser, *Second Skins*, 67–69.

from this perspective, the "chains" in the song are those of the "wrong" body or the "wrong" gender assigned at birth or interpreted by others in a gender-normative society. The "spirit" is the self one truly is. In this way supposedly "gender-straight" country music becomes transgendered in the film. The music is resignified with reference to the experiences, histories, feelings, bodies, lives, and realities of transgender people.

Any kind of music might be transgendered in this way, depending on whose voice we are listening for. For example, such popular songs as "A Boy Named Sue" by Johnny Cash or "If I Were a Boy" by Beyoncé certainly construct different meanings around a transperson than a non-transperson. Yet country music is especially open to transgender readings because of its direct emotionality; its celebration of the real stories of ordinary, often somehow disenfranchised people; and its central themes of loss, sorrow, searching, and transformation. The film's strategy of transgender appropriation of country music can be considered structurally similar to how the LGBTIQ (lesbian, gay, bisexual, transgender, intersex, and queer) communities appropriate country music—and popular culture in general: the communities make country music their own by resignifying it from the point of view of queer life and experiences and by redefining its meanings for purposes of their own.

One example of the film's transgender appropriation of country music and its construction of an acoustic space for transgender subjectivity is when Bree is shown in the hospital, heading for the operation that will end her transition and complete her arrival "home" in her body. Simultaneously, we hear Lucinda Williams tenderly singing "Like a Rose," which contains phrases that sound like Bree's inner voice calming herself in a nurturing acoustic envelope of music:

> It's okay, you don't have to be afraid.
> There's nothing to worry about....
>
> It's all right here, it's safe and warm.
> It's okay to feel good;
> That's the way it should be.

The music of a quest, of soul-searching and transformation, also conveys the theme of outsiderness, common in archetypal cowboy mythology, country music, and transgender life. "Gender outlaws"[16] are often relegated to the frontiers of society, "lonesome cowboys far from home." Director Duncan Tucker has also mentioned the theme of the outsider in discussing the film's music, pointing to the "outlaw" and the "alternative" nature of the many bluegrass, folk, and country musicians heard in the film.[17]

All of these points apply not only to the country music compiled for the film, but also to Mansfield's rootsy original music, which conveys a sense of travel and soul-searching.

[16] Cf. Kate Bornstein, *Gender Outlaw: On Men, Women, and the Rest of Us* (New York: Routledge, 1994).

[17] See Craig Shelburne, "Gender Identity and Country Music Merge in *Transamerica*," *CMT News*, March 3, 2006, at http://www.cmt.com/news/articles/1525363/20060303/parton_dolly.jhtml?headlines=true (accessed February 9, 2010).

The original music includes acoustic guitar–based country music with bluegrass, folk, and gospel elements. The timbre of different kinds of guitars together with mandolin, banjo, and violin dominates the foreground, and the easy, flowing sound often has a plaintive, reflective feeling, a mixture of hopefulness and melancholy, drive and restraint, strength and fragility, on certain occasions echoing the compiled songs heard in the film.

Diversity of Identities

The music in *Transamerica* helps render the setting American and, most important, also emphasizes the characters as American. The Americana music implies that a transgender woman and a teenage male prostitute who wants to break into the gay porn industry are "just two more Americans."[18] The title of the film suggests that it is an American thing to be "trans." The music indicates that these characters are not freaks or abnormal or people to be shocked about; they are simply Americans, even archetypal Americans, because they are on the road, driving from New York through Virginia, Kentucky, Arkansas, Texas, New Mexico, Arizona, and on to California.

Indeed, a range of American music is heard in the film: mountain music, old-time music, jug band music, bluegrass, yodeling, gospel, Texas cowboy music, Nashville pop, Native American, and Mexican music. This diversity of American musical traditions ("musical roots") signifies the richness of identities in America, and the film's strategy of deploying them on the sound track is a political choice, to fuse the richness of musical identities with the richness of gender identities.

Gender variance is particularly celebrated in a scene depicting a transgender gathering at the Texas home of Mary Ellen (Bianca Leigh), to which Bree and Toby have come to sleep one night. Country music plays in the background. At one point Mary Ellen sings "Home on the Range" ("Oh, give me a home"), and the group of transpeople sing along with the refrain. The patriotic song, which during the nineteenth century was adapted by settlers and cowboys across the United States in various forms, praises the American West and celebrates the idea of an idyllic home ("where seldom is heard a discouraging word / And the skies are not cloudy all day"). In this scene the song is adopted as a kind of anthem of transgender pride, performed with camp affection, as wholehearted as it is ironic. The home in the song can be heard as representing a transsexual person's sense of, or wish for, "homecoming" to her/his/hir true body: the right for a happy ending after years spent in itinerant gender transition and the right to define one's own gender identity and "settle in a home" as one is. The special power of the scene is derived

[18] This has also been emphasized by Tucker. See Shelburne, "Gender Identity and Country Music Merge in *Transamerica*."

from the fact that all but one of the actors playing the party participants are themselves transgendered; there is real and intense transpresence in the scene.[19]

A diversity of identities is portrayed also in a ranch scene, the home of Calvin Many Goats (Graham Greene), a Native American man whom Bree has met at a roadside bar and for whom she seems to be developing feelings. One night, sitting outside on the porch, Calvin sings "Beautiful Dreamer" to Bree—a Native American cowboy-farmer singing a well-known sentimental serenade to a white transwoman. Intense dreaming (of another life) is a central aspect of translife, especially during pretransition or preoperative life. The scene constructs an acoustic space—beautiful and dreamy—for transgenderness. This sense of transgender utopia is accentuated by the fact that many Native American cultures have three or four social genders in which "two-spirit" people blend the feminine and masculine.[20] When on the next day Calvin drives Bree and Toby to Phoenix, we hear Joanne Shenandoah—an Iroquois musician—singing "I May Want a Man" in Iroquois, as if continuing the theme of Bree's transgender utopia. Furthermore, the oppressed and disenfranchised position of Native Americans in the United States throughout its history could be thought of as mirroring the plight and life experiences of transgender people.

Marginal Whiteness

"Race" and ethnicity are important themes in the film's music. In addition to the predominantly "white" country music and the Native American music mentioned previously, Latin music plays a significant role. An early scene shows Bree at work cleaning dishes in a Mexican restaurant and now and then swaying her hips to the sounds of guitar, maracas, and trumpet in the tango "Maldito Cabaret" by Los Pamperos. At the end of the film we see Bree back at work after the operation, waitressing in a Mexican dress. It is Christmas, and a multilingual and cross-cultural "Tex-Mex" version of "Silent Night" by Tish Hinojosa (a Texan folksinger of Mexican ancestry) is heard.

As Sean Brayton notes, Bree works in the type of bottom-rung job that is racialized in the United States as "Mexican" and that often passes unacknowledged in white bourgeois culture, just as its workers do.[21] Latin music affirms the Hispanic setting of Bree's life, but it also draws parallels between racism and transphobia. This is especially clear in the scene in which Bree and Toby are hitchhiking after being robbed in the New Mexico desert. They succeed in getting a ride on the back of a pickup truck with some poor

19 This is pointed out by Tucker in the director's commentary on the DVD release of the film.

20 Stryker, *Transgender History*, 11; see also Sue-Ellen Jacobs, Wesley Thomas, and Sabine Lang, eds., *Two-Spirit People: Native American Gender Identity, Sexuality, and Spirituality* (Urbana: University of Illinois Press, 1997).

21 Sean Brayton, "'Mexican' Labor in the Hollywood Imaginary," *International Journal of Cultural Studies* 11 (2008): 459.

Mexican farmworkers. Simultaneously, we hear the melodramatic "Soy Infeliz" ("I Am Unfortunate"), sung by the famous Mexican ranchera singer Lola Beltrán. By this congruence of visual and sonic images, the gendered other and outsider (Bree) is compared to racial others and outsiders. The images suggest that the problems transgender people face in the world are structurally parallel to problems of racism, poverty, and other systemic injustices.

The racializing of Bree's space, work, and life reflects her position on the margins of society and also on the margins of white culture. The use of Latin music aligns Bree's identity with marginal whiteness, deviance, and social displacement. As Brayton points out, as a dishwasher or a waitress in a Mexican restaurant, Bree not only does the work of the ethnic other, but she is even employed by the ethnic other. She is also learning Spanish. In this way the film deconstructs the normativity of whiteness; it destabilizes the hegemonic forms of white culture and offers a critique of white middle-class bourgeois—and gender-normative—culture. As Brayton notes, it "allows the film to re-articulate whiteness within a nuanced multicultural framework" and creates a potentially progressive space for intersectionality by "translating ethnic and gender difference into the shared idiom of class."[22] It is precisely Hispanics as well as Native American people, not white people, who accept Bree as she is. The white people in the film are often more prejudiced and untrustworthy. This is highlighted in the scene at Bree's old childhood home.

Bree and Toby visit Bree's weird (white) parents in their luxury house in Phoenix, Arizona. Bree's mother (Fionnula Flanagan) is a self-centered, oddly behaving woman who neither accepts, acknowledges, nor even recognizes Bree's womanhood or transgenderness, but she is ecstatic about discovering she has a grandson, a "normal" boy to foster. Compared to her outrageous mother and her sympathetic ex-alcoholic sister (Carrie Preston), who lives with her parents, Bree seems to be the most normal and balanced woman in the family. The only music heard in the scenes portraying bourgeois whiteness is empty, nondescript cocktail music played in the restaurant where the (un-) united family has a catastrophic dinner. The music seems to reflect the unsubstantial, even nonexistent, nature of the support Bree receives from her childhood family and the hollowness of the lives of white, upper-middle-class families.

Travelin' Thru

By the end of the film Bree has had her operation. She has also received a promotion in her restaurant job, from dishwasher to waitress: she has transitioned from the kitchen to the dining room, a change that symbolizes her greater sense of confidence, safety, and connectedness with people and social situations. Toby has landed a part in a gay porn

22 Brayton, "'Mexican' Labor in the Hollywood Imaginary," 468–470.

film. But Bree and Toby have not seen each other since Bree revealed that she is in fact Toby's father. Bree has deeply missed her son and suffered from their parting.

Then we see Bree at home, and Toby comes to visit her for the first time since learning the truth. The scene suggests that Toby has come to terms with the fact that Bree is his father (or mother; Bree uses both words in the film). Both Bree and Toby have undertaken huge journeys to arrive at this moment in their relationship and to make it work by accepting themselves and one another. At the precise moment when the audience is made aware of this acceptance and the journeys behind it, the music begins. Dolly Parton hums, with some drumming and guitar picking. The image fades, and the closing credits start to roll just as the song lyrics begin. The song is called "Travelin' Thru," and Parton created it specifically for the film. It begins:

> Well I can't tell you where I'm goin', I'm not sure of where I've been.
> But I know I must keep travelin' till my road comes to an end.
> I'm out here on my journey, tryin' to make the most of it.
> I'm a puzzle, I must figure out where all my pieces fit.

Once again the film uses the familiar country music imagery of traveling, soul-searching, and redemption to portray Bree's journey.[23] The arrangement is simple, so that the voice—as carrier of the story and subjectivity—is very much front and center. The music has a lively beat and uplifting mood; it conveys a sense of coming home or feeling at home, of self-acceptance despite the aches and pains of life. Indeed, it is an empowering and comforting piece of music that may give strength to anyone who has been through hard times.

The song rounds up the themes in the film: a journey toward a more whole self, crossing borders, being in a state of transition and coming home, growing and healing, finding a place in the world somehow. It also further creates an acoustic, symbolic space for transgender subjectivity—a space that continues to flow after the story is over, because the song is heard over the closing credits: an inspirational transgender vision (of a progressive future). At the end of the film the song beautifully emphasizes with unusual eloquence and beauty the rightness and happiness of transsexual or transgender transitions and life. That is certainly remarkable in the history of cinematic transgender representations: a happy ending for a transgender character. The musical transgender utopia—the space of possibility—created during the meditative ritual of the closing credits prolongs the film's gender-political message beyond its story.[24]

[23] The music here and elsewhere can also be heard as portraying Toby's journey, hard times, overcoming of traumas, and search for a better life and home.

[24] I am here indebted to Michel Chion's discussion of the ritualistic and "religious" nature of the modern film's closing credits. Chion, *Film, a Sound Art*, trans. Claudia Gorbman (New York: Columbia University Press, 2009), 158–160. Musical spaces for transgender subjectivity can be heard in the closing credits of other mainstream films featuring transgender characters: queer country icon k. d. lang sings Irving Berlin's "Always" in *Normal*, and Lyle Lovett sings Tammy Wynette's country (queer) standard "Stand by Your Man" in the *Crying Game* (dir. Neil Jordan, 1992), followed by the film's title song, sung by gay celebrity and gender-blender Boy George.

Significant transgender political power here is gained from the fact that Dolly Parton is a trans icon (just as she is a gay icon). Her ultrafeminine style reminds us what hard work—and joy—it is to construct femininity and of the right to define oneself and freely express one's gender. In queer culture, the pop diva occupies an important consoling and empowering position. The queer fan identifies both with the power (the musical virtuosity) and the vulnerability (the personal life) of the diva. As a source of cathartic identification, the diva in a sense incorporates and embodies the sorrows of the fan while reflecting these attributes back in a "divinely" beautiful or sublimated form.

Identifying the Audience

The strategy of employing roots styles that communicate universal themes is an effective means to articulate transgender subjectivity while simultaneously addressing the film's mainstream audience. It is above all the music that makes the film's central themes of travel, inner transformation, soul-searching, existential ache, and life change, as well as the broader themes of love and acceptance, more palpable and within the emotional reach of people belonging to different audience demographics. The mainstream audience is not alienated from the film's transgender protagonist, but rather can identify and sympathize with the protagonist thanks to the appealing, demystifying music. The music helps to make transgenderness a matter of the art of living, illuminating in general what it is to be a human being, rather than casting transgenderness as some strange medical (and psychiatric) condition.

There might also be some gentle queer irony in the choice of American country music, traditionally considered very conservative and normative, as the music of transgenderness. Indeed, the film manages to address two distinct audiences at the same time, the mainstream and the transgender.[25] Country music in the film appeals first to the transgender audience, because the subject matter of the songs so aptly matches trans experience. Second, it may appeal to a trans audience in light of the practices and history of country music's appropriation within queer country subculture. In the twenty-first century queered country imagery has been visible and audible to a larger audience in other mainstream films too, such as the tragic gay Western *Brokeback Mountain* (dir. Ang Lee, 2005), released in the same year as *Transamerica*.[26]

[25] By transgender audience I mean not only transgender people, but also people with knowledge of and close ties to the transgender culture or community.

[26] Naturally no audience, be it mainstream or subcultural, is unified. For example, in LGBTIQ communities there are also people who do not endorse the queer country trend, because they consider country music the voice of straight, conservative, white society with old-fashioned values that are easily tipped over into intolerance (trans- and homophobia, racism), even a glorification of those "who enforced segregation in the South and destroyed Native American society in the West." Tina Gianoulis, "Country Music," in *The Queer Encyclopedia of Music, Dance & Musical Theatre*, ed. Claude J. Summers (San Francisco: Cleis Press, 2004), 63.

Although more alternative country than mainstream country is heard in *Transamerica*, the music is not particularly or specifically "queer" as such (as it exists outside the film's context). Aside from the scene showing the transgender (pride) gathering and the use of Dolly Parton's music and song, there are no other direct references to queer country culture: no other singers with significant queer followings (such as Patsy Cline or Tanya Tucker); no openly queer singers or musicians (such as k. d. lang or Chely Wright) or performers with other kinds of significant bonds to LGTBIQ culture or activism; no music that is specifically about queer life (such as "Cowboys Are Frequently, Secretly [Fond of Each Other]") or that carries notably queer interpretation traditions (such as "Stand by Your Man"); and no scenes of country evenings in gay, lesbian, and transgender clubs. But the country music heard is neither mainstream rock nor pop country; there are no big hits or established stars the mainstream audience will know in advance (superstar Dolly Parton is an exception here, too).

It is precisely this combination of alternative and "straight" country (transgendered in the film's context), together with country music's general queer overtones, which are audible to the more knowing audience, and a few explicitly queer musical moments (such as Parton and the "transgender choir") that create the film's gender-political strategy of double-coding to cater to the tastes of two discrete audiences. In effect, this double strategy can be considered a far-reaching solution, suggesting that films with transgender content should target not only the transgender audience, but also the mainstream audience, and vice versa. Transgenderness touches and affects the whole of society, not just a small and marginal part of it. It could be said that Parton's "Travelin' Thru," which ends the film, crystallizes this double strategy by allowing simultaneously both a mainstream interpretation and a more nuanced reading.

In short, the queer potential of country music is used very subtly in *Transamerica*. It can even be argued that if specifically queer country music had been more dominant in the film, such references might easily have been interpreted as lesbian, gay, and bisexual allusions that point to the sexual orientation minority instead of the gender minority, because the former dominates the mainstream discourse about LGBTIQ people. In that case the (trans)gender-political message of the film might have been obscured by being lumped together with the known categories of lesbian, gay, and bisexual, which in turn reinforces the prevailing ideology of binary gender. The presence of the category of transgender has a marked destabilizing effect on binary forms of thinking because of the way its audiovisual enactments in the film refuse to fit neatly into existing stereotypical categories.

Finding a Voice

Voice is a critical issue in the gender-normative mainstream culture; it is a gender cue and crucial to one's passability as a woman or a man. Transwomen often undertake voice therapy to acquire a feminine-sounding voice, and for many it is a difficult challenge.

Bree's voice encapsulates her journey of transsexuality, from the very first scene of voice training and by her constant efforts to control her voice. As background to the voice-training program, we hear Jules Massenet's "Meditation" from the opera *Thaïs* (1894) in an arrangement for violin and piano. We might read the serene, steady, and graceful sound of the solo violin as the ideal feminine voice that Bree strives for. Its presence further suggests the amount of rehearsal and work the gender transition involves and the performative nature of gender. It is apt that operatic music is used as an example of the ideal voice, because opera demands an extremely disciplined vocal culture, a rigid system of norms and gendered voice types that are anything but "natural" or "normal." Yet opera is also a powerful cultural platform for gender transgression, from the history of the castrati to trouser roles and opera queens. The operatic music in the film reminds audio-viewers that the gendering of voice is conventional, cultural. We change our voices to match the ideals and norms we want to express; we learn to perform gender by using "appropriate" vocal registers.[27]

Following her voice training, Bree turns off the television and turns on the stereo, which plays music by the renowned South African singer and human rights activist Miriam Makeba. The percussive and lively piece is called "Jol'inkomo," a traditional song of encouragement for young warriors going into battle. As she listens to the song, Bree prepares for the day, for her personal "battle" at the local psychiatrist's office, where she has to endure and pass a psychiatric interrogation to procure the psychiatrist's signature on the referral for genital surgery. She changes her robe to a suit jacket, puts on her makeup, varnishes her fingernails, and brushes her hair. The viewer sees Bree's face fully for the first time only when she is putting the finishing touches on her makeup. The first scene in the film is thus unmistakably based on the construction of gender. The music gives Bree power, providing her with strength to face the day and defend herself as she is; this function is emphasized by having the music overlap with dialogue between Bree and the psychiatrist for several seconds, an auditory cue that began already in the previous shot as Bree walked to catch a bus to the psychiatrist's office. The music also suggests a parallel between racial injustices and the injustices faced by transgender people and reminds us that transgender rights are human rights.

After her therapist has refused to sign the referral for the operation,[28] Bree returns home, where she listens to a recording of Dido's aria, "When I Am Laid in Earth" (from Henry Purcell's opera *Dido and Aeneas*, 1689). This is music of profound sorrow, a melodic lament underpinned by a chromatically descending ground bass (sung by

[27] Suzanne G. Cusick, "On Musical Performances of Gender and Sex," in *Audible Traces: Gender, Identity, and Music*, ed. Elaine Barkin and Lydia Hamessley (Zürich: Carciofoli Verlagshaus, 1999), 29–33.

[28] There are some problematic details in the story when it comes to the gender confirmation process in the United States and many other countries. One is the therapist's withholding of legal permission for a vaginoplasty operation that is already settled and scheduled to take place within a week's time. In real life such matters are agreed on very much in advance—as much as a year. Another such detail is the therapist's exercise of power in blocking the process on the basis of a particular course of action desired by the therapist; this would be highly unethical.

Dido, the queen of Carthage, just before she commits suicide at the end of the opera). As Bree listens, she makes the voice lower and misshapen, "monstrous," by slowing down the record with her hand, a kind of inversion of her voice-training exercises. It is as if she makes the soprano's voice match the depressed image of her preoperative self as "misshapen" and in so doing makes the void of depression even more overwhelming. To be denied the operation feels to Bree like death. The aria could also be interpreted as a reminder of the high rates of suicide among transsexual people who have no possibility of receiving gender confirmation treatments.

Gender-political Questions

Later we learn that Bree does not have the courage to sing, at least in social situations; one can say that she has not found her singing voice. But to be more precise, we do hear Bree attempt a singing of sorts at the beginning. Home alone one evening, she takes her hormones, looks at herself in the mirror, and goes to sleep singing, or rather muttering rhythmically with some changes in pitch, a kind of variation of the Scottish folk song, "Loch Lomond": "You take some hormones / And I'll take some hormones / And I'll be a woman before ye / You make me happy."

For many in the transidentified audience, Bree's singing "I *will be* a woman" (which she repeats at the psychiatrist's office) may sound problematic, because she already is a woman. The transexperience is understood as having always been cross-gendered, from the moment life began (not the moment a person discovers her/his/hir transgenderness, and whether or not a person transitions or is at any stage in the transition process); in the transition process it is the body and the social presentation that are altered to *fit* one's internal body image, gender identity, and self-concept. Bree *is* a woman. The vaginoplasty surgery she is anticipating will alter only her genitals, which is just one (possible) part of a transsexual's gender confirmation process, though experienced as central by many male-to-female transsexuals (many other parts of Bree's body have already been subjected to modifications). The problem here is that these small words by Bree might easily be misread by the mainstream audience as strengthening the gender-normative, even sexist, and altogether erroneous conception of equating being a woman with having a vagina (meaning that genitals would define gender).[29]

On the other hand, Bree's phrase ("*I'll be* a woman") can be interpreted as reflecting the status of the body to a transsexual, the body as being formative of the core self: it emphasizes the importance of the somatic, material dimension (the flesh) in the transsexual experience, "an experience of the body that cannot simply transcend the literal."[30] Bree feels incomplete before her operation. Only after her actual body has been

[29] This corresponds to the cultural prejudice and pressure on transsexual women: "one cannot be a 'real woman' as long as one has a penis" (Bornstein, *Gender Outlaw*, 119).

[30] Cf. Prosser, *Second Skins*, 59, 65, 176.

reconciled as completely as possible to her internal body image can she feel herself a "complete," "full" woman. As Jay Prosser writes, genital surgery "promises the ultimate passing—a passing in the flesh"; it allows a transsexual to pass and live as a nontranssexual and nontransgendered.[31] In this sense the film can be read as portraying a "conventional" form of transgenderness (and in many ways Bree is a conservative woman), evidencing a form of transsexuality that, in a sense, can be restored, normalized, and returned to the normative binary gender system—in the sense of transsexuality that after transition goes "stealth", that is, "blends in" without revealing a person's transgender history.

This conventional model of transsexuality (and transgenderness) in *Transamerica* is probably more easily acceptable to a mainstream audience than a presentation of openly alternative genders not definable with reference to the binary gender system or the medical models of "classic" transsexuality,[32] such as the butch main characters of the film *By Hook or by Crook* (dir. Harriet [Harry] Dodge and Silas Howard, 2002) or some other examples of independent queer/transgender cinema. On the other hand, there is no universal means of representing transsexual or transgender subjectivity,[33] and the factual transitions, choices, and journeys of all transsexual and transgender people are just as radical, given the strictures of the dominant binary gender system.[34] In this sense, films like *Transamerica* can improve the public's acceptance of gender variance by raising awareness and tolerance outside transgender communities.

Perhaps a more serious gender-political question that *Transamerica* raises concerns the casting of a traditionally gendered (cis)woman—a person who the audience knows very well is nontransgender—to play a transgender protagonist. Certainly Huffman does a great acting job, but this casting might also be considered a "safe" solution. The mainstream audience is not forced to confront a real transperson or to experience personal insecurity about the gender of the actor; the audience knows that the actor only *plays* a transgender person, so there is no "actual threat" that would cause the gender trouble to be confronted for real. This choice can be seen as complying with Hollywood's fixed practice, which subjects the liberal message to the commercial interests of maximizing the audience. Solutions too radical are avoided for fear of alienating the mainstream (mass) audience, which the entertainment industry resolutely considers prejudiced.

However, it should be emphasized that in *Transamerica* there is real transpresence, in considerable numbers in the scene of the transgender gathering as well as on the voice-training video, unlike in many other mainstream films about transgenderness, such as *Boys Don't Cry*. Remarkable also is the fact that *Transamerica* does not conform to the usual Hollywood formula of a tragic conclusion for queer characters.

31 Prosser, *Second Skins*, 89.

32 Today many transgender individuals choose only some of the available physical and social modification procedures of transsexuality, or none at all. Furthermore, transgender individuals may not identify themselves as man or woman, but specifically as both, between or beyond man and/or woman.

33 Cf. Judith Halberstam, *Female Masculinity* (Durham, N.C.: Duke University Press, 1998), 148–149.

34 Cf. Girshick, *Transgender Voices*, 12.

Although the emancipatory or queer potential of any transgender media representation may be debatable—because media representations are always *multidiscursive*[35] and subject to different and even contradictory readings—a major change has nevertheless occurred in the cinematic representation of transgenderness. Since the dawn of the new millennium, transgender identities have gained new visibility and have attracted serious, nonjudgmental interest on the part of mainstream films, art films, and queer/transgender cinema, of which *Transamerica* is one example. In the twenty-first century the choice "either a man or a woman" no longer provides the only or self-evident manifestation of genderness in society, audiovisual media, and academia.

References

Altman, Rick. "General Introduction: Cinema as Event." In *Sound Theory/Sound Practice*, edited by Rick Altman, 1–14. New York: Routledge, 1992.

Bornstein, Kate. *Gender Outlaw: On Men, Women, and the Rest of Us*. New York: Routledge, 1994.

Brayton, Sean. "'Mexican' Labor in the Hollywood Imaginary." *International Journal of Cultural Studies* 11 (2008): 459–476.

Butler, Judith. *Gender Trouble: Feminism and the Subversion of Identity*. New York: Routledge, 1990.

Chion, Michel. *Film, a Sound Art*. Translated by Claudia Gorbman. New York: Columbia University Press, 2009.

Cusick, Suzanne G. "On Musical Performances of Gender and Sex." In *Audible Traces: Gender, Identity, and Music*, edited by Elaine Barkin and Lydia Hamessley, 25–48. Zürich: Carciofoli Verlagshaus, 1999.

De Lauretis, Teresa. *Technologies of Gender: Essays on Theory, Film, and Fiction*. Bloomington: Indiana University Press, 1987.

Gianoulis, Tina. "Country Music." In *The Queer Encyclopedia of Music, Dance & Musical Theatre*, edited by Claude J. Summers, 62–63. San Francisco: Cleis Press, 2004.

Girshick, Lori B. *Transgender Voices: Beyond Women and Men*. Hanover, NH: University Press of New England, 2008.

Halberstam, Judith. *Female Masculinity*. Durham, N.C.: Duke University Press, 1998.

Halberstam, Judith. *In a Queer Time and Place: Transgender Bodies, Subcultural Lives*. New York: New York University Press, 2005.

Jacobs, Sue-Ellen, Wesley Thomas, and Sabine Lang, eds. *Two-Spirit People: Native American Gender Identity, Sexuality, and Spirituality*. Urbana: University of Illinois Press, 1997.

Prosser, Jay. *Second Skins: The Body Narratives of Transsexuality*. New York: Columbia University Press, 1998.

Shelburne, Craig. "Gender Identity and Country Music Merge in *Transamerica*." *CMT News*, March 3, 2006, at http://www.cmt.com/news/articles/1525363/20060303/parton_dolly.jhtml?headlines=true (accessed February 9, 2010).

[35] The term derives from Rick Altman, "General Introduction: Cinema as Event," in *Sound Theory/Sound Practice*, ed. Rick Altman (New York: Routledge, 1992), 9–10.

Stryker, Susan. "(De)Subjugated Knowledges: An Introduction to Transgender Studies." In *The Transgender Studies Reader*, edited by Susan Stryker and Stephen Whittle, 1–17. New York: Routledge, 2006.

Stryker, Susan. *Transgender History*. Berkeley, Calif.: Seal Press, 2008.

The Filmography

Transamerica. Directed and written by Duncan Tucker. Original music by David Mansfield, music supervisor Doug Bernheim, supervising sound editor Louis Bertini. Belladonna Productions, 2005.

CHAPTER 23

SOUNDSCAPES OF ISTANBUL IN TURKISH FILM SOUNDTRACKS

MERI KYTÖ

THE city of Istanbul has served as a versatile and inexpensive outdoor studio for hundreds of films and their constructed soundscapes. It is said that Turkish cinema itself might be referred to as "Istanbul cinema," because that city has always been at the center of the film industry. According to one estimate, at least 70 percent of all Turkish films have been shot in Istanbul[1] —five thousand of the roughly seven thousand titles. Watching Turkish daytime television or leafing through books such as *100 Istanbul Films*[2] or *Istanbul in Turkish Cinema*[3], one realizes that the city itself is often a central narrative character. Istanbul becomes the locus for urban dreams, border crossings, and liminalities, all of which are interwoven through the historical and cultural encounters of its millions of inhabitants. Nobel prize winner Orhan Pamuk has described in one of his books a personal memory from his childhood, a moment when he saw a film crew set up on a street in the Cihangir neighborhood, shoot a love scene in 10 minutes flat, and then leave so quickly it was as though they had never been there. Only years later, when he happened to see one of these black-and-white films on television, did he realize the true subject was not the love affair raging in the foreground, but the Bosphorus glittering in the distance.[4] One doesn't need to search very far to find sequences of rolling landscapes by the Bosphorus strait or scenes in which the usually male protagonist raises his head, stares into the distance, and addresses the city with a monologue: "O

[1] Burak Göral, "Perdelerde kalan İstanbul," *İstanbul* 18 (1996). 89; İbrahim Altınsay, "Sinemanın orta yeri İstanbul'du," *İstanbul* 18 (1996): 74.

[2] Semra Kır, *İstanbul'un 100 filmi* (Istanbul: İstanbul Büyükşehir Belediyesi Kültür A. Ş. Yayınları, 2010).

[3] Agâh Özgüç, *Türk sinemasında İstanbul* (Istanbul: Horizon International, 2010).

[4] Orhan Pamuk, *Istanbul—Memories of a City,* trans. Maureen Freely (London: Faber & Faber, 2005), 77.

beautiful Istanbul, your thousand years of beauty is still not ruined!" or "You whore of a city, I'll conquer you yet!"[5]

This chapter examines relationships among sounds, locations, and their cultural meanings in Turkish film. My purpose is to track how Turkish films have changed in recent years, with particular reference to the sonic representations of their acoustic environments. Soundscapes require a listener and a cultural context to be comprehensible. On a semantic continuum from speech to music to soundscape (the last composed of all three systems of acoustic communication), soundscape is most dependent on context.[6] Two recent films, *11'e 10 kala* (*Ten to Eleven*, dir. Pelin Esmer, 2009) and *Uzak* (*Distant*, dir. Nuri Bilge Ceylan, 2002), allow us to consider in detail how articulations of *urbanity* and *privacy* are constructed through film soundscapes. These two films represent the auteur vein of new Turkish cinema;[7] both feature subtle and delicate sound design, use very little music, and evidence a form of heightened realism that stands in contrast to traditional approaches. Although the locations of both of these films, as well as their characters and aspects of their audiovisual aesthetics, are remarkably similar, their soundtracks differ markedly in how they render the experience of the urban soundscape and, through this, the experience of urbanity and privacy.

Before discussing these newer sonic representations of Istanbul, it is important to review the historical context of the praxis of Turkish film sound.

Istanbul on Soundtrack: A Brief Historical Overview

As for most national cinemas, establishing a definitive periodization of Turkish film history is problematic, through its various genres from melodramas to kebab westerns, political dramas, and sex films. For the purposes of this chapter, it is useful to consider some of the main trends and changes through practices in film music. Beginning with the first Turkish sound film, *İstanbul sokaklarında* (*In the Streets of Istanbul*, dir. Muhsin Ertuğrul, 1931), Sadi Konuralp singles out four main periods. The first, the musical melodrama and operetta period (1931–1938), dominated by the theater director Muhsin Ertuğrul, featured interludes of ballads and tangos after the fashion of American and

[5] From the films *Ah güzel İstanbul* (*O Beautiful Istanbul*, dir. Atif Yılmaz, 1966) and *Gurbet kuşları* (*Birds of Exile*, dir. Halit Refiğ, 1964), respectively.

[6] Barry Truax, *Acoustic Communication*. 2nd ed. (Westport, Conn.: Ablex Publishing, 2001), 49–55.

[7] Asuman Suner breaks down the differences between the two lines in new Turkish cinema as follows: "popular," big budget movies that have stars as actors and actresses, large media campaigns, and wide distribution networks in Turkey, and "art" cinema, with small budgets, auteur directors, amateur or unknown actors and actresses, and smaller scale distribution in Turkey but successful at national and international film festivals. *Hayalet ev: Yeni türk sinemasında aidiyet, kimlik ve bellek* (Istanbul: Metis 2006), 33.

European musicals; some films had "upholstery music," a loose mixture of music from available recordings. From 1938 to 1950, the most common practice was to rescore and add performance scenes to musicals imported from Egypt and India. New advantageous tax reforms in 1948 that affected filmmaking started the decade of the producers (1950–1960), including the first attempts at using composed film music. This period also initiated what has been called the golden era of the Yesilçam (the Turkish equivalent of Hollywood) industry, producing at its peak almost three hundred films annually. The fourth period (1960–1990) continued the tradition of "upholstery music" and witnessed the emergence of several key composers, visits from popular and folk musicians, and electronic experiments.[8] Following a steady drop in production attributed to the spread of television in Turkey, the declining Yesilçam gave way to new Turkish cinema in the 1990s, with a new generation of film music composers.

The challenge for studying environmental sound in Turkish film is that starting in the 1940s films were shot without location sound of any kind; all soundtracks were added in postproduction. This practice remained entrenched in the Turkish film industry until the late 1990s. Because there are only about a dozen pre-1940 films, all of which were produced primarily in a theater-like studio setting, not much material is available from this period. Of course location sequences in post-1940s films were not silent, but the aesthetic ambitions for film sound were dictated by economic constraints, including a minimum of crew members and very tight schedules, which meant that filmmakers could give almost no emphasis to coloring locations with soundscapes other than music. Sound engineer and dubbing actor Levent Dönmez recalls hurried timetables and films that had to be produced with only a few days' notice, in inadequate studios with DIY soundproofing. But he also writes about the ingenious schemes that emerged as a result of these confounding issues: solutions that saved time, film stock, and money wherever possible.[9] Until the decline of the Yesilçam industry, the audience had to put up with dubbed dialogue, music, Foley, and the odd sound effect, all of which rendered the soundtracks hollow at times, lacking in presence, tactility, and coherence of acoustic space. But as Savaş Arslan incisively points out, going out to see a film became a family carnival involving meeting and catching up with friends, as well as eating:

> How important was the illusion or realism of a diegetic world, both in terms of soundtrack and image track for such spectatorship within the distraction of open-air summer theaters that constituted half of the theaters in Turkey during the golden age of Yesilçam cinema?[10]

Indeed, there may well have been more urban soundscape present for audiences than what could be heard from the loudspeakers alone.

[8] Sadi Konuralp, *Film müziği tarihçe ve yazılar* (Istanbul: Oğlak, 2004), 63–73.

[9] Levent Dönmez, "Türk sinemasında seslendirme," *Yeni Sinema* 27 (2010): 41–45.

[10] Savaş Arslan, *Cinema in Turkey: A New Critical History* (New York: Oxford University Press, 2011), 123.

Setting aside the social occasion of attending a film screening, this leaves us with those representations of Istanbul that dialogue, diegetic music, and sound effects were able to create. Both intended and unintended accents found in dubbed dialogues would sometimes indicate characters' localities in confusing ways. Earlier dubbing artists declaimed in the tradition of the City Theater of Istanbul, with a cosmopolitan Istanbul accent, regardless of the background of the character.[11] Later, most of the professional dubbers hailed from outside Istanbul and could imitate the various accents matching the characters' backgrounds. Sometimes the dialogue had a comic effect. The accent of the character would change at various points in the film if musical performances were involved, because the artist performing the songs might use yet another dialect or have a distinctly different voice.[12]

Music has been part of the representation of Istanbul as a place of urbanity, whether one is discussing Turkish art music for the romantic *flâneur*,[13] contemporary rap songs criticizing globalization,[14] or *arabesk* popular music portraying the city as a femme fatale devouring the Anatolian migrant.[15] Whereas the early theatrical films of Muhsin Ertuğrul mixed snippets of Western classical music and music from other films, Yesilçam-era Istanbul films drew from a plethora of musical genres. The music came from the record shelves and album collections of the sound engineers, who were knowledgeable about the local hits of the day, including light Western entertainment music, jazz, and pop.[16] Royalty fees for source music weren't legally introduced until 1983, so sound engineers had a financial free hand when it came to finding catchy music for films.

Some of the conventions of diegetic music can be puzzling for a listener-viewer familiar only with Hollywood movies. *Yusuf ile Kenan* (*Yusuf and Kenan*, dir. Ömer Kavur, 1979) provides an example of mixed musical meanings. Two orphan boys, Anatolian villagers who have just arrived in Istanbul, wander the cobblestone streets, amazed by all the sounds (a street vendor with a chiming bell, radios, TVs) and unconventional-looking people (namely homosexuals) in the urban mix. They are lured into a churchyard by the sound of an organ puffing out chromatic chords (reminiscent of the music in Dracula's castle in Hollywood movies). When the music suddenly changes to a Bach chorale, the boys run away in fear of this strange religious soundscape that they have never before encountered. According to Sadi Konuralp, the film industry deployed Bach not only to

[11] Arslan, *Cinema in Turkey*, 118.

[12] Mustafa Sözen, *Sinemada ses kullanımı* (Ankara, Turkey: Detay yayıncılık, 2009), 164–166.

[13] Fahriye Hazer Sancar, "City, Music and Place Attachment: Beloved Istanbul," *Journal of Urban Design* 8, no. 3 (2003): 269–291.

[14] Thomas Solomon, "Listening to Istanbul: Imagining Place in Turkish Rap Music," *Studia musicologia Norvegica* 31 (2005): 46–67.

[15] Martin Stokes, "Sounding Out: The Culture Industries and the Globalization of Istanbul," in *Istanbul Between the Global and the Local*, ed. Çağlar Keyder (Oxford: Oxford University Press, 1999), 121–139. A contemporary look at the musical scenes of Istanbul, presenting the various genres, is presented in Fatih Akın's music documentary *Sound of Istanbul: Crossing the Bridge* (2005).

[16] Levent Dönmez, "Türk sinemasında seslendirme," *Yeni Sinema* 27 (2010): 41–52.

depict church soundscapes and Christianity, but also Nazis and other dangerous or fearsome situations.[17]

One of the all-time favorite shooting locations is the Bosphorus, sonic representations of which conventionally include such sounds as shrieking gulls and *vapur* whistles. The *vapurs* (literally meaning "steam") are the passenger ferries that crisscross the Bosphorus, like the *vaporetti* of Venice's waterways. They have been carrying passengers in the Bosphorus since the 1850s[18] and are considered an emblem of Istanbul's bridgelike character. Countless location sequences have made the *vapur* whistle the sine qua non acoustic prop for any film taking place in Istanbul. The cynic might call it a cliché, but the whistle nevertheless is a key "soundmark" of the city's seaside soundscape, underlining the location of the city between two continents. Soundmarks are sound signals that have historical importance in acoustic communities and have gained a special status because of their strong association with long-term memories that create continuity with the past.[19] The sound of the *vapur* in films has changed, along with the actual ferries, from steam-operated whistles to the electric horns heard on the modern gas-powered ferries.

Curiously, one consistent feature distinguishes the soundscapes intended to depict Istanbul that are heard in films produced in Turkey from those that are made outside the country. The Bond movie *From Russia with Love* (dir. Terence Young, 1963); another adventure movie, *Topkapi* (dir. Jules Dassin, 1964), produced in the United States; the Finnish production *Zombie ja Kummitusjuna* (*Zombie and Ghost Train*, dir. Mika Kaurismäki, 1991); and the French *Monsieur Ibrahim et les fleurs du coran* (*Monsieur Ibrahim and the Flowers of the Koran*, dir. François Dupeyron, 2003) all locate Istanbul as the gateway to the Orient, with the undulating call-for-prayer, *ezan*, signaling Oriental exoticism to the Western ear.[20] Even though the call-to-prayer is an inseparable part of the city's sound culture, setting the rhythms for everyday life, the relationship it has with film sound is troublesome.

Until the 1990s the call-to-prayer was almost impossible to find in Turkish productions, and even nowadays it is not a regular ingredient. The film industry in Turkey originated as a modern Western art form. For the Turkish audience, Istanbul represents the urban West, and religion, considered a private matter, is not the stuff musical melodramas are made of. The use of the call-to-prayer as a locational effect per se would have been seen as backward looking and even orientalist, alluding to the pre-republican era of Ottoman rule. The self-orientalizing sonic modulations found in Turkish films seem to be reserved for rural migrants' folk or *arabesk* music.[21] Savaş Arslan has argued

[17] Konuralp, *Film müzigi tarihçe ve yazılar*, 113.

[18] Nejdet Ertuğ, *Osmanlı Döneminde İstanbul Deniz Ulaşım ve Kayıkcılar* (Ankara, Turkey: T. C. Kültür Bakanlığı, 2001), 259

[19] Truax, *Acoustic Communication*, 67.

[20] To be more precise, *Topkapi* didn't involve an *ezan* at all but an *ağıt*, or lament song, which was obviously close enough vocally to convince most Hollywood audiences, but suspension of disbelief would instantly have been compromised for any Muslim in the audience.

[21] Stokes, "Sounding Out," 121–139.

that from its beginning, Turkish cinema has struggled with problematic strategies of "Turkification" associated with a series of reforms and changes related to the modernization and Westernization of Turkey.[22] Sonic representations of urbanity and privacy lie at the core of these struggles.

A Closer Reading: *11'e 10 kala* and *Uzak*

11'e 10 kala (*Ten to Eleven*, dir. Pelin Esmer, 2009) and *Uzak* (*Distant*, Nuri Bilge Ceylan, 2002) present the everyday, heterogeneous soundscapes of contemporary Istanbul. Their story lines and soundtracks are realistic, focusing on diegetic sound. The only nondiegetic sound in *Uzak* is a few bars of the second part of Mozart's *Sinfonia concertante* (K364, Andante in C minor) and an intermittent musical transformation of a wind chime. There are two short sequences in which we visit the dream worlds of the main characters, but other than that the soundtracks are diegetic, realistic, and rewarding. Both films are filled with subtleties when listened to with an ear familiar with the sound culture of Istanbul.

11'e 10 kala tells the story of a retired octogenarian engineer, Mithat, who has a passion for collecting small mundane items such as newspapers, clocks, the paper labels on bread, and vodka bottles. He is a middle-class, educated *Istanbullu* living alone with his fastidiously organized collection in his apartment. The new *kapıcı* or concierge of the apartment building, Ali, is a thirty-something working-class man from an Anatolian village who is trying to make it in the big city so that he can reunite with his family in Istanbul. Ali starts running small errands for Mithat for extra cash. After their fragile building is marked for demolition due to the threat of earthquakes, these two men develop a quiet and discreet friendship. The movie ends with Ali finding his way out of the confining ground-floor apartment to a life in the city, leaving Mithat with the ultimate piece for his collection, the eleventh part of the *Istanbul Encyclopedia*, a symbol of his obsession with preserving time and memories of the city.

In *Uzak*, the main character, Mahmut, is a photographer who is quite bored with his unchallenging work at a tile factory. He has lost his motivation to work in art and has emotionally unsatisfactory relationships with women. He misses his ex-wife, who is newly married. Yusuf, his younger relative from the village, comes to stay with him in his apartment while searching for a job at the docks. The urbanite Mahmut grows annoyed with the presence of Yusuf and his rural mannerisms. During the few weeks they live together, Mahmut makes Yusuf feel uncomfortable by insinuating that Yusuf has stolen his watch. Eventually Yusuf leaves without saying good-bye and Mahmut is left alone, sitting by the shore staring out at the Bosphorus.

[22] Arslan, *Cinema in Turkey*, 44–46.

These films are firmly wedded to the visual tradition of Istanbul cinema. Both were marketed with posters showing the main character(s) in the foreground and in the background the Bosphorus with boats and the silhouette of Istanbul, including the Beyazıt tower and Süleymaniye mosque.[23] Pelin Esmer, who not only directed but wrote the screenplay, coproduced, and coedited *11'e 10 kala*, has made her career in documentary film. This is her first fiction feature, and it is based on an earlier documentary about her uncle, Mithat Esmer, playing a character based on himself in the fiction film.[24] Likewise, Nuri Bilge Ceylan not only directed *Uzak* but also wrote, produced, and coedited it and was the cinematographer.[25] These films have enjoyed success at various festivals; Ceylan is the more internationally acclaimed of these directors, having won several important prizes at Cannes, and *Uzak* won the Cannes Grand Prix in 2003.

Apart from the similarities in character and story—small lives and loss being played out in the realm of the ordinary—there are also similarities in how the films set the stage during their opening scenes. In both films the first indication of the city comes from the soundtrack, followed after the titles by an identifiable image on a black background. A ship's horn welcomes the listener-viewer at the very beginning of *11'e 10 kala*, accompanied by the bustle of the ferry pier. There is also the introduction of static long shots in *Uzak*, common in Ceylan's cinematographic aesthetics, of Yusuf leaving his home village. During the titles the silent ambience of the village transforms into the nighttime ambience of Istanbul, again with the sound of a ship's horn.

In addition to environmental sounds, recordings are an integral part of the story of *11'e 10 kala*. Mithat, the obsessive collector, keeps a trove of tape recordings of radio programs and telephone conversations, which he transcribes with great care (see figures 23.1b and 23.1c). The film starts with Mithat walking away from a ferry pier (see figure 23.1a). He runs his errands in the crowded Eminönü, the city center, haggling for a dynamo flashlight, then he converses with a man selling eyeglasses at Galata bridge; later we see him walking through crowds, the camera staying at a respectful distance, blending him into the crowd. In the course of these scenes we hear the soundscape of the ferry pier, the horn, the gulls, children's voices, electric toys, all the dialogue, and the continuous urban rumble of crowds and traffic.

When Mithat returns to his apartment, which is full of newspapers and memorabilia, the urban soundscape persists. The camera slowly glides around the piles of his beloved collection, revealing dozens of clocks. The faint ticking of the clocks rises to the fore: once the camera stops moving, we realize that all the urban sound has been coming from a small portable tape recorder situated in the middle of the screen. Mithat has recorded everything taking place on his walk in order to include it in his collection—a

[23] There are two official posters of *Uzak*, both showing Mahmut by a shore: one on the Bosphorus and the other on the Haliç (the Golden Horn). I am describing the first one, which has a less Photoshopped silhouette and closely resembles the *11'e 10 kala* poster silhouette.

[24] The sound recording in *11'e 10 kala* was by Kasper Munck-Hansen, sound editing by Umut Şenyol, and mixing by Marc Elsner, and the Foley artist was Peter Drexler.

[25] *Uzak*'s sound recording and editing were done by Ismail Karadaş and the mixing by Erkan Aktaş.

collection not only of the bric-à-brac of the city's material life, but also of its sonic, immaterial life. The incongruity of the 360-degree tracking shot in the claustrophobic, crammed apartment with the outdoor soundscape seems to underline the sentimental value of Mithat's collection, his devotion to Istanbul, and his striving to preserve time. Only after Ali rings the doorbell to collect the evening trash does Mithat turn down the

FIGURE 23.1: a) Opening scene of Mithat near a Bosphorus ferry pier; b) Mithat listening to his tape archives of telephone conversations; c) Mithat taking notes of the tape.

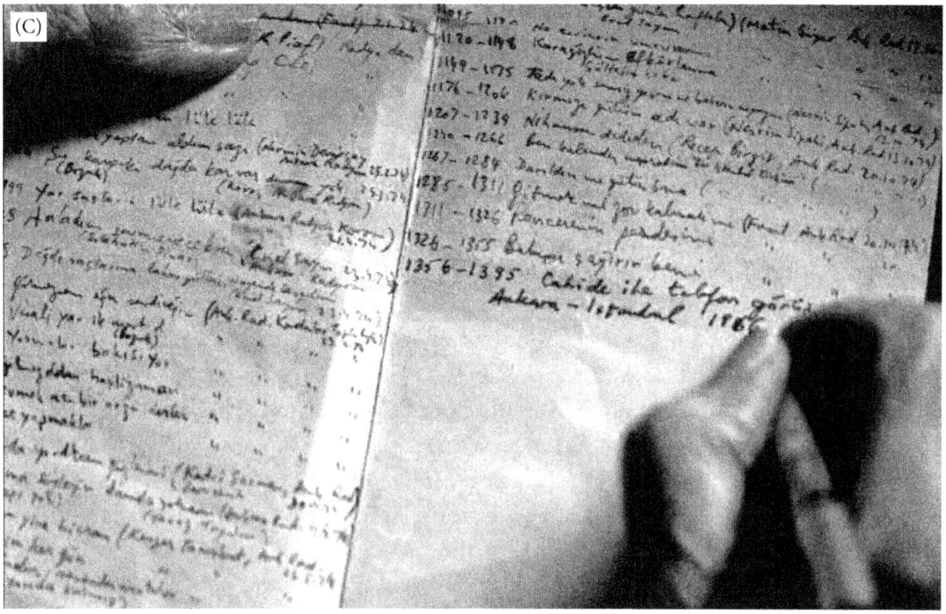

FIGURE 23.1: (Continued)

volume to answer the door, and we hear the empty apartment with the presence of Ali. Ali, who has no experience of the city or any emotional attachment to it, is presented standing in silence in the corridor amid the rustle of plastic bags and the barking of a neighbor's dog.

In interviews, Esmer has indicated that right from the start, she wanted to place equal emphasis on sound design and narration by adding the recordings to Mithat's collection: "Sometimes we forget how things looked like but there are sounds we never forget."[26] An example of an unforgettable sound looming in the cultural memory is a recording Mithat has of the radio announcement of the 1960 military coup d'état.[27] In the film a repairman and Mithat try to rewind the tape on the broken recorder and listen to the announcement once more, but because the machine is broken and won't rewind, they only hear it once. Feride Çiçekoğlu notes that during the first screening of the film at the Istanbul International Film Festival, "the audience in the packed movie theater rejoiced at this moment with laughter and applause, filling in the subtext of the film."[28] The broken tape recorder was proven a wonderful gesture of nose-thumbing against Turkey's history of military takeovers.

[26] Senem Aytaç, "Pelin Esmer, süreklilik sağlamaya calışan bir cambaz," *Altyazı* 87 (2009): 25.

[27] The radio announcement of the 1960 military coup d'état is also found as an extra feature in the DVD edition, together with the 1980 coup announcement.

[28] Feride Çiçekoğlu, "Modernity as a Collector's Item in Pelin Esmer's Film 10 to 11," 2010, at http://www.11e10kala.com/images/press_clip/feride_cicekoglu.html (accessed April 3, 2011).

The Acoustic Horizon of Privacy and Transphonic Trouble

Sound in both of these films is instrumental in revealing the story occurring inside the protagonists' apartments. The new generation of sound designers and the possibilities offered by changing sound technology have shifted the focus of sonic Istanbul from public space to providing more detail for personal and private spaces. We spend a lot of time indoors in the apartment homes of Ali and Mithat in *11'e 10 kala* and of Mahmut in *Uzak*; a number of sequences contain minimal dialogue and focus on the ambient sonic environments that describe the characters' domestic routines—those that construct their private soundscapes. About half of each film takes place indoors in apartment buildings (see table 23.1).

The soundscape of Mithat's apartment abounds with details that circumscribe this retiree's private world. In one of the longest scenes in *11'e 10 kala*, he watches the Turkish version of the game show *Who Wants to Be a Millionaire* and calls on his comprehensive knowledge of trivia to comment on the questions. He ignores Ali's repeated ringing of the doorbell; when he finally turns off the TV, the silence exposes dozens of ticking clocks in his apartment. He shuffles, coughing, to the window, clicks it open, and takes a deep breath of fresh air seasoned with traffic hum, a solitary car horn, and a street dog barking. Closing the window, he slowly goes to bed, turning off the lights click by click and squeezing his dynamo flashlight with its characteristic whir. The camera is left in the dark living room with the tick-tock of his clocks as we hear him sitting on his creaking bed, scanning the radio for the national broadcasting company's eleven o'clock news announcer. The camera shifts to his bedroom, and we see him making some notes to include in his collection (the clock ticking on his night table has lost 10 minutes in 193 days—hence the title of the film). He slowly writes, the pencil brushing the surface of the paper, places the paper next to the radio, then scans a new channel and lies down on his bed, the springs of the bed squeaking and bed linen brushing against him. He drifts into sleep, listening to a ricocheting *kanun* melody. The use of all these sound effects creates the loneliness of his

Table 23.1 Minutes spent in different locations in *11'e 10 kala* and *Uzak*.

11'e 10 kala (1'51")	Minute	*Uzak* (1'45")	Minute
Mithat's home	38	Mahmut's home and studio	53
Ali's home	18		
Other apartments	1	Other apartments	4
Building corridor	8	Building corridor	5
Street in front	2	Street in front	6
The cellar	5		
Indoor Istanbul	21	Indoor Istanbul	9
Outdoor Istanbul	18	Outdoor Istanbul	19
		Outside Istanbul	9

domestic space without any dialogue. This scene depicting the everyday routine of going to bed tells us about Mithat's sense of private space and the control he exercises over it.

"Privacy" is a cultural construct based strongly on the values and concepts of the individual.[29] In apartment life, the privacy of the soundscape, or acoustic privacy, can be seen as an indicator of the degree of autonomy the person possesses. Soundscapes of apartments in dense urban environments have a porous quality. The sounds of neighbors and traffic from the street seep in through walls, open doors, and windows, creating layered spaces connecting the life of the individual to the lives of others. The connection between street and private space is indeed clearly heard in Ali's ground floor apartment. Cars drive by and dogs bark even when the window is closed. The acoustic horizon of his flat and the distance over which he can hear[30] do not end at the walls, but extend into the street. In Ali's case, these seeping sounds do not give him feelings of belonging; quite the contrary. In addition to the flow of the external world, the sounds that compromise his privacy include those made by his neighbors. When Ali wakes up he is chagrined by the sound of the plumbing flushing waste from an upstairs tenant right through his living room (see figure 23.2a). As a concierge he is also expected to be available through the intercom to run errands (see figure 23.2b). The demands seem to be dripping from the intercom, regardless of the time of day.

In the course of the film we see Ali engaging in his concierge duties: collecting the trash, delivering groceries from the market, and washing the corridor floor. The relationship between the tenants and the concierge is "upstairs–downstairs," emblematic of a social class division. Living in the ground floor flats of apartment buildings, concierges, usually migrant families from Anatolia, are not expected to assimilate into the modern middle-class urban culture. Cultural researcher Gül Özyeğin has analyzed how apartments and middle-class homes construct a physical and social space for the confrontation of classes caused by their close proximity in daily life. Ongoing self-reflective processes can be detected in the behavior of the tenants and the concierge family in their feelings of class guilt, distrust, or contempt, which appear to result in a variety of strategies for receiving and providing domestic help. The inhabitants negotiate their relationship with urbanity while constantly scrutinizing their emotions and actions. These apparently trivial social arenas of everyday life are in fact full of anxiety.[31] Reflecting the social realities of class negotiations, Ali's home becomes a liminal soundscape between

[29] As a historical concept, privacy is heavily related to the formation of the bourgeois family in Western civil society. Privacy can also mean controlling access to information and thereby also the autonomy of the individual; in this respect it becomes a precondition for the formation of social order in a democratic society. See Jürgen Habermas, *Julkisuuden rakennemuutos: Tutkimus yhdestä kansalaisyhteiskunnan kategoriasta*. Trans. Veikko Pietilä (Tampere, Finland: Vastapaino, 2004/1990), 213–236; and Juha Räikkä, *Yksityisyyden filosofia* (Helsinki: WSOY, 2007), 85.

[30] Truax, *Acoustic Communication*.

[31] Gül Özyeğin, "The Doorkeeper, the Maid and the Tenant: Troubling Encounters in the Turkish Urban Landscape," in *Fragments of Culture: The Everyday of Modern Turkey*, ed. Deniz Kandiyoti and Ayşe Saktanber (London: Tauris), 43–72, 42, 65.

public work and private living. Just as Mithat persists in ignoring troublesome neighbors who arrive at his door, Ali gradually learns how to set boundaries on his own soundspace. Mithat has placed him correctly in this regard: the concierge does have rights, and he should learn about them. Later in the film, Ali begins to adopt a more middle-class posture in the social dynamics of the apartment; while talking on the telephone with his

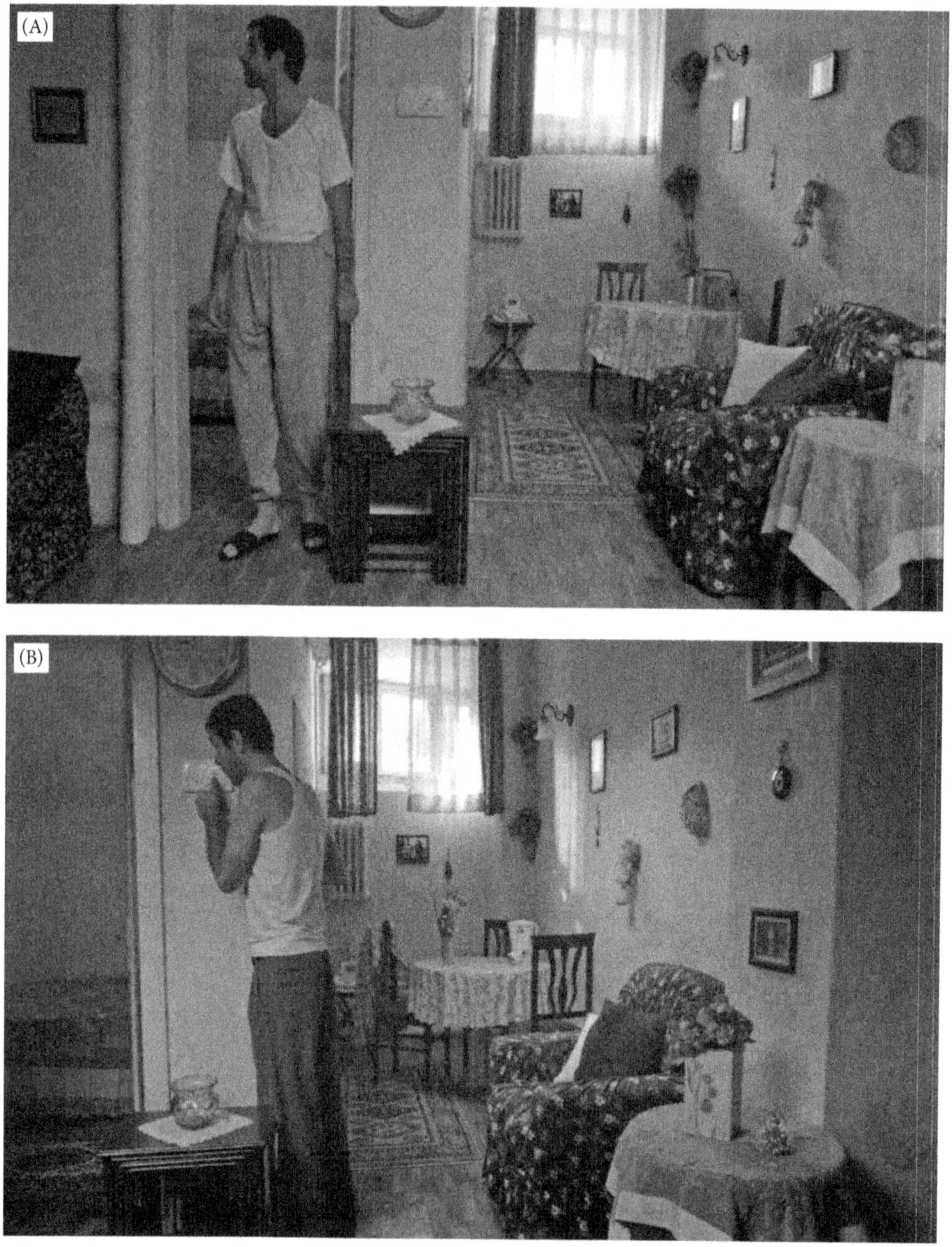

FIGURE 23.2: a) Ali hearing an upstairs toilet being flushed; b) Ali talking through the intercom; c) Ali phoning his wife and ignoring the intercom call.

FIGURE 23.2: (Continued)

wife, he ignores the "Ali! Ali?" calls from the intercom and places his own privacy ahead of walking the dog for the upstairs tenant (see figure 23.2c).

Transphonic sounds, those that are electrically reproduced and dispersed,[32] create spaces of embarrassment and unexpected encounters in private soundscapes. One of Mithat's tape recorders plays an important role in his friendship with Ali. When he is unable to make it work, he asks Ali to take it to a repairman. Ali goes, and while returning with the now functioning pocket device he records everything on the way, just as Mithat did at the beginning of the film, but this time accidentally. Realizing that Ali has recorded over his own sonic memories, Mithat is at first angry with him, but then understands that he has learnt things about Ali that he would not have asked about directly, including personal and family issues. Listening to the tape further, he comes

[32] The term "transphonia" points to the same phenomenon of the electrical reproduction of sound as "schizophonia" by R. Murray Schafer and Barry Truax, but without the negative, albeit intentionally polemical, connotation. As Heikki Uimonen points out, the context for schizophonia is heavily linked with the Benjaminian aesthetic concepts of the technical reproducibility of artworks, Pierre Schaeffer's notions of acousmatic art, and Bauhausian ideals for avoiding the possible "mechanical anarchy" occasioned by inconsiderate use of reproduced sound. Thus the more neutral term transphonia, used in Finnish soundscape studies, is more applicable when analyzing the roles that the electrical reproduction of sound plays in acoustic environments. Heikki Uimonen, *Ääntä kohti. Ääniympäristön kuuntelu, muutos ja merkitys* (Tampere, Finland: Tampere University Press, 2005), 60–62; see also Jonathan Sterne, *The Audible Past: Cultural Origins of Sound Reproduction* (Durham, N.C.; London: Duke University Press, 2003), 20–22; and Steven Feld, "From Schizophonia to Schismogenesis: On the Discourses and Commodification Practices of 'World Music' and 'World Beat,'" in *Music Grooves*, ed. Steven Feld and Charles Keil (Chicago: University of Chicago Press, 1994), 258.

across a discussion that Ali has had with a friend of his; Ali has discovered information about Mithat's past as well. This unexpected interlude brings the men closer together on a personal level, because the tape recorder removes some of the mannerisms of correct conduct that are assigned by their different positions in the class divide. Ali's city experience is now also a part of Mithat's collection; through the collection Ali becomes part of the city and is no longer an outsider. Again Mithat must acknowledge that time cannot be reversed and that the city keeps on evolving on its own, no matter how precisely he keeps track of it.

In contrast, the relationship between Mahmut and Yusuf in *Uzak* builds on different transphonic dynamics. Living under the same roof is difficult; Mahmut finds it hard to tolerate Yusuf's presence. Mahmut's interpersonal difficulties are manifested in the way that he uses the telephone. He doesn't answer a message his mother has left on his answering machine. Only after a follow-up message from his sister informing Mahmut that their mother is in the hospital does Mahmut react to his distant family. When he screws up the courage to call his ex-wife, he takes his phone into the most private room in the apartment, the bathroom, to be certain that Yusuf will not hear him (see figure 23.3a). Yusuf also feels uneasy in the apartment, hiding at the other end of the flat while phoning his mother and almost whispering during the call. The men eavesdrop on each other's telephone conversations (see figure 23.3b). Their strained negotiations and lack of sonic privacy create a distressed soundscape in which the characters struggle with the unpleasant closeness of the other. The awkwardness spreads to the

FIGURE 23.3: a) Mahmut talking in the toilet to his ex-wife; b) Mahmut eavesdropping on Yusuf; c) Yusuf talking to his mother.

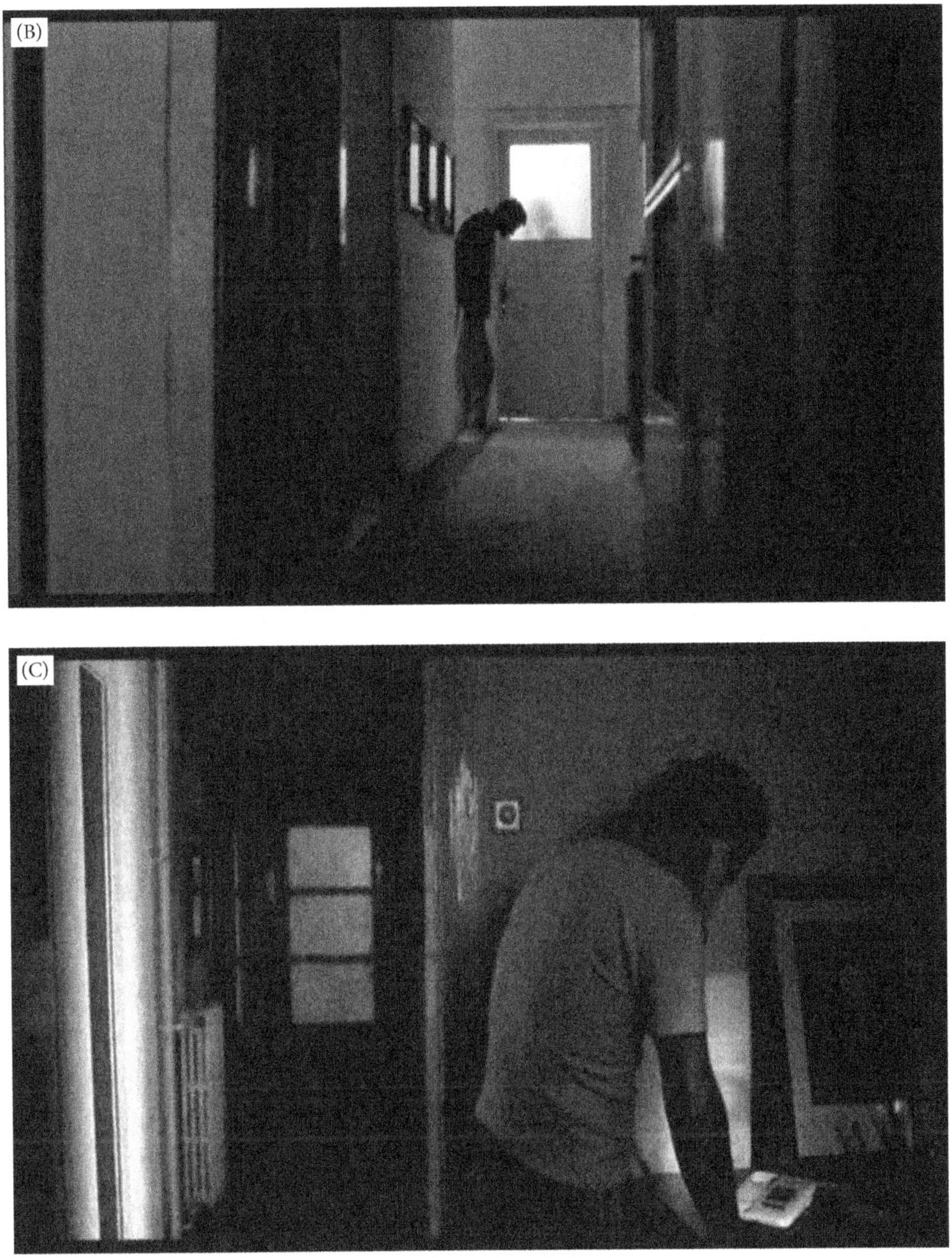

FIGURE 23.3: (Continued)

listener-viewer by means of the static long shots of the somber corridor of the apartment (see figure 23.3c). In the process, Ceylan makes eavesdroppers of us.

The relationship between Mahmut and Yusuf reflects tensions in the contemporary Turkish mindset originating in the socioeconomic changes that have taken place in Turkey in recent decades, where urban-identified people treat rural migrants as second-class citizens.[33] These processes of othering and the negotiation of identities are complicated by the fact that 70 percent of people in Istanbul were born elsewhere.[34] The film invokes musical taste to express class differences: when Yusuf tries to chat with Mahmut, asking if he has any albums by Sezen Aksu, a very popular Turkish singer, in his music collection, Mahmut grunts "no." He claims he only has music such as Bach ("Who is this Bak anyway," asks Yusuf).[35] Yusuf doesn't share Mahmut's taste in cultivated music or Tarkovsky films, and he fails to understand Mahmut's implicit message: that Yusuf does not belong in Istanbul.

Transcoding of Soundmarks

In following the trajectories of the films' younger and poorer protagonists, Yusuf and Ali, we hear two very different experiences of the city. In *Uzak* Yusuf prefers to walk in the snow and slush; in the empty streets he is followed by the sounds of jackdaws, cooing doves, crows and sparrows, barks and meows. The city seems to offer no contact with other people. The growls of the *vapurs* reversing at the Galata bridge remind him of the job that he cannot seem to find (see figure 23.4c). There are few places where he feels welcome. Unlike Mahmut, who enjoys a glass of tea by the Bosphorus at sunset with the gulls and the horns of *vapurs* (see figure 23.4a), Yusuf takes his tea with the fishermen, who are listening to the *arabesk* artist Ibrahim Tatlıses on the radio (see figure 23.4b).

Feride Çiçekoğlu identifies an important distinction between *Uzak* and *11'e 10 kala*:

> Striking cinematographically, yet sharing with films of the 1950s and 1960s the same traumatic clash with the city, *Uzak* looks at Istanbul as a distant dream, just as its title ["distant"] suggests. [On the other hand] Pelin Esmer represents a fresh viewpoint in this sense, since she presents the city neither as a distant skyline, nor as an intimidating persona but as a lively organism with its crammed streets, street-vendors, second-hand shops, and the ongoing buzz of its soundscape.[36]

In *11'e 10 kala* the public soundscape is made up of interactions with other people. For Ali, the city emerges as a place in which to discover new possibilities and acquaintances. While running errands, he visits shops, meets people, and asks directions. He also uses public transport and enjoys tea by the Bosphorus. An almost identical image of solitary tea-drinking by the waterfront is present in *Uzak* with Mahmut. These images of

[33] Hasan Akbulut, *Nuri Bilge Ceylan sinemasını okumak: Anlatı, zam, mekan* (Istanbul: Bağlam, 2005), 28.

[34] *Istanbul between the Global and the Local*, ed. Çağlar Keyder (Oxford: Oxford University press, 1999).

[35] Akbulut, *Nuri Bilge Ceylan*, 155.

[36] Çiçekoğlu, *Modernity as a Collector's Item*.

ephemeral standstills in the busy center bring out the autonomous urban individualities of these two men, manifested in the peaceful *keyif* (pleasure) of a glass of tea.

The traditional soundmarks discussed previously, the *vapur* whistle and the horn and the *ezan*, or call-to-prayer, are represented in both *Uzak* and *11'e 10 kala*, demarcating

FIGURE 23.4: a) Mahmut by the Bosphorus; b) Yusuf at the fishermen's café; c) Yusuf at the snowy Galata bridge.

FIGURE 23.4: (Continued)

a shift in register from the traditional context. In *11'e 10 kala* we hear the *ezan* briefly as a timely accompaniment to Ali's sunset tea by the Bosphorus. This sound of religion, though very rare, does not appear to stand for anything in particular in the film. The *ezan* is as ubiquitous as the constant murmur of traffic and beeping car horns. What it appears to do is to contest the religiosity of the soundmark, making it more of an indicator of communal time, comparable to the tolling of a church bell. The *ezan* in this context transforms the soundscape of Istanbul from the Turkish sound design tradition of evading religious sound making to a more blended attitude on communality, articulating meanings of urbanity with tolerance.

In *Uzak* the traditional *vapur* horn is replaced by a sound effect akin to a cargo ship's foghorn, which is first heard during the opening titles. The foghorn is not the confident ferry whistle that would tie Yusuf to the daily life of the city; the cargo ship would once again take him away from the slushy and dripping soundscape that he would experience if only he were given the job. The ship sounds its mournful horn to warn others of a potential collision, struggling to move ahead, carrying with it an overwhelming feeling of displacement. Orhan Pamuk explains the danger of the gloomy horns on foggy nights: "For those who wake up in the night in Istanbul... most get back to sleep by counting the horn blasts. And perhaps in their dreams, they imagine themselves on a ship moving through the fog to the brink of disaster."[37] Through

[37] Pamuk, *Istanbul*, 192.

this subtle transcoding of environmental sounds the city is made present for Ali and far away for Yusuf, who drifts even further with the radio music that he hears at the fishermen's café.

The City Lives in Sonic Detail

The soundscapes of films do reflect soundscape reality. If we were to ask people what their favorite sounds in Istanbul are, the most common answers would probably be, emblematically, the *vapur* whistle and the gulls. In the study *One Hundred Finnish Soundscapes*, people were asked to recall their most meaningful soundscapes in Finland.[38] One woman born in Istanbul but living in Finland wrote that every time she heard the steam whistle of a local cruise ship, she felt transported to Istanbul; she saw her life rolling before her eyes "like a film" and could almost smell the salt from the Bosphorus shore.[39] Even though the steam whistles have changed to electrical horns, the sound hasn't evaporated from everyday experience. With the popularity of old domestic films on television and streaming portals on the Internet, the whistle remains a persistent part of the collective memory of Istanbulites.[40]

Local soundscapes are important identity markers. By relying on the soundscape competence of the listener-viewer, films provide the pleasures of identification. Anahid Kassabian, writing about the assimilating identificatory mechanisms of film music, points out that using compiled music that already resonates with the perceivers' own experiences may cause a "threat of history," bringing external associations into their engagements with the film.[41] Similarly, assimilating identifications occur within the reconstructed soundscapes: based on experience, the sound designs of *11'e 10 kala* and *Uzak* use the soundscape competence of the audience and their contextual knowledge of the sonic environment. As a result we can enjoy innovative transformations of space and partake in constructing and contributing to imagined soundscapes.

In a popular episodic film from 2005, *Anlat Istanbul* (*Istanbul Tales*, dir. Ümit Ünal, Kudret Sabancı, Selim Demirdelen, Yücel Yolcu, and Ömür Atay), the last sequence is a music-video-like collage of the fairy-tale-like stories that take place in the film. An improvisatory introduction played by the clarinetist Hüsnü Şenlendirici gives way to small vignettes of sonic detail mixed into the rest of the music. These tiny urban

[38] Helmi Järviluoma, Ari Koivumäki, Meri Kytö, and Heikki Uimonen, eds., *Sata suomalaista äänimaisemaa* (Helsinki: SKS, 2006).

[39] Järviluoma, Koivumäki, Kytö, and Uimonen, *Sata suomalaista äänimaisemaa*, 101.

[40] For collective memory and soundscape, see Helmi Järviluoma, "Soundscape and Social Memory in Skruv," in *Acoustic Environments in Change*, ed. Helmi Järviluoma, Meri Kytö, Barry Truax, Heikki Uimonen, and Noora Vikman (Tampere, Finland: TAMK University of Applied Sciences, 2009), 138–153.

[41] Anahid Kassabian, *Hearing Film: Tracking Identifications in Contemporary Hollywood Film Music* (London: Routledge, 2001), 2–3, 141–143.

FIGURE 23.5: a) Pigeons; b) tea glass; c) *simit* seller; d) bootblack.

FIGURE 23.5: (Continued)

elements—pigeons flapping their wings, the clinking swirl of a teaspoon in a traditional tulip-shaped glass, a *simit* (sesame bagel) seller tapping on glass with a coin, a bootblack fluffing his brushes (see figures 32.5a–d)—are all closely miked, as if to suggest to the listener-viewer that this is a personal hearing experience that is happening just a few feet away. The proximity of these sound events gives the sounds a personal dimension connected with everyday experiences in the city. This kind of clarity and detail is possible only because of new sound technology, Dolby-equipped theaters, and more ambitious and sophisticated audio aesthetics. Michel Chion notes that Dolby enriches intimate scenes of dialogue, affecting us physically in a way that this kind of scene could not have done in earlier times. He also argues that the *silences* in the soundtrack, made possible by Dolby, expose us to our own sensitized listening.[42]

Balancing among fluent sound narration, silences, and the local color of soundscapes like those present in *Uzak* and *11'e 10 kala* gives richness to sonic representation and to the entire film-viewing experience. Tuukka Tomperi has written appreciatively about the concrete humanism of such films, suggesting that the most challenging objective for realistic cinema might be simply to show the meaningfulness of the everyday without indulging in naiveté, platitudes, or clichés. He asks if it is not essential in the context of such realism to show precisely that: What is revealed of the world, what is brought to light as deserving of scrutiny while not betraying its dignity? [43] When emerging from a movie theater in Istanbul into the present sonic reality of the city, experiences of imagined soundscapes in the movie just might amplify our affective sense of place and awareness of our own relationship with its soundscape.

References

Akbulut, Hasan. *Nuri Bilge Ceylan sinemasını okumak: Anlatı, zam, mekan*. Istanbul: Bağlam, 2005.

Altınsay, İbrahim. "Sinemanın orta yeri İstanbul'du." *İstanbul* 18 (1996): 73–75.

Arslan, Savaş. *Cinema in Turkey: A New Critical History*. New York: Oxford University Press, 2011.

Aytaç, Senem. "Pelin Esmer, süreklilik sağlamaya calışan bir cambaz." *Altyazı* 87 (2009): 25.

Chion, Michel. "The Silence of the Loudspeakers, or Why with Dolby Sound It Is the Film That Listens to Us." Translated by John Howe. In *Soundscape: The School of Sound Lectures*, edited by Larry Sider, Diane Freeman, and Jerry Sider, 150–154. London: Wallflower Press, 2007 [2003].

Çiçekoğlu, Feride. "Modernity as a Collector's Item in Pelin Esmer's Film 10 to 11." 2010, at http://www.11e10kala.com/images/press_clip/feride_cicekoglu.html (accessed April 3, 2011).

[42] Michel Chion, "The Silence of the Loudspeakers, or Why with Dolby Sound It Is the Film That Listens to Us," trans. John Howe, in *Soundscape: The School of Sound lectures*, ed. Larry Sider, Diane Freeman, and Jerry Sider (London: Wallflower Press, 20072003), 150–154, 151–152.

[43] Tuukka Tomperi, "Konkreettinen humanismi ja tekemisen taito, elokuvarealismin magiasta," *Niin & näin* 69 (2011): 125.

Dönmez, Levent. "Türk sinemasında seslendirme." *Yeni Sinema* 27 (2010): 41–52.
Ertuğ, Nejdet. *Osmanlı Döneminde İstanbul Deniz Ulaşım ve Kayıkcılar.* Ankara, Turkey: T. C. Kültür Bakanlığı, 2001.
Feld, Steven. "From Schizophonia to Schismogenesis: On the Discourses and Commodification Practices of 'World Music' and 'World Beat.'" In *Music Grooves*, edited by Steven Feld and Charles Keil, 257–289. Chicago: University of Chicago Press, 1994.
Göral, Burak. "Perdelerde kalan İstanbul." *İstanbul* 18 (1996): 89–90.
Habermas, Jürgen. *Julkisuuden rakennemuutos: Tutkimus yhdestä kansalaisyhteiskunnan kategoriasta.* Translated by Veikko Pietilä. Tampere, Finland: Vastapaino, 2004 [1990].
Järviluoma, Helmi, Ari Koivumäki, Meri Kytö, and Heikki Uimonen, eds. *Sata suomalaista äänimaisemaa.* Helsinki: SKS, 2006.
Järviluoma, Helmi. "Soundscape and Social Memory in Skruv." In *Acoustic Environments in Change*, edited by Helmi Järviluoma, Meri Kytö, Barry Truax, Heikki Uimonen, and Noora Vikman, 138–153. Tampere, Finland: TAMK University of Applied Sciences, 2009.
Kassabian, Anahid. *Hearing Film: Tracking Identifications in Contemporary Hollywood Film Music.* London: Routledge, 2001.
Keyder, Çağlar, ed. *Istanbul Between the Global and the Local.* Oxford: Oxford University Press, 1999.
Kır, Semra. *İstanbul'un 100 filmi.* Istanbul: İstanbul Büyükşehir Belediyesi Kültür A. Ş. Yayınları, 2010.
Konuralp, Sadi. *Film müziği tarihçe ve yazılar.* Istanbul: Oğlak, 2004.
Özgüç, Agâh. *Türk sinemasında İstanbul.* Istanbul: Horizon International, 2010.
Özyeğin, Gül. "The Doorkeeper, the Maid and the Tenant: Troubling Encounters in the Turkish Urban Landscape." *Fragments of Culture: The Everyday of Modern Turkey*, edited by Deniz Kandiyoti and Ayşe Saktanber, 43–72. London: Tauris, 2002.
Pamuk, Orhan. *Istanbul—Memories of a City.* Translated by Maureen Freely. London: Faber & Faber, 2005.
Räikkä, Juha. *Yksityisyyden filosofia.* Helsinki: WSOY, 2007.
Sancar, Fahriye Hazer. "City, Music and Place Attachment: Beloved Istanbul." *Journal of Urban Design* 8, no. 3 (2003): 269–291.
Solomon, Thomas. "Listening to Istanbul: Imagining Place in Turkish Rap Music." *Studia musicologia Norvegica* 31 (2005): 46–67.
Sözen, Mustafa. *Sinemada ses kullanımı.* Ankara, Turkey: Detay yayıncılık, 2009.
Sterne, Jonathan. *The Audible Past: Cultural Origins of Sound Reproduction.* Durham, N.C.; London: Duke University Press, 2003.
Stokes, Martin. "Sounding Out: The Culture Industries and the Globalization of Istanbul." *Istanbul Between the Global and the Local*, edited by Çağlar Keyder, 121–139. Oxford: Oxford University Press, 1999.
Suner, Asuman. *Hayalet ev: Yeni türk sinemasında aidiyet, kimlik ve bellek.* Istanbul: Metis, 2006.
Tomperi, Tuukka. "Konkreettinen humanismi ja tekemisen taito, elokuvarealismin magiasta." *Niin & näin* 69 (2011): 121–125.
Truax, Barry. *Acoustic Communication.* 2nd ed. Westport, Conn.: Ablex, 2001.
Uimonen, Heikki. *Ääntä kohti. Ääniympäristön kuuntelu, muutos ja merkitys.* Tampere, Finland: Tampere University Press, 2005.

CHAPTER 24

AUDIOVISUAL OBJECTS, MULTISENSORY PEOPLE, AND THE INTENSIFIED ORDINARY IN HONG KONG ACTION FILMS

CHARLES KRONENGOLD

In a 2006 interview, director Johnnie To (Du Qifeng) reflected on "the change and sense of loss Hong Kong has experienced since the 1997 handover":

> It's a very rare event in any part of the world. A historical change of this scale, one entailing changes in culture, economy and, frankly, the quality of people, is too heavy for Hong Kongers. How do you cope with things you once refused to identify with? How do you identify and adapt?

"[T]he changes were fundamental and to do with the very nature of things," he continued, commenting on the context of his recent film, *Election* (2005):

> In 2004, the situation was still unclear although more than seven years had elapsed.... People's thinking is bound to change with the times. *Election* is about the handover of authority and political change. But what about things that have always been there? What about buses? Will money be the same?[1]

Switching registers from the deepest questions about the "quality of people" and the "very nature of things" to the seemingly banal matters of buses and money, To's sketch of post-1997 Hong Kong depicts the pressures on ordinary life as a bewildering diversity of effects that

[1] Lawrence Pun, "Johnnie To on *Election*," in *Milkyway Image, Beyond Imagination*, ed. Lawrence Pun, 306–314, 306, 310 (Hong Kong: Joint, 2006).

aren't fully knowable. This diversity works as both a too-muchness and a "sense of loss." We can't understand these broad historical shifts, To seems to suggest, without considering how they are imprinted on the thought patterns of individual human subjects moving through the city, caught up in the flow of capital, engaging in simple transactions, trying to hold onto whatever they can identify with in the swirl of activity around them. To's picture approaches the ungraspable "world of intensified economic and social volatility" that Lauren Berlant has limned, in which people are "stuck in what we might call survival time, the time of struggling, drowning, holding on to the ledge, treading water, *not-stopping*." For Berlant, "[t]his is a way of describing the specificity of the experience of ordinariness... in its visceral temporality today."[2] But To frames his remarks as an observation on his "creative process." What sorts of influence might these broad and deep changes have on a director's work and on cinema more generally? Do these new kinds of people and things actually show up in the films? How might their emergence be bound up with the nature and techniques of digital cinema? And how might the action film, To's principal genre, accommodate these new people and things?

This chapter seeks to address these questions, focusing on audiovisual practices. Simply put, the techniques of audiovisual intensification that mark digital cinema grew up alongside the "fundamental" changes in Hong Kong life after the 1997 handover, and the post-1997 Hong Kong action film, subject to new geopolitical, commercial, and aesthetic pressures, has been compelled to deal with both sets of transformations. Declining local audiences for action films, shifts in distribution patterns outside Hong Kong, and the pressures and possibilities of mainland and Western markets have unsettled the genre.[3] In the ruthless market of global action cinema, heightened audiovisual techniques both provide the means for a film to stand out (or opt out) and themselves become a site for competition among films. One might expect such practices to govern the fight sequences and other big set pieces, the montages of unfettered movement through space, perhaps even the intimate moments of strong emotion. But—and this is the question that led me to focus on To—what happens when these techniques bleed into minor or transitional scenes of everyday life, when people are just eating, walking, or hanging around?[4] Why would these films spend time showing people experiencing the world in ordinary ways?

2 Lauren Berlant, "Nearly Utopian, Nearly Normal: Post-Fordist Affect in *La Promesse* and *Rosetta*," *Public Culture* 19, no. 2 (2007): 273–301, 279.

3 For a director like To, whose depictions of mainland people and policies make clear he's not seeking that market, the Western festival circuit has acquired a particular importance. See Laikwan Pang, "Postcolonial Hong Kong Cinema: Utilitarianism and (Trans)local," *Postcolonial Studies* 10, no. 4 (2007): 413–430; on To specifically, see 425–426.

4 David Bordwell's important article "Intensified Continuity" (*Film Quarterly* 55, no. 3 [2002]: 16–28) points out that "even ordinary scenes are heightened to compel attention and sharpen emotional resonance" (24); but the examples he provides show he is still referring to scenes of clear, heightened emotionality. While Bordwell's essay provides a grammar for my investigation here, its relatively small number of relevant techniques is too restrictive to delineate the style I am discussing. At the same time, Bordwell made a point early on of connecting To with the "intensified" style. See his "Louder Than Words: The Films of Johnnie To," *Artforum* (May 2003): 154–157 and "Transcultural Spaces: Toward a Poetics of Chinese Film," in *Chinese-Language Film*, ed. Sheldon Lu and Emilie Yeh, 141–162, 148 (Honolulu: University of Hawai'i Press, 2005).

A few short scenes from Johnnie To's *Breaking News* (*Dai si gin*, 2004) show how the audiovisual practices of new digital cinema have broadened the forms of attention a film makes possible. To's films have given more and more space to heightened depictions of materiality, temporality, and the ordinary. We experience this in the heavy, smoky air; the multisensory impact of food; the emphasis on ordinary behaviors; and little exchanges between people in which a common object plays a mediating role. Sonic materiality—of dialogue, music, Foley effects, and ambient sound—becomes essential to this work. Against the speed of "a world that is visually and physically crowded, both overwhelming and underwhelming in its assault, allowing little time to luxuriate in its sounds, tastes and smells,"[5] To's films give weight to, and allow time for, a range of multisensory experience that is both "ordinary" and hard to access. With Berlant's dark picture as a backdrop, we can say that anything capable of *registering* audiovisually can create a multisensory experience that follows a different cultural logic. It creates a slowdown, carves out a discrete space, makes an ordinary cinematic object seem real, or marks a quiet moment. In this way To's action films increase the weight and dimensionality of the human in a manner that is posthumanist, extranarrative, and specific to Hong Kong. But the effects of this experience are transient, limited, and contingent.

This chapter is part of a smaller project. In a way, I want to focus on just one short scene, which I discuss later: a nine-second shot of the main cop and his partner eating sandwiches in their car. I think you could say everything you wanted about the ordinary, the city, genre, modes of thinking, and means for continuity in post-1997 Hong Kong action cinema by a thorough consideration of this unimportant moment. To's statements encourage this focus on "little things," which he says "[h]uman relationships are built on."[6] This project is small also in its concern with the micro-gesturality or -viscerality of thinking by means of the senses. Throughout I point to ordinary multisensory experience in scenes that use heightened audiovisual techniques (and deemphasize dialogue): What does it mean to sense a silent character thinking onscreen?

Multisensory Experience and Audiovisual Objects

To's intensified ordinary emerges sharply against more conventional Hong Kong film practice. A preliminary example, from Benny Chan's *Divergence* (*Saam cha hau*, 2005), shows the heightened ordinary working in service of a very clear goal.[7] As such it puts

[5] Berlant, "Nearly Utopian," 280.

[6] Rather, that is, than "on declarations of love or paying some kind of price." "Author's Interview with Johnnie To," in Stephen Teo, *Director in Action: Johnnie To and the Hong Kong Action Film* (Hong Kong: University of Hong Kong Press, 2008), 215–244, 241.

[7] Chan served as To's assistant director in the mid-1980s.

us in a better position to consider several To scenes in which the aims are less certain. A moment between two of *Divergence*'s big action sequences demonstrates how heightened audiovisual techniques can depict multisensory experience, especially in the absence of dialogue. Suen (Aaron Kwok) is a cop on the edge, chasing Koo, an assassin (Daniel Wu). A foot chase leads to an indoor food market. Suen loses Koo in the crowd inside. He doubles over as if he's fighting a side-stitch as the rhythmic musical cue gives way to a cascade of shoppers' voices. Suen stands in the middle of things, huffing and puffing; this creates a moment of repose, partly because he needs to catch his breath, partly because he doesn't know where to look for Koo anyway. This uncertainty about how to proceed underscores the *work* of thinking—both decision making and less-than-conscious apprehension of multisensory stimuli. The activity in the market has an energy that makes Suen's heightened state seem average: one shopper's excited calls for attention match and parallel Suen's intensity. Suen walks forward slowly with the shoppers streaming around him; point-of-view (POV) shots tell us he's scanning for Koo. So when our eyes are drawn toward the edges of the frame by individual shoppers pointing and gesticulating with vigor, we imagine Suen as similarly led from one part to another of his perceptual field. Indeed the sound, mise-en-scène, and editing show us how Suen's attention shifts among points of activity that might captivate *anyone* thrown into the midst of this busy scene. Sound plays a key role; Foley effects here mostly precede their visual correlatives, suggesting that sound leads Suen's vision. The assertive bone-chopping, fish-scaling, and knife-sharpening sounds connect to striking images of hanging chickens, whole fish, and pig bones. These audiovisual objects are irrelevant to Suen's pursuit, but the way they draw his attention makes perceptual sense. A tall guy in a black trench coat, shown from behind, catches Suen's eye (as we see in a reaction shot). When we cut back, we see the man must be a fishmonger. But the camera, still representing Suen's point of view, can't turn away; it follows the man's gloved hand as he reaches down and lifts up a fish to discuss it with another worker. Rational thought is thus shown to lag behind less-than-conscious mental processes: a black trench coat doesn't necessarily indicate criminality, but try telling that to your amygdala.[8]

At this moment Suen stops walking forward; he just more passively takes in what is happening around him. He starts to register the sounds of the market. Extreme close-ups, wipe-bys, and slow motion underscore Suen's more deliberate perceptual work; but even more than before, the flow of his attention is defined by the sound, which becomes highly stylized. The ambient sound is reduced to quiet, reverb-heavy reminders of the shoppers' voices, while the soundscape's foreground is dominated by Foley sounds representing what a particular shot focuses on: a close-up of live chickens in crates, a medium shot of a blowtorch tracing the contours of a ghostly white pig carcass, extreme close-ups of a fish getting scaled and an ice pick chipping away, and a butcher's cleaver chopping off a joint that then bounces away (at twenty frames per second). Each

[8] On the amygdala and the brain's fear system, see Joseph LeDoux, *Synaptic Self: How Our Brains Become Who We Are* (New York: Penguin, 2002), 61–64.

of these shots thus has a unique sonic profile as well as a way to register the work of the other senses; this gives extra weight to these sites as discrete sources of multisensory information. The Foley sounds are panned aggressively to reflect the position of Suen's head as his focus shifts among these sites, meaning that his physical position in relation to these sites also colors the film's depiction of its reality. Finally the chicken, ice pick, and reverbed crowd sounds swell together and recede. We then hear only the heavy breathing of an unseen figure; the nondiegetic music reenters to confirm that Suen's listening exercise has led him to Koo. What this 90-second sequence doesn't quite spell out audiovisually is also important: that Suen's perceptual work concerns not only what is out there around him, but also *his own body*. An awareness of his own labored breathing reminds him that *anyone* would be out of breath, and therefore Koo also must be. Rather than any special perceptiveness or physical ability, it is what Suen holds in common with Koo—and many other people—that serves as a ground for this heightened depiction of the senses. (In a clever touch, we see a POV shot from Koo's perspective before Koo himself does. So again, it seems more important that a character *could* experience a particular stimulus than that he actually *does*.)

Intensified audiovisual techniques are employed here to depict body/brain processes of the most basic sort. Why would an action film devote screen time to showing a silent character, moving slowly, just looking and listening as he catches his breath? In its broad outlines this scene is an unproblematic instance of successful detective work, but it plays as an odd literalization of the cliché that detectives search for things. The film slows down and zooms in—literally and more than literally—as if it wants to reveal what's going on in Suen at the neurophenomenological level. Its focus on this micro-experiential level has three entailments we should register. It reveals (1) the *vividness of what's experienced* (how stimuli can draw our attention even when they are unimportant); (2) the *materiality of what exists* (including not only bodies and objects, but light, sounds, breath, thoughts, and so forth); and (3) the *strangeness of the ordinary*. The vividness has a lot to do with set designer William Chang Suk Ping's transformation of the space; as Chan jokes in the DVD extras, "Uncle redecorated." We tend to picture the everyday as what is always happening, but here it wasn't, because this market had been shuttered for years. Maybe we perceive this constructedness, on some level, in the comportment of the extras, the recesses of the space, the look of the fauna. For Hong Kongers this ordinariness may enfold memories of the "real" faded public space. All this serves to heighten the intensity of the experiences we see onscreen. Thus the scene and its setting read as *ordinary* only because they are *vivid*—more real than real.

In the texture of this sequence we note an insistence on the materiality of what is depicted onscreen—not only of the ice, the live chickens, and the very dead pigs, but of smoke, breath, the vivid red light fixtures, and even the workings of the character's body/mind. One thing we can learn from this scene's emphasis on materiality and the multisensory is that we need to pay attention to the ways that perception is mediated. Think about how we are asked to confront the *media* and *work* of perception here: the scene shows Suen trying to push his perceptual focus *past* water, glass, and his own labored breathing; he is trying to see and hear *around* crowds and loud chickens. What does it matter that Suen's thinking/sensing is compromised by fatigue and sensory overload? Through concerted audiovisual means this scene renders ordinary experience as particularly intense and concrete. So this scene is ordinary not only because it fails to provide "action," but also because it insists on the fallibility and contingency of perception; it grounds the characters' behaviors in ordinary weaknesses we share rather than in heroic attributes we see as a character's specific property.

This scene demonstrates what I mean by the *strangeness* of the ordinary. The "ordinary" and the "intensified" intertwine in many ways: the market's ordinariness against its stylized constructedness; the average animals made strange audiovisually; the nonspecificity and silence of the main characters versus the heightened, "detailed" depiction of extras; ordinary perception shown in intensified ways, and maybe *not* quite ordinary because exaggeratedly impinged on and affect laden. The scene says both "this is how body/mind thinking works under these fraught conditions" and "this is just how the world *is*—it's, you know, *odd*." Thought gains materiality—almost a sense of friction or grain—through the concreteness of objects, sounds, light, and space. Multisensory perception and an insistence on the materiality of objects, settings, thoughts, and gestures, and indeed of the gaps *between* them, add a dimensionality that action-film reality normally flattens out. This sense of materiality means we see what's *producing* thoughts: the film shows how "*thoughts... are made of the same stuff as things are*."[9] Heightened depiction of Suen's point of view means his thought of an object is the same as the object. "Realness" and strangeness become inseparable as cinematic effects.

We are starting to consider how the ordinary can be constructed, worked, or heightened; how it is necessarily dynamic and historical; and how it is contingent, if not precarious. In the market sequence from *Divergence* this constructed ordinary serves a clear narrative function; the emphasis on materiality, the ordinary, and the texture of thinking works in service of, and is enfolded within, a big set piece. In To's films this depictive strategy starts to change the cinematic economy, shifting the balance toward his "little things,"[10] what's "unimportant," and other elements that do not advance the plot or fulfill the action genre's requirements. This strategy raises questions about what a film will contain or emphasize, what can move it forward, and how its temporality works. Moreover, the greater the emphasis on the small and unimportant, the harder it is for a film to deliver broad themes and grand statements.

We can get closer to To's distinct picture of the ordinary by examining scenes that operate outside their films' plots and themes. In *Breaking News* one scene of nearly 90 seconds concerns roasted yams. At the end of the sequence that precedes it, Inspector Cheung, the lead cop, makes his partner nervous by announcing he is hungry. This yam sequence begins with a shot of his team's cars pulling up to the curb and two shots of Cheung's partner, Hoi, getting out of the car and circling aimlessly in the middle of the street; the last of these shots pans to Cheung, seen through the windshield, apparently

[9] William James, *Writings 1902–1910* (New York: Library of America, 1987), 1158; italics in original. (See also 1156–1157.)

[10] See note 6.

talking under his breath. The next three shots each last 11 seconds or more, and they are notable partly for the range of things they include. The first shows Cheung busting out of the car in long shot and walking with purpose toward what we soon see is a yam vendor; making eye contact with the vendor and gesturing toward the yams, hearing but not responding verbally to the vendor's pitch; taking a yam and splitting it open with his hands (underscored by a surprisingly loud Foley effect and digital enhancement that makes the orange color glow); and taking a bite from each half as he turns back toward the car without having paid, as the vendor is on the point of calling out to him and the rest of the cops are getting out of their cars. Cheung walks to the car while his men are approaching the vendor. As the men stream past him on both sides in what almost looks like a choreographed formation, while Hoi is left to pay, Cheung gestures with the half-yam in his right hand, first over his right shoulder, then over his left, as if to say, "You people on my *right* should get a yam, and you people on my *left* should get a yam." This is a subtly funny move that perhaps only a comic actor like Cheung would come up with, but it nevertheless presents an interesting way of providing direction or conveying authority. This scene may not have a narrative goal that advances the plot, but it shows different kinds of directed motion—people and cars in changing configurations—along with gestures and objects that seem capable of carrying the film forward.

This 15-second shot alone is sufficient to suggest that this scene is treated as a *mission*, if not quite an action sequence. One *could* say this sequence helps establish Inspector Cheung's character by demonstrating that he is directed and resolute. He knows what he wants, he doesn't play games—see how he doesn't stop to pay for the yam, look how his men follow him—but the movie has already shown us these elements of his character. Plus it's all about yams, so the more weight we place on it, the funnier and odder it becomes. What stands out more are formal qualities—of motion, and even of the yam itself. Indeed, the yam is an audiovisual object par excellence, all the more because its multisensory effects reach beyond sight and sound to taste, smell, and touch. It is easy to note the choreography of the camera, the bodies, and the cars as the feel of the sequence tautens once Cheung jumps out of his car. We can see this sequence as tracing lines through space, with Cheung's yam as a moving center of gravity.

Each of the five longer takes changes a lot as the camera moves from a single to a two shot to a group, from long to medium shot to close-up, from generous depiction of the background to an emphasis on objects like the yams. We sometimes catch Cheung alone in the frame, occasionally through an anamorphic lens that exaggerates the extent of empty space around him. He appears to be thinking, looking at his split yam as he's eating it. The materiality of the yam (as food, but also as an audiovisual object) thus becomes, strangely, the fulcrum for both movement and thinking. Sound helps achieve these effects. It is typical of To's films that the sound designer goes crazy Foleying in the breaking of the yam. This loud sound contrasts with characters talking silently to themselves (like Cheung in his car), *not* quite talking (like the vendor about to say, "Hey, you never paid!"), and communicating nonverbally (Cheung using the yam as a pointer). Perhaps because it is "pointless," this scene becomes capable of showing us something about the ways people think, interact with objects, and move through space. This is so all the more because it is suddenly interrupted by the plot. These eight shots begin to show how To's action films register the ordinary: (1) The scene presents a variety of affects and behaviors that change rapidly and work contrapuntally. (2) The choreographed motion of multiple figures and the circulation of audiovisual objects, along with the narrative structure of a mission, establish a *multiparametric line* that governs the temporality of and functions as scaffolding for the contrapuntal weave[11] and (3) create a flow that keeps us in the moment rather than wondering why we're suddenly watching the "pursuit of the yam." (4) These cinematic modes "elevate" and intensify the ordinary objects and behaviors the scene depicts. This adds up to a sense that (5) a range of human experience can be captured in a scene like this, even though (6) beyond being ordinary and uneventful, it is also transitional, not to say unstable and incomplete.

Thus if this film is using the performances of its characters to tell us something about them, it is to show us what *people* are like, what human activities look like, and not necessarily anything about *these characters*. Crucially, the film is more specific about Hong Kongers and mainlanders *as broad types*—how they think, how they move—than it is about any particular characters. Partly this is because these depictions remind us how much about being human happens at a less-than-conscious level. So what does a scene like this say about To's methods, cinematic economy, and relation to action cinema? We have seen the ordinary rendered as concrete, partly by depicting multisensory experience with the aid of camera movement and Foley sound. Food and eating play important roles; by contrast, what dialogue there is doesn't work to define the scene's mood or function. *Breaking News* can help us ask what it means to put nonverbal thinking in the foreground. For one thing it encourages consideration of the impersonal forces that impinge on thinking, that work both collaboratively and antagonistically to create the "ordinary." The film's cinematic economy puts its themes, plots, and schemes (narrative, visual, sonic) into a swirl that does not guarantee prominence for any single strand and makes characters, genres, places, images, and sounds fight it out for a moment in the spotlight.

Following Lines

But *Breaking News* does not lack traditional narrative drive. The cops-and-robbers plot certainly churns like a police procedural's ought to. Indeed, the film begins on the later side of medias res and takes place over the course of a single day, which gives the narrative a strong sense of forward motion. Another major strand competes with the film's depictions of the ordinary. As the title hints, images of the news media prove equally capable of providing narrative and thematic material: led by the young Commissioner

[11] What I call a (single) multiparametric line is the aggregate effect of what's easiest to follow, moment to moment, in the progress of this contrapuntal weave—like moving from the local highpoint in one line to the highpoint in whatever line next asserts one, and so on. I discuss an example below.

Rebecca Fong, the cops battle the crooks in the old and new media. This strand also connects with the film's broader exploration of *mediated* communication, especially human–technology interaction.

Given this description of the film's plot and themes, a focus on ordinary scenes rather than big set pieces may seem counterintuitive. But To's films encourage this focus through their sheer number of ordinary sequences, their working of the ordinary into even the climactic scenes, and their use of ordinary spaces for major action sequences.[12] To's status as a director of the ordinary has to do with these and other compensatory strategies: the way he uses slo-mo during sped-up moments, heightened visual intensity during scenes of repose, and so on. One example of these compensatory strategies—and a sequence whose function in the plot conveys almost nothing of its qualities—is the film's amazing, endless opening shot. Because it smoothly enfolds a shootout after beginning more discursively, it gives the sense that action sequences can blossom unpredictably from more "ordinary" scenes. In addition, we can see the opening shot as fulfilling the action genre's demands *early*, so To can do whatever he wants afterward; he is building up credit. What does he spend it on? On notably ordinary sequences like the yam purchase, I would suggest. But it is important that a tour de force like the opening shot shares techniques and approaches with the ordinary little scenes I am drawing attention to. In particular, the opening shot provides a clearer example of the multiparametric lines I mentioned in connection with the yam scene, and it does so through audiovisual means that are useful to look at in some detail. These multiparametric lines rely on both *the techniques of digital cinema* and *the multisensory nature of perception*, and they are an essential part of how this film depicts its people.

This much-noted opening shot presents a line traced across parameters: a modest Hong Kong skyline followed by a wandering melodic line, a fast-moving crane shot, a newspaper carried by the wind, cliché dialogue, a car driving down the street, a figure walking, and so forth. The sense of line derives principally from the continuous, vigorous camera movement, and receives confirmation from a guitar melody that comes in and out of aural focus. But this shot allows for other parameters to project a sense of line; this line is notably intermedial and multisensory. And the fact that it is a single take of nearly seven minutes is essential to the creation of this line, simply because of the time element: a single shot encompassing all this stuff requires more screen time than would multiple shots. It means the film has to spend time moving *between* points that would work as places for discrete setups in a more conventional sequence. Like the choreographed qualities of the yam scene, this opening shot's flow depends on the careful coordination of bodies and cars in relation to camera movement. This shot goes much further, however. Designed explicitly as an experiment, this sequence was extremely difficult to film: beyond the two months' location scouting and one month to mock up the set, three days of rehearsal convinced the filmmakers that they would have only one

[12] Especially in *Exiled*; see Vivian Lee, *Hong Kong Cinema Since 1997: The Post-Nostalgic Imagination* (London: Palgrave Macmillan, 2009), 96–97.

chance at a single take.[13] To wanted this scene to accomplish an additional pedagogical function. Because neither of the leads had worked in an action film, To thought it would help to "have them involved throughout the whole sequence... and feel what a gunfight on a Hong Kong street would be like. Even when they're not in the scene they'll still be acting because the camera hasn't stopped."[14] Again, it seems plausible to suggest that something of what we see and hear in this sequence manages to *register the effort* behind the spatial/temporal movement through the scene. "Line" and materiality connect through the feeling of effort or friction associated with motion.

The multiparametric line works as follows: the first sounds we hear are street noises—jackhammers, a metal saw, voices—but the line is prepared by the unison attack of a crotale, a synth chord, and a low-frequency rumble as the title card appears against a black background. (The subsonic shaking could be naturalized as the vibrations given off by a heavy truck, but its source and nature are unclear, and its temporal/rhythmic placement performs useful work: it shows the soundtrack's wide ambitus and signals the haptic, visceral effects sound is capable of.) Next a classical guitar presents its wandering melody, which initiates the sense of a line: the entrenched metaphor of melodies as "lines" makes melody essential to the creation of these multiparametric structures. As the guitar begins its second phrase, the film fades up to the first shot, a skyline. The camera soon begins to move, tilting down along a tall, thin building, while the guitar's melody starts to lose its distinctiveness. Because the guitar ornaments its melody, then ad-libs and becomes noodly before nearly disappearing altogether, it seems to pass the line off to the visual domain, first giving a sense of line to the camera's tilt down, then allowing a car moving in from the back of the frame to pick up the line. The car comes forward literally and as an object of our attention, partly because it is underscored by a slightly too-present Foley sound as it gets close to the foreground. Once it passes under the camera, we notice a long-haired guy (who turns out to be Long, the main crook Yuen's right-hand man) walking forward near the center of the frame, swinging his arms; we catch him in close-up as he turns into a building and starts up the stairs before disappearing from view. That he has been carrying the line becomes clear when the camera "follows" him up the side of the building (a tilt underscored with its own Foley sound that swells into a crotale attack as the camera accelerates). We continue with repeated knocks on the door, then the guitar's main melody returns. As Yuen looks out the window, the wind-gusts increase and blow a newspaper off the roof; we watch it trace a graceful path until it lands on the windshield of Cheung's car. After Cheung reaches out the window to pull it inside the car, he and Hoi trade a few lines of typical bored-cops-on-a-stakeout dialogue. Camera movement then reasserts itself as something to follow. This goes on, for another four and a half minutes, even as the tension increases and the gunfight begins. So this shot presents a multiparametric line that

[13] To also wanted everything to be accomplished manually, without using any special effects. Teo, "Author's Interview," 234–235.

[14] Teo, "Author's Interview," 235.

depends on audiovisual objects and the directionality of melody, as well as on sinuous camera movement.

In the creation of this line and otherwise, this sequence presents an impressive variety of Foley effects that work toward differentiation. As in the celebrated mall shootout in To's *The Mission*, every gun here has its own sonic profile (report, falling casings, trail, sound on impact); the cars, jackhammers, and offscreen voices are also highly individuated. There is also a range of extradiegetic Foley sounds: the whoosh of the camera as it tilts up to follow Long inside; a lower-register wind gust that coincides with Yuen's face appearing full frame in the light, sticking his head out the window; the swell of a bowed gong accompanying Yuen's exit from the building; a thunder effect when one of the uniformed cops notices a suspicious bag in the car; a quiet, low-register wind gust as the camera pulls back to a long shot of the street; and finally a whine that could be naturalized as a vapor trail, but works as a sonic correlative to the swish-pan it is synched with. These ways of underscoring movement show, again, the *friction* that resists motion; motion thus requires *effort*. Granting the camera its own Foley sound doesn't always register its capacity to "swoop," "prowl," or "rove," to stand in as an "agent"; it can have more to do with showing the materiality of "empty" space. Whenever there's motion, these Foley sounds suggest, there's resistance. These sounds provide a way of adding weight or substance, a material feel, to the world they help depict. Mobility we already have; this gives us what slows it down. Lines seem to require friction.

We have established that this opening scene's continuity derives from more than just its being a single shot: it is important that there is a multiparametric line available to follow. The mixed composition of such lines shows that every cinematic parameter can carry the line and thus move the film forward. But the multiparametric line of the sort I am describing can also be hard to trace. It works differently for different viewers, and it is contingent on how the film is diffused. It can dead-end or fall apart. And even when it succeeds, it may constitute nothing more than a wandering arabesque: nothing says it will *take us anywhere*, that it's *worth* following. Nor can we say beforehand how such a line will affect the depiction of characters. The roles and limits of these multiparametric lines can make us think about the relative importance of narrative and other goal-driven modes of continuity. By making the continuity tenuous and refusing to guarantee the value of any narrative or extranarrative mode of continuity, these films can interest us in the *mechanisms* of continuity, including aural mechanisms. Placing weight on the idea and the *work* of following a line adds a degree of concreteness to the characters' movement through the plot and through Hong Kong spaces. Moreover, it can give the film a way of emphasizing its characters' thoughts and efforts, particularly in the performance of ordinary activities.

In other words, first we can trace a multiparametric line through the long opening shot, encouraged by the guitar's melody and the moving camera; then we witness the characters working to follow various sorts of line. Cheung discovers a blood trail leading from the crooks' abandoned police van. He points the way with his yam, and his men walk his path toward the yam vendor, then pick up the trail of the crooks. We watch the characters following different lines of reasoning—Where would the crooks hide out? What are the cops thinking?—moving in linear formations, chasing vehicles, tracing cell-phone calls, and so forth. Music/sound sometimes helps hold these lines together; one notes, for example, that the guitar melody of the opening returns once Cheung sees the drops of blood leading away from the police van. But it can also frustrate the characters' (and viewers') attempts to follow a line, such as when the sound of a conversation or a TV news report isn't granted the aural foreground. In either case, music and sound are essential to the film's sense of forward motion. Heightened Foley effects help create audiovisual objects that can shape our paths through the film. Ambient sound becomes a continuous stream, itself capable of projecting lines we can follow. Music plays a special role in this regard. Melodies can jut out of an audiovisual texture. And a musical cue always has multiple temporal levels and usually several textural strata; each musical stratum can have its own material, trajectory, and temporality. This can aid in the construction of a counterpoint of lines.

Music, Specifically

Music's role depends on the emotionality and directionality of melodic lines. Equally important is the very materiality of sound. Enhanced sonic materiality has been one entailment of a broad, slow convergence of music production and film sound design. These production practices are marked by an aesthetic emphasis on concreteness and specificity, particularly in the work of finding, processing, and deploying sounds. In the background is music's multitemporality and its possibilities as a medium uniquely able to deliver cultural memories without spelling out their meanings or demanding notice. It is also important for To's work that Hong Kong films are shot with virtually no direct sound, and that composers and sound designers are asked to work extremely quickly, on small budgets. The focus on melody and sonic materiality, in the context of Hong Kong production practices and alongside the musicalized sound design, defines the approach to music in To's films. Melody comes first, but in an *object-oriented* musical approach wherein the cues are built up from a heterogeneous group of particularized fragments (sometimes melodic, sometimes not) that come and go, interacting with the musicalized Foley and ambient sound.

The little montage scene I mentioned as encapsulating To's Hong Kong ordinary derives much of its effect from the musical cue that accompanies it, even though it uses Western instrumentation and a groove-driven approach that signifies Anglo-American popular music. As such it is worth considering from a specifically musical perspective, particularly in relation to questions of line. Here the principal melody emerges from the bass in an arrangement that also includes voices, synthesizer, and several electric guitar parts. The 45-second sequence begins like a typical driving-through-the-city montage. This sequence is underdetermined by the plot, but it reads clearly enough as a depiction of Cheung and Hoi searching for the crooks. The musical cue takes over from a blanket of semidiegetic car horns and continues into the following scene. The montage sequence divides into two halves: the first half shows their car moving against a gray sky, gray buildings, and electronics stores, all shot in an intensified style, whereas in the second half the car is shown motionless against a suddenly brighter blue sky. The second half begins with a fast-moving crane shot that parallels the car's path, continuing the sense of motion even though the car has stopped. But the dolly shot that slowly circles the rear of their average (now stationary) Honda, from left to right, shot with an anamorphic lens that also captures a bus traversing the rear of the frame right to left, takes us beyond what we would expect from a conventional driving montage. This gives way to the shot that best emblematizes the sort of scene I am trying to attend to: a nine-second shot through the windshield in which the men are eating sandwiches, underscored by Foley sounds of chewing that are clearly audible above the groove-oriented musical cue. The camera tracks slowly from Hoi to Cheung. They don't talk, they don't really acknowledge each other, they don't even seem to be looking in the same direction. They're just eating the same kind of sandwich, sitting together, perfectly fitting the interior space of the Honda's front seat. What we see is nothing more or less than a mode of being-with that allows these guys to occupy the same point in space and time, doing the same thing in two different, highly particularized ways. Cheung's purposeful mode of inhabiting himself contrasts with Hui's gently scrambly comportment. There is something perfect about this shot, but it's hard to say what, beyond its ordinariness. It depends on the specificity of Hong Kong's urban spaces and on the shot's depiction of snacking, the quintessential Hong Kong activity. But partly it is the way the scene captures how people really behave, including the strangeness, the improvisatory character, of ordinary activities, along with the weight of the immediate environment—the car's interior, the cityscape, the light, and the diegetic sound.

This scene emblematizes the use of heightened audiovisual techniques for presenting ordinary experience. We can learn something from this quiet, slowed-down depiction of being-with; one basic point is that such depictions seem to need the physical, affective, and cultural density that food, music, and urban space provide here. What does the musical cue contribute to this scene? A melodic hook projects from instrumentation that includes electric guitars and what sounds like electric bass (although it's probably a digital sample played on a keyboard). The functions and meanings of guitars thus play a role, as they often do in the music for To's films. Guitars provide a cultural thread as well as melodic lines: the guitar has served as a mode and emblem of cultural exchange, bound up with the histories of trade, imperialism, colonialism, neocolonialism, and Americanization. As this cue's heavily distorted lead-guitar part reminds us, the *electric* guitar embodies rock culture's peculiar imbrication of amplification, sex, drugs, collectivity, and commodification. In timbral terms the guitar is extraordinarily malleable, capable of both a percussive attack and sustained melodic lines, and of course it can play both melody and harmony. Culturally it is attractive to film composers and arrangers because it can efficiently code specific comportments—think about how quickly a power chord or a classical-guitar flourish can do its cultural work.[15] Plus it is also portable, inexpensive, and can give good results in any sort of recording studio; competent guitarists are never hard to find. An obvious point bears saying: when a guitar seeks the foreground, it is propelled by a host of sonic, cultural, and practical forces.

But what does it mean that this cue's main melody appears on what sounds like a *bass* guitar? A bass line doesn't normally stand alone, even when it is doing something melodic, even when it presents a texture's only melody; it is almost always part of a rhythm arrangement wherein it interacts with at least the drums and usually other rhythm-section instruments. In Anglo-American popular music and whatever derives from it, a bass-line-driven song tends to signify "black music." This more Afrocentric musical economy means that the rhythm section can bear all of a song's weight. When the bass leads, arrangements can be built from the bottom up, without requiring an emphasis on chord changes. One typical way to do so, which we hear in this cue, is to have the rhythm guitar double the bass an octave up;[16] this underscores the bass line as something to follow while at the same time keeping the rhythm guitar from taking up too much space in the arrangement. The solidity of the bass line can also allow stratified textures to emerge: other instrumental and vocal parts can come and go, each forming a discrete stratum, as the bass line maintains the groove along with the drums. Here the texture includes five such elements: a breathy middle-register male voice presenting a singable melody, a whispering male voice, the distorted lead guitar, a synthesizer melody in the mid-high register, and (briefly) a female singer ad-libbing in a sort of UK-soul style. Any of these parts *could* occupy the foreground, if they were mixed a little hotter and hung around a little longer, but the arrangement makes them subsidiary to the doubled bass line (see example 24.1).

The particularities of this bass part can influence our experience of the scene. It is constructed like a typical funky bass line in a number of ways.[17] First, it contrasts syncopation with emphasized strong beats. Second, it has a striking "freeze" on the second

EXAMPLE 24.1: Funky bass line that repeats throughout the montage sequence.

[15] And more subtly: the guitar can carry a melody and signal a style, but for cultural as well as timbral reasons, it can sometimes be read as just noodling or otherwise unworthy of attention; it therefore differs from instruments like the dizi (Chinese flute) in To's avowedly inter-Asian film *Fulltime Killer*, which can only occupy the foreground.

[16] From time to time it also harmonizes the bass line in tenths, which is also common, especially in soul, funk, and disco.

[17] This cue does not come directly from 1970s funk itself, but derives from canto-pop's connections with UK synth-pop and "new romantic" artists (like Duran Duran), whose borrowings from disco gained them access to features of funk.

half of beat 3, creating space in the first half of beat 4; in the second measure it is silent for the whole of beat 4. This also serves as a reminder that funky bass lines in general leave space—because they need to interlock with other parts, and because in classic funk basically *all* melodies leave space. Third, it has an antecedent/consequent structure, without benefit of tonic/dominant polarity, thereby working more in the manner of traditional "call and response." Fourth, it uses the lowered 7th scale-degree to reinforce the tonic (rather than a dominant chord); in a minor-mode context, at a moderate or slower tempo, this itself starts to make things funky. Fifth, all its pitches fit into a pentatonic minor collection (including only scale-degrees 1, 3, 4, 5, and 7), which allows it to be fleshed out with minor-blues harmony (that is, by using the raised 6th degree). Specifically, the bass line moves from the 1st scale-degree to scale-degree 4; its repetition creates the smooth oscillation between i and IV often found in funk, soul, and disco. Beyond these rhythmic and melodic/harmonic features are the bass line's rhetorical insistence and dry, percussive sound, both of which are enhanced by the rhythm guitar. These last two features help the bass line interact with the drum pattern in a way that funk demands. They heighten the effect of the freeze at the end of beat 3 and deepen the interaction with the bass drum; perhaps they invite the 16th-notes in the hi-hat. They also bring out the sedimentedness of this bass line's musical materials—the way these materials participate in a racialized history of Anglo-American popular music and reveal the historicity of the performing body/mind. This bass line, along with the drum pattern and the rhythm-guitar part, tells us this is bass-line-driven, groove-oriented, "urban" music in an African American tradition.

This cue isn't highly original, notably well-played or -produced, or otherwise especially lovable. The bass line is an average pastiche, a small musical object made in the studio and then sampled and looped; everything in the arrangement around it could be considered clichéd. More important, this music will provoke a range of responses, depending on a viewer/listener's familiarity with African American popular genres.[18] But I have described its features because—being this but not that, happening now but not then—they necessarily pressure the scene. Whether their genericity hits home or not, these features still color the scene's temporality, its depictions of urban space, and indeed the people who inhabit this time and place. Experiencing this 45-second montage *without* and then *with* its soundtrack can show how the down-tempo groove structures the viewer's sense of motion; how the bass line's accents and empty spaces allow visual details to emerge; and how the music's multitemporality almost grids out the space, attaching specific visual elements to corresponding rhythmic strata. I would suggest further that timbral particularity, in this slow, bass-line-driven musical environment, can signal an emphasis on concreteness in the image. So the music lends a slower speed to the follow shot of the car than the car's velocity and the urgency of the mission might imply; by contrast, the groove adds a sense of movement to the slow tracking shot across the car's front seat, which would otherwise seem nondirectional. The music

[18] Those who get that this cue is (derived from) "black music" *do* gain access to an additional layer of meaning, however.

"guides" a little point of light playing across Cheung's face and makes it an agent. When the reflection of an apartment building does a slow cartwheel across the windshield, the groove helps us see/hear it as a lilting phrase, coming and going like the snatches of melody above the bass line. Furthermore, because the groove-oriented, bass-line-driven arrangement renders the cue's vocal parts superfluous, the traditional weight and insistence of the voice must contend with the mixing board's rough justice. This compromised or contingent vocality, along with the possibilities for hearing—and failing to hear—the music's cultural references, makes the music a party to the film's broader uncertainties of identity and recognition.

Thus there are two main things this musical cue can tell us. First, the multiple pressures the cue exerts on the other parameters of the scene show how the film confronts us with a constant swirl of audiovisual elements and cultural meanings. The music works with and against other sets of strands, some of which we have access to (like the play of light), some of which we experience in highly mediated ways (like the consumption of sandwiches), and others we have to intuit (like a silent character's stream of thought). More generally we can see the way a single line—a color scheme, a visual motive, dialogue, a melody—will move in and out of focus as it contends with other streams and forces. Similarly, things come in and out of narrative roles: they sometimes advance the plot or contribute to character development and sometimes don't. This variety of functions (ranging from clear to vague) can suggest the importance of preserving or creating a space for what *doesn't need to matter*—often through an emphasis on materiality. Music, especially carefully rendered music we might not be inclined to care about, provides such a space. This scene is resolutely ordinary, free of dialogue, unable to advance the plot; it is sustained by music that is itself part of the commons. But audiovisually it is still rich, dense, slow, and particularized. The music can give everything in the image, every millisecond's worth of the characters' movements, gestures, and thoughts, something to hang on to. But the second point is this: when the music swells in this film, its *own* voices are trying to come forward. The music wants to perpetuate itself; it is not always working on behalf of the characters or the drama. The characters too must struggle for attention; their identities too are uncertain, incomplete, and experienced in ebbs and flows. What does it mean if the characters are just part of the film's audiovisual swirl?

To's Audiovisual People

My final question is, therefore, what this approach says about the characters and about To's people in general. Why would the film suggest that its people matter *sometimes* but not always? Why would it refuse to clarify whether its characters are specific or generic? And how does the intensified ordinary—including its audiovisually heightened sounds, objects, and spaces—affect the film's depictions of people? Though mostly drawn from the stock of action-film types, To's people are governed by an unusual regime. Four aspects in particular interact with heightened audiovisuality: To's interest in "little things," his sense that criminals have "more feelings than an ordinary person," his interest in showing "many groups," and his disturbing admission that he "can't describe women."[19] The director's claim that "[h]uman relationships are built on little things" emerges in a description of a scene borrowed directly from Kurosawa, in which the heroine helps the hero put on his shoe; this underscores the importance for To of actual little objects in mediating human interactions or revealing character. But To says more strongly: "It's scenes like this, fragments of human feelings.... [T]his is what society is."[20] Like this emphasis on "fragments," To's idea that criminals have "more feelings" doesn't require deep or fully drawn characters. It has only to do with moment-to-moment intensification, a kind of emotional compression: the criminals "may have more feelings than an ordinary person because they know they don't have tomorrow."[21] This desire to amass collections of "little things," meaning both objects loaded with emotionality and moments of intense feeling, reflects a cataloging impulse that provides the key to To's depiction of people. Thus he is interested in "groups" not only because he sees the "group as a microcosm of humanity," but also because he wants to "experiment and find out just how many groups I can make films about."[22]

The "experimental" accumulation of "little things" is partly why a female character's interaction with an audiovisual object can produce a heightened moment of singularity. Only once she has taken hold of a dead crook's cell phone does Commissioner Rebecca Fong become singular. Fong finds this cell phone and uses it to track Yuen to a nearby street corner. Again the film demonstrates a marked insistence on materiality and multisensory experience, especially because Fong is dealing here with visual, aural, haptic, and olfactory stimuli in the aftermath of an explosion. Her relation to the cell phone as an object is shaped by the same insistence. She gains access to the phone first by hearing it and then by bending down to pry it out of the dead man's bloody hand.[23] She quickly realizes it's an open connection to another crook on the move, who turns out to be Yuen. Another of the film's many examples of characters following lines, Fong's work here is rendered as careful listening to a series of audiovisual objects. This is how Fong's skill and character are revealed. She hears four main things coming from the cell phone: static, then street sounds, followed by an ice-cream truck in motion (its typical tune subjected to the Doppler effect), and finally a traffic signal for the visually impaired. This creates a sequence moving toward narrower focus and greater clarity of meaning and also toward more sparse and synthetic sounds. Most important, it homes in. Fong attends to progressively quieter, smaller, more discrete objects; the sound emanates from ever more specific sources. First it is just plain sound on the other end, a live connection; then simply "outside," "on the street"; then we can tell Fong realizes it's

[19] Teo, "Author's Interview," 242. And further: "I'm no good at fathoming women."

[20] Teo, "Author's Interview," 241 (ellipsis in original), referring to his *Throwdown* and Kurosawa's *Sanshiro Sugata*.

[21] Teo, "Author's Interview," 238.

[22] Teo, "Author's Interview," 221.

[23] Her effort to grasp the cell phone is—needless to say?—underscored by concerted Foley sound.

the ice-cream truck moving along *this particular* street; then she hears the sound of the traffic light on *that* particular corner. This is all revealed by the camera in increasingly plain ways: the static carries no implication of a visible source whatsoever; the street sounds aren't granted any specific visual correlative, just Fong going outside and looking around; then from Fong's perspective we see tracking shots of the ice-cream truck in motion; and finally, after several shots of Fong running toward a point she has triangulated on, there is an abrupt cut to an extreme close-up of the traffic light's speaker, which we hear (close-miked) emitting its synthetic beeps.

She is hearing these sounds mediately, of course—something this film has emphasized all along. Again, *Breaking News* thematizes "the media" and gives mediated communication, broadly defined, a huge share of the audiovisual economy. Phones in general and especially mobile phones play a big role in this: more than half a dozen pieces of business concern cell phones as objects.[24] Usually these images not only show the communication of information but also problematize the transmission itself. But all these transactions help this scene restore a sense that it is strange and wonderful how these little boxes can (also) carry *sound* from one place to another—not information, just sound. In To's post-1997 films the ordinary is a constellation of actually existing freedoms (of movement, behavior, thought) as they are impinged on by material, local, geopolitical, and world-historical forces and shaped by the work of the senses. It is precisely focused interactions like this one that serve as the point at which these forces meet the senses: this is the intensified ordinary. The specificity and generality of people, objects, and places thus emerge in odd, particularly audiovisual ways. An assertion of sound's uncanny materiality enables a display of an enigmatic lead character's thinking. This character is bound up with digital communication, but she ultimately connects with the world through an "analog" engagement with the corpse's clenched hand.[25] Similarly, this scene's narrower and narrower focus on audiovisual objects reveals a world that is more and more Hong Kong specific, culminating in the traffic light that couldn't be anywhere else.

All of To's people are products of this audiovisual regime. To often uses actors like Kelly Chen, with cosmopolitan backgrounds and atypical careers in film.[26] One might ask whether these experiences are written into her character. More important, are they written on Chen's *body*, are they *palpable* in the way she moves? Fong is constituted as a subject by the forces working through her, including cinematic, technological, sexual, affective, and material ones. This way of rendering people not only represents a posthumanist investment in a more dispersed sort of personhood, one that is tactful enough

[24] Many of To's post-1997 films make significant use of cell phones; *PTU* is an especially good example, as noted by Michael Ingham in *Johnnie To Kei-Fung's PTU* (Hong Kong: Hong Kong University Press, 2009), 46, 74–75, 83–84 and Jeff Smith in "*PTU*: Johnnie To and the Clockwork Metropolis" (in *Milkyway Image*, ed. Pun, 230–234, 238).

[25] And also soon after, when she and Yuen are tethered together—an irreducibly face-to-face connection.

[26] Chen has lived in Hong Kong, Japan, and the United States, receiving a degree from the Parsons School of Design in New York; her success as a singer has made her an inter-Asian star.

not to require depths up front; it also makes personhood more precarious—more dependent on impersonal forces and the audiovisual swirl. We are interpellated by these characters' interactions with objects, sounds, and spaces. We entrain to a character's behaviors, including semivoluntary sorts: tearing up, chewing, fumbling, talking under one's breath. We can feel we're in the middle of something "real" when we experience these characters' silent, arm's-length takings in of one another.

Perhaps To wants to keep in play both the generality and the specificity of people. He seems to care a lot about showing every *kind of person* he can, especially as he has lost interest in creating traditionally "deep" characters. The work of demonstrating what people hold in common, in all its variety, suggests a desire to illuminate everything evenly. To wants to put the whole world in italics. His own statements imply that he believes this variety is necessary to understanding the totality, or more precisely *completing the inventory*. In politics we would be nervous about someone who cared about humanity in general but nobody in specific.[27] But To's work might demonstrate that it is not paradoxical to focus on everyone. Maybe his task lies in showing the Hong Kong ordinary and creating an archive of human activities. When he wonders "how many groups" he can possibly show in his films, he is asking how much humanly experienced reality the world contains. William Empson famously wrote that it was "one of the assumptions of pastoral... that you can say everything you want about complex people through a complete consideration of simple people."[28] To seems to be suggesting, rather boldly, that by saying a precise little bit about complex characters, and just as much about the extras and everybody else on screen, you can say everything about people in general.

Bibliography

Berlant, Lauren. "Nearly Utopian, Nearly Normal: Post-Fordist Affect in *La Promesse* and *Rosetta*." *Public Culture* 19, no. 2 (2007): 273–301.

Bordwell. David. "Intensified Continuity." *Film Quarterly* 55, no. 3 (2002): 16–28.

Bordwell. David. "Louder Than Words: The Films of Johnnie To." *Artforum* (May 2003): 154–157.

Bordwell. David. "Transcultural Spaces: Toward a Poetics of Chinese Film." In *Chinese-Language Film*, ed. Sheldon Lu and Emilie Yeh, 141–162. Honolulu: University of Hawai'i Press, 2005.

Empson, William. *Some Versions of Pastoral*. New York: New Directions, 1974.

Ingham, Michael. *Johnnie To Kei-Fung's PTU*. Hong Kong: Hong Kong University Press, 2009.

James, William. *Writings 1902–1910*. New York: Library of America, 1987.

LeDoux, Joseph. *Synaptic Self: How Our Brains Become Who We Are*. New York: Penguin, 2002.

Lee, Vivian. *Hong Kong Cinema Since 1997: The Post-Nostalgic Imagination*. London: Palgrave Macmillan, 2009.

Margalit, Avishai. *The Ethics of Memory*. Cambridge, Mass.: Harvard University Press, 2002.

[27] As Dostoyevsky suggested; see Avishai Margalit, *The Ethics of Memory* (Cambridge, Mass.: Harvard University Press, 2002), 33.

[28] William Empson, *Some Versions of Pastoral* (New York: New Directions, 1974), 137.

Pang, Laikwan. "Postcolonial Hong Kong Cinema: Utlilitariansim and (Trans)local." *Postcolonial Studies* 10, no. 4 (2007): 413–430.

Pun, Lawrence, ed. *Milkyway Image, Beyond Imagination*. Hong Kong: Joint, 2006.

Smith, Jeff. "*PTU*: Johnnie To and the Clockwork Metropolis." In *Milkyway Image*, ed. Lawrence Pun, 230–234. Hong Kong: Joint, 2006.

Teo, Stephen. "Author's Interview." In *Director in Action: Johnnie To and the Hong Kong Action Film*, 215–244. Hong Kong: Hong Kong University Press, 2008.

PART V

EMERGING AUDIOVISUAL FORMS

MUSIC VIDEO AND BEYOND

CHAPTER 25

MUSIC VIDEO'S SECOND AESTHETIC?

CAROL VERNALLIS

How different is a Lady Gaga video from one by A Flock of Seagulls? MTV's first broadcast was thirty years ago. Music video has since undergone shifts in technologies and platforms, periods of intense cross-pollination with other media, financial booms and busts, and changing levels of audience engagement. While music videos hit a low point in the 00s as budgets dried up, they have reemerged as a key driver of popular culture.[1] Music video's moment of resurgence resembles MTV's first moment: there seems to be a question of what music video can do and where it fits.

What does it mean to look back on this thirty-year history? A comparison of the beginnings and the present might show vast differences in performance style, formal conceits, editing, depictions of space, and the showcasing of new technologies—or it might not. Might we track the changes from 1979 to 2012? Should we follow the arrivals of new technologies or the migrations to new venues and platforms—from low-res video production in the eighties, to high-gloss 35-millimeter in the nineties, to flexible digital technologies in the 2000s; from BET, MTV- and late-night TV to YouTube, Vimeo and Vevo? We might instead follow the cycles of maturation (in genres like rap and metal), or auteurs' interests and influence and the ways audiences participate with music video. Or we might track the image's response to pop music's changing production practices and vice versa, or the larger cultural turn toward the audiovisual.

Such a project would be too ambitious for a single chapter. Instead, I treat a narrower topic, providing a frame and focusing on some videos from today and from the eighties. Looking back to the eighties and comparing them with the present moment makes sense: new technologies and changing platforms have shaped video making in both

[1] Music video is financially viable again, as directors and musicians embed product placement in clips, and YouTube clips link directly to the industry-driven site VEVO. A version of this chapter appears in my book *Unruly Media: YouTube Music Video, and the New Digital Cinema* (New York: Oxford University Press, forthcoming).

moments. A variety of styles, genres, tropes, and treatments of space marks both the eighties and today. This chapter aims to provide a sense of whether the genre has become savvier and more open to experimentation or more ossified, and what this thirty-year history might add up to.

What is a music video? At one time we knew, but no longer; part of the change has to do with media contexts. In the eighties and nineties, music videos were primarily seen on a few satellite services—like MTV, BET or VHI—or in a countdown on broadcast television late at night, and it was difficult for record companies to get their clips on the air. To make the MTV rotation, clips were first vetted by a board of ten, then had to clear the Standards and Practices division. Consciously or unconsciously, directors and artists tailored their work for these committees. Standards and Practices was an especially difficult hurdle, seemingly wielding as much power as the Hays Office in the 50s. Directors and musicians could never predict which constraints would be enforced. For example, no alcohol or product placement was supposed to appear on MTV (unless you were Guns N' Roses). Some forms of smooching and T&A were okay, others not.[2] Most submissions to the station never aired, and those that did possessed a high degree of uniformity, probably resulting from the cat-and-mouse games between censors and directors. Today music video clips are dispersed across a number of commercial Web sites (Vevo, Hulu, Launch, MTV, Pitchfork), as well as YouTube. There is little vetting of clips. Except for concerns about copyright violations (a constant struggle), prosumers feel free to upload a range of material that confounds genres. For example, many clips with full-frontal nudity remain up even though YouTube viewers can flag them.[3]

We used to define music video as a product of the record company in which images are put to a recorded pop song in order to sell the song. None of this definition holds any more. On YouTube, individuals as much as record companies post music video clips, and many prosumers have no hope of selling anything. The image can be taken from a variety of sources and a song recorded afterward; a clip might look like a music video, but the music might be neither prior nor preeminent. In addition, the song might not be a pop song but something similar (ambient, electronic) or very different (jazz or opera). Clips can range from ten seconds to several hours; no longer is there a predictable four- to five-minute format.[4] All sorts of interruptions can occur (an insertion of a trailer clip or someone talking), and material from other genres may infiltrate (commercials, sportscasts). Music videos appear in new and unexpected media, interactive games and iPhone apps. A dizzying array of user-based content ranges from vidding and remixes to mashups. It still makes sense to call all these music videos.

We might thus define music video, simply and perhaps too broadly, as a relation of sound and image that we recognize as such. YouTube especially makes it hard to draw a

[2] At least the Hays Office distributed a highly codified list of what was disallowed.

[3] A prosumer is a consumer who does production. The work can be semiprofessional.

[4] TV On the Radio's album-length music video collection; R. Kelly's opera-length "Trapped in the Closet," at http://www.youtube.com/watch?v=_Ch4dKpBJmU and Kanye West's "Runaway," at http://www.youtube.com/watch?v=Jg5wkZ-dJXA] (accessed October 11, 2011).

line between what is a music video and not. We might keep all of the attributes that once made up music video hovering like a shadowy constellation, calling on them to help us read the new clips. We might also strengthen the definition to include the requirement that the images seem engaged with showing off the soundtrack to some extent. But even adding this corollary provides little assistance. Music, sound, and image can be so tightly interwoven in some segments of contemporary film that we might see them as music video sequences; once these appear on YouTube they can seem indistinguishable from other clips. In large segments of today's films, too, the soundtrack may be more striking than the image. Conversely, on YouTube some sleepy music videos have such a passive soundtrack that there's almost nothing to show off, but these clips are nothing if not music videos.[5]

At the same time that we define music video inclusively and expansively, we may wish to restrict the focus. In the thirty years of music video, various sorts of "canon" have emerged. We can see why it is useful to flag some musicians' and directors' bodies of work, as well as particular historical moments. It is hard to be rigorous about what exactly is within this genre, and what is an outlier. Wittgenstein's idea that genres are made up of family resemblances might prove helpful here. For example, games can share a number of features, but not all; they can be related but very different (chess and hopscotch are both games, for example). This may also hold true for music video and music video-like aesthetics.

Recent studies have embraced analytic methods that better encompass this larger body of materials and more deeply consider what music videos were then and are now. Nicholas Cook has defined three types of interaction between music and images: complement, conformance, and contrast. The first shows off or brings to light; the second matches or replicates; and the last differs or works against. He also notes that one medium can fill in the gap of another's. Michel Chion's concept of added value, wherein the image seems to absorb or take on the attributes of the music, as well as the notion of empathetic and anempathetic relations, can also apply to music video. Claudia Gorbman's model, holding that music seeks out attributes in the image, is another helpful approach. There is also my own, which considers the ways sound and image reflect individual parameters such as narrative, teleological drive, harmony, timbre, rhythm, and so forth.[6]

But a broader picture of music video may require a new model. Because music videos place song and image in a relation of copresence, I suggest that we consider them as

[5] The definition of music video I advanced in *Experiencing Music Video* also seems obsolete. There I argued that music video image seeks to sell a song by showing off musical features in a serial fashion (because one can't reveal all of them simultaneously). This careful tracking of musical features largely holds true for the industry-funded music videos of big-name artists, but not for today's music videos more broadly. Carol Vernallis, *Experiencing Music Video: Aesthetics and Cultural Context* (New York: Columbia University Press, 2004), 68.

[6] Nicholas Cook, *Analysing Musical Multimedia* (New York & Oxford: Oxford University Press, 1998), 98–106. Michel Chion, *Audio-Vision: Sound on Screen* (New York: Columbia University Press, 1994), 5. Claudia Gorbman, in "Aesthetics and Rhetoric," *American Music* 22, no. 1 (Spring 2004): 14–26, cites Bernard Herrmann's famous quote, drawing from Cook's *Analysing Musical Multimedia*, 104. Gorbman's *Unheard Melodies: Narrative Film Music* (London: BFI [1987], 2, 57) is considered the first major scholarly work on film scoring. She discusses many topics, including what music does in the movies and how it does it. She notes that music relaxes the "psychic sensor" and provides interpretive assistance

partners: we might sit them on the couch and imagine them in couples therapy. As analysts, we might consider each spouse in turn. What kinds of behavior does this persona exhibit, what attitudes, dispositions, traits, and ways of functioning? In what ways is each able to listen to or shoulder the requests of the other? Are there examples of pushing and shoving, stifling, or mutual admiration? Asking each to articulate needs in classic therapeutic language is not too farfetched: "when you do this, I feel this," or "if you do this, I will be better able to do this." We can assume there are issues of dominance and subservience, passivity and aggression. In music-image relations, one medium often seems to be pushing the other to do something, acting as the driver. Each suffers from not being able to show all it has. If only it had a different partner! Some new entity or quality emerges from the couple's relationship, and we respond more to that quality than to either individual in the pair. This aspect is surely contingent and constructed, but it feels so densely colored. Similarly, we may think of the music–image relationship as a new hyper-being.[7]

Two short examples will show how audiovisual relations in music video might be structured this way. Sigur Rós's and Floria Sigismondi's clip "Untitled" presents itself immediately as stoic, abject, and vulnerable. The song and imagery show some overlapping traits: the visual track suggests the schoolchildren are charming, tender, oppressed, and innocent. The music is also sympathetic to these children's circumstances, but it is witnessing: it's not going to step in and help them. (This stance is literalized when at one moment a teacher's hand runs down a child's hair, but both adult and child remain unresponsive to the other. Music takes no note here, simply coursing on.) Establishing the unresponsiveness between sound and image early in the clip is important. Later the children go out in gas masks to play in a dark, burnt-out, post-apocalyptic wasteland where blackened dust falls like snow.

Lady Gaga's "Born This Way" and Kanye West's "Power," on the other hand, project a superfluidity of emotion: energy flows from the music and image together. These two videos, both alone in relationship with their music and image and together as dynamic multimedia clips, feel like good corporate entities. Each stares side by side like two contenders in a beauty pageant. Both feature the star placed at the center of an outwardly expanding vortex.[8]

Asking what the music and image are saying to one another, how they act as players and performers, can reveal a music video's persuasiveness or allure. "Born This Way"

to combat the ambiguity of visual cues. Nevertheless, what I value most is the ways she considers what music and image do together and apart. Drawing on film scenes, for example, bicyclists on a holiday in Truffaut's *Jules and Jim*, she queries the ways music shapes our attention to the image.

[7] Kay Dickinson's approach which considers music-image relations that have gone bad seems particularly relevant here. See her book *Off Key: When Film and Music Won't Work Together* (New York & Oxford: Oxford University Press, 2008).

[8] Sigur Rós, "Untitled," at http://www.vevo.com/watch/sigur-ros-1/untitled/GBK680300010; Lady Gaga, "Born This Way," at http://www.vevo.com/watch/lady-gaga/born-this-way/USUV71100098?source=ap and Kanye West, "Power," at http://www.vevo.com/watch/kanye-west/power/USUV71001422?source=ap (all accessed October 11, 2011).

and "Power" suggest that the first imperative is cultural work rather than fine musical or formal relations. Music video's main goal here may be simply to pull us out of the recession and sync us up with one another. And why shouldn't music video step into the breach? I argue elsewhere that if we can get coordinated around a hook (a syllable like "ga," a visual stutter, a "beep beep beep" buzzy tone, or a simple image like that of a kiss), perhaps we'll be attuned enough to address corporate domination and environmental disaster. According to Siegfried Kracauer, Busby Berkeley's musicals with lines of chorines helped keep capitalism going.[9] Why not music video today?

Let us begin a comparison of eighties videos with present-day ones, focusing in both periods on videos produced by the large record labels., I adopt a parametric approach, considering elements like form, color, editing, technology, and performance. (In a few cases—editing, performance—I'll add a brief historical overview.) The chapter ends with a return to the wider definition of music video and my suggestion of an *interpersonal* method for understanding music-image relations to help compare the two historical moments.

It is my hope that an interpersonal method will help us assess this history of heterogeneous audiovisual materials. Music video is difficult to evaluate. The genre possesses an odd particularity—is comprised of intangibles that have analogs to pop music like syncopation, rubato, articulation, and grain; it's fragile.[10] I will float the claim that many eighties videos possess more charm, allure or power than their contemporaries today, not only because a community cared about them, and the work was so novel, but because the audiovisual relations were special. In eighties videos, directors were trying to discover how to get the new technology of videotape to catch up with the song. This effort is literalized in a video like A-Ha's "Take on Me," where the rotoscoped (animated) hand reaches up to the (live-action) woman as the lead singer sings "up." Similarly there is something fragile and earned about the intimacy of U2's "With or Without You" and George Michael's "Father Figure." Both videos are haunted, as the performers and supporting characters press forward through hazy diffusion, stoically aiming to make a connection that may not happen. This lost-versus-found relation is endearing; it may remind us of our own fraught relations and our desires for what might be. Today's attempts, such as Beyoncé's "1 + 1," a supercharged, hypersexualized video ("make love to me as the war rages"—even the lyrics are jacked up), can seem jaded compared to U2's "With or Without You."[11] Perhaps the eighties were a fortuitous moment when our knowledge of technology, culture, music and image produced some special tension or frisson. But then again, today's moment has its own special newness. Directors are struggling with surprising limitations and possibilities. While budgets

9 Siegfried Kracauer, "Girls und Krise," *Frankfurter Zeitung*, May 27, 1931.

10 Pam Belluck, "To Tug Hearts, Music First Must Tickle the Neurons," *New York Times*, April 18, 2011.

11 A-Ha, "Take on Me," at http://www.youtube.com/watch?v=djV11Xbc914; U2's "With or Without You," at http://www.youtube.com/watch?v=XmSdTa9kaiQ&ob=av3e; Andy Morahan and George Michael's "Father Figure," at http://www.vevo.com/watch/george-michael/father-figure/GB0200202150; and Beyoncé, "1 + 1," at http://www.youtube.com/watch?v=KaasJ44O5lI (all accessed October 11, 2011).

have been drastically curtailed, new technologies enable all kinds of new configurations. Changes in methods of pop songwriting along with new audio and video recording and producing technologies may free music videos from the classic, strongly demarcated verse-chorus alternation, making possible a new emphasis on shifting intensities and textures.[12] Learning how to enact these new modes is exciting for practitioners. Many have been in the industry a long time, sometimes working in film when music video budgets were low, but coming back for love of the genre. Their knowledge informs this generation of clips.

Audiovisual Relations in the Eighties and Today

Technology

Do technologies call attention to themselves now more than in the past? Mathias Korsgaard celebrates the recent foregrounding of visual effects like the video trail, kaleidoscope, stamped multiples, and sinusoidal designs. He claims these digital technologies show off music's plurality.[13] But one could argue that similar effects occur just as frequently in eighties videos, like David Byrne's "Once in a Lifetime," Prince's "When Doves Cry," and Queen's "Bohemian Rhapsody." It is true that the technological devices in these videos are not quite as riveting or hallucinogenic as today's. There is something a bit more insistent in recent clips—friskier. But perhaps this is occurring now because MTV cast a conservative shadow, and the wider number of venues, from YouTube to Vevo, has loosened things up a bit. Another question concerns the history and the incorporation of technologies in music video. Why do some become popular at certain points and not others? It has been noted that new visual technologies often appear first in music video. (Examples include the snorkel cam in Steve Winwood's "Roll with It" and the Quantel in Cutting Crew's "I Just Died in Your Arms Tonight.") [14]

[12] I'd like to thank John Richardson for coining this phrase. For more on contemporary audiovisual aesthetics see his *An Eye for Music: Popular Music and the Audiovisual Surreal* (New York & Oxford: Oxford University Press, 2011).

[13] Mathias Korsgaard, "Creation and Erasure: Music Video as a Signaletic Form of Practice," *Journal of Aesthetics & Culture* 4 (2012), at http://www.aestheticsandculture.net/index.php/jac/article/view/18151/22823 (accessed October 11, 2011).

[14] David Byrne, "Once in a Lifetime," at http://www.youtube.com/watch?v=I1wg1DNHbNU; Prince, "When Doves Cry," at http://www.slack-time.com/music-video-6416-Prince-When-Doves-Cry; Queen, "Bohemian Rhapsody," at http://www.vevo.com/watch/queen/bohemian-rhapsody/GB0400201412; Steve Winwood, "Roll with It," at http://www.youtube.com/watch?v=fWptXUblA4E; and Cutting Crew, "I Just Died in Your Arms Tonight," at http://www.youtube.com/watch?v=Ua26qTEK25U (all accessed October 11, 2011).

As I write, Right now kaleidoscopes are popular, for example in Selena Gomez's "Naturally," Beyoncé's "1 + 1," and Gnarls Barkley's "Crazy." Perhaps they match today's musical materials, or they are nostalgic, or they pick up some musical feature that has recently become popular. The trails and kaleidoscopes might also project well on cell phones. Back in the eighties, the frame was frequently fractured into quadrants or blocks (as in Michael Jackson's "Billie Jean"). Today that is a familiar effect, but in the eighties it was tremendously exciting.[15]

This makes sense: music videos were higher profile then, but had lower costs and fewer aesthetic constraints. Today, with so many media forms and venues, innovations may appear elsewhere first. Not all visual effects have been useful for music video. Michael Jackson's "Black or White" was the first to employ morphing, for example, but it did so only during the song's break. Then the device nearly vanished from use. Perhaps morphing is so engaging that it draws attention away from the music; it's also relatively continuous and seamless, so may provide a poor complement to musical transformations. Bullet time, on the other hand, has remained popular (appearing for example in Lady Gaga's "Bad Romance"). This technique may be engaging because it makes music's time strange.[16]

In the eighties, technological gizmos were often used to foreground a song's form. Multiples might quickly carry us from a sparser verse into a thickened chorus. (One device favored then was using multiple instruments wedged into the frame's edges, such as The Police's "Every Breath You Take.") Perhaps directors have discovered how to produce strong audiovisual relations through many parameters, most strikingly through the use of color. So today's technologies do not need to do as much work. (Note the kaleidoscopes in Beyoncé's "1+1;" though they are musical, they seem to appear more for their local charm than as a means to assert large-scale structure.)

Can technologies help change our understanding of space and time? The trails in today's OK Go "WTF" and the pixelation in Kanye West's "Welcome to Heartbreak" help to suggest a Bergsonian present: we are aware that the present is like a saddle, with the past streaming behind us and the future yet to arrive. But I would argue that David Bowie's 1980 "Ashes to Ashes" with its image solarization seems to do an even better job of this. Surely these devices respond in part to the pop song's arrangement, lyrics, and their relation to the image-scape.[17]

[15] Selena Gomez and the Scene, "Naturally," at http://www.vevo.com/watch/selena-gomez-and-the-scene/naturally/USH5V0920974; Gnarls Barkley, "Crazy," at http://www.youtube.com/watch?v=7W2KR_z9PoM; and Michael Jackson, "Billie Jean," at http://www.vevo.com/watch/michael-jackson/billie-jean/USSM20301088. Other examples of quadrants include Asia's "Heat of the Moment," at http://www.youtube.com/watch?v=wlTvWvfEMxE (all accessed October 11, 2011).

[16] Michael Jackson, "Black or White," at http://www.vevo.com/watch/michael-jackson/black-or-white/USSM20300985; and Lady Gaga, "Bad Romance," at http://www.vevo.com/watch/lady-gaga/bad-romance/USUV70903493 (accessed October 11, 2011).

[17] The Police, "Every Breath You Take," at http://www.vevo.com/watch/the-police/every-breath-you-take/GBF060300032; OK Go, "WTF?" at http://www.youtube.com/watch?v=12zJw9varYE; Kanye West,

We may also track subtle flows of artistry and influence. In the spring of 2011, there were numerous 1000-hit alternative (non-commercial) videos that foregrounded technological gimmicks. Suddenly by the summer's end, it seemed mainstream directors had capitalized on them. (Such a fast turn! How can we guess where music video will be in a year?) Handmade, low-cost devices and techniques have always appeared alongside their more expensive siblings, often with equally striking results. In the eighties when directors were using the Quantel box to produce prism effects, others were holding beveled mirrors before the camera to produce kaleidoscopic patterns. Today, Michel Gondry has made low-tech his stylistic signature. And other music video directors on small budgets find alternatives: without fancy software like After Effects (which can produce prisms in the background), directors simply paste Xeroxed sheets of paper on the wall (such as Azis's "Bulgaria +18 [Tits and Penis]").[18] The role of the technological gimmick differs between large-budget mainstream clips and alt-independent siblings. For mainstream clips, digitally distorted effects tend to be narrativized and the performer's body and face remain legible. For example, kaleidoscopes and mirroring in Linkin Park's "Iridescent" are naturalized by a Gothic landscape that seems out of Lang's *Metropolis*. Similarly, Selena Gomez's "Naturally" has multiples, but it also harks back to Busby Berkeley's art deco look. Gomez looks dressed up for the prom, and the mirroring might suggest the fancy hotel where she and her boyfriend first paint the town. [19]

In what ways are today's visual schemes, with their sinusoidal waves, meant to complement the digitally enabled, buzzy soundtrack? Perhaps we cannot discern how much the digital image is driven by its technological context, and how much it is responding to musical features, like qualities of tempo, rhythm and timbre.[20] We might note that the weightlessness of the sinusoidal and the buzzy has a long history: music videos have long used light shows and visual micro-articulations, and these may help to disarticulate objects and performers from their settings. Today we might consider Radiohead's "House of Cards" or OK Go's "WTF," but earlier films and videos like Erasure's "A Little Respect" and Michael Jackson's "Rock with You" also became weightless.[21] The similarity among these examples—changing colored light—suggests that highlighting shifting

"Welcome to Heartbreak," at http://www.youtube.com/watch?v=wMHoe8kIZtE; and David Bowie, "Ashes to Ashes," at http://www.youtube.com/watch?v=CMThz7eQ6Ko&ob=av2n (all accessed October 11, 2011).

[18] Azis, "Bulgaria +18 [Tits and Penis]," at http://www.youtube.com/watch?v=78g5AAWtRQw (accessed October 11, 2011).

[19] Linkin Park, "Iridescent," at http://www.youtube.com/watch?v=xLYiIBCN9ec&ob=av2e (accessed October 11, 2011); and Selena Gomez and the Scene, "Naturally," at http://vimeo.com/61429208 (accessed June 11, 2013).

[20] I've argued in *Experiencing Music Video* for the ways the image reflects music's processual nature and its heterogeneity. Vernallis, *Experiencing Music Video*, 68.

[21] Radiohead, "House of Cards," at http://www.youtube.com/watch?v=8nTFjVm9sTQ; Erasure, "A Little Respect," at http://www.youtube.com/watch?v=65lyoDUDWQg; and Michael Jackson's "Rock with You," at http://www.vevo.com/watch/michael-jackson/rock-with-you/USSM20301087 (all accessed October 11, 2011).

musical features like timbre and time passing is more relevant than showcasing technological advances.

From another perspective, however, these showy technological effects just work aggressively. Not musicality, but rather visual or aural novelty, may be what catches a viewer's attention. (Or do these technologies work like musical hooks drawing her into the music?) Technological gimmicks, or showboating, can highlight the question of what kinds of images go with what kinds of music. Perhaps sync only needs to be good enough, and then music and image can each independently go about its business.

Color and Digital Intermediate

In the eighties and nineties, music video was a hotbed of color experimentation, even though directors could not change each pixel's color through digital intermediate (DI). Even before the 1994 Gatorade commercial,[22] elements in the frame were cordoned off and given lurid color; rotoscoping also gave the image fine detail through hand-tinted, frame-by-frame animation (e.g., The Outfield's "Since You've Been Gone" and INXS's "What You Want").[23] Telecine could amp up a color across the image, and directors would shoot to exploit this. For example, it was common to see very bluish diaphanous cloth from drapery and orange tints from fire or candlelight in eighties and nineties videos (e.g., David Fincher's and George Michael's "Freedom," or Bonnie Tyler's "Total Eclipse of the Heart"). With DI, however, color management provides a much wider range and more detailed possibilities for shading. Music video today is loudly proclaiming its capacity for hyper-control in many ways. Think of all the videos that proclaim, "We have color!" In the Coldplay video "Every Teardrop Is a Waterfall," buckets of paint are spray-painted onto the characters, the background walls, and tenement buildings' facades; the lead singer then comes forward wearing a deeply purple T-shirt. Painting on walls has always been a music-video trope, but in the Coldplay video it occurs on so many different planes—even on a virtually-configured epoxy sheet placed in front of the camera. There are also new videos that foreground party drinks. Every plastic cup is separated out and given a different shade, as if the drinks had become elixirs and then everything suddenly turns black-lit and fluorescent. Colors in videos also seem to be conversing about the latest fashions, as if trends were quickly streaming by, and some videos might miss the boat. Recently some wan-looking yellows, pinks, and greens have appeared, one suspects because others flaunt the same hue. Colorist David Hussey

22 The Gatorade commercial—in black and white except the Gatorade—made its debut in 1994. See http://articles.chicagotribune.com/1994-04-13/business/9404130237_1_isotonic-beverage-boston-chicken-fluid-absorption (accessed October 11, 2011).

23 The Outfield, "Since You've Been Gone," at http://www.vevo.com/watch/the-outfield/since-youve-been-gone/USSM20400831; and INXS, "What You Need," at http://www.youtube.com/watch?v=vSME53nL8tg. Belinda Carlisle's "I Get Weak," at http://www.youtube.com/watch?v=nmMCXLdNrz8&ob=av2n, is another video that uses the isolation of color for expressive effects (all accessed October 11, 2011).

claims that few practitioners today want to work with magenta, because it reminds viewers of the eighties. I've seen it creep slightly back in, by way of a hot pink (see Dave Meyers and Rihanna's "Where Have You Been" and recent T-Mobile ads).

The control of color opens up many new possibilities. Music video now can go very dark, as dark as the darkest night, and then suddenly become sharply lit (like David Guetta's video featuring Ludacris's and Taio Cruz's "Little Bad Girl"). Varied types of footage can be more readily combined, as in Katy Perry's "E.T.," which blends super-8-like footage with digital projections onto blue screen. Streaks of light and color can also be added to the frame, complicating and enriching it, suggesting that the music and the people have been touched by sonic waves, God's touch, or aliens—we never know.[24]

DI can serve as a focal point or pivot. Directors put a lot of time into what Jonas Akerlund calls "beauty work," retouching the star in post production (Akerlund likes to digitally enhance a performer's mouth so that it opens wider, for example). Directors often change the color of the eye's iris from shot to shot. In Gaga's "Judas," her eye color turns from green to blue. Akerlund's videos take much care with expressive fingernail polish (notice the black with white stripes, the circled silver, and the American flags—like in "Telephone"). Imagine you have modified the star's iris and fingernails. From there you can start turning her into pure color: consider Mika's "We Are Golden," Lady Gaga and Beyoncé's "Telephone," Madonna's "Ray of Light," and Britney Spears's "Hold It Against Me."[25]

In mainstream music videos, color is usually thematized (painting on buildings, drinking from cups); even when color serves as a backdrop (as in Hype Williams's clips), it cannot just be free. Independent videos sometimes suggest that it can. Color's historical trajectory in music video overlaps with and diverges from its treatment in cinema. Eighties video seemed to be predominantly scaped in blue, whereas in the nineties videos were golden and red. These colors were independent of cultural fashions. The popularity of these colors may have been tied to timbre and production practices. Colors were certainly tied to race, genre and gender.[26] Color provides new possibilities in terms of experience, culture and ideology. Floria Sigismund, tired of all the silver and gray cars, decides to imagine her technofuture world tinted with feminine gold, pink and lavender in Katy Perry's "E.T." But first Perry flies down in a uterine, hibiscus, purple-blue-fuchsia world. Such painterly effects can make us feel that, like Perry, we too are in utero.[27]

[24] Katy Perry featuring Kanye West, "E.T.," at http://www.youtube.com/watch?v=t5Sd5c409UM&ob=av2e; and David Guetta featuring Ludacris and Taio Cruz, "Little Bad Girl," at http://www.vevo.com/watch/david-guetta/little-bad-girl/GB28K1120016 (both accessed October 11, 2011).

[25] Lady Gaga, "Judas," at http://www.youtube.com/watch?v=wagn8Wrmzuc&ob=av2e; Mika, "We Are Golden," at http://www.youtube.com/watch?v=hEhutIEUq8k&ob=av2e; and Britney Spears, "Hold It Against Me," at http://www.youtube.com/watch?v=-Edv8Onsrgg&ob=av2e (all accessed October 11, 2011).

[26] See Vernallis, *Experiencing Music Video*, 125.

[27] Katy Perry featuring Kanye West, "E.T.," (see n. 24).

Materiality and Microrhythms

Fine, changeable and tangible things of the world—dust, water, smoke, and clouds—may be more insistently depicted today because digital cameras have become so adept at capturing detail. As Chion notes, visual microrhythms function well within audiovisually rich media, because they resemble musical processes.[28] As sound waves decay, they exhibit granular detail (through an oscilloscope, one can see these sound waves breaking into fractal patterns). Today these help show off features in pop songs. Producers arranging for low bit-rates choose musical objects sharply differentiated through timbre—for example, buzzy versus smooth. Grain and its absence then come to the fore: music video directors often respond to these production choices by picking highly differentiated visual detail.[29] Of course, earlier music video directors also foregrounded such effects. One of the best music videos of the eighties, U2's "With or Without You," worked with delicate projections of shadows of tree branches and water. But consider Adele's 2011 "Rolling in the Deep," with the dust motes that surround her and the water glasses on the floor that shimmy their contents as the music marks the beat. Each element is marked off so clearly it is almost as if we were examining the video's detail through a magnifying glass.[30]

With digital intermediate, smoke and clouds can become performers. Beyoncé's "Best Thing I Never Had" contains little performance, except that she sings in her bra and underwear (okay, maybe that's a lot) and then slowly gets into a wedding dress. But behind her there's a lot of business. The sky sometimes shifts color slowly, sometimes very quickly, so that the clouds themselves maintain our interest. Clouds have long been foregrounded in music video, as in Herb Ritts's videos for Chris Isaak, "Wicked Games." But today, a finer grain of control allows clouds to come to the fore for much greater lengths of time. David Fincher claimed for film that the first thing viewers track is light, the play of light and shadow. With music video we track the play of light and shadow against sound.[31]

[28] Michel Chion, *Audio-vision: Sound on Screen*, trans. Claudia Gorbman (New York: Columbia University Press, 1994), 16.

[29] Janet Jackson's "Make Me," at http://www.youtube.com/watch?v=ZwQyUTkGOew (accessed October 11, 2011), foregrounds the way director Michael Hales isolates and brings to the fore various musical elements—easier to do now with digital technologies.

[30] U2, "With or Without You," at http://www.youtube.com/watch?v=XmSdTa9kaiQ&ob=av2e; and Adele, "Rolling in the Deep," at http://www.youtube.com/watch?v=rYEDA3JcQqw&ob=av2e. The Human League's "Human," at http://www.vevo.com/watch/the-human-league/human/GB1200301690, is another eighties example. Janet Jackson and Busta Rhymes's "What's It Gonna Be," at http://www.youtube.com/watch?v=P4PFClnMkOU, is a nineties one. (All links accessed October 11 2011.)

[31] Beyoncé, "Best Thing I Never Had," at http://www.youtube.com/watch?v=FHp2KgyQUFk&ob=av2e (accessed October 11, 2011); and Chris Isaak, "Wicked Games," at http://www.youtube.com/watch?v=UAOxCqSxRDo (accessed October 11, 2011). Conversation with director, Spring 1998.

Rhythmic Subtlety

Rhythmic subtlety in the eighties was often difficult to create: clips were mostly edited on video, some without timecode (e.g., found footage). Frame counts were inaccurate;; even with timecode, an editor would suffer a one- or two-frame slip. A sequence of tight, brief edits might take forever. Forms of rhythmic articulation seen today were nearly impossible to achieve then. While I've only seen a few recent examples that really strike me as both virtuosic and unachievable by earlier technologies, they point to what the future might yield. Ke$ha's and Taio's "Take a Dirty Picture of Me," for example, foregrounds a sense of speed-ramping, of acceleration and deceleration, as a sports car revs against passing telephone poles and mountains, and the music also whip-pans between accelerando and diminuendo. The clip suggests a new experience of frenetic tautness. Consider Akerlund's and Pink's "Sober." The shot lengths and the editing are surprising and exact; nothing this precise existed before. It took not only the advent of the digital, but also a few years of practice, to change the way shot lengths worked in music video.[32]

Shots and Editing

Have shots and editing in music video become more sophisticated or better able to reflect musical features? I begin here with a few historically situated styles that point to larger stylistic shifts. As mentioned, in the eighties, figures moved and suddenly froze as still frames, or were suddenly startled by hard edits as if through electric shocks. The boomy synth sucked up the frequency range; sounds weren't quite assimilated into pop song writing (or much else).[33] Director Matt Maturin's strange gaps from shot to shot often seemed like non-sequiturs: what are the images saying to one another, and the viewer? In the late eighties, Mark Pellington discovered how to project a series of staccato-shots composed of two to three frames, alongside incorporated bits of text with strong graphic values. Marcus Nispel created "dolly within dolly" moves in which the camera's motion constantly circled. Tarsem Singh made videos with a lot of leader and flash-frames, raising the question of what counts as an edit. In the early nineties Hype Williams used wide-angle lens and strange sets to distort the characters into loveable, superhero, cartoon-types. Videos for hip-hop artists like Biggie Smalls showcased a relaxed style, wherein the long shots' edits would fall off the beats and one couldn't predict where they would land. In the 2000s Floria Sigismondi employed edgy, hard edits, attenuating narrative drive. Later Alan Ferguson

[32] Taio Cruz, "Take a Dirty Picture of Me," at http://www.youtube.com/watch?v=RgnXl7fzoBc; and Pink, "Sober," at http://www.youtube.com/watch?v=nJ3ZM8FDBlg (both accessed October 11, 2011).

[33] This aesthetic was both technologically and musically driven. A video with different concerns, R.E.M.'s "Driver 8," showcased folk guitar and nostalgia and featured grainy super-8 footage of trains.

established an all-over technique wherein every single musical element might be picked up within the frame.[34]

Some types of framing and editing we see today could not have been done in the eighties. Jonas Akerlund likes to use an extreme wide-angle shot of the setting and then cut quickly to an extreme close-up. Without digital cameras and new postproduction techniques, I doubt this shift would make much sense. He may also cut three or four fast shots around the face at well-judged off-angles. These are hard to see; viewers likely don't register them as a cubist realization, but just experience deeper immersion with a character.

Framing too has changed. A musically saturated culture (iPods everywhere), a long period of the public shooting with cell phones (so visual literacy has risen), lighter cameras, and a history of music-video practices have all contributed to an image no longer framed four-square, flush along a horizon on a tripod. In music video today one can see much freer framing, as in Melina Matsoukas's and Rihanna's "Rude Boy." Here off-kilter shapes come into the frame from all sides. Layers build up and we're not sure where they will stop. And then while all this is going on, a beautiful moment arrives. Instead of following Rihanna's gorgeous moves, the instruments, or the engaging Warholian graphics of grenades and pineapples, my eye drifts to a slow black stain seeping slowly from the top of the frame. Contrast "Rude Boy" with INXS's "What You Need." Too four-square! Though "What You Need" looks contemporary—animation has long contributed to the most vanguard music videos—the camera's framing and the way images build toward the chorus reflect an earlier period.[35]

Some of today's videos flaunt off-angled and elongated forms on the bias streaking past the lens, like Skrillex's "First of the Year." Cars skidding and horses galloping (sometimes together in the same clip) often suggest both multi-temporality and freedom.

Narrative and Large-Scale Forms

I have described visual elements such as color, microrhythms, and editing before narrative, because these are the things that come to the fore today and feel like a shift from the

34 The clips include Mark Pellington and Pearl Jam's "Jeremy," at http://www.youtube.com/watch?v=MS91knuzoOA&ob=av2e; Marcus Nispel and C&C Factory's "Everybody Dance Now,"at http://www.youtube.com/watch?v=N2VQQEoWlTg; Amy Grant's "House of Love," at http://www.youtube.com/watch?v=aXxXj7rzZy4&ob=av2n; Tarsem Singh and R.E.M.'s "Losing My Religion," at http://www.youtube.com/watch?v=if-UzXIQ5vw&ob=av2e; Hype Williams and Missy Elliot's "The Rain (Supa Dupa Fly)," at http://www.youtube.com/watch?v=hHcyJPTTn9w; The Notorious B.I.G.'s "Big Poppa," at http://www.youtube.com/watch?v=phaJXp_zMYM; Floria Sigismondi and Marilyn Manson's "The Beautiful People," at http://www.youtube.com/watch?v=YpkvoHeUvTc&ob=av2e; and Alan Ferguson and Cee-Lo's "Open Happiness," at http://www.youtube.com/watch?v=Cxfkg3RaRjs (all accessed October 11, 2011).

35 Rihanna, "Rude Boy," at http://www.youtube.com/watch?v=e82VE8UtW8A&ob=av2e; and INXS, "What You Need," at http://www.youtube.com/watch?v=vSME53nL8tg (both accessed October 11, 2011).

eighties. But narratives have changed too: they have become more subtly worked and therefore more transparent, allowing surface detail to come forward.

Though most videos today, both indie and mainstream, seem to hew to familiar forms, a handful of examples suggest other possibilities. Lady Gaga's and Beyoncé's "Telephone" is a remarkable one.[36] While Hitchcock once quipped that film was life with all the boring bits cut out, "Telephone" feels like a feature with all of *its* boring bits cut out. One senses a complete film residing behind the clip. We can find ways of explaining why we have only now come across this new formal conceit. Like Michael Jackson's "Thriller" and Akerlund's "Paparazzi," "Telephone" has a substantial introduction. (Satellite services like MTV didn't approve of long beginnings, and screening "Thriller" took much arm-twisting.) "Telephone" presents one long segment of narrative exposition and a medley-like number from a musical, with tiny bits of interlocking business between. There is also something about the video's suggestion of time, the characters, and their offscreen behavior that is new and striking: we sense they're constantly up to important business, shenanigans we've most likely missed and even right now do not quite grasp. "Telephone" 's heightened storytelling is enabled by the end of censorship. Stakes are high—poisonings, murder, and sexual betrayal. The songs themselves might make narrative more possible. "Telephone" is more cellular and fragmented than the average pop song, facilitating more interrupted moments in the images' unfolding. With these short segments and interruptions, the work stretches like an archipelago and only in retrospect seems peculiar. Why is Lady Gaga wearing that leopard print and shimmying in front of the Jeep at night? Is she the limousine driver? And why is Beyoncé wearing that Sergeant Pepper's military dress in her hotel room, hopping up and down all by herself as if she were a windup doll, while behind her we catch glimpses of kitschy Louis XIV furniture and painted cinderblock walls? And let's not ignore the over-the-top stuff of Gaga's hair in rollers fashioned from coke cans, and sunglasses made of lit cigarettes. The prison block is really a gay dance hall; "telephone for Lady Gaga" rings out. The harp in the soundtrack is very sweet, and its return may enable Gaga's and Beyoncé's final getaway (the women and the credits outstrip the story). Earlier music videos like Madonna and David Fincher's "Bad Girl" or his and Aerosmith's "Janie's Got a Gun" also are constructed through musical but segment-oriented narratives.[37] Romanek's videos were often set as tableaux that implied worlds behind the videos. Akerlund's videos suggest a synthesis of these approaches.

Floria Sigismondi's "E.T." also has a density of causes that seems to exceed what we normally experience in a music video. Is it Kanye West, the Wall-E doll, Katy Perry, the

[36] Lady Gaga and Beyoncé, "Telephone," at http://www.youtube.com/watch?v=EVBsypHzF3U (accessed October 11, 2011).

[37] Madonna and David Fincher, "Bad Girl," at http://www.youtube.com/watch?v=JUII7DTACf4; and Aerosmith and David Fincher, "Janie's Got a Gun," at http://www.youtube.com/watch?v=bvFeqUQcBOE (both accessed October 11, 2011).

deer, or the CD that enables the sci-fi creatures to have sex and repopulate? The chain of Proppian helper agents is never made clear, but the narrative still feels sensible.[38] In a different way, Laurieann Gibson's and Lady Gaga's "You and I" may present a wider range of characters than traditional music videos. In her 1987 book *Rocking Around the Clock*, Ann Kaplan identified a "Madonna 1" and "Madonna 2" in Madonna's "Papa Don't Preach." The protagonist vacillates between two forms of identity that never integrate: a Jean Seberg good girl, working-class type and a vamp.[39] But the range of Gaga types in "You and I" is much broader. The clip explores transgendered identity (again, freedom from censorship may have made more representations possible) in a richer way than we have seen before. Gaga is a fashionista-type, Addams-family Morticia, a mermaid, a girl next door, a male James Dean type, a horror monster (flash-frame), a dancing troll-like doll, a wood sprite, and a fairy queen.

Some directors have become savvier about how to construct character in music video. Directors I have interviewed have stated that returning to music videos after directing feature films has helped them develop character. Technology helps, as does a whole history of music video. In Francis Lawrence's "Bad Romance," both the large-scale changes—Lady Gaga as sheik, prostitute, and revenge artist—and the many fine shifts as well (including a kewpie doll and a French chanteuse) are richer than in any eighties video I can recall.[40] Digital intermediate plays a role too: you really need to know you can easily shift from those whites to hot red, with the reptilian green in between.

Performance

In *Experiencing Music Video* I note what might be considered bad acting for the camera. Sometimes eighties musicians seem as if they have been shot with an elephant tranquilizer; they move woodenly through space until forced to a halt by a freeze-frame.[41] Such mannequin-like deportment may have occurred because performers hadn't yet figured out music video's language, or there may be something in the music itself; those big enormous synth sounds have sucked up most of the frequency range once filled by

[38] Vladimir Iakovlevich Propp, *Morphology of the Folktale*, trans. T.R. Laurence Scott (Austin: University of Texas Press, 1968).

[39] Gibson and Lady Gaga, "You and I," at http://www.youtube.com/watch?v=X9YMUoWeBwU&ob=av2e (accessed October 11, 2011); and Madonna, "Papa Don't Preach," at http://www.youtube.com/watch?v=RkxqxWgFEz4&ob=av2n (accessed October 11, 2011); E. Ann Kaplan, *Rocking Around the Clock: Music Television, Post Modernism and Consumer Culture* (New York & London: Routledge, 1987), 130.

[40] Lady Gaga and Francis Lawrence, "Bad Romance" http://www.youtube.com/watch?v=qrO4YZeyloI

[41] See Vernallis, *Experiencing Music Video*, 286. Gary Numan's "Cars," at http://www.youtube.com/watch?v=Ldyx3KHOFXw (accessed October 11, 2011), is one example.

rich instrumental arrangements.[42] The new sounds may have overwhelmed performers' bodies. Stasis also represented a turn away from seventies disco: dancing was no longer cool.[43] Maybe the stance was just a haughty, chic pose that now looks a bit too obvious. But at the same time, eighties videos possess some of the best performance moments in music video history. Since there was often not much going on but the camera and the barren set, the body had to carry weight, unlike now, when a performer knows that a flurry of post-production business may appear suddenly behind her might alter her expressions in post.[44] Eighties videos convey an intimacy and vulnerability that is forever lost; its sweetness may resemble the beginnings of film, as when Robert Flaherty's actor Nanook smiles for the camera. Look at some Tears for Fears videos or the Pet Shop Boys: such charged but ambivalent sincerity! A high point in the history of music video performance might include Sinead O'Connor's "Nothing Compares 2U," with her solo face and shaved monkish head, floating against a black background. Hype Williams's extreme wide-angle shots, with foregrounded performers mugging against cartoonish scapes, often gave a sense of the performers as blowup dolls. Francis Lawrence's and Justin Timberlake's "Cry Me a River" marked the first time I felt that music video performance might project the same amount of intimacy and realism as cinema.[45] In retrospect, however, that was an unusual video. Today so much is built around the character that it can seem as if less acting and dancing is unfolding. Music videos have their own ways of working with a star performer and supporting figures, as I argue in *Experiencing Music Video*.[46] Perhaps directors have become more savvy about ways of working with characters who have no dialogue and appear only briefly on camera. Consider the stone-faced man wearing a single black eye-patch who appears as an interstitial cutaway in Ph.D.'s "Little Susie's on the Up" in relation to the dead women and other assorted characters in Lady Gaga's "Paparazzi." The latter better integrate into the video and carry much more narrative weight.[47]

Today music-video image fractures into the smallest bits. In the digital era the face often bifurcates: eyes versus mouth, each heading off in different directions. Performers

[42] Think of seventies' Earth, Wind, and Fire's "After The Love Is Gone," at http://www.youtube.com/watch?v=BolpityVOiE compared to the eighties' The Human League's "Don't You Want Me," at http://www.youtube.com/watch?v=uPudE8nDogo&ob=av2e (both accessed October 11, 2011).

[43] Though there are some exceptions, like Young MC's "Bust a Move," at http://www.youtube.com/watch?v=tZQQGX24Teg (accessed October 11, 2011).

[44] See Jean Pierre Geuens's chapter on the coming of digital intermediate and the end of art, "Angels of Light," in *Oxford Handbook of Sound and Image in Digital Media*, ed. Carol Vernallis, Amy Herzog, and John Richardson (New York: Oxford University Press, forthcoming).

[45] Sinead O'Connor, "Nothing Compares 2U," at http://www.youtube.com/watch?v=iUiTQvToW_0; and Justin Timberlake, "Cry Me a River," at http://www.youtube.com/watch?v=DksSPZTZES0&ob=av2e (both accessed October 11, 2011). And sure enough Timberlake became an actor—but I'd argue his best performance was in this music video.

[46] Vernallis, Experiencing Music Video, 54-72.

[47] For description of background characters in feature films, see Will Straw, "Scales of Presence: Bess Flowers and the Hollywood Extra." *Screen* 52 (2011), 121-127. PhD, "Little Susie's on the Up," at http://www.youtube.com/watch?v=JKgzYLBV_cc; Lady Gaga, "Paparazzi," at http://www.youtube.com/watch?v=d2smz_1L2_0. (Both accessed June 11, 2013.)

have found that eyes particularly must hail and capture the camera, but the mouth still needs to carry the text (as in Nicole Scherzinger's "Poison").[48] The hyper-focus on the face is complemented by today's musical arrangement, lyrics, and production. One thing that has changed is an intense focus on the processing of the voice and the ways it is brought forward—the voice might be chorused, faded in and out, autotuned, or shadowed by other timbres created through plugins. (Listen to the kind of fine work done in Katy Perry and Kanye West's "E.T.")

Dancing is worth tracking as well. Early hip-hop videos, like those with Chaka Khan, display a kind of freedom. When it first appeared in music videos, break-dancing seemed fresh and alive. In the eighties and nineties performers often moved in sync in what felt like robotic simulacrum, and that practice continues today. Jonathan Dayton's, Valerie Faris's and Steve Winwood's "Higher Love" in the eighties, with its stylized dance moves in gypsy costumes, was the music video that captured my attention and has kept me watching all along.[49] Today, Beyoncé's "Countdown" has lovely dancing in it, too (borrowed from experimental choreographer Anne Teresa De Keersmaeker).

Settings

I have claimed that images wafted along or buoyed against a soundtrack are musical.[50] In music video, the origins of such levitation are uncertain, lending more authority to the song. But music videos also at some point tend to "touch ground," to reveal the floor or the earth. The ways music videos depict figures within space can reflect technical acumen, musical style, or fashion. For example, one typical eighties scenario showcased a night scene at a smoky bar, shot from overhead, often with a ceiling fan cresting the frame. But often this image would not give the viewer an integrated kinesthetic sense of the floor, feet dancing, the walls, and ceiling in a way that bound these elements to the music (examples include Simple Mind's "Don't You [Forget About Me]" and Wang Chung's "Dance Hall Days," though I can provide several exceptions).[51] In eighties videos, high heels, long legs, thick shoulder pads, and blow dried, waxed, or sculpted hair styling often pulled everything away from the floor, perhaps because the big glossy synth

[48] Nicole Scherzinger, "Poison," at http://www.youtube.com/watch?v=9joqPp3peLg (accessed October 11, 2011).

[49] Steve Winwood, "Higher Love," at http://lockerz.com/u/20542314/decalz/6159090/steve_winwood_higher_love (accessed October 11, 2011).

[50] See Vernallis, *Experiencing Music Video*, 32.

[51] Wang Chung, "Dance Hall Days," at http://www.youtube.com/watch?v=V-xpJRwIA-Q&ob=av2e; and Flock of Seagulls, "I Ran," at http://www.youtube.com/watch?v=o_PqoxYr3L4. Paula Abdul, "Cold Hearted Snake," at http://www.youtube.com/watch?v=o7aShcmEksw&ob=av2e, is a good example: staged as a Bob Fosse number, it draws from traditional dance editing. Lionel Ritchie's "Dancing in the Streets" similarly references the musical. (All accessed October 11, 2011.)

sounds provided the "true" ground.[52] In nineties hip-hop videos, the floor was essential, but it was implied, not displayed. The low-slung camera framed as a tracking wide-angle shot seemed always to be three feet above.[53]

There may be something "musical" about repressing footage of the floor, yet today, for the first time, we find directors concertedly working to create a three-dimensional space that combines the ceiling, walls, and floor. Does the music seem to call for this approach, or have directors finally figured out how to do it? Perhaps arrangements built up with digital sounds on the computer rather than through live playing create a sense of absence that must be compensated for; hence a more completely articulated space is established. Simultaneously the concrete and object-like qualities of the digital sounds may also demand clearer containers. In Justin Bieber's "I Need Somebody to Love" and Justin Timberlake's "Rock Your Body," there's a series of low-angle shots up through a glass floor—the video moves from shots of feet, toward the performer's torso, then up toward the wall, the bent background, and finally the ceiling. Francis Lawrence's "Bad Romance" articulates ceiling, walls, and floor very carefully.[54] I find Jonas Akerlund's hybrid spaces particularly charming.

Sculptural Spaces

Most music videos today need to project both on large screens and on cellphones. One way to accommodate this range is to foreground a dramatic shift in scale between figure and set. In the nineties director Mark Romanek was the master of building sets that looked simultaneously enormous and miniature, as in En Vogue's "Free Your Mind," but today there has been a renaissance. The sloping and accordion-ribbed spaces in Rihanna's "Who's That Chick?" or the Serra-like iron constructions in Nicole Scherzinger's "Whatever U Like" can be seen as canny extensions of Romanek's practice.[55,56] This rich play of figure and environment may well reflect an accrued understanding of the genre to be deployed and developed into the future.

[52] "En Vogue, "Free Your Mind" at http://www.youtube.com/watch?v=i7iQbBbMAFE; Rihanna, "Who's That Chick?" at www.youtube.com/watch?v=jbghbznr26U (accessed October 11, 2011).

[53] In hip hop videos, the expensive, fancy car coming in in slow motion with a focus on the hubcaps was a common trope. Ron Isley and R Kelly, "Down Low," at http://www.youtube.com/watch?v=fXdu3pwT4ps&ob=av2e (accessed October 11, 2011) is a good example.

[54] Justin Bieber, "Somebody to Love," at http://www.youtube.com/watch?v=SOI4OF7iIr4&ob=av2e. Justin Timberlake, "Rock Your Body," at http://www.youtube.com/watch?v=TSVHoHyErBQ&ob=av2e. Francis Lawrence, "Bad Romance," at http://www.youtube.com/watch?v=qrO4YZeyloI (all accessed October 11, 2011).

[55] En Vogue, "Free Your Mind at http://www.youtube.com/watch?v=i7iQbBbMAFE (accessed October 11, 2011). Rihanna, "Who's That Chick?," at http://www.youtube.com/watch?v=D4_U2ZqFLeM (accessed October 11, 2011).

[56] Nicole Scherzinger, "Whatever U Like," at http://www.youtube.com/watch?v=JX-1q_Lpzp8&ob=av2e (accessed October 11, 2011).

Packing the Frame

In many eighties videos, you could often see the seams of the barren film stage-set or television studio; a cookie-cutout scrim produced a silhouette of a window against the wall; and a figure might be draped in silky cloth, obscured by some smoke. There weren't many items in the frame. When performers and supporting characters moved in a spookily stilted way and the blocky editing unpredictably turned harsh, there was something magical about the image with the music (for example, Kim Carnes's "Bette Davis Eyes").[57] Now, we have the reverse: with digital cameras and digital intermediate, directors can put an unprecedented number of objects in the frame, and delineate them through color, texture and lighting. Even small objects toward the back of the frame possess distinct textures, whether they are made of softer, more malleable plastic or harder acrylic. Digital intermediate helps these elements come forward—objects pop. We can also track the shifts in spots of color from mauve to burgundy and the modulation from dark to light. Rihanna's videos seem to do this more than others. Is it her voice? Her beauty? Her Amazonian presence? In many of her videos everything projects forward. This visual strategy complements the musical scapes designed for headphones: hooks are finely manicured, stacked up, and distributed around the space. (Consider her "Who's That Chick?" "Rude Boy," and "Umbrella.")[58]

Multiples and Crowds

Music video's prismatic proliferation of objects reflects both the digital signal and music's inherent polyphony. The image becomes buzzy as technical devices jack it up to speak to both music video's new digital technology and its nature as a polyphonic form. Also, as never before, we feel the pressure of the crowd around us as billions on the planet (many who are online at the same time) compete for the same jobs and natural resources. As Les Brill might argue, the images of multiples in the frame reflect human crowds.[59] Then again, music video has always drawn on images of multiples. Think of the crane shots that pass like wind over a field of wheat in the eighties stadium videos

57 Kim Carnes, "Bette Davis Eyes," at http://www.youtube.com/watch?v=EPOIS5taqA8&ob=av2e (accessed October 11, 2011).

58 Rihanna, "Who's That Chick?" at http://www.youtube.com/watch?v=vDgTokR6770&feature=fvwrel (accessed October 11, 2011); Rihanna, "Umbrella," at http://www.youtube.com/watch?v=PXvauXKo2hU (accessed October 11, 2011). Stan Hawkins has written about what he calls the "hyperembodiment" of the figure. Each thing including bodies seems more extremely realized.

59 Lesley Brill, *Crowds, Power, and Transformation in Cinema (Contemporary Approaches to Film and Television)* (Detroit: Wayne State University Press, 2006), 3.

for rock and heavy metal, or a video like Peter Gabriel's "Sledgehammer," in which a white-speckled-on-black animated figure opens the door and walks out into a field of stars.[60]

In Depth and on the Horizontal

The tracking shot has been an essential technique, because it supports the music's pace in relation to the video's environment and provides a respite from rapid editing. But, surprisingly, music videos have backed away from the tracking shot—and when they do deploy it, it is frequently less showy than in the past. Directors rather have started exploiting other spatial techniques, like placing performers and objects twisting from within an expanding whorl. (Examples include Justin Timberlake's "Let Me Talk to You/ My Love" and Katy Perry's "E.T.")[61] Today music videos are also staged more in depth and on the horizontal. Perhaps the new cameras create a greater three-dimensionality, and digital intermediate can more easily separate objects from the background, bringing some objects close while leaving others in the far distance (but all remain clearly visible through strong color demarcation). Directors shooting for the scale of cell phones, too, may coax objects to pop. With YouTube in mind, they may sharply define edges to compete with everything around the frame. These videos may tap into primitive "fight or flight" responses: objects coming from a distance or entering from the side can seize a viewer's attention, holding her within the clip, rather than letting her dally with other engaging Web attractions outside the frame. Directors and viewers may also be starting to imagine their projects in 3D, because so many media are set for release in that format. Some visual objects are also designed for music that has been spatialized and often redistributed (panned from ear to ear) for headphones. Just as likely, the whorl could appear because it works as an inverted mirror of our lived experience: we sit at the computer and feel our presence radiating out from the mouse, through the screen, to other screens beyond it. Or it could simply be that this technique is the latest trick directors and musicians have stumbled on, a novelty to exploit, but I doubt it. Such a strong hook—something barreling down an unfurling path, calling to us, cloth whirling from an abyss at a distance—is a very powerful image. It suggests control, authority, magic, and magnetism. It claims this video is the center of our attention and the Internet.[62]

[60] Peter Gabriel, "Sledgehammer," at http://www.youtube.com/watch?v=hqyc37aOqTo (accessed October 11, 2011). George Michael's "Monkey," at http://www.youtube.com/watch?v=CHb2XYeXcJI&ob=av2e (accessed October 11, 2011), is a good example of a crane shot documenting a stadium performance with masses of concertgoers.

[61] For example, Lady Gaga's "Bad Romance," at http://www.youtube.com/watch?v=qrO4YZeyloI&ob=av2e, and "Telephone," at http://www.youtube.com/watch?v=EVBsypHzF3U&ob=av2e (both accessed October 11, 2011), use very discreet tracking shots.

[62] It appears in Floria Sigismondi and Katy Perry's "E.T.," at http://www.youtube.com/watch?v=t5Sd5c4o9UM&ob=av2e, Kanye West's "Power," at http://www.youtube.com/watch?v=L53gjP-TtGE&ob=av2e, and Lady Gaga's "Born This Way," at http://www.youtube.com/watch?v=wV1FrqwZyKw&ob=av2e (all accessed October 11, 2011), for example.

Haptics

Do music videos today elicit a heightened sensation of touch or a greater sense of kinesthetic engagement? Whereas objects in recent videos may seem concrete, three-dimensional, and isolated in space, objects from earlier clips seemed more capable of existing in a generous, cohabitable space—where we might reach out and be a part of them. They seemed to belong more to the world of film critic André Bazin.

We can contrast these approaches by comparing some recent videos, like Nelly's "Just a Dream" and Justin Timberlake's "My Love," with earlier ones like Matt Mahurin and R.E.M.'s "Orange Crush" or Mark Romanek and Macy Gray's "I Try."[63] Perhaps the older "generosity" derives from the fact that it wasn't as easy in the eighties and nineties to create a tactile sense in the image as it streamed alongside the music, so directors worked hard to find ways of using hands and objects that were expressive. In Mahurin's "Orange Crush" the hand in close-up digs into rich dirt and clasps a piece of wood. Romanek's "I Try" shows Gray holding a bouquet of flowers that perches in the frame's center for much of the video. The extra friction or work required to project a person in relation to an object may now be unnecessary. Now objects may simply be hurled at us; there is less charm in setting them off against everything else. It may also be that digital sound and image is a bit harsh, while video is softer and more capacious.[64]

In *Experiencing Music Video* I describe how objects in music videos become odd.[65] They project their own aura or voice that we recognize from the real world, but they nevertheless seem strange. It's almost as if you had inadvertently encountered your pet, suddenly feral, as it was trolling through the park, or as if you peered at a stick as seen underwater, now twisted and bent. Objects in these videos remain strange: ring, car, violin, flower, stick and dirt. But in recent videos, objects often seem to retain more of their real-world ordinariness, and it is difficult to pinpoint why. Perhaps each sound dutifully seeks out an object in the frame; each newly formed sound-image object is more fully rendered and separate than in the past. The sound–image connections don't seem surprising. Do we recognize these amalgams now more simply as commodities? Consider the car and ring in Nelly's "Just a Dream": they look grand and they float, but there's less sense of wonder. Directors may only now be discovering how to work with low bandwidth and a small frame in a way that compensates for what could be seen as a brittleness of the digital soundtrack and image. In "Wish You Were Here," Avril Lavigne holds

[63] Nelly, "Just a Dream," at http://www.youtube.com/watch?v=N6O2ncUKvlg&ob=av2e; Justin Timberlake, "My Love," at http://www.youtube.com/watch?v=OVvIWkgJ12g; Matt Mahurin and R.E.M., "Orange Crush," at http://www.youtube.com/watch?v=_mSmOcmk7uQ&ob=av2n; and Mark Romanek and Macy Gray, "I Try," at http://www.youtube.com/watch?v=LzvbiFR95gM&feature=related (all accessed October 11, 2011).

[64] Marshall McLuhan argued that the television screen elicited a greater sense of touch than sight. McLuhan, "The Playboy Interview: Marshall McLuhan," *Playboy Magazine* (March [1969] 1994), 11. Perhaps a combination of factors at any historical moment shapes our relation to space and objects.

[65] Vernallis, *Experiencing Music Video*, 99.

a burning flower, to little effect, but such instances when a hand holds an object may carry great weight soon.[66]

Some objects do still seem strange, their uncanniness created through savvy use of color. In Jonas Akerlund's "Paparazzi" the video's color arc finally leads us to Lady Gaga as a musketeer dressed in black and yellow, pouring a poisonous substance into a pale pink fizzy liquid. Suddenly everything turns uncanny. Perhaps it's because we are surprised that the video's opening spring promise—a beautiful, pale pink rose and a rich magenta orchid, both linked to Lady Gaga—has turned sullen. The bits of purple at the video's opening and close suddenly become tainted with sickly yellow, green and black; this shift, as well as a new motor-rhythmic pulse, pushes the video into some sort of hyper-dreamland where murder becomes contagious and licit.[67]

Elements in music production also have tended toward the distinct, so that they will project well on MP3s and YouTube. The attacks have become shorter, and careful equalization has sharpened the separation between sounds. Perhaps songs and images are triggering each other: the sharply defined objects in the image encourage music producers to seek sharply defined qualities in the music, and vice versa—both seem to seek a greater dimensionality. Here low-register attacks boom, each sonic event suggesting a three-dimensional object the listener can trace in space. Visually, too, we can sense the other sides of objects in the frame. Like Caravaggio's chiaroscuro, in which shadows suggest fuller forms, performers now have "backs."

Sometimes a sound effect and an object can become so tightly synced that they become a three-dimensional amalgam. Look at the Dan Flavin-like fluorescent lights blinking and listen to the thumps and variously pitched cowbells in Timberlake's "Let Me Talk to You," or the exhortation of "heartbeat" and the lurid 3D modeling of a pumping heart in Enrique Iglesias's "Heartbeat."

Intertextuality

Music video has always been self-reflexive, as well as intertextual with nearby forms and genres; the Buggles' "Music Video Killed the Radio Star" inaugurated music video's first broadcast in 1979, and as the song's title suggests, staked its claim against other media. My favorite historically based intertextual videos include Paula Abdul's "Rush Rush," which pays homage to *Rebel Without a Cause*, and the Blues Travelers' "Runaround," which reenacts *The Wizard of Oz*. But videos today want to say, "music video is back!" and do so in many ways. Musicians can place clips of their earlier videos in a recent one, as if to say, "I'm still around." "Know your music video history!" suggest Britney Spears's "Hold It Against Me" and Eminem's and Dr. Dre's "I Need a Doctor." Another way is to

[66] Avril Lavigne, "Wish You Were Here," at http://www.youtube.com/watch?v=VT1-sitWRtY&ob=av2e (accessed October 11, 2011).

[67] Lady Gaga, "Paparazzi," at http://www.youtube.com/watch?v=d2smz_1L2_0&ob=av3e (accessed October 11, 2011).

intersperse references to other videos, as in Hanson's 2011 "Thinking 'Bout Somethin'."[68] The clip plays with speed; characters move a bit too fast or slow, which makes the clip seem very up-to-date, but it's also filled with a thousand references for those in the know—to Blues Brothers films, *West Side Story*, Spike Jonze's and Weezer's music video "Buddy Holly" (an homage to the television show *Happy Days*), a Gap commercial, and every other "dancin' in the street" video, like the already nostalgic LMFAO's "Party Rock Anthem" and Lionel Ritchie's "All Night Long." It seems jokingly to say, "Hanson was always retro, remember when they did 'Mmmbop?' but we'll really test your knowledge of retro." Many other examples include Katy Perry's "Friday Night," which contains cameos by eighties music video stars Kenny G and Debbie Gibson and recent YouTube viral Web star Rebecca Black. And Weezer's "Pork and Beans" video is a mashup of YouTube one-hit wonders.

Remediation

Music videos frequently remediate material. They adopt images from earlier sources (films, commercials, paintings, posters) and often juxtapose them with others in the video.[69] In MTV's first half-hour in 1981, two clips exhibited extensive remediation, perhaps more than we tend to see today. Todd Rundgren's "Time Heals" featured images from paintings by Magritte, and Ph.D.'s "Little Susie's on the Up" borrowed from Fred Astaire movies. The practice of remediation continues today. In The Strokes' "Taken for a Fool," the singer wears a T-shirt with an American flag on it, while behind him flicker shadowy electric trees, lit as if they might serve as Christmas ornaments, and then the band rotates to the left as if it's on a lazy Susan.[70] We might say that the video points to multiple media: lithography (the flag stamped on the T-shirt); the coming of electricity and capitalism (electric trees); and records, record culture, and moving media (the electrified lazy Susan). The materials sort of combine into something new. A patriotic Christmastime snow globe? Whatever the intent, it is evocative and it looks good.

Music videos may remediate materials to work like poetry. In poems, words or phrases not normally placed together form new relations. The brain can experience a flooding, or an affective overload. In music, images serve the same function as words

[68] Paula Abdul, "Rush Rush," at http://www.youtube.com/watch?v=yqyIaNWPoTo; Britney Spears, "Hold It Against Me," at http://www.youtube.com/watch?v=-Edv8Onsrgg&ob=av2e; and Hanson, "Thinking 'Bout Somethin'," at http://www.youtube.com/watch?v=TmGoDqhfDbY (all accessed October 11, 2011).

[69] Korsgaard suggests that more of this takes place in the digital era than did in the past. This is an interesting claim, but it might be hard to prove. Mathias Korsgaard, "Creation and Erasure"

[70] Ph.D., "Little Susie's on the Up," at http://www.youtube.com/watch?v=JKgzYLBV_cc; and The Strokes, "Taken for a Fool," at http://www.youtube.com/watch?v=oU_jGVEKr9s&ob=av2e. Queen and David Bowie's "Under Pressure," at http://www.youtube.com/watch?v=xtrEN-YKLBM, is another example of an eighties video that uses much remediation. Lady Gaga, "Paparazzi," at http://www.youtube.com/watch?v=d2smz_1L2_o&ob=av2e (all accessed October 11, 2011).

in poems, and the sense of overload becomes amplified by music's affective qualities, forming a potent amalgam. In the era of multitasking and the remix, our brains may more strongly crave these interactions. Remediation also makes accessible certain features of music-audiovisual relations. As Nicholas Cook and Philip Tagg argue, music presents conflicting attributes simultaneously. Music is often said to create the sense that it's immediately affective; even before culture, it goes "directly to the heart" without explanation. But in a contradictory fashion, music in an audiovisual context seems "cultural." Cook argues that music is willing to pick up associations with almost anything it encounters; it is "sticky."[71] One remembers a song because its halo of memories always trails it. All the modes of dress, performance, and paraphernalia surrounding music—its concerts, album covers—can shape our relation to a piece of music. Remediation reminds us that music still pierces us, but also that almost anything can work in an audiovisual context. One image might make associative chains with the music it is coupled with, but another might do as well.

The Fragment

Nicki Minaj sings, "boom da da da, boom da da da, super bass," and that's what the video is about. Her hands flutter, her hips pound, and speakers quiver on ice. Stuttering hooks have long been important in popular music, but earlier examples have never been so pointed, piercing, insistent. Lady Gaga sings, "Ga-ga." Enrique Iglesias sings, "listen to my heart beat," and we hear a "boom," "boom," "boom," as we peer through his illuminated body's insides to a synchronized red heart beating.[72] Today's instances may reflect new possibilities for pinpoint control, a competitive urge with YouTube, a claim for listening now, or a desire to sync up everyone.

* * *

This chapter has embarked on a comparison of music videos from the eighties and today. I want to conclude first with a claim for the artistry of the past: with small and then adequate budgets, and with forgiving, inexpensive video incorporated into the production process, an eighties director might create a delirious environment that moved beautifully against the human figure. Video's visual softness and loose sync actually supported the big, stripped-down sound of the eighties; here, pop music production and video technology may have tightly fitted one another. The record industry also actively sought out experimental visual artists across many fields, including the graphic arts

[71] See Nicholas Cook, "Theorizing Musical Meaning," *Music Theory Spectrum* 23, no. 2 (Autumn 2001): 170–195 and Philip Tagg, "Gestural Interconversion and Connotative Precision," *Film International* 3, no. 13 (January 2005): 20–31.

[72] Nicki Minaj, "Super Bass," at http://www.youtube.com/watch?v=4JipHEz53sU&ob=av2e (accessed October 11, 2011); and Enrique Iglesias, "Heartbeat," at http://www.youtube.com/watch?v=NVk4vENObiI&ob=av2e (accessed October 11, 2011).

and filmmaking. Directors reported being excited by audience responses. The field was open: new programming was needed, costs could be low, and fast production schedules obliged many directors to improvise and rapidly review their ideas.

The present era also presents many exciting opportunities for music video. With digital technologies, fine sync between sound and image becomes realizable, frame by frame and pixel to pixel; more malleable, flexible relations have become possible. Though budgets have dropped, directors still find means to produce glossy work, as cameras and recording media have become cheaper. Shooting on green-screen or against a studio's cyclorama (cyc) background and paying technicians to animate backgrounds and edit on Final Cut rather than shooting on location keep costs low. Placing products in videos can also raise a budget by twenty per cent. On the other hand, today's audiences and their favorite venues are fragmented. Directors often feel they don't know whom they are shooting for. The relaxation of censorship rules creates new and sometimes freeing possibilities.

Which period, the eighties or today, seems richer? This chapter began with the argument that in the eighties music and image had to work to find one another, and there was something plaintive about this (like a relationship). Some of the resistance could be found in the sync of sound and image on videotape. I suspect finer control of sync may not always be freeing today. Although today's technologies might seem capable of producing a music video sublime, where the image in its voluble fluidity can be as responsive as the song, we may not want our music video images to be so flexible that they cross over into the realm of pure animation. Rather, we may enjoy the weight of the human figure and real objects in space, in relation to more painterly elements. Technologically, today there may be less friction in creating the image or music, and it's not as exciting.

One might argue that bodies still have plenty of inertia and the digital offers all kinds of new possibilities, particularly with color. Some directors, like Romain Gavras and Melina Matsoukas, have stayed with film; others, like Mark Pellington, have embraced the digital. Even today, different approaches and aesthetics are most suited to particular technologies.

Sync may be important only for some genres of music video. On one hand, the most popular clips on Vevo today still work "classically," hewing to the familiar mode of carefully tracking the song. On the other hand, many YouTube and Vimeo clips with 1,000-500,000 hits may foreground first a technical gimmick or disjunctive sound-image connections (to seem different from corporate-sponsored clips). Audiovisual aesthetics may not be as essential as we had once assumed; sync can be good enough. Directors with great visual flair can make wonderful videos even when their musicality isn't immediately apparent. Other directors, with highly developed chops in shaping music-image relations, tend to be appreciated more by connoisseurs (like director Alan Ferguson). This may boil down to taste; I like videos that encourage repeat viewings (and these tend to track the song), whereas other viewers may be drawn to punchiness or beauty in but one domain: image, music, or text.

We might also be able to evaluate the eighties and the present day by considering the roles of experimentation and innovation. There are some strong early examples. In the eighties, MTV vee-jay Mark Goodman announced, "This is a wild one from R.E.M.," and then screened, both upside-down and scrolling to the left, footage of a stone quarry and bolded lyrics for the song "I'm Falling"—that's all. MTV also played clips that surprised its audience, like Peter Gabriel's "Mercy Street," which dealt with incest and suicide but lacked strong performers or identifiable figures. Today's equivalents might include clips that disrupt narrative expectations (e.g., Jonas Akerlund's clips for Lady Gaga's "Paparazzi" and "Telephone"). Some videos experiment with hybrid forms—videos built for cellphone apps, teasers or long-playing quasi-musicals (e.g., the work of Bjork, Britney Spears and Kanye West), or with interactive elements that help them approach video games.[73]

But what about videos that leave us completely lost—that might reflect postclassical values, like those that have reconfigured cinema (*Eternal Sunshine of the Spotless Mind, Moulin Rouge*), or technical approaches that really stun us? I *could* claim that music video remains conservative. As noted previously, it has long showcased an image heightened by technical effects. Today, mainstream, corporate-funded music videos may cannibalize YouTube's and indie clips' technologically showy devices (trails, kaleidoscopes, sinusoidal waves) and then incorporate them as passing moments—as a means to lead into the chorus, fill in gaps among verses, or kick off the intro. But the performer's face and body must remain legible and accessible. When these effects appear, the clips find ways to explain or narrativize the devices (e.g., the trippy effects might be part of a karaoke show or a performer's hallucination as he drives his car at night, or the whole video might adopt an art-deco sheen as if it were a segment from a Busby Berkeley musical).[74] There are some exceptions (Kanye West's "Welcome to Heartbreak," Chairlift's "Evident Utensil," and MGMT's "Time to Pretend"), but these are few and even they could be said to remain what I'd call classical.[75]

We *could* argue that mainstream music video has always been progressive and experimental, even before digital technologies saturated production practices. Music video began in the era of video editing. The technology was cumbersome and the sync was poor, but with a four- or five -minute piece, and so few constraints, a director could move material around and experiment. Techniques applied to the frame, like

[73] See Mathias Korsgaard, "Music Video Transformed," chapter 28 in this volume; and Nicola Dibben, "Inventing the App Album in Björk's Biophilia," in *Oxford Handbook of Sound and Image in Digital Media*, ed. Carol Vernallis, Amy Herzog, and John Richardson (New York: Oxford University Press, forthcoming).

[74] Here my argument follows David Bordwell's understanding of post-classical cinema. For Bordwell intensified continuity is tamed and rationalized in traditional Hollywood films, which retain their traditional character arcs and three-act structures. Similarly, music videos in corporate clips assimilate novel techniques while still focusing on showing off features of the song. David Bordwell describes "intensified continuity" in *The Way Hollywood Tells It: Story and Style in Modern Movies* (Berkeley: University of California Press, 2006), 120–121. Selena Gomez and the Scene, "Naturally" at http://vimeo.com/61429208 (accessed June 11, 2013).

[75] KanyeWest,"WelcometoHeartbreak,"athttp://www.youtube.com/watch?v=wMHoe8kIZtE&ob=av2e and MGMT, "Time to Pretend," at http://www.youtube.com/watch?v=B9dSYgd5Elk&ob=av2n (both accessed October 11, 2011).

animation, frame-by-frame rotoscoping, and visual software and hardware, provided frisson.[76] Predigital videotape was already pretty weightless and buzzy. Music video is a short-form genre, and its underlying material—the pop song—has not gone through any radical transformations since the late eighties.

But then I check myself. Suddenly, anew, mainstream music video is true for me again. Beyoncé's and Adria Petty's "Countdown," Rihanna's and Jonas Akerlund's "Who's That Chick," Katy Perry's and Floria Sigismondi's "E.T.," Lady Gaga's and Francis Lawrence's "Bad Romance," and Kanye West's and Hype Williams's "All of the Lights" are as strong as or stronger than anything I have seen.

Why are these clips seductive? A sizeable cohort of music video directors have been directing for ten to twenty years and have developed a well-honed method and mature handling of materials. Their knowledge informs these clips. Music video has also experienced competitive pressures that have forced quick adaptation, in response to both economic shifts and developments in other newly emergent media, rendering some videos tough and fleet. Mainstream music video needs to compete with or respond to indie clips that appear on sites like Pitchfork and Vimeo and have their own innovations. Their music is often brutalist, compressed for the MP3 aesthetic, and the image seems overtaken by jittery, colorful, sinusoidal waves and mirroring effects that are rendered by algorithms. Surprise might play a role, too: How do Rihanna, Lady Gaga, or Katy Perry and their directors treat performance and editing when any feature can be distorted in postproduction, including an expression? Doesn't this create some uncertain tension, a new relationship among artists, practitioners and directors? Suddenly music video has the right scale for today, and perhaps the right mode for a competitive global market (tied but loosely to language, it easily crosses national borders).

I have intimated that some of the strongest music videos arise from a nexus of evolving audiovisual relations. The image responds to pop songwriting and vice versa. Perhaps we are now witness to a new type of songwriting, and directors are laboring to keep up. Some musicologists have noticed the appearance of "the soar." Many hit songs, like Katy Perry's "Teenage Dream," rely on a tiered chorus, which draws on principles of layering and "buildups" that have long been a staple of electronic dance music. Unlike a traditional pop song chorus, its chorus builds in stages. The song begins with a relatively basic, perhaps even sparse, texture, then repeats a second time with added layers that usually thicken the rhythm, along with an included propulsive dance beat. This is effectively a two-part chorus, and as the listener moves through it, she experiences a rapidly building textural crescendo. To add to this layering effect, many of these recent pop songs feature a fairly active verse that then intentionally scales back at the beginning of the prechorus or chorus, so it can make the textural layering and buildup of the chorus even more dramatic. Examples include Katy Perry's "Firework," Ke$ha's "We R Who We R," and Britney Spears's "I Wanna Go" and "Till the World Ends."[77]

[76] Like the Quantel and the toaster in the eighties, and the flame in the nineties.

[77] I'd like to thank Theo Cateforis for describing "the soar" for me.

Many musicologists don't like "the soar."[78] They feel listeners are forced into an automatic response—hectored into the ecstatic high of the chorus. The listener feels obliged to raise her hands (or hail the DJ). But in a music video context the new songwriting technique may offer new possibilities. Against the song's regimented structure, color can adopt a contrapuntal voice, or project its own phrasing, possibly even to break free from other visual elements and the music. Watch the patches of reds, pinks, yellows, and blues in some recent videos featuring the soar, like The Black Eyed Peas' "I Gotta Feeling" and Jennifer Lopez's "On the Floor."[79] We don't know enough about how YouTube, music video, and digital cinema are influencing one another. Nor are we sufficiently tracking the ways directors draw on these media, incorporate, and refashion them while they respond to music video's history. We need to think more about this, but for now I'll say that music video is back with a vengeance.

References

Auslander, Philip. "Sound and Vision: The Audio/Visual Economy of Musical Performance." In *The Oxford Handbook of New Audiovisual Aesthetics*, edited by John Richardson, Claudia Gorbman, and Carol Vernallis. New York: Oxford University Press, forthcoming.

Belluck, Pam. "To Tug Hearts, Music First Must Tickle the Neurons." *New York Times*, April 18, 2011.

Bordwell, David. *The Way Hollywood Tells It: Story and Style in Modern Movies*. Berkeley: University of California Press, 2006.

Brill, Lesley. *Crowds, Power, and Transformation in Cinema. Contemporary Approaches to Film and Television*. Detroit: Wayne State University Press, 2006.

Chion, Michel. *Audio-Vision: Sound on Screen*. New York: Columbia University Press, 1994.

Cook, Nicholas. *Analysing Musical Multimedia*. New York: Oxford University Press, 1998.

Dibben, Nicola. "Inventing the App Album in Björk's *Biophilia*." In *The Oxford Handbook of Sound and Image in Digital Media*, edited by Carol Vernallis, Amy Herzog, and John Richardson. New York: Oxford University Press, forthcoming.

Dickinson, Kay. *Off Key: When Film and Music Won't Work Together*. New York: Oxford University Press, 2008.

Geuens, Jean. "Angels of Light." In *The Oxford Handbook of Sound and Image in Digital Media*, edited by Carol Vernallis, Amy Herzog, and John Richardson. New York: Oxford University Press, forthcoming.

Gorbman, Claudia. *Unheard Melodies: Narrative Film Music*. Bloomington: Indiana University Press; London: BFI, 1987.

Gorbman, Claudia. "Aesthetics and Rhetoric." *American Music* 22, no. 1 (2004): 14–26.

[78] See Simon Reynolds, who also connects "the soar" to dance music, at http://www.guardian.co.uk/music/musicblog/2011/apr/14/balearics-ibiza-pop (accessed October 11, 2011); and Daniel Barrow's critique of the soar, at http://thequietus.com/articles/06073-a-plague-of-soars-warps-in-the-fabric-of-pop/ (accessed October 11, 2011).

[79] The Black Eyed Peas' "I Gotta Feeling," at http://www.youtube.com/watch?v=uSD4vsh1zDA; and Jennifer Lopez and Pitbull's "On The Floor (featuring Pitbull)," at http://www.youtube.com/watch?v=t4H_Zoh7G5A (both accessed October 11, 2011).

Kaplan, E. Ann. *Rocking Around the Clock: Music Television, Postmodernism and Consumer Culture*. New York: Routledge, 1987.
Korsgaard, Mathias. "Creation and Erasure: Music Video as a Signaletic Form of Practice." *Journal of Aesthetics & Culture* 4 (2012), at http://www.aestheticsandculture.net/index.php/jac/article/view/18151/22823.
Korsgaard, Mathias. "Music Video Transformed." Chapter 28 in this volume.
Kracauer, Siegfried, "Girls und Krise." *Frankfurter Zeitung*, May 27, 1931.
McLuhan, Marshall. "The Playboy Interview: Marshall McLuhan." *Playboy Magazine* (March 1969). ©1994 by *Playboy*.
Propp, Vladimir I., and T. R. Laurence Scott. *Morphology of the Folktale*. Austin: University of Texas Press, 1968.
Vernallis, Carol. *Experiencing Music Video: Aesthetics and Cultural Context*. New York: Columbia University Press, 2004.
Vernallis, Carol. *Unruly Media: YouTube, Music Video, and the New Digital Cinema*. New York: Oxford University Press, forthcoming.

CHAPTER 26

AESTHETICS AND HYPEREMBODIMENT IN POP VIDEOS: RIHANNA'S "UMBRELLA"

STAN HAWKINS

In the vast majority of pop music videos, a repertoire of norms disciplines the body through stark imagery and processed sound. This is the underlying tenet of this essay, which attempts to situate the gendered body as musically constructed. A claim is made for the representational politics and mechanisms that shape artistic production. The chapter argues that the analysis of performance in music videos relies on recognizing the visual representation of gender as part and parcel of entertainment, because in the majority of pop videos the body-on-display is about flamboyant virtuosity, which normalizes notions of beauty. This comes down to the technological manipulation of the artist's image and her or his aestheticization on screen. Through a process of "getting bodied," the pop artist sets out to evoke a specific mood,[1] and this provides us with a discursive space for understanding the sonic interplay between the body and technology within the context of the entertainment industry.

My close reading of the music video "Umbrella" (2007) aims to demonstrate the synchronization of sound and image, especially with reference to the body. Processes of viewing and listening involve bridging sound and image, so what we see and hear

[1] Robin James, "'Robo-Diva R&B': Aesthetics, Politics, and Black Female Robots in Contemporary Popular Music," *Journal of Popular Music Studies* 20, no. 4 (2008): 402–423. In a study that considers Beyoncé's 2007 BET performance and Rihanna's "Umbrella" video, James draws attention to the complexity of the gaze and the homology between control and loss of control. Specific emphasis is placed on the political and aesthetic implications of black women presented as robots. James argues that the robo-diva highlights white patriarchy's anxieties about technology, especially in terms of black female sexuality. Race-gender politics in Anglo-American pop music is critiqued and deconstructed by James in a fascinating insight into black female R&B singers.

is about opening an imaginary space. This ultimately defines the musical experience. Music thus highlights subject positions according to our expectations, assessment, and understanding of the subject. Accordingly, the structuring of subjectivity is convoluted by the complex vectors of visual embodiment, which completely transform the original audio recording. Locking into the music during a music video, the very sight of an artist performing affords a new rendition of the audio recording, the emphasis falling on the mannerisms of the body. In contrast to real-time performance, the video creates its own domain for musical representations as it sets out not only to entertain, but also to promote the artist. Starting with the initial recording session, at which the original tracks are laid down, the audiovisual process involves mixing, engineering, mastering, and directing the performance. Only by following on from the final stage of production does the viewer become involved in the experience of the music video, wherein, as Carol Vernallis puts it, "[i]n a fraction of a second, we have the entire sweep of the changes that occur in all of the parameters of music video."[2]

I argue here that the disciplining of the body in the "parameters of music video production" conveys much about traditions and conventions, and in "Umbrella" a range of signifiers overtly objectifies the female. Transgressive in terms of its representational function, Rihanna's powerful and erotic imagery frequently exceeds the limits of what is acceptable for emancipated girls playing out the "sinful" or "bad." This strategy is in itself a critical point for contemplation throughout this chapter. Not only are the pop artist's physical responses to the music significant in that they foreground the viewing experience,[3] but they also reveal much about the demands that are placed on artists by the music industry. Throughout the relatively brief history of the pop video, there is ample evidence that the fragmented imagery of the body accrues meaning through the contingency of the music, which operates as a continuum for bodily movement.

Pop videos are generally glossy productions stylized to titillate the viewer, aestheticizing what we see and desire. Notwithstanding their main aim to promote a performer or band, videos also provide entertaining sociocultural commentaries on trends and aesthetic preferences at any particular point in time. This returns us to the task of working out an artist's agency: if the display of the body is to exert its own force, its authority then lies in the controlling of the audiovisual space. Controlling, in this sense, involves editing, camera work, and the specific choice of gestures. Legs, face, hands, and torso are meticulously edited and enhanced by everything from airbrushing to lighting, costume, makeup, choreography, and stage props. The body's disparate representations from one frame to the next form part of a larger structure that gains currency through its virtuosic show. Above all, the visibility of the artist's body is intended to encourage multiple

[2] Carol Vernallis, *Experiencing Music Video: Aesthetics and Cultural Context* (New York: Columbia University Press, 2004), 56.

[3] See Michel Chion, *Audio-Vision: Sound on Screen*, trans. Claudia Gorbman (New York: Columbia University Press, 1990), for one of many compelling arguments dealing with the temporality of sound in audiovisual contexts, where sound serves to track movement and motion in a process of gradual diffusion.

viewings, its fetishistic appeal being culturally specific and based on many variants of the gaze, not least of all that of the director.

Enter the director (predominantly white and male), who wields control over the body in performance mode, making decisions about how the music picks up on the body's varied surfaces. Consider the face alone. In an earlier study of Annie Lennox, I debated the determining role of close-up facial features in a video's expressive realm by giving consideration to the varied shots of a performance.[4] Magnifying Lennox's eyes, lips, and hair contributed a major trajectory in the interpretation of her body, directly leading to an understanding of psychic identification on the part of the artist, director, and spectator. There can be little doubt that screening the face in all its minute detail adds a high dose of emotional value, escorting us into the music via the act of singing. As did Lennox's video "Money Can't Buy It," "Umbrella" consists of facial shots that tell us much about the director's strategies. In no uncertain terms, Rihanna is stylized largely according to the director's tastes and preferences. Vernallis maintains that pop videos signify "strong personal realizations of space," where successful directors generally tend to develop their "trademark styles" in a manner that operates in confluence with the video's "transitoriness, incomprehensibility, and speed."[5] Inevitably the politics of representation reflect the director's as much as the artist's intentions, demands, and aspirations. From this perspective, we might say that the body showcases the star through the gaze of the director. In turn, this raises a host of questions linked to packaging, reception, and marketing ploys.

Unraveling audiovisual components is a necessary task for the scholar intent on considering subjectivity. From a musicological standpoint, however, this field of study is still relatively undeveloped. It is worth stressing that in pop videos the intense framing of the body through music is quite unique (e.g., in ways not encountered in film). The "magic" of the video is founded on an unusually potent visual and musical relationship that is all about making a song meaningful—turn the sound off, and the image is nonsensical. I also argue that the most palpable aspect of most video performances is the *suggestive positioning* of the body, whose stylized display signifies that which is well beyond the bounds of "normal" everyday experience. This helps explain how hyperembodiment redefines reality, where the body's technological constructedness constitutes a prime part of the show. With these ideas in mind I now turn to the details of Rihanna's performance in "Umbrella."

Rihanna: "Umbrella" (2007)

Rihanna's representation in "Umbrella" epitomizes hyperembodiment, entailing a beautification process that takes the aesthetics of pop to an extreme. This is commonplace

[4] Stan Hawkins, "Perspectives in Popular Musicology: Music, Lennox and Meaning in 1990s Pop," *Popular Music* 15, no. 1 (1996): 17–36.

[5] Vernallis, *Experiencing Music Video*, 136.

among megastar pop contemporaries: Madonna, Mariah Carey, Janet Jackson, Alicia Keys, Britney Spears, Gwen Stefani, Lady Gaga, Beyoncé, Christina Aguilera, and Katy Perry. Highly constructed pop videos, like pop songs, might well prove contentious for many scholars, and Rihanna is one in a long line of female artists at the onset of the twenty-first century whose act steadily meets the eyes of a porn-fixated culture. Certainly her commercial success is indisputable. By the time she was twenty-three, sales exceeding twenty million albums and sixty million singles had made her one of the top-selling female artists of all time.

In "Umbrella" her airbrushed body has its corollary in the gloss of the produced sound, establishing the sonic conditions for stylizing corporeality in terms of gender, ethnicity, and generation.[6] With this in mind, I suggest that the aesthetics of Rihanna's act are predicated on the reassemblance of the body audiovisually. In this process, hyperembodiment becomes a by product of sound production, offering itself up to the multifaceted gaze in numerous ways. From this we might ask: How does the body assume its positioning through technological manipulation? If agency in videos operates through hyperembodied structuring, what is the function of the sound recording? How might one comprehend the qualities of bodily stylization through the audio experience? Perhaps the answers to these questions lie in understanding the processes of transformation, wherein the essentials of the artist's look, her erotics, her sex appeal, are heightened cosmetically by the intricacies of her sound.

Performance and Direction

Written by Jay-Z, Christopher Stewart, Kuk Harrell, and The-Dream for Rihanna, the song "Umbrella" was released to instant commercial success in March 2007. As one of the biggest hits from the album *Good Girl Turned Bad*, it featured Jay-Z on the introductory rap verse. The sparkling arrangement is dominated by hi-hats, synthesizers, a muddy bass-line, and Rihanna's semiflanged, tough cyborg voice. Stylistically the song falls under the categories of R&B, hip-hop, and pop. A standard verse, chorus, middle section structure defines the song's form.

With over two hundred videos already to his credit when he directed "Umbrella," American music video director Chris Applebaum has explained the huge pressure he was under to shoot the video in only one day. Drawing his inspiration from other artists he had worked with—Madonna, Britney Spears, and Kid Rock, to name a

[6] James, "Robo-Diva R&B." James argues that Rihanna's robo-diva aesthetic in "Umbrella" serves to "throw in white patriarchy's face what it most fears—black women and black femininity," 417. The stereotype of black women as "closer to nature" is, broadly speaking, embedded in neocolonial patriarchal discourse, which James describes as the "classic 60s myth." James's notion of hyperembodiment has a resonance in Eshun's *More Brilliant Than the Sun*, differing somewhat from mine in that I perceive Rihanna's subjectivizing of the posthuman body as primarily nonemancipatory.

few—Applebaum came up with a concept that Rihanna readily accepted. At first he was concerned about whether she would agree to the most daring sequence in the video, in which her naked body is painted silver from top to bottom (see figures 26.1a and b). Indeed, this became the climactic point in the visual narrative. With feline grace she gently lowers herself onto her haunches in a crouched and contorted position, avoiding the camera's gaze. The intimacy of this heightened eroticism, Applebaum has explained, involved closing the set just to him, Rihanna, and the camera assistant, because she stripped naked before being covered in paint. The smearing of the female subject with paint, however, is nothing new, and historically this has an obvious referent in the contemporary art piece by Yves Klein, *Anthropométries de l'époque bleue*, in which, under Klein's direction, three nude women applied blue paint to their bodies to become a work of art.[7] This radical happening was highly controversial in 1960.

Particularly relevant is the screenplay's treatment[8] in "Umbrella." During its making Rihanna requested that in one of the scenes she dance *en pointe*, which Applebaum consented to. Allegedly the video performance involved junctures of negotiation among the director, the rest of the production team, and Rihanna, who played out her various roles with great zest.

Complementary to Klein's piece, Rihanna's persona in "Umbrella" has its genealogy in other texts that deal with rain, such as music videos (Björk's "It's Oh So Quiet," Peabo Bryson's "Can You Stop the Rain," and Anne Peebbles's "I Can't Stand the Rain") and film musicals (*Singin' in the Rain, Cabaret, Les Parapluies de Cherbourg*). In all cases, the glamorous female artist takes center stage in a cultural and social setting that is far more male controlled than one might assume. Overtly sexy and tarted up, Rihanna's performance in "Umbrella" belongs to a long tradition of older men directing young girls, which would seem consistent with her media coverage offstage. Yet lines of control in any performance are easily blurred. Philip Auslander has argued that the success of pop artists lies in their ability to perform their personae "across a multitude of platforms," which feels like "a direct performance of a persona unmediated by character."[9] This is especially true in Rihanna's case, where, despite her changes from one song or video to the next, something remains consistent in her own authoring that affords her authority. This is because, as Auslander insists, the pleasure derived by fans "consuming the personae" of their pop idols is inseparable from the music. So to the music we now turn.

[7] See Jon Refsdal Moe, "Aesthetic and Performative Considerations of Christina Milian's Music Video *Dip It Low*," in *Essays on Sound and Vision*, ed. John Richardson and Stan Hawkins (Helsinki: University of Helsinki Press, 2007), 327–360. Moe provides a close reading of Christina Milian's music video "Dip It Low" as an unintended reenactment of Yves Klein's "Happening," *Anthropométries de l'époque bleue*. Moe sets up two power arrangements by juxtaposing Klein and Milian, emphasizing how the latter's sexualized imagery objectifies representational politics in pop culture.

[8] Treatment refers to the step-by-step draft of the screenplay, which includes the detailed synopsis in a directorial style.

[9] Philip Auslander, "Musical Persona: The Physical Performance of Popular Music," in *The Ashgate Research Companion to Popular Musicology*, ed. Derek B. Scott (Farnham: Ashgate, 2009), 308–309.

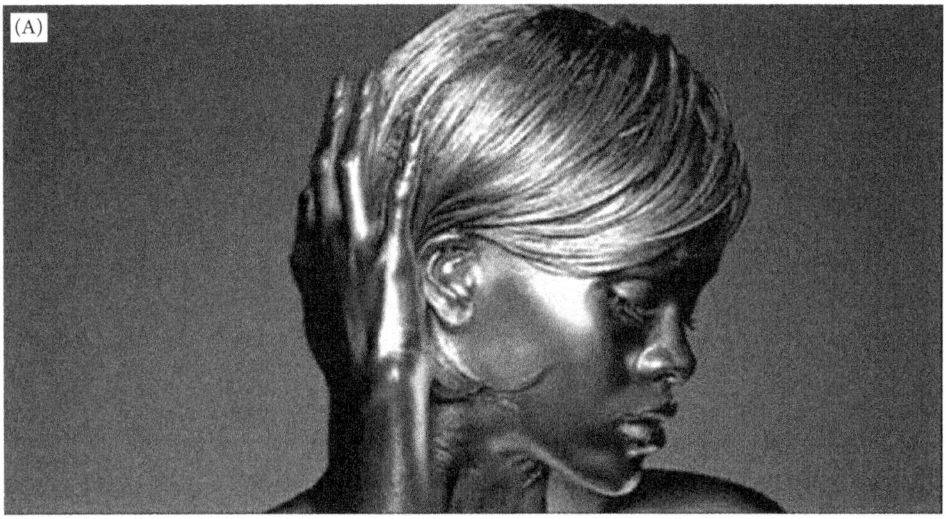

FIGURES 26.1A AND 1B: Rihanna, hyperembodied in silver-coated paint (2:03–2:45).

Musical Form: Vocal and Beat Structures

Editing, production, and technology construct the body in pop videos, and the processes deployed are contingent on the music. The audiovisual flow of a pop video invariably mediates a range of conventions that say much about an audience's expectations and reception of an artist. Auslander makes the point that audiences take on board "the same means of expression of popular musicians"[10] through their responses to them and

[10] Auslander, "Musical Persona," 315.

their performance. In other words, audiences learn much about themselves from watching others perform. Hence, pop videos signify not just musical performances, but also a complex range of representational issues that impinge on patterns of reception.

The video "Umbrella" lasts just over four minutes, with the song's formal structure consisting of a verse introduction (with guest rap by Jay-Z), verse 1, chorus 1, verse 2, chorus 2, bridge, chorus 3, and outro with fade-out. Various features characterize the rhythmic flow and groove from one section to the next. The groove comprises a medium slow, funk drum loop;[11] open-closed cymbals on first beats that dominate the kit's reverbed sounds; and a muddy synth bass-line.[12] Rhythmic textures and timbres consist of flurries of sixteenth notes on different parts of the kit, while an abundance of applied effects and edits serves to establish a strong sense of spaciousness in the mix. With a strong rhythmic undertow, this rich material energizes the groove. In fact, all the way through there is a sense that the groove extracts Rihanna's vocal track, accentuating her melodic interjections and incessant hook vowels, "eh" and "ella" (from the word "umbrella"). These vowel sounds are subjected to a style of vamping, typical of rap, heightening the lyrical poignancy while at the same time contributing to the tapestry of musical events. Complementing this are Rihanna's vocal dynamics, which merge with the programmed kit components, the cymbals, snares, and bass drum. Charged with rhythmic vitality, Rihanna's vocal track works the beat and overlays the groove. Yet underlying her vocal tone is something nonchalant, mechanical, and indifferent that strengthens her resolve. Primarily, the "umbrella" hook with the preachy repetition of the word's vowels becomes a central musical trope. Hypnotically seductive, this hook becomes the song's mantra: "come under my umbrella-ella-ella-eh-eh-eh-eh-eh-eh."

Throughout, a sense of urgency underlies the chilly vocal expressiveness of Rihanna's style. African American in its influence, her style is predicated on the poetics of rap and hip-hop. Throughout the song the "umbrella" hook offers a moment of repose, reflection, and temporal paucity as the singer's voice nestles within the arrangement. Rihanna's vocal affectations on the hook are wistful, with the tempo changing its feel due to the melodic and harmonic rhythm of her utterances on the word "umbrella." There is a sense that time is suspended during this passage. Her speech-like phrasing of the plaintive melodic hook gives her voice authority, as her musical performance shapes what we see and imagine. All this is coded in a message that is open-ended and static. Heavily compressed in the mix, her vocal sound forms an integral part of her hyperembodiment, articulated by a timbre that is processed digitally, making it suppressed, taut, and deformed. The flanged vocals fluently conjoin the materiality of the musical events through the body, as from start to finish the detailed editing in the instrumental backing supports a quivering voice, which teeters hysterically on the verge of its own reality.

[11] This groove pattern is from Apple's GarageBand drum loop software (Vintage Funk kit 03).

[12] Serge Lacasse has suggested to me that this bass-line's effect arises from the overcompressed effect of the drum loop (especially the bass drum), which introduces a degree of distortion into the lower frequency range.

Virtual Reality and Structuring Ethnicity

The video "Umbrella" is a slick production, and this is attributable to Rihanna's imagery as much as her performance, all of which is the result of intricate production devices. The gloss of any pop video is located in stylized imagery and musical expression and helps frame a sense of virtual reality through the musical flow and the imaginary world we enter into. John Richardson has examined how virtual reality is created "in terms of spatial representations of the musicians in the mix, which intersect in significant ways with attendant visual representations."[13] In considering Rihanna's "attendant" visuality, it would seem that her playfulness, her robo-diva construction, tells us most about the musical narrativity. And although her sound might be chilling and cyborg-like, it is the combined effect of this with her imagery that articulates a specific aesthetic, the technicalities of which I now dwell on.

Positioned in line with an array of other internationally successful female pop stars, Rihanna's look is highly individualized and teasing. Her ethnicity alone opens up the categorization of European-African-American, her Barbadian parentage being African Guyanese (on her mother's side) and Barbadian Irish (on her father's side). Ethnicity is crucial in the marketing of any pop star. Andrea Elizabeth Shaw has addressed the discourse associated with nonwhite women in terms of gendered and racial embodiment: "Unlike the choice of national bird or national dish, the country's beauty queen represents the gendered and racialized identity that a nation decides to assume." With the recent entry of black women into mainstream culture, Shaw argues, "whiteness is no longer the zenith of Western beauty and femininity." There is a subtler foregrounding of whiteness in popular culture at the start of the new millennium, where "despite a black genetic heritage," this is reflected through a paradigm that "would find little room to aesthetically value an overweight, dark-skinned woman."[14] Arguably, Rihanna's look complies with Shaw's critical observations; high cheekbones, light eyes, straight nose, thin lips, and a trained, slender body shape an image that sells. With very few exceptions (Queen Latifah, Missy Elliott, Angie Stone, Bessie Smith, and Aretha Franklin), the slender, light-skinned black diva's passage into mainstream pop culture is navigated through a social context of multiethnicity that still remains under the controlling glare of the white gaze. Following Shaw's tack, one might say that Rihanna's construction obeys the rules of a corporeality that idealizes it. And it is idealized by a process of hyperembodiment. The political backdrop to this exposes an anxiety about color, size, and weight, which in developed, industrialized countries has privileged performative contexts in which technological innovation perpetuates the conventions of beauty. "Umbrella" thus profiles the "body beautiful" to its utmost advantage. The video is a reminder that desirability is associated with the beauty and sexiness of youthfulness,

[13] John Richardson, "'The Digital Won't Let Me Go': Constructions of the Virtual and the Real in Gorillaz' 'Clint Eastwood,'" *Journal of Popular Music Studies* 17, no. 1 (2005): 15.

[14] Andrea Elizabeth Shaw, *The Embodiment of Disobedience: Fat Black Women's Unruly Political Bodies* (Oxford: Lexington Books, 2006), 6–7.

the phenomenon of which can also include marginalization or, worse, mutilation (think of the late Michael Jackson). Yet the modalities of aesthetic beauty also raise issues of "girl power" and the construction of femininity the popular way.[15] It is worth noting that "Umbrella" is from an album with the title *Good Girl Gone Bad*.[16] This is hardly anything new in popular culture. Consider the genealogy of Josephine Baker's banana-clad body, Madonna's vogue period, Britney Spears's slut-play, Lil' Kim's porn antics, and Christina Aguilera's bionic cyberplay. In all these instances, the transgression of "safe" norms (good girl turning bad) also panders to the male gaze. The point I am arriving at is that no reading of Rihanna can circumvent the troublesome politics of voyeurism. Through her extensive media exposure, Rihanna has had much to say about her own staging and haute couture. She acknowledges that replicating the body in various guises and playing the role of the bad, tough girl is instantly appealing, entertaining, and, at best, addictive.[17] So how might one critique such a strategy and situate it historically in terms of gender and ethnicity?

In a study that picks away at the incisive parody found in Tina Turner's image and performance, Susan Fast employs a model of signifying to illustrate how normative male practices can be turned around. Back in the late 1960s Turner's tough persona was not only sexually provocative, but also ethnically problematic, as she pandered to stereotypes associated with black identity. There are striking similarities between Turner and Rihanna in their performance strategies; an energetic toughness in their sound and iconography raises the issue of female masculinity. In the case of Turner, as Fast explains, this operates through "a de-emphasis on curves in Tina's body type, which in addition to the often angular movements in the stage show, work against the softness associated with traditional femininity. Tina's is a hard body."[18] Significantly, the choreography that shaped Turner's moves, at least since her performances with the Ikettes in the 1960s, showed off the scantily clad body. Notably, the physical discipline of her dance movements also posed a potential threat. In contrast to many other black women of the day, who were restrained physically, Tina and the Ikettes (Fast maintains) "were creating physical spectacle that made them culturally other—that made them black(er) and,

[15] See Dafna Lemish, "Spice World: Constructing Femininity the Popular Way," *Popular Music and Society* 26, no. 1 (2003): 17–29.

[16] See Leslie M. Meier, "In Excess? Body Genres, 'Bad' Music, and the Judgment of Audiences," *Journal of Popular Music Studies* 20, no. 3 (2008): 240–260, for an important study of body genres, exploring some of the debates regarding musical "badness" and the uncomfortable excesses that traverse boundaries linked to gender-oriented cultural expectations. Meier's Bourdieuan contention is that certain performers who play with gender and explicit sexual content are targeted by the censorship of social conservatives. This has a resonance in many of the negative reactions I have noted toward Rihanna's overtly sexualized display. See my earlier study, "Dragging Out Camp: Narrative Agendas in Madonna's Musical Production" in *Madonna's Drowned Worlds: New Approaches to her Cultural Transformations*, ed. Santiago Fouz-Hernández and Freya Jarman-Ivens (Aldershot: Ashgate, 2004), 3–21.

[17] As many Internet searches have revealed at the time of writing, countless references to Rihanna's views on fashion and style demonstrate the star's preoccupation with clothes and her look.

[18] Susan Fast, "Bold Soul Trickster: The 60s Tina Signifies," in *She's So Fine: Reflections on Whiteness, Femininity, Adolescence and Class in 1960s Music*, ed. Laurie Stras (Farnham: Ashgate, 2010), 232.

I would argue, that also 'masculinised' them, since some of their male counterparts—James Brown, Sam and Dave—engaged in similarly unrestrained physical movement."[19] Ostensibly the powerful signifying practices of Turner's defeminization, or for that matter her masculinization (in stereotypical terms), paved the way for the next wave of female performers, black and white.

Hyperembodiment and Musical Fetishization

On the phenomenon of the type of human performance detected in an artist such as Rihanna, Steve Dixon has researched hyperembodiment and hypersexuality as part of his interdisciplinary approach to interpretation. He points out that the "body beautiful" in the late twentieth century could be perceived as a "Cartesian triumph of mind over matter," wherein the "the willful mind is the invisible but overwhelming sign, the ultimate agenda."[20] Digitalized bodies, edited down to the tiniest detail, can therefore be interpreted as profound manifestations of the mind transcending the body, and more. Dixon argues that in digital performance the "mind-body split is generally at complete odds with the practice of artists and performers." This is because performers explore and enact their "holistic autonomies and interiorities (gendered, spiritual, emotional, and political)," not merely their corporeality. The point is, as Dixon insists, that the performing virtual body is no less authentic than the live one, "nor is it disembodied from the performer."[21] What then are the implications of fetishistic manipulation, and why is this integral to mainstream pop videos? In addressing this question, I consider the sonic manipulation of the body through audio engineering.

Space hardly permits any full-blown discussion of the microstructures of production behind "Umbrella," but it is worth highlighting several processes. Commenting on his approach to the sound engineering in the track, Manny Marroquin explains that his biggest challenge was to get the mix "right."[22] To start with, he sought a sound that was as "warm as possible" yet aggressive; to achieve this he worked a lot with the synth lines he describes as "purely eq." A major task was to break down the sound from the rough mix he started with. Describing the prevalence of delays in the mix, Marroquin clarifies his use of the technical details when manipulating the sound. Using the Waves doubler plug-in and the return of his delay and reverb, he created a phasing effect with the delays—a stereo delay panned hard left, and the right involved hardly any feedback, while the left side contained feedback. The result of this was a lushness in the sound, further enhanced by the use of the doubler and the AMS reverb and Lexicon 480-L

19 Fast, "Bold Soul Trickster," 233.

20 Steve Dixon, *Digital Performance: A History of New Media in Theater, Dance, Performance Art, and Installation* (Cambridge, Mass.: MIT Press, 2007), 213.

21 Dixon, *Digital Performance*, 215.

22 See Manny Marroquin's account of the mixing of the "Umbrella" video at http://www.youtube.com/watch?v=L5MWmif7teM (accessed February 10, 2011).

classic reverbs; the effect was to create the sensation of "things swimming in a weird way." For the bass part, Marroquin used an R-bass plug-in for capturing what he called the "real sub"; this comes into full force at the entry point of the first chorus (0:57–1:39). Rihanna's vocals were also enhanced in many different, easy ways, not least through the use of a meta-flanger, which provided the nostalgic effect of vintage tape flanging and phase emulation.

From Marroquin's account it becomes clear that the juncture between digitalized musical and visual performance shapes a specific cinematic aesthetic. In pop videos the act is always virtual, and as Richardson points out (in his analysis of the Finnish singer-songwriter, Maija Vilkkumaa, and her video "Kesä"), the role of cinematography is significant in the coding of a pop video. Essentially, the singer needs to come across as assured, and this depends on a convincing synchronization of music and visuals, "in the use of a restless to-ing and fro-ing of camera angles, unexpected zooms, cuts, and swish pans, and in the apparent inability of the camera to stay in focus."[23] In Richardson's analysis of Vilkkumaa, the camera's tracking provides its own narrative on the music. In much the same way, the tension and release in Rihanna's movements through variable camera angles converts into a visual commentary on the rhythm, timbre, and texture in the audio recording. Hence the digitalization of her image and sound occurs within a context where she becomes a reflexive mirror for human vanity, her body fragmented into close-up facial shots, full body shapes, and components (limbs, torso, hair, breasts, and so forth). Ultimately then, digital production traverses the imaginative and dramatic entity of the artist's animation frame by frame. From this one might say that the performative dimension is exaggerated to the point of parody: costume changes are rapid, movements are considerably varied, and the makeup is altered continuously in conjunction with lighting and props. Moreover, the supporting dancers (all females in the introduction, all males in the finale) make implicit her gendered position.

Digitally realized, the music is constructed around a simple beat that generates different layers of instrumental activity. For example, the percussion, in particular the hi-hat, and the resonant bass synth line play a main role in determining the aesthetics of Rihanna's voice. Rihanna visually brings to life everything that is encoded in these groove-based instruments. The elegance of her solo and ensemble shots is blended with ease into the sound production.

Vernallis has stated that videos cast the singer in an "overseeing role," where role-playing is governed by the star's look, charm, and charisma. Ostensibly the singer knows little about the outcome while making the video, because the "whole never becomes an issue, nor does the fact that the background figures seem attentive or sensitized to the singer's voice."[24] Yet having shot numerous videos, Rihanna is well aware that her fragmented body parts are critical in making fluid the final mix: in the end it is

[23] John Richardson, "Double-Voiced Discourse and Bodily Pleasures in Contemporary Finnish Rock: The Case of Maija Vilkkumaa," in *Essays on Sound and Vision*, ed. John Richardson and Stan Hawkins (Helsinki: University of Helsinki Press, 2007), 425.

[24] Vernallis, *Experiencing Music Video*, 61.

the seamlessness of the audiovisual flow that accounts for its magical quality. This brings us to one of the other main features of a pop video: the details of movement, especially through dance.

The majority of pop videos include dance movements. Dance assists continuity and draws the viewer's attention to the music. Vernallis claims that dance teaches us not only how music is experienced through the body, but also "how we should feel about our bodies within a certain cultural epoch."[25] There can be little doubt that Rihanna sports a cultural agency through the way she dances. Significantly, her physical movements encourage engagement on the part of the viewer, with the choreography revealing aspects of the artist's persona (see table 26.1). Rihanna's dance sequences are varied, ranging from strict lockstep and full synchronization to a freestyle that veers away from tracking the rhythmic impulse of the groove. Of course many elements define dance, and it is difficult to distinguish between standard learned step routines and physical movements made simply in response to sound. Given that dance is the bodily response in the form of movement to sound, it depends on conventions and social entities.

Seldom do music videos contain full-length choreographed dance sequences, and in "Umbrella" the visual display of Rihanna in action embraces short spurts of motion in a variety of ways that capture the spirit of the song's narrative. For the purpose of this analysis, I restrict my discussion to the following three sections to verify a number of points: chorus 1 (0:57–1:39), verse 2/chorus 2 (1:40–2:24), and chorus 3/outro (3:08–4:11) (see table 26.2).

In chorus 1 Rihanna's movements are improvised and characterized by turns and swirls, with close and long shots of her in a Monroe-esque white dress, with full-skirted halter. Although gestures in these frames might be read as coquettish, oblique, and affected, as she looks demurely into the camera, they are also graceful and assured. Iconography of this kind is about intimacy and charisma and is heightened by slow-motion digitalization. What we are exposed to is an eroticization of the star to the music. The set is a simple monochromatic backdrop with added computerized edits that suggest buckets of water, slowed down, hitting her from both sides, her body responding by moving from side to side.

Quite unexpectedly, a costume and scene change takes place halfway through (1:18), on the umbrella rant, "ella, el, la, el, la," where Rihanna is depicted in a black wet-look minidress with frills. The focus falls on her legs, while the screen comps involve fluorescent droplets of rain falling down. Ostensibly the computer-generated imagery (CGI) illuminates Rihanna's movement in all the frames. The wet look of the set not only highlights the song's narrative, but also adds to the details of Rihanna's choreography. Indeed, the varying levels of movement are intended to elicit an emotional rapport with the viewer.

In the second sequence, verse 2/chorus 2 (1:40–2:24), a further shift occurs from free movement to choreographed dance. With this comes a change in costume to a black

[25] Vernallis, *Experiencing Music Video*, 71.

Table 26.1. Structural Divisions: Audiovisual Events and Narrative in "Umbrella"

Form	Musical and Lyrical Events	Visual Details
Introduction (0:00–0:32)	Jay-Z guest raps in the intro. Spacious drums and vocal rap dominate the mix, with Rihanna interjecting with "eh" sounds. Jay-Z's final phrase is: "Jay, rain man is back with little Miss Sunshine, Rihanna where you at?"	The video starts with shots of Rihanna looking seductively into the camera. She is posed sitting with one leg up: the camera roams her body. Six sexy female dancers flank Jay-Z.
Verse 1 (0:33–0:56)	Rihanna takes over from Jay-Z. Instrumentation remains the same. She declares her love: "You had my heart, and we'll never be worlds apart." Echo and reverb is applied at the end of lines to emphasize the rhyme.[26]	The entire section consists of long and close-up shots of Rihanna. A jerky, blurring effect is used for titillation.
Chorus 1 (0:57–1:39)	Bass, strings, and synthesizers help pad out the chorus, forming a luscious backdrop for the vocals. Rhythmic intensity increases with a plaintive vocal rhyme play on "Under my umbrella—ella ella eh eh eh."	Rihanna's "rain dance" is juxtaposed with lashings of water hitting her in slo-mo. Swirling movements merge with *en pointe* ballet. (see Table 2)
Verse 2 (1:40–2:02)	Rihanna's voice continues to dominate the mix, with added echo effect. A buildup to the chorus occurs just before the end of verse 1, with the bass and strings entering at 1:59.	The shots are taken in an opulent interior, suggestive of eighteenth-century French gilt decoration, with Rihanna, as dominatrix, using an umbrella as a prop in her dance routine.
Chorus 2 (2:03–2:45)	Dynamics increase, with fuller instrumentation than chorus 1. Vocals are compressed, and echo effects are more expanded. Rihanna's voice is chorused on key words: "shine together," "be here forever," "more than ever," "under my umbrella."	The interior scene continues to 2:26, where the visual highlight of the video starts, with Rihanna's body painted silver. Crouched and feline-like, her movements are languid and erotic (see figure 1b)
Bridge (2:46–3:07)	A shift in tonal center occurs. The rhythmic textures and timbre in the mix are relaxed as Rihanna's voice is left exposed and intimate: "I'll be all you need and more." The final phrase entails a fast crescendo, heightening the dramatic effect.	Most of this section consists of close-up shots of Rihanna's face as she looks directly into the camera. The closing seconds are of her with a troupe of male dancers, dancing and singing in the rain. This functions as transitory material.

[26] See Serge Lacasse, "'Listen to My Voice': The Evocative Power of Vocal Staging in Recorded Rock Music and Other Forms of Vocal Expression" (PhD diss., University of Liverpool, 2000), for an in-depth discussion of the use of echo, reverb, phasing, and reiteration in the produced voice (167–236).

Form	Musical and Lyrical Events	Visual Details
Chorus 3 (3:08–3:52)	The song's climactic moment is achieved through a full use of effects and many textural layers. The ecstatic lead vocals are reinforced by a more elaborate harmony.	There is rapid editing of shots from all angles. This scene involves a dark backdrop with digital stabs of light (matrix-like) raining down.
Outro (3:53–4:16)	Rihanna sings: "It's raining, raining, You can always come into me." "It's pouring rain."	With beckoning hand gestures, Rihanna faces the camera.

bathing suit with halter neck, long black gloves, and high stilettos. Rihanna's makeup is thicker and more pronounced, her hair strictly tied back, framed by a closed umbrella that functions as a prop. Her look is now that of the sexy hotel maid, framed against a change in lighting to a warmer and golden indoor space; long shots are angled to depict her slenderness, bottom, and long legs. Erotically charged, this scene depicts her movements as more sensual and controlled. One of the main functions of this scene is to provide respite from the rain outside, the effect of which dramatizes her representation. Halfway through this sequence, on the words, "when the sun shines we'll shine together," the lighting changes to a whiter shade on the top half of the setting. This color contrast serves to emphasize her black costume against her light skin, all of which is intensified by a musical crescendo. Rihanna's movements vary in tempo—her twists, arches, and contorted stretches operate as a striking trajectory to the music. Central to this effect is the use of an umbrella as a dance prop. Possibly the most obvious historical referent to this in a dance sequence is Gene Kelly's celebrated routine in the comedy musical film *Singin' in the Rain* (1952). In the legendary number from that musical, "Singing in the Rain," he sings and dances and does not mind getting drenched, because he's infatuated with Kathy Selden (Debbie Reynolds). At the start of the sequence there is a deliberate heaviness to the choreography (which arguably highlights the link between sport and dancing), in which Kelly hunches his shoulders at the same time that he awkwardly positions his knees. But in using the umbrella, his dancing gradually becomes more nimble, with shots of him swinging from a lamppost, placing one foot in the gutter and the other on the curb, and then gleefully jumping up and down in a large puddle. Flirtatiously, Kelly uses the umbrella as a dance partner, which then becomes a juggling prop as he throws it high up in the air and catches it. Toward the middle of the sequence he even strums the umbrella as if it were a banjo or guitar. With the aid of the umbrella in this dance routine, Kelly succeeds in opening up the street scene expansively, making full use of camera angles and movements. This provides him with a wealth of directions to move within. Enhanced by an athleticism and muscularity that is nevertheless graceful, Kelly is depicted as an everyday guy. And through the combination of tap and other agile step movements, the umbrella becomes a vehicle for expressing the joy and exhilaration of live dance in a deceptively casual way.

Table 26.2 Rihanna's Choreography in "Umbrella"

Sections	Movement Shots
Chorus 1 (0:57–1:39)	
Verse 2 (1:40–2:24)	
Chorus 3 (3:08–4:11)	

In contrast to Gene Kelly, more than fifty years later, Rihanna's disciplined dance sequence substitutes the umbrella for something quite different, the dominatrix's stick, which adds authority to her movements within an erotic zone that is heavily fetishized. As an object of desire, the umbrella is malleable and used sensually in moves that include single and double handclasps, rotations, insertions between the legs, and slides around and up along Rihanna's body. Finally, in the final moment of this scene, the umbrella opens up. Functioning as phallic signifier, Rihanna's use of the umbrella steers much of the choreography, adding symbolic weight to the dance routine. Nonchalantly, she looks at us square on, her defiant gaze locking with the camera's lens. In these moments the expressive resource of her eye contact with the camera (and us as viewers) is fully tapped.

The last scene to be considered commences in the bridge bars between the final verse and chorus 3, serving as a transition into the final section of the song. This marks a climactic point in the video, in which Rihanna is joined by a troupe of male dancers. In the tradition of the grande finale of the musical, the dance routine here is elegantly executed, with black umbrellas as props, with laser shots raining down and dispersing into real water shots on the stage. During this sequence the shot is multiedited by a variety of techniques that ease in the passage of visual continuity: low- and high-angle shots, crane shots, slo-mo, jump cuts, defocusing, mixing speeds, and so forth. Against a backdrop of visual pyrotechnics, Rihanna leads her troupe with great panache and control, and as in all the sequences, her centeredness in each frame is accentuated by lighting and camera angles that compel us to look on. As I see this, the variations in her dance and movements not only ritualize her subjectivity, but also hold our attention all the way through because of the rapidity in image changing. In fact, it is the steady increase and buildup in musical and visual textures that makes viewing compelling: the mix is denser, the dynamics are escalated, and the dazzling effect of rain falling down is rapid, all of which alternates with angle shots of Rihanna. Ending with a musical fade, Rihanna is shot dramatically lifting her umbrella up (now closed) to the skies. The effect is mesmerizing.

Final Reflections

Hyperembodied display implies an obsession with the look that is governed by the technologies of musical production as much as the decisions that go into directing the video. It is as if every frame in "Umbrella" negotiates its own terms for lending weight to Rihanna's representation. Musically, the genre of this song typifies early twenty-first-century mainstream pop and hip-hop videos, in which the body is anchored in a digitalized arcadia. Most of all, videos of this kind are about utopian escapism. Cunningly they turn the present into virtual reality, signifying a hedonistic fantasy that becomes a foil for everyday life. Undoubtedly, though, the audiovisual representations of Rihanna's performance raise crucial issues about inscriptions of ethnicity, gender, age, class, and, most important, agency. After all, pop artists are viewed in terms of desire as much as identification. Intriguingly, the pop video is itself an ambiguous text: it resists while it conforms to normative categorization through the seamlessness of audiovisual flow.

To convert the virtual into the actual is a sociopolitical process that induces erotic desire and intimacy. What does it mean to confer one's desire through the multifaceted gaze? And how does the visualization of sexuality and gender objectify the body in the cause of entertainment? The answers lie in how the audiovisual representation of the body operates. One of the most potent signifiers of hyperembodiment is the ever-changing technologized domain, and Rihanna's construction is a consequence of broader cultural matters. "Umbrella" is a fitting example of performers positioned in relation to the categories of the "posthuman" in a PlayStation-fixated social sphere. In sum, then, Rihanna's body symbolizes a new form of dissonance in the politics of representation. While it remains the object of entertainment, its titillation will always be characterized by a high degree of ambiguity and agitation.

References

Auslander, Philip. "Musical Persona: The Physical Performance of Popular Music." In *The Ashgate Research Companion to Popular Musicology*, ed. Derek B. Scott, 303–315. Farnham: Ashgate, 2009.

Chion, Michel. *Audio-Vision: Sound on Screen*. Translated by Claudia Gorbman. New York: Columbia University Press, 1990.

Dixon, Steve. *Digital Performance: A History of New Media in Theater, Dance, Performance Art, and Installation*. Cambridge, Mass.: MIT Press, 2007.

Fast, Susan. "Bold Soul Trickster: The 60s Tina Signifies." In *She's So Fine: Reflections on Whiteness, Femininity, Adolescence and Class in 1960s Music*, ed. Laurie Stras, 203–234. Farnham: Ashgate, 2010.

Hawkins, Stan. "Perspectives in Popular Musicology: Music, Lennox and Meaning in 1990s Pop." *Popular Music* 15, no. 1 (1996): 17–36.

Hawkins, Stan. "Dragging Out Camp: Narrative Agendas in Madonna's Musical Production." In *Madonna's Drowned World: New Approaches to Her Cultural Transformations*, ed. Santiago Fouz-Hernández and Freya Jarman-Ivens, 3–21. Aldershot: Ashgate, 2004.

James, Robin. "'Robo-Diva R&B': Aesthetics, Politics, and Black Female Robots in Contemporary Popular Music." *Journal of Popular Music Studies* 20, no. 4 (2008): 402–423.

Lacasse, Serge. "'Listen to My Voice': The Evocative Power of Vocal Staging in Recorded Rock Music and Other Forms of Vocal Expression." PhD diss., University of Liverpool, 2000.

Lemish, Dafna. "Spice World: Constructing Femininity the Popular Way." *Popular Music and Society* 26, no. 1 (2003): 17–29.

Meier, Leslie M. "In Excess? Body Genres, 'Bad' Music, and the Judgment of Audiences," *Journal of Popular Music Studies* 20, no. 3 (2008): 240–260.

Moe, Jon Refsdal. "Aesthetic and Performative Considerations of Christina Milian's Music Video *Dip It Low*." In *Essays on Sound and Vision*, ed. John Richardson and Stan Hawkins, 327–360. Helsinki: Helsinki University Press, 2007.

Richardson, John. "'The Digital Won't Let Me Go': Constructions of the Virtual and the Real in Gorillaz' 'Clint Eastwood'." *Journal of Popular Music Studies* 17. no. 1 (2005): 1–29.

Richardson, John. "Double-Voiced Discourse and Bodily Pleasures in Contemporary Finnish Rock: The Case of Maija Vilkkumaa." In *Essays on Sound and Vision*, ed. John Richardson and Stan Hawkins, 401–441. Helsinki: Helsinki University Press, 2007.

Robin James. "'Robo-Diva R&B': Aesthetics, Politics, and Black Female Robots in Contemporary Popular Music." *Journal of Popular Music Studies* 20, no. 4 (2008): 402–423.

Shaw, Andrea Elizabeth. *The Embodiment of Disobedience: Fat Black Women's Unruly Political Bodies*. Oxford: Lexington Books, 2006.

Vernallis, Carol. *Experiencing Music Video: Aesthetics and Cultural Context*. New York: Columbia University Press, 2004.

CHAPTER 27

THE EMANCIPATION OF MUSIC VIDEO: YOUTUBE AND THE CULTURAL POLITICS OF SUPPLY AND DEMAND

PAULA HEARSUM AND IAN INGLIS

In June 2005, when Chad Hurley, Steve Chen, and Jawed Karim launched YouTube, they had relatively modest ambitions for the new enterprise. The three had met in 2000 while working at PayPal's offices in San Mateo, California, and initially conceived a broad vision of a video-sharing Web site that could effectively function as an online dating agency, allowing individuals to upload footage of themselves to be viewed by prospective partners. Originally named Tune In Hook Up, the site attracted little interest or attention after it appeared in April 2005; its first video ran for 19 seconds and showed Karim in front of the elephant house at the San Diego Zoo, explaining that "the cool thing about these guys is that they have really long trunks."[1] However, the founders' enthusiasm for a user-friendly Web service that would enable global audiences to share in-demand images that were dramatic and/or sensational (confirmed by the huge interest in television pictures of Janet Jackson's bared breast during the 2004 Super Bowl half-time show and cell phone video footage of the Indian Ocean tsunami in the same year)[2] remained intact.

YouTube was not alone in seeking to solve the considerable technological obstacles to public video sharing, including the prohibitive size of video files and the need for different media players. However, its success in attracting early investment funding (including $8.5 million from Sequoia Capital in November 2005) gave the company a financial

[1] Jawed Karim, "Me at the Zoo," at http://www.youtube.com/watch?v=jNQXAC9IVRw (accessed March 25, 2012).

[2] Frederick Levy, *15 Minutes of Fame: Becoming a Star in the YouTube Revolution* (New York: Alpha Books, 2008), 1.

advantage that helped it create an accessible and attractive platform for potential users that quickly outdistanced its competitors (including Singingfish, Google Video, blinkx, and Yahoo! Video):

> Technically, YouTube has three major characteristic features: bandwidth and memory restrict video length to ten minutes; the url code for any clip can easily be embedded in other sites so that access to the clip can be from any online location; thirdly, it is officially not possible to download YouTube videos to your own hard drive. Other technical features include standard search capabilities and some social network functions.[3]

Assisted by publicity stemming from various forms of media response—ranging from a favorable review on the business/technology site Slashdot to threatened legal action from NBC Universal after an uploaded clip from *Saturday Night Live* attracted more than five million viewers in less than three months[4]—YouTube rapidly emerged as the dominant participatory media channel and most popular entertainment Web site of the new millennium. Its provision of a free, global broadcasting platform was embraced equally by amateur, grassroots video makers and professional, mainstream media producers. The speed of its uptake exceeded all expectations. By mid-2006 100 million clips were being viewed and 65,000 new videos uploaded daily.[5] In October 2006 YouTube was purchased by Google for $1.65 billion. By April 2008 it held more than 85 million videos.[6] In October 2009 it was claimed that YouTube was achieving more than a billion views per day.[7] By May 2010 this figure had risen to two billion.[8] On its fifth birthday, it was reported to be the world's third-most-visited Web site (after Google and Facebook), with imminent predictions of more than a million uploads per day.[9] It has been an astonishing period of expansion for a company whose promotional message to its users in 2005 encouraged them to "show off your favorite videos to the world... take videos of your dogs, cats and other pets [and] show videos to your friends and family around the world." In many ways, its exponential rate of growth through overlapping social networks is reminiscent of the chain letter activity of generations of schoolchildren. Indeed, Penenberg has identified it—along with eBay, PayPal, MySpace, Flickr, and Twitter—as an archetypal example of the phenomenon of a "viral loop": a company that grows "because each new user begets more users... just by using a product they spread it."[10]

[3] Martin Lister et al, *New Media: A Critical Introduction*, 2nd ed. (London: Routledge, 2009), 227.

[4] Jean Burgess and Joshua Green, *YouTube: Online Video and Participatory Culture* (Cambridge, UK: Polity, 2009), 2–3.

[5] Levy, *15 Minutes of Fame*, 19.

[6] Burgess and Green, *YouTube*, 2.

[7] Miguel Helft, "YouTube: We're Bigger Than You Thought," *New York Times*, October 9, 2009, at http://bits.blogs.nytimes.com/2009/10/09/youtube-were-bigger-than-you-thought/ (accessed March 25, 2012).

[8] Randall Stross, "YouTube Wants to Sit and Stay Awhile," *New York Times*, May 28, 2010, at http://www.nytimes.com/2010/05/30/business/30digi.html (accessed March 25, 2012).

[9] Patrick Barkham, "YouTube: Five Years On," *Guardian*, April 23, 2010, at http://www.guardian.co.uk/technology/2010/apr/23/youtube-five-years-on (accessed March 25, 2012).

[10] Adam L. Penenberg, *Viral Loop: The Power of Pass-It-On* (London: Sceptre, 2009), 11.

At the same time that the volume of videos on YouTube has escalated, so, too, has the range of its content, to routinely include TV and movie trailers, news and current affairs, educational clips, online marketing, live concerts, political campaigning, sporting events, and personal video blogs.[11] One of the principal functions that YouTube has served throughout its short history has been to engender a real process of democratization in the creation of music video, through which the traditional constraints of budget, time, and equipment have been challenged by the efforts of many thousands of casual music and video makers, who possess little or no professional expertise, but are motivated by a desire to display their work to as wide an audience as possible. The practice—or at least the thinking that lies behind it—is not new, but reflects criticism, distrust, or rejection of traditional media suppliers. Indeed, commenting on the appearance of "do-it-yourself" (DIY) media activities more than three decades earlier, Lewis offered a description that could stand as a blueprint for the interactive culture of YouTube:

> [As] the technology became available—cheap, lightweight, and easy to use—an ever-growing number of people learned how to make audio or video recordings (perhaps becoming involved just for fun at first).... They began to see through the professional mystique, realise the inadequacies of what was officially on offer, and explore new uses for media themselves.[12]

Long recognized as "the most pervasive and significant form of musical audiovisual text,"[13] the music video (which grew out of an initial desire to use short promotional films that would allow TV audiences to see a pseudo-performance of a song in the absence of a live appearance) experienced a decisive shift in development in 1983, when the 14-minute video for Michael Jackson's "Thriller" (directed by John Landis) became the first with a budget that reached $1 million. Its impact led to a pattern of rapidly spiraling production costs as video makers sought to focus attention on their particular product in an increasingly congested market, which itself had been substantially reshaped by the launch of MTV in August 1981. Russell Mulcahy's video for Duran Duran's "Wild Boys" in 1986 cost $1.2 million; Michael Jackson's "Bad" (dir. Martin Scorsese, 1987) cost $2.2 million; the budget for Guns N' Roses' "Estranged" (dir. Andy Morahan, 1993) was $4 million; Madonna's "Bedtime Story" (dir. Mark Romanek, 1995) cost $5 million; and in the same year, Michael Jackson and Janet Jackson's "Scream," also directed by Romanek, cost $7 million.

[11] Indeed, there is a fast-growing literature of research and/or manuals related to many of these areas. See, for example, Michael Miller, *YouTube for Business* (Indianapolis, Ind.: QUE, 2008); Thomas E. Rudolph and James T. Frankel, *YouTube in Music Education* (Milwaukee, Wis.: Hal Leonard, 2009); Morley Winograd and Michael D. Hais, *Millennial Makeover: MySpace, YouTube and the Future of American Politics* (New Brunswick, N.J.: Rutgers University Press, 2009); Greg Jarboe, *YouTube and Video Marketing* (Indianapolis, Ind.: Wiley, 2009); and Michael Sean Kaminsky, *Naked Lens: Video Blogging and Video Journaling to Reclaim the You in YouTube* (New York: Organik Media, 2010).

[12] Peter M. Lewis, *Whose Media?* (London: Consumers' Association, 1978), 134.

[13] Roy Shuker, *Understanding Popular Music Culture*, 3rd ed. (London: Routledge, 2008), 107.

The financial and stylistic extravagance of these, and many other, videos throughout the 1980s and 1990s had a number of direct consequences. The production of videos was predictably, and effectively, controlled by those major record companies that had the financial resources to meet mounting production costs; performers seeking exposure became dependent on internal marketing and promotional decisions about their commercial viability and "camera-friendly" attributes; and audiences were restricted by the programming policies of MTV (and its competitors), which, in their role as gatekeepers, determined which videos would and would not be broadcast. It has been argued that by the late 1990s the cumulative effect of these tendencies had ensured that the generation and circulation of music video was largely stripped of creativity:

> Program services like MTV exercise control by requiring submitted music videos to comply with their standards policies [and] regularly compromise the artistic independence of recording artists and clip directors by requiring changes in video images or song lyrics.... Record companies regularly encourage producers and directors to pander to MTV by imitating the style and visual effects of popular videos played on the channel in the past, hoping that MTV will play these clips. This pressure often leads to a bland conformity in videos that are loaded with hackneyed visual clichés.[14]

Although this may have been true, it has to be acknowledged that the recording industry—even in the 1990s—has always found space for auteurs, mavericks, and "outsiders" to create idiosyncratic texts that do not conform to the preferred templates. A list of such music videos includes, for example, those produced for Devo's "Whip It,"[15] George Harrison's "Got My Mind Set on You,"[16] Baz Luhrmann's "Everybody's Free to Wear Sunscreen"[17] and Neil Young's "This Note's for You."[18] However, the dominant trajectory of video makers undoubtedly did follow MTV's routine expectations.

This is not to deny the power that viewers have to decipher and employ texts in any way they choose. Kaplan has noted that "the level of any one text's production—in which individuals might have artistic ambitions and an aesthetic (or even an anti-aesthetic) end in mind—is completely irrelevant once a video is accepted by MTV.... It is completely out of the hands of the original producers and of the performers as well."[19] In this sense, the "meaning" of a text is always contingent, fluid, and open to negotiation. In the case of music video, this remains true whether it is screened on MTV or watched on YouTube,

[14] Jack Banks, *Monopoly Television: MTV's Quest to Control the Music* (Boulder, Colo.: Westview Press, 1996), 196.

[15] Devo, "Whip It," at http://www.youtube.com/watch?v=Xbt3oUnzRWw (accessed March 25, 2012).

[16] George Harrison, "Got My Mind Set on You," at http://www.youtube.com/watch?v=6GdeUoww4zy (accessed March 25, 2012).

[17] Baz Luhrmann, "Everybody's Free to Wear Sunscreen," at http://www.youtube.com/watch?v=sTJ7AzBIJoI (accessed March 25, 2012).

[18] Neil Young, "This Note's for You," at http://www.youtube.com/watch?v=KSSvzCNBvlQ&ob=av2e] (accessed March 25, 2012).

[19] E. Ann Kaplan, *Rocking Around the Clock: Music Television, Postmodernism And Consumer Culture* (New York: Methuen, 1987), 52–53.

whether it falls into one of the dominant categorizations discussed by Frith ("performance," "narrative," or "conceptual");[20] or whether, as Kinder suggests, it combines, with differing emphases, components of "performance," "narrative," and "dream-like visuals" in its search for visual intensity.[21] But this discussion has less to do with the cultural politics of "meaning," and more to do with the cultural politics of supply and demand and their implications for the internal contours of music video. At the turn of the century, when MTV was supplying music television to an estimated 342 million homes around the world and generating an annual revenue of more than $3 billion, producers and consumers (real or aspirational) were restricted by material and ideological codes that appeared resistant to change. Within a few years, however, YouTube provided a vehicle through which many of those apparently entrenched codes were actively confronted and challenged:

> By providing a distribution channel for amateur and semi-professional media content, YouTube incites new expressive activities.... Having a shared site means that these productions get much greater visibility than they would if distributed by separate and isolated portals. It also means that they are exposed to each other's activities, learn quickly from new developments, and often find themselves collaborating across communities in unpredictable ways.[22]

Taken together, these new opportunities have substantially reshaped traditional understandings—industrial, ideological, and technological—of the "music video aesthetic"[23] (although, as Vernallis makes clear in her comment that "music video *is* irreducibly strange," that aesthetic has never been regarded as straightforward or unproblematic).[24] Nonetheless, in the same way that skiffle in the 1950s and punk in the 1970s enabled "new expressive activities" to shape the performance of popular music by abandoning conventional requirements of musicianship, expertise, and technical ability, so too has YouTube in the twenty-first century provided a place in which those without formal training, up-to-date equipment, and professional qualifications can actively engage in the audiovisual representation of popular music.

Unsurprisingly, the most common DIY music clips on YouTube mimic, and thus reproduce, the conventions of the "performance" model, which has led some critics to question their radical credentials and to see them instead as "interchangeable, bite-sized [and]

[20] Simon Frith, *Music for Pleasure* (Cambridge, UK: Polity, 1988), 205–225.

[21] Marsha Kinder, "Music Video and the Spectator: Television, Ideology and Dream," *Film Quarterly* 38, no. 1 (1984): 2–15.

[22] Henry Jenkins, *Convergence Culture: Where Old and New Media Collide* (New York: New York University Press, 2006), 274–275

[23] See John Mundy, *Popular Music on Screen: From Hollywood Musical to Music Video* (Manchester, UK: Manchester University Press, 1999), 224–239.

[24] Carol Vernallis, "Strange People, Weird Objects: The Nature of Narrativity, Character and Editing in Music Videos," in *Medium Cool: Music Videos from Soundies to Cellphones*, ed. Roger Beebe and Jason Middleton (Durham, N.C.: Duke University Press, 2007), 111.

formulaic."[25] Moreover, the extension of opportunity has led many to protest against the resultant diminution of quality in the films and videos on public display. Queenan has likened YouTube to "an online jumble sale.... [T]here are tons of schlock, cult films, trash, direct-to-video overstock, and tongue-in-cheek vanity projects."[26] Keen has complained of the inanity and absurdity of its content. "Nothing seems too prosaic or narcissistic for these videographer monkeys. The site is an infinite gallery of amateur movies showing poor fools dancing, singing, eating, washing, shopping, driving, cleaning, sleeping, or just staring into their computers."[27]

Although these attacks may not be without foundation, they are reminiscent of the professional elitism that has characterized the response to many similar increases in access or shifts in policy, ranging from the "more is worse" opposition to university expansion in the United Kingdom through the 1960s[28] to the annual condemnation of contemporary conceptual art directed at the Turner Prize by traditional artists and their supporters since the early 1990s.[29] Attempts to undermine unfamiliar artistic practice seem to reflect a belief that such outputs infringe upon established consensus about what is aesthetically pleasing. However, this assumed consensus is not fixed: Juhasz's investigation of the site concluded that "what defined YouTube as good entertainment [was] its compelling lack of depth and expertise, and its all but disappeared procedures of coherence, order, and forced attention."[30] In addition, as Wolff has pointed out, "there is nothing sacred and eternal about the aesthetic."[31] This is especially pertinent for music video, where rapid advances in the technological determinants of production have combined with fragmented, interrupted, and temporary conditions of consumption to render past assumptions about the reception of images largely irrelevant. In effect, YouTube presents new kinds of texts to be watched by new kinds of viewers. The problem of how this might be interpreted has been neatly summarized by Connor:

> Uniqueness, permanence and transcendence seem in the reproducible arts of film and video to have given way irrevocably to multiplicity, transience and anonymity. At the same time, both film and video seem to offer certain possibilities of a reawakened radical impetus, and the emergence of avant-garde video art is evidence

[25] Alex Juhasz, quoted in Henry Jenkins, "Learning from YouTube: An Interview with Alex Juhasz," *Confessions of an Aca-Fan*, at http://henryjenkins.org/2008/02/learning_from_youtube_an_inter.html (accessed March 25, 2012).

[26] Joe Queenan, "YouTube Movies: The Diamonds among the Debris," *Guardian*, January 14, 2010, at http://www.guardian.co.uk/film/2010/jan/14/youtube-movies-joe-queenan (accessed March 25, 2012).

[27] Andrew Keen. *The Cult of the Amateur* (London: Nicholas Brealey, 2008), 5.

[28] See, for example, C. B. Cox and A. E. Dyson, eds., *The Black Papers on Education* (London: Davis-Poynter, 1971).

[29] In 2002, Culture Minister Kim Howells declared, "If this is the best British artists can produce, then British art is lost. It is cold, mechanical, conceptual bullshit." See Nicholas Watts, "Bottom Marks for Turner Prize as Culture Minister Vents His Spleen," *Guardian*, October 31, 2002, at http://www.guardian.co.uk/uk/2002/oct/31/arts.turnerprize2002 (accessed March 25, 2012).

[30] Juhasz, in Jenkins, "Learning from YouTube."

[31] Janet Wolff, *The Social Production of Art* (London: Macmillan, 1981), 141.

of this. As such, TV and video encompass, like film, the two worlds of mass culture and minority avant-garde culture.[32]

When two worlds collide, the structural and cultural repercussions supply new perspectives from which to consider old debates and also introduce new themes and topics for analysis.

For many years music video analysis ranged across two competing perspectives that were broadly, and controversially, grounded in either visually based theory (film studies) or aurally based theory (popular music studies). The resulting differences of emphasis were largely unresolved. For example, an early attempt to overcome such a binary opposition was made by Kaplan, who sought to deconstruct music video from a postmodernist stance that allowed her to examine both production and consumption at a time when the principal platforms and contexts of music video delivery were undeniably determined by the dominance of MTV.[33] However, the approach was questioned by Goodwin's doubts over the definition and deployment of postmodernism as a suitable perspective; in addition, though acknowledging that "pop has always stressed the visual as a necessary part of its apparatus—in performance, on record covers, in magazine and press photographs, and in advertising,"[34] he cautioned against the elevation of visual analysis over aural. This in turn led other writers to point out that to neglect visual analysis is to ignore the space created by the relationship between the two and to suggest a way forward through a synesthetic analysis of music video.[35]

One immediate effect of YouTube has been to reignite this discussion and replace the substantive comparisons of visual/aural components with theoretical issues that center around its "participatory turn, its embrace of mashup culture, its openness to textual destabilization and radical recontextualization, and its fundamental reliance on user-generated content."[36] The concepts so easily applied by Raymond Williams to understand "televisual flow"[37] no longer stand the test of new technology platforms. So, for example, while YouTube's music video output offers, as does MTV's, a loss of "grand narrative structures" through intertextuality and pastiche,[38] the parallel ends at the former's ability to place industry-standard content next to homemade musical

[32] Steven Connor, *Postmodernist Culture: An Introduction to Theories of the Contemporary* (Oxford: Basil Blackwell, 1989), 158.

[33] Kaplan, *Rocking Around the Clock*.

[34] Andrew Goodwin, *Dancing in the Distraction Factory: Music Television and Popular Culture* (Minneapolis: University of Minnesota Press, 1992), 8.

[35] See, for example, Kay Dickinson, "Music Video and Synaesthetic Possibility," in *Medium Cool: Music Videos from Soundies to Cellphones*, ed. Roger Beebe and Jason Middleton (Durham, N.C.: Duke University Press, 2007), 13–29.

[36] William Uricchio, "The Future of a Medium Once Known as Television," in *The YouTube Reader*, ed. Pelle Snickars and Patrick Vonderau (Stockholm: National Library of Sweden, 2009), 24.

[37] Raymond Williams, *Television: Technology and Cultural Form* (New York: Routledge, 1974), 77.

[38] Goodwin, *Dancing in the Distraction Factory*, 8.

movies. Thus, the painstaking and expensive choreography of John Landis's "Thriller" sits alongside spontaneous home and party versions that imitate Michael Jackson's moves, at negligible cost to the camera operator and immeasurable humiliation to any participants who may not have signed up for worldwide ridicule. A single copy of a URL into an e-mail, and one drunken moment of reenacting the "Thriller" shuffles is spread virally through contact directories. And though the impact of many DIY videos may be comic, the absence of rigorous monitoring procedures leaves open the opportunity to discern darker possibilities embedded in their inception and reception: the spate of "baby parody" videos (e.g., compare the two versions of "Telephone" by Lady Gaga and Baby Gaga) poses uncomfortable questions about child exploitation and abuse.[39]

Similarly, the "gatekeeping" commentary of a TV-studio-based video jockey has been replaced in YouTube by the open access equality of user-generated commentary. Hurley's stated aim to "democratize the entertainment process"[40] has been questioned by users, music industry professionals, and academics alike. Although emancipation from former restrictions lies at the heart of any shift in the direction of cultural participation, Van Dijck has suggested that in this particular instance, Hurley's democratic ideal is somewhat disingenuous, given the apparent secrecy surrounding the Google rating algorithms running behind the YouTube site.[41]

The potential power of the "viral loop" noted previously was amply illustrated in 2006, when OK Go's "Here It Goes Again"[42]—a quirky video of choreographed treadmill dancing—quickly achieved fifty million views. Since that moment, consideration of the "virality" (a new term for "word of mouth" or "pass it on") of a music video through YouTube has become an essential component of directorial strategies and approaches. Adam Sadowsky, president of Synn Labs,[43] has commented on the difficulties created by the success of "Here It Goes Again" for the creation of OK Go's next video, "This Too Shall Pass."[44] The eventual solution was to move from the relative simplicity of treadmill dancing to the design and construction of a Rube Goldberg machine, whose movements had to coincide with the tempo and rhythms of the song and to provide some of its musical functionality. In both cases, however, the video's obligation to promote itself

39 Lady Gaga and Beyonce, "Telephone," at http://www.youtube.com/watch?v=GQ95z6ywcBY&ob=av2n; and Baby Gaga, at http://www.youtube.com/watch?v=v1hNuoR1v7U (accessed March 25, 2012).

40 Ben McGrath, "It Should Happen to You: The Anxieties of YouTube Fame," *New Yorker*, October 16, 2006, at http://www.newyorker.com/archive/2006/10/16/061016fa_fact (accessed March 25, 2012).

41 Jose Van Dijck, "Users Like You? Theorizing Agency in User-Generated Content," *Media Culture & Society* 31, no. 1 (2009): 52.

42 OK Go, "Here It Goes Again," at http://www.youtube.com/embed/XJulhGUh8vU (accessed March 25, 2012).

43 Adam Sadowsky, "Adam Sadowsky Engineers a Viral Music Video," at http://www.ted.com/talks/adam_sadowsky_engineers_a_viral_music_video.html (accessed March 25, 2012).

44 OK Go, "This Too Shall Pass," at http://www.youtube.com/watch?v=qybUFnY7Y8w (accessed March 25, 2012).

as a topic for discussion—within viral video charts[45] or via simultaneous broadcast—is equally emphatic. The resultant trajectory is toward music "super-distribution," whereby music comes to the consumer rather than the consumer searching for the music.

The social and emotional dynamics associated with the circulation of music video are often unexpected and unpredictable. The history of the competing versions of Sick Puppies' "It's All the Same" supplies a pertinent example. The original record-company-produced footage presents, lavishly and slickly, a (stereo)typical narrative of "boy meets girl and has tempestuous relationship." However, this quickly fell into music video anonymity when the band's guitarist, Shimmon Moore, met performance artist Juann Mann in 2006 and was moved to create a different video to the song as a "sympathy v-card" for Mann, who had recently lost his grandmother. The new video circulated virally through its YouTube link and gave Mann's Free Hugs Campaign an enormous boost. To date, this "campaign version" has attracted some sixty million viewings—thirty times more than the record company's original video.[46] Each user's decision to open an e-mail, select those people likely to enjoy the music and/or video, and transmit the information has thus become an additional element of the video itself. It substantively adds new layers of communication that work in similar ways to "videos of affinity," whose main function is "to keep the lines of communication open to certain social networks, large or small, by sharing informal experiences."[47] Indeed, when picked up and played by the "aural viewer," the video message not only bears the imprint of a relationship between sender and receiver, but also introduces a connection between the new viewer and the video maker that is one of the more compelling attractions of YouTube music video culture.

Whereas MTV offered the world 24-hour music videos with *dual* functionality (to listen and to watch), YouTube offers 24-hour *multiple* functionality (to listen, to watch, to select, to read, to add comments, and to participate). It is ironic that in the period of YouTube's initial impact and rapid growth, MTV's emphasis on music broadcasting began to contract; in accounting for this, Middleton and Beebe have suggested that starting around 2004, the public appetite for music video was not declining per se, but new opportunities and locations from which to consume it (smart phones and handheld devices with an integrated reconfiguration for YouTube) fundamentally changed the experience.[48] Some of these strip away elements of interactivity and refocus attention on aural and visual components (although even that is being rewired for the next

45 See, for example, "Viral Video Chart," *Guardian*, at http://www.guardian.co.uk/technology/series/viralvideochart (accessed March 25, 2012).

46 Sick Puppies, "It's All the Same," at http://www.youtube.com/watch?v=okjxe8VWQPo; and "Free Hugs Campaign," at http://www.youtube.com/watch?v=vr3x_RRJdd4 (both accessed March 25, 2012).

47 Patricia G. Lange, "Videos of Affinity on YouTube," in *The YouTube Reader*, ed. Pelle Snickars and Patrick Vonderau (Stockholm: National Library of Sweden, 2009), 77.

48 Roger Middleton and Jason Beebe, eds., *Medium Cool: Music Videos from Soundies to Cellphones* (Durham, N.C.: Duke University Press, 2007), 1–2.

generation of devices). In a smaller and more mobile way, technology has thus brought the relationship between producer and consumer full circle.

In this context, it may be appropriate to consider Chion's description of TV as "illustrated radio." His belief that "television is fundamentally a kind of radio, 'illustrated' by images"[49] implies that the models employed to analyze the audiovisual nature of the medium are equally applicable to music video. But an understanding of "environment" is essential in the assessment of technological shifts and their impacts on consumption; as Vernallis has asked, "Do technological changes in the musical or the visual realm affect one another? And are these effects seamless or disjunctive?"[50] In the case of YouTube, this can be seen most clearly as control shifting from the industry to the consumer, who with the click of a mouse (or touch of the mobile screen) can "turn on, tune in (and drop out)"; here, there is no disc or video jockey to construct and direct the narrative. The playlist is personal. It is also political. Although surges of usage have alarmed an industry desperate to retain its grip on distribution, it is precisely this cross-fertilization of mutual interest that has driven the YouTube community—and the music video with it—back into our daily consciousness. In the classroom, for example, students can access, and illustrate, the worldwide history of popular music's aural and visual aesthetics in ways that inspire a new appreciation of the role and functions of video. In effect, the existence of a comprehensive audiovisual archive has transformed the ability of fans, researchers—and musicians themselves—to compare and contrast standards and strategies of musical performance over previous generations.

These changes in the position of the audience serve to consolidate the power of the musical community over the musical industry and also illustrate some of the issues created by the wider media fragmentation from broadcast to narrowcast. In 2009, after lengthy negotiations, Google and the Performing Rights Society reached an interim three-year, multi-million-dollar agreement under which the PRS received an undisclosed lump copyright sum for songwriters, composers, and publishers.[51] This was all the more unusual at a time when the rest of the industry was continuing to struggle with the old "pay-per-view/listen" structures. Intriguingly, it mirrors the long-standing relationship between the PRS and television companies and explicitly acknowledges YouTube's elevated status. YouTube has become an important place to be seen and heard, as much for the multinationals (Sony, Universal, and EMI, who in the wake of the PRS agreement reinstated their premium videos in the United Kingdom) as for amateur music video makers and independent labels, although the relationship is not without its problems.[52]

[49] See Michel Chion, *Audio-Vision: Sound on Screen* (New York: Columbia University Press, 1994), 165.

[50] Carol Vernallis, *Experiencing Music Video: Aesthetics and Cultural Context* (New York: Columbia University Press, 2004), 288.

[51] Emma Barnett, "YouTube Music Industry Video Agreement Is 'a Landmark Deal,'" *Daily Telegraph*, September 3, 2009, at http://www.telegraph.co.uk/technology/google/6128362/YouTube-music-industry-video-deal-is-a-landmark-deal.html (accessed March 25, 2012).

[52] However, tensions remain near the surface, and relationships have been continually renegotiated. In September 2006 the Warner Music Group (WMG) was among the first of the major labels to agree to

It is a challenging task to overturn decades of musical practice and put demand before supply. Nevertheless, in a culture built around instant images, sound bites, and celebrity presence, new narratives are required. For Susan Boyle, the "music video" was the television performance; her rendition of "I Dreamed a Dream" on ITV's *Britain's Got Talent* was the most watched YouTube clip of 2009. More important, it was a global news event. Although the three-minute clip superficially conforms to the conventions of a performance video, there are many points of divergence (the lack of choreography, the mundane stage setting, the inattention to costume, the singer's static pose, the evident under-rehearsal) that clearly distance it from the assumed characteristics of the genre.[53] Her brief audition has received more than 300 million views and led to ITV's decision to set up its own channel on YouTube to recapture its share of the audience, if not its lost revenue (variously estimated to be between £500,000 and £1.5 million in the two-week period following Boyle's initial appearance)—although the international publicity and increased number of viewers tuning into the program in subsequent weeks to follow her progress may have provided some compensation.[54]

The manner in which many of the videos (including Boyle's) placed on YouTube deviate from long-standing definitions of the video maker's art, aesthetics, and applications is perhaps its most significant aspect. For example, a recent discussion of music videos as musical texts contains the following assertions:

> Their most obvious characteristic is their similarity to advertisements, making them part of a blatantly consumerist culture.... Different styles of video utilize different conventions: heavy metal videos, for example, make considerable use of wide-angles lens and zoom shots in keeping with their emphasis on a "live concert" format.[55]

Although both statements may offer plausible descriptions of the industry-created videos seen on MTV, they are wholly misleading accounts of the home-produced videos seen on YouTube. (In passing, it should be noted that Mundy has suggested that the real significance of music videos lies less in their role as advertisements than in the various continuities they help to establish between popular music and the screen, and in particular, their contribution to the "visual economy" of popular music).[56] Very few

a relationship with YouTube, allowing users to include WMG music in their own videos to "embrace the power and creativity of user-generated content... enabling its artists to connect with a vast new audience in an entirely new way," only to renege on the agreement over the issue of royalties in December 2008 and remove or block its recordings. In September 2009 WMG agreed to a new relationship with YouTube and launched its own WMG channel.

[53] Susan Boyle, "I Dreamed a Dream," at http://www.youtube.com/watch?v=9lpOIWv8QZY (accessed March 25, 2012).

[54] Caroline Davies, "ITV Misses Out as Susan Boyle Conquers Web," *Observer*, April 26, 2009, at http://www.guardian.co.uk/media/2009/apr/26/susan-boyle-youtube-itv (accessed March 25, 2012).

[55] Shuker, *Understanding Popular Music Culture*, 108.

[56] Mundy, *Popular Music on Screen*.

DIY videos are there to promote or advertise another text, such as an album, a single, or a movie; on the contrary, their principal function is *self*-referential. The realization that "an increasing practice of self-staging and self-stylization is... a trademark of digital mass culture"[57] applies just as much to the videos on YouTube as it does to the personal home pages on Facebook or MySpace. For the twenty-first-century descendants of Tom Wolfe's "me generation"[58] growing up in Christopher Lasch's "culture of narcissism,"[59] YouTube has expanded "opportunities for self-expression well as self-promotion [and] has provided a new forum for self-portraiture."[60] Furthermore, these home-produced music videos disregard—deliberately or unwittingly—the conventions linking specific genres of music to particular visual approaches.[61] Indeed, one of the principal freedoms enjoyed by amateur music video makers is the ability to work outside the constraints imposed by the adoption of familiar patterns and assumptions. This freedom may be born of necessity—stemming from a lack of tangible (money, equipment) or intangible (time, expertise) resources—but there is no doubt that the "look" and "sound" of such videos departs dramatically from those themes and traditions initially established in the 1970s, and confirmed in the decades since, by the music video industry. The bedroom, the kitchen, the yard, and the suburban street have displaced the arena, the surreal landscape, and the exotic location as settings for musical performances and their accompanying narratives; poor lighting, unsteady camera work, and uneven sound quality contrast with meticulous and detailed music and vision editing; the whimsical has replaced the ostentatious; and everyday clothing, props, and accessories are substitutes for grandiose, spectacular, and flamboyant studio sets. In this respect, the inclusive nature of YouTube's library typifies the changing relationships between "elite" and "popular" forms of entertainment, including "the volume of their production, the sophistication of their delivery systems, the kind of education necessary to appreciate them, and the sort of consumer dynamics which factor into their acquisition."[62]

Significantly, the scarcity of resources underpinning many DIY videos has presented no obstacle to their subsequent impact. Aspiring musicians who have uploaded self-made clips have been rewarded with lucrative recording contracts, as the virality of their YouTube exposure has alerted industry gatekeepers. Ysabella Brave was signed to Cordless Recordings in 2007 after posting several videos of her songs (and spoken commentaries)

[57] Kathrin Peters and Andrea Seier, "Home Dance: Mediacy and Aesthetics of the Self on YouTube," in *The YouTube Reader*, ed. Pelle Snickars and Patrick Vonderau (Stockholm: National Library of Sweden, 2009), 188.

[58] See Tom Wolfe, "The Me Decade and the Third Great Awakening," in *Mauve Gloves and Madmen, Clutter & Vine* (New York: Farrar, Straus & Giroux, 1976), 117–150.

[59] Christopher Lasch, *The Culture of Narcissism: American Life in an Age of Diminishing Expectations* (New York: W. W. Norton, 1979).

[60] Matt Ferranto, "Digital Self-Fashioning in Cyberspace: The New Digital Self-Portrait," in *A History Of Visual Culture*, ed. Jane Kromm and Susan Benforado Bakewell (Oxford: Berg, 2010), 356.

[61] See Kaplan, *Rocking Around the Clock*, 49–88.

[62] Jim Collins, *High-Pop: Making Culture into Popular Entertainment* (Oxford: Blackwell, 2002), 29.

from her home in California;[63] Dutch teenager Esmee Danters was offered a contract by Tenman Records following the videos she made (in her bedroom) of her performances of Justin Timberlake's "What Goes Around"[64] and Natasha Bedingfield's "Unwritten";[65] in May 2010 12-year-old Greyson Chance signed with Interscope Records after the clip of him performing Lady Gaga's "Paparazzi"[66] on the piano in his school hall in Edmond, Oklahoma, became a YouTube hit; and in June 2010 Kim Yeo-Hee secured a recording contract with Dream High Entertainment after her iPhone versions of Beyonce's "Irreplaceable"[67] and Lady Gaga's "Poker Face"[68]—both filmed in the living room of the family apartment in South Korea—appeared on YouTube.

Music remains at the heart of the site's popularity. Responding to the finding in 2009 that 75 percent of the top fifty searches on YouTube were for music, Niamh O'Reilly, Sony Music's head of digital sales, was able to claim that "this research shows the extent to which something like MTV has been displaced and YouTube has taken its place as a channel to view music videos."[69] Of course issues of quality and improved technology may determine future audience allegiances. In the same way that social networking choice shifted from Friends Reunited to Facebook, new alignments (such as that between Apple and Vimeo, or among Sony, Universal, EMI, and Vevo) may shape future trends and allow the established corporations back into a restructured marketplace. Vevo's promises of a significant improvement in quality alongside a revenue stream of branding and advertising are especially attractive at a time of financial strain across the industry as a whole.[70]

Notwithstanding these possibilities, the cultural politics of supply and demand that revolve around YouTube have broken the equation that assigns supply to the producers, and demand to the consumers, of music video. Of course this should not be overstated. The list of the most viewed music clips, compiled by YouTube itself,[71] is still dominated

[63] See, for example, Ysabella Brave, "What a Wonderful World," at http://www.youtube.com/watch?v=e1qw6duAJjo and "Blue Bayou," at http://www.youtube.com/watch?v=pEkhmONEOFc (both accessed March 25, 2012).

[64] Esmee Danters, "What Goes Around," at http://www.youtube.com/watch?v=69Grnh7Qin8 (accessed March 25, 2012).

[65] Esmee Danters, "Unwritten," at http://www.youtube.com/watch?v=cndPHeBiM3s (accessed March 25, 2012).

[66] Greyson Chance, "Paparazzi," at http://www.youtube.com/watch?v=VGe2cwsR-IQ (accessed March 25, 2012).

[67] Kim Yeo-Hee, "Beyoncé's Irreplaceable," at http://www.youtube.com/watch?v=X3WiI9nT9Uo (accessed March 25, 2012).

[68] Kim Yeo-Hee, "Poker Face," at http://www.youtube.com/watch?v=nzh2UygPwDU (accessed March 25, 2012).

[69] See Eamonn Forde, "Take the Tube for Music," *Music Week*, February 14, 2009, 9.

[70] Vimeo is currently being promoted as a clearinghouse for producers and *the* place for music video makers to hold their material. Interestingly, "Here It Goes Again" is held on both YouTube and Vimeo, although the quality (visually and aurally) is substantially better on Vimeo, viewing numbers have yet to reach sixty thousand. Although YouTube is presently unable to match its new rival in terms of quality, it retains a proven ability to link dispersed musical communities. However, it may be significant that the TV advertisements to launch Apple's iPad in June 2010 specifically endorsed Vimeo.

[71] See http://www.youtube.com/charts/videos_views/music?t=a&p=1 (accessed March 25, 2012).

by professional videos showcasing sales leaders such as Miley Cyrus, Eminem, Lady Gaga, and Justin Bieber—although it is noteworthy that Bieber was signed to Island Records in 2008 on the basis of DIY music videos he had uploaded from his home in Ontario.[72] Nevertheless, in the dispersed YouTube community, the producers are the consumers; supply and demand are not separate enterprises, but part of a single process. Such media democratization is not unique. Over the past few decades numerous examples have appeared in the expansion of local and regional publishing, freelance film and TV, independent record production, and community radio. But such enterprises still tend to retain a degree of exclusivity based on the possession of certain skills and qualifications, without which it remains difficult to gain entry. By contrast, YouTube offers opportunities for a "networked individualism" that allows all to participate on equal terms:

> The most important role of the Internet in structuring social relationships is its contribution to the new pattern of sociability based on individualism.... Networked individualism is a social pattern, not a collection of isolated individuals. Rather, individuals build their networks, on-line and off-line, on the basis of their interests, values, affinities, and projects.[73]

Those interests and projects have led to new examples, understandings, and approaches to the aesthetics of music video. While the industry's preference for multi-million-dollar productions may not have vanished completely—as the lavishly produced and erotically charged videos in 2010 of Lady Gaga and Beyonce's "Telephone"[74] and Christina Aguilera, Lil' Kim, Mya, and Pink's "Lady Marmalade"[75] clearly demonstrate—it has been (at least temporarily) reduced. So, too, has its reliance on a narrow and complacent catalog of visual representations, drawn from a list that includes "beautiful Caucasian women, cars, high-heeled shoes, hotel rooms, fog, leather, snow, detectives, and beautiful Oriental women—the comic-book fantasies of adolescent males and James Bond fans."[76]

In its brief history, YouTube has provided an accessible site from which these kinds of clichés—and the political and professional ideologies that underpin them—may be questioned. Though its ability to attract and retain huge numbers of participant-consumers is self-evident, there is no guarantee that its radical potential will endure; after all, the popular culture industry has, over many decades, learned to skillfully absorb successive "threats" or "revolutions" into its commercial operations.[77]

72 See, for example, Justin Bieber, "Cry Me a River," at http://www.youtube.com/watch?v=KJWZsEkCrAM (accessed March 25, 2012).

73 Manuel Castells, *The Internet Galaxy* (Oxford: Oxford University Press, 2001), 130–131.

74 Lady Gaga and Beyoncé, "Telephone."

75 Christina Aguilera, Lil' Kim, Mya, and Pink, "Lady Marrmalade," at http://www.youtube.com/watch?v=RQa7SvVCdZk (accessed March 25, 2012).

76 Richard Gehr, "The MTV Aesthetic," *Film Comment* 19, no. 4 (1983): 39.

77 See George Melly, *Revolt into Style* (London: Allen Lane, 1970).

Furthermore, the emancipatory properties of any technology (including YouTube) only become fully effective when they are allied with other liberating forces:

> For engagements with the media to be truly transformative, the fact of expanded access to its production and exhibition is only one in a set of necessary conditions that also includes a critique, a goal, a community, and a context.... [O]ne of my great fears about YouTube is that it consolidates media action to the video production and consumption of the individual.[78]

Nevertheless, YouTube's (imperfect) achievement has been to supply individual music and video makers with opportunities for experiment, expression, and empowerment that, for the moment at least, continue to lie outside the rigid controls of a popular music hierarchy.

References

Aguilera, Christina, Lil' Kim, Mya, and Pink, "Lady Marrmalade," at http://www.youtube.com/watch?v=RQa7SvVCdZk (accessed March 25, 2012).

Banks, Jack. *Monopoly Television: MTV's Quest to Control the Music*. Boulder, Colo.: Westview Press, 1996.

Barkham, Patrick. "YouTube: Five Years On." *Guardian*, April 23, 2010, at http://www.guardian.co.uk/technology/2010/apr/23/youtube-five-years-on (accessed March 25, 2012).

Barnett, Emma. "YouTube Music Industry Video Agreement Is 'a Landmark Deal.'" *The Daily Telegraph*, September 3, 2009, at http://www.telegraph.co.uk/technology/google/6128362/YouTube-music-industry-video-deal-is-a-landmark-deal.html (accessed March 25, 2012).

Bieber, Justin, "Cry Me a River," at http://www.youtube.com/watch?v=KJWZsEkCrAM (accessed March 25, 2012).

Boyle, Susan, "I Dreamed a Dream,"at http://www.youtube.com/watch?v=9lpOIWv8QZY (accessed March 25, 2012).

Brave, Ysabella, "Blue Bayou," at http://www.youtube.com/watch?v=pEkhmONEOFc (accessed March 25, 2012).

Brave, Ysabella. "What a Wonderful World," at http://www.youtube.com/watch?v=e1qw6duAJjo (accessed June 4, 2013).

Burgess, Jean, and Joshua Green. *YouTube: Online Video and Participatory Culture*. Cambridge, UK: Polity, 2009.

Castells, Manuel. *The Internet Galaxy*. Oxford: Oxford University Press, 2001.

Chance, Greyson. "Paparazzi," at http://www.youtube.com/watch?v=VGe2cwsR-IQ (accessed March 25, 2012).

Chion, Michel. *Audio-Vision: Sound on Screen*. New York: Columbia University Press, 1994.

Collins, Jim. *High-Pop: Making Culture into Popular Entertainment*. Oxford: Blackwell, 2002.

Connor, Steven. *Postmodernist Culture: An Introduction to Theories of the Contemporary*. Oxford: Basil Blackwell, 1989.

Cox, C. B., and A. E. Dyson, eds. *The Black Papers on Education*. London: Davis-Poynter, 1971.

[78] Juhasz, in Jenkins, "Learning from YouTube."

Danters, Esmee, "Unwritten," at http://www.youtube.com/watch?v=cndPHeBiM3s (accessed March 25, 2012).

Danters, Esmee, "What Goes Around," at http://www.youtube.com/watch?v=69Grnh7Qin8 (accessed March 25, 2012).

Davies, Caroline. "ITV Misses Out as Susan Boyle Conquers Web." *The Observer*, April 26, 2009, at http://www.guardian.co.uk/media/2009/apr/26/susan-boyle-youtube-itv (accessed March 25, 2012).

Devo. "Whip It," at http://www.youtube.com/watch?v=Xbt30UnzRWw (accessed March 25, 2012).

Dickinson, Kay. "Music Video and Synaesthetic Possibility." In *Medium Cool: Music Videos from Soundies to Cellphones*, edited by Roger Beebe and Jason Middleton, 13–29. Durham, N.C.: Duke University Press, 2007.

Ferranto, Matt. "Digital Self-Fashioning in Cyberspace: The New Digital Self-Portrait." In *A History of Visual Culture*, edited by Jane Kromm and Susan Benforado Bakewell, 356–366. Oxford: Berg, 2010.

Forde, Eamonn. "Take the Tube for Music." *Music Week*, February 14, 2009, 9.

Frith, Simon. *Music for Pleasure*. Cambridge, UK: Polity, 1988.

Gehr, Richard. "The MTV Aesthetic." *Film Comment* 19, no. 4 (1983): 37–40.

Goodwin, Andrew. *Dancing in the Distraction Factory: Music Television and Popular Culture*. Minneapolis: University of Minnesota Press, 1992.

Harrison, George. "Got My Mind Set on You," at http://www.youtube.com/watch?v=6GdeUoww4zy (accessed March 25, 2012).

Helft, Miguel. "YouTube: We're Bigger Than You Thought," *New York Times*, October 9, 2009, at http://bits.blogs.nytimes.com/2009/10/09/youtube-were-bigger-than-you-thought/ (accessed March 25, 2012).

Jarboe, Greg. *YouTube and Video Marketing*. Indianapolis, Ind.: Wiley, 2009.

Jenkins, Henry. *Convergence Culture: Where Old and New Media Collide*. New York: New York University Press, 2006.

Jenkins, Henry. "Learning from YouTube: An Interview with Alex Juhasz." *Confessions of an Aca-Fan*, February 20, 2008, at http://henryjenkins.org/2008/02/learning_from_youtube_an_inter.html (accessed March 25, 2012).

Kaminsky, Michael Sean. *Naked Lens: Video Blogging and Video Journaling to Reclaim the You in YouTube*. New York: Organik Media, 2010.

Kaplan, E. Ann. *Rocking Around the Clock: Music Television, Postmodernism and Consumer Culture*. New York: Methuen, 1987.

Karim, Jawed. "Me at the Zoo," at http://www.youtube.com/watch?v=jNQXAC9IVRw (accessed March 25, 2012).

Keen, Andrew. *The Cult of the Amateur*. London: Nicholas Brealey, 2008.

Kinder, Marsha. "Music Video and the Spectator: Television, Ideology and Dream." *Film Quarterly* 38, no. 1 (1984): 2–15.

Lange, Patricia G. "Videos of Affinity on YouTube," in *The YouTube Reader*, edited by Pelle Snickars and Patrick Vonderau, 70–88. Stockholm: National Library of Sweden, 2009.

Lasch, Christopher. *The Culture of Narcissism: American Life in an Age of Diminishing Expectations*. New York: W. W. Norton, 1979.

Levy, Frederick. *15 Minutes of Fame: Becoming a Star in the YouTube Revolution*. New York: Alpha Books, 2008.

Lewis, Peter M. *Whose Media?* London: Consumers' Association, 1978.

Lister, Martin, Jon Dovey, Seth Giddings, Iain Grant, and Kieran Kelly. *New Media: A Critical Introduction*. 2nd ed. London: Routledge, 2009.

Luhrmann, Baz. "Everybody's Free To Wear Sunscreen" http://www.youtube.com/watch?v=sTJ7AzBIJoI (accessed March 25, 2012).

McGrath, Ben. "It Should Happen to You: The Anxieties of YouTube Fame." *New Yorker*, October 16, 2006, at http://www.newyorker.com/archive/2006/10/16/061016fa_fact (accessed March 25, 2012).

Melly, George. *Revolt into Style*. London: Allen Lane, 1970.

Jason Beebe, and Middleton, Roger, eds. *Medium Cool: Music Videos from Soundies to Cellphones*. Durham, N.C.: Duke University Press, 2007.

Miller, Michael. *YouTube for Business*. Indianapolis, Ind.: QUE, 2008.

Mundy, John. *Popular Music on Screen: From Hollywood Musical to Music Video*. Manchester, UK: Manchester University Press, 1999.

OK Go. "Here It Goes Again," at http://www.youtube.com/embed/XJulhGUh8vU] (accessed March 25, 2012).

OK Go. "This Too Shall Pass," at http://www.youtube.com/watch?v=qybUFnY7Y8w (accessed March 25, 2012).

Penenberg, Adam L. *Viral Loop: The Power of Pass-It-On*. London: Sceptre, 2009.

Peters, Kathrin, and Andrea Seier. "Home Dance: Mediacy and Aesthetics of the Self on YouTube." In *The YouTube Reader*, edited by Pelle Snickars and Patrick Vonderau, 187–203. Stockholm: National Library of Sweden, 2009.

Queenan, Joe. "YouTube Movies: The Diamonds among the Debris." *Guardian*, January 14, 2010, at http://www.guardian.co.uk/film/2010/jan/14/youtube-movies-joe-queenan (accessed March 25, 2012).

Rudolph, Thomas E., and James T. Frankel. *YouTube in Music Education*. Milwaukee, Wis.: Hal Leonard, 2009.

Sadowsky, Adam. "Adam Sadowsky Engineers a Viral Music Video." (2010), at http://www.ted.com/talks/adam_sadowsky_engineers_a_viral_music_video.html (accessed March 25, 2012).

Shuker, Roy. *Understanding Popular Music Culture*. 3rd ed. London: Routledge, 2008.

Sick Puppies, "Free Hugs Campaign," at http://www.youtube.com/watch?v=vr3x_RRJdd4 (accessed March 25, 2012).

Sick Puppies, "It's All the Same," at http://www.youtube.com/watch?v=okjxe8VWQPo (accessed March 25, 2012).

Stross, Randall. "YouTube Wants to Sit and Stay Awhile." *New York Times*, May 28, 2010, at http://www.nytimes.com/2010/05/30/business/30digi.html (accessed March 25, 2012).

Uricchio, William. "The Future of a Medium Once Known as Television." In *The YouTube Reader*, edited by Pelle Snickars and Patrick Vonderau, 24–39. Stockholm: National Library of Sweden, 2009.

Van Dijck, José. "Users Like You? Theorizing Agency in User-Generated Content." *Media Culture & Society* 31, no. 1 (2009): 41–58.

Vernallis, Carol. *Experiencing Music Video: Aesthetics and Cultural Context*. New York: Columbia University Press, 2004.

Vernallis, Carol. "Strange People, Weird Objects: The Nature of Narrativity, Character and Editing in Music Videos." In *Medium Cool: Music Videos from Soundies to Cellphones*, edited by Roger Beebe and Jason Middleton, 111–151. Durham, N.C.: Duke University Press, 2007.

Watts, Nicholas. "Bottom Marks for Turner Prize as Culture Minister Vents His Spleen." *Guardian*, October 31, 2002, at http://www.guardian.co.uk/uk/2002/oct/31/arts.turnerprize2002 (accessed March 25, 2012).
Williams, Raymond. *Television: Technology and Cultural Form*. New York: Routledge, 1974.
Winograd, Morley, and Michael D. Hais. *Millennial Makeover: MySpace, YouTube and the Future of American Politics*. New Brunswick, N.J.: Rutgers University Press, 2009.
Wolfe, Tom. "The Me Decade and the Third Great Awakening." In *Mauve Gloves and Madmen, Clutter & Vine*, 117–150. New York: Farrar, Straus & Giroux, 1976.
Wolff, Janet. *The Social Production of Art*. London: Macmillan, 1981.
Yeo-Hee, Kim, "Beyoncé's Irreplaceable," at http://www.youtube.com/watch?v=X3WiI9nT9Uo (accessed March 25, 2012).
Yeo-Hee, Kim, "Poker Face," at http://www.youtube.com/watch?v=nzh2UygPwDU (accessed March 25, 2012).
Young, Neil. "This Note's for You," at http://www.youtube.com/watch?v=KSSvzCNBvlQ&ob=av2e (accessed March 25, 2012).

CHAPTER 28

MUSIC VIDEO TRANSFORMED

MATHIAS BONDE KORSGAARD

WHAT is happening with music video? Once the sole content of channels like MTV and the generator of much academic attention, music videos have experienced a decline, both on television and in academia. With a few notable exceptions, scholarship on music video has been in short supply since the 1990s.[1] However, research is now increasing, perhaps because of recent shifts in the genre: music video has embraced wild new forms in the last five years or so. This chapter explores recent changes in music video, asking what it is now that it has proliferated online. I catalog five new types of music videos: participatory/interactive, user-generated content, remakes/remixes, alternate lengths, and hi/low definition. These categories, however, seem insufficient: many music video types are difficult to place, with some occupying a gray area between music video and another genre. They also often transgress traditional music video boundaries by reversing the production process in which "music comes first."[2] At the same time they may foreground familiar functions like the tendency toward visual multiplication and

Links to many of the music videos and related forms mentioned in this chapter can be found at the book's accompanying website. ▶

[1] The first wave of scholarly work on music video seems to have reached its end in the early 1990s, with Andrew Goodwin's book *Dancing in the Distraction Factory: Music Television and Popular Culture* (Minneapolis: University of Minnesota Press, 1992) and the volume edited by Goodwin with Lawrence Grossberg and Simon Frith, *Sound and Vision: The Music Video Reader* (London & New York: Routledge, 1993). The "few notable exceptions," that is, some of the few relevant publications in the period between the early 1990s and today, include Carol Vernallis's book *Experiencing Music Video: Aesthetics and Cultural Context* (New York: Columbia University Press, 2004) as well as a book by Kevin Williams, *Why I (Still) Want My MTV: Music Video and Aesthetic Communication* (Cresskill, New Jersey: Hampton Press, 2003). Some of the more recent works are Henry Keazor and Thorsten Wübbena, *Rewind, Play, Fast Forward: The Past, Present and Future of the Music Video* (Bielefeld: Transcript Verlag, 2010); Diane Railton and Paul Watson, *Music Video and the Politics of Representation* (Edinburgh: Edinburgh University Press, 2011); and Joachim Strand, *The Cinesthetic Montage of Music-Video: Hearing the Image and Seeing the Sound* (Saarbrücken: VDM Verlag Dr. Müller, 2008).

[2] Vernallis, *Experiencing Music Video*, x.

modulation (e.g., the use of digital imaging effects and multiple images). Music videos thus both "visualize music" and "musicalize vision"—here, popular music's multitracking engenders music video's "multitracked visuality." They also remediate[3] content more actively than almost any other media form.

I propose an understanding of music video as an intermedial and remediated phenomenon defined through constant transgression of its own medial borders.[4] Through a focus on interactive music videos, particularly Arcade Fire's "We Used to Wait" and Björk's app album *Biophilia*, I aim to answer the following question: Does the emergence of these new forms mark music video's decline or its expansion? The advent of these new forms in turn raises many questions: What constitutes a music video? Why are these new forms appearing now? Are they only foregrounding technological change—the latest technological wizardry? Or are they now only free from the constraints of MTV? Are they competing with rivals, like video games? Do they express broader changes in society and the media landscape? Or do the new music video types, particularly the interactive ones, enable audiovisual experiences that engage the user in new physical and emotional ways?

New Types of Music Videos

In music video's post-televisual period, several new types of video have appeared both via mainstream satellite services and online. Some are similar to traditional music videos, while others work harder to push the limits of the medium. Following is my list of new music video types:

Participatory/interactive

- The interactive music video (e.g., Arcade Fire, "Black Mirror")
- The music video app (e.g., Polyphonic Spree, "Bullseye")
- The music video game (e.g., Team Me, "Chemicals and Weathervanes," released as the video game *Get Home*)
- Clikthrough.com videos: music videos that contain hyperlinks, allowing viewers to purchase items depicted on screen (e.g., Lady Gaga, "Poker Face" via clikthrough.com)
- Sites involving manipulation of source materials (e.g., Yooouuutuuube.com, a site that allows users to upload any YouTube or Vimeo video and play it back in multiple windows at once with a short delay between each window, while moving, dragging, and stretching the images. It transforms traditional music videos into interactive ones)

[3] Jay David Bolter and Richard Grusin, *Remediation: Understanding New Media* (Cambridge, Mass. and London: MIT Press, 2000 [1999]).

[4] This is true not only for contemporary music video, but historically as well; from its earliest incarnations in "visual music" and visual jukeboxes (such as Soundies and Scopitones), to the pre-MTV video promos and the formative MTV years, and all the way to today's digital experiments, music video is premised on resisting any finite shape.

User-generated content

- The fanvid: amateur videos that mix a song with footage from either a film or a TV series (e.g., Arcade Fire, "My Body Is a Cage," set to footage from Sergio Leone's *Once Upon a Time in the West*)
- Video mods: music videos in which characters from computer games perform the song of a popular artist, as seen on the former MTV2 show *Video Mods* (e.g., Franz Ferdinand, "Take Me Out," performed by characters from the game *Star Wars Episode III: Revenge of the Sith*)
- The music video contest: contests proposed by bands in which fans are encouraged to make videos for a song or an album (e.g., Radiohead's contest via aniboom.com for the album *In Rainbows*, or the contests staged via genero.tv)
- Videos featuring concert footage shot by fans on handheld devices (e.g., Bloc Party, "Ares [Villains remix]")

Remakes/remixes

- Music video remixes and mashups (e.g., Eclectic Method, "Lock Up Your Videos")
- The music video parody (e.g., The Key of Awesome!'s parody of Ke$ha's "We R Who We R")
- Lipdubs: groups of people, often university or college students, lip-synching to a song (e.g., "I Gotta Feeling" at l'Université du Québec à Montréal)
- Literal versions: videos in which the lyrics have been replaced by alternate lyrics that comment directly on the video images (e.g., Bonnie Tyler, "Total Eclipse of the Heart")
- "Shreds": videos in which the sound track has been replaced, often by music in a conflicting genre or by a re-recording of the music that suggests that the musicians are playing a faulty version of the song (e.g., Kings of Leon, "Shreds—Their Worst Performance Ever")
- "Autotune the news" and similar phenomena: news reports or other kinds of documentary footage in which the voices of people speaking have been autotuned and set to music, originally invented by the Gregory Brothers (e.g., Carl Sagan ft. Stephen Hawking, "A Glorious Dawn [Symphony of Science]")
- Music videos without music: music videos that have had the music removed and are then redubbed with sounds that diegetically match the music video in question (e.g., Macklemore, "Thrift Shop," redubbed by Mikolaj Gackowski)

Alternate lengths

- The music video album: entire albums with one or more videos for each song (e.g., Liars, *Drum's not Dead*—each song has a total of three videos)
- The album music video: an entire album in one music video (e.g., Dum Dum Girls, "*Only in Dreams* [Full Album Stream]")

- Long-form videos (e.g., Kanye West, "Runaway")
- Two or more songs in one video (e.g., Justin Timberlake, "Let Me Talk to You/ My Love")
- The blip: a short form that does not feature an entire song, but only a short part of it—or no music at all (e.g., various blips for the Radiohead album *Kid A*)[5]
- The music video teaser (e.g., ultrashort teasers for the Britney Spears video "Hold It Against Me")

Hi/low definition

- 3D music videos (e.g., Deerhunter, "Primitive 3D")
- Music visualization: videos with auto-generated imagery created via visualization software. Media player software often generates these clips (e.g., Pepepiano, "Flesh Rails")
- Viral lo-def videos (e.g., OK Go, "Here It Goes Again [The Treadmill Video]")
- Intimate lo-def live performance videos, shot in everyday locations with handheld cameras (e.g., Vincent Moon's *Concerts à emporter/Take-away shows*)

Although extensive, this list is by no means complete; new music video–like phenomena take shape all the time through a bewildering proliferation of practices, which are too numerous to follow. Moreover, some of these new types are actually not new at all, including fanvids, long-form, and interactive videos, all of which have a pre-online history.[6] Although the Internet is not necessarily the origin of these music video types, it has surely accelerated their development: these new forms can now be more readily produced, circulated, and accessed. Several of the forms mentioned here also even upset the categorizations I propose; for example, several of the "remakes/remixes" rely on "user-generated content," thus fitting equally well into these two categories.

These music video types are diverse and tend to offer experiences that can be intensely joyful and encapsulating. Perhaps the most striking—and my main focus here—are the interactive videos. I address these in more detail and offer two close readings. First, however, I briefly describe some of the other main types from the list. The videos in the first two categories, those based on *user-generated content* and the *remakes/remixes*, range from amateur fan productions and humorous reworkings of source material to more fully realized remixes and mashups. The pairing of the visuals for Radiohead's "Lotus

[5] Joseph Tate, "Radiohead's Anti-Videos: Works of Art in the Age of Electronic Reproduction," in *The Music and Art of Radiohead*, ed. Joseph Tate (Burlington: Ashgate, 2005), 103–117.

[6] On fanvids see Julie Russo, "User-Penetrated Content: Fan Video in the Age of Convergence," *Cinema Journal* 48, no. 8 (2009): 125–130. Long-form precursors are manifold (e.g., Michael Jackson's videos); some of Weird Al Jankovic's videos might be thought of as early parodies, while interactive music video forerunners include the video game *Vid Grid* from 1995 for the Atari Jaguar; the Hell Is for Heroes' video for "You Drove Me to It," which incorporated the television remote control; and some of the content of the music CD-ROMs of the 1990s.

Flowers" with Beyoncé's song "Single Ladies," and "The Grey Video" with one of the tracks from Dangermouse's infamous *Grey Album* are two of many examples. Fanvids often display potent pairings of image and music sources; in these cases the videos offer a double reading of both the musical and the visual source material, in which one sheds new light on the other. In a similar fashion, some remixes and mashups map out connections between different visual and musical styles that are both obvious and unforeseen. The "shreds," literal versions, and autotune forms instead disrupt their sources' meaning by substituting or transforming elements, thereby creating new associations. Other fan productions incorporate user-generated footage to mimic the look of concert imagery shot on cell phones. Arguably, these videos take part in a new lo-def aesthetic, where the noisiness of the pixillated imagery intensifies the feeling of actually "being there" at the concert.

A similar lo-def aesthetic can be traced in some of the video types belonging in the category *hi/low definition*. Vincent Moon's *Take Away Shows* create a feeling of being in close proximity to the musicians performing, which is due to the pared-down acoustic performances together with the use of everyday locations, handheld cameras, extreme close-ups, and a grainy and haptic image quality. Some of the viral music videos (such as some of OK Go's videos) similarly hint at a lo-def, home-video aesthetic. The hi-def videos at the other end of this category, for example the 3D videos, aim at a heightened sense of visual depth and definition.

Perhaps the least problematic new videos are those in the final category, videos with *alternate lengths*. With a longer or shorter duration than normal, they interrogate the structural role of the song. When a clip is too short or too long, is it a music video? Do the teasers for Britney Spears' "Hold It Against Me" constitute 10-second music videos? Is Kanye West's "Runaway" a 35-minute music video, or something else? As do most of the other forms discussed, these occupy a position in between media forms and deviate somewhat from traditional music video.

My main interest in this article is the category of *interactive/participatory* videos. The interactive video for Arcade Fire's "Neon Bible," released in August 2007, was the first of this kind, and it was quickly followed by a wide variety of other interactive music videos. These fall into two groups: those that are only visually interactive (e.g., MGMT's "Electric Feel") and those that are audiovisually interactive (allowing one to influence both image and music, such as Cold War Kids' "I've Seen Enough"). Obviously the visual interaction aims to provide some level of user immersion in the image: in some videos, users navigate through virtual 3D spaces (e.g., The Broken Bells, "October"; Labuat, "Soy Tu Aire"; and Rome, "Three Dreams of Black"). In others, users are able to direct the camera 360 degrees within the visual environment (e.g., Pendulum, "360"; DEVO, "What We Do"; Steye & The Ottowanians, "Wonderful"; or Craig Wedren, "Are We"). Still others allow users to switch among camera positions or image layers (e.g., Pitchfork's POV series; MGMT, "Electric Feel"; Mobley, "Ego Is"; Shihad, "Sleepeater"; or The Bynars, "How Does It Feel to Be in Love?"). Others let users upload their own content, whether it be images or text (e.g., Hoobastank, "My Turn"; Who Made Who, "Every Minute Alone"; Robyn, "Killing Me"; or Will.i.am, "Hope. Act. Change"). Finally, some incorporate users' webcam footage, thereby directly engaging the user as a videographer (e.g., Lost Valentinos, "Nightmoves"; C-Mon & Kypski, "More Is Less"; or Sour, "Mirror," which also includes the user's Facebook and Twitter accounts, Google Maps imagery, and YouTube). These all demonstrate music video's strong tendencies to remediate.

Interactive videos empower the user in ways that traditional clips do not. Many leave it up to the user to edit the images or control the camera, while a few others allow the user to mix the sound. Others allow users to feed their own content into the video, via either upload or footage shot by the webcam *in* the video. These devices encourage the viewer to feel active in the midst of an environment that projects authority through rhythm, flow, and pattern, as Carol Vernallis has argued.[7] It also means that these interactive clips are potentially different each time users play them. Some allow the user to make new narrative choices each time (e.g., Andy Grammer's "Keep Your Head Up"), others are frequently updated with new user-frames (C-Mon & Kypski's "More Is Less"), and yet others make it possible to group the various user-generated frames according to their visual style (Johnny Cash's "Ain't No Grave"). Interactive videos can also extend the role of advertising. They all promote the musicians and the director, but some also sell additional products: the site clikthrough.com provides the opportunity to purchase the instruments played and the clothes worn by the performers, and K.I.Z.'s "Neuruppin" allows the participant to buy band merchandise.

Interactive clips emphasize mediation and image multiplication. Most achieve a sense of visual multiplicity by operating in multiple windows or by dividing the screen, a typical hypermediated strategy. For example, some interactive videos feature numerous windows that pop up and move around the screen (see OK Go's "All Is Not Lost" and Sour's "Mirror"). These create new kinds of visual multiplicity and provide an increased sense of visual polyphony that complements popular music's heterogeneity through multitracking. These pop-up windows also subtly point to the video's commercial allegiances; as Vernallis observes, they remind us of the experience of being continually inundated with pop-up ads online.[8]

[7] See Vernallis, *Experiencing Music Video*. According to Vernallis, interactive video may offer the possibility of a new type of viewer engagement, somewhere between acting *and* tracing or following. It may reside somewhere between the experience of video games, narrative film, and music video. If the clip's unfolding becomes too much like a game or narrative film, the participant may stop attending to the music. The pop-ups and actions may help break this flow, making it possible for the viewer to become once again sutured to the image and the song. Carol Vernallis and I remediate one another's work. See chapter 25 for a sense of how this has worked. This footnote is Vernallis's turn. With the Internet, publishing online, and scholars who Skype and travel internationally, research may become more synergetic.

[8] Advertising on the Web remains in flux. When we click on a link we may subtly brace for an encounter with an ad. Music video's relation to advertising has not yet solidified. Clips often showcase products within them, and YouTube and Vevo stream ads within and around them. A click within a music video may suggest the appearance of an ad more than it might with other media, according to Vernallis.

Although some of the video types discussed are only gimmicks, many employ their technological novelty to produce poignant experiences that actively address and engage the user or prompt a physical or emotional response. Interactive videos, music video games, and music video apps all rely on users' active engagement with their audiovisual material, and in this way they differ from videos of the past. Fanvids, lipdubs, many of the music video parodies, and contests all draw on contributions made by fans or amateurs. As with other areas of contemporary culture, music videos have long been involved in processes of media convergence and "participatory culture"; they have also accessed different media technologies, hybridized with other media forms, and functioned as part of cross-promotional processes. But the new forms accelerate trends latent in the past.[9]

What Is a Music Video?

Before attempting to understand how these new music video types transgress traditional borders, a definition of music videos is in order. Bente Kristiansen proposes a commonsense definition of a music video: "Music videos are short video productions that are made as a visual accompaniment to pop and rock music. The videos function as commercials for the musicians and as entertainment to the audience."[10] We can organize Kristiansen's definition into the following characteristics: (1) brevity: (2) a combination of visuals and music; (3) pop and rock music as the sound track; (4) the song preceding the visuals; (5) and having a dual scope, both commercial and entertaining. And we might include two more traits, not mentioned by Kristiansen: (6) no incisions are made in the song's structure; its length determines the video's length; and (7) the image illustrates features of the song in order to sell it.[11]

In many instances today, we recognize an object as a music video, yet some trait has been subverted in one way or another. A definition of music video might thus perhaps best be approached via Wittgenstein's notion of *family resemblances* (*Familienähnlichkeiten*); there is no one single trait that ties together the entire family of music videos, but rather a range of traits, not all of which might appear at the same time. Likewise, Derrida's notion of "participation" versus "belonging" in relation to genre classifications is helpful.[12] To Derrida, texts do not "belong to" as much as "participate in" genres; similarly, the music video–like phenomena discussed here participate in an interrogation of music video without necessarily belonging to it. These music videos engage in an active exploration of the genre's

[9] Henry Jenkins, *Convergence Culture: Where Old and New Media Collide* (New York and London: New York University Press, 2006).

[10] Bente Kristiansen, "Musikvideo," in *Analyser af TV*, ed. Ralf Pittelkow (Copenhagen: Medusa, 1985), 147 (my translation).

[11] Vernallis, *Experiencing Music Video*, 156.

[12] Jacques Derrida, "The Law of Genre," *Critical Inquiry* 7, no. 1 (1980): 55–81.

potential and often directly challenge mainstream music videos. Kristiansen's definition fails to describe the entire range of music videos today. Along similar lines, some of the better-known categorizations of music video, such as Marsha Kinder's division of music video into the categories of performance, narrative, and "dream,"[13] tell us very little about the way these new forms work. A more flexible or expansive definition of the form is now called for. Carol Vernallis proposes to define a music video "as any relation of sound and image that we recognize as such."[14]

In place of the old definitions, I propose approaching the music video through the concept of remediation, allowing for a much more flexible definition of its medial functions and providing a better understanding of its new forms. Music videos can be said to follow the logic of remediation on many different levels. Bolter and Grusin argue that music videos generally operate via "immediacy through hypermediacy." Their hybridized and intense stylistic expressions "create an immediate and apparently spontaneous style."[15] Many music videos engage in very concrete acts of remediation; they "represent one medium within another." Music videos routinely resemble other media forms, including silent cinema (Smashing Pumpkins' "Tonight, Tonight"), televised news programs (R.E.M.'s "Bad Day"), computer games (Xiu Xiu's "Boy Soprano"), Google's search engine (M.I.A.'s "The Message"), concerts (any number of performance videos), and others.

The music video has always incorporated and repurposed elements of other media. And in a feedback loop, other media borrow aspects from music video. As Michel Chion argues, music video "has invented and borrowed an entire arsenal of devices,"[16] while Michael Shore claims that music videos both "mirror and extend popular culture."[17] Thus, not only does music video borrow from other media, but at the same time its audiovisual language may meld with the media it borrows from. For example, the rock concert and the music video mutually remediate each other, as Philip Auslander suggests.[18] Similarly, it is easy to imagine music video having some sort of stylistic influence on postclassical cinema, as John Richardson and others have shown.[19] Another example includes the new music video types that foreground viewer–participant interactivity. This incorporation of interactivity can be understood as an act of remediation—here, music videos appropriate a function associated with new digital media. Some of the new

[13] Marsha Kinder, "Music Video and the Spectator: Television, Ideology and Dream," *Film Quarterly* 38, no. 1 (1984): 4–7.

[14] Carol Vernallis, "Music Video's Second Aesthetic?," in *The Oxford Handbook of New Audiovisual Aesthetics*, ed. John Richardson, Claudia Gorbman and Carol Vernallis (New York and Oxford: Oxford University Press, 2013).

[15] Bolter and Grusin, *Remediation*, 9.

[16] Michel Chion, *Audio-Vision: Sound on Screen* (New York: Columbia University Press, 1994 [1990]), 166.

[17] Michael Shore, *The Rolling Stone Book of Rock Video. The Definitive Look at Visual Music from Elvis Presley—and Before—to Michael Jackson—and Beyond* (London: Sidgwick & Jackson, 1985), 99.

[18] Philip Auslander, *Liveness: Performance in a Mediatized Culture* (London and New York: Routledge, 1999), 31.

[19] John Richardson, *An Eye for Music: Popular Music and the Audiovisual Surreal* (New York and Oxford: Oxford University Press, 2011), 57–59.

forms also mutually remediate music videos and video games: some share the feature of interactivity with games; others have a gamelike structure, presenting a virtual universe to be explored or tasks to be completed before the participant can unlock extra features or enable a download of additional content (e.g., Björk's "Crystalline" app, K.I.Z.'s interactive video for "Neuruppin," and Spleen United's "Sunset to Sunset" puzzle). Some are even actual games that should be completed before the song ends (Team Me's "Chemicals and Weathervanes" or the platform game *Get Home*).

More generally, every video can be said to function through a specific kind of audiovisual remediation. Any music video operates by visually remediating music (recasting a preexisting song visually), but also by musically remediating the image (structuring the image according to musical logic). As Vernallis points out, letting the images show "responsiveness to musical features"[20] is common in music video, and vision itself thereby becomes musical. The image takes on new functions, challenging the usual perceptual hierarchies of audiovisual forms.[21]

I argue also that music videos often demonstrate a tendency toward visual multiplications and image modulation in general. In order to respond to the multitrack recording processes of popular music, the image is often multiplied or modulated, thereby being liberated from representational duty. Michel Chion points to the rapid succession of shots in music videos that can create "a sense of visual polyphony,"[22] but other common tropes include the use of images-within-the-image, frames-within-the-frame, split-screen, double exposure, digital compositing, rear projection, and a vast array of digital imaging effects (morphing, data-moshing, kaleidoscopes). Indeed, such multiplications seem to have been a stable feature of music videos since the 1980s. Already in 1987 E. Ann Kaplan noted that "[a]ll kinds of framing within the frame are now common."[23] So the remediation of music by visual means often leads to a proliferation of image layers to make the image as compelling and multifaceted as the music.

Arcade Fire, "We Used to Wait"

From a certain perspective, interactive videos are problematic as music videos, because the interactive images risk stealing the attention from the music. This is a familiar complaint that has often been leveled against music videos in general, especially in the early

[20] Vernallis, *Experiencing Music Video*, 44.

[21] See also Alf Björnberg, "Structural Relationships of Music and Images in Music Video," in *Reading Pop: Approaches to Textual Analysis in Popular Music*, ed. Richard Middleton (Oxford: Oxford University Press, 2000), 247–278; Strand, *The Cinesthetic Montage of Music Video*; Williams, *Why I (Still) Want My MTV*.

[22] Chion, *Audio-Vision*, 166.

[23] E. Ann Kaplan, *Rocking Around the Clock: Music Television, Postmodernism, and Consumer Culture* (New York: Methuen, 1987), 37.

MTV days, as recapitulated by Stan Hawkins and John Richardson.[24] Many of the interactive videos have this problem; interacting with their imagery diverts attention from the music, threatening to let the music lapse into the role often assigned to film music.[25] (As many people I have shown them to also note, users become so absorbed with the image that they forget the music.) A central question is whether this mode of engagement is musical. If the interactive part functions poorly, it becomes a gimmick. But when it functions well, a video can provoke a strong symbiosis among music, image, and lyrical content, leading to an enhancement of the music. Arcade Fire's interactive music video, "We Used to Wait," is one example.

This video was released in 2010 under the title "The Wilderness Downtown," so named after a fragment from the song's lyrics. Before starting the video, the user is asked to submit his or her childhood address. This address is then used to gather data from Google Maps and Street-View, and then the data are integrated into the video. When the user presses "play," a browser window with an image of a person running down city streets pops up as Arcade Fire's song begins. During the video different browser windows pop up while others close, and the user is free to drag, close, minimize, or resize individual windows. The windows show either the running person, the image data collected from Street View and Maps, a digitally animated flock of birds (controllable via the computer mouse), machinery, or quickly growing trees. At one point a window pops up and asks the participant to write a letter of advice to "the younger you that lived there then." Here the user can either type words using the keyboard or draw lines using the mouse (see figure 28.1). The video thus employs many different kinds of imagery at once: computer-animated images, actual footage, satellite images (the Google Maps images), and images combining two or more of these.

The video obviously aims to give each user a customized experience; however, a bit more is at stake. First of all, this video shows that in today's convergence culture, a product can have many commercial functions. The video fulfills the traditional function of selling both the music and the director, but it is also a commercial for Google Street View, Google Maps, and especially Google's browser, Chrome. If users attempt to access the video via another browser, they encounter a text that advises them to download Google Chrome to get "the best viewing experience." Thus, the concrete remediation of Google Street View and Google Maps (i.e., "the representation of" these in the video) serves not only an aesthetic but also a commercial purpose.

In some instances the video stages close interactions between music and image: some of the windows pop up or close in time with the music, and at several points the lyrics and the images work in concert. The lyrics introduce a theme of writing letters, which extends into the letter that the video asks its user to write. The "past" culture

[24] Stan Hawkins and John Richardson, "Remodeling Britney Spears: Matters of Intoxication and Mediation," *Popular Music and Society* 30, no. 5 (2007): 605.

[25] As most prominently put into words by Claudia Gorbman: the role of film music is often to remain unheard; see Claudia Gorbman, *Unheard Melodies: Narrative Film Music* (Bloomington: Indiana University Press, 1987).

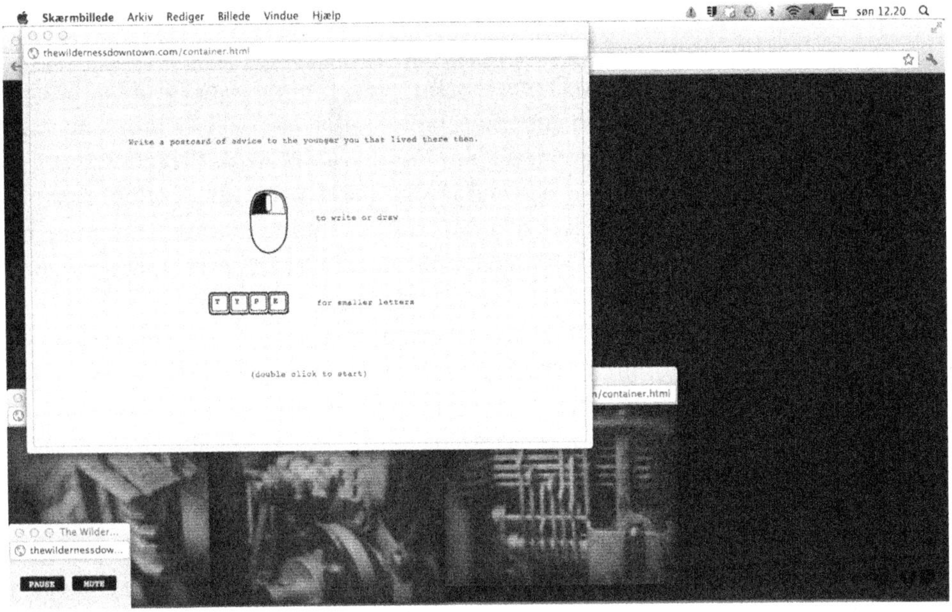

FIGURE 28.1: Arcade Fire, "We Used to Wait/The Wilderness Downtown." Directed by Chris Milk, 2010. The interactive video for "We Used to Wait" lets you write a letter of advice to yourself.

of handwritten letters (evident in the lyrics' use of the past tense: "I *used* to write.") is opposed to a present culture of change ("Now our lives are changing fast."). "Past" culture is presented as a culture in which "we used to wait"; the new culture involves haste, immateriality, and loss of identity ("I used to sign my name."). Thus the lyrics seem to criticize modern digital culture and its apparent impatience. Such a view is hardly surprising, because Arcade Fire's lyrics often criticize modern (American) popular culture, marked by excess and speed. Modern culture is incapable of "waiting for it," as the lyrics suggest (significantly, the band rhymes "MTV" with "World War Three" in another of its songs, "Windowsill").

The opposition between an old culture of "waiting" and a new culture of "haste" is also expressed musically. Interspersed among some of the song's verses is an extra half-measure that makes the verses seem "too long"—an expression of "musical waiting." Another section that prominently features strings builds tension by repeating the same bass note. Here, we know that a chorus is on its way (like a letter), but we are not entirely sure when it will arrive; again the section seems "too long," and we either lose count or fail to predict exactly when the chorus will come.

This musical waiting, heard mostly in the song's first half, is countered by a "musical haste" that appears in the outro—the musical aspects of the song thus express the same movement from waiting to haste as do the lyrics. In the outro, there is a measure "too little," not a half-measure too much. This section seems to repeat itself just a little too rapidly, while building tension through rising dynamics and faster harmonic rhythm;

we expect the chord progression to start over a little later than it actually does. Moreover, the tension that builds never fully finds a resolution: we expect a dynamic release of some kind, for instance a return to the chorus. Instead the music stops abruptly, the only resolution being the echoing remnants of the tonic chord played solo by the piano, as in the beginning of the song. Thus we never get "the chorus again" as the lyrics promise. ("We used to wait for it. Now we're screaming sing the chorus again.") Ultimately this lack of musical resolution, in the lack of a final chorus, communicates that waiting for something is a quality in itself—even waiting for something that never arrives, whether a chorus or a letter.

Paradoxically, the images seem to reflect a similar critique while simultaneously celebrating the possibilities of the HTML5 browser. Toward the end of the video all the windows are filled up by the ominous birds and the erupting trees that break through the asphalt: nature reclaims the city. The video thereby plays up a longing for things past, for an ideal situation that is now irretrievably gone, "childhood" or "the old times." The album from which the song is taken, *The Suburbs*, lyrically deals with the experience of growing up in the suburbs. By drawing on childhood experience in one's own suburb, the video activates a sense of mediated nostalgia; it is very concretely "a walk down memory lane."

In doing this, however, the video also indicates some of the changes brought about by new global media and some of the limits of mediation. My own experience of watching the video suggests how. As I entered my childhood address, I was confronted with the following text: "Your address doesn't contain enough Street View and/or Google Maps data to 100% enjoy this experience." The place where I grew up, the small village Lysabild in Denmark, has yet to be photographed and converted into Street View data, so some of the windows do not appear when I watch the video. Today the suburbs have also been digitally redefined, as areas where Google Street View is not yet a reality. My experience of the video differs depending on whether I enter my childhood address or my current address: the latter does indeed "contain enough data." My sense of nostalgia is less "real" or fulfilled, because my hometown does not fully exist in the virtual world. Even when I enter my current address, I am reminded that reality still moves at a quicker pace than virtuality; within the short amount of time that has passed since my street was photographed by Google's cars with mounted cameras, it has changed significantly, as new buildings have been constructed just across from where I live (see figure 28.2). These buildings are still under construction in the video, whose imagery is thereby caught in the past.

Significantly, "We Used to Wait" is not presented as a music video, but as "an interactive film." Is it not a music video, then? In some senses "We Used to Wait" is different from traditional music videos, mainly in that it is interactive and thus presents each user with a personal version; as many possible versions exist as there are addresses in the world. In other ways, however, it still feels like a music video. The song is still the structural unit that determines the video's length, and the video performs the familiar function of staging close relations among music, image, and lyrics. Ultimately, "We Used to

FIGURE 28.2: Arcade Fire, "We Used to Wait/The Wilderness Downtown." Directed by Chris Milk, 2010. The video operates in multiple windows that can be dragged, resized, or minimized at will.

Wait" provides a potent emotional experience, and as John Richardson points out, it truly "captures the changing landscape of audiovisual expression,"[26] not just in characterizing the changing nature of music videos, but of audiovisual culture as a whole.

Björk's *Biophilia*

Music videos often seek to present something new to stand apart from competitors. As interactive music videos have become relatively widespread, music videos have also begun appearing as apps for smart phones and tablet computers. Some of these music-video–like apps are more similar to video games than to music videos (e.g., Gorillaz's "Escape to Plastic Beach"), while others are more similar to interactive music videos (e.g., The Polyphonic Spree's "Bullseye"). The most ambitious musical app project yet is without a doubt Björk's "app-album" *Biophilia*, each song of which is an app that can be accessed via iPad or iPhone (again, indirectly selling not only the music but also Apple's products).

[26] Richardson, *An Eye for Music*, 293.

Biophilia sits in between various phenomena: the app, the album, the song, the music video, the instrument, the video game, and even academic writing. One thing that unites most of these phenomena is that they can be *played* in one way or another, encouraging direct physical action. In its overall scope, *Biophilia* attempts to redefine several musical formats (or "media," in the absolutely widest sense of the term): *the song* comes in different versions, depending on how one accesses or purchases it; *the album* is released both in the app version and as a traditional album and limited special editions; the interactive content of the apps can be understood as an expansion of *the music video* (traditional music videos have also been made for some of the songs); some of the apps function as *instruments* that allow the user to generate new sounds; and in *concert*, *Biophilia* is a multimedia show that is installed in a given venue for longer periods of time, utilizing new and unusual instruments constructed specifically for this event (large pendulums, a "gameleste"—a hybrid between a gamelan and a celeste—and a Tesla coil), the last involving educational sessions in which children can try the instruments and learn about musicology. At one point *Biophilia* was also imagined as a film album, and even as a house in which each song would have its own room. The original ambitions of the project thus extended not only beyond traditional ways of approaching music, but also into the realms of filmmaking and architecture.

All the apps share the same structure. They contain a menu with five options: "Play," "Animation," "Score," "Lyrics," and "Credits." Apart from these five selections, each app is also accompanied by a musicological essay written by Nicola Dibben, who has written extensively on Björk before.[27] When selecting "Credits" or "Lyrics," the user is simply presented with written text containing this information. Selecting "Score" plays back the song in an alternative instrumental arrangement (one instrument playing the melody and one playing the accompaniment) as a traditional musical score rolls horizontally across the screen in time with the music. The option "Animation" functions in a somewhat similar way: the song is played in its entirety with a visual supplement functioning as an alternate kind of notation that is more spatially oriented than a traditional musical score. In its use of colored geometrical shapes to represent different musical tracks (circles, lines, dots, bars), this "animation" is reminiscent of the tradition of "visual music" (see figure 28.3). If the "animation" sections are regarded as a kind of music video, then they mark a return to the prehistory of music video. They echo original pieces of "visual music" made by Oskar Fischinger and his peers, often considered the first music videos *avant la lettre*.[28]

By selecting "Play," the user gets what is arguably the core of the apps: the song plays with an interactive visual accompaniment. The "Crystalline" app, for example, lets users

[27] See, for example, Nicola Dibben, *Björk* (London: Equinox, 2009).

[28] See, for example, Saul Austerlitz, *Money for Nothing: A History of the Music Video from the Beatles to the White Stripes* (London & New York: Continuum, 2007), 13; Even Ruud, *Musikk for øyet. Om musikkvideo* (Oslo: Gyldendal Norsk Forlag, 1988), 34; Shore, *The Rolling Stone Book of Rock Video*, 20; Peter Weibel, "Von der visuellen Musik zum Musikvideo," in *Clip, Klapp, Bum: Von der visuellen Musik zum Musikvideo*, ed. Veruschka Bódy and Peter Weibel (Köln: DuMont, 1987), 54.

FIGURE 28.3: Björk, "Cosmogony" (Animation), 2011. In the apps, the function "animation" brings reminiscences of the tradition of visual music.

play a game in which they control a crystal flying through tunnels of different colors by tilting the device used to access the app (see figure 28.4). The game's "goal" is to collect colored crystals attached to the sides of the tunnels, in particular orders, to unlock new paths through the tunnel system. Each tunnel corresponds to a section of the song; the red tunnels are the choruses, and the tunnels of other colors are the various verses. In the app, users can thus chart their own way through the tunnel system and through the song, joining tunnels/song sections in various combinations, thereby creating new arrangements or infinite loops.

If the apps are considered music videos, many present a visual environment that exists independently of the song. In many of the apps, users can select an option called "instrument" and "touch" elements to provoke different sounds. This visual setting often looks similar to the one accessed via the "play" function, the only difference being that the music is not playing. Similarly, some of the interactive online music videos also establish a setting that is not fully dependent on the song. In Rome's "Three Dreams of Black," users can "stay" in the video's visual space after the song stops playing and further explore the virtual universe. "Knight of Wands" presents an interactive coloring book in which the user is encouraged to color objects within the frame while the music unfolds. However, after the song ends the user can continue coloring. Hence, these videos and the Björk apps demonstrate that the song no longer singlehandedly delineates the music video space.

FIGURE 28.4: Björk, "Crystalline app," 2011. The app for "Crystalline" presents you with a navigable tunnel system in which each tunnel corresponds to a song section.

Biophilia's use of touchpad-based devices activates the sense of touch in a way normal music videos do not. Both the images and sounds of the "music video" apps can be "touched" and thereby altered. This allows for a more tactile way of experiencing music *and* images. Here, *Biophilia* delivers the promise of online interactive videos that hint at tactile experiences by letting users stretch, change, and rearrange images via the mouse or keyboard.

Is it reasonable to think of these apps as music videos? In an interview, Björk raised doubts about the status and future of traditional music videos and at the same time opined that "the apps are videos."[29] Generally, the "play" function of each app contains something quite similar to a music video, an instrument, or a video game, with no absolute borders separating these three. In ways both obvious and subtle, the apps thus depart from the traditional music video, as in their incorporation of interactivity and gamelike structures, and in not holding the song to a finite shape or length. But in other ways they perform some of the functions of traditional music videos, for instance in being "music plus images" and in that they stage close interrelations between music and image.

[29] In Brandon, "Stereogum Q&A: Björk talks *Biophilia*." June 9, 2011 (11:37 a.m.), at http://stereogum.com/744502/stereogum-qa-bjork-talks-biophilia/top-stories/lead-story (accessed December 8, 2011).

Alive and Well?

So what is contemporary music video? Perhaps Lev Manovich is right in stating that music video "has served as a laboratory for exploring numerous new possibilities of manipulating photographic images made possible by computers."[30] Certainly music video has always provided ample room for audiovisual experimentation: it constantly explores the possible relations between musical sounds and moving images and continues to do so in the digital realm. For now the musical multiplication of images in music videos has adopted new multi-windowed shapes in interactive video forms. Though it might be on the verge of becoming something new—mutating into something else, hybridizing with other forms—it remains a medium with a great deal of audiovisual vitality.

The new music video types enable new forms of audiovisual experience. They provoke strong emotional reactions that engage the user in a kinetic experience. This mediated embodiment may be a response to the coldness and dematerialization of digitality. The videos can be characterized by their sensory overload, not just because of their rich engagement of music, images, and words, but also because of something more—in the case of Björk, a physical involvement, and in the case of Arcade Fire, a personal involvement. Three features in the new types come to the fore: remediation, interactivity and multiple frames, and the question of advertising (What is being sold? Who is funding these clips? Is this an indie or a corporate thing?). Although some traditional music video functions remain (such as the close interaction between music and image, visual multiplicity, and the tendency toward remediating other media), other elements are added or transformed (interactivity, touch-related functions, gamelike structures, length, the song no longer being the structural unit, an interrogation of the "sound first" principle).[31] In other words, many of the new music video types are no longer brief, the song does not necessarily come first, and the advertising function is not always a straightforward matter. But on the other hand they showcase musical features, market the song, and still *feel* like music videos. As such, music video may already be in the process of disintegrating and being surpassed by new forms. At the very least, we can say that the field of music video has opened up to a range of transformations. But if we accept that music videos are intermedial and remediational by nature and that music video continually defines itself by stretching beyond its own territory, then its time is not over. It is highly likely that it has only just begun.

30 Lev Manovich, *The Language of New Media* (Cambridge, Mass. and London: MIT Press, 2001), 311.

31 Whether or not these new music-video-like forms are music videos is thus difficult to answer. To return to Derrida's distinction, they surely all participate in the medium of music video, without necessarily belonging to it.

References

Auslander, Philip. *Liveness. Performance in a Mediatized Culture*. London; New York: Routledge, 1999.

Austerlitz, Saul. *Money for Nothing: A History of the Music Video from the Beatles to the White Stripes*. London; New York: Continuum, 2007.

Björnberg, Alf. "Structural Relationships of Music and Images in Music Video." In *Reading Pop: Approaches to Textual Analysis in Popular Music*, edited by Richard Middleton, 347–378. Oxford: Oxford University Press, 2000.

Bolter, Jay David, and Richard Grusin. *Remediation—Understanding New Media*. Cambridge, Mass.; London: MIT Press, 2000 [1999].

Brandon. "Stereogum Q&A: Björk talks *Biophilia*." June 9, 2011 (11:37 a.m.), at http://stereogum.com/744502/stereogum-qa-bjork-talks-biophilia/top-stories/lead-story (accessed December 8, 2011).

Chion, Michel. *Audio-Vision: Sound on Screen*. Translated by Claudia Gorbman. New York: Columbia University Press, 1994 [1990].

Derrida, Jacques. "The Law of Genre." Translated by Avital Ronell. *Critical Inquiry* 7, no. 1 (1980): 55–81.

Dibben, Nicola. *Björk*. London: Equinox, 2009.

Frith, Simon, Andrew Goodwin, and Lawrence Grossberg. *Sound and Vision: The Music Video Reader*. London; New York: Routledge, 1993.

Goodwin, Andrew. *Dancing in the Distraction Factory: Music Television and Popular Culture*. Minneapolis: University of Minnesota Press, 1992.

Gorbman, Claudia. *Unheard Melodies: Narrative Film Music*. Bloomington: Indiana University Press, 1987.

Hawkins, Stan, and John Richardson. "Remodeling Britney Spears: Matters of Intoxication and Mediation." *Popular Music and Society* 30, no. 5 (2007): 605–629.

Jenkins, Henry. *Convergence Culture: Where Old and New Media Collide*. New York and London: New York University Press, 2006.

Kaplan, E. Ann. *Rocking Around the Clock: Music Television, Postmodernism, and Consumer Culture*. New York: Methuen, 1987.

Keazor, Henry, and Thorsten Wübbena. *Rewind, Play, Fast Forward. The Past, Present and Future of the Music Video*. Bielefeld: Transcript Verlag, 2010.

Kinder, Marsha. "Music Video and the Spectator: Television, Ideology and Dream." *Film Quarterly* 38, no. 1 (1984): 2–15.

Kristiansen, Bente. "Musikvideo." In *Analyser af TV*, edited by Ralf Pittelkow, 147–166. Copenhagen: Medusa, 1985.

Manovich, Lev. *The Language of New Media*. Cambridge, Mass.; London: MIT Press, 2001.

Railton, Diane, and Paul Watson. *Music Video and the Politics of Representation*. Edinburgh: Edinburgh University Press, 2011.

Richardson, John. *An Eye for Music: Popular Music and the Audiovisual Surreal*. New York and Oxford: Oxford University Press, 2011.

Russo, Julie. "User-Penetrated Content: Fan Video in the Age of Convergence." *Cinema Journal* 48, no. 4 (2009): 125–130.

Ruud, Even. *Musikk for øyet. Om musikkvideo*. Oslo: Gyldendal Norsk Forlag, 1988.

Shore, Michael. *The Rolling Stone Book of Rock Video. The Definitive Look at Visual Music from Elvis Presley—and Before—to Michael Jackson—and Beyond.* London: Sidgwick & Jackson, 1985.
Strand, Joachim. *The Cinesthetic Montage of Music-Video: Hearing the Image and Seeing the Sound.* Saarbrücken: VDM Verlag Dr. Müller, 2008.
Tate, Joseph. "Radiohead's Antivideos: Works of Art in the Age of Electronic Reproduction." In *The Music and Art of Radiohead*, edited by Joseph Tate, 103–117. Burlington: Ashgate, 2005.
Vernallis, Carol. *Experiencing Music Video: Aesthetics and Cultural Context.* New York: Columbia University Press, 2004.
Vernallis, Carol. "Music Video's Second Aesthetic?." In *The Oxford Handbook of New Audiovisual Aesthetics*, edited by, John Richardson, Claudia Gorbman, and Carol Vernallis. New York and Oxford: Oxford University Press, 2013.
Weibel, Peter. "Von der visuellen Musik zum Musikvideo." In *Clip, Klapp, Bum. Von der visuellen Musik zum Musikvideo*, edited by Veruschka Bódy and Peter Weibel, 53–164. Köln: DuMont, 1987.
Williams, Kevin. *Why I (Still) Want My MTV: Music Video and Aesthetic Communication.* Cresskill, New Jersey: Hampton Press, 2003.

Music Videos

Andy Grammer. "Keep Your Head Up," directed by Interlude, at http://vevo.com/videoevolved/andy-grammer/keep-your-head/ (accessed December 10, 2011).
Arcade Fire. "Black Mirror," directed by Olivier Groulx and Tracey Maurice, at http://www.rorrimkcalb.com/ (accessed December 10, 2011).
Arcade Fire. "My Body Is a Cage," directed by J. Tyler Helms, at http://www.youtube.com/watch?v=Pyp34v6Lmcc (accessed December 10, 2011).
Arcade Fire. "Neon Bible," directed by Olivier Groulx and Vincent Morisset, at http://www.beonlineb.com (accessed December 10, 2011).
Arcade Fire. "Sprawl 2," directed by Vincent Morisset, at http://www.sprawl2.com/. (accessed December 18, 2011).
Arcade Fire. "We Used to Wait"/*The Wilderness Downtown*, directed by Chris Milk, at http://www.thewildernessdowntown.com (accessed December 10, 2011).
Au Revoir Simone. "The Knight of Wands," directed by Eli Stonberg, at http://theknightofwands.com/ (accessed December 10, 2011).
Björk. *Biophilia*. Downloadable app-suite for iPad, iPhone, or iPod Touch.
Bloc Party. "Ares (Villains Remix)," director unknown, at http://www.youtube.com/watch?v=QPe7tk58S8Y (accessed December 10, 2011).
Bonnie Tyler. "Total Eclipse of the Heart (Literal Version)," original directed by Russell Mulcahy, alternate lyrics by David A. Scott, at http://www.funnyordie.com/videos/f03d464867/total-eclipse-of-the-heart-literal-video-version-original (accessed December 10, 2011).
Britney Spears. "Hold It Against Me (Teaser #1)," directed by Jonas Åkerlund, at http://www.youtube.com/watch?v=leKlV1WiynU (accessed December 10, 2011).
Broken Bells. "October," directed by Richard Lehmann and Matthew Hollister, at http://www.brokenbells.com/october/ (accessed December 10, 2011).
The Bynars. "How Does It Feel to Be in Love?" directed by Shaun Clarke, at http://thebynars.ccoom/hdif-video.htmlm/hdif-video.html (accessed December 10, 2011).

Carl Sagan Featuring Stephen Hawking. "A Glorius Dawn (Symphony of Science)," directed by John Boswell, at http://www.youtube.com/watch?v=zSgiXGELjbc (accessed December 10, 2011).

C-Mon & Kypski. "More Is Less," directed by Joel Wouters and Jonathan Puckey, at http://oneeframeoffame.com/frameoffame.com/ (accessed December 10, 2011).

Cold War Kids. "I've Seen Enough," directed by Sam Jones and Dustin Califf, at http://coldwarkids.com/iveseenenough/ (accessed December 10, 2011).

Craig Wedren. "Are We," directed by Tim Nackashi, at http://craigwedren.com/arewe/index.html (accessed December 10, 2011).

Dangermouse. "The Grey Video," director unknown, at http://www.youtube.com/watch?v=3zJqihkLcGc (accessed December 10, 2011).

Deerhunter. "Primitive 3D," directed by R. J. Bentler, at http://3d.pitchfork.com/e/1/deerhunter (accessed December 10, 2011).

Devo. "What We Do," directed by Gerald Casale, at http://www.wired.com/underwire/2011/04/devo-what-we-do-video (accessed December 10, 2011).

Dum Dum Girls. "*Only in Dreams* (Full Album Stream)," directed by unknown, at http://www.youtube.com/watch?v=TSoVQp3nN9g (accessed December 10, 2011).

Eclectic Method. "Lock Up Your Videos," directed by Eclectic Method, at http://www.eclecticmethod.net/2008/12/02/lock-up-your-videos (accessed December 10, 2011).

Franz Ferdinand. "Take Me Out" (video mod-version), directed by unknown at http://www.youtube.com/watch?v=2p2L2fnKTw4 (accessed December 10, 2011).

Gorillaz. "Escape to Plastic Beach." Downloadable app.

Hoobastank. "My Turn," directed by Paul Brown, at http://myturn.hoobastank.com/ (accessed December 10, 2011).

Johnny Cash. "Ain't No Grave"/*The Johnny Cash Project*, directed by Chris Milk, at http://thejohnnycashproject.com/ (accessed December 10, 2011).

Justin Timberlake. "Medley: Let Me Talk To You/My Love," directed by Paul Hunter, at http://www.youtube.com/watch?v=xjpe7EGyiw8&ob=av2e (accessed December 10, 2011).

Kanye West. "Runaway," directed by Kanye West, at http://www.youtube.com/watch?v=O7WoDMAx8FY (accessed December 10, 2011).

The Key of Awesome! "Ke$ha: 'We R Who We R'—Music Video Parody," directed by Tom Small, at [http://www.youtube.com/watch?v=HFepINobQAM (accessed December 10, 2011).

Kings of Leon. "Shreds—Their Worst Performance Ever," directed by unknown, at http://www.youtube.com/watch?v=NOF1FJ7wGhw (accessed December 10, 2011).

K.I.Z.. "Neuruppin," directed by Kubikfoto³, at http://kiz-neuruppin.de/ (accessed December 10, 2011).

Labuat. "Soy Tu Aire," directed by Rafa Soto and Roman Rodriguez (no longer available online).

Lady Gaga. "Poker Face" (clikthrough-version), directed by Ray Kay at http://www.clikthrough.com/theater/video/13 (accessed December 10, 2011).

"LIPDUB—I Gotta Feeling (Comm-UQAM 2009)," directed by Luc-Olivier Cloutier and Marie-Ève Hébert, at http://www.youtube.com/watch?v=-zcOFN_VBVo (accessed December 10, 2011).

Lost Valentinos. "Nightmoves," directed by Crucial by Design, at http://lostvalentinos.com/ (accessed December 10, 2011).

Macklemore. "Thrift Shop," redubbed by Mikolaj Gackowski (original video directed by Jon Jon Augustavo, Ryan Lewis, and Ben Haggerty), at http://www.youtube.com/watch?v=9rpjlA-z08o (accessed June 10th, 2013).

MGMT. "Electric Feel," directed by Ray Tintori (no longer available online).
Mobley. "Ego Is," directed by Straight Creative, at http://www.mobleytheband.com/egois/ (accessed December 10, 2011).
OK Go. "All Is Not Lost," directed by Trish Sie, at http://www.allisnotlo.st/ (accessed December 10, 2011).
OK Go. "Here It Goes Again (The Treadmill Video)," directed by OK Go and Trish Sie, at http://www.youtube.com/watch?v=dTAAsCNK7RA&ob=av2e (accessed December 10, 2011).
Pendulum. "360," directed by Dan Rutely, at http://www.pendulum.com/360 (accessed December 10, 2011).
Pepepiano. "Flesh Rails," directed by Asha Tamirisa, at http://vimeo.com/23693259 (accessed December 13, 2011).
Pitchfork. *POV Series*, at http://pitchfork.com/tv/pov/ (accessed December 10, 2011).
Polyphonic Spree. "Bullseye." Downloadable app.
Radiohead. "*Kid A* Blips," directed by The Vapour Brothers or Shynola! at http://www.vimeo.com/28222629 (accessed December 10, 2011).
Radiohead. "Lotus Flower (Single Ladies Edition)," directed by Anthony Dimeiri, at http://www.youtube.com/watch?v=9Eo7ttIKdfQ (accessed December 10, 2011).
Robyn. "Killing Me," directed by Mary Fagot, at http://robyn.com/killingme/ (accessed December 10, 2011).
Rome. "Three Dreams of Black," directed by Chris Milk, at http://www.ro.me/ (accessed December 10, 2011).
Shihad. "Sleepeater," directed by Sam Peacocke, at http://sleepeater.co.nz/ (accessed December 10, 2011).
Sour. "Mirror," directed by Masashi Kawamura, Qanta Simishu, Sagooshi, and Hiroki Ono, at http://sour-mirror.jp/ (accessed December 10, 2011).
Spleen United. "Sunset to Sunset (Puzzle Game)," directed by Hello Monday,at http://sunsettosunset.com/ (accessed December 10, 2011).
Steye & The Ottowanians. "Wonderful," directed by unknown, at http://inacabinwith.com/wonderful/ (accessed December 10, 2011).
The Streets. "The Longest Video Ever," directed by Mike Skinner,at http://video.google.com/videoplay?docid=3920953731128671811 (accessed December 10, 2011).
Team Me. "Chemicals and Weathervanes," released as the game *Get Home*, directed by jorgnsn, at http://www.teammegame.com/ (accessed December 10, 2011).
Vincent Moon. *Les concerts à emporter / Take-Away Shows*, concert documentary series, directed by Vincent Moon, at http://www.blogotheque.net/serie/concert-a-emporter/ (accessed December 10, 2011).
Who Made Who. "Every Minute Alone," directed by Good Boy! Creative, at http://everyminutealone.com/ (accessed December 10, 2011).
Will.i.am. "Hope. Act. Change," directed by Syrup, at http://www.hopeactchange.com/ (accessed December 10, 2011).

VIDEO, FILM, AND INSTALLATION ART

CHAPTER 29

"BETWIXT AND BETWEEN" WORLDS: SPATIAL AND TEMPORAL LIMINALITY IN VIDEO ART-MUSIC

HOLLY ROGERS

THE first wave of video art, which began in 1965 in New York, was highly interactive. The newly available technology enabled artists and composers to produce intermedial spaces in which image and music were simultaneously created, projected, and received. As a result, pieces were often site specific and performative. In May 1969 the Howard Wise Gallery in New York opened *TV as a Creative Medium*, one of the first American exhibitions devoted entirely to television and video work. Although it included work by Nam June Paik and Aldo Tambellini, it was *Wipe Cycle*, by Ira Schneider and Frank Gillette (see figure 29.1), that best embodied the interactive proclivities of early video work. Nine monitors, stacked three-by-three, were positioned in front of the elevator that brought people into the gallery. The screens presented a mixture of prerecorded video footage and live closed-circuit images taken from a camera videoing the visitors as they stepped from the elevator into the exhibition space: "The most important function," wrote Schneider, "was to integrate the audience into the information."[1] After eight seconds the newly recorded image appeared on two screens, and after sixteen on two others, before the delayed images switched axes. The outer four screens showed prerecorded images; according to a predetermined cycle, the monitors were intermittently wiped blank, and the process began again.

[1] Ira Schneider, quoted in Roy Ascott, *Telematic Embrace: Visionary Theories of Art, Technology, and Consciousness*, ed. Edward A. Shanken (Berkeley: University of California Press, 2007), 58.

FIGURE 29.1: *Wipe Cycle* by Frank Gillette and Ira Schneider, at the Howard Wise Gallery, New York City 1969.

Wipe Cycle embodied many of the aesthetic tropes common to early video work. Used as raw compositional material, visitors were drawn into the center of the video sculpture and thus became both receivers and creators. The work became site specific and resistant to commodification, because it only existed as long as it was being performed (and was thus difficult to "collect"). Nevertheless, although visitors were physically immersed in the work, they were not transported *into* it, because the materiality of the art form was constantly in sight: the video apparatus, the speakers, and the gallery walls were a vital part of the piece.

More recent work demands a more complex process of identification. Emerging from a period of radical technological, aesthetic, and institutional change, contemporary video work from the early 1990s is less sculptural and more cinematic than its forebears. For example, *Ocean Without a Shore*, Bill Viola's contribution to the 2007 Venice Biennale, was conceived for the tiny sixteenth-century Venetian chapel, the Church of St Gallo (see figure 29.2). A triptych of plasma screens surrounded by six speakers was mounted on the three altars, each screen showing a black-and-white image of a person walking in extreme slow motion toward the camera. Viola describes the screens as a "cross between a tomb and an altar": "These altars, actually, are a place where the dead…reside and

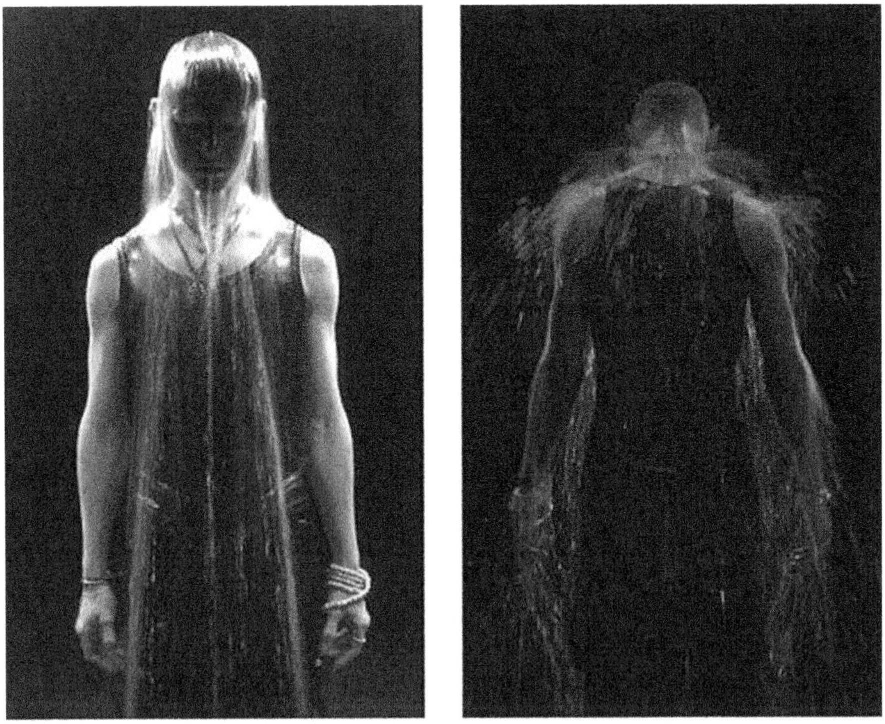

FIGURE 29.2: *Ocean Without a Shore* (2007) by Bill Viola.

connect . . . with the living." The figures on each of the three screens remain calm until their approach brings them to a wall of hitherto invisible water. As each form passes through the "invisible threshold," water cascades around it, and the images transform into high-definition color, a change that propels the characters into the visitor's space with alarming acuity. The wall, explains Viola, indicates "the fragility of life: the borderline between life and death is not a hard wall, it's not to be opened with a lock and key, it's actually very fragile, very tenuous . . . you can cross it . . . in an instant."[2] The fragility of these borders is also articulated through the passage of each of the characters, who represent various ethnicities and ages; for instance, one man emerges from his watery baptism in drag, a faint smile of relief on his face.

Although this piece thrums throughout, both visually and audibly, with the ambience of the chapel, the type of site specificity activated by the architectural fusion differs considerably from that produced by *Wipe Cycle*. The audience of *Ocean Without a Shore*, although feeling thoroughly immersed in the work and its context, is not asked to participate physically. Although the work is certainly influenced by its audience, as is every performance, it is not *performative*; instead, its narrative is predetermined,

[2] Bill Viola, "Bill Viola: Ocean Without a Shore—Venice Biennale 2007," at http://www.youtube.com/watch?v=6-V7in9LObI (accessed March 4, 2012).

which allowed the installation to be re-created with great accuracy at the James Cohan Gallery in New York City later that year. Projected onto flat screens, often in darkened rooms, more recent pieces such as *Ocean Without a Shore* tend to be more physically self-contained, initiating what Claire Bishop has described as a process of "mimetic engulfment."[3] Although context is vital to both styles of video work, the activation of space and the audiovisual relationships enabled within it are nevertheless articulated and activated in very different ways. These differences, I suggest, can be productively theorized in terms of two contrasting forms of liminality.

With its roots in the Latin *limen*, the concept of the liminal was introduced in anthropology (in 1909 by Arnold Van Gennep and later popularized by Victor Turner) to refer to a sensory threshold or an intermediate stage.[4] The term was first used to describe a rite of passage, a ritual that Gennep split into a period of separation, a liminal period (or what Turner refers to as a "gestation" period), and the act of reassimilation.[5] During such a ritual a person hovers "betwixt and between" (Turner) different social and existential spaces, and it is here that the person becomes acutely aware of his or her social and cultural positioning.[6] This temporary "gestation" period, writes Turner, is characterized by a "fructile chaos," acting as "a storehouse of possibilities, not by any means a random assemblage but a striving after new forms."[7] Turner points out that "liminality is frequently likened to death, to being in the womb, to invisibility, to darkness, to bisexuality, to the wilderness, and to an eclipse of the sun or moon."[8] The liminal has also been used to describe other transitional phases, such as the process of self-realization in Jungian theory, a period characterized by the breakdown of the persona before individualization is initiated; it can also refer to concrete places of indeterminate status, such as borders, crossroads, or disputed territories. However, the authors of *Mapping Liminalities* point out that "although the underlying metaphor is spatial, liminality is about process, it is always dynamic and is diachronic as well as synchronic. Liminality entails doubleness and is ultimately fluid and unfixable."[9] When blues guitarist Robert Johnson made his mythical pact with the devil at the crossroads, for instance, he mapped his physiological transformation—the moment he was able to exist physically in this world, while temporarily seeing into and conversing with the supernatural one—onto a physical space of equal directional ambiguity. His pact was such that he remained suspended in a "fluid

[3] Claire Bishop, *Installation Art* (London: Tate Publishing, 2005), ch. 3, 82–101.

[4] Arnold Van Gennep, *The Rites of Passage* (1960; repr., London: Routledge, 2004).

[5] Victor Turner, *The Forest of Symbols: Aspects of Ndembu Ritual* (Ithaca, New York : Cornell University Press, 1967), 96.

[6] Victor Turner, "Betwixt and Between: the Liminal Period in Rites of Passage," in *The Forest of Symbols*, 93–111.

[7] Victor Turner, "Dewey, Dilthey, and Drama: An Essay in the Anthropology of Experience," in *The Anthology of Experience*, ed. Turner and Edward Bruner (: Champaign, Illinois: Illinois University Press, 1986), 42.

[8] Victor Turner, "Liminality and Communitas," in *The Performance Studies Reader*, ed. Henry Bial (New York: Routledge, 2004), 80.

[9] Lucy Kay, Zöe Kinsley, Terry Phillips, and Alan Roughley, eds., *Mapping Liminalities: Thresholds in Cultural and Literary Texts* (Bern: Peter Lang, 2007), 8.

and unfixable" liminal space, unable to reintegrate into society once he had severed his ties in exchange for unusually dextrous fingers.

Characterized by fluidity and a lack of stability, liminality can take many forms. In video work, these forms vary greatly between early and more recent practice. Early work can be read as occupying the transitional, "gestational" phase in the evolution of video practice: a temporal, historical threshold. The technology first became available to the general public in 1965 and was quickly appropriated as a creative material by artists seeking to give sound to their images and by musicians eager to visualize their sounds. Set against a historical backdrop of intense experimentation that ranged from the conceptual work of Duchamp and the performance-based practices of Allan Kaprow on the art side to the heightened spatialization of Stockhausen and the aleatoric procedures of John Cage in the arena of music, video technology provided a new means to expand traditional practice. As an electromagnetic technology, video enabled music and image to be recorded and transmitted simultaneously for the first time, allowing an unprecedented level of creative syncretism and audiovisual synergy. Previous audiovisual practices, such as lantern shows, music theater, opera, synesthetic experimentation, and early direct film, were intermedial primarily at the level of reception. Although early experimental filmmakers such as Hans Richter, Oskar Fischinger, and Stan Brakhage had already explored the possibilities of single-authored visual music, film stock demanded a period of "deliberation" (Belton 1996) between musical and visual creativity.[10] Video enabled those working with the medium to produce sound and image tracks concurrently, at the moment of a work's inception, its electromagnetic scanning process ensuring that the image was continually "in the process of coming into being," as in *Wipe Cycle*.[11]

Because it was so immediate, early video work could easily be combined with other disciplines: for example, Carolee Schneeman included video in her performance art and Joan Jonas in her dance. The easy reproducibility of the video format, together with its capacity for instantaneous projection, offered these artists a way not only to articulate current creative concerns, but also to do so with sound. In a similar way, video's ability to simultaneously record and transmit music and image offered musicians an easy way to visualize their music. As a result, those working with early video were often musically trained; Nam June Paik (experimental composer), Steina Vasulka (classical violinist), Robert Cahen (electro-acoustic composer), and Tony Conrad (member of the *Theatre of Eternal Music*) are just a few examples. Initially, then, the use of the medium as a creative tool produced a unique moment in audiovisual history: the video practitioner, newly equipped to produce a form of visual music at an intermedial level, could become an artist-composer.

[10] John Belton, "Looking Through Video: The Psychology of Video and Film," in *Resolutions: Contemporary Video Practices*, ed. Michael Renov and Erika Suderburg (Minneapolis; London: University of Minnesota Press, 1996), 65.

[11] Belton, "Looking Through Video," 67.

Given that artists could thus use video to give sound to their visual work, while composers and performers could visualize their music from within their immediate acoustic space, the first wave of video can be considered the coming together of music and art spaces, the physical audiovisuality of the medium allowing these two histories to meet. At a material level the technology was able simultaneously to digest and project music and image; when received, this duality was situated in the intermedial space between music, sculpture, painting, drama, and film. Importantly, this space could be navigated by a single person, the artist-composer, who had to engage with the performance, manipulation, transmission, process, and feedback of both audio and visual tracks. It is important, however, not to over-romanticize the notion of the singular artist, when in fact many video artist-composers working in the 1960s used video as a tool to produce communal, improvisatory and expansive forms of creativity.

Much of Steina Vasulka's work demonstrates the expanded capabilities of video's audiovisuality. After graduating from the Prague Music Conservatory, she became a violinist with the Icelandic Symphony Orchestra. She left in 1965 for the life of a freelance musician in New York, where she became interested in visualizing her performances and turned to the video camera for help in creating a continuous experience or modality of crafting and remediating image-and-soundscapes:

> My background is in music. For me, it is the sound that leads me into the image. Every image has its own sound and in it I attempt to capture something flowing and living. I apply the same principle to art as to playing the violin: with the same attitude of continuous practice, the same concept of composition. Since my art schooling was in music, I do not think of images as stills, but always as motion.[12]

From her earliest work with Woody, her artist husband, Vasulka's installations were concerned with imaging sound. Initially the Icelandic artist fragmented the traditional gallery area not only by bringing music into the normally silent space, but also by replacing the fixed viewpoint of an artwork with a rotating table. In *Allvision* (1976), for example, two video cameras and a mirrored sphere revolved on a turntable in the middle of the space. Their scanning images were transmitted to four monitors, initiating an immediate fragmentation of the performance area. William Judson, the curator of the 1982–1983 installation at the Carnegie Museum of Art in Pittsburgh, described the piece in terms of the physical and temporal expansions it enabled:

> Upon entering the gallery, one is presented with three versions of space: the three dimensional gallery space which one shares with the machine and monitors as sculptural objects; the space which one sees mirrored in the sphere; and the "whole" space which is taken in by the cameras and presented in flattened version on the monitors. These versions of space correspond to three quite different ways of understanding "reality": as a physical material presence verifiable by touch; as

[12] Steina Vasulka, quoted at http://www.vasulka.org/Steina/Steina_Orka/Orka.html (accessed March 29, 2011).

FIGURE 29.3: Charlotte Moorman performs Nam June Paik's *TV Cello*.

> a visual perception, in which the material world may be rearranged or distorted but which is nevertheless comprehensible as an optical entity, like a painting or photograph; as a concept, in which an abstract system must be taken into account before the reality it presents is understood.[13]

In *Allvision* the focus was on the physical processes of video recording and projection and its ability to shatter the gallery space. Such emphasis on process resulted in a work that was site specific and highly transitory, less an artifact on display and more of a performance that used space, time, and the audience as its raw material, yielding a contextuality that Catherine Elwes has described as a "dismantling [of] the box itself."[14] A similar aesthetic was promoted in numerous other works of the period, including Paik's *TV Cello* (1971), in which a performer (Charlotte Moorman) played an instrument made from three television monitors (see figure 29.3). Connected to the monitors, the cello's strings distorted and fragmented the images when sounded, creating a visual music that included performer, artist, audience, and the space in which they interacted. As in *Allvision*, the focus lay beyond the screen, as context was the primary material for each performance.

The multidisciplinary possibilities afforded by video led many to believe that the format would open up a new era for creativity. And yet it is a tricky business to pinpoint

[13] http://www.vasulka.org/archive/ExhFOUR/Carnegie/Carnegie.pdf (accessed November 11, 2012).
[14] Catherine Elwes, *Video Art: A Guided Tour* (London: University of the Arts, 2005), 150.

the "birth" of the new medium. Although "liminal" has not been used in this context directly, several theorists have arrived at ideas that evoke this sense. André Gaudreault and Philippe Marion, for instance, use film to illustrate their thesis that a new creative practice must establish itself in relation to preexisting disciplines before it can articulate its own media specificities: it must define itself contextually before developing into a discrete art form.[15] According to their theory, only when film developed its medium specificity could it do this: "It wasn't until cinema's practitioners arrived at a reflexive understanding of the medium and until the cinema achieved a certain degree of institutionalisation that the medium became autonomous."[16] The first wave of video work is an excellent example of this theory, as it was particularly slow in consolidating its media specificity—a protraction that Yvonne Spielmann argues may more productively be referred to as its "integrating birth."[17] Site specific, performative, and structured around sound, early video repelled the easy commodification of art: as transient acts, the works could be neither repeated nor collected. Hans-Peter Schwarz, one of the founding directors of the Zentrum für Kunst und Medientechnologie, Karlsruhe (ZKM, Germany), described their ephemerality as setting off an "explosive charge" at the gates of traditional art establishments.[18] At first this "explosive charge" was blocked by major galleries because of curatorial problems (how to include sound and performance in a gallery space, temporal modes of perception fundamentally at odds with the traditional gallery experience), aesthetic issues (video's relationship to mass media such as television and untraditional modes of artistic discourse), and financial concerns (how to sell or keep something that is unrepeatable).[19] Artist Lynn Hershman Leeson articulates many of these problems when she recalls that "in 1972, the University Art Museum in Berkeley closed an exhibition of mine because I used audio tape and sound in a sculpture entitled *Self Portrait as Another Person*. The museum curators claimed that electronic media was not art and most certainly did not belong in a museum."[20] These ideological

[15] André Gaudreault and Philippe Marion, "The Cinema as a Model for the Genealogy of Media," *Convergence* 8, no. 4 (2002): 12.

[16] Gaudreault and Marion, "The Cinema as a Model for the Genealogy of Media," 2.

[17] Yvonne Spielmann, *Video: The Reflexive Medium* (Cambridge, Mass.; London: MIT Press, 2008), 117.

[18] Hans-Peter Schwarz, "Discourse 1: Media Museums," in *Media Art History*, ed. Rebecca Picht and Birgit Stöckmann (New York: Prestel, 1997), 11.

[19] The similarity of video's communicative strategies to the easily consumed domesticity of television, combined with the format's technological and spatial requirements, challenged the aesthetic (and ideological), financial, and physical operations of institutional exhibition. Although all three challenges are interlinked, the ideological concerns were voiced most strongly by curators, concert promoters, and significantly, artists themselves. Ten or so years after the first use of video as artistic material, for example, Allan Kaprow assessed the form, arriving at a less than encouraging conclusion. Video environments, he claimed, were little more than "a lavish form of kitsch" that resemble "world's fair 'futurama' displays with their familiar nineteenth-century push-button optimism and didacticism." Allan Kaprow, "Video Art: Old Wine, New Bottle (1974)," in *Essays on the Blurring of Art and Life*, ed. Jeff Kelley (Berkeley; Los Angeles; London: University of California Press, 1996; expanded ed. 2003), 152.

[20] Hershman Leeson, quoted in Pierre Restany, "San Francisco and the Grand Dame of Digital Art," *Domus* (June 1999): 114.

incompatibilities were also acknowledged by many video artists and composers, who rejected the methods of funding and exhibition favored by the larger institutions, preferring to perform their work in alternative spaces, such as people's houses or lofts; public spaces; and small, privately owned galleries. Two major exhibitions in the early 1980s signaled a change in the relationship between video artist-composer and institution. The Whitney Museum of American Art was one of the first American galleries to exhibit video work, with a retrospective of Nam June Paik in 1982; this was followed five years later by a Bill Viola retrospective at the Museum of Modern Art. Clearly video has gained institutional acceptance, with the Tate Modern currently constructing phase two of a multi-million-dollar wing that will house video and performance work.

Initially used as a component of other creative events, such as happenings and multimedia performance art, video was first used to bring together other disciplines, and it was not until the 1980s that the format could be considered an "aesthetically independent genre" (Spielmann 2008), or to return to the anthropological model I described at the outset, a *reassimilated* mode of audiovisual discourse. Viewed in this way, video's "integrating birth" can be mapped onto the "gestation process" of the rite-of-passage ritual. The audiovisual possibilities of the technology initiated a "withdrawal from normal modes of socialization" or artistic discourse and hovered for almost a decade in a state of intermediality "betwixt and between" disciplines, audiences, and modes of expression. Put another way, video enabled music and art practices to leave their established arenas and enter a period of intense flux. During this threshold stage, artists and musicians converged at the metaphorical crossroads, looking, like Robert Johnson, in two directions. Only once these two histories were fully integrated did video become an "aesthetically independent genre." But how has this institutional acceptance—or video's reassimilation—manifested itself in terms of creativity? What are the media specificities that have developed since video left the arena of intense communal creativity and entered the institutional fold? And how have these changed the nature of video's audiovisuality? In other words, now that the rite of passage is complete, how has video's temporal liminality transformed into a spatial one?

We can find examples of "aesthetically independent" video pieces by younger video artists and composers who, working from the late 1990s onward, developed the cinematic, self-contained style that articulates the more subtle audiovisual relationships in *Ocean Without a Shore*. As previously noted, these pieces were often projected onto flat screens. At first glance the differences in levels of performativity, interactivity, and site specificity activated by the two waves of video work are vast. If we understand the first wave as musicians visualizing their work with a heightened sense of materiality and contextualization, we can see the second wave, although often still installational, as moving toward a more sutured, cinematic mode of discourse that attempts to blend with its environment. But despite the initial performative and material changes between the two waves, is there a common aesthetic thread that connects early and recent work? Should we read contemporary pieces as simply a more polished way of articulating the same audiovisual problems?

Recognizing that the differences stem from the ways in which each wave of video interacts with its environment, let us take Spielmann's reading of early video a step further. During video's liminal "integrating birth," the audiovisual synergy enabled by the new technology allowed music and art to move into each other's realms, as in *TV Cello*. Once an "aesthetically independent genre" emerged during video's second wave, however, practitioners reworked audiovisuality into a more immersive, insular, and self-reflexive style, as articulated in many of Viola's installations. It was here that a second form of liminality was initiated. This time the threshold did not exist as a temporal and historical period of confinement, because as we have seen, video was by then thoroughly assimilated into the art world. Rather, the historical "gestation" period was replaced by a conceptual liminality that operated not temporally but spatially. More recent video forces its audience into a state of critical self-awareness that positions it in the *existential* space of Gennep's transitional phase. But what happened to make the two sets of sensibilities of early and more recent video work so radically different?

Spatial Liminality

The answer is twofold and lies somewhere between technological innovation and institutional acceptance. Rapid developments in video technology have blurred the distinctions between media specificities. Rather than being used contextually as part of a Happening or site-specific event, video worked toward, not against, the syncretism of the cinematic. Whereas Paik was preoccupied with the television monitor as a sculptural object, the later work of Viola and others repositioned attention from the apparatus of display onto, or rather into, the two-dimensional screen, which was enjoying rapid gains in resolution throughout the 1980s and 1990s.[21] Viola now works predominantly with high-definition video that is shown either via rear projection onto a screen, as in *Emergence* (2002), or on wall-mounted plasma displays, as in *Two Women* (2008). Elwes has articulated this shift between "contrasting spatial dynamics" as "[t]he emergence of the video image from its cuboid container."[22]

The move from context to content has been hailed as "a new beginning" for video work.[23] Although practitioners continue to refer to themselves as video artists, it is clear that those working with the medium have outgrown the technological confines inherent in the name. (Viola has been particularly vocal about the material emphasis of the term "video artist," for example, insisting that his work highlights content rather than the materialities of display.) Not only has the quality of video improved so much that it is difficult to distinguish it from

[21] As with all attempts at categorization, the edges of definition are blurred. For example, instances of the expanded screen aesthetic that characterizes the second wave of video can occasionally be found in earlier work, such as Vito Acconci's almost televisual, single-screen *Theme Song* (1973).

[22] Elwes, *Video Art*, 153.

[23] Elwes, *Video Art*, 153.

film, but by the turn of the twenty-first century digital technologies had all but destroyed the divide between video and film, prompting a move into what Michael Rush describes as a post-medium world.[24] The ready interchange between media can be seen in the various sections of Matthew Barney's *Cremaster Cycle* (1994–2002), which were shot on different video systems but later transferred to 35mm film stock. Michel Gondry demonstrated a similar post-medium sensibility in his recent installation with Pierre Bismuth, *The All-Seeing Eye (The Hardcore Techno Version)* (2005), in which video footage is transferred to DVD and shown on a television set.

Technological advances have allowed artists and composers working with video from its earliest days to expand on their initial ideas while resisting the temptation to reassimilate into art culture. Paik, although initially expressing reluctance to embrace technological media ("I use technology in order to hate it more properly"), moved from work with video and tape technology to satellite extravaganzas in the 1980s, even as his underlying aesthetic remained consistent.[25] *Wrap Around the World* (1988), for example, a video work seen by more than fifty million people, celebrated the then-forthcoming Seoul Olympic Games. Using satellite technology, Paik mixed live performances by David Bowie; La, La, La; Human Steps; and Merce Cunningham in America with contributions by Ryuichi Sakamoto, the Viennese Art Orchestra, and an elephant football match in locations as diverse as China, Brazil, France, Germany, Israel, and Japan. The synchronous manipulation of image and sound introduced in *TV Cello* also lay at the heart of *Wrap Around the World*, albeit on a globally magnified scale. The aesthetic and conceptual basis remained the same, but the method of voicing became more spectacular.

Vasulka also embraced technological innovation to hone and intensify the intermedial connections that informed her earliest experimentation. Working with her husband in 1978, she embarked on a series of works known as *Violin Power*, which explored the possibilities of sending audio signals directly into a video recorder without using a camera. As she played her violin, the sounds were channeled directly into the video signal, enabling her to manipulate her own image, which was being projected onto a screen via a closed-circuit feed. Unlike Paik, whose similarly performative works, such as *TV Cello*, were only performed several times before he abandoned them, Vasulka continued to work on *Violin Power*, describing it as "an ongoing continuous project with an ever increasing 'repertoire.' So far I have made five videodisks and I change the program for every performance."[26] Starting in 1991 she replaced video with computer technology, which allowed her more precise control over the visual manipulations as she performed:

> In 1991, after having experimentally interfaced my acoustic violin with a variable speed video cassette player, I bought a MIDI violin and a Pioneer Disk Player. Interfacing these instruments with a computer gave me an instant access to any

[24] Michael Rush, *Video Art* (London: Thames and Hudson, 2007).

[25] Paik, quoted in Elwes, *Video Art*, 35.

[26] Vasulka, quoted at http://www.vasulka.org/Steina/Steina_ViolinPower/ViolinPower.html (accessed March 29, 2011).

> frame of video on the disk as well as access to fast/slow and forward/backward movements.[27]

Developing software that was later utilized by video jockeys looking to merge sound and image, the Vasulkas' electric ZETA violin could assign specific functions to different strings or individual notes. This enabled her to change the speed or direction of a visual sequence, repeat prerecorded progressions, or control the actions of other performers. The computer technology used in *Violin Power* enabled a more versatile form of audiovisuality, because a single idea could be continually revoiced in a variety of contexts.

Whereas both *Wrap Around the World* and *Violin Power* retained their emphasis on context common to the first wave of video artist-composers, the younger generation has used technological advancements to move attention away from the edge of the frame and into the diegesis. It can be argued that the move toward two dimensionality in recent video work simply reflects technological advancement. The use of multiple screens to create multidimensional narrative spaces mirrors the emergence of technological "non-places" promoted by new media expansions of "simulation, immersion, telepresence and surveillance," which, as Alison Butler has argued, has had "profound anthropological effects, breaking down distinctions between local and global, interior and exterior, here and elsewhere, and, ultimately, self and other."[28] Anne Friedberg has been more specific in her understanding of the reasons behind the profound "paradigm shift in visual address" toward a more complex form of audiovisual engagement, arguing that it is in response to the proliferating virtual windows found in most digital interfaces over the last thirty years, which encourage engagement with multiple screens and activate distributed attention.[29] Interestingly, Dennis Waskul has described these "proliferating virtual windows" of the Internet as "a natural environment for liminality," because they suspend the ordinary life that surrounds the computer screen; it follows that the user is prevented from engaging too fully in any one virtual world.[30]

Bishop has reformulated the opposing spatial dynamics identified by Butler and Friedberg in terms of audience engagement, suggesting that the first wave of video art-music encouraged an "activated spectatorship." In contrast, more recent, flat-screen works promote a more cinematic "mimetic engulfment," as they operate through what Liz Kotz describes as a "seductive immateriality."[31] Although this phrase initially seems to suggest a compatibility with the illusory modes of discourse commonly found in cinema,

[27] Ibid.

[28] Alison Butler, "A Deictic Turn: Space and Location in Contemporary Gallery Film and Video Installation," *Screen* 51, no. 4 (2010): 306.

[29] Anne Friedberg, *The Virtual Window: From Alberti to Microsoft* (Cambridge, Mass.: MIT Press, 2006), 3.

[30] Dennis Waskul, "Ekstasis and the Internet: Liminality and Computer Mediated Communication," *New Media and Society* 7, no. 1 (2005): 47.

[31] Liz Katz, "Video Projection: The Space Between Screens," in *Art and the Moving Image: A Critical Reader*, ed. Tanya Leighton (London: Tate Publishing, 2008), 379.

video actually entails a very different form of engagement. Like Paik and Vasulka, many second-wave video practitioners use *themselves* as raw material, yet unlike earlier video artist-composers, their audiovisuality has been revoiced in terms of contemporary music culture. During the 1990s, for instance, the inclusion of popular musical elements into video self-portraits became increasingly common, ensuring that the relationship between sound and visuals remained at the forefront of both creation and reception. In *I'm Not the Girl Who Misses Much* (1996), Swiss artist Pipilotti Rist delivers a parody of the John Lennon song "Happiness is a Warm Gun" (1968) that can be read as a commentary on the (particularly visual) representation of women in popular music. But as she delivers the song directly to the camera, her own voice and image are fragmented through fast-forward and extreme slow motion, distortions that highlight the materiality of the video medium. Anne McGuire's nostalgic *I Am Crazy and You're Not Wrong* (1997) articulates a different relationship between technology and sound. Here the San Francisco–based artist performs Kennedy-era lounge songs to a disinterested camera. Highlighting what Elwes has described as a "struggle for self-expression within the mimetic confines of the musical vernacular," the video style moves away from the performative intermedialities of *Violin Power* and *TV Cello* toward the prerecorded style of music video. In *I'm Not Crazy*, the "hysteria, drug addiction and madness that were always simmering under the performances of iconic figures like Judy Garland and Billie Holliday" (Elwes) are suppressed by preexisting musical structures, producing the opposite effect to Rist's energized performance, which manages visually to break apart Lennon's song.[32]

A similar preoccupation with visualizing music can be found in the work of Young British Artists Gillian Wearing and Sam Taylor-Wood. Wearing's 1995 piece, *Dancing in Peckham* (a 25-minute video shown on a television monitor), for instance, shows the artist dancing in a shopping center to a soundtrack that remains to us unheard (see figure 29.4); the silence could be read as a nod to the much-theorized "inaudibility" of many film scores. With no music to connect viewer to screen, the performer's movements appear unsettling and ensure a distance between the visitor and the work. Taylor-Wood's *Killing Time* (1994) articulates a contrasting form of audiovisual rupture by presenting four people miming badly to arias from Richard Strauss's *Elektra*. Out of time with the recording and frequently distracted from their task, the miming characters again emphasize the materiality of the medium by critiquing the "realist" audiovisual synchronicity of film. The flat-screen projection can be considered as seductively immaterial, as attention is placed *within* the frame rather than on its mode of display, yet at the same time the self-conscious and reflexive audiovisuality produces a ruptured depiction of reality that prevents the visitor from feeling fully absorbed into the fictive space. This duality activates the hinterland between the location of display and the "seductive immateriality" of the video. These single-screen videos, then, use different strategies to produce similar effects. In each piece sound and image are pitted against one another: the artists mime or sing from within a restricted technological or aesthetic framework, producing

[32] Elwes, *Video Art*, 165.

FIGURE 29.4: *Dancing in Peckham* by Gillian Wearing.

disquieting audiovisual fissures very different from the intermedial procedures found in *TV Cello* and *Violin Power*. The visitor, at once lured into and repelled by the diegesis, hovers in the liminal space "betwixt and between" gallery and video world.

This relationship between work and viewer can also be found in recent installational video works. In the Tate Modern retrospective of Finnish artist Eija-Liisa Ahtila (April 30–July 28, 2002), videos were spread through a series of blackened rooms, each with a multiple-screen installation. Most of the pieces were in triptych formation; Ahtila described them as representing "human dramas."[33] With the exception of *Consolation Service* (1999), none of the works had a timed entry, as the "human dramas" unraveling in each darkened room resisted linear and cumulative trajectories. Of course many examples of narrative fragmentation can be found in mainstream cinema culture as well, either through multiple story lines, as in *Crash* (Paul Haggis, 2004), in which several tales unfold as the result of a single event, or through the actual split screen of the television series *24*, in which four segments of activity are stitched together by the ticking of a real-time clock. Despite the split narrative and screens, however, shot-reverse-shot sequences and offscreen audio position the audience safely within the diegesis. In both examples the music (by Mark Isham and Sean Callery, respectively) succeeds in dispelling the potential

[33] Eija-Liisa Ahtila, quoted at http://www.paolocurti.com/ahtila/ahtila.htm (accessed March 29, 2011).

rupture that such multiple viewpoints could cause by smoothing the boundaries between frames and the geographical distances between concurrent events. Isham's insistent electronic score for *Crash* is particularly successful in drawing attention away from the materiality of the editing, to ensure that filmgoers remain fully engrossed in the fiction.

As we have seen, recent video pieces often reject such suture. Although Elwes refers to contemporary video as operating within a "newly radicalised cinema space," the aesthetic intentions of both film and early video have been challenged by the spatial ruptures of recent pieces. In Ahtila's piece *Anne, Aki and God* (1998; Tate Modern 2002), a large screen, framed by television monitors, shows five men auditioning for the main part. The installation is based on a true story. The artist explains: "Aki V resigned from his work as a computer application support person at Nokia Virtuals, became schizophrenic and isolated himself in his one-room flat. His mind started to produce a reality of its own in sound and vision."[34] This "reality" included an imaginary girlfriend called Anne, the hearing of voices, and a vision of God that hovered above his bed. Ahtila's piece, installed as part of her 2002 retrospective, was divided into two sections: one a "passive" space that includes Aki's bed, five television monitors, and a large projection of God, played by both a man and a woman; the other an "active" area, in which a chair, reading lamp, and table are positioned facing another large projection screen.[35] On the television monitors appear five men "auditioning" for the part of Aki. Each is seen and heard reciting the same lines, which describe, at varying speeds, the character's relationship with the imaginary Anne. "The simultaneous delivery of the same lines by different voices," as the exhibition catalog explains, prevents the viewer "from attaching identity to any single young man" and thus emphasizes "his schizophrenic state."[36] The large screen in the "active" area is more like a documentary, presenting seven women who are auditioning for the part of the imaginary Anne explaining how they feel about the character and why they want to play her.

The result is rather overwhelming. Fragmented visual representations are accompanied by a dislocated audio track, a cacophony of voices that coagulate into a nonlinguistic mode of signification, or noise-music, preventing absorption into any one screen. Wherever we look, the voices, out of sync with one another, provide a constant reminder of the edge of each screen, of other characters competing for attention, and of the space that the installation occupies. In this spatial sense, *Anne, Aki and God* resembles early video pieces, such as *TV Cello* and *Violin Power*. However, although thoroughly immersed in the multidimensional and intensely audiovisual work, the audience is no longer an *active*, inclusive participant. It is not used as visual or audio material and remains unable to change the physical progression of the piece, only its place in relation to it. At the same time, the installation rejects the fictive immersion common to cinema, as meaning and narrative become increasingly ambiguous.

34 Ahtila, quoted at http://www.tate.org.uk/whats-on/tate-modern/exhibition/eija-liisa-ahtila-real-characters-invented-worlds http://www.tate.org.uk/modern/exhibitions/ahtila/room9.htm (accessed March 29, 2011).

35 Terence Riley, *Eija-Liisa Ahtila: Cinematic Works* (London: Crystal Eye, 2003), 136–139.

36 Riley, *Eija-Liisa Ahtila*, 138.

At first glance the recent spatial dynamic apparent in Ahtila's work appears to promote a move away from the experiential interactivity of the 1970s. However, the move is actually toward an immersive, sensorial experience that demands a type of audience engagement that is different from but equally as radical as that of earlier video pieces. The visual "mimetic engulfment" of *Anne, Aki and God* is countered by its multiplane soundtrack, which prevents full immersion into the competing dialogues. As a result, audio-viewers experiencing the work remain suspended between gallery space and the video's diegesis. Dislocated from the gallery by the numerous portals into Aki's mind—yet prevented from identifying with any one strain of thought because of the antagonistic musical syntax of the babbling chorus—we find ourselves held in a *spatial* liminality, rather than sutured absorption, among work, gallery, and audience. Butler's distinctions between "interior and exterior, here and elsewhere, and, ultimately, self and other" do not dissolve, but rather coexist. Like Robert Johnson, we are able temporarily to look into both worlds.

During its "integrating birth," then, video work occupied a historical, temporal liminality as its practitioners temporarily left their artistic or musical backgrounds and moved into a transitory arena of intense intermedial experimentation. This gestation period is characterized by the merging of art and music histories, which like the physically, perceptually, and conceptually reimagined gallery space in Vasulka's *Allvision*, exists in a state of high instability. Once video became established as an "independently aesthetic genre" through a process of technological change and institutional acceptance, it entered into a process of "reassimilation." It is here that temporal liminality has been replaced by a spatial one. The flat screens create a "newly radicalized cinema space" in which works negotiate the aesthetic divide between film and early video installation, between being sewn into the diegesis and retaining an acute sense of self. The works discussed previously promote a transitional, spatial liminality, a temporary "fructile chaos" of distributed attention that asks the visitor to reassess his or her relationship with artwork, music, fellow spectators, and the arena in which they collide. The visitor is then free to leave, to reassimilate into society, perhaps not with a new social role or status as suggested by Gennep, but hopefully with a refreshed understanding of intermedial discourse and his or her own position within it.[37]

By contrast, early work exists in a state of perpetual liminality, rejecting reincorporation into the social structure or the institutional fold. In 2010 The Tate Liverpool hosted Paik's first major retrospective since his death in 2006, an elegantly curated collection of his most famous and radical pieces. Among the works assembled was *TV Cello*; however, in the absence of both Paik and Moorman, the instrument reclined on a pedestal, separated from the visitor by a thick white line. On its screens were not live, closed-circuit images of the audience, but prerecorded footage from other events, and from its speakers came the sound of old news footage rather than "TV Cello Sounds."[38] The refusal to let the Cello play—to let it fragment and re-create its environment—brought Paik's

[37] Bjorn Thomassen, "Liminality," in *Routledge Encyclopedia of Social Theory*, ed. Austin Harrington, Barbara L. Marshall, and Hans-Peter Müller (London: Routledge, 2006), 322.

[38] Charlotte Moorman described the sounds of the installation as "TV Cello sounds" in an interview in 1984, at http://www.youtube.com/watch?v=r9hTdaFz36c

piece to the end of its historical gestation period by defusing its "explosive charge" at the traditional gallery and its modes of display. The moment the performative, interactive intermediality of its threshold stage was removed, once it was transported into the traditional gallery arena, it became an artifact; its "fluid and unfixable" nature was silenced and immobilized.

Bibliography

Elwes, Catherine. *Video Art: A Guided Tour.* London: University of the Arts, 2005.

Gaudreault, André, and Philippe Marion. "The Cinema as a Model for the Genealogy of Media." *Convergence* 8. no. 4 (2002): 12–18.

Hall, Doug, and Sally Jo Fifer, eds. *Illuminating Video: An Essential Guide to Video Art.* New York: Aperture Press, 1991.

Knight, Julia, ed. *Diverse Practices: A Critical Reader on British Video Art.* Luton: University of Luton/Arts Council England, 1996.

Meigh-Andrews, Chris. *A History of Video Art.* Oxford: Berg, 2006.

Schneider, Ira, and Beryl Korot, eds. *Video Art: An Anthology.* New York: Harcourt Brace Jovanovich, 1976.

Spielmann, Yvonne. *Video: The Reflexive Medium.* Cambridge, Mass.; London: MIT Press, 2008.

Youngblood, Gene. *Expanded Cinema.* New York: E. P.Dutton & Co., 1970.

References

Ahtila, Eija-Liisa. "Eija-Liisa Ahtila: Past Exhibitions," at http://www.paolocurti.com/ahtila/ahtila.htm (accessed March 29, 2011).

Ahtila, Eija-Liisa. "Real Characters, Invented Worlds," at http://www.tate.org.uk/whats-on/tate-modern/exhibition/eija-liisa-ahtila-real-characters-invented-worlds (accessed March 29, 2011).

Ascott, Roy. *Telematic Embrace: Visionary Theories of Art, Technology, and Consciousness.* Edited by Edward A. Shanken. Berkeley: University of California Press, 2007.

Belton, John. "Looking Through Video: The Psychology of Video and Film." In *Resolutions: Contemporary Video Practices*, edited by Michael Renov and Erika Suderburg, 61–72. Minneapolis; London: University of Minnesota Press, 1996.

Bishop, Claire. *Installation Art.* London: Tate Publishing, 2005.

Butler, Alison. "A Deictic Turn: Space and Location in Contemporary Gallery Film and Video Installation." *Screen* 51, no. 4 (2010): 305–323.

Elwes, Catherine. *Video Art: A Guided Tour.* London: University of the Arts, .

Friedberg, Anne. *The Virtual Window: From Alberti to Microsoft.* Cambridge, Mass.: MIT Press, 2006.

Gaudreault, André, and Philippe Marion. "The Cinema as a Model for the Genealogy of Media." *Convergence* 8, no. 4 (2002): 12–18.

Gennep, Arnold Van. *The Rites of Passage.* 1960; repr., London: Routledge, 2004.

Kaprow, Allan. "Video Art: Old Wine, New Bottle (1974)." In *Essays on the Blurring of Art and Life*, edited by Jeff Kelley, 148–153. Berkeley; Los Angeles; London: University of California Press, 1996; expanded ed. 2003.

Kotz, Liz. "Video Projection: The Space Between Screens." In *Art and the Moving Image: A Critical Reader*, edited by Tanya Leighton, 371–385. London: Tate Publishing, 2008.

Kay, Lucy, Zöe Kinsley, Terry Phillips, and Alan Roughley, eds. *Mapping Liminalities: Thresholds in Cultural and Literary Texts*. Bern: Peter Lang, 2007.

Restany, Pierre. "San Francisco and the Grand Dame of Digital Art." *Domus* 816 (June 1999): 114.

Riley, Terence. *Eija-Liisa Ahtila: Cinematic Works*. London: Crystal Eye, 2003.

Rogers, Holly., *Sounding the Gallery: Video and the Rise of Art-Music*. (Oxford: Oxford University Press, 2013).

Rush, Michael. *Video Art*. London: Thames and Hudson, 2007.

Schwarz, Hans-Peter. "Discourse 1: Media Museums." In *Media Art History*, edited by Rebecca Picht and Birgit Stöckmann, 11. New York: Prestel, 1997.

Spielmann, Yvonne. *Video: The Reflexive Medium*. Cambridge, Mass.; London: The MIT Press, 2008.

Thomassen, Bjorn. "Liminality." In *Routledge Encyclopedia of Social Theory*, ed. Austin Harrington, Barbara L. Marshall, and Hans-Peter Müller, 322–323. London: Routledge, 2006.

Turner, Victor. "Betwixt and Between: The Liminal Period in Rites of Passage." In *The Forest of Symbols: Aspects of Ndembu Ritual*, 93–111. New York: Cornell University Press, 1967.

Turner, Victor. "Dewey, Dilthey, and Drama: An Essay in the Anthropology of Experience." In *The Anthropology of Experience*, edited by Victor Turner and Edward Bruner, 33–44. Illinois: Illinois University Press, 1986.

Turner, Victor. "Liminality and Communitas." In *The Performance Studies Reader*, edited by Henry Bial, 79–87. New York: Routledge, 2004.

Vasulka, Steina. "Violin Power: The Performance," at http://www.vasulka.org/Steina/Steina_ViolinPower/ViolinPower.html (accessed March 29, 2011).

Vasulka, Steina. "Orka," at http://www.vasulka.org/Steina/Steina_Orka/Orka.html (accessed March 29, 2011).

Viola, Bill. "Bill Viola: Ocean Without a Shore—Venice Biennale 2007," at http://www.youtube.com/watch?v=6-V7in9LObI (accessed March 4, 2012).

Waskul, Dennis. "Ekstasis and the Internet: Liminality and Computer Mediated Communication." *New Media and Society* 7, no. 1 (2005): 47–63.

CHAPTER 30

SOUND EVENTS: INNOVATION IN PROJECTION AND INSTALLATION

MAUREEN TURIM AND MICHAEL WALSH

LET us start with with silence, films that eschew sound. Our discussion of sound events in avant-garde film, video, and installation begins with the resurgence of American avant-garde filmmaking in the 1950s and 1960s and asks what survives of that period's silent aesthetic today. This was a moment when a new emphasis on visual exploration led artists to privilege a silence thought to mark the image as self-sufficient. Filmmakers such as Stan Brakhage felt that silence was needed to fully concentrate on images and to allow their visual rhythms and even their suggestion of visual music to emerge. "I now see/feel no more absolute necessity for a sound track than a painter feels to exhibit a painting with a recorded musical background," wrote Brakhage in 1966.[1]

The years when silent avant-garde films were so often listed in catalog and exhibition entries with the parenthetical words (b&w, silent) or (color, silent) were also when art houses, film societies, and museums showed films from the silent era without accompanying sound, sometimes at a "silent projection speed" of eighteen frames per second. Artists bathed in these visual rhythms from the past in the space opened anew by silence, although in most cases the original projections had been accompanied with diverse music and sound effects, sometimes even had voiced narration, and were hand-cranked at varying speeds.

Although there is a history of sound experiments by avant-garde filmmakers reaching back into the 1920s, the American renaissance of the avant-garde in the 1950s and 1960s was strongly associated with films experienced in silence. Stan Brakhage made more than 350 films of various lengths, with only twenty-seven using sound, and some

[1] *Brakhage Scrapbook: Collected Writings* (New Paltz, N.Y.: Documentext, 1982), 49.

of those using it only minimally. For example, *Fire of Waters* (1965) gives us a highly reworked use of recorded sound at three key instances in a film that is largely silent.[2] Other factors contributing to this silence were financial (avoiding the added costs of striping an optical sound track on a film print), technical (synchronizing a separate magnetic sound track on a dual-band projector was often awkward), and attitudinal (individual subjectivity was valued over collaboration with others in composing, sound recording, editing, and scriptwriting). Yet those collaborations, and those artists who had either come to filmmaking with musical or sound recording backgrounds or had acquired such skills, were critical in establishing a renewed interest in avant-garde film sound tracks.

The subsequent uses of sound in avant-garde film, video, and installation are so many and so various that they make us think of Badiou's definition of being as an inconsistent multiplicity, itself composed of multiplicities,[3] or equally of his characterization of Deleuze as a philosopher for whom everything is an event.[4] Yet the idea that being is multiple and everything is an event does not prevent either Badiou or Deleuze from observing many regularities in the world. This chapter makes no claim to exhaustivity, but rather focuses on a number of specific tendencies, listed below. Note that some artists count as participants in several different tendencies, and that while there certainly is such a thing as medium specificity, some aesthetics readily cross over among film, video, and installation:

1. Silence (Stan Brakhage, Maya Deren and Alexander Hammid, Larry Gottheim, Bill Viola, Douglas Gordon)
2. Tone and drone (Tony Conrad, Paul Sharits, Michael Snow, Bruce Conner, Andy Warhol)
3. Antic, aleatory (Ken Jacobs, Jack Smith, Andy Warhol, Christian Marclay)
4. Multilayering, cacophony (Peter Kubelka, Michael Snow, Larry Gottheim, Abigail Child, Christian Marclay)
5. Work with voices (Hollis Frampton, Su Friedrich, Abigail Child, Bruce Nauman, Gary Hill, Janet Cardiff and George Bures Miller)
6. "Modern antiquity," or the legacies of classical cinematic exhibition (Douglas Gordon, Janet Cardiff and George Bures Miller, Christian Marclay, Bruce High Quality Foundation)
7. Resonant spaces in galleries and museums (Eija-Lisa Ahtila, Bill Viola, Isaac Julien)

[2] Maureen Turim, "Sound: Beyond Distinctions between Music, Noise, and Speech: A New Process, A New Ordering," in *Abstraction in Avant-garde Films* (Ann Arbor, Mich.: UMI Research Press, 1985), 30.

[3] Alain Badiou, *Being and Event* (London: Continuum, 2005), 33.

[4] Alain Badiou, "The Event in Deleuze," *Parrhesia* 2 (2007): 37–44, at www.parrhesiajournal.org/parrhesia02/parrhesia02_badiou02.pdf (accessed August 17, 2011).

An intriguing instance of the question of silence and sound in the avant-garde film may be seen in the history of Maya Deren and Alexander Hammid's *Meshes of the Afternoon* (1946). The film was originally shot silent, but was transformed in 1959 when Deren added an innovative musical score by her then husband, Teiji Ito. Today the film is usually shown with the Ito sound track, which is scored for Japanese instruments and seeks percussive and lyric correspondences to the beats of the film's visual rhythms, while at other times anticipating them provocatively. Another late 1950s film with variable sound is Shirley Clarke's film *Bridges Go-Round* (1959), which was screened with two alternative sound tracks, Louis and Bebe Barron's electronic music and Teo Macero's jazz.

Deren and Clark's initiatives may be seen as antecedent to later films that examine structural sound and image segments. Speaking about the making of *Mouches Volantes* (1976), Larry Gottheim elaborates on the frame-by-frame notation of complex graphs of events on both image and sound track.[5] Indeed, he transferred his sound, portions of a narration by Angelina Johnson on the story of the life of her husband, blues great Blind Willie Johnson, to 16mm magnetic tape to be able to mark the sound off frame by frame. Gottheim wanted to show each section of the image track both silently and with sound; he decided on a palindromic structure in which sections 1 through 7 would first appear in order, then be seen in reverse order from 7 back to 1. This play with units of image montage correlated with different units of sound continues in Gottheim's *Four Shadows* (1978), in which four image sections are repeated four times, each time with a different sound section, so that each group of images is heard with each group of sounds (one of which is silent), creating sixteen variations in all. The 64 minutes of this film become an exploration of how image events seem to differ in correspondence with new sound events. For example, the chimpanzees seen cavorting imaginatively across their tightly framed cage create visual trajectories that read differently when heard against the richly captured ambient sound of the zoo than when combined with passages from Debussy's *Pelléas et Melisande*. Conjunctions and disjunctions become determinant on an abstract rhythmic plane. The paradigm also works to transform signifiers by new sonic associations, so that different connotations attach to visual elements and their movements. To so foreground conjunction and disjunction of sound and image as a compositional principle becomes a rich element of filmic experimentation. Michael Snow worked in a related vein in this same period, and in the twenty-five sequences of the 267-minute *Rameau's Nephew by Diderot (Thanx to Dennis Young) by Wilma Schoen* (1974) he produced a virtual encyclopedia of possible relationships between recorded image and recorded sound.

Another way of approaching the innovative function of sound in avant-garde film is to look at the minimalist composers who collaborated with filmmakers. Examples are Steve Reich's phased loop track for Gunvor Nelson's *My Name Is Oona* (1969), and Terry

[5] Scott MacDonald, *A Critical Cinema: Interviews with Independent Filmmakers* (Berkeley: University of California Press, 1998), 93–97.

Riley's compositions for both Tony Conrad's *Straight and Narrow* (1970) and Bruce Conner's *Crossroads* (1976).[6] Tony Conrad was himself a musician, collaborating with John Cale, Angus MacLise, La Monte Young, and Marian Zazeela in the "Theatre of Eternal Music." Conrad's *The Flicker* (1966) joins a synthesized drone to its rapid alternation of black and clear frames, introducing an aesthetic of repetitive tonal alternation that found many variations. Conner's *Crossroads* is composed of static framings from various angles of the Bikini Atoll test of the atomic bomb. The first view is accompanied by sound from the distant site at which the image was taken, so that the sound of the explosion is delayed with respect to the formation of the mushroom cloud. In all subsequent views the sound is electronically reworked, first to synchronize with the image of the explosion in the image and then to reorganize and abstract. These reiterations and recompositions of an ultrafamiliar image pose important questions about the iconization of historical events.

The introduction of high-quality portable sound recording with Nagra III NP recorders in 1962 was a boon both to 16mm portable news recording and to sound work in avant-garde practice. Increasingly, avant-garde filmmakers composed and recorded their own sound, and live recorded sound quickly became its own way to innovate. This meant avoiding the patterns of sound editing exemplified by the more conventional Hollywood sound tracks, although isolating and emphasizing those more innovative moments found in Hollywood and world cinema would become an inspiration. Certainly the sounds and editing practices that artists were hearing in Italian neorealism, in newly imported Japanese films, and in the French New Wave could be seen as forming a new sound context for these inventive artists, who tended to flock to cities where they could see such films and each other's works.

Yet Ken Jacobs mines his antique record collection and a reflexive voice-over in *Little Stabs at Happiness* (1959–1963). To create the sections, one of which includes his own voice-over commentary, Jacobs joined 100-foot rolls, which he says "timed well with music on old 78s."[7] In his *Blonde Cobra* (1959–1963), the performative chaos that was Jack Smith unfurls on both image and sound tracks, which are nonetheless kept disjunct, as emphasized by the black leader that punctuates the images while the voice continues. Both image and sound free-flow toward an imaginative self-invention sliding along the edge of despair. Further aleatory, further antic, was the following instruction to the projectionist: "VERY IMPORTANT: A live radio, loud and clear, is to interject talk two times." Compare Barbara Rubin's *Christmas on Earth* (1963): "A radio must be hooked up to your P. A. system with a nice cross-section of psychic tumult, like an AM rock station turned on and played loud."[8]

[6] Rebecca Marie Doran Eaton, "*Unheard Minimalisms: The Functions of the Minimalist Technique in Film Scores*" (PhD diss., University of Texas at Austin, 2008).

[7] Ken Jacobs, "Blonde Cobra," in *New York Filmmakers' Cooperative Catalog No. 7* (New York: New American Cinema Group, 1989), 268.

[8] Barbara Rubin, "Christmas On Earth," New York Filmmakers' Cooperative Catalog No. 7 (New York: New American Cinema Group, 1989), 416.

Sound events could be tied to minimalism, repetition, duration, phasing, and droning on one hand, or to excessive layering, density, and a richness verging on cacophony on the other. Peter Kubelka's *Unsere Afrikareise* (1966), an intense 12-minute montage distilled from 3 hours of actuality footage of Europeans hunting big game in Africa, is sound-tracked with a staccato of animal noises, German voices, rifle shots, running water, and brief snatches of crooners and classical music. All of these sounds can be associated with images that we see in the film, and at moments we hear sounds that go directly with what we are seeing. Yet this is only incidental; the film as a whole juxtaposes a montage of sounds with a montage of images for a memorably jarring account of postcolonial tourism.

Michael Snow famously described *Wavelength* (1967) as "a continuous zoom which takes 45 minutes to go from its widest field to its smallest and final field."[9] Yet the meditative calm this suggests is inapt for an image track alive with abrupt cuts and lighting changes, red frames, purple frames, fogged frames, color negative, colored gels, frames jumping in the gate, end-roll light flares, superimpositions, and dissolves. It is a little more fitting for a sound track that begins with synch sound (traffic noise, men moving a bookcase, a woman's footsteps, "Strawberry Fields Forever" on a tinny radio), then switches after about 8 minutes to an electronic sine wave, gradually rising from 50 to 12,000 cycles per second. This tone continues to the end of the film, though it is twice interrupted by returns to synch sound, first for some scraping and banging that can be interpreted as a shooting, then for a phone call in which a woman says she is frightened by the dead body on the floor. As early commentators pointed out, *Wavelength* contains the elements of a murder mystery, but these are displaced by the substitution of sine wave for synch and literally excluded by the journey of the lens across the room, so that the film in effect stages the repudiation of conventional narrative by the avant-garde.

Percussive, aggressive sound finds its champion in Paul Sharits, first in his *Ray Gun Virus* (1966), which amplifies the sound of the projector itself into a static-loaded buzz and instructs the projectionist to turn the sound to maximum. Sharits's *Shutter Interface* was first seen in 1975, then not revived until 2001, in a two-screen version for the Whitney Museum's *Into the Light* exhibition, and again in 2009, in a full four-projector installation at New York's Greene Naftali Gallery. The four projectors, placed side-by-side on large black pedestals, project partially overlapping frames of different colors, creating color mixing that results in a horizontal band of changing hues on infinite loop. Interspersed into each filmstrip are single black frames, creating punctuating flashes. Each projector also offers its own high-frequency tone, with the sound blending into a varied drone, as the image blends into an exuberant strip of varied light.

Filmmakers such as Hollis Frampton, Yvonne Rainer, and Su Friedrich based some of their most remarkable sound track work on playing with voices. Frampton's *Zorns Lemma* (1970) cleverly uses the reading of texts in both its opening and closing sections

[9] Michael Snow, "A Statement on Wavelength for the Experimental Film Festival at Knokke-le-Zoute," *Film Culture* 46 (1967): 1.

to bookend its long silent central section, a famous, highly subsegmented montage that uses an alphabet to organize a series of twenty-four sequences of gestural images. The performance of both verbal texts (*The Bay State Primer* and Robert Grosseteste's "On Light: The Ingression of Forms") abstracts the words as spoken sound elements, turning enunciation into sound composition in a verbal scansion of rhythmic form, leaving the signification ironic and floating. Yvonne Rainer's *Journeys from Berlin/1971* (1980) uses a casual political dialogue between a man and a woman, displaced over its quite disjunct visual narration. Here the conversation also floats, though it simultaneously anchors the images by providing a debate on the historical context presented in the film in the form of textual inserts annotating the activities of the Baader-Meinhof group. Su Friedrich's *Sink or Swim* (1990) uses a marvelously inventive and poetic narration for its voicing of memories by a daughter of her father's words and actions. If voice-over can be too bland, too heavy-handed when simply added to a film, the alternative these films represent is to treat the voice as a compositional element that troubles the categories of poetics on the one hand, and music or song on the other. Sound composition that uses the spoken word in all its textual complexity calls on the type of theorization Trevor Wishart's *On Sonic Art* suggests when it looks at the verbal as an example of music less dependent on pitch as its defining parameter.

Abigail Child's sound tracks are marked by excess and overlay, as well as second-by-second precision of juxtaposition between sound collage and image collage. Child's sounds are active, disjunct, independent, cutting into the immediate associations one might have with her images. A combination of improvisation and sampling, her sound tracks mock and interrupt. "Edgy, sharp, ironic" are terms that Maureen Turim has used to describe Child's sound, noting that *Mayhem* (1987) "draws its fetishes comparatively, cutting them together to ask why these images draw us in despite their displacement."[10] *Mayhem*'s meta-commentary includes a climactic scream that lacks any narrative motivation; the scream seems to hover over the entire film as a marker of intensity removed from any specific precipitating cause, but calling on us to pay attention. One line in *Covert Action* (1984), "My goal is to disarm my movie," may be key to understanding how Child's sound tracks work. They can be a violent assault on the listener, with antecedents in Sharits's most imposing efforts to make sound confrontational. Yet disarming such violence as play is also part of Child's strategy; she avoids the insistent repetition and drone of past sonic scores in favor of variation, including beguiling rhythms and musical cuts that lure more than they attack. That this is an intensive sound space, layered so densely that repeated listening highlights entirely different components, is also part of the bet she is making.

In the late 1960s, early video coupled direct sound with low-resolution images and difficulties in editing, technical properties that actively informed sound/image

[10] Maureen Turim, "A Look at the Violence of Female Desire," in *Women and Experimental Filmmaking*, ed. Jean Patrolle and Virgina Wright Wexman (Urbana: University of Illinois Press, 2005), 79.

innovations such as Bruce Nauman's *Stamping in the Studio*, *Bouncing in the Corner no. 1*, and *Bouncing in the Corner no. 2* (all 1968), in which simple performed actions provide the sound beats that punctuate the intriguingly framed movements of the artist's body. Here the performative event is as much a sound event as it is a conceptual movement of the framed body. Nauman's *Lip Sync* (1969) contests the live synchronization typically associated with video by combining an upside-down close-up of the artist's mouth repeating the words "lip-synch" with sound that remains ironically out of phase. The comic literalization is furthered by the fact that at the beginning of each iteration of the phrase, the artist touches his lip with his tongue.

Lest this aesthetic be misunderstood as a mere artifact of early video technology, we should note its continuation in the late 1970s and 1980s by artists such as Bill Viola and Gary Hill. Hill's *Soundings* (1979) studies a series of procedures that affect the skin of an audio speaker playing back the sound of the artist's voice. His *Meditations* (1986) also focuses on an audio speaker, onto which his hand sprinkles sand, wedding sonic to visual transformations. In other words, artists' video revitalizes a minimalism in which the sound event and the image event are not only closely tied to direct recording, but can be the exploration of a causal relationship, with the sound event the raison d'être of the image. As Bill Viola has said, "I have always recorded simultaneous sound and picture, which you can do with video as opposed to film; it's a part of the same machine."[11]

Histories of video art often begin with the first availability of video equipment to artists in the mid-1960s. Often cited is Nam June Paik's fall 1965 purchase of a Sony Portapak, though as Tom Sherman has pointed out,[12] what Paik is supposed to have done with this camera (shoot the New York visit of the Pope from the back of a taxi) would not have been possible with a 1965 Portapak, which still needed to be plugged into an AC power outlet. So at least one of the creation myths of American video art is apocryphal, or as Gene Gort suggests, can be understood as the jape of a Fluxus artist.[13] Less frequently mentioned, though much less disputable, and as a remedial lesson in sound–image relations more aesthetically memorable, is the early combination of film and video in Andy Warhol's *Outer and Inner Space*, shot in August 1965 using an Auricon film camera and video equipment on loan from Phillips Norelco. The Auricon was a sound-on-film camera; that is, it recorded optical sound onto the same filmstrip as the images, and was typically used for TV news.

Outer and Inner Space was Warhol's first double-screen presentation and is made of two 33-minute rolls of 16mm film, which both show twenty-two-year-old Edie Sedgwick sitting and talking in front of her own prerecorded image on a TV monitor. The glamorous but troubled Sedgwick, who was "girl of the year" in 1965 but died of an overdose in 1971, is seen on the monitor to the left of the 16mm frame, in profile

[11] http://www.bbc.co.uk/radio3/johntusainterview/viola_transcript.shtml (accessed November 14, 2012).

[12] Tom Sherman, "The Premature Birth of Video Art," at www.experimentaltvcenter.org (accessed July 27, 2010).

[13] Gene Gort, e-mail to Michael Walsh, July 30, 2010.

and in tight close-up; her heavily made-up eyes look up and out of frame to the right. On the right of the frame is the more frontal filmed Edie, chandelier earrings dangling, also mostly in close-up, though awkward adjustments of a zoom lens create some variations in apparent camera distance. The face of the filmed Edie cuts across the left edge of the TV image, so that the TV Edie seems to be speaking directly into the right ear of the filmed Edie. The film image is starkly lit, without much fill, like much of Warhol's cinema of the 1960s; the TV Edie is brighter, paler, and larger, and subject at times to electronic distortion. When the two rolls are projected side-by-side, the result is a kind of frieze in which the four faces of Edie figure and follow each other across the space of a widescreen ratio; the four eyelines never meet, but do align in parallelograms across the frame, while the four voices chatter away, mostly unintelligibly.

Warhol's paintings of the 1960s were mediations of mediations—his gridded and serial images of figures like Jackie Kennedy and Elizabeth Taylor began life as press photographs; they were transmitted on wire services, printed in newspapers, stenciled for silk-screening, and then squeegeed onto canvas. Like these, *Outer and Inner Space* presents an image of an image, a film of a video, an optical sound recording of an electronic sound recording, that seems by duplication to comment on or recede into itself. The sound is distorted and difficult to follow, so much so that one programmer has hired a speech therapist to make a transcript.[14] But even without such help, we can make out some of what is said: "I can't even remember what I did today... about ten o'clock... I think we're gonna.... How can I think about clothes or anything else.... O dear... it could be done... it's just an idea... we had a better time than anyone else." However, even when we can understand the words, we never know what is being talked about. One reason is that Sedgwick is apparently in dialogue with someone off-camera, which is to say that we are hearing only one side of a conversation. Second, the sound is self-interfering. As Callie Angell has pointed out,[15] there are moments when all four Edies are speaking at the same time; we are listening to two simultaneous sound tracks, both of which also contain re-recorded TV monitor sound, all in glorious mono. Occasionally one of the Edies is actually in sync with what we are hearing. According to Angell, the audio levels of both the video monitor and the film camera were being adjusted during shooting, so part of the problem is sheer audibility. Anyone who has seen other Warhol sound films of the period knows very well the gossipy triviality typical of the "superstars," so there is a sense in which it doesn't much matter that we can't really understand the film's sound. In another sense, our incomprehension is the point; it is wholly characteristic of Warhol that a technical limit should read as a critique of conventional cinematic practice. This "doesn't matter" element in Warhol has always bothered some, but is clearly intrinsic to his work. Interviewed by *Tape Recording* magazine

[14] Lisa Dillon Edgitt, "What Edie Said in *Outer and Inner Space*," in *From Stills to Motion and Back Again* (Vancouver: Presentation House Gallery, 2003), 27–39.

[15] Callie Angell, "Doubling the Screen: Andy Warhol's *Outer and Inner Space*," *Millenium Film Journal* 38 (2002), at http://mfj-online.org/journalPages/MFJ38/angell.html (accessed July 20, 2010).

in 1965, Warhol seems not to have even known that videotape can record a broadcast signal without a camera.[16] *Outer and Inner Space* was shown a few times in the 1960s, then vanished from circulation for nearly 30 years; it is one of the few newly canonical films to have thus far emerged from the joint project of the Whitney and the Museum of Modern Art to restore and reissue Warhol's films.

If Warhol's first use of video is one way of dating the beginning of American video art, the reissue of his films coincides with another turning point, less widely recognized but arguably as important: the moment in the late 1990s at which it ceased to be exceptional, in fact became routine, to go into galleries and museums and find motion picture or projected image work on show. This development was simultaneous with the emergence of both new media (i.e., digital) art and of what Eric de Bruyn has called "the museum of attractions," full of screens, large-scale projection rooms, and competing sound tracks.[17] This moment also saw the rise of figures like Douglas Gordon, Stan Douglas, Janet Cardiff, and Tacita Dean, whose work is inconceivable without film and video, but who are not primarily understood as filmmakers and/or video artists. Something comparable had happened in the 1980s with the emergence of a postmodern photography that replaced the modernist idea of a "photographer" with that of "an artist working with photography" (Louise Lawler, Cindy Sherman, Barbara Kruger).

The place of sound in this new world of installation is, as noted previously, multiple and various. Some work retains the code of silence characteristic of Brakhage, whereas other pieces verge on sound art per se. In between is work whose sound is carefully crafted and essential to meaning, yet not significantly different from what can be heard in contemporary commercial film sound tracks. The next few pages focus on artists who consciously engage with the modern environment of recorded sound (records, radio, movie sound tracks). These are the artists who cover the gallery floor with vinyl records (Marclay), or redeploy the sound and image tracks of Hitchcock (Gordon), or reimagine the neighborhood movie theaters of the mid-twentieth century (Cardiff), or document the shutdown of the last Kodak film-manufacturing plant in Europe (Dean). These are the artists for whom twentieth-century sound cinema constitutes what Peter Scheldhjal has called "modern antiquity."[18]

The code of silence is exemplified in Douglas Gordon's much-discussed *24 Hour Psycho* (1993), which differs from its Hitchcock original (1960) by playing at two rather than twenty-four frames a second, being on video rather than on film, being projected onto a translucent screen in the middle of the room so that the viewer can walk around behind and see the images inverted left to right, and being completely silent. As if to complement this, *Feature Film* (1999), another Gordon creation, extracts or subtracts

[16] Quoted in J. Hoberman, "Nobody's Land: *Inner and Outer Space*," in *From Stills to Motion and Back Again* (Vancouver: Presentation House Gallery, 2003), 22.

[17] Eric de Bruyn, "The Museum of Attractions: Marcel Broodthaers and the *Section Cinéma*," in *Art and the Moving Image: A Critical Reader*, ed. Tanya Leighton, 112–121. London: Tate/Afterall, 2008).

[18] Peter Scheldhjal, "Lessness: The Whitney Biennial," *New Yorker*, March 17, 2008, at www.newyorker.com (accessed July 27, 2010).

the score of Hitchcock's *Vertigo* (1959). This piece exists as a book with accompanying CD, as a 35mm theatrical film, and as a video installation. In the last, we see on one wall close-ups of the face and hands of James Conlon conducting the Paris Opera Orchestra in a performance of Bernard Hermann's music. On another wall is a video projection of *Vertigo* itself. The sound from the musical performance is dominant, but when the film reaches an unscored sequence the orchestra falls silent, and we can hear the dialogue and sound effects from the original film; meanwhile, the camera in the concert film cuts away from the conductor and roams the hall. Gordon is a film-educated artist whose work has used elements from Preminger's *Whirlpool* (1949) and Scorsese's *Taxi Driver* (1976), who has acknowledged both his debt to and the elusiveness of Warhol with *Bootleg Empire* (1997), and who has had the structural wit to simply superimpose *The Song of Bernadette* (1943) onto *The Exorcist* (1973). The result, *Between Darkness and Light* (1997), suggests that the two are in some sense the same film—both the child who sees the Virgin and the child who is possessed by the devil are ringed around by concerned family and clergy. But it is the pair of Hitchcock homages, the one suppressing the film's sound, the other singling it out, that are most relevant to our topic.

Close to sound art per se is Christian Marclay, much of whose career has directly engaged with the materiality of recorded sound. Marclay has played a turntable with a Jimi Hendrix record on it as though it were a guitar, he has brought people together to "play" vinyl records by scratching them with their fingers and rubbing them on their clothes, he has collaged album covers, he has built sculptural cubes out of vinyl records, he has wrapped a violin in magnetic recording tape, he has created scores from musical notation found on wrapping paper and T-shirts, he has posted music paper on the streets and treated any marks people made on it as a score, and he has paved the floor of the gallery with CDs as well as with vinyl discs. In his video piece *Looking for Love* (2008), we see an extreme close-up of a stylus that is dropped onto a variety of vinyl records that all have the word "love" in the lyrics. We stay for no more than 90 seconds with any one record, skipping repeatedly back and forth over phrases like "let me love you," "can't quit your love," "they say that falling in love is wonderful," and "you shouldn't have laughed at my love." We hear from Marvin Gaye, Roxy Music, James Brown, and the Bee Gees. The fact that it is so easy to find records that contain the word "love" is one of the deadpan points of the piece.

The much more antic *Video Quartet* (2002) is similarly easy to understand in principle, but cuts and flows quickly enough to be dizzying in practice. In this swirling, stuttering, 14-minute, four-screen montage of scenes from more than seven hundred films of people playing musical instruments, singing, tap-dancing, or sometimes just making a sound (knocking on a door, screaming), all sound is synch, and all four sound tracks are heard at once. The piece is structured by topic (classical orchestras, scat, tap, pop, pianos, harps, trumpets, bugles, voices) and by associational montage, both visual and aural. At moments the four screens all show piano players or all show harpists, but more typically images and sounds tumble one on top of the next. Footage of Arthur Rubinstein, Mahalia Jackson, Maria Callas, Dizzy Gillespie, Ella Fitzgerald, Charlotte Moorman, and Jimi Hendrix in live performance is intercut with fictional portrayals of actual musicians (Forrest Whitaker as Charlie Parker, Dennis Quaid as Jerry Lee Lewis), with actors portraying fictional musicians (Denzel Washington as Bleek Gilliam in *Mo' Better Blues* [1990]), and with musical moments from fictional nonmusicians (Dustin Hoffman as Ratso Rizzo playing the xylophone in *Midnight Cowboy* [1969]). Operatic divas are aurally matched with the scream of Sissy Spacek from the climactic scene in *Carrie* (1976), as well as with performance footage of Cab Calloway and Johnny Rotten. Eric Dolphy on flute is cheek-by-jowl with Sean Penn on guitar; Jo Ann Greer's voicing of "Bewitched, Bothered, and Bewildered" from *Pal Joey* (1957), surely a sly commentary on our experience of the piece, is matched with the finger-popping youths from *West Side Story* (1961); the banjo and guitar conversation from *Deliverance* (1972) is simultaneous with Harpo Marx, the whistling of a bellboy, and what seems to be a demonstration of the theremin.

Structured by topic and by associational editing, *Video Quartet* is punctuated by curiosities (Fred Astaire behind a drum kit) and sight gags (a woman holding her hands over her ears). But it has a clear center of gravity in classic Hollywood cinema. This is even more the case in Marclay's earlier *Telephones* (1995), another montage piece that freely combines clips from dozens of movies from the 1930s to the 1980s, but looks to have been made up exclusively of Hollywood films. The seven-and-a-half minute *Telephones* has a basic throughline, beginning with Martin Balsam in the phone booth from *Psycho* (1960) and ending with Barbara Stanwyck in the phone booth from *Sorry, Wrong Number* (1948). In between, we get glimpses of Tippi Hedren, Joan Fontaine, Cary Grant, Whoopi Goldberg, Charles Bronson, Tom Hanks, Clark Gable, Katharine Hepburn, and many others. At the outset we hear something like twenty "hellos," followed by half a dozen "yeahs" and "yesses." There follow a few names ("Felix," "Dave," "Jenny," "Jeff") and a hint of melodrama (mention of a dead girl, dialogue from an intense woman who can think only of the one she has called). A series of shots of characters listening to the person on the other end lead us to just one "Good night" and one "Bye-bye" and (at the very end) a couple more "Hellos" (the sort we understand as indicating that the other person has hung up). The picture track favors melodramatic shots of characters crossing the room toward the phone as though some matter of life and death is at stake, close-ups of ringing phones, medium shots of people on the phone in bed, dozens of medium close-ups of talking heads, and about two dozen shots of people putting the phone down. The fractured conversation is comic but also ominous, with Jimmy Stewart from *Rear Window* (1954) apparently speaking with Geena Davis from *The Accidental Tourist* (1988), while Clint Eastwood from *Play Misty for Me* (1971), Brian O'Halloran from *Clerks* (1994), and the emergency operator from *The Shining* (1980) all hang up in quick succession.

At the time of writing, Marclay has begun showing a truly monumental montage project, the 24-hour-long *The Clock* (2010), made up of thousands of movie clips that either show clocks or contain spoken mentions of the time. This piece is synchronized with standard time wherever it is shown. That is, when it is 2:11 a.m. in *The Clock*, it is actually 2:11 a.m. in the screening room—though of course, what is meant by "actually 2:11 a.m." is just the question; Marclay immerses us in what Bergson might call the difference between mathematical time and pure duration, or what Lacan might call the difference between reality (time as conventionally measured) and the real (time as an impossible beyond). *The Clock* is a festival of false eyeline matches, false action matches, and false audio cues, assembling moments from instantly recognizable films (*Metropolis* [1927], *Rear Window* [1954], *Taxi Driver* [1976]) and less familiar ones (*The Gentle Gunman* [1952], *A Private's Progress* [1956], *Buffalo 66* [1998]). Events in *The Clock* are sequenced to the conventional day (at 5:00 p.m. we see people leaving work; at 1:00 a.m. we see insomniacs turning on bedside lamps), and they faithfully follow the story time of the original—that is, a representation of 8:03 a.m. is shown at 8:03 a.m. in *The Clock*, though in many cases (e.g., interiors), it would be easy enough to substitute an original from 8:03 p.m. Thematically appropriate sound bites emphasize lateness, earliness, and urgency, while the piece plays with obviously apposite titles (*Chimes at Midnight*, *Rock Around the Clock*) and sequences (a bungled attempt by British Army officers to synchronize watches). With an average shot length of 3 to 4 seconds, *The Clock* is paced like a feature and is projected in a 1.85 to 1 ratio. But these factors, which recall theatrical exhibition of films, are countered by the fact that the audience is seated on rows of couches, evocative of the domestic experience of television.

Also close to sound art is Janet Cardiff. Her *40 Part Motet* (2001) reconfigures the "Spem in Alium" of Thomas Tallis by providing a single speaker for each of the voices in the piece, with the listener free to walk among them. Her various sound walks (e.g., Rome 1998, São Paulo 1998, London 1999) send visitors wearing headphones on preplanned itineraries with Cardiff's recorded voice in their ears. Her *Opera for a Small Room* (2005) consists of a tumbledown shack full of record players and stacks of vinyl records, its protagonist represented by a megaphone and a shadow. *Feedback* (2004) consists of a guitar amplifier, wah-wah pedal, and speaker; when the gallery-goer steps on the pedal, she or he is blasted by the sound of "The Star-Spangled Banner" played in the style of Jimi Hendrix. This last is a one-liner, but for anyone who has ever played air guitar, which is to say most males born after 1945, it is a good one.

The Muriel Lake Incident, jointly credited to Cardiff and her partner, George Bures Miller, consists of an unpainted wooden box on metal legs, with a rectangular window allowing spectators to look inside, and three pairs of headphones. The interior is a miniature movie theater, in matte black, with rows of empty seats, lengths of picture frame to represent balconies, an oakleaf rosette above the proscenium, and a 20-inch TV set showing images in black and white. Like so many video installations, *The Muriel Lake Incident* is looped, replaying every 7 minutes or so, and the specifics of the design recall the classic Hollywood era of continuous performances in neighborhood movie theaters.

The headphones provide sound from two sources. Much of what we hear (car engines, ringing telephones, ominous piano notes, various elements of dialogue) is synched with the actions and characters that we see on the screen, but another whole register of sound (crunching popcorn, coughing, shushing, and half a dozen remarks from a female voice) belongs to an unseen audience. Perhaps we are expected to populate the empty theater with an imaginary audience; perhaps we are expected to imagine ourselves as part of that the audience. Add to this that the three dozen shots that we see on the screen are economical and evocative rather than redundant and direct, and the result is that it probably takes two or three run-throughs to piece together the basic scenario.

Yet the fiction is not complex. At dawn, a couple on the run (played by the makers) set off for a house by the eponymous lake. Next a ponytailed hit man is woken by a phone call and agrees to "take care" of the fugitives. At the lake house the woman dances in slow motion to a beaten-up LP on an ancient portable record player. The woman is in a black slip and heels, framed from the shoulders down, and the record is piano, violin, and vocal, a tango or gypsy sound. Outside, by a driftwood fire on the lake beach, is a man in a cowboy hat, whose musing voice-over and handgun suggest that he is a bodyguard. Cut to the hit man in profile, advancing through the woods toward the fire.

All this is like a new wave take on film noir; Muriel Lake is said to be near Cardiff's childhood home, but it may just as well be intended to evoke Resnais. The opening shot in a moving car, the dreamlike dance, and the musings of the bodyguard are suffused with romanticism, though this is undercut by the no-nonsense demeanor of the hit man. So we are moving toward a fairly conventional climax. Now, however, comes a twist. The shooting that we are anticipating on the screen in fact seems to happen in the audience. That is, the woman whom we have heard asking if there is any more popcorn, commenting that she's not sure if this is the right film, remarking that the slow dance reminds her of a dream she had the night before, expressing her concern about a strange man seated nearby, and finally being shushed by another spectator, ends by saying, "I'm going down now; he's supposed to be seated in the second row." The fire on the beach suddenly becomes a fire in the gate of the projector, and the invisible audience hoots with dismay. We hear shots, shouts, running feet, and finally a man's laugh.

The ambiguity here is studied; it is possible that there is shooting in both the film and the theater, as in *The Man Who Knew Too Much* (1934 and 1956). But there is little doubt that there is shooting in the theater; we can't otherwise make sense of the sounds of shouts and the running feet. In other words, the fiction has shifted registers; the real action is not with the on-screen characters that we have been watching, but with the unseen characters that we have been hearing. The woman in the audience, who has been set up as talkative, as vulnerable, as partly annoying and partly endearing, as more active than the typical moviegoer but still basically passive, turns out to be an unlikely femme fatale, in distant conformity with noir conventions. *The Muriel Lake Incident*, like a number of other Cardiff pieces, plays a sophisticated game with the imaginary investments of the spectator—so much so that we need to explain that "spectator" here means the viewer of the piece, not the woman in the audience within the fiction.

The piece also condenses a whole history of image cultures. The lengths of picture frame that form the proscenium suggest painting, while the TV monitor simultaneously evokes both the Academy ratio of classic Hollywood cinema and the postclassical experience of watching movies on TV. The woman's chattiness underscores this point, because she is that annoying person who brings into the theater behavior more appropriate to watching TV at home. The design of the theater is spare, yet the wooden rosettes on walls and ceiling are just decoration enough to suggest that we may be in the kind of neighborhood theater that took some of its architectural cues from the movie palaces.

Also returning us to the neighborhood movie theater is the Bruce High Quality Foundation (BHQF). Specializing in a satirical version of institutional critique, BHQF is a Brooklyn arts collective whose members choose to remain anonymous. "Bruce High Quality" is a fiction, a "social sculptor" who is supposed to have died on 9/11. Since 2004 BHQF has staged a number of interventions. In 2005, when a group representing the estate of Robert Smithson posthumously realized his idea of towing a floating island of parkland around the island of Manhattan, BHQF followed with their own boat, carrying a model version of the orange gates installed in Central Park that year by Christo and Jeanne-Claude. The BHQF piece for the 2010 Whitney Biennial, *We Like America and America Likes Us*, was a montage reminiscent of Bruce Conner, Josef Beuys, and Ant Farm, projected from the interior of an ambulance/hearse onto a widescreen windshield. The sound was a female voice-over discussing "America" as though it were a problematic family member or personal partner.

But the BHQF piece in which sound is most salient and effective is *Isle of the Dead*, their contribution to "This World and Nearer Ones," a Creative Time project for Governors Island in New York harbor in the summer of 2009. Governors Island was for two hundred years a base for the U.S. Army and Coast Guard and has only recently been ceded to the city of New York; thus it has a lost-in-time feeling, where 5 minutes from Wall Street one can walk through picturesque village streets and greens. BHQF showed its piece in the island's own small cinema, an army standard-plan, wood-portico, brick building from 1936. BHQF outlines the piece thus: "The basic arc of *Isle of the Dead* is that the art world has died (literalizing its economic death), that it rises from the dead in search of an alternative space (Governors Island), and that, once installed there, it spends its time looking at its own past nostalgically."[19]

The piece begins with broadly comic newspaper headlines about the market crash of 2008 ("Art World Collapses: Hundreds Perish") and moves on to show the corpse-strewn exteriors of the Guggenheim and Metropolitan Museums. One corpse is reanimated as a zombie, and in a mini-dress and silver heels wanders the lower Manhattan art districts of Chelsea and the East Village. She boards the ferry for Governors Island and slowly makes her way to the very theater in which the film is being shown, now filled with six hundred extras face-painted Halloween-style as the living dead. So far so cleverly self-referential; anyone in the audience is by implication a zombie of the art world, dutifully trudging around the venues. So we are hardly surprised when a video-within-the-video appears on the screen. This is a "morning in America" montage with kids, dogs, fast-motion blooms, a clip of Morgan Freeman from *The Shawshank Redemption* (1994), and the smiling face of Barack Obama, all cued to music appropriated from Carter Burwell's score for *Miller's Crossing* (1990), itself adapted from the Irish traditional "Lament for Limerick." This music is sardonic in the original, because its keening pipes and swelling orchestrations seem more appropriate to an uplifting television documentary on immigration than to the Coen brothers' vicious gangsters.

[19] Bruce High Quality Foundation, "Isle of the Dead," http://vimeo.com/7311523 (accessed June 5, 2013).

But the most effective use of sound is yet to come. The video-within-the-video comes to an end, and we return to scanning the zombie audience. Slow bass drums, synth washes, single notes on the piano, gongs and snares, surging string sections, and six hundred amateur voices start to sing along uncertainly to "Summer of '69," Bryan Adams's sub-Springsteen heartland rock hit of 1985. This is perfectly pitched, its funereal arrangement and hesitant singing both ludicrous and moving, and surely ranks among the great pop song détournements, along with the Sid Vicious version of "My Way" and David Lynch's appropriation of Roy Orbison's "In Dreams" for *Blue Velvet* (1986). *Isle of the Dead* (name of both an 1880 Böcklin painting and a 1945 Lewton/Tourneur film) is an antinostalgia trip, explained by the artists in one interview as a critique of the way in which the market crash led the art world to anticipate a return of practices encountered in the wake of previous crashes, when in fact new circumstances require a new kind of response.[20] The contradiction here is that BHQF, in this and in other pieces, seem most adept precisely in conjuring a past.

Sound in installations, and even in single channel works shown on monitors or projected, extends into a space beyond the individual work, so that some installations need rooms of museums or galleries entirely devoted to them. They reconstitute the movie theater inside the museum, yet often only accommodate some fifteen to twenty spectators at a time. That many of these spectators are transient, rather than patiently watching the entire work, is often another factor of reception; sound, along with fragments of visual narrative, beckons the audience, suggesting that they stay with the work longer than they otherwise might.

Such is the case with the remarkable sound work of three installation artists with whom this chapter closes: Bill Viola, Eija-Lisa Athila, and Issac Julien. Viola's large-scale works on simple dramatic actions of the human body, sometimes articulated against a landscape or a built environment, sometimes against an abstract ground, are still accompanied, as were his first videos, by sounds matching the actions depicted: water rushing, fire crackling, footsteps, and the like. These are comparable to what Hollywood calls "sound effects" of discrete diegetic actions. However, since Viola's actions are reduced to their isolation and singularity and staged against silence, and the sound effects are heavily amplified and sometimes electronically reworked, these sound events become dramatic swooshes and swirls, sounds that seem to be worlds in and of themselves, punctuating the visuals. In *Five Angels for the Millennium* (2001) the visual events tied to the appearance of each angel are timed in alternation with the others, so that the sounds of each angel departing, ascending, engaged with birth, fire, or creation, pull us toward the climactic instance in that angel's visual evolution.

[20] "Bruce High Quality Foundation: Isle of the Dead," *Creative Time*, at http://www.youtube.com/user/creativetimenewyork (accessed July 27, 2010).

Eija-Lisa Ahtila's installations explore disjunct narratives, often linked to interior states of mental disturbance or fantasy, across multiple screens, so that two, three, or four different projected images give us varied views on an event or different related events. Sound can move from one screen to another, or conversely float over all of them, disembodied. Sound-on of a particular image is sound-off for the others. Attention in her installations is thus constantly in relay, moving between one sound-image and another. In *The Wind* (2002) the central female character suffers from sound hallucinations; inside her house, she is haunted by sounds from distant elsewheres.

Architecture or landscape, and the movement of figures in space (dancers, actors, green-screened goddesses) play a prominent role in Issac Julien's recent installations. Some sounds in his *Baltimore* (2002) seem to have a strong relationship to Viola's sounds, with the piece opening in the Walters Art Museum on the sound of Vanessa Myrie's high-heeled boots striking a marble floor and echoing in the empty interior courtyard, while three separate images relay elements of this action, and Melvin Van Peebles is seen watching her. Electronically generated tones begin to intervene extradiegetically, prefiguring the action shifting to the imaginary floating of the Myrie character through space. Julien rechoreographs the gestures of the black action genre, reworking its cinematic sound into selective, emphatic installation sound.

In the nine-screen *Ten Thousand Waves* (2010), Julien begins with actuality sound of British emergency services receiving a call that a group of Chinese shellfish pickers have been cut off by a rapidly rising tide; only one of twenty-three survives. The topic connects with Julien's established interest in global migration (his own family left St. Lucia for Britain, a journey traced in *Paradise Omeros* [2002]) and is the starting point for a physically beautiful reverie on an imaginary China, from the mountain valleys and flying goddess-warriors of a mythological past, through the streetcars and cheongsams of the 1930s, to the spectacular cityscapes of twenty-first-century Shanghai. The beatific presence of Maggie Cheung suggests contexts of Chinese popular cinema and the films of Wong Kar-Wai, while the laying bare of the devices of wired flight (green screen, steadicam, cables, and technicians) points in a more Brechtian direction. The sound, as in *Paradise Omeros*, is a mix of poetic voices; ambient tonal music; and a selective, seductive synch that isolates and emphasizes certain sounds (wind, waves, streetcar wheels, and bells).

Installations such as these of Viola, Ahtila, and Julien use sound in ways that recall our filmic experience of sound effects and voices, but also use fragmentation, isolation, spatial placement, and repetition in ways unique to installation. Placement of the sound event and the re-sounding of the sound in space finally is the common element that beckons the spectator/auditor. Sound in the artist's film, video, and installation pointedly selects events, often self-consciously aware of their electronic reproduction. As it plays out in relationship to visual space, the sound echoes with contemporary theories of the way the time-based arts work.

References

Angell, Callie. "Doubling the Screen: Andy Warhol's *Outer and Inner Space*." *Millennium Film Journal* 38 (2002), edited by Bill Jeffries, at http://mfj-online.org/journalPages/MFJ38/angell.html (accessed July 20, 2010).

Angell, Callie. "Andy Warhol: Outer and Inner Space." In *From Stills to Motion and Back Again. Texts on Andy Warhol's Screen Tests and Outer and Inner Space*, 13–17. Vancouver, B.C.: Presentation House Gallery, 2003.

Autelitano, Alice, ed. *The Cinematic Experience: Film, Contemporary Art, Museum*. Udine, Italy: Camponotto, 2010.

Badiou, Alain. *Being and Event*. Translated by Oliver Feltham. London: Continuum, 2005.

Badiou, Alain. "The Event in Deleuze." *Parrhesia* 2 (2007): 37–44, at www.parrhesiajournal.org/parrhesia02/parrhesia02_badiou02.pdf (accessed August 17, 2011).

Beck, Jay, and Tony Grajeda, eds. *Lowering the Boom: Critical Studies in Film Sound*. Urbana: University of Illinois Press, 2008.

Bloemheuvel, Marente, ed. *Cinéma Cinéma: Contemporary Art and the Cinematic Experience*. Eindhoven: Stedelijk Van Abbemuseum; Rotterdam: NAi Publishers, 1999.

Brakhage, Stan, and Robert A. Haller. *Brakhage Scrapbook: Collected Writings, 1964–1980*. New Paltz, N.Y.: Documentext, 1982.

Bruce High Quality Foundation. "Isle of the Dead", at http://vimeo.com/7311523 (accessed June 5, 2013).

Conrad, Tony. "Inside the Dream Syndicate." *Film Culture* 41 (1966): 5–8.

Creative Time. "Bruce High Quality Foundation: Isle of the Dead," at http://www.youtube.com/user/creativetimenewyork (accessed July 27, 2010).

De Bruyn, Eric. "The Museum of Attractions: Marcel Broodthaers and the *Section Cinéma*." In *Art and the Moving Image: A Critical Reader*, edited by Tanya Leighton, 112–121. London: Tate/Afterall, 2008.

Dyson, Frances. *Sounding New Media: Immersion and Embodiment in the Arts and Culture*. Berkeley: University of California Press, 2009.

Eaton, Rebecca Marie Doran. "Unheard Minimalisms: The Functions of Minimalist Technique in Film Scores." PhD diss., University of Texas at Austin, 2008.

Edgitt, Lisa Dillon. "What Edie Said in *Outer and Inner Space*." In *From Stills to Motion and Back Again*, 27–39 (Vancouver, B.C.: Presentation House Gallery, 2003).

Hoberman, J. "Nobody's Land: *Inner and Outer Space*." In *From Stills to Motion and Back Again* (Vancouver, B.C.: Presentation House Gallery, 2003).

Jacobs, Ken. "Blonde Cobra." In *Filmmakers' Cooperative Catalog No. 7*, 268. New York: New American Cinema Group, 1989.

Joseph, Branden W. *Beyond the Dream Syndicate: Tony Conrad and the Arts After Cage*. New York: Zone Books, 2008.

Kahn, Douglas. *Noise, Water, Meat: A History of Sound in the Arts*. Cambridge, Mass.: MIT Press, 1999.

Kelly, Caleb. *Sound: Documents of Contemporary Art*. London: Whitechapel Gallery; Cambridge, Mass. MIT Press, 2011.

Kim-Cohen, Seth. *In the Blink of an Ear: Towards a Non-Cochlear Sonic Art*. New York: Continuum, 2009.

Kittler, Friedrich. *Gramophone, Film, Typewriter*. Stanford: Stanford University Press, 1999.

Labelle, Brandon. *Background Noise: Perspectives on Sound Art*. London: Continuum, 2006.

Labelle, Brandon. *Acoustic Territories: Sound Culture and Everyday Life*. London: Continuum, 2010.

Leighton, Tanya, ed. *Art and the Moving Image: A Critical Reader*. London: Tate/Afterall, 2008.

Licht, Alan. *Sound Art: Beyond Music, Between Categories*. New York: Rizzoli, 2007.

MacDonald, Scott. *A Critical Cinema: Interviews with Independent Filmmakers*. Berkeley: University of California Press, 1988.

Nancy, Jean-Luc. *Listening*. New York: Fordham University Press, 2007.

Ragona, Melissa. "Hidden Noise: Strategies of Sound Montage in the Films of Hollis Frampton." *October* 109 (2004): 96–118.

Ragona, Melissa. "Paul Sharits' Cinematics of Sound." In *Lowering the Boom: Critical Studies in Film Sound*, edited by Jay Beck and Tony Grajeda, 171–182. Urbana: University of Illinois Press, 2008.

Ragona, Melissa. "Impulse, Types, and Index: Warhol's Audio Archive." In *Warhol Live: Music and Dance in Andy Warhol's Work*, edited by Stéphane Auquin, 130–135. Montreal: Museum of Fine Arts, 2008.

Rubin, Barbara. "Christmas on Earth." In *Filmmakers' Cooperative Catalog No. 7*, 416. New York: New American Cinema Group, 1989.

Schafer, R. Murray. *The Soundscape: Our Sonic Environment and the Tuning of the World*. Rochester, Vt.: Destiny Books, 2003.

Scheldhjal, Peter. "Lessness. The Whitney Biennial." *New Yorker*, March 17, 2008, at www.newyorker.com (accessed July 27, 2010).

Sherman, Tom. "The Premature Birth of Video Art." *Experimental TV Center*, January 2, 2007, at www.experimentaltvcenter.org (accessed July 27, 2010).

Snow, Michael. "A Statement on Wavelength for the Experimental Film Festival of Knokke-le-Zoute." *Film Culture* 46 (Autumn 1967): 1.

Sterne, Jonathan. *The Audible Past: Cultural Origins of Sound Reproduction*. Durham, N.C.: Duke University Press, 2003.

Turim, Maureen. *Abstraction in Avant-garde Films*. Studies in Cinema, no. 32. Ann Arbor, MI: UMI Research Press, 1985.

Turim, Maureen. "A Look at the Violence of Female Desire." In *Women and Experimental Filmmaking*, edited by Jean Petrolle and Virginia Wright Wexman, 71–90. Urbana: University of Illinois Press, 2005.

Uhlin, Greg. "Sound and Speech in Andy Warhol's Films." *Quarterly Review of Film and Video* 26 (2009): 322–338.

Voegelin, Salome. *Listening to Noise and Silence: Towards A Philosophy of Sound Art*. London: Continuum, 2010.

Wishart, Trevor. *On Sonic Art*. New York: Routledge, 1996.

GAMING

CHAPTER 31

CONTEXTUALIZING GAME AUDIO AESTHETICS

ROB BRIDGETT

INTRODUCTION

I have worked in the video game industry for 10 years—not long—and like many others in the field of audio, I have found myself working in many varied roles: as a composer, sound designer, recording engineer, voice director, dialogue editor, sound implementer, mixer, mastering engineer, and just about everything else in between. Since 2003 I have worked primarily as an audio director, a position that demands an understanding of the entire production process, aesthetic direction, and technical implementation of the game soundtrack. It further requires the ability to connect an overall vision with an eye for minuscule details. This holistic view brings together all the elements of music, sound effects, and dialogue with the game play and the image, and it is to me an analog of what the acclaimed film editor and sound designer Walter Murch means by the role of the *sound designer* in film[1]—which is essentially an analog in itself of the film's production designer/director of photography.

[1] Walter Murch and Ben Burtt were the first film sound personnel to be given the credit "sound designer," both in 1979, on *Apocalypse Now* and *American Graffiti*, respectively. The term has been the cause of much confusion and contention ever since among movie directors and other sound personnel, with a popular misconception being that the sound designer only has a technical role and makes strange sounds mainly with plug-ins via synthetic manipulation. However, the traditional role, as it was performed by Burtt, Murch, and others (most notably Randy Thom) in collaboration with the film's director during the writing and production stages of a film, is still the closest analogy in film production to the role of the sound director in gaming production.

Video game sound—at least in terms of cinematic, triple-A console titles—has advanced quickly from being a one-man home-studio operation to Hollywood-scale production, and most projects today comprise elements of both. I am interested in how the relatively advanced production practices of digital film sound can be transferred to video game sound production, to improve quality, simplify the process, and elevate the role of sound in storytelling by paying greater attention to the fidelity of source sounds. A further concern is the role of sound in serving interactivity in visual game media. The use of sound in film is a constant reference point for me in my working day. To some extent this is due to the kind of games I work on: broadly speaking, third-person action adventure titles. No matter what the genre, however, film and game audiences share enough cultural currency to make the storytelling vernacular relevant to both genres. This has prompted me to consider the wider context in which games, films, and other media exist, and how exactly the dialogue among those contexts is managed, edited, and directed.

Vernacular of Filmic Reality

The brief aesthetic history of games has been dominated by technical change. Games now are less challenged than in the past by the aesthetic limits of technology (sound chip synthesis), and as content creators we have at our disposal the same array of styles and sonic colors available with any sound media. Games have begun to lean extensively on the aesthetic language of film (among other media). This reliance is certainly not in any sense plagiaristic—it is impossible to plagiarize an aesthetic—but is more a process of referencing, reimagining, and juxtaposing an aesthetic palette. This process of quotation operates in a very similar way to exclusively visual cultures; for example, the way graphic designers embed their influences directly in their work. The referenced work is often not immediately apparent to observers, particularly those who are not accustomed to picking apart those same cultural and aesthetic references; however, it does form part of a common media vernacular, an audiovisual syntax, that exists across games, film, radio, television, and music. The aesthetic of game sound, at least in narrative games, could be characterized as one of *adaptation* and *quotation*, be it from previous games or from the styles, scenes, conventions, and tropes of cinema, television, and music. In much the same way, film itself can be considered an "adaptation medium," relying as it does on literature and theater, and to some extent due to the inherent production culture of adapting written scripts into audiovisual stories. Games exist more as nodes of popular culture than as isolated cultural entities. This is an often underdiscussed aspect of video game sound that I believe both content creators and audiences alike "get," and which the former actively engage with to create meaningful content.

Because of the presence of such a shared vernacular between film sound and game sound, similar layers of realism and exaggeration can be articulated as the means for building up a video game soundtrack. As in film, games require an element of "convincing" reality. Sound elements such as Foley and background ambience sell a scene in a movie and also make an interactive environment in a game believable. Without these basic realities of sound, the game would likely feel "broken" or somehow lacking. Once these realistic elements are established, game creators can layer in a more cinematic reality without it being questioned. Players buy into this arrangement because of the conceit of its synchronization with their actions and its simultaneous presence alongside these more realistic elements. In this way, sounds that are in fact much "larger" than the sounds one would expect to hear when a weapon is fired or when a punch connects with an enemy can be used to dramatically heighten emotion and engagement and to cinematize the experience for the player.

The Role of the Audio Director

When considering the differences, similarities, and connections between the production environments of game sound and film sound, it is apparent that the responsibilities for overseeing the entire soundtrack—and in a sense for defining the overall sound from the technical to the aesthetic tone—are very similar from film to games. There are, however, some slight nuances in the differing job titles that need to be understood. The role of the audio director (also called the sound director, or sometimes even the audio lead) in games is very similar to the role, which Walter Murch first defined, of the sound designer in film.[2] In an ironic twist, the role of sound designer has a very different implication in games. More often than not, the role of the technical sound designer is to both create and implement the game's sound effects (i.e., using tools and programming script to get the sounds to play back in association with game events); the closest analog to this in the film production world would be the sound editor. This is probably the definition of sound designer that film is attempting to fight against, in an attempt to reclaim the notion that a sound designer is the gatekeeper of the overall vision and tone of the entire film soundtrack (with the possible exception of the tone and feel of the score, which is controlled almost exclusively by the director and the composer).

The audio director in games, then, is responsible for the technical and artistic direction of the *entire* soundtrack, which includes dialogue, ambience, sound effects, *and music* (both licensed, if any, and composed score). As I have said, my feeling is that games do not really have a unique audio aesthetic or direction that stands on its own, but they imply more a nexus of references, and it is these references and how well they resonate with the audience at the time the game is released that will determine the success

[2] Feature design is essentially the creation of game-play features and actions that the player uses and combines to create game-play; for instance, a sniper zoom feature on a particular weapon allows the player to target and shoot distant enemies. This would be known as a feature of the game, and the player would be given certain specific challenges and opportunities in order to make the most of this feature to complete certain sections of the game.

of the project. The role of audio director includes a more technical side, in that she or he works closely with the audio programmers in establishing, designing, and implementing the desired technical requirements and direction of the audio *playback*, as well as with the wider design and art team in augmenting and leading "feature design."[3] This requires expertise, and arguably experience, in each and every area of the soundtrack, from artistic to technical, and of course a deep understanding of what will and won't work and how to balance all the elements across the game in its entirety.

On a day-to-day basis, the role of the audio director changes dramatically through the many phases of production, depending on what is necessary at various stages. The audio director also has to plan out the work that will be done in the production as a whole. In addition, she or he must foresee how many additional people will be required to perform this work. Creating schedules, writing design documents, preparing preview material, testing out implementation and ideas with placeholder sound content,[4] directing, and liaising with composers and voice directors are all tasks that require detailed involvement and yet also allow for creative freedom and input from the various team members. Give and take with others on the project is a vital part of the work of an audio director. This everyday, hands-on, and social work needs to continue while maintaining a thousand-foot view of the overall vision and tone of the game, as well as a profound awareness of where the game sits within popular culture. Every dialogue line, music cue, and individual sound effect must ultimately build, brick by brick, the overall effect. This higher level vision often comes down to the audio director's individual taste (cultural reference points); it is frequently based on instinct and feel for the material and almost always is the result of some limiting aesthetic factors that are imposed by the nature of the game's content and art direction.

An example I often cite is the sonic universe of the *Scarface* video game (itself based on the 1983 movie directed by Brian De Palma), on which I worked as sound director. For the title's overall tone, the effects needed to either participate in the 1980s retro vibe of the movie or make the audience feel like the movie's character Tony Montana—perhaps a more potent strategy—and the latter ultimately overruled the authenticity angle. It was often a careful balancing act to maintain enough of the feel of the movie and still have sound that could live outside the original movie, through use of sound effects (loyal to the movie's aesthetic of "dirty," realistic, gritty, and lacking low end),

[3] Temporary sounds are put into the game to demonstrate the playback of those sounds in conjunction with the features. They allow the audio director or sound designer to get a feel for how the implementation works, before eventually reconsidering those sounds and creating final assets. This is somewhat similar to the practice of using "temp" sounds or music in film production, in that sounds that are used as placeholders will often end up in the final game. This occurs because there is often too little time in the postproduction phase to fully reconsider all the effects. If the effects "work" technically, they are likely to remain "low risk" and unaddressed.

[4] For this important and prominent sound in the video game, I chose the use of filmic "synchresis" over the more convincing "reality" of the original film material. This improved the feeling given to the player during game-play.

spoken dialogue (authentic Cuban and Hispanic accents and dialect), and music (retro synth score). For example, some weapon sounds were far larger and meatier than those of the weapons used in the film,[5] but their qualities conjured with greater potency the over-the-top feeling of the personality of Tony Montana. Similarly, in the use of licensed music, the choice of tracks was balanced against authenticity of the period (early 1980s) and location (Miami, Cuba, and surrounding islands), as well as acknowledging the huge recognition that the hip-hop community had given to the movie over the years, much of whose output imprinted a feeling of what *Scarface* really meant in contemporary popular culture. The overall idea was to recontextualize *Scarface* within the popular culture of two decades after the film. Much of the film's soundscape is now perceived as a camp pleasure—for example, the original Giorgio Moroder score and some aspects of the performances. But these somewhat rococo elements all needed to be included and referenced in the game for it to *feel* right. The audio direction considered *Scarface* as part of a cultural continuum; arguably in video games, because so much importance is placed on immersion, "fun," and entertainment, we could not have overlooked this angle through a dogged loyalty to the static context of the original movie. As a cultural artifact, this was very much a video game released in 2006 rather than a movie released in 1983, and the audio direction embraced this distinction. Our approach mirrors closely what De Palma did himself when updating the movie from the original in the 1980s.

Sound Design and Implementation

Turning to some smaller technical differences between game sound and film sound, and perhaps considering sound as a continuum and consisting of smaller, molecular moving parts,[6] I want to clarify the role of the "sound designer" in games and the ways this role has changed in the last few years. (Recall that this role is different from the film sound designer; in games the audio director takes that role.) These recent changes are certainly influenced by shifting technology, but they have arisen largely because of the need for the audio director to think at a higher supervisory level.

As the sheer amount of audio content in games has increased, the need for the audio director to become less "hands-on" has become apparent. On smaller projects much of the sound effects design and content would have been created by the audio director;

[5] I hold the perspective that every single sound is essentially a part of a larger semiotic continuum that is learned by engaging in a culture's mediated output.

[6] Audio tools are the computer programs that are used by the sound designers to get sounds, music, and dialogue to play back in the game. They act essentially as interactive sound sequencers in which the entire soundtrack is mixed and balanced. A good example of a third-party audio tool is Audio Kinetic's Wwise.

however, with larger titles and more intense production, coupled with a larger available freelance pool, the work of contract sound designers and implementers is now more likely to be outsourced than to be done in-house by a full-time employee. Under the guidance and review of the audio director, the process of designing sound effects for a game has gone through significant changes with the arrival of new technologies. The title "sound designer," and the role itself, have changed significantly over the past decade or so to encompass very firmly the implementation stage as a crucial part of the sound design process. By this I mean that sourcing, creating, and mixing sounds together to make the actual wave files for the sound effect is now coupled with creating and setting up the rules and behaviors under which those sounds will be played back in the game. Perhaps five to ten years ago, with more limited memory available on the older console systems (PlayStation 2, GameCube etc.), if we were designing the sound of a gunshot in a game, the simultaneously heard elements of the sound—the shot, the shell casing, the tail, and any mechanical elements of the machinery itself—would more than likely be mixed down into one single wave file. This single "mixed-down" entity would therefore be implemented to play back when the weapon is fired, a technique that is still used today when economic factors dictate. In the past freelance sound designers would create sound effects based on a "list," knowing nothing of game context. This practice is falling out of favor because of the higher levels of scrutiny and expectations of audio quality that surround the release of video game titles today. New approaches incorporate all of the separate elements of the gunshot and trigger them separately in the game's action: for example, the shell-casing could well have a separate visual effect, so the shell sound is coupled exclusively with that, the gunshot itself is bonded to the firing of the weapon, and the choice of different tails of the shot sound is determined by the environmental context in which the weapon is fired. This newly focused attention to detail allows a more dynamic and interactive sound design to occur, and it allows more freedom for either realism or fantastical exaggeration.

So increasingly, at least on this atomic level, thoughts about implementation are becoming integral to the sound design process, and technical realization has become inseparable from artistic ends. Run-time, which refers to the combinatory contexts of actual game usage, is the only time when all the various sound elements are heard together. The use of enhanced audio tools[7] that allow content to be tweaked, tuned, and mixed at run-time is changing the creative process in a way that furthers these new aspirations. Allowing sound effects to be replaced while the game is still running is becoming an increasingly important part of this process. During implementation the variants for each sound, variation in pitch and volume, the distances over which sound will remain audible, and how much environmental reverb is added to them are all specified. It is no longer acceptable to use only a fixed laundry list of effects, because context in the new modes of production is everything, even at the atomic level of individual sound events.

[7] This are essentially software-based reverberation, delay, and filter effects running in real time to affect the sound in desirable ways.

On Aesthetic Goals

It is a challenge to generalize broadly about sound style in video games. Numerous clichés spring to mind, but these are perhaps more representative of old technologies and specific older games that are part of the cultural fabric than they are of current video games. Titles such as *Pac-Man* and *Space Invaders* give rise to the common stereotype of "game sound," but the sounds of these older aesthetic references are defined almost entirely by antiquated chip-based synthesis technology. Another cliché of game sound style is repetitiveness, often found in fighting games of the 1990s, in which the same sound effect or the same vocal sample is used over and over again when retriggered in connection with a common game-play action, such as punching. Again, this is a sound trope that emerged from the limitations of a technology rather than in connection with a conscious design aesthetic.

Current gaming audio is actually defined by an enormous breadth and depth of styles and genres. The former dependency on synthesis technology for sound playback is gone, and it is now simply one of many aesthetic choices available to the sound director. Knowledge of genre and the general tone of the game play perhaps the most important parts in defining the overall function of the soundtrack in supporting game play as well as conveying the mood of the title. This tone resonates across sound effects, dialogue, and performance styles as well as music. Because the relationship of gaming to cinema is arguably closer than to any other medium, form of entertainment, or art, sound design in gaming will frequently imitate the general auditory tones of film soundtracks. This is done during production; the team will use examples of dialogue, clips, and movie scenes as models for the tones of particular scenes or moments in a game, and they can also directly reference films and actually use existing sound elements from them. It is difficult to imagine, for example, an underwater combat scene that doesn't make reference to the bullet whiz-bys in the movie *Saving Private Ryan*.

Cinema is a constant reference point for games, the assumption being that the audiences of both media share a common cultural vernacular. So much needs to be communicated without a moment's hesitation in games, particularly where storytelling is abbreviated so the gamer can proceed to the action (and interaction) without delay. This means relying heavily on preexisting tropes and clichés. It must also be admitted, however, that these references frequently fail to convince, whether because of their poor execution or because of poor or tasteless recontextualization.

A great many more granular technical elements are involved in the conception of gaming sound, including environmental factors related to the mode of play and the number and interaction of players. Establishing whether the game is to be played in a "cinematic context," meaning a single-player experience where there is no interruption from other people in the room, or as a party game for multiple users to play at the same time in a noisy room, can affect the amount of output compression the game will require. For example, in the party environment, subtlety may well be relinquished in favor of attention-grabbing arcade-type sounds. Whether reference is made to an action movie, cartoon, or any other preexisting medium, game sound, just like the other expressive elements employed in gaming, is often like a magpie, insofar as it freely adopts and adapts to different styles from various media and merges them with the gaming experience. It seems that game art directors, and equally sound directors, are increasingly becoming "editors," a definitive twenty-first-century media skill of both graphic and sound artists, rather than creators in the traditional sense, tapping into a familiar cultural reservoir of sights and sounds as a means of making the experience more compelling and immersive.

The Final Mix

The audio director must have an intimate understanding of these atomic implementation processes in order to make, or suggest, smaller-level tweaks that contribute to higher level audio effects. The ability to suggest and implement time- and memory-saving production techniques for sounds, music, or dialogue that may have a similar *feel* but use significantly more modest resources is a skill that is frequently called upon in the closing stages of game development. The audio director sees these small details in the much wider context of the entire soundtrack and is therefore able to prioritize between what is essential to the whole and what is a mere detail. Given that the clock is always ticking and only a finite amount of production and implementation time is ever available, a top ten list of features will often turn into a top three must-have list.

In a sense, the final mix in both cinema and games is where all the elements that belong in a soundtrack will interrelate for the first time. It is only at this point that the larger questions about these interrelationships can be addressed. In the premixing of films and games alike, each discipline of those working on the soundtrack—backgrounds (ambiences), dialogue, sound effects, Foley, and music—receives a premix in which some artistic decisions are made about the importance of certain sounds to the overall effect of the image. In games, each of these is treated more broadly, with sound effects including both Foley and backgrounds, but similarly, dialogue and music are treated as areas to be given consistency and quality passes prior to reaching the final mix. In technical matters, the two media differ significantly. In film the mixes are "recorded" against the time-code of the image and re-recorded to a final print master. In games, however, various interactive, real-time strategies are implemented to change the levels and attenuation of sounds as the game runs. Perhaps the most common interactive mixing concept is currently the mixer "snapshot," in which a snapshot of fader values (containing volume, pitch, panning, and digital signal processing attributes) is installed to coincide with an action occurring in the game. Again using the example of a gunshot, whenever a gun is fired by the player, a mixer snapshot brings about a smooth transition that decreases the volume of other sounds in the game, such as other less relevant enemy gunfire, so that the important gunshot may be foregrounded. This is all done as the game simulation runs on the console, and the player, in a sense, *initiates* these sound mixes through his or her actions in the game.

At a higher level, aesthetic direction, the final mix offers an opportunity to foreground the artistic elements of the sound direction at specific moments of game play. Again, the processes involved are in the nature of a continuum—implying constant change, with events triggered at any given moment—more than a fixed timeline. In essence, the goals of the game mix are precisely the same as those of a film mix: to highlight and bring into focus what is important to the listener and to gracefully orchestrate a dance among music, sound, and voice as servicing the ends of the story or game play. The only difference is that instead of locating mix decisions along a fixed timeline, the mix decisions are attached to predetermined events that are triggered by the player's actions.

In Conclusion

I argue in this chapter that every sound, line of dialogue, and musical cue fits into the overall context of a game. Similarly, the game itself is part of a much wider media landscape that involves not only other games, but also film, music, and television content spanning decades. Writing this has chapter been an exercise in reflection: trying to conceptualize and reflect on how I work on a conscious level, when so much of the work I do as a sound designer, sound director, and mixer happens unconsciously. My hope is that this will become part of a two-way exchange in which academics pay closer heed to the experiences of practitioners, and practitioners in turn learn something about their craft from the analytical rigor and level of reflection that academics bring to discussions of sound. Sound studies is an arena involving both academics and practitioners, in which the role of *sound* (comprising music, voices, and a good deal else besides) will be highlighted as a more active participant in the production and storytelling process.

CHAPTER 32

IMPLICATIONS OF INTERACTIVITY: WHAT DOES IT MEAN FOR SOUND TO BE "INTERACTIVE"?

KAREN COLLINS

VIDEO games, mobile phones, and other modern digital media alter the traditional relationships between creator and consumer, audience and performance when the audience takes a participatory role in instigating sound events. When using such media audiences may, through their actions, be responsible for evoking sounds, selecting them, altering or shaping them, or creating new sounds, thus playing an active role in the composition of their own soundscapes. This active role of the audience raises interesting questions about the ways in which we theorize sound in media. What does it mean to interact with sound? Who is the audience, and who is the creator of such co-creative, interactive sonic constructions? How does interacting with sound change our relationship to that sound? How do we begin to discuss these changes in relationship? As I tried to work through these questions, I asked a group of students in a music class at McGill University to consider the diagram in figure 32.1. Each corner of the triangle represents a different relationship a participant has to music or sound design: creation, performance, and reception.[1]

The students and I agreed that there is considerable overlap among these positions. A composer generally performs the music while in the process of composing, and of course he listens to it as well. A performer will listen to a song as she plays, to time her part or to catch mistakes. A listener may choose to sing harmony or play air guitar along with a piece of music, thus becoming, in part, creator (or at least orchestrator)

[1] There is no real equivalent today to the musician/performer in the field of sound design. Perhaps the closest is the Foley artist, who creates sounds "live" in the studio. In the early days of film, the traps person was the closest to this role.

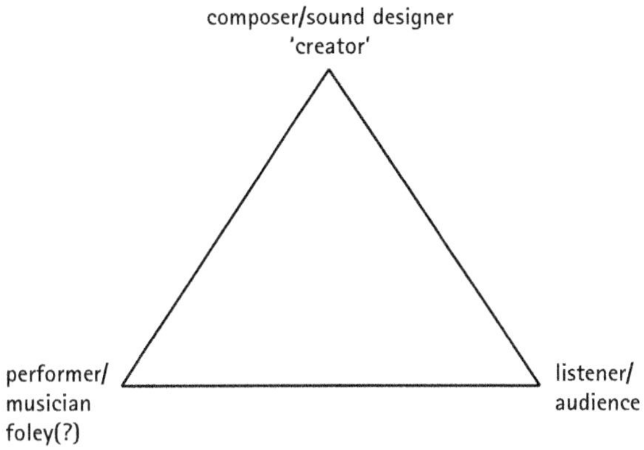

FIGURE 32.1: Relationships to music and sound design.

and performer (even if a silent one). In other words, these roles cannot be considered entirely distinct. Nevertheless, the diagram helps us discuss the impact of interactivity on our traditional ways of perceiving our relationships to sound and music.

I asked the students where they would place interactive video game sound on the diagram. If a player can create the overall soundscape through her game play or rearrange the music cues based on her characters' movements by changing instrumentation or sequencing, or by triggering generative music parts, is she not in some way the creator of the overall sound experience? If she is constantly "performing" sound by triggering the emitter of that sound (pushing buttons, swinging the Wii remote) or altering sonic events through action, is she not also part performer? And if she is listening to the sounds as she plays (critical for some games), is she a listener/audience as well? Again, we can never consider these roles as separate, but if there is considerably more overlap among them than in most other forms of music and sound, where do our interactions with game sounds belong on the diagram? Ultimately most of the students decided that interactive sound belongs somewhere in the middle of the triangle, but the longer we discussed the problem, the more the corners of our triangle became rounded, and we entered into John Cagean discussions of what it means to create art/music, especially in light of the often nonlinear, aleatory, and generative nature of game sound.

Although we arrived at no definitive answers, it was clear from our discussion that most scholarship on music and sound design privileges a single perspective at any given time (usually that of the composer), often disregarding the performers' and audience's complementary roles in a piece of music or sound design. Thus, when it comes to a type of sound or music that fits somewhere in the middle of our triangle, there is little scholarship to develop an understanding of interactive sound, nor is there adequate language to discuss the participant's active role in the sonic experience. In this chapter I explore the differences between interactive and noninteractive sound, focusing on video games, although I also refer to contemporary digital slot machines because they have some common features.

This chapter raises several central questions. What makes interactive sound different from noninteractive sound? Where does *interacting with* sound fit into our understanding of our experience of sound and music in media? And how do we begin to approach interactive sound from a theoretical perspective? Elsewhere[2] I have begun to explore video game sound by drawing on film theory. Indeed, other scholars have also approached game sound from a film-theoretical framework,[3] although this has certainly not been the only approach taken.[4] In some ways film theory is an obvious starting point from which to discuss game sound, as games share many qualities of films. Like films, games usually have a narrative and contain cinematic sequences,[5] and cross-marketing (as well as coproduction) has also grown between the game and film industries. Recent scholarship has adapted useful concepts from the study of film sound and music to the study of games.[6] But as I have argued, film theory seems to fall short in many respects when applied to game sound; notably, film studies does not account for the sound that is directly controlled by the player and for the distinctly different experience that this embodied control of sound involves. I contend that to study interactive sound we need to expand our scholarly horizons and look farther afield to computer science, interaction design, and cognitive psychology, all of which have dealt for some time with the phenomenon of interactivity with sound and other modalities.

Defining Interactivity

Defining interactivity is a tricky business, because of the variety of types of interaction with media texts that can occur. In *The Language of New Media* Lev Manovich states, "All classical, and even more so modern, art is 'interactive' in a number of ways. Ellipses in literary narration, missing details of objects in visual art, and other representational 'shortcuts' require the user to fill in missing information." [7] We can argue that a

[2] Karen Collins, "An Introduction to the Participatory and Non-Linear Aspects of Video Games Audio," in *Essays on Sound and Vision*, ed. John Richardson and Stan Hawkins (Helsinki: Helsinki University Press, 2007).

[3] For instance, Anahid Kassabian, "The Sound of a New Film Form," in *Popular Music and Film*, ed. Ian Inglis (London: Wallflower, 2003); and Zach Whalen, "Play Along: An Approach to Videogame Music," *Game Studies: The International Journal of Computer Game Research* 4, no. 1 (2004).

[4] See, for example, Mark Grimshaw, "*The Acoustic Ecology of the First Person Shooter*" (PhD diss., University of Waikato, 2007).

[5] See Karen Collins, *Game Sound: An Introduction to the History, Theory and Practice of Video Game Music and Sound Design* (Cambridge, Mass.: MIT Press, 2008), 5–6, for an expanded comparison of film and video game music and sound practice.

[6] In particular, for example, Michel Chion's chapters on the audiovisual scene and phantom audiovisual in *Audio-Vision: Sound on Screen* (New York: Columbia University Press, 1994); and Philip Tagg's approach to music semiotics in *Kojak: Fifty Seconds of Television Music* (New York: Mass Media Music Scholars' Press, 2000).

[7] Lev Manovich, *The Language of New Media* (Cambridge, Mass.: MIT Press, 2001), 56.

paperback book is interactive on a psychological level. Indeed, Manovich and others have argued that the act of *participating* or *active reception* is the same as interacting. It may therefore be best to think of interactivity as a spectrum of activities, from the psychological to the physical. However, we can also say that although we *act* with a book, it does not respond to our actions: it does not *interact* with us. There is no feedback from the book based on our actions. Those actions do not alter the book, merely our perception of it, and therefore we lack control or agency over the book. For the purposes of this chapter, then, I suggest that a book is not interactive because it lacks two fundamental elements: control and feedback.

Interactivity need not take place only between a user and a text (e.g., a reader and a book), of course. A variety of different types of interactivity characterize media such as video games, even including interpersonal interactions mediated by a game.[8] For example, in online multiplayer games, players interact with each other through speech or play virtual instruments in ad hoc or planned jam sessions. More widescale interactions may also occur, including the social and cultural interactions that take place on a much vaster and temporally longer scale. For example, a game's plot or aesthetics may inspire a movie director, or fans may modify ("mod") and then spin off a new series of fan-authored games. These may be released as official versions, based on the modifiable game engines and code provided by the original game's manufacturer, or "hacked" versions of games, such as *Kaizo Mario* (also known as *Asshole Mario*),[9] a fan modification of *Super Mario World* (Nintendo 1990) designed to be nearly impossible to play. All of these works may then become part of a larger cultural dialogue about games, film, art, and so forth. Although these types of interactions are culturally significant and interesting, they lie outside the scope of this chapter.

Here I focus on the interactivity between a game and the player(s), which might range from game content or events based on in-game parameters, where the player has little control; to generative or artificially intelligent content; to interaction with prefabricated scripts; to entirely open, unscripted interaction in a multiplayer game. A game may be fluid in its degrees of interactivity and may afford different degrees of interactivity at different times. The correspondence between action and speed of the response to the player, the number and types of characteristics that the player can exert control over or modify in a game, as well as the number and type of inputs that afford agency all influence the degree to which a game is interactive.[10]

As discussed previously, many theorists, particularly outside of the humanities, agree that central to the idea of interactivity are *feedback* and *control*. As Bert Bongers notes,

[8] See Sally J. McMillan, "Exploring Models of Interactivity from Multiple Research Traditions: Users, Documents, and Systems," in *Handbook of New Media*, ed. Leah A. Lievrouw and Sonia Livingston (London: Sage, 2002).

[9] Douglas Wilson and Miguel Sicart, "Now It's Personal: On Abusive Game Design," in *Proceedings of Future Play 2010* Vancouver, Canada, May 6–7.

[10] See Matthew Lombard and Jennifer Snyder-Duch, "Interactive Advertising and Presence: A Framework," *Journal of Interactive Advertising* 1, no. 2 (2001).

"Interaction between a human and a system is a two way process: control and feedback.... The system is controlled by the user, and the system gives feedback to help the user to articulate the control, or feed-forward to actively guide the user."[11] Here, then, I use the term "interactive" with this idea of control and action as the core, to refer to physically acting, with agency (control), with media that in some way respond to the action (feedback). The rest of this chapter explores what feedback and control mean in our understanding of sound in media such as video games.

Implications of Interactivity: Sound as Feedback

Sound in nature provides us with continuous feedback. We constantly receive information about the status of our surroundings, from the state of the weather to the direction of moving objects and approaching dangers. It is not surprising, then, that when it comes to games (which may aspire to some degree of verisimilitude), sound has continued to fulfill this same role. Over time music has also been developed in games (perhaps to a lesser extent) to provide feedback to the player, from signaling enemies nearby to indicating the character's status.

Most sound in early video games was designed specifically to provide feedback to the player to indicate that he had taken an action (fired a gun, jumped, bumped into a wall), that he had earned points, or that there was a change in game-state (e.g., he was beginning a new level). Sonic feedback or prompts were also used to alert the player to take an action: that her spaceship was under attack, that an encounter with an enemy was imminent, or that time was running out. An item in *Electronic Games* in July 1983 advised the player of Adventure Vision's *Super Cobra*: "Super Cobra makes use of a range of sound effects to enhance the play. Listen to these special tones since they frequently warn you of what type of enemy the helicopter will face next."[12] About Adventure Vision's *Space Force*, the same guide notes: "Pay close attention to the sound effects. The approach of alien ships are [*sic*] signaled by alien cannon fire. This alerts you to be prepared to shoot."[13]

I have defined *dynamic audio* in games as audio that reacts to changes in the game-play environment *or* in response to a user.[14] I distinguish two types of dynamic audio: *interactive* (sound events occurring in reaction to game play, which respond to

[11] Bert Bongers, "Physical Interfaces in the Electronic Arts—Interaction Theory and Interfacing Techniques for Real-Time Performance," in *Trends in Gestural Control of Music*, ed. Marcelo M. Wanderley and Marc Battier (Paris: IRCAM–Centre Pompidou, 2000), 41–70.

[12] Joyce Worley, "Adventure Vision: Inside the Hardware," *Electronic Games* (July 1983): 116.

[13] Worley, "Adventure Vision," 118.

[14] Collins, "Introduction to the Participatory and Non-Linear Aspects of Video Games Audio," 265.

the player directly) and *adaptive* (sound that reacts appropriately to game play and even anticipates it, rather than responding directly to the player). Adaptive audio is closely related to interactive audio in that it is preemptively interactive, implying that there will be a response from the player (after the sound event has taken place). As this chapter discusses feedback, it may be useful to consider interactive and adaptive audio as a series of events that are generated by the system (adaptive audio) or the player (interactive audio). A *player-generated event* is an event that the player initiates, such as the click of a mouse or the pressing of a controller button, and hence is *interactive*. Interactive sound is primarily player-generated; the player initiates an event through an input device (button, controller), and there is a system-controlled response. A *system-generated event* is initiated by the software, such as a timer running out or a spaceship flying overhead at random intervals. System-generated events tend to be adaptive audio events. We could say, then, that interactive audio is always in some form of causal relationship with an event and with a player.

Games map sound to events in a number of ways and for a variety of purposes. Sometimes, for variation in sound effects, an entire collection of sounds might be mapped to a single event; only one sound file from the collection connects to the event at run-time. For example, to make sure I don't hear the same gunshot shell casing fall the same way every time I shoot a weapon, there may be a folder of shell-casing-fall sounds from which a single one is randomly selected. Thus, when I shoot the weapon my action can create a slightly different sound each time. As noted previously, the mapping of sound to an event in video games has historically been motivated to provide immediate feedback to the player, either directly in response to a player action or to instigate one. Turning the sound off in a video game can be detrimental; in fact, there is ample objective evidence that having the sound on enhances the ability to play the game.[15]

Today's game sound typically provides many types of feedback to the player.[16] These fall into seven overlapping categories:

1. *Preemptive attention and alert sounds*: Preemptive sounds are usually a call to attention ("you need to take an action"). For example, they can be musical cues that serve as a warning that an enemy is around the corner and that you need to pull out your sword. Notably, in games *acousmatic sound*—that is, sound with no clear origin visually—may inspire the player to look in the direction of a sound, to "incite the look to go there and find out."[17] The term was first adopted from

[15] See, for example, Kristine Jørgenson, "Left in the Dark: Playing Computer Games with the Sound Turned Off," in *From Pac-Man to Pop Music: Interactive Audio in Games and New Media*, ed. Karen Collins (Aldershot: Ashgate, 2008).

[16] I take the first four areas from Alan Dix, Janet Finlay, Gregory Abowd, and Russell Beale, *Human-Computer Interaction* (London: Prentice Hall, 1998), 24. The last three are arguably "feedback," but I believe they contribute to the communication (hence information/feedback) process and so include them here.

[17] Chion, *Audio-Vision: Sound on Screen*, 71, 85.

ancient Greek usage by French composer Pierre Schaeffer and was later used by Michel Chion to describe sounds in film that have no visible source onscreen. Even if we cannot compel the camera to go where the sound seems to come from, we mentally look there. Acousmatic sound is actually far more pronounced in games, as sound gives the player cues to head in a particular direction or to run the other way. And unlike in film, preemptive and alert sounds prompt an active response from the listener. When your character is dehydrated and running out of health points, the sound of a waterfall may draw you in one direction, whereas adjacent gunfire might scare you away. These cues (particularly acousmatic sounds) provide the most information about the environment.

2. *Confirmation sounds*: Confirmation sounds verify that an event has been carried out ("you have taken an action"). Most player-generated sound effects in video games are confirmation sounds: "you have taken a step," "you have jumped up," "you have fired your weapon." Because these player-generated sounds are mapped to input events (button presses, etc.), they tend to be repetitive. Contemporary game sound designers therefore often spend a lot of time making variable sound effects for these events, as in the shotgun shell casing example. Footstep sounds are now often randomly selected from a series of samples or even generated in real time using a variety of synthesis methods.
3. *Status feedback*: A status sound is an often continuous sound or musical cue that provides information about status ("you are taking an action"). In a game, such sounds commonly take the form of health status information, notably when the player is running out of health (e.g., a steady beeping or sped-up musical cue) or is temporarily invincible.
4. *Navigation and orientation*: Navigation sounds and music indicate where the player is in a level or the larger game matrix. Spatial sound, for example, gives feedback about proximity or direction of objects, and occlusion effects can provide feedback about barriers. Music and ambient sound help to tell you where you are in the game (both in terms of environment and the overall game matrix).
5. *Peripheral information*: In addition to the more direct feedback in the game, sounds can provide input about the brand, the genre or style, and aesthetic information. This is particularly notable when the game uses recognizable intellectual property such as music. Familiarity with a television show, film, person, place, musical act, or sport is likely to entice players to various slot machines, for example. "Players may find [them] more enjoyable because they can easily interact with the recognizable images and music they experience."[18]
6. *Affective feedback*: Sound in games can provide feedback of an affective nature. For example, music in a game, particularly musical leitmotifs, can give information about the state of your own character or nonplaying characters in a

[18] Mark Griffiths and Jonathan Parke, "The Psychology of Music in Gambling Environments: An Observational Research Note," *Journal of Gambling Issues* 13 (2005): 5.

game. In addition to providing feedback about the emotional states of characters, sound and music can influence the player, through what has been termed *mood induction*. This sound "changes how one is feeling, while communication of meaning simply conveys information. One may receive information depicting sadness without him or herself feeling sad."[19] Game music commonly deploys tempo for mood induction; different musical genres can also affect the player's success rates. Yamada studied the impact of different genres of music on the player (in addition to playing without music) and found "that the no-music condition showed the best rate of success. Moreover, a 'mixed' musical excerpt added 'unpleasantness' to the game and, in turn, resulted in a negative effect on the success rate. Increasing the speed increased the 'potency' of the game, but did not affect the success rate, systematically."[20]

7. *Reward and punishment*: Reinforcement sounds (positive and negative) are very common in video games and provide feedback to the player about the consequences of her actions. Digital slot machines are a clear example. Sound effects govern a variety of reward and feedback systems in slot machines.[21] You can hear coins falling into the hopper—even though credits are usually substituted for physical coins in today's machines. These false coin sounds can portray wins much larger than the actual win, giving deceptive feedback to the player. Of course positive, winning sounds are key to the machines, and sounds of losing are rarely heard, emphasizing positive experiences over negative ones. Verbal reinforcement also takes place: computer-generated voices tell players that they are "cool" or "a genius." Parke and Griffiths note that verbal reinforcement is designed to raise self-esteem, give hints and guidance, and even provide friendship or company.[22]

Sonic rewards are also fairly common in video games. They have considerably more losing sounds than slot machines—think of the sounds for player character death. Winning sounds—gaining points, gathering a special object, and so on—are of course very common and offer sonic rewards to the player. When it comes to casual games (games usually consumed in short time periods, with a smaller barrier to entry and less involvement), some games go over the top with reward sounds and, as do slot machines,

[19] Cited in Annabel. J. Cohen, "Music as a Source of Emotion in Film," in *Music and Emotion: Theory and Research*, ed. Patrick N. Juslin and John A. Sloboda (Oxford: Oxford University Press, 2001), 42.

[20] Masashi Yamada, "Can Music Change the Success Rate in a Slot-machine Game?" in *Proceedings of the Western Pacific Acoustics Conference* (Beijing, China, 2009).

[21] See Karen Collins, Holly Tessler, Kevin A. Harrigan, Michael J. Dixon, and Jonathan Fugelsang, "Sound in Electronic Gambling Machines: A Case Study of Player Interaction," in *Game Sound Technology and Player Interaction: Concepts and Developments*, ed. Mark Grimshaw (London: IGI Global, 2011).

[22] Jonathan Parke and Mark Griffiths, "The Psychology of the Fruit Machine: The Role of Structural Characteristics (Revisited)," *International Journal of Mental Health and Addiction* 4 (2006): 171.

aim more at making the player feel good about playing the game than providing any critical feedback about status or location.

Implications of Interactivity: Sound and Control

The other key element of interactivity is control. Because the player has some control over many of the audio events in video games, she participates in that sound. The player directly triggers some sound events through her input device, and her actions nearly always affect the overall soundscape of the game. Often she may have a gestural interaction with that sound. From an arbitrary button-press to more sophisticated racket swings of the Wii remote, the player has a unique physical and gestural connection to the sound events. These technological changes alter the player's relationship to that sound. This self-produced sound distinguishes the game experience from that of most other media, which often disconnect the player from her physical self, and the sonic events do not respond to her physical actions.

Chion proposes the term "ergo-audition" to refer to how we hear ourselves taking an action, noting that "this concept extends the concept of feedback to incorporate the subjective experience of one's impact on the world."[23] One might argue that in everyday life we have a greater connection to self-produced sounds because we have a deeper understanding of their causes and effects. For example, I draw on the sounds of my fingers tapping on my keyboard as I type to determine if I managed to hit the keys, and I know that the harder I hit the keys, the louder the sounds will be. The connection between the physical action and the sonic reaction is arguably much stronger when it comes to self-produced sounds. Indeed, this control over sound events is vital to our perception of sounds in the environment. For instance, when given control over noise, people are more likely to accept sound, as anyone who has control over his own stereo as opposed to a neighbor's will attest. Even the *illusion* of control over a sound alters the ways in which we perceive it. [24]

Many of today's video games offer options for customizing sound elements, including music, voice-over, and sound effects. Though not all games are completely flexible, it is increasingly the case that they allow for some degree of customization beyond the volume or equalization found in most audio playback devices. The customization of sound, however, may not always be a conscious attempt to alter sounds. For example, you may

[23] Michel Chion, *Le Son: Traité d'acoulogie* (Paris: Editions Nathan, 1998), 79–86.

[24] See, for example, Julie Hatfield, R. F. Job Soames, Andrew J. Hede, Normal L. Carter, Peter Peploe, Richard Taylor, and Stephen Morrell, "Human Response to Environmental Noise: The Role of Perceived Control," *International Journal of Behavioral Medicine* 9, no. 4 (2002).

customize the overall soundscape through your choice of avatar or weapon. If you choose a tiny elf as your avatar, different sound effects are likely to accompany it than if you choose a giant ogre, so the sonic experience of the game will depend on your choice. You may also customize the overall playback of sounds, as many games allow players to enter menu or options screens and individually adjust the volume (thus overall mix) of sound effects, ambient levels, speech, and music.

Moreover, modern game consoles like the Xbox 360 allow users to insert their own music into games as they play. Some games even allow the player's input music to directly impact the level maps of the game, such as *Vib Ribbon* (SCEI, 1999) and *Phase* (Harmonix Music Systems Inc., 2007). Advertising research suggests that we have a different relationship to media that we select than to media chosen for us, which implies that we may have a different relationship to games than to media for which we cannot customize sound.[25] A pilot study recently carried out by one of my students on players' selection of music in games found that players consciously choose music to alter their affective state—for example, to relieve anxiety—as well as to increase their immersion. Players could in fact change their anxiety levels by using their own music rather than the precomposed game music. A particularly important finding is that their personal music choices could alter their game-play tactics, notably speed of play. But perhaps most relevant to the discussion here is that players' control over music influenced their enjoyment of the game.[26]

Our study also found that familiar music controlled by the player could be used to help her overcome frustration and increase her immersion. This phenomenon might be best described using Csikszentmihalyi's concept of *flow*, characterized by concentration on the task at hand, a sense of control, merging of awareness and action, temporal distortion, and a loss of self-consciousness.[27] It may be the case that control over music and sound in general leads to a more immersive experience, because we become a part of the process rather than being external to it, although this remains unexplored. Roccheso and Bresin argue, "The possibility of using continuous interaction with sounding objects allows for expressive control for the sound production and, as a result, to higher engagement, deeper sense of presence, and experiential satisfaction."[28]

Although research into the effect that control has on video game players remains limited, there has been some research into control—and the illusion of control—when it comes to playing modern video slot machines. Modern slot machines bear many

[25] Paul A. Pavlou and David W. Stewart, "Measuring the Effects and Effectiveness of Interactive Advertising: A Research Agenda," *Journal of Interactive Advertising* 1, no. 1 (2000).

[26] Andrew Wharton and Karen Collins, "Subjective Measures of the Influence of Music Personalization on Video Game Play: A Pilot Study," *Game Studies: The International Journal of Computer Game Research* 11, no. 2 (2011).

[27] Mihalyi Csikszentmihalyi, *Flow: The Psychology of Optimal Experience* (New York: Harper Perennial, 1990).

[28] Davide Rocchesso and Roberto Bresin, "Emerging Sounds for Disappearing Computers," in *The Disappearing Computer, Lecture Notes in Computer Science 4500*, ed. Norbert Streitz, Achilles Kameas, and Irene Mavrommati (Berlin: Springer-Verlag, 2007), 241.

similarities to video games, and the industries share game designers as well as composers. Until the 1990s, slot machines had fairly standard mechanical or electromechanical reels and parts. The digitization of slot machines has brought considerably more complex elements to slot machine game play. Many of these elements have been adapted from video games; for example, cut scenes, bonus rounds, secret functions, and specialist plays[29] are designed to increase what the industry calls "time on device."[30] A simple bonus or increased (illusory) skill component leads to an increased psychological involvement on the part of the player.[31] Control is key to the player's involvement, and many elements are designed to give players the illusion of control (e.g., by presenting a choice even when the outcome is predetermined). Players are far more engaged and will spend longer on the game when they feel that they have some control over the outcome. Some of these elements of game play are hinted at by the sound (as in the *Simpsons* EGM, in which Krusty the Clown says, "Here's a clue for ya, Jack.").[32] We can extrapolate the findings from slot machine research to video games and make the assumption that the more control a player has, the more engaged he becomes. When it comes to sound, this *could* mean that players are more engaged with the sound, which could have implications in areas such as memorability and branding.

Conclusion

Feedback and control are two of the key distinctions that make interactive audio a unique experience for its audience. I have only touched on these issues here, hinting at what might be found by more empirical research into the impact of interactivity on audience experience. Both feedback and control, I have hypothesized, alter the relationship that an audience has with music or sound in interactive media. We have seen that feedback provides important information to the player about a variety of game elements, and that without sound, the player increasingly relies on visuals to gain that information. In the most vital cases, sound provides preemptive warnings to the player to take an action. Control over the sonic environment may immerse the player more deeply in the game.

Not only do feedback and control influence audience experience, but as I have suggested, production practices must also be different. The nature of a feedback-based medium means that sounds tend to be more repetitive, requiring considerations for

[29] There are also, of course, some notable differences between video games and slot machines, the most obvious being the betting of money on the outcome, but effectively slot machines today are video games.

[30] Natasha Dow Schull, "Digital Gambling: The Coincidence of Desire and Design," *The Annals of the American Academy of Political and Social Science* 597 (2005): 67.

[31] Parke and Griffiths, "Psychology of the Fruit Machine," 176.

[32] Parke and Griffiths, "Psychology of the Fruit Machine," 157.

variability. Player participation in some instances has meant that composers completely relinquish control to the player's choice of music. Moreover, increased unpredictability in the overall soundscape must constantly be negotiated, as players may alter the overall aesthetic with a variety of choices in not only music but also sound effects and dialogue.

I began the chapter with a series of questions: What makes interactive audio different from noninteractive audio? Where does interacting with audio fit into our understanding of sound and music in media? How do we begin to approach interactive audio from a theoretical perspective? Drawing on research from a variety of disciplines, I have indicated some of the related literature that hints at methodologies as yet unexplored that may be particularly useful when it comes to interactive audio, such as advertising, interaction design, gambling studies, and cognitive psychology. Moreover, our understanding of not just interactive sound, but sound in audiovisual media in general, may be enhanced by expanding our scope of research into the areas that have been underutilized by scholars of music and sound in media. It is evident that we lack research into the influence that interactivity has on player experience as well as production practice. In particular, empirical research is needed in a variety of areas so that we may better understand what, exactly, it means to interact with sound.

References

Bongers, Bert. "Physical Interfaces in the Electronic Arts—Interaction Theory and Interfacing Techniques for Real-Time Performance." In *Trends in Gestural Control of Music*, edited by Marcelo M.Wanderley and Marc Battier., 41–70. Paris: IRCAM–Centre Pompidou, 2000.

Chion, Michel. *Audio-Vision: Sound on Screen*. New York: Columbia University Press, 1994.

Chion, Michel. *Le Son: Traité d'acoulogie*. Paris: Editions Nathan, 1998.

Cohen, Annabel. J. "Music as a Source of Emotion in Film." In *Music and Emotion: Theory and Research*, edited by Juslin, Patrick N. and John A. Sloboda, 249–279. Oxford: Oxford University Press, 2001.

Collins, Karen. "An Introduction to the Participatory and Non-Linear Aspects of Video Games Audio." In *Essays on Sound and Vision*, edited by John Richardson and Stan Hawkins, 263–298. Helsinki: Helsinki University Press, 2007.

Collins, Karen. *Game Sound: An Introduction to the History, Theory and Practice of Video Game Music and Sound Design* Cambridge, Mass.: MIT Press, 2008.

Collins, Karen, Holly Tessler, Kevin. A. Harrigan, Michael. J. Dixon, and Jonathan Fugelsang. "Sound in Electronic Gambling Machines: A Case Study of Player Interaction." In *Game Sound Technology and Player Interaction: Concepts and Developments*, edited by Mark Grimshaw, 1–21. London: IGI Global, 2011.

Csikszentmihalyi, Mihalyi. *Flow: The Psychology of Optimal Experience.* New York: Harper Perennial, 1990.

Dix, Alan, Janet Finlay, Gregory Abowd, and Russell Beale. *Human Computer Interaction.* London: Prentice Hall, 1998.

Friberg, Johnny, and Dan Gärdenfors. "Audio Games: New Perspectives on Game Audio." In *Proceedings of the ACM International Conference on Advances in Computer Entertainment Technology*, 148–154. Jumanji, Singapore, June 3–5 2004.

Griffiths, Mark, and Jonathan Parke. "The Psychology of Music in Gambling Environments: An Observational Research Note." *Journal of Gambling Issues* 13 (2005), at http://jgi.camh.net/doi/full/10.4309/jgi.2005.13.8 (accessed November 12, 2012).

Grimshaw, Mark. "The Acoustic Ecology of the First Person Shooter." PhD diss., University of Waikato, New Zealand, 2007.

Hatfield, Julie, R. F. Job Soames, Andrew J. Hede, Normal L. Carter, Peter Peploe, Richard Taylor, and Stephen Morrell. "Human Response to Environmental Noise: The Role of Perceived Control." *International Journal of Behavioral Medicine* 9, no. 4 (2002): 341–359.

Jørgenson, Kristine. "Left in the Dark: Playing Computer Games with the Sound Turned Off." In *From Pac-Man to Pop Music: Interactive Audio in Games and New Media*, edited by Karen Collins, 163–176. Aldershot: Ashgate, 2008.

Kassabian, Anahid. "The Sound of a New Film Form." In *Popular Music and Film*, edited by Ian Inglis, 91–101. London: Wallflower, 2003.

Lombard, Matthew, and Jennifer Snyder-Duch. "Interactive Advertising and Presence: A Framework." *Journal of Interactive Advertising* 1, no. 2 (2001), at http://www.jiad.org/article13 (accessed November 12, 2012).

Manovich, Lev. *The Language of New Media*. Cambridge, Mass.: MIT Press, 2001.

McMillan, Sally J. "Exploring Models of Interactivity from Multiple Research Traditions: Users, Documents, and Systems." In *Handbook of New Media*, edited by Leah A. Lievrouw and Sonia Livingston, 162–182. London: Sage. 2002.

Parke, Jonathan, and Mark Griffiths. "The Psychology of the Fruit Machine: The Role of Structural Characteristics (Revisited)." *International Journal of Mental Health and Addiction* 4 (2006): 151–179.

Pavlou, Paul A., and David W. Stewart. "Measuring the Effects and Effectiveness of Interactive Advertising: A Research Agenda." *Journal of Interactive Advertising* 1, no. 1 (2000), at http://jiad.org/article6 (accessed November 12, 2012).

Rocchesso, Davide, and Roberto Bresin. "Emerging Sounds for Disappearing Computers." In *The Disappearing Computer, Lecture Notes in Computer Science 4500*, edited by Norbert Streitz, Achilles Kameas, and Irene Mavrommati, 233–254. Berlin: Springer-Verlag, 2007.

Schull, Natasha Dow. "Digital Gambling: The Coincidence of Desire and Design." *The Annals of the American Academy of Political and Social Science* 597 (2005): 65–81.

Tagg, Philip. *Kojak: Fifty Seconds of Television Music*. New York: Mass Media Music Scholars' Press, 2000.

Whalen, Zach. "Play Along: An Approach to Videogame Music." *Game Studies: The International Journal of Computer Game Research* 4, no. 1 (2004), at http://www.gamestudies.org/0401/whalen (accessed November 12, 2012).

Wharton, Andrew, and Karen Collins. "Subjective Measures of the Influence of Music Personalization on Video Game Play: A Pilot Study." *Game Studies: The International Journal of Computer Game Research* 11, no. 2 (2011), at http:/gamestudies.org/1102/articles/wharton_collins (accessed November 12, 2012).

Wilson, Douglas, and Miguel Sicart. "Now It's personal: On Abusive Game Design." *Proceedings of Future Play 2010*. Vancouver, Canada, May 6–7, 2010 .

Worley, Joyce. "Adventure Vision: Inside the Hardware." *Electronic Games* July (1983), at http://www.handheldmuseum.com/BooksMagazines/Mag-EG_0783/EG0783_16.htm. (accessed November 12, 2012).

Yamada, Masashi. "Can Music Change the Success Rate in a Slot-machine Game?" In *Proceedings of the 10th Western Pacific Acoustics Conference*. Beijing, China, September 21–23, 2009.

CHAPTER 33

MULTICHANNEL GAMING AND THE AESTHETICS OF INTERACTIVE SURROUND

MARK KERINS

For many of us old enough to remember a time when video games were a novelty rather than a commonplace, the phrase "video game sound" brings to mind the lo-fi bleeps of pioneering classics like *Pong* and *Asteroids*, or perhaps the synthesized music loops of Atari 2600, Commodore 64, and NES titles. Modern game sound bears little resemblance to the nostalgia-inducing, simple sound tracks of such systems. Today's home gaming consoles and PCs pack more power than even the highest-end arcade machines of a few years ago, while the high-definition graphics and multichannel, DVD-quality sound tracks of contemporary games rival those of television and feature films. If, as one game sound designer put it, "we're trying to catch up to the movies," that goal is growing ever closer.[1]

In terms of sound playback, game technology has already caught up with the cinema. Most contemporary games rely on the same high-quality sound encoding and playback schemes as the film industry, using digital surround systems such as Dolby Digital and DTS. These systems—introduced to theaters in the early 1990s and now the standard for HDTV, DVD, and Blu-ray as well—employ a "five point one" (5.1) multichannel configuration, which places three distinct channels of sound in front of the viewer (left, center, and right) and two surround channels behind the viewing position (left surround and right surround), then adds a low-frequency effects (LFE) channel (the "point one" of "five point one") for added power in the bass frequencies. Support for outputting premixed 5.1-channel sound first appeared in home game consoles in the early 2000s, and as gaming systems have grown more powerful, their surround capabilities have improved dramatically; the two most advanced current-generation consoles

1 Mark Petty, interview by Mark Kerins, July 7, 2010.

as of this writing, Sony's PlayStation 3 and Microsoft's Xbox 360, both feature real-time 5.1-channel (or better) mixing capabilities.[2]

Yet while the impressive technical capabilities of modern video game sound have been well documented, the *uses* of those capabilities have been given scant attention even as game sound design has grown increasingly complex and varied. Particularly curious, given how much of the scholarly work on gaming focuses on the role of the player in an interactive medium, is the lack of attention paid to gaming's use of surround sound, a technology inherently designed to bring the onscreen environment out into the game player's listening space. At least one experimental study has shown that playing a game in surround rather than in stereo significantly improves players' enjoyment of the experience, suggesting that the type of sound playback used can have as much of an impact on the game-play experience as other facets that have received far more attention.[3] In fact, for all the attention paid to the ever-improving quality of game visuals, this same study found that although 5.1 sound enhanced player ratings of engagement, realism, and enjoyment, no such differences were found between standard-definition and high-definition play.[4] Clearly the role of multichannel sound in gaming deserves more attention than existing research indicates that scholars have given it.

This chapter begins to fill that gap through an overview of gaming surround aesthetics. Specifically, it examines the varying manners in which games structure the three-way relationship among the multichannel soundtrack, the onscreen visuals, and the game play itself. Because many elements of aural and visual design, including surround usage, are highly dependent on the specific type of game in question—a given set of aural and visual strategies can accommodate some forms of gameplay but not others—gaming genres serve as a useful structure for this investigation. That said, a comprehensive survey of all types of games is beyond the scope of a single chapter. I have therefore chosen to explore four genres that together demonstrate both the breadth of surround design approaches found in current gaming and the varying ramifications of different surround usage strategies for the gaming experience.

Platformers and Screen-Centric Mixing

Platform games or "side-scrollers," as one of the oldest and most successful game genres, provide a useful place to begin this study thanks to the clarity of their approach to surround mixing. In a traditional side-scrolling or "2D" platformer—*Super Mario Bros.*

[2] Nintendo's Wii, the other current-generation gaming system, uses a simpler surround system, Dolby Pro Logic II. This system allows for playback over a 5.1-channel sound system, but uses a matrix encoding process that limits the possibilities for how sounds can be placed throughout the soundscape. For more see Jay Beck, "A Quiet Revolution: Changes in American Film Sound Practices, 1967–1979" (PhD diss., University of Iowa, 2003).

[3] Paul Skalski and Robert Whitbred, "Image versus Sound: A Comparison of Formal Feature Effects on Presence and Video Game Enjoyment," *PsychNology Journal* 8, no. 1 (2010): 67–84, 78.

[4] Skalski and Whitbred, "Image versus Sound," 76–80.

is perhaps the best-known example—the player controls an onscreen character who moves left and right (and at times up and down) through a "flat" 2D world toward some endpoint or objective, avoiding obstacles and often acquiring powers or bonuses along the way. This genre adopts a conservative, screen-centric approach to surround mixing, keeping all gameplay sounds in the front three channels and reserving the surround channels for different types of ambience and nondiegetic sounds such as music. In most cases the surround channels contain little unique content; rather, they simply provide an outlet for the sounds of the game to bleed out into the player's environment even as all essential sounds remain in the plane of the 2D game world. A surround system thus provides a more enveloping gaming experience, but no qualitative change to the gameplay.

This mixing strategy mirrors common early usage of surround sound in the cinema. As detailed in my book *Beyond Dolby (Stereo): Cinema in the Digital Sound Age*, Hollywood feature films have historically deployed surround sound in two primary ways. The first is the screen-centric model employed by most surround films prior to the advent of 5.1 surround technology (and still common in the 5.1 era, for reasons explained later in this chapter). This model deploys surround sound primarily for different types of ambience, expanding the onscreen environment, but not the action, into the space of the theater. Mixes using this approach keep dialogue in the front center channel and pan sound effects across the three front channels to correspond to the position of their onscreen sources. Dialogue and effects are rarely moved out into the surround channels regardless of their implied position in the diegetic world.

A visually based conception of cinema tends to drive this screen-centric approach to film mixing; as one surround-phobic director explains, "[T]he movie's on the screen. I'm hearing all this sound out here, but the movie's on the screen. I want to focus on the screen."[5] Regardless of the merits of this argument as applied to the cinema, it does offer a strong rationale for keeping game sounds onscreen in side-scrollers. Literally the entire world of a 2D platformer resides in the same two-dimensional plane as the screen, so it makes perfect sense for the genre to rely on front-heavy sound mixes and employ the surrounds in only a limited fashion. Thus even contemporary side-scrollers featuring 5.1 sound tracks, like *Little Big Planet* (figure 33.1), generally keep all game-play sounds in the front three speakers and use the surround channels solely for different types of ambience and nondiegetic sounds such as music.

This screen-centric mixing style is not unique to platform games. Other types of games in which all the game action is onscreen—that is, where it is understood that nothing important is happening "behind" the implied camera position—frequently adopt this approach as well. Many sports games, for instance, keep all play-related sounds in the front speakers even if atmospheric noises (such as crowds) and elements not originating within the field of play (e.g., music, or comments by the announcers in the *Madden* series) spread more completely around the entire soundscape. The same basic mixing logic holds for variations on the side-scroller genre: if the main action is always onscreen, then

[5] Quoted in Mark Kerins, *Beyond Dolby (Stereo): Cinema in the Digital Sound Age* (Bloomington: Indiana University Press, 2010), 159.

FIGURE 33.1: In a traditional side-scroller like *Little Big Planet*, the surrounds are reserved for non-game-play sounds.

the surround channels should be limited to sounds not directly affecting game play. *Lego Harry Potter* (figure 33.2) offers a good example of how this strategy comes into play in a side-scroller variation. This game is one of many that could be considered an "expanded" 2D side-scroller; it allows players limited movement in depth through a pseudo three-dimensional onscreen world, but otherwise functions as a traditional side-scroller. On the surface this game seems to deviate from the mixing strategy described previously, as it sometimes pans important diegetic sounds into the surround channels.

Most notably, it places the sounds of offscreen enemies in the appropriate surround channel, essentially making the stereo surround speakers function as "far left" and "far right" channels that warn the player ahead of time about upcoming adversaries. This expanded use of the surround channels seems appropriate for a game world that is not quite flat. Even this panning of upcoming enemies into the surrounds, however, still holds to the traditional side-scroller approach to mixing: because offscreen enemies cannot harm the player, panning their sounds to the surround channels has a minimal effect on gameplay itself. Just as in a true 2D platformer, anything that can immediately affect the game or the player is kept onscreen both visually and aurally.

Shooters, Active Surrounds, and the "Exit Door" Effect

The *Lego Harry Potter* example suggests that games with 3-D worlds in which off-screen action can have a major effect on the gameplay could employ a different model

FIGURE 33.2: *Lego Harry Potter* allows its characters to move in-depth within the onscreen world, but as with a traditional side-scroller, this world does not extend into the foreground beyond the implied camera position. Here the surround channels are used to hint at upcoming enemies or items rather than to truly extend the space toward the player.

of surround use. In particular, titles in which the active game world extends not just out to the sides of the screen, but also out in front of the screen (into the space of the player's environment), might be almost *expected* to take a much more aggressive approach to surround mixing. One category of games perfectly suited to, and often deploying, such an aggressive mixing style is the first-person shooter (FPS) genre, best known for classics like *Wolfenstein 3D*, *Doom*, and *Quake*. In this style of game, what the player sees onscreen is literally what one of the in-game characters is seeing (hence the term "first-person"). In 5.1-equipped FPS titles, this visual aesthetic is usually mirrored with an aggressively "first-person" approach to the sound design that pans all sounds around the 5.1 soundscape to correspond with their position around the player's avatar; for example, sounds that originate in the diegetic world from somewhere behind and to the left of the avatar are played through the left surround speaker.

If the surround mixing model employed by side-scrollers mimics that of pre-digital-era cinema, that of FPS titles similarly resembles that of later, 5.1-equipped films. After 5.1-channel digital sound was introduced to movie theaters, some filmmakers exploited the new technology's enhanced surround capabilities by abandoning the screen-centric mixing strategies common to earlier surround films in favor of a more aggressive mixing style (and corresponding visual strategies, such as quick cutting and heavy reliance on close-ups with limited use of master shots). Dubbed "diegetic immersion," this aesthetic approach to filmmaking—impossible with earlier surround technologies—visually and aurally places the audience in the midst of the onscreen action. One key element of this style is that in contrast to earlier strategies of reserving the surround channels for different types of ambience and music, virtually all diegetic sounds (sometimes excepting dialogue, sometimes not) are panned around the 5.1 soundscape so that their aural locations correspond with their positions in the filmic world relative to the implied camera.

First-person shooters with 5.1-channel soundtracks adopt a similar approach, panning sounds throughout the multichannel soundscape to correspond to their sources' locations in the diegetic environment relative to the onscreen view from the player/avatar's position. In *Bioshock 2*, for example, careful spatialization of sonic elements within the 5.1 soundscape keeps players aware of what is happening on all sides of their avatars (figure 33.3). Yet while the surround mixing strategy of FPS games mimics the cinematic strategy of diegetic immersion, one major difference between the two is their relative prevalence in their respective mediascapes. In the cinema, the screen-centric surround mixing style of the previous era still remains common two decades after the debut of 5.1 digital surround, even as 5.1-channel sound has emerged as the standard release format for nearly all varieties of audiovisual content. Modern FPS games, however, almost all employ heavily spatialized mixes. This difference reflects a number of dissimilarities between film and gaming. For instance, the two media privilege dramatically different types of listening positions. A motion picture soundtrack needs to play well to a large number of seating positions—more than five hundred in the largest theaters—even though multichannel mixes sound best from a limited range of positions, and the size of this ideal listening location or "sweet spot" shrinks with increasing numbers of sound channels. One reason filmmakers continue to employ screen-centric mixes while using the surround channels principally for different types of ambience is that keeping all important sounds in the plane of the screen ensures that

FIGURE 33.3: In *Bioshock* 2, careful spatialization of sonic elements within the 5.1 soundscape keeps players aware of what is happening on all sides of their avatars.

their soundtracks will sound acceptable from a wide variety of positions.[6] Though the same "sweet spot" limitations apply to game sound design, they are less important in the latter realm because game players generally sit in a well-defined area directly in front of the screen. Game designers, unlike filmmakers, can thus employ heavily spatialized mixes with the comfort of knowing that players will be seated in, or very near, the sweet spot.

Game designers have another advantage over their filmmaker brethren in creating fully spatialized sonic environments: the relative ease of doing so. Film mixers have to manually pan every sonic element (effect, dialogue, music, etc.) to its appropriate location in the 5.1 environment—and each cut, camera movement, or movement of a sound-emitting object onscreen means sounds must be painstakingly replaced in their proper locations. This is no easy feat under the tight budgetary and timeframe pressures usually accompanying the final mixing process. In contrast, the diegetic environments of a three-dimensional game are built from the ground up inside a computer. The computer "knows" exactly where each sound source exists relative to the player avatar, the implied camera, and other sounds, and can place sounds in the 5.1 soundscape accordingly during game play.

Visual aesthetics—specifically the lack of cutting—also play a role in promoting spatialized soundtracks in first-person shooters. As a rule of thumb, sound designers in all media aim to create "continuous" soundtracks, in which careful editing and mixing hide aural cuts, keeping the soundtrack from drawing attention to itself and smoothing over cuts in the image track. One of the unusual features of the diegetic immersion model in cinema is that it inherently violates this strategy: sounds jump from one channel to another precisely *at* cuts in the image track, as this is where sound-emitting objects jump from one place to another relative to the implied camera position in the diegetic world. These sonic discontinuities can draw attention to cuts, highlighting the cinematic apparatus, which is one reason not all filmmakers are comfortable with the diegetic immersion aesthetic. This issue, though, is not a problem for first-person shooters. During FPS gameplay, the visuals show the view through an in-game avatar's eyes. A cut in the image track would mean the character teleported (an event one would expect to be accompanied by an abrupt change in the soundtrack as well), so in normal gameplay the image track *cannot* cut—and thus neither can the soundtrack, which is spatially matched to the image track. Sounds may move from one channel to another as the in-game avatar moves, but they cannot make the troublesome jumps between channels that inhibit use of diegetic immersion in the cinema.

One final factor may bear more responsibility than any other for the greater prevalence of aggressively spatialized sound mixes in FPS games than in movies: the difference between filmmakers and game designers in their perceptions of how surround may distract audiences or players. Filmmakers have worried since the introduction of surround sound about the "exit door effect": the possibility that audience members will

[6] Kerins, *Beyond Dolby*, 280–281.

misinterpret attention-drawing sound effects in the surround channels as originating from occurrences in the theater itself and turn their attention from the screen to look behind them. Even today, when audiences have decades of experience with surround sound, fears of the exit door effect still lead many filmmakers to push for conservative, screen-centric surround mixes regardless of whether aggressive surround mixing might be more appropriate for the scene at hand.

Game designers building first-person shooters, however, are less concerned about the exit door effect. Indeed, in the gaming world offscreen sounds that draw a player's attention away from the screen can serve a valuable purpose. To be sure, game designers, like filmmakers, do not want their players/audiences to think that sounds mixed behind the viewing position are coming from sources in the viewing space rather than from the diegetic world. But in games, designers often *want* players to pay specific attention to sounds originating behind them. As one game director points out, 5.1 sound can "give players information that cannot be visually described on-screen... allowing them to anticipate key plot points or enemies approaching from different directions."[7] Panning sounds to the surround channels, in other words, allows designers to intentionally draw a player's focus to nonvisible elements of the game world; the simple fact that a significant sound comes from the surround channels makes it stick out.[8] If, for example, an enemy is shooting at a player from behind, those gunshot sounds *should* come from the rear speakers—thus drawing the player's conscious attention—because this spatial information aids the gameplay decision of whether to shoot back and, if so, where to aim.

Of course, taking advantage of these spatial cues requires the player to recognize those sounds as originating from the game world rather than from the listening environment. Film sound designers realized long ago that the opening minutes of a movie shape audience expectations about that film's aesthetic approach and that using the surrounds aggressively early in a film lowers the probability of activating the exit door effect later by teaching the audience to *expect* surround effects.[9] Game sound designers appear to have taken this lesson to heart. Most modern FPS games begin with some sort of "training" sequence at the start of the game, where the player learns how to use the controller and what to expect from the gameplay. In surround-equipped games, these segments also offer a ready-made opportunity to train the player about the game's approach to surround mixing. For example, in the training sequence that opens *Call of Duty: Modern Warfare 2*, players go through an abbreviated military boot camp course that not only teaches them how to play the game, but also acclimates them to the game's highly spatialized sonic environment. Throughout this segment the voice of a drill sergeant (who offers instructions about how to play) is panned within the

[7] "Dolby Digital 5.1 Turns Up the Volume for SEGA's Holiday Xbox Line-Up," August 20, 2002, at http://www.thefreelibrary.com/Dolby+Digital+5.1+Turns+Up+the+Volume+for+SEGA%27s+Holiday+Xbox+Line-Up-a090541313 (accessed June 15, 2009).

[8] Petty interview.

[9] Kerins, *Beyond Dolby*, 173–180.

5.1 soundscape to match his position relative to the player avatar, including points when his voice comes solely from the surround channels to indicate that he is standing directly behind the player. This sequence effectively accustoms players both to hearing diegetic sounds from all directions and to gleaning useful information from those sounds.

With the surround design of a first-person shooter—unlike that of a side-scroller—conveying potentially strategy-altering information, game play in a first-person shooter can differ radically depending on whether the game is played in surround or mono. Game designers know that not everyone has a 5.1 system, and they work hard to ensure that their products will remain playable and enjoyable regardless of a user's home setup. Indeed, in some cases they pair aggressively spatialized surround mixes with visual localization cues, such as arrows or other indicators, showing the direction from which the player is being attacked. Yet while such techniques allow players without surround sound systems to visually acquire spatial information normally conveyed by the surroundscape, they still cannot acquire it as quickly as those who have a 5.1 surround setup. In single-player games, this difference has minimal effect; at worst, a game becomes somewhat more difficult when played in a nonsurround environment. But in an online multiplayer battle—a staple of the FPS genre—someone using only a monophonic or two-channel stereo sound system faces a distinct disadvantage when playing against a competitor equipped with a 5.1 sound system, because the latter player can locate the source of enemy fire in the three-dimensional game world more quickly. During a firefight in which an extra second can make the difference between killing or being killed, this advantage cannot be overstated.

In the end, how much heavily spatialized sound design actually affects gameplay varies, depending largely on the number of distinguishable sonic elements playing at one time—and somewhat counterintuitively, the busier the sonic environment, the *less* useful the 5.1 environment becomes to the player. This is not to say that busier soundscapes somehow make surround sound irrelevant; complex multichannel environments can certainly increase the sense of reality and immersion in a game world, which may make a game seem better or more fun. But as the number of sounds present at any given time grows larger, surround sound becomes less valuable as a tool for helping a player locate objects or characters in the diegetic world, because it becomes increasingly difficult to pinpoint any one sound in the cacophony. Essentially, the fewer enemies or other sound-emitters in an area, the more useful the 5.1 soundscape becomes in guiding the player to key points of focus. Spatialization of sound effects in the 5.1 environment tends to be more helpful in games—whether first-person shooters like *Bioshock* or third-person shooters like *Dead Space*—in which enemies often appear alone or in small groups than in games such as *Call of Duty* or *Halo*, which are dominated by frenetic, heavily populated battles. In terms of multiplayer gameplay, this suggests that the advantage of a player with a surround sound system over one without may diminish as more players enter the game—and that a player without a surround system can minimize that disadvantage by playing in games with lots of players rather than in small groups or one-on-one matches.

Third-person Gaming, Perspective, and Image–Sound Disparity

In narrative feature film, point-of-view segments tend to feature atypically aggressive surround mixing.[10] Thus it is unsurprising that first-person shooters—which are essentially game-length point-of-view scenes—feature heavy sonic spatialization. Third-person action-adventure and shooter games present an interesting corollary to the FPS genre. These titles in many ways resemble first-person shooters, in that players control avatars moving through a three-dimensional world to achieve game objectives, often with combat elements and weaponry similar to FPS games (indeed, some third-person shooters even switch to a literal first-person perspective when using certain weapons, such as sniper rifles). In third-person games, however, the onscreen view is not that of the avatar character per se, but that of an omniscient viewer *near* the avatar, usually slightly above and behind, or over his or her shoulder.

Because the player's view is not intrinsically tied to that of the avatar, these games usually include an element missing from the FPS genre: camera controls allowing the player to alter the onscreen view independently of character movement. This addition significantly complicates the image-sound-player relationship. In the first-person genre, image and sound are always tightly connected to the perspective of a character in the game world: a player sees and hears what would be heard from the avatar's actual position in the game world. In a third-person game, on the other hand, a player can move the game camera to acquire visual information about objects or enemies not visible to the onscreen avatar. Third-person gaming thus ontologically separates the player's *perspective* of the game from the diegetic *gameplay*. In other words, in an FPS game changing the onscreen view (and soundscape orientation) moves the player's avatar, directly affecting the in-game world, but in a third-person game the particular spatial orientation of the visual and sonic environment is not intrinsically tied to anything in the game itself. Third-person gaming therefore requires players to identify with and control avatars from which the aesthetic design intrinsically distances them.

This foregrounding of the distinction between the player and the onscreen avatar, quite different from the precise match between player and avatar experience in a first-person shooter, blurs the role of surround sound and sonic spatialization. Although surround sound in third-person gaming still functions to put the listener in a specific place (as in first-person games), it becomes unclear what exactly that place is—it could be the camera's position behind the avatar, the body of the avatar, or even the listening space itself. Such uncertainty about the aural perspective to be rendered is reflected in the array of surround design approaches taken by third-person titles, in marked contrast to the largely uniform strategy of aggressive surround use in the FPS category. On

[10] Kerins, *Beyond Dolby*, 181.

the less surround-intensive end of the third-person spectrum, we find games such as *Assassin's Creed,* which spreads environmental sounds and different types of ambience into the surrounds but rarely pans attention-drawing sounds out of the front channels; in this screen-centric approach, the surround channels expand the diegetic space beyond the screen but offer little additional spatial information. This mixing strategy situates the player "in" the diegetic environment, but at a remove from the action.

Such an ultraconservative mixing style is relatively uncommon in contemporary games, perhaps because it does not exploit the capabilities of 5.1 surround technology to the degree that tech-savvy gamers who have doled out thousands of dollars for their home entertainment systems expect. More commonly, third-person games adopt a moderately immersive surround design, keeping attention-grabbing elements in the front channels but correctly positioning atmospheric sounds and effects with clear in-game sources—that is, those unlikely to trigger the exit door effect—around the 5.1 surroundscape. *Demon's Souls,* for example, builds an enveloping 5.1-channel environment out of wind and eerie spirit sounds and incorporates panned "fly-by" effects in cases where the sounds' diegetic sources are clear. When an arrow flies past a player, for example, the sounds of the arrow move through the appropriate channels; similarly, when the player runs by a campfire, the flame sounds move from the front to the back, then die off. But the game avoids using surround effects to guide players' attention to unseen enemies, restricting these gameplay-driving sounds to the front channels. Ultimately this mixing strategy uses the capabilities of 5.1 to draw the player into the environment and makes the world *feel* spatialized by panning carefully chosen elements throughout the soundscape, but acknowledges that the player's perspective is not literally that of the onscreen avatar and avoids using multichannel in any way that could draw the player's attention offscreen and out of the game world.

Finally, some third-person titles exploit the 5.1 configuration to create fully spatialized surround mixes as aggressive as those heard in first-person shooters. *Batman: Arkham Asylum,* one example of this class, places virtually all sounds—including even much of the dialogue—in their appropriate locales around the 5.1 soundscape. Sounds are positioned relative to the game camera, so if a player rotates the camera, the soundscape rotates with it to maintain correct matching between sounds and their onscreen (or implied offscreen) sources. Figure 33.4, for example, shows a gameplay still in which the player has rotated the game camera to face the Batman avatar. The result is that the 5.1 soundscape heard by the player is nearly 180 degrees opposite the one the in-game Batman would actually hear. This type of lockstep matching between visual and aural orientation produces conflicting, and sometimes competing, effects when used in the third-person genre. On the one hand, it creates a sense of immersion, making the onscreen environment feel like a living, inhabited place with things happening on all sides and allowing the player to explore that world in all directions via the camera controls. On the other hand, this setup highlights the player's distance *from* the game world. Whenever a player takes control of the camera and uses it to look around without moving the onscreen character, the pairing of a shifting visual and aural perspective with the static onscreen avatar serves as a reminder that here—unlike in FPS games, where

FIGURE 33.4: In this gameplay still from *Batman: Arkham Asylum*, the player has rotated the game camera to face the Batman avatar. The result is that the 5.1 soundscape heard by the player is 180 degrees opposite that the in-game Batman would actually hear.

the player essentially *is* the in-game character—the player remains forever an outside observer.

Rhythm Games and Static 3D Soundscapes

The final game genre I consider here—"rhythm games" like *Guitar Hero, Rock Band,* and *Dance Dance Revolution*—similarly highlights the disparity between the gameplay experience of the player and the action within the game itself. Alternately known as music games or performance games, titles in the rhythm genre require the player to complete prescribed actions (dance steps, guitar strums, and so on) in time with music and onscreen instructions. Given the music-driven nature of these games and the long-running debate in the music industry about how best to employ surround sound (some argue for "performance" mixes, placing the direct sounds of the band in the front channels and using the surround channels solely for ambient sounds that create a sense of space; others prefer an "in the band" approach, spreading direct performance sounds around the entire soundscape), one might expect that rhythm games as a genre would display a similarly varied approach to multichannel mixing.

In actuality, rhythm games are surprisingly uniform in their mixing strategies, more or less adopting the music industry's "performance" approach to surround mixing. They mix the music itself to the three front channels, reserving the rear channels for crowd sounds and reverb. In a sense this is a curiously conservative approach in the gaming world, as most non-rhythm games freely mix music into the surrounds. To be clear, this mixing strategy does not mean that music is entirely absent from the rear channels in rhythm games—often the surround channels help create a sense of space through echoes and reverberations of the music, even while all the direct musical sounds are mixed to the front speakers. Nor does it mean that the surrounds are used only for unimportant different types of ambience (as in most screen-centric cinematic mixes): in many rhythm games, the crowd sounds in the rear channels serve as crucial components of the sound and game design, with applause, boos, or singing each providing signals about the quality of the players' performances.

But for the many rhythm games of the *Guitar Hero* type, in which the gameplay involves players "creating" the music, this highly specified mixing strategy puts players in an odd implied position. Because the music all comes from in front of the players, and the crowd sounds all emerge from behind them, the game seems to indicate that the players are facing the onstage band from some limbo between the band and the crowd, rather than actually being part of either. To be sure, the gameplay itself leaves no doubt that players are supposed to *be* the band members—the players' unique onscreen avatars are on stage playing, while the gameplay involves hitting correct "notes" on an instrument-shaped controller. Yet this makes it doubly curious that the music originates from *in front of* the real-world players rather than from all *around* them, and that the crowd sounds come from the rear rather than from the front, as the actual first-person perspective of the onscreen band members would yield precisely the opposite sonic orientation.

Clearly this case resembles that of the third-person adventure games described previously, in which players have a different sonic perspective than their avatars. In rhythm games based on playing music, though, this disconnect between the viewing/listening experience of the player and that of the player's avatar within the game is compounded by the way the musical elements are spread across the front three audio channels. As an example, consider *Rock Band 2*, a music performance game in which up to four players at a time can each control a different instrument (guitar, bass, drums, or vocals). Though the character and presence of the sounds making up the mix change during gameplay—poor performance by a player results in scratchy or missing notes from that player's instrument—many elements of the mix, including the placement of each instrument in the multichannel environment, are predetermined. Some songs, for example, place the guitar track in the front left channel and the bass track in the front right, a configuration that remains the same regardless of the number of simultaneous players or which player chooses which instrument.

This preset orientation can create confusing spatial mismatches in certain gaming conditions. In the simplest example of such an issue, two players each use a guitar controller. After one player selects to play guitar or bass, the other player is obliged to play the unchosen instrument. Instructions for each instrument (e.g., what guitar frets to hold) are presented side-by-side across the width of the screen. Which set of instructions appears on the left of the screen and which on the right depends on the assigned controller numbers; instructions relating to whichever guitar controller is designated (via menu) as controller number 1, for example, will always be on the left of the screen—whether the player using it is playing guitar or bass—and those for controller 2 (or any higher number) will be on the right. Depending on which player selects which instrument, then, the guitar instructions could end up on the left of the screen, with the bass instructions on the right, or vice versa.

Since the guitar sounds are always panned to the same respective channels, but the visual instruction placement varies, roughly half the time the instrument sounds will be spatially mismatched with the onscreen instructions (as well as with the players, who usually move to the side of the screen with their own instructions to read the cues more easily). The guitar instructions, for example, may appear on the right-hand side while the guitar sounds are panned to the left. Conceptually, this configuration creates a disconnect between the player and the sound of the game. More important, it can hinder the actual game play, which requires that players be able to hear their own instruments to tell if they get ahead of or behind the beat. This means that it is often nearly impossible for whoever plays the bass to hear that instrument if the bassist is on the wrong side of the room, because the (relatively loud) guitar sounds coming from right in front of that player easily drown out the (subtler) bass music emanating from the speaker on the opposite side. If one player always plays bass and another always plays guitar, they can avoid this problem by setting the controller numberings appropriately, but as *Rock Band* is a "party" game in which players often switch controllers and/or instruments between songs or setlists, this is simply an impractical solution for most real-world gaming sessions, and mismatches occur quite frequently.

Adding one more layer to the already complicated spatial relationships among the players' avatars, the players themselves, the sound mix, and the onscreen instructions are the background onscreen visuals, which change fairly independently of the other elements. Unlike the image tracks of any of the genres previously discussed, those of rhythm games are *discontinuous*. While the stream of instructions to the player about what keys to press (or notes to sing, or dance steps to do) flows continuously during a performance, the visuals of the on-stage performance of the player's avatar do not. Instead, following common concert video practice, every few seconds they cut to a different view of the performance. And unlike the editing in most narrative filmmaking, the cutting here does not adhere to any particular spatial logic. In music performance games like *Rock Band* or *Guitar Hero*, successive shots may include close-ups of band members (as seen in figure 33.5, where a player's avatar is facing out toward the player), wide shots of the whole stage from over the crowd, and shots from behind the band looking out at the crowd. Meanwhile, even as the visuals present several significantly different spatial orientations, the orientation of the multichannel soundscape remains constant (music in front, crowd in surrounds)—perhaps taking a cue from traditional cinematic practices, in which the continuous sound track deemphasizes cuts in the image track.

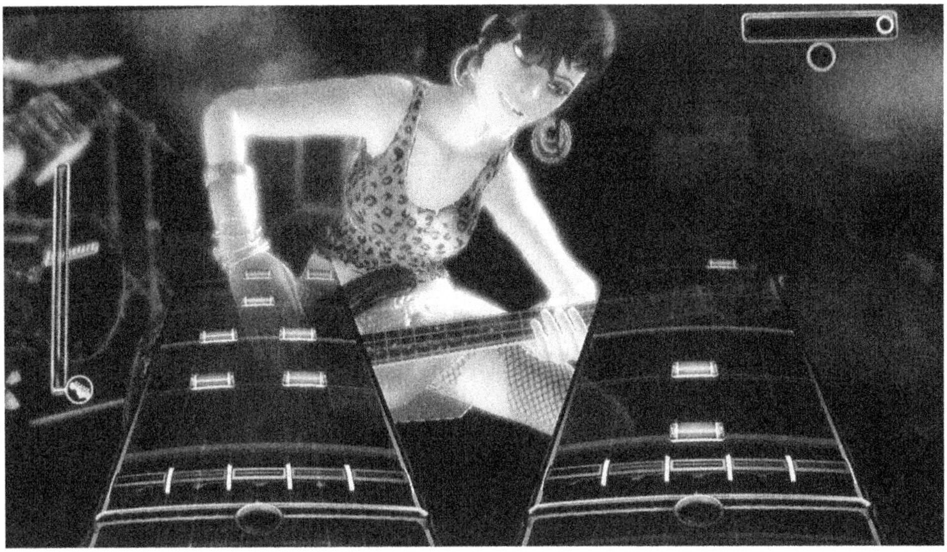

FIGURE 33.5: Two sets of instructions—guitar and bass—appear in front of one of the player avatars during *Rock Band 2* game play; all three of these visual elements can spatially mismatch both the orientation of the soundscape and the actual players' positions.

This approach to the image–sound relationship might at first appear similar to the traditional screen-centric cinematic mixing model described previously, in which sounds do not move from speaker to speaker just because the image cuts to a new shot with a different orientation. In the cinematic version of this strategy, however, reorientation of the sonic space is unnecessary, as all important sounds remain in front of the audience regardless of the onscreen shot. This differs dramatically from rhythm games, in which the multichannel sonic environment has a definite, specific three-dimensional orientation: performance in the front channels, audience in the rear channels. By pairing a discontinuous image track with a consistent three-dimensional sonic space, heard in a consistent orientation, rhythm games highlight—perhaps more than any other common media form—the constructed artificial nature of both multichannel soundtracks and the image tracks that accompany them.[11] The music-performance subgenre in particular epitomizes this split. Its image track presents one spatial configuration, its onscreen instructions another, and its multichannel soundtrack a third, offering the player at least three distinct and unrelated spatial configurations simultaneously.

[11] Music videos and the musical sequences of film musicals present the closest film-style counterparts to rhythm games. Music video, however, remains a two-channel stereo medium, while the limited number of musicals released in the 5.1 era have taken a variety of approaches to surround mixing. The 2007 musical *Hairspray* even varies the surround mixing of its musical sequences depending on whether they are really occurring in the diegesis or just fantasies. See Kerins, *Beyond Dolby*, 307–315.

The Complexity of Gaming Surround

Even though I have covered only a small sampling of genres, my overview of surround sound in gaming has illustrated the breadth of approaches the video game medium has taken to surround mixing and has explained some of the factors leading to such varying approaches. Most significantly, I hope I have shown how complex game sound aesthetics can be, and that they offer a fertile scholarly field of study. Although some elements of sound design may span all audiovisual media, clearly game sound (and game surround) differs dramatically in some ways from that of film, television, or indeed any other media form. These differences trace their roots to a number of factors, many of which I discussed in this chapter. The most significant is the peculiar fact of gaming being—uniquely among mass media—inherently interactive: where film and television require the audience to sit back and take in a predesigned piece of artwork, video games are based on the concept that players/audiences can affect both their audiovisual experiences and what actually happens within the game. This interactivity fundamentally alters the sound design process in games, adding a layer of complexity beyond that faced by sound designers in film and television; choices made by game designers about how aggressively first- and third-person shooters spatialize their soundtracks, for instance, are partially decisions about how much offscreen elements should affect gameplay.

Of course game sound design choices are not dictated solely by gameplay considerations; the various factors that influence surround mixing decisions in other media have an impact on games as well. Visual aesthetics play a role, such as when the lack of visual cuts in first-person shooters eases concerns about the exit door effect, encouraging more aggressive surround mixing. The type of diegetic environment portrayed matters, such as when the flat, two-dimensional worlds of platform games suggest screen-centric multichannel mixes. And as with any media form, technological and industrial constraints can have as significant an effect on sound design strategies as anything else, even if their influence often remains invisible to the end user. Game sound designers have to deal not only with the same budgetary and production timetable limitations as film sound crews, but also with challenges unique to the game medium. These include physical limits on how quickly data can be read off a disc or drive; battles over how to allocate console processor resources among video, sound, and other needs; and the inherent "nonlinearity of the creative process" in a medium where changes in the mix cannot simply be made and immediately heard, but rather must be coded, compiled, and then evaluated in test gameplay.[12]

These issues all deserve further study. Here I have endeavored not to provide a comprehensive study of surround's role in video games or the factors affecting surround usage, but rather to lay the groundwork—and suggest likely productive directions—for

[12] Petty interview.

further work spanning a variety of scholarly methodologies. For one, as made clear in this chapter, surround sound functions differently in different game genres, and empirical work exploring audience responses to surround sound in a variety of genres could help determine whether and how strongly any effect of multichannel on the player experience depends on how a given game deploys the soundtrack's multichannel capabilities. Indeed, the study cited previously that found surround sound increased audience enjoyment and engagement in gameplay exemplifies the importance of genre awareness. Its results were based on experiments with a single game title—a first-person shooter, the only genre discussed here in which the presence or lack of a surround sound system can exert a direct impact on gameplay.

For those scholars interested more in industrial practices than in quantitative research, specific investigations into the effect of technological and commercial limitations on game sound design would also be valuable. They could ask, for example, how often aggressive surround mixing plans end up compromised by limits on how much processing power is available for audio, or how designers approach the task of sound mixing, an incredibly controlled and precise process in the film world, given the interactive nature of their medium. And as yet a third potential scholarly approach, historically minded researchers could trace the impact of multichannel soundtracks on game design itself. How has the use of surround changed as game makers have gained more experience with it, and how, if at all, have they altered their design practices to better exploit it?

I have suggested but a small sampling of the many questions about game surround that scholars can, and should, investigate. In the end, that may be the most important point made in this chapter: sound design in general, and surround sound in particular, is an integral element of game aesthetics, and it deserves as much attention as any other aspect of the game medium. As the emerging scholarly field of game studies matures, those working in this realm must ensure that it avoids the mistake made by cinema studies, which for decades treated film as a solely visual medium (and often still does). Instead, we need to study gaming as the intensely audiovisual medium it is. Only in this way can we understand this medium and its technological, cultural, and artistic impact.

References and Further Reading

Beck, Jay. "A Quiet Revolution: Changes in American Film Sound Practices, 1967–1979." PhD diss., University of Iowa, 2003. (surround sound)

Brandon, Alexander. *Audio for Games: Planning, Process, and Production.* Berkeley, CA: New Riders Games, 2004. (gaming sound)

Chion, Michel. *Audio-Vision*: Sound on Screen. Translated by Claudia Gorbman. New York: Columbia University Press, 1994. (image–sound relationship)

Collins, Karen. *Game Sound: An Introduction to the History, Theory, and Practice of Video Game Music and Sound Design.* Cambridge: MIT Press, 2008. (gaming sound)

Cook, Nicholas. *Analyzing Musical Multimedia*. Oxford: Oxford University Press, 2000. (image–sound relationship)

Kerins, Mark. *Beyond Dolby (Stereo):* Cinema *in the Digital Sound Age*. Bloomington: Indiana University Press, 2010. (surround sound)

Kerins, Mark. "Understanding the Impact of Surround Sound in Multimedia." In *The Psychology of Music in Multimedia*, edited by Siu-Lan Tan, Annabel Cohen, Scott Lipscomb, and Roger Kendall, 361–384. Oxford: Oxford University Press, 2013. (surround sound)

Marks, Aaron. *The Complete Guide to Game Audio for Composers, Musicians, Sound Designers, and Game Developers*. Oxford: Focal Press, 2009. (gaming sound)

Skalski, Paul, and Robert Whitbred. "Image versus Sound: A Comparison of Formal Feature Effects on Presence and Video Game Enjoyment." *PsychNology Journal* 8, no. 1 (2010): 67–84. (surround sound and gaming sound)

PART VI

AUDIOVISUALITY IN PERFORMANCE AND DAILY LIFE

CHAPTER 34

SOUND AND VISION: THE AUDIO/VISUAL ECONOMY OF MUSICAL PERFORMANCE

PHILIP AUSLANDER

A current debate in computer music touches on a fundamental question about the audiovisual economy of musical performance. Audiences at musical performances using traditional instruments are assumed to understand the underlying cause-and-effect relationships between what they see and what they hear (e.g., if I see a musician press a key on a piano or even reach inside it, I understand the sound that follows to be the result of the action I witnessed). By contrast, audiences of music that uses relatively unfamiliar digital devices such as various MIDI interfaces or laptop computers as instruments cannot be assumed to understand the relationships between the performers' actions and the resulting sounds (unless, of course, they are fully conversant with the particular technologies and techniques in use). As Caleb Stuart points out, "With the laptop, there is no [cause-and-effect] connection. From the point of view of the audience, the computer is an inanimate object; it sits there while the performer acts surreptitiously behind the screen.... The audience in general does not know exactly what it is that the performer is doing and most do not know how the sound is produced or with what."[1] (See figure 34.1; and video clip 34.1.⊙)

This masked production of sound challenges the understanding of the relationship between musician and audience that I call the "traditionalist" view. W. Andrew Schloss outlines aspects of this position: "[T]his relationship is based on many factors, most significantly on trust, and also on the audience *understanding* what the performer is doing on stage."[2] Those engaged in the debate about computer music agree that new musical

[1] Caleb Stuart, "The Object of Performance: Aural Performativity in Contemporary Laptop Music," *Contemporary Music Review* 22 (2003): 61.

[2] W. Andrew Schloss, "Using Contemporary Technology in Live Performance: The Dilemma of the Performer," *Journal of New Music Research* 32 (2003): 239. Emphasis in original.

FIGURE 34.1: Patrick K.-H. and Oleg Makarov, live-acousmatic performance, LoveLiveElectronic Festival, November 27, 2009. Camera: Ivan Savchenko, "OK-films" studio. Source: http://www.youtube.com/watch?v=VIVFmIoMpt4.

technologies challenge the traditional relationship of audience to performance, but view this challenge differently. Schloss, who represents the traditionalist side, insists to computer musicians that "[a] visual component is essential to the audience, such that there is a visual display of input parameters/gestures" that clarifies the nature of causality in the performance.[3] Stuart, on the other hand, argues that "[t]he performativity of the music is to be found in the act of listening and the performance of the audience in relationship to the sound they hear. There is no need then for us to see a performer physically interacting with an instrument to engage in this aural performativity: we need only listen and engage in the act of listening."[4]

Although this debate is driven by the accelerating incursion of digital technologies into the live performance of music, the underlying issues are not new. The current debate is a chapter in the ongoing argument over what Pierre Schaeffer, who was central to the development of *musique concrète* beginning in the 1940s, called "acousmatic sound," defined by Jonathan Sterne as "sounds that one hears without seeing their source."[5] The idea that the audial and visual dimensions of musical performance are distinguishable "tracks," and the question of how the relationship between these tracks should be understood and configured in performance, has come up in many different contexts at least since recording technology made it possible to experience sound apart from vision.[6] The

[3] Schloss, "Using Contemporary Technology," 242.

[4] Stuart, "Object of Performance," 64.

[5] Sterne summarizes the discussion about this concept and its implications briefly in *The Audible Past: Cultural Origins of Sound Reproduction* (Durham, N.C.: Duke University Press, 2003), 20–22.

[6] See Dave Laing, "A Voice Without a Face: Popular Music and the Phonograph in the 1890s," *Popular Music* 10 (1991): 1–9.

understanding of this relationship, which dominated twentieth-century thinking and continues to exert a powerful influence, falls in line with the well-documented Western privileging of the sense of sight.[7]

The traditionalist view acknowledges the importance of "the visual communication of musically relevant information" and generally limits this category to the gestures and facial expressions musicians make while performing.[8] For Schloss, musical performance entails a display of the musician's effort on the audience's behalf, which betokens both an expenditure of physical energy and an ethical commitment "to what one is doing."[9] Stan Godlovitch, who provides a more detailed traditionalist model of musical performance, includes in a list of conditions that have to be met for an event to be considered a musical performance that the event is "the immediate output of some musical instrument" (which does not include computers), involves "the exercise of skilled activity," and is "the outcome of appropriately creditworthy physical skill."[10] Both Schloss and Godlovitch locate the essential aspects of musical performance in things that are not directly apprehensible from sound alone. Godlovitch refutes the idea that listeners who close their eyes at concerts experience "all that is musically significant," because "musical sound alone is not sufficient for performance."[11] One cannot *hear* the musician's effort or skill; one must be able to *see* the "bulging veins in the neck of the trumpeter blasting a high C" to fully appreciate her effort.[12] And one cannot be certain that the musician's sound is a direct product of his skill unless one witnesses him in the act of producing the sound. It is worth noting that musical audiences, for the most part, probably do not have a very fine-grained sense of instrumental causality. As Michael Schutz observes about wind instruments, "changing pitches requires complex interactions between embouchure and fingertips that are far from transparent to audiences."[13] Therefore, the traditionalists' emphasis on visible causality in musical performance is best understood as ideological. In most cases the musical audience does not really understand exactly how the sound is produced, but wants to believe it does nevertheless.

From the traditionalist perspective, anything that inhibits the audience's ability to perceive the musician as the skilled causal agent of the performance, including

[7] The literature on the ocularcentrism of Western culture is vast. One classic study of both ocularcentrism and its critiques is Martin Jay, *Downcast Eyes: The Denigration of Vision in Twentieth Century French Thought* (Berkeley; Los Angeles; London: The University of California Press, 1994).

[8] Michael Schutz, "Seeing Music? What Musicians Need to Know about Vision," *Empirical Musicology Review* 3 (2008): 86, at http://hdl.handle.net/1811/34098 (accessed November 15, 2012). Although I have borrowed the phrase "musically relevant information" from Schutz, I do not consider him a representative of the traditionalist position.

[9] Schloss, "Using Contemporary Technology," 240.

[10] Stan Godlovitch, *Musical Performance: A Philosophical Study* (London; New York: Routledge, 1998), 49. Godlovitch explicitly excludes computers from the realm of musical instruments on page 101.

[11] Godlovitch, *Musical Performance*, 14–15.

[12] Schloss, "Using Contemporary Technology," 240.

[13] Schutz, "Seeing Music?" 101. Theodore Gracyk makes a related point when critiquing Godlovitch in "Listening to Music: Performances and Recordings," *The Journal of Aesthetics and Art Criticism* 55 (1997): 145.

sound recording, distracting spectacle, or the use of digital technologies that obscure cause-and-effect relations, threatens the integrity of musical performance.[14] Godlovitch, for example, argues that "whatever we hear on a recording is not itself sufficient to ground judgments of the player's real role and true merit," because the listener cannot know from the recording itself precisely how it was produced.[15] Even if one believes a performance on a sound recording to reveal virtuosity or hears things that seem to suggest effort and commitment on the musician's part (e.g., pianist Glenn Gould's famous vocal interjections or guitarist Alvin Lee's yelps and exclamations on Ten Years After's recording of "Boogie On"), one would have to have witnessed the performance directly to be able to conclude that the recorded sounds mean what they seem to mean.

When a new technology or media form, including radio, sound recording, music video, and the use of computers in performance, threatens to render this visual verification moot, traditionalists become anxious. Musical traditionalists share this anxiety with theorists of acousmatics, who, as Sterne points out, "assume that face-to-face communication and bodily presence are the yardsticks by which to measure all communicative activity" and fear that certain technologies and performance practices decontextualize "sound from its 'proper' interpersonal context."[16]

In *Liveness: Performance in a Mediatized Culture*, I hypothesize that the category of "liveness" was first used to distinguish some performances from others (the *Oxford English Dictionary* dates the earliest usage of this kind to 1934) in response to such anxiety, brought on at that time by the dominance of radio. Early sound recording technologies did not problematize the distinction between live and recorded sound: if you put a record on your gramophone and listened to it, you knew exactly what you were doing, and there was no possibility of confusing the activity of listening to a record with that of attending a concert. But radio is a blind medium that makes it impossible to verify the source of the sounds being heard. The resolution of this crisis was to create the labels "live" and "recorded" with which to discursively distinguish live broadcasts from recorded material, thus allowing radio listeners to know whether they were hearing the immediate results of musicians' skilled activity or a recording.[17]

More recent manifestations of this anxiety include Godlovitch's concern that digital technologies will eventually displace "real" musical instruments and skills; Schloss's worry that the illegibility of cause-and-effect relations in musical performances involving interfaces with which most listeners are unfamiliar will alienate the audience; and the fear expressed by Thompson, Graham, and Russo that a range of phenomena, including the imagery of music video, spectacular pop music performance, and air

[14] For rhetorical purposes, I am treating the traditionalist view as if it were monolithic. It is not, of course. People who espouse traditionalist values certainly may subscribe in various degrees to the orthodoxy I am positing.

[15] Godlovitch, *Musical Performance*, 26.

[16] Sterne, *Audible Past*, 20–21.

[17] Philip Auslander, *Liveness: Performance in a Mediatized Culture*, 2nd ed. (London: Routledge, 2008), 59–60.

guitar, will replace or draw the audience's attention away from "musically relevant" visual information.[18]

A growing body of research on musical perception and cognition in experimental psychology lends some support to the traditionalist view and its concerns. Studies of hearing suggest that sound perception is multimodal, in that both our visual and auditory senses contribute to it, and that the human brain seeks always to construct causal links between a heard sound and a visible source.[19] Experimental studies of musical performance show that its visual dimensions decisively influence what we hear.[20] However, the *values* attached to the two sensory modalities associated with musical experience—hearing and seeing—and hierarchical relationships between them are not produced by human biology, but rather are cultural in origin.

Although all musical perception is multimodal, it is only in some cultural contexts that audiences demand that the relationship between modalities be structured to reveal the musician's effort and confirm her agency. Although such transparency is imperative to traditionalists, it seems quite clear that the majority of the audiences for the Black Eyed Peas or Lady Gaga, for example, are not in the least bit concerned that their uses of digital technology to produce both instrumental and vocal sounds in performance do not readily allow for identifiable cause-and-effect connections between musical sound and the means used to produce it. Godlovitch explicitly bases his model for musical performance on the classical recitalist, and though Schloss does not identify the genre of music with which he is primarily concerned, his career as a percussionist and computer musician bridges jazz, rock, Latin music, and contemporary composition.[21] It is just as plausible that audiences of classical music and contemporary composition with traditional values would want to see and understand how the music they are hearing is produced as it is that audiences of pop and dance music that employs digital technology do not necessarily share those values.

On the other hand, musicians and their audiences in these latter contexts do not necessarily reject traditionalist values, either. The desire to maintain the transparent relationship between musician and audience is not limited to art music; it is also central to the ideologies of most forms of rock, jazz, blues, country, folk, and other genres of popular music. In work based on ethnographic study of Berlin club DJs, Mark J. Butler observes:

> [T]o the extent that they are expected to convey liveness in performance, musicians must also communicate connections between physical gestures and resultant sounds to their audiences. This is especially important in an electronic dance music context,

[18] William Forde Thompson, Phil Graham, and Frank A. Russo, "Seeing Musical Performance: Visual Influences on Perception and Experience," *Semiotica* 156 (2005): 221–224.

[19] Schutz, "Seeing Music?" 85.

[20] For an overview of this work, see Schutz, "Seeing Music?" For a more detailed account of several experiments, see Thompson, Graham, and Russo, "Seeing Musical Performance."

[21] University of Victoria School of Music, "W. Andrew Schloss," at http://finearts.uvic.ca/music//faculty/Bios/aschloss.shtml (accessed June 27, 2010).

> in which many of the musicians' interactions with interfaces may be invisible, and the unfamiliarity of the instruments renders their performance techniques gesturally opaque to most audience members.[22]

The DJs therefore strive for "legibility" in their uses of technology. In *Liveness* I discuss the way rock's ideology of authenticity entails the audience accepting that the musicians before them, whether on stage or on record, are the agents responsible for making the sounds they are hearing (paralleling Godlovitch's analysis of classical music). Any doubt on this score (e.g., over the use of recorded material in concert [e.g., lip-synching] or session players in the studio) can discredit the music in question as authentic rock. But the authenticity of the sound cannot be verified in and for itself—audiences can effect such verification only by observing the musicians and drawing conclusions from the perceptible relationship between their actions and the sounds produced.[23]

Nevertheless, even performers operating within genre contexts in which traditional values generally hold sway sometimes challenge them by manipulating the relationship between the auditory and visual aspects of musical performance in ways that go against the traditional (or traditionalist) grain. The remainder of this chapter examines one such performance practice: the use of light shows in both psychedelic rock and classical music concerts.

Liquid Light

One very direct challenge to traditionalist beliefs was the practice by a number of prominent psychedelic rock bands of the 1960s, including the Doors and Jefferson Airplane, of performing portions of their concerts in darkness, thus replicating one way people listened to records and implying that musical sound is self-sufficient and requires no visual verification.[24] Jefferson Airplane considered the point important enough to include the track "Turn Out the Lights" on the album *Bless Its Pointed Little Head*, a live recording made at the Fillmore East and Fillmore West in 1968. On it, members of the group can be heard imploring stage management to dim the stage lighting; their pleas become an improvised instrumental number with a corny country feel. But careful listening reveals that the group does not see performing in the dark as an end in itself. Rather, they are concerned that their audience be able to see the accompanying light show.[25]

[22] Mark J. Butler, "Playing with Something That Runs: Technology, Improvisation, and Composition in Electronic-Music Performance" (unpublished manuscript, n.d.).

[23] Auslander, *Liveness*, 91.

[24] Philip Auslander, *Performing Glam Rock: Gender and Theatricality in Popular Music* (Ann Arbor: University of Michigan Press, 2006), 18.

[25] Jefferson Airplane, "Turn Out the Lights," *Bless Its Pointed Little Head* (RCA Records 4133-2-R, CD).

Light shows were staples of rock concerts during the psychedelic era. The Airplane engaged the services of San Francisco–based Glenn McKay; his Headlights, who had performed frequently at the Fillmore Auditorium, later known as the Fillmore West, became their exclusive light show group from 1967 through 1972.[26] The Fillmore East in New York City had a troupe of resident light artists under the direction of Joshua White, known collectively as the Joshua Light Show.[27] Clearly the Airplane wanted their audience to get the benefit of their arrangement with Headlights, but their demand for darkness also had other implications.

As a performance to which two sets of artists contribute in different media, the rock concert with light show can be analyzed as an instance of musical multimedia (IMM), for which Nicholas Cook has provided a theoretical framework. Cook distinguishes types of multimedia events according to the character of the relationships among the media. These can be of three types: conformance, complementation, and contest. *Conformance* describes situations in which other media are consistent with the music (and vice versa); *complementation*, those cases in which music and other media complete one another to form a whole expression; and *contest*, those situations in which music and other media are in conflict or competition with one another.[28] As Cook wisely suggests, these are not best treated as discrete categories: "A more sensitive application will distinguish between the different roles played by different media within any IMM and will categorize the relative preponderance of conformance, complementation, and contest."[29]

Concerts with psychedelic light shows were complex and multifaceted instances of musical multimedia. Descriptions often indicate that the movements of lights, shapes, colors, and images "were based on the underlying rhythm of the music" and established a "direct

[26] Jeff Tamarkin, *Got A Revolution: The Turbulent Flight of Jefferson Airplane* (New York: Atria Books, 2003), 146.

[27] See Gregory Zinman, "The Joshua Light Show: Concrete Practices and Ephemeral Effects," *American Art* 22 (2008): 17–21; and Edwin Pouncey, "Laboratories of Light: Psychedelic Light Shows" and "I Never Stopped Loving the Light: Joshua White and the Joshua Light Show" in *Summer of Love: Psychedelic Art, Social Crisis and Counterculture in the 1960s*, ed. Christoph Grunenberg and Jonathan Harris (Liverpool: Liverpool University Press and Tate Liverpool, 2005), 155–162 and 163–178. For accounts that place the Joshua Light Show and related phenomena into cultural context, see Chrissie Iles, "Liquid Dreams" in *Summer of Love: Art of the Psychedelic Era*, ed. Christoph Grunenberg (Liverpool: Tate Liverpool, 2005), 67–83; and Christoph Grunenberg, "The Politics of Ecstasy: Art for the Mind and Body," in *Summer of Love: Art of the Psychedelic Era*, ed. Christoph Grunenberg (Liverpool: Tate Liverpool, 2005), especially 21–35.

[28] In "Music Video and Synaesthetic Possibility," Kay Dickinson critiques analyses that treat audiovisual formats "as a parade with one leader [rather than] a thoroughfare with two-way traffic," in *Medium Cool*, ed. Roger Beebe and Jason Middleton (Durham: Duke University Press, 2007), 15. It is worth noting in this context that whereas Cook's notion of multimedia does depend on clear distinctions among media and the senses to which they appeal, only the category of conformance entails "leader" and "follower" media. Contest is a condition of tension among the media making up an IMM rather than the dominance of one by another, and complementation does not imply any hierarchical relationship among media.

[29] Nicholas Cook, *Analysing Musical Multimedia* (Oxford; New York: Oxford University Press, 2001), 106.

link between the visual and aural effect."[30] On this basis, the concerts could be described as instances of conformance, where the lights conformed to the music's rhythmic or thematic structure. David Snyder, however, who performed as Revelation Lights, insisted that he did not want the audience to think that the lights followed the music, but rather that the lights and the music constituted simultaneous interpretations of the composition.[31] Thus understood, the concert with light show could be an instance of what Cook describes as "triadic conformance": music and other media are in mutual conformance with a third entity (in this case the musical composition).[32]

It is also often suggested that psychedelic rock and light shows sought to enhance or simulate the experience of an acid trip. McKay states, "Even if you weren't tripping, [the light show] gave you another trip."[33] On "Turn Out the Lights," a member of Jefferson Airplane jokingly threatens the stage crew to "send Owsley to get you" if the lights are not turned down, a reference to Owsley Stanley, the preeminent provider of LSD in San Francisco at the time. Sheila Whiteley describes the London psychedelic music scene: "[L]ong, improvisatory passages and electronically produced sound effects resonated with stroboscopic lighting to bring about a feeling of freedom analogous to the effect of acid: the 'piling up of new sensations,' the associations with changed perspectives and color."[34] In this connection, the concerts could be considered instances of complementation, in which music replicated or stimulated the aural portion of the synesthetic LSD experience while light shows provided the hallucinatory visual dimension of the same experience. Performances in visual and aural media combined in the psychedelic rock concert to deliver a full replication of an LSD trip that neither could produce on its own.[35]

Psychedelic light shows can be understood as instances of complementation even apart from the context of psychedelic drug experience, however. Headlights' relationship with the Jefferson Airplane was unusual (at least in the United States).[36] Light artists

[30] Sheila Whiteley, *The Space Between the Notes: Rock and the Counter-Culture* (London; New York: Routledge, 1992), 28–29.

[31] "Virgil Fox Heavy Organ," at http://www.youtube.com/watch?v=gIPCx3Te-BA (accessed June 26, 2010).

[32] Cook, *Analysing Musical Multimedia*, 101.

[33] Quoted in Jesse Hamlin, "Painting Live with Light and Music," *San Francisco Chronicle*, January 31, 1999, at http://articles.sfgate.com/1999-01-31/entertainment/17677751_1_mckay-s-work-paintings-mckay-s-head-lights (accessed June 24, 2010).

[34] Whiteley, *Space Between the Notes*, 33.

[35] It is worth noting in the present context that Whiteley takes up the question of whether Pink Floyd's trippy "Astronomy Dominé" was psychedelic in itself or depended on the presence of the light show to create a psychedelic effect. After weighing the evidence, Whiteley concludes that the song is psychedelic in purely musical terms. Whiteley, *Space Between the Notes*, 31–33.

[36] Barry Miles indicates that "the psychedelic light show developed differently in Britain than in the States. In America, the light-show teams operated independently, as if they were groups themselves, and would be hired to provide a show for all the groups playing that evening, whereas in Britain any band wanting a light show tended to develop their own." *Hippie* (New York: Sterling Publishing, 2004), 170. Although this is not entirely the case, because there clearly were British light shows that worked independently for multiple bands (see Iles, "Liquid Dreams," 79), this tendency may partly account for why Sheila Whiteley, writing on the London psychedelic scene, states that the light shows followed the rhythm of the music, while Joshua White, speaking of his work in New York, says that the light shows were "arrhythmic" (both are quoted in the main text).

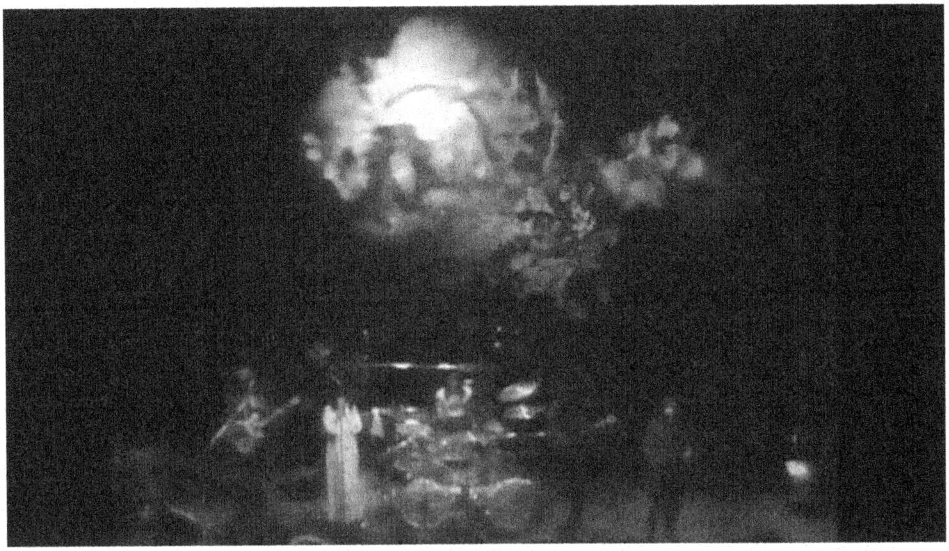

FIGURE 34.2: Jefferson Airplane performing "Wooden Ships" at the Fillmore East, New York City, November 28, 1970. Source: http://www.wolfgangsvault.com/jefferson-airplane/video/wooden-ships_2146595451.html.

usually worked for the venue rather than the musicians. As the resident light show at the Fillmore East, the Joshua Light Show was employed by Bill Graham, the impresario behind the Fillmores East and West, not by the bands with whom they worked, and they provided light shows for all the artists Graham booked into the hall (except for those who refused to work with them). These light shows were not collaborations between the light artists and the musicians (although the light artists would cooperate with specific requests from the musicians), and they did not necessarily rehearse together. White emphasizes the live, improvisational, and "manual" (as opposed to automated) aspects of the lights shows and suggests that for the most part there was little effort to achieve close synchronization between the music and the lights. He describes the light show as "arrhythmic[,] and therefore it was the audience and the musicians which gave it a rhythm."[37] The assumption underlying these concerts was that musicians and light artists shared a sensibility, a sense of their countercultural context, and an awareness of what their audience wanted. They all worked toward a common goal, but not through any formal alignment of sound and vision. (See figure 34.2.)

Although Cook presents his schema for musical multimedia as a quasi-objective, structuralist vocabulary for identifying relationships among the elements constituting a given IMM, I argue that the choice (or emphasis) of one of his categories over another reflects the ideology, bias, or interests of the analyst more than the inherent properties of the IMM. As the examples I have cited suggest, it seems likely that the musicians

[37] Quoted in Pouncey, "I Never Stopped," 175.

and light artists involved in producing psychedelic concerts and their audiences would have considered the relationship between music and light show to entail conformance or complementation, or both. They probably perceived the lights as following or illustrating the music or the music and lights as paralleling one another (either of which is an instance of conformance), or, because the counterculture of which psychedelic rock concerts were a part emphasized synesthetic experience, they may have understood the aural and visual media to be working together to create a total event, whether the event was understood as a simulation of an LSD trip or as a celebration of countercultural aesthetics.

From the traditionalist perspective I have described here, however, the psychedelic rock show can be understood only in a quite different way: as an instance of *contest* between the aural and visual elements of the concert. This characterization derives not from the relationship between these elements, but from the nature of the visual elements themselves. A traditionalist presumably would have no objection to a performance in which the visual and musical elements conformed to one another or complemented one another; in either case, they would be working together to communicate musical information, as long as the visuals in question were "musically relevant." In psychedelic light shows, however, musicians' performing bodies were interwoven with moving images, colors, and patterns, some abstract and some representational, in ways that obscured their gestures and facial expressions.

For the sake of historical accuracy, it is important to distinguish the early light shows in San Francisco from slightly later East Coast practices. In mid-1960s San Francisco, where musical performances by psychedelic rock bands were staged as dances rather than concerts, the light shows provided immersive visual environments that suffused musicians and audience alike. (See video clip 34.2. ▶) Later East Coast light shows, especially at the Fillmore East, relied more on rear projection on screens that appeared behind the musicians and obscured them less.[38] (See video clip 34.3. ▶) In the former case, the light show erased the musicians' gestures and facial expressions; in the latter, the light show provided distracting, spectacular competition for the musicians. The effect of distraction was intentional. Joshua White attributes his opportunity to create light shows at the Fillmore East to Bill Graham's decision "that the audience needed to have something to look at besides a bunch of musicians in street clothes tuning up."[39] In both cases, even if the visual effects followed the rhythm or structure of the music and thus conveyed musical information to the audience, the light show also inevitably impeded the audience's

[38] Joshua White ascribes the origins of the East Coast light show to a weeklong event in Toronto in 1967 for which Bill Graham wished to re-create the San Francisco scene. The venue, however, was a traditional proscenium theater rather than an open ballroom like the Fillmore Auditorium. Graham approached White and his company about devising a way to re-create the ballroom atmosphere in a conventional theatrical space, which White accomplished through the use of rear projection on the stage and atmospheric lighting in the auditorium. Although White did not provide the actual light shows for this event, he became immersed in their imagery through his involvement. Ultimately it was from the adaptation of the techniques and imagery of the San Francisco light show to a theater space primarily through the use of rear projection that the East Coast light show was born. See Pouncey, "I Never Stopped," 167–169 and Del Signore, "Joshua White, the Joshua Light Show."

[39] Quoted in Del Signore, "Joshua White, the Joshua Light Show."

ability to see or focus on the very things valorized in the traditionalists' model of musical performance: the musicians' physical actions in producing the sound. Audiences were thus deprived of what traditionalists believe they need to perceive the musicians' effort and skill and to verify the authenticity of their performance. The light show was guilty of the same crime of which traditionalists sometimes accuse music videos: "substituting the gestures of a performer with other visual content necessarily changes perceptual and affective co-regulation, distorting and diluting the communication between performers and listeners through a literal distancing of the performer from his or her audience."[40]

Although I am framing the rock concert with psychedelic light show as a performance practice that challenged the traditionalist view of musical performance and the values inherent in it, it is difficult to determine with certainty whether psychedelic rock bands like Jefferson Airplane understood their own use of light shows as a statement of defiance against such a view or were simply adhering to the performance conventions of their genre, social milieu, and historical moment. There is evidence of some tension surrounding the recourse to visual spectacle within psychedelic rock. Chuck Beale, lead guitarist for the Canadian band The Paupers, was quoted as saying, "We are trying to create a total environment with sound alone.... Sound is enough. We don't use lights or any gimmicks. When we record we don't double track or use any other instruments. What the four of us can do is the sound we make. That's all."[41] This remark was probably directed at the Airplane, whom The Paupers reportedly outplayed when they shared a bill at the Café Au Go Go in New York City in 1967. It suggests that the community of psychedelic rock musicians was not monolithic, that there were factions, including a traditionalist faction that dismissed "musically irrelevant" visuals alongside recording studio trickery in favor of focusing on the musicians, the sound, and their unvarnished skill in creating it.

During the psychedelic era, from the mid-1960s through the early 1970s, light shows were not restricted to rock concerts: both the Joshua Light Show and Headlights worked with classical musicians as well. The organist Virgil Fox, a Bach specialist, began a series of what he called "Heavy Organ" concerts with a performance at the Fillmore East in 1970; the show also featured Joe's Lights, an offshoot of the Joshua Light Show. In 1971 Fox toured the Heavy Organ with Pablo Lights and performed with them at Winterland in San Francisco. In 1972 he teamed up with Revelation Lights. Posters for Fox's concerts gave the light shows equal billing, in the manner of contemporaneous posters for rock concerts; Fox also brought David Snyder, the "lumierist" (as he called himself) behind Revelation Lights, out on stage for a bow at the end of the concert. Fox made several live Heavy Organ recordings during this period, including *Bach Live at Fillmore East* (1971) and *Bach Live in San Francisco* (1972), recorded at Winterland. Whereas the sleeves of many of Fox's earlier albums (he began recording in 1941) had the staid look associated

[40] Thompson, Graham, and Russo, "Seeing Musical Performance," 222.

[41] Quoted in Michael Lydon, *Flashbacks: Eyewitness Accounts of the Rock Revolution 1964–1974* (New York; London: Routledge, 2003), 26.

with classical music, the sleeves for the *Bach Live* albums looked like they were designed for rock albums and partook of the visual styles associated with the counterculture. The cover for the album recorded at Winterland even listed Pablo Light Show as part of its title.[42] (See video clip 34.4. ▶)

Whatever the precise motivations of the psychedelic rockers who chose to intertwine their music and bodies with powerful visual effects, it is clear that Fox's reconfiguring of the classical organ recital as a rock concert, including his use of light shows and his embrace of countercultural visual style, was a gesture of rebellion against the performance conventions of a musical genre in which traditionalist values held sway. Addressing an audience, he declared himself to be "in open warfare with a gang of creeps who call themselves purists."[43] He regularly used the language of drug experience to describe his concerts, calling them "trips." During a Boston Pops concert in 1974 that was broadcast on PBS, he held up his experiences at the Fillmore East and Winterland as models of what a concert should be, saying, "This is the kind of a trip where there is bright sunlight, magnificent uplift, true inspiration." He encouraged the Pops audience to clap along with Bach and dance in the aisles, as had the "kids" at the Fillmore East and Winterland, and the audience obliged.[44]

Although Fox's insertion of rock showmanship into the performance of classical music is an example of a musician intentionally using the visual dimensions of performance to challenge both traditionalist tenets regarding what counts in musical performance and the cultural position of classical music, it is somewhat ironic that Fox was an organist, because historically organists had always been at a disadvantage in meeting traditionalist criteria for performance. D. C. Somervell describes the organist's predicament (with tongue firmly in cheek) in an essay of 1943 entitled "The Visual Element in Music": "Here...there is nothing to see. The organist is hidden away in the organ-loft and even if you could see him you would not get much idea of what he was doing. The great stacks of organ pipes stand as impassive as ever. There is a grand impersonality about organ performance."[45] Somervell's description suggests that since organists are generally invisible and their playing does not reveal clear cause-and-effect relationships between visible effort and auditory output anyway, they cannot provide the kind of performance described by Schloss and Godlovitch.

Fox's solution was to perform on a Rodgers electronic touring organ (called "Black Beauty" and at two tons, the "heavy organ" of the concerts' collective title) that was specially designed and built for him. This technology enabled him to perform in halls like

[42] The information in this paragraph derives from several sections of The Virgil Fox Legacy Web site, including "Biography," "Chronology," "Discography," and "Virgil Fox Promotional Materials," at http://www.virgilfoxlegacy.com (accessed June 26, 2010).

[43] "Virgil Fox Heavy Organ," at http://www.youtube.com.

[44] "Virgil Fox Legacy |Bach| Gigue Fugue|Virgil Fox Legacy |Bach| Gigue Fugue|Virgil Fox Legacy |Bach| Gigue Fugue," at http://www.youtube.com/watch?v=ogRBCAdC7wI&feature=related (accessed June 26, 2010).

[45] D. C. Somervell, "The Visual Element in Music," *Music & Letters* 24 (1943): 47.

the Fillmore East or Winterland, which did not have built-in pipe organs, and to place his instrument downstage at an approximately 55-degree angle to the edge of the stage so that his hands were as clearly visible as possible as he worked the keys and stops. This, coupled with his flashy attire (a 1974 article in *Time Magazine* draws attention to the "overblown poppies bloom[ing] in Oriental splendor in the organist's iridescent paisley jacket" and "his rhinestone-decorated black suede shoes") and special effects, such as his disappearing "in a puff of smoke" at the concert's end, places Fox alongside Liberace (with whom he once shared billing on a television program), Jerry Lee Lewis, Keith Emerson, Elton John, and Lady Gaga, among others, in the lineage of flamboyant keyboard artists, a category usually restricted to those performing in rock and pop.[46] Embracing the conventions of rock performance, Fox brought the organist out of the loft and into the spotlight, an act that in itself aligned performance on that instrument more closely with traditionalist values. However, his use of psychedelic visual effects to challenge what he saw as overly rigid conventions of interpretation and performance decisively distanced his Heavy Organ performances from traditionalist values.

Conclusion

It is clear that technological change is the backdrop for the audiovisual economy of musical performance described here. Technologically driven developments that have challenged traditionalist values, which emphasize the importance of maintaining clear cause-and-effect relationships between the visual and auditory aspects of musical performance, include sound recording, radio broadcasting, and the use of computers and digital instruments in live performance, as well as such recent cultural forms as music video and air guitar. On balance, the evidence suggests that traditionalist anxiety about these developments is misplaced. However much the aesthetics of current popular music performance seem to be dominated by pure visual spectacle, the traditionalist belief that we require visual verification of musical sound maintains its ideological grip. As new ways of making music arise, their practitioners more often than not find ways to assimilate them to traditionalist values. This is evident on one side of the debate about computer music with which I began. As a further elaboration of that example, consider an e-mail invitation I received on January 9, 2010, to an evening of live-coded music at the Anatomy Museum, King's College, London. The invitation explains, "Live coders expose and rewire the innards of software while it generates improvised music and/or visuals" (live coding is also called "on-the-fly programming"). [47] The invitation goes on to assure us, "All code manipulation is projected for your pleasure," making it clear that

[46] "Music: Heavy Organ," *Time Magazine*, January 7, 1974, at http://www.time.com/time/magazine/article/0,9171,910977-1,00.html (accessed June 30, 2010).

[47] Princeton University Computer Science, "On-the-fly Programming: Using Code as an Expressive Musical Instrument," at http://on-the-fly.cs.princeton.edu/ (accessed June 30, 2010).

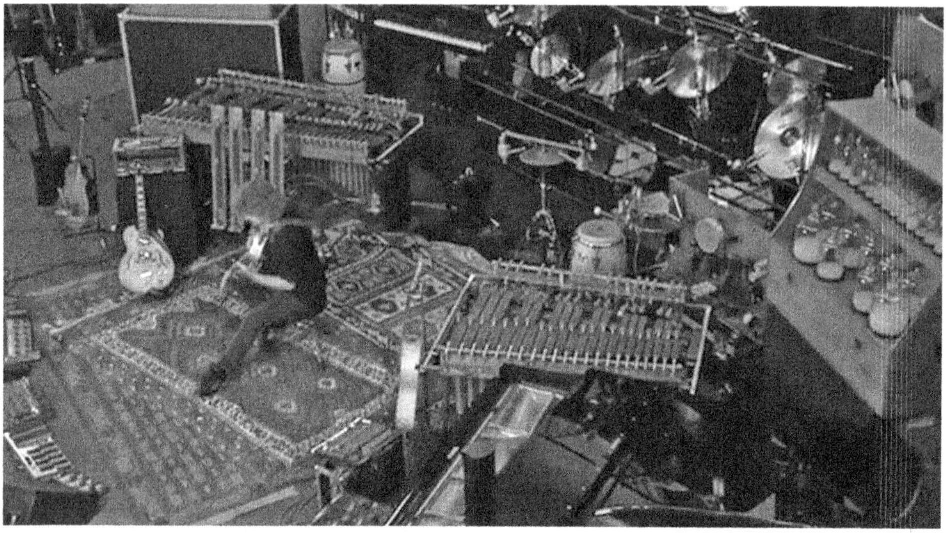

FIGURE 34.3: Pat Metheney and The Orchestrion. "Pat Metheney—The Orchestrion EPK." Source: http://www.youtube.com/watch?v=9VymAn8QJNQ.

even in this rarefied, technologically advanced musical context, the traditional assumptions hold sway: the audience must be *shown* how the sound is made in whatever way possible.

Much the same issue arose recently about jazz guitarist Pat Metheny's performances with the orchestrion, an elaborate array of robotic musical instruments, primarily stringed and percussion, that he developed, controlled by a computer and MIDI interface, which accompanies his guitar playing. (Metheny is the only "human" performer onstage at these concerts; see figure 34.3; and video clip 34.5. ◉) Ben Ratliff's review of Metheny's 2010 orchestrion concert at Town Hall in New York City interestingly traces the way the concert appeared to be structured to clarify what was going on for an audience steeped in traditionalism. Ratliff begins by noting that Metheny played solo guitar at first, something his audience was used to and in which the visual cause-and-effect relationships between what he was doing and the sounds produced were clear. Suggesting that the audience would have "riot[ed]" had Metheny not provided it with some understanding of what was going on, Ratliff notes that he moved into a section of the concert in which "it seems that the specificity of your attack on the guitar—whether and how you strum a chord or pick a note—determines the texture of the orchestral sounds that result from it. How it all works remains unclear, but the audience understands it better.... It's quite possible that a listener is thinking, for the first time that evening, 'I could do that.' "[48] Ratliff's description implies that to make his performance using unfamiliar

[48] Ben Ratliff, "If Not 76 Trombones, Everything Else a One-Man Band Can Handle," *New York Times*, May 23, 2010, at http://www.nytimes.com/2010/05/24/arts/music/24metheny.html (accessed June 30, 2010).

music palatable to a traditionalist audience, Metheny followed Schloss's suggestion, quoted previously, that he provide "a visual display of input parameters/gestures" to clarify the relationship between gesture and sound and allow the audience to believe it understood what was going on.

Although there is no reason to suppose that traditionalist values will be dethroned in musical performance any time soon, consideration of the historically uneven relationship between sound and vision in musical performance shows that the "audiovisual" is not to be understood in this context as seamlessly unified, but as syncretic, and probably better rendered as "audio-visual" or "audio/visual." In the cultural contexts of rock, classical, jazz, and computer music to which I have referred here, the audiovisual is always divided into two tracks, which are treated as discrete and can be placed in various relationships to one another. These relationships are configured as power relationships, in which one track is thought to dominate and set the context for the other. The traditionalist position, which remains dominant, entails a complex relationship between these tracks. On the one hand, the sound is thought to be the more important track, because the goal of the performance is precisely to play the music. On the other hand, sound alone is incapable of providing the audience with all of the information it needs to assess the musician's skill and effort; it is thus dependent on the visual track for verification. In that sense, the true locus of power is in the visual track, and it is this track that the musicians I discussed here who sought to challenge traditionalist values and performance conventions manipulated by using lighting effects, including darkness and psychedelic light shows, that both obscured their own actions as they produced musical sound and allowed spectacular visual effects to dominate their performances.

References

Auslander, Philip. *Performing Glam Rock: Gender and Theatricality in Popular Music.* Ann Arbor: University of Michigan Press, 2006.

Auslander, Philip. *Liveness: Performance in a Mediatized Culture.* 2nd ed. London; New York: Routledge, 2008.

Butler, Mark J. "Playing with Something That Runs: Technology, Improvisation, and Composition in Electronic-Music Performance." Unpublished manuscript, n.d.

Cook, Nicholas. *Analysing Musical Multimedia.* Oxford; New York: Oxford University Press, 2001.

Del Signore, John. "Joshua White, the Joshua Light Show." *The Gothamist*, April 2, 2007, at http:/ gothamist.com/2007/04/02/interview_joshu.php (accessed November 6, 2010).

Dickinson, Kay. "Music Video and Synaesthetic Possibility." In *Medium Cool*, edited by Roger Beebe and Jason Middleton, 13–19. Durham, N.C.: Duke University Press, 2007.

Godlovitch, Stan. *Musical Performance: A Philosophical Study.* London; New York: Routledge, 1998.

Gracyk, Theodore. "Listening to Music: Performances and Recordings." *The Journal of Aesthetics and Art Criticism* 55 (1997): 139–150.

Grunenberg, Christoph. "The Politics of Ecstasy: Art for the Mind and Body." In *Summer of Love: Art of the Psychedelic Era*, edited by Christoph Grunenberg, 11–43. Liverpool: Tate Liverpool, 2005.

Hamlin, Jesse. "Painting Live with Light and Music." *San Francisco Chronicle*, January 31, 1999. at http://articles.sfgate.com/1999-01-31/entertainment/17677751_1_mckay-s-work-paintings-mckay-s-head-lights (accessed June 24, 2010).

Iles, Chrissie. "Liquid Dreams." In *Summer of Love: Art of the Psychedelic Era*, edited by Christoph Grunenberg, 67–83. Liverpool: Tate Liverpool, 2005.

Jay, Martin. *Downcast Eyes: The Denigration of Vision in Twentieth Century French Thought*. Berkeley; Los Angeles; London: The University of California Press, 1994.

Jefferson Airplane. "Turn Out the Lights." *Bless Its Pointed Little Head*. RCA Records 4133-2-R, 1969. CD.

Laing, Dave. "A Voice Without a Face: Popular Music and the Phonograph in the 1890s." *Popular Music* 10 (1991): 1–9.

Lydon, Michael. *Flashbacks: Eyewitness Accounts of the Rock Revolution 1964–1974*. New York; London: Routledge, 2003.

Miles, Barry. *Hippie*. New York: Sterling Publishing, 2004.

"Music: Heavy Organ." *Time Magazine*, January 7, 1974, at http://www.time.com/time/magazine/article/0,9171,910977-1,00.html (accessed June 30, 2010).

Pouncey, Edwin. "I Never Stopped Loving the Light: Joshua White and the Joshua Light Show." In *Summer of Love: Psychedelic Art, Social Crisis and Counterculture in the 1960s*, edited by Christopher Grunenberg and Jonathan Harris, 163–178. Liverpool: Liverpool University Press and Tate Liverpool, 2005.

Pouncey, Edwin. "Laboratories of Light: Psychedelic Light Shows." In *Summer of Love: Psychedelic Art, Social Crisis and Counterculture in the 1960s*, edited by Christopher Grunenberg and Jonathan Harris, 155–162. Liverpool: Liverpool University Press and Tate Liverpool, 2005.

Princeton University Computer Science. "On-the-fly Programming: Using Code as an Expressive Musical Instrument." Princeton: Computer Science, 2002, at http://on-the-fly.cs.princeton.edu/ (accessed June 30, 2010).

Ratliff, Ben. "If Not 76 Trombones, Everything Else a One-Man Band Can Handle." *New York Times*, May 23, 2010, at http://www.nytimes.com/2010/05/24/arts/music/24metheny.html (accessed June 30, 2010).

Schloss, W. Andrew. "Using Contemporary Technology in Live Performance: The Dilemma of the Performer." *Journal of New Music Research* 32 (2003): 239–242.

Schutz, Michael. "Seeing Music? What Musicians Need to Know about Vision." *Empirical Musicology Review* 3 (2008): 83–108, at http://hdl.handle.net/1811/34098 (accessed November 14, 2012).

Somervell, D. C. "The Visual Element in Music," *Music & Letters* 24 (1943): 42–47.

Sterne, Jonathan. *The Audible Past: Cultural Origins of Sound Reproduction*. Durham, N.C.: Duke University Press, 2003.

Stuart, Caleb. "The Object of Performance: Aural Performativity in Contemporary Laptop Music." *Contemporary Music Review* 22 (2003): 59–65.

Tamarkin, Jeff. *Got A Revolution: The Turbulent Flight of Jefferson Airplane*. New York: Atria Books, 2003.

"The Virgil Fox Legacy," at http://www.virgilfoxlegacy.com (accessed June 26, 2010).

Thompson, William Forde, Phil Graham, and Frank A. Russo. "Seeing Musical Performance: Visual Influences on Perception and Experience." *Semiotica* 156 (2005): 203–227.

University of Victoria School of Music. "W. Andrew Schloss," at http://finearts.uvic.ca/music//faculty/Bios/aschloss.shtml (accessed June 27, 2010).
"Virgil Fox Heavy Organ," at http://www.youtube.com/watch?v=gIPCx3Te-BA (accessed June 26, 2010).
"Virgil Fox Legacy | Bach | Gigue Fugue," at http://www.youtube.com/watch?v=ogRBCAdC7wI&feature=related (accessed June 26, 2010).
Whiteley, Sheila. *The Space Between the Notes: Rock and the Counter-Culture.* London; New York: Routledge, 1992.
Zinman, Gregory. "The Joshua Light Show: Concrete Practices and Ephemeral Effects." *American Art* 22 (2008): 17–21.

CHAPTER 35

FOREGROUND FLATLAND

JOSEPH LANZA

Music Loses Its Shadow

Background music in public spaces was once a subtle counterpoint to daily life, but attention-hogging foreground music has taken its place, robbing us of a dimension or two in the process. Hints of this change surfaced in 1984, when many wondered whether (or how much) George Orwell's dystopian vision of Big Brother had come to pass. That year the UPC code tattooed most of our products, cable television spread its multiple channels and 24-hour news cycles into more homes, the infomercial masquerading as news came of age, the B-actor president who scared us about the "evil empire" had his reelection locked up as he waved to his wife from a giant screen at the Republican National Convention, and oh, yes, Muzak celebrated its fiftieth anniversary.

Despite what some might assume, Muzak was the least Orwellian (i.e., technologically manipulative) of all these examples. For half a century Muzak's melodies wafted through our public spaces to quell our moods, propel our purchasing decisions, and of course make riding elevators less scary, but their relatively mild sounds and modest power to influence our lives had none of the baleful effects that folks like Yehudi Menuhin griped about when initiating an anti-Muzak campaign via UNESCO in 1969. Elevator music did not silence the cultural and social upheavals of the 1960s and 1970s.

On the contrary, the elevator music seemed to complement the seismic shifts with its toned-down counterpoint. While the Beatles hollered out their rock and intoned their psychedelia, as Donovan sang about an electrical banana, and as Bob Dylan worked his nasal passages with his paeans of protest, the elevator music songbook expanded—precisely because these artists were leaving melodic trails that were ripe for reinterpretation not only by the orchestras in Muzak's studios but by a record industry that profited from easy-listening instrumentalists like Percy Faith, Paul Mauriat, and the Hollyridge Strings. Like the Muzak arrangers, the easy-listening maestros had an uncanny knack for covering pop and rock songs shortly after the originals appeared, revealing tunes that were just as engaging as those from the Tin Pan Alley era.

But a *Newsweek* article from September 1984 commemorating Muzak's fiftieth anniversary revealed one disturbing sign of what was to come.[1] Muzak's then-president Tony Hirsh mentioned a new plan to broadcast "original artist music," or "foreground music." This would have jarring consequences. Instead of encountering an orchestral version of "Mellow Yellow" designed as an unobtrusive background, supermarket shoppers would soon amble through the produce aisle to the sound of Donovan's actual voice from the Top 40 hit. With foregrounding, the songs would no longer have a shadow identity; they would instead induce people to listen more actively, as if they were blasting the AM radio in their cars.

One of the motives for this shift was generational. A new crowd was coming into power: aging baby boomers clinging to remnants of hipness and seeking new choices. By 1973 easy-listening albums by Mantovani, Ferrante and Teicher, Roger Williams, and Ray Conniff were dropping off *Billboard*'s album charts, whereas just two years before they still had impressive showings. Such a change suggests an age shift at record companies as well, with younger CEOs coddling the recording artists they favored and nudging out the old guard of mood maestros.

When Variety is Monotony in Drag

In the late 1970s radio stations that played easy-listening instrumentals, sometimes referred to as "beautiful music," started the foreground frenzy soon known as "adult contemporary," a format emphasizing "middle-of-the-road" tracks by vocalists ranging from Frank Sinatra to James Taylor. From then on the trend against background music accelerated. Muzak, which made elevator music its livelihood, was relatively late in this transition when it launched its Foreground Music One channel in 1985. Competing companies like Yesco (which later merged with Muzak) had already started foregrounding a few years earlier.

Foreground music's momentum coincided with lifestyle research trends. In 1978 SRI International conducted research studies, based on computerized data from questionnaires, that resulted in values and lifestyles strategies geared to predict the kinds of products that consumers, particularly the post-hippie hyper-individuals, would prefer according to their habits and cultural premises. A decade earlier the counterculture was too busy rebelling against suburban conformity to realize that they too would become market-prone consumers, their unprecedented forays into self-expression ultimately creating new selling niches.

After finding out the desires of these budding shoppers, ad agencies were quick to provide this segment of the maturing boomer population with a want list that might

[1] David Gates and Patrice Johnson, "Muzak's Five Decades of Art-Free Melody," *Newsweek*, September 10, 1984, 9–10.

have seemed vast, but was ultimately far from infinite. In short, former hippies could be had, because companies found a way to produce a fresh line of products that even former college Maoists could like. If in 1964 Herbert Marcuse conceived of "one-dimensional" consumers grasping at what was then a relatively limited "free choice between brands and gadgets,"[2] he would have cringed at the "lifestyles" science that, at the time of his death, packaged the nonconformist spirit with what seemed like lots of variety, but with stealth monotony at its core.

The foreground virus spread into the 1980s. Actor Robert Urich (famous for his title role in the popular series *Spenser: For Hire*) became an adult contemporary spokesman, appearing on television ads urging people to go back to the easy-listening dial but to "forget what they used to play." Philadelphia's EAZY 101, for instance, altered its instrumental format to favor performers like Neil Diamond, the Eagles, and some ex-rockers like Michael McDonald, who went on to record "power ballads."

A Mirage of Options in a Desert of Din

However, foreground music, despite what seemed an opportunity for change, created an irony. As in-store channels expanded and classifications varied, the customer, underling employees, and public passersby had no choice in the programs. Decisions about what to play were left to the tastes and whims of on-site proprietors. People could now go into a Duane Reade drug store and hear adult contemporary music in the afternoon but hip-hop in the evening, depending on who was manning the shift. Also, the music tended to be distracting and often louder than the elevator music, which after all was meant to complement and not compete with the public's routines.

When a company like Muzak played its single elevator music channel, the proprietor merely turned it on and didn't have the added authority of dictating the program content. There was just one default option and one style of default music. Christopher Case, a former Muzak programmer, expressed the difference to me in the early 1990s when I was doing research for my book *Elevator Music*:

> When musicians are left to themselves to make art for the sake of art, not considering public taste, demographics or psychology, they will put together something that won't please everyone.... My task is to amalgamate tastes. Imagine trying to please 80 or 90 million different viewpoints of the way things should be.[3]

Foregrounding's à la carte approach, which current Muzak publicists like to refer to as "audio architecture," gives business proprietors the privilege of acting as life coaches, second-guessing what is good for our ears and what mood best suits the sounds (and

[2] Herbert Marcuse, *One-Dimensional Man* (Boston: Beacon Press, 1964), 7.

[3] Lanza, Joseph. *Elevator Music: A Surreal History of Muzak, Easy Listening, and Other Moodsong*, 2nd ed. Ann Arbor: Michigan University Press, 2004, 149.

corresponding images) of a business setting. Foregrounding puts the music into the center of existence, reinforcing what some in the retail world call company "branding."

Under this assumption, urbanites might feel more urban when hearing jazz selections at a Starbucks, with the added value of being able to purchase CDs of the same music at the frappuccino checkout. But those with a different idea of the appropriate caffeine concerto are left feeling alienated. A place like The Gap might want to impose a hip-hop ambience, but a heavy metal fan taking the time to try on various pairs of jeans might feel irritated. And a high-toned New York City bistro might try to slather on a layer of "class" by piping in classical music, but not everyone likes classical (whether brunch baroque or romantic Tchaikovsky). Classical has even proven to be a human repellent, such as when New York's Port Authority blasted it to scare away loiterers.

Those who don't care for the establishment's foreground style, which usually plays much more assertively than conventional background music, are prone to resent this more tailored environment in ways they likely would not if the music were the softer elevator material, which purposely avoided any connotations of lifestyle, age group, social class, or even musical genre. As soon as people replace elevator music with anything other than the now-impossible dream of silence, they risk remonstrance from those with differing tastes. When businesses patronize patrons by giving them what they think they want, bedlam can break out.

This foreground dilemma brings to mind what author Barry Schwartz calls "the tyranny of overwhelming choices."[4] In *The Paradox of Choice*, he observes that a world of "multiple alternatives makes it easy for us to imagine alternatives that don't exist.... And to the extent that we engage our imaginations in this way, we will be even less satisfied with the alternative we end up choosing."[5]

Foreground music providers have attempted to offer business owners a long menu of musical options, but the longer the list gets and the more varied the titles are, the more finite the choices seem. This can make us feel as if we are being shoehorned into preexisting identities, inhabitants of a museum displaying dioramas of borrowed selves. The souls we think we are, or the identities we hope to inhabit, look more like a marketer's fantasy of necromantic scenarios dreamt up by infomercials repackaging the past. We can be the coffeehouse bohemians of bebop, relive the "innocence" of Motown, groove with the soundtrack to the Summer of Love, and shake our booties once again under the disco-era's ball of mirrors.

The Aural Depth of Field

In contrast, elevator music, for those who took the time to listen, offered an *audio depth of field*: the opportunity to take in a shadow version of a song we liked or at least

[4] Barry Schwartz, *The Paradox of Choice: Why More Is Less* (New York: Ecco, 2005), 79.

[5] Ibid., 122–123.

recognized. The original lingered as a haunting memory while the background tune wafted through our minds. This meant a deep-focused listening whereby both songs could simultaneously play in our imaginations. Conversely, with only the foreground, we are in a world comparable to the one Edwin A. Abbott described in his fantasy *Flatland*;[6] in this case, we are stuck in a two-dimensional existence where we cannot conceive of music that exists beyond the hard, egotistical edges of its original recording artists. Here the star is the centerpiece of our lives at all times, and we are just subordinate drones.

Today Muzak publicists are likely to downplay (even scorn) their elevator music past in order to brag about their growing list of channels. At the same time, digital cable and satellite radio companies bedevil us with a hydra-head of options. Xfinity, formerly known as Comcast, offers almost limitless versions of jazz (smooth jazz, "Singers and Swing," blues), Contemporary Christian, "True Country," "Today's Country," "Classic Country," "Classical Masterpieces," "Light Classical," "Toddler Tunes," "Kidz Only," "Party Favorites," "Solid Gold Oldies," "Soft Rock," "Alternative," "Adult Alternative," "Classic Alternative," "Rock," "Retro Rock," "Soft Rock," "Classic Rock," "R&B Classics," "R&B Soul," "Hip-Hop Classics," "Dance/Electronica," "Rap," "MC MixTape," "Hip-Hop and R&B," "Throwback Jamz," "Musica Urbana," "Pop Latino," "Mexicana," and so forth. To be fair, there is one easy-listening channel offering elevator airs. The fact that it's just one choice in a sea of options suggests a rich palette lurking in its narrow band: colors and shades reflecting an amalgam of influences from classical to rock that have always made easy-listening instrumentals the most eclectic and textured music in pop history.

One sentence in my book *Elevator Music* has struck a provocative chord over the years: "Not every musician should be obligated to reassure us that we are not zombies."[7] That sentiment is truer now more than ever. If we are already expressive or passionate beings, we don't need hot and busy music to keep us motivated or to remind us that we are alive. The old elevator music, which was to some the best compromise, now seems both civically and aesthetically right. Civic music should complement civic environments. This is among the few instances when a one-size-fits-all policy makes sense. When entering a public sphere like a supermarket or a mall, shoppers are entitled to an aural escape, a sound mark to delineate the safe shopping environment from the more cacophonous and unwieldy world outside.

Years ago, when I started writing about this subject, I was not too alarmed about the prospect that the foreground would gobble up the background. Part of me didn't think it could really happen. I was also more preoccupied with pointing out how the popular notion that elevator music is mass manipulation has been a delusion, a canard preventing people from seeing how their own favorite forms of music and other mass-produced pleasures are much more manipulative. I suspect that many younger people would be less averse to hearing background music's shadow world. Some might be pleasantly

[6] Edwin A. Abbott, *Flatland: A Romance of Many Dimensions* (New York: Perennial Library, 1983).

[7] Lanza, *Elevator Music*, 2.

flabbergasted to discover the melodic nuances in a James Last cover version of Lady Gaga's "Bad Romance" (even if they need to ignore his singers).

When the current stress is foreground, the music is louder, and paradoxically, the illusion of musical "choices" leaves many of us feeling limited in a sea of cacophony that no longer even attempts to comfort or indulge us. The clash of musical tastes that wages from speakers all around us can instead make us feel irritated, and worse, dumb or numb. I think of those blank, confused expressions on the faces of people on the streets and in subways as they listen to their iPod playlists through earbuds. Elevator music was never a threat to individuality, whereas foreground music drowns it out. Thinking about the matter from this angle, we can suspect that the less elevator music we hear, the more unreal we become.

References

Abbott, Edwin A. *Flatland: A Romance of Many Dimensions*. New York: Perennial Library, 1983.

Gates, David, and Patrice Johnson. "Muzak's Five Decades of Art-Free Melody." *Newsweek*, September 10, 1984, 9–10.

Lanza, Joseph. *Elevator Music: A Surreal History of Muzak, Easy Listening, and Other Moodsong*, 2nd ed. Ann Arbor: Michigan University Press, 2004.

Marcuse, Herbert. *One-Dimensional Man*. Boston: Beacon Press, 1964.

Schwartz, Barry. *The Paradox of Choice: Why More Is Less*. New York: Ecco, 2005.

CHAPTER 36

REMAKING THE URBAN: THE AUDIOVISUAL AESTHETICS OF IPOD USE

MICHAEL BULL

> I find that my iPod "colors'" my surroundings quite significantly; as it's on shuffle I don't know what's coming up next, and it often surprises me how the same street can look lively and busy and colorful one moment and then—when a different song starts—it can change to a mysterious and unnerving place. (Andy)

> [The iPod] has dramatically changed the way I listen to music. I use my iPod every day, generally for four to six hours a day. I listen to it at work, at home, in my car; on the subway.... [T]he iPod has become a necessity. When I leave the house, I now check my pockets for four things: my wallet, my keys, my mobile phone, and my iPod. I never go out without all four on my person. (iPod user)

WHAT people mostly want from public space is to be alone with their personal network.[1]

In a well-known passage from the *Dialectic of Enlightenment*, Adorno and Horkheimer analyze a section from Homer's *Odyssey* in which Odysseus pits his wits against the Sirens. Their singing evokes, "the irresistible promise of pleasure as their song is heard.... Even though the Sirens know all that has happened, they demand the future as the price of that knowledge."[2] In Homer's tale, all who hear the Siren's song perish on the rocks, to which their alluring sounds draw the desirous yet hapless sailors. Odysseus plans to outwit the Sirens by being lashed to the mast of his ship while the oarsmen have their ears blocked with wax—all so he can hear the tempting sound of the Sirens. The oarsmen, in contrast, can hear neither the Sirens' song nor Odysseus's desperate orders to steer the ship onto the rocks. Adorno and Horkheimer rightly note that

[1] Sherry Turkle, *Alone Together: Why We Expect More from Technology and Less from Each Other* (New York: Basic Books, 2011).

[2] Max Horkheimer and Theodor Adorno, *The Dialectic of Enlightenment* (London: Penguin, 1973), 33.

Odysseus's desire for pleasure is sublimated into aesthetic experience; he can hear the song, but he can do nothing about it. They also correctly point to the historical moment in which aesthetic experience becomes class bound. The oarsmen merely row; their ears are closed, and they do not get to share Odysseus's aesthetic experience, yet they provide the means for it to take place.

Paradoxically, Adorno and Horkheimer fail to discuss the spatial and specifically auditory nature of Odysseus's confrontation with the Sirens. The sound of the Sirens' song originates beyond Odysseus; it is the Sirens who construct his soundscape.[3] However, Odysseus intervenes in the very nature of this soundscape by having the crewmen's ears blocked with wax, in an early example of technological intervention that transforms the very nature of sonic space. The soundscape that Odysseus experiences now encompasses only himself and the Sirens; it exists only between him and them. Socially speaking, Odysseus occupies his very own sound-world, a technologically constructed sound bubble. This passage from Homer is the first description of the privatization of experience through sound.

Equally significant is the role that this experience plays in Odysseus's personal narrative. Odysseus is a traveler who makes himself through his journey; in outwitting the Sirens he furthers his self-development, in effect becoming an early "tourist of experience" in search of an aestheticized and personalized world.[4] The Sirens constitute an aesthetic presence in Odysseus's biography, representing in part the draw of the "exotic" and the forbidden that he encounters in his travels and masters through his intellect. Homer's tale shows that aesthetics, sound, and control are embedded in Western culture from its very outset. It also points to a potential theoretical framework within which we may situate contemporary practices of iPod users as they move through urban space. Odysseus is sonically immersed in the world with a force that differs from the other senses.[5] The tale also presages the powerful motivation of iPod users to organize their relationship to space and place through sound. As I explain further, sound *colonizes* iPod users while simultaneously enabling them to actively re-create and reconfigure the public spaces they occupy. Odysseus repossesses space to make it conform to his desires in much the same way that contemporary iPod users do. His experience of the Sirens points to the reconfiguring role that sound can have on the relational qualities of experience—the cognitive, aesthetic, and moral makeup of social space as enacted by iPod users.

This chapter investigates the aesthetic strategies and tactics undertaken by Apple iPod users as they navigate through their days accompanied by the music contained in their iPods. To date, over 50 percent of Western populations have the ability to create their

[3] Murray Schafer, in *The Tuning of the World* (New York: Knopf, 1977), uses the term "soundscape" to describe the fully experienced acoustic environment. This includes all noises: musical, natural, and technological.

[4] Tzvetan Todorov, *On Human Diversity: Nationalism, Racism, and Exoticism in French Thought* (Cambridge, Mass.: Harvard University Press, 1993).

[5] See George Simmel, *Simmel on Culture: Selected Writings. Ed. David Frisby and Mike Featherstone* (London: Sage, 1998).

own privatized sonic bubbles through the use of either dedicated MP3 players, such as the Apple iPod, or mobile phones with MP3 capability. The present analysis focuses on Apple iPod users and is based on primary research into the daily behavior of iPod users globally. The research was undertaken mainly through qualitative Internet interviews and exchanges. Users responded to requests for interviews placed in the *New York Times*, *Wired News*, *Guardian Online*, and *BBC News Online*. Respondents were mostly adults from North America, the United Kingdom, and the EU and from social classes one and two.[6]

Use of iPods represents the culmination of over a century of media use in which our ability to control our sound-world through a process of sensory filtering has become second nature to many, from early radio users who listened privately through headphones in their living rooms, to users of transistor radios, to those hermetically sealed listeners in automobiles.[7] Everyday urban experience has become increasingly mediated by an array of technologies, which, to pursue the thought of Walter Benjamin, have both trained and conditioned the human sensorium.[8]

The age of mechanical reproduction is characterized by increasing sonic saturation in which urban space, both public and private, is colonized. Throughout the twentieth and twenty-first centuries, we have increasingly experienced daily life in the home, in the street, or at work mediated through music.[9] In this chapter I analyze forms of sonic mediation through the filter of technologies that afford a set of disparate responses among city dwellers. These technologies are divided into the categories Fordist, post-Fordist, and hyper-post-Fordist.

Fordist technologies are those provided by companies such as the Muzac Corporation. The point about these technologies is that they are collectively experienced, voluntarily or not; social space tends to be indiscriminately colonized by them. Examples of Fordist sonic experience are myriad; from radio programs such as "Music Whilst You Work," transmitted by the BBC to factories during and after World War II in Britain, to the use of a sound system in Jonestown, Guyana, where all who lived there could not escape the interminable 24-hour monologues of the Reverend Jim Jones.[10] Contemporary

[6] Social class one includes senior managers in large companies and higher professionals, such as those working in the university sector. Social class two includes lower managerial and technical staff, as well as those working in the non-university sector of education.

[7] See Kathleen Geurts, *Culture and the Senses: Bodily Ways of Knowing in an African Community* (Berkeley: University of California Press, 2002) ; and Jonathan Sterne, The Audible Past: Cultural Origins of Sound Reproduction (Durham, N.C.: Duke University Press, 2003).

[8] Walter Benjamin, *Illuminations* (London: Penguin, 1973).

[9] See Michael Bull, *Sounding Out the City: Personal Stereos and the Management of Everyday Life* (Oxford: Berg, 2000); Michael Bull, *Sound Moves. iPod Culture and Urban Experience* (New York and London: Routledge 2007); Ito, M., Okabe, and M. Matuda, *Personal, Portable, Pedestrian: Mobile Phones in Japanese Life* (Cambridge, Mass.: MIT Press, 2005) and Marek Korczynski, "Music at Work: Towards a Historical Overview," *Folk Music Journal* 8, no. 3 (2003): 314–334.

[10] Deborah Layton, *Seductive Poison. A Jonestown Survivor's Story of Life and Death in the People's Temple* (New York: Random House, 1998).

examples are sound systems in sports stadiums and music transmitted throughout shopping centers.

Post-Fordist forms of music production relate to niche marketing. An example is music played in specific shops, such as music that is thought to provide the correct ambience for purchasing expensive designer jeans. The history of radio is very much about the provision of niche music channels for a selective listening public.[11]

Hyper-post-Fordist modes of listening refer to technologies like the Sony Walkman and the Apple iPod, through which, with the aid of a pair of headphones, users create individualized soundscapes for themselves. For example, the iPod user can superimpose her own soundscape above the one provided by Fordist and post-Fordist technologies or indeed any sound activity of others. It is important to note that these three modes of sound experience exist in parallel. The trend toward a hyper-post-Fordist model does not deny the significance of the other two modes of sonic experience. The following analysis predominantly investigates a range of aesthetic strategies employed by iPod users in their everyday experience of urban life. It assumes, rather like Odysseus, that we take our urban predispositions wherever we travel; iPod users have described taking their iPods to Yellowstone Park, on whaling expeditions in the Pacific Ocean, and on deserted beaches while on holiday.[12] The analysis of the aesthetic practices of iPod users is treated as a set of affordances in the following pages. Users move from one set of affordances to another as they listen to music on their iPods. Use appears to offer a glimpse into the internal workings and strategies engaged in by users in their management of themselves, others, and urban space by engaging in a series of self-regulatory practices through which they habitually manage their moods, volitions, and desires. In its inherent fluidity music appears to correlate with a Bergsonian model of consciousness based on duration, in which the notes of a tune melt into one another.[13] The iPod users appear to be embracers of a Bergsonian world of free consciousness, in which consciousness is inherently mobile, fluid, and in flux.[14]

The mundane world of the city becomes more adventurous in the privatizing sound-world of the iPod user. The contingency of the street in which one moves with others, dependent on their ebb and flow, becomes manageable and potentially pleasurable. The subject is simultaneously "pacified" and "energized" as he wends his way through the street. Walter Benjamin, in his analysis of city life, was attentive to the role that technology played in the navigation of the urban subject through the city; iPod users become reminiscent of the urban subject, whom Benjamin described as "[plunging] into a crowd as into a reservoir of electric energy...a kaleidoscope equipped with consciousness."[15] The iPod user has moved on technologically since Benjamin's

[11] Susan Douglas, *Listening In: Radio and the American Imagination* (Minneapolis: University of Minnesota Press, 2004).

[12] Henri Lefebvre, *The Urban Revolution* (Minneapolis: University of Minnesota Press, 2003).

[13] Henri Bergson, *Introduction to Metaphysics* (London: Kessinger, 1998).

[14] Bergson, *Introduction to Metaphysics*.

[15] Benjamin, *Illuminations*, 171.

observation, accompanied by music, which drives both mood and his relationship to the spaces passed through. Enhancement relates to the mood of the user or, and sometimes also, the environment passed through, which in turn feeds back into the cognition of the user.

The Privatizing of Audiovisual Aesthetics

William Gibson understood the radical transformative possibilities that lay in a relatively simple everyday technological device, the Sony Walkman; as he remarked, "the Sony Walkman has done more to change human perception than any virtual reality gadget. I can't remember any technological experience since that was quite so wonderful as being able to take music and move it through landscapes and architecture."[16] Gibson noted the radical transformation that technology can make to the human sensorium. Historically the ears have been interpreted as both passive and democratic—passive inasmuch as the ears are open to all sounds, and democratic for the same reason. Walkman and iPod use is neither passive nor democratic, but rather discriminating and distinctive. The passivity of the ears appears to be merely a historical effect, now technologically superseded through the development of earpieces, which empower users so that they can choose what they wish to hear, screening out the urban soundscape to create a private auditory universe. In doing so they transform their relationship to the social world in which they live.

Just as Odysseus immersed himself in the sound of the Sirens, so iPod users' desire for immersive experience embedded in a wide range of iPod practices is intimately connected with the eradication of the preexisting spatial sound-world. Frances Dyson recently commented on the intimate relationship between sound technologies and immersion:

> Sound is the immersive medium par excellence. Three-dimensional, interactive, and synaesthetic, perceived in the here and now of an embodied space, sound returns to the listener the very same qualities that media mediates: that feeling of being here now, of experiencing oneself as engulfed, enveloped, enmeshed, in short, immersed in an environment. Sound surrounds.[17]

Use of the iPod valorizes the "here and now." Sound both colonizes the listener and actively re-creates and reconfigures the spaces of experience. Through the power of a privatized sound-world, the world becomes intimate, known, and possessed.

[16] William Gibson, *Time Out* 6 (October 1993): 49.

[17] Frances Dyson, *Sounding New Media: Immersion and Embodiment in the Arts and Culture* (Berkeley: University of California Press, 2009), 4.

Fordist and Hyper-Post-Fordist Aesthetics of the City

Some years ago I was visiting the ancient Buddhist sanctuary of Koyasan in Japan. The center is perched high up in the mountains near Osaka, engulfed in ancient forests. Late one afternoon I took a walk through the old and rambling Okuno-in cemetery in the heart of the Koyasan complex, with nothing but the sound of my feet and the birds to accompany my reveries. At 7.00 p.m. on the dot my thoughts were interrupted by the sound of what appeared to me to be celestial "shopping music" emanating from a concealed system of speakers attached to the trees throughout the graveyard. The serene and peaceful surroundings of the graveyard were suddenly transformed into a scene reminiscent of one in David Lynch's *Twin Peaks*, a suspense/horror television series I had watched a few years earlier. This personal anecdote illustrates the power of music in the transformation of our sense of place and space. It is a story of "colonization." I involuntarily experience the sounds of "celestial shopping music" that I cannot ignore—in this sense the experience is a "Fordist" experience, insofar as all people walking through that space will hear the same involuntarily imposed sounds, to which they nevertheless respond individually. The character of this particular audiovisual aesthetic is multiply mediated through the associated technology of the particular sound system in Koyasan and my own media experience. This example also represents the increasingly universal cultural imperative to provide sound accompaniment wherever one might go.

If my sonic experience of Koyasan was essentially Fordist in nature, then the privatizing aesthetic of the use of mobile technologies like the iPod represents a hyper-post-Fordist moment of urban culture in which the city is individually consumed and re-created. My Koyasan experience exemplifies a modernist urban world of the city wherein it was the subject who was traditionally embedded in the electronic lights and billboards of the city; the subject becomes colonized by the enticements of the city, interiorizing the utopian dreams fabricated by the image. The representational spaces of the city were perceived as engulfing subjectivity:

> Illuminated words glide on the rooftops, and already one is banished from one's own emptiness into the alien advertisement. One's body takes root in the asphalt, and, together with the enlightening revelations of the illuminations, one's spirit—which is no longer one's own—roams ceaselessly out of the night and into the night.[18]

Kracauer's understanding of the urban colonization of the subject, in which the dominating rhythms of the city create the cadences within which all citizens walk, is essentially Fordist. Urban experience becomes mediated through the advertising

[18] Siegfried Kracauer, *The Mass Ornament: Weimar Essays* (Cambridge, Mass: Harvard University Press, 1995), 332.

technologies of commodity culture and the empowered dreams associated with the very act of movement itself. IPod use reverses this phenomenon. The user is rather saturated with the privatized sounds of the iPod; the cultural imperative, fully commoditized, lies in the contents of the iPod itself, not in the city street. The world is drawn into the user's "individual" narrative rather than the street drawing the user into its realm: "It's as though I can part the seas like Moses. It gives me and what's around me a literal rhythm, I feel literally in my own world, as an observer. It helps to regulate my space so I can feel how I want to feel, without external causes changing that" (Susanna). The experiences of the city described by Kracauer and those of the iPod user remain deeply mediated and commoditized. Both sets of descriptions are filmic in character. Kracauer's urban stroller lives in the polyrhythmic, audiovisual world of the street, which presents itself to him as a spectacle in which the street becomes a commodified dream. In contrast, iPod users construct a monorhythmic aesthetic narrative to the street deciphered from the sounds of the culture industry emanating from the iPod. Theirs is a hyper-post-Fordist street of potentially multiple audiovisual scenarios—with each iPod user constructing her own singular, mediated dream-world simultaneously. Whereas Kracauer's subject is diminished, made smaller by the enormity of the street and its illuminated signs, iPod users such as Sophie, a marketing manager from London, describe their iPod experiences as "making the world look smaller—I am much bigger and powerful listening to music. The world is generally a better place, or at the very least it is sympathetic to my mood.... [Y]ou become part of the music and can take on a different persona."

The iPod user might be seen as uniquely individualizing social space, in the manner of Odysseus, creating her own unique and unrepeatable audiovisual aesthetic of the city. Each journey is unique yet personal. Public space is made up of parallel individualizing trajectories as each user is absorbed in her own sound-world: "I enjoy having a soundtrack for New York streets. Having my own rhythm. I commute two hours a day. When I'm on the subway people listening to music on headphones often surround me. We each inhabit our own realities" (Karen). Use of the iPod represents a world in which each person is locked into her own interiority, moving to her own rhythm and motivated by her personalized auditory sound track to urban life:

> Sometimes it seems to look a lot more hectic and almost like I'm in my own slow world, going only at the speed of the music I'm listening to. The lack of day-to-day sound effects totally changes living in a city. (Adam)

> I keep some slow music that gives me a calm, peaceful feeling when I'm in busy or chaotic settings, like on the subway. Norah Jones is a great example. Then, I also like really upbeat, dance-style music. This is good not only for the gym, but also when I'm just walking around the city—puts me in an upbeat mood. Like, Britney Spears (who I normally don't listen to) has some good new dance songs, like "Toxic." They have great rhythm, very upbeat. (Samantha)

Increasing numbers of urban dwellers are sounding out the sensory environment of the city, plugged into their earphones and listening to their own auditory soundtracks.

The Filmic City: The Aesthetic Strategies of iPod Users

The imagination of iPod users is mediated through the sounds of the device, which become an essential component of their ability to imagine at all. Users frequently construct an aesthetic narrative to the city deciphered from the sounds of music emanating from their iPods. The world is brought into line through a privatized, yet mediated, act of cognition. Users often describe their city experiences in filmic terms, whereby the world is experienced as a movie script in which the user takes command. The world and the user's experience within it gain significance through her enveloping and privatized sound-world:

> The world looks friendlier, happier, and sunnier when I walk down the street with my iPod on. It feels as if I'm in a movie at times. Like my life has a soundtrack now. It also takes away some of the noise of the streets, so that everything around me becomes calmer somewhat. It detaches me from my environment, like I'm an invisible, floating observer. (Berklee)

> I find when listening to some music choices, I feel like I'm not really there. Like I'm watching everything around me happening in a movie. I start to feel the environment in the sense of the mood of the song and . . . find that I . . . start to love a street that I usually hate, or feel scared for no reason. (Susan)

> I'll pick music that complements the weather, and that can alter the outlook on the world around me. I can take joy in otherwise gloomy, rainy, dank weather by putting on something wonderfully gloomy and dank, something I love to hear. It's a fine synergy of the visual and auditory environments. It makes me feel like I'm walking through my own movie, with my own soundtrack. The people around me look like extras on the set. I see myself in the third person. (Angie)

Although the conditioning of the filmic in the creation of a personalized audiovisual aesthetic is prominent in these accounts of iPod use, it is useful to interpret the dynamic of aesthetic appropriation in some detail. For the most part, users claim that the aesthetic principle tends to depend on the use of their iPods. Users will pick playlists or fast forward to the music track that suits either their mood or their surroundings. In Berklee's account, the environment is transformed by the music played; indeed, the environment becomes a function of individualized sound: the listener becomes an auditory spectator. Yet as in Susan's account, the iPod user is also dependent on the music to re-create specific moods or images within her urban experience. Equally, Angie picks music that will enhance the environment, that suits her mood. It is important to recognize the cognitive strategies being employed here. The world is being aesthetically reproduced in conformity to the user's mood or the mood of the music listened to. The iPod users' overriding aim is to create a privatized sound-world that is in harmony with their mood, orientation, and surroundings, enabling them to re-create their urban experience through a process that might be described as solipsistic aestheticization. Rather than reaching out to understand or see the "otherness" of the city *as* "otherness," as represented by the traditional practices of the *flaneur*, for example, iPod users aim to habitually create an aesthetically pleasing urban world for themselves in their own image. Theirs is a strategy of bringing the world in line with their cognitive predispositions, as an act of mimicry. This aesthetic appropriation of urban space is a prominent cognitive strategy in their attempt to create seamless webs of mediated and privatized experience in their everyday movement through the city, enhancing virtually any chosen experience in any geographical location at will.

Strategies of sonic transcendence are multifaceted, but central to that transcendence is the construction of urban space as a "seamless space." IPod users possess the ability and have the desire to unify urban space as they move from home, to the street, to the automobile, and to work, thereby denying the heterogeneity of the urban landscape passed through. The use of the iPod appears to bind the disparate threads of urban movement together, both "filling" the spaces "in-between" communication or meetings and structuring the spaces thus occupied. In the often-repressive "realm of the ever-same,"[19] or the "ever-always-the-same,"[20] iPod users attempt to achieve a level of autonomy over time and place through the creation of privatized auditory bubbles. They often refer to the magical nature of carrying their entire music collection with them wherever they go, thus giving them an unprecedented amount of choice of music to listen to. In this deroutinization of time lies both the unalloyed pleasure of listening and the management or control of their thoughts, feelings, and observations as they manage both space and time. Time and experience are increasingly micromanaged through the technological potential of the iPod. Jean, a 35-year-old bank executive, scrolls though her song titles looking for a particular song to listen to that suits her mood at that particular moment, and while listening to that song, she scrolls through her list for her next choice—her musical choices thus merge seamlessly into one another during her journey. She describes her journey time evocatively as possessing "no dead air." The ability to continually adjust music to mood while on the move, with such sophistication and precision, is relatively new, if indeed the desire to do so is not. Thus users "fine-tune" or "shape" their relationship among cognition, space, and music.[21] This distinguishes iPod users from previous generations of personal stereo users, who were confined to the fixed contents of the tape or CD. IPod users are more akin to sophisticated "listening selves," attuned to the transient nature of cognition while simultaneously attempting to "fix" their relationship to public space:

> I like to crank angry, loud music at night; the city seems so much more dark and brutal in the dark if I do that. Walking home, I sometimes listen to more soaring; passionate melodies and they make me see things differently. I listen to rhythmic and pulsating music sometimes, which makes me feel confident and secure—I don't have to be anything but "following the beat," so to speak.... Delirium's music always

[19] Theodor Adorno, *The Culture Industry: Selected Essays on Mass Culture* (London: Routledge, 1991).

[20] Benjamin, *Illuminations*.

[21] Richard Coyne, *The Tuning of Place: Sociable Spaces and Pervasive Digital Media* (Cambridge, Mass.: MIT Press, 2010).

> strikes me in this emotional, soul-searching way, and elevates even the smallest details to some greater significance; every moment of the people in the streets seems spiritual and sacred. (Brian)

The iPod gives users an unparalleled micromanagement of mood, environment, and sound that allows the successful management of the self through the contingencies of the user's day:

> There are times where I will put on one song, and then ½ way through it I will change my mind and switch it to another song because my mood changed or the song wasn't capturing my mood correctly. (Heather)

> I almost always keep the setting on "shuffle" so that the songs come up randomly. If a song starts that doesn't suit my mood at the moment, I just hit "next." (Karen)

These hyper-post-Fordist practices of iPod users appear to resemble the utopian remaking of the city envisaged by De Certeau, Lefebvre, and Debord.[22] Yet this initial viewpoint is problematic. The individualizing practices of iPod users, though transcendent in nature, also appear to deny central facets of urban experience articulated by De Certeau and others. Henri Lefebvre, for example, described walking through the city as being immersed in its polyrthyms: "[H]e who walks down the street... is immersed in the multiplicity of noises, murmurs, rhythms."[23] From this perspective, the urban citizen is primarily a "listening" subject, more or less open to the cultural diversity of the city. The subject actively immerses herself in the sounds of the city, deciphering it to make sense of its multiplicity and confusion. The loud, polyrhythmic nature of city sounds is seductive, chaotic, and unrhythmic nature brought to order by the attentive ear, enabling the subject "to separate out, to distinguish the sources, to bring them back together by perceiving interactions."[24] The image of sensory richness of the urban derives from the observations of city centers of Paris, Berlin, New York, and Vienna.[25]

The positive evaluation of an open sensory sensibility to urban experience equates the vast array of sensory delights confronting the citizen with providing the tools for self-realization. Self-realization, from this viewpoint, is gained by the understanding of "difference," of "otherness" offered by the multicultural city. Even in its apparent sensory and physical chaos, the city provides nourishment for subject's sense of displacement, seductively experienced as something to be desired.[26]

[22] Michel De Certeau, *The Practice of Everyday Life* (Berkeley: University of California Press, 1988); Henri Lefebvre, *The Production of Space* (Oxford: Blackwell, 1991) Henri Lefebvre, *The Urban Revolution*; Henri Lefebvre, *Rhythmanalysis. Space, Time and Everyday Life* (London: Continuum Press, 2004); Guy Debord, *Society of the Spectacle* (Detroit, MI: Black and Red, 1977).

[23] Lefebvre, *Rhythmanalysis: Space, Time and Everyday Life*, 28.

[24] Lefebvre, *Rhythmanalysis*, 27.

[25] Benjamin, *Illuminations*; De Certeau, *Practice of Everyday Life*; Musil, *Man Without Qualities*; Simmel, *Simmel on Culture*.

[26] De Certeau, *Practice of Everyday Life*; Lefebvre, *Rhythmanalysis*.

This privatizing of urban experience through technologies like the Apple iPod appears rather to represent a potentially dystopian moment in urban theory, one in which the subject responds to the urban with strategies of retreat, neutralization, or aestheticization. These dystopian responses are located theoretically in the perceived sensory oppressiveness of the urban crowd, in the neutralizing architectural spaces of the city, and in the values and disposition of the urban subject. The present analysis of iPod use stresses the tension that exists between the utopian and dystopian nature of aestheticized urban experience. In essence, use shifts between them and is articulated through a range of disparate strategies that transform or negate. Each user might use a range of utopian or dystopian strategies to navigate the city.

Aesthetically Derealizing the Other?

IPod users never willingly interact with others while engaged in solitary listening. The iPod becomes a "gating" technology that draws circumscribed circles around the subject, both physical and metaphorical. This is one of the historical legacies of the values of individualism and its concurrent demand for privacy: an overriding desire to be left alone while in urban culture. The perception of face-to-face communication in public spaces as a threat to this desired privacy has a lengthy cultural history, embodied in the use of communication technologies, which separate out, and mediate, the subject from others. These technologies simultaneously connect people together, enabling them to socialize with one another in new ways, and separate them from others—much mobile phone use exemplifies this duality. Although the focus of this chapter primarily concerns the way in which "solitary" individuals weave their way through everyday life, the use of technologies like the iPod simultaneously connects users to their auditory histories, the culture industry, and newly imagined scenarios within the spaces they move through. One significant tactic of iPod users, for example, is to aestheticize other people:

> For some reason, Talking Heads seems to work best for this. Like, I will look at an old woman with a cane, and imagine her singing one lyric. Then move on to a hip-hop style teenage boy, and have him sing the next line. My imagination really can take off. It sometimes makes me laugh and smile to myself—especially if a particularly amusing line comes up. It really does transform my surroundings—I sort of feel like I'm in my own music video. (Karen)

> On my walk to work, I'm leaving downtown, and walking across a river into a neighborhood of small shops and restaurants, so it's quite pleasant. The music helps me feel like I'm leaving dreary downtown and going someplace happy. On my way home, it transforms my path from "the path home" into "the path to whatever I'm going to be doing." Sometimes, I'll use it to ignore homeless people, because they're always asking for change, and I carry none. (John)

City life is invariably about surfaces, the superficial reading and the transitory clues involved in our observations of others, hence the overriding dominance of the visual in urban culture. Connectivity—if it occurs at all—is often "virtual" for iPod users. The "personalization" of the user's sound-world imbues the street and others with its own atmosphere, in which the world appears intimate and endowed with significance. Karen gives roles to others while listening to Talking Heads—the world mimics and moves to the rhythm of the music. Other users refer to the absent-derealized nature of others as they view them through their own sound-worlds:

> It removes an external layer. I see people and things as inanimate or not-fully-connected. It seems that I have an external connection they lack. It's quite odd, actually.... When I look at the people around me, they appear to be two-dimensional and without significance. (Jonathan)

Use of the iPod represents a desire for uninterrupted and continuous experience as a central facet of the user's urban experience. This desire for a subjectively empowered sense of continuousness is enabled by and facilitated through iPod use, which links disparate places and moods through the temporal immediacy of sounds.

From the *Flâneur* to the iPod User: The Interiorization of Cosmopolitanism

The *flâneur* was interpreted as integral to the cosmopolitan city. The cosmopolitan image of city life is at least partially a function of life on the street.[27] Through interacting with and being open to experience, the urban citizen contributes to the rich fabric of city life. Yet while many iPod users report enjoying city life, theirs is a mediated experience of the pleasures of the city. The city is frequently viewed through the products of the culture industry in the form of music, talking books, and of course, the iPod itself:

> I refer to my iPod as my pace maker, it helps me find that place. I almost exclusively Travel to NYC when not in London. I have a dedicated playlist called "NY State of Mind." This includes a lot of New York rap music and NY/ East coast Jazz. Something With N.Y. in the lyrics, but also the sophistication, edge and energy of the place. (Sami)

> It makes NY City feel like a happy place—a place where taxi's don't honk...also, it always helps adjust my mood—if I'm listening to John Denver, I am happy go lucky—If it is AC/DC, I'm feeling like a New Yorker. (Susie)

The meaning of city spaces for these users derives from their playlists. Cosmopolitanism becomes a fictional reality existing in the often-eclectic mix of music contained in the iPod: in the user's music collection itself. For many iPod users the pleasure of the city

[27] Simmel, *Simmel on Culture*; Ann Gleber, *The Art of Taking a Walk: Flanerie, Literature and Film in Weimar Culture* (Princeton, N.J.: Princeton University Press, 1999).

comes not from interacting with others, who "disrupt" and "distract" their energy, but rather from listening to music, which might remind them of what it is to live in a city. This becomes a form of mediated cosmopolitanism that is encased in the user's iPod.

Although the audiovisual is dominant in iPod use, the evidence from the data I have collected suggests that this not a form of *flânerie*; rather, iPod users aim to create a privatized sound-world that is in harmony with their mood, orientation, and surroundings, enabling them to respatialize urban experience through a process of solipsistic aestheticization. In doing so, they create an illusion of omnipotence through mediated proximity and "connectedness" engendered by the use of their iPods.

From a Fordist to a Hyper-Post-Fordist Aesthetic

For many theorists from Auge to Sennett, this denuded and privatized social space is thought to reside in the streets we walk through; the buildings we pass by; the modern shopping centers we are inevitably drawn to; the anonymous spaces of airports, train stations, and parking lots; and the endless motorways that many of us progressively live on as we shuttle backward and forward in our cars or on public transport. Auge, in his analysis of urban space, used the term "nonspace" to describe an urban culture of semiologically denuded spaces, of shopping centers, airports, motorways, and the like. He thought of these spaces as if they had been dropped onto the urban landscape at random, as invariably architecturally bland.[28] Who can tell one shopping center from another, for example? Urban spaces from this perspective increasingly function as the endless transit zones of urban culture, emblems of the increasingly mobile nature of urban culture.

However, iPod use transforms any urban space into a nonspace. The defining feature of the user's relationship to urban space is not necessarily how culturally situated he might be. For iPod users, urban "nonspace" is not dependent on the "anthropological" nature of the space itself, but increasingly on the technologically empowered subjective response to that space, or indeed, the prior negation of that space through the cognitive predilections of the subject. Just as the placing of earphones over the ears empowers the ear, so the urban subject is free to re-create the city in his own image through the power of sound, as the following iPod user so aptly describes: "When I plug in and turn on, my iPod does a 'ctrl+alt+delete' on my surroundings and allows me to 'be' somewhere else" (Wes). Users can control and manage their urban experience. In doing so, time becomes subjectivized, and speed is brought into the rhythm of the user:

> I view people more like choices when I'm wearing my iPod. Instead of being forced to interact with them, I get to decide. It's almost liberating to realize you don't have to

[28] Marc Auge, *Non-places: Introduction to Anthropology of Supermodernity* (London: Verso, 1995).

> be polite or smile or do anything. I get to move through time and space at my speed [and] my pace. (Andrea)

Use of the iPod potentially furthers the existing isolation of urban citizens, who are articulated and embedded in a range of technologies that enables them to carry out many traditionally public tasks with little or no interpersonal contact. This furthers the architecture of isolation articulated in the work of Sennett and others. Exchanges are increasingly taking place between subjects and machines in urban culture, making interpersonal exchange increasingly obsolete. Cognitively, consumers often expect, feel comfortable with, and desire no direct interpersonal communication while out in public:

> I then started wearing it [the iPod] while shopping. I did it to control my environment and desensitize myself to everything around me. What I found interesting was that the more I wear my iPod, the less I want to interact with strangers. I've gotten to the point where I don't make eye contact. I feel almost encased in a bubble.... I view people more like choices when I'm wearing my iPod. (Zuni)

The construction of privatized sonic landscapes permits users to control the terms and condition of whatever interaction might take place, producing a web of asymmetrical urban relations in which users strive for control.

Retreat has become a dominant urban metaphor to describe strategies whereby citizens attempt to maintain a sense of "self" through the progressive creation of distancing mechanisms from the urban "other." Richard Sennett describes urban space as "a bland environment [that] assures people that nothing disturbing or demanding is happening 'out there.' You build neutrality in order to legitimize withdrawal."[29] Urban retreat as a means to maintain a subjective sense of balance or equilibrium can be traced back to the work of Georg Simmel, who described the urban subject as constructing a blasé attitude toward the physical nature of the city in order to achieve this aim.[30] The blasé attitude negates difference through distancing itself from that which surrounds it:

> [T]hings themselves are experienced as insubstantial. They appear to the blasé person in an evenly grey tone, no one object deserves preference over any other.... The self-preservation of certain personalities is bought at the price of devaluing the whole objective world.[31]

Simmel in effect was the first thinker to propose that a rich and full interiority was prefaced on negating the urban environment that confronted the individual. Thus, the dystopian image of urban life is prefaced on a rejection of difference, and indeed of physical presence. Urban life, from this perspective, becomes a dialectical process of

[29] Richard Sennett, *The Conscience of the Eye* (London: Faber, 1990), 65.

[30] Simmel, *Simmel on Culture*, 143

[31] Simmel, *Simmel on Culture*, 179.

freedom and insecurity whereby the urban citizen progressively retreats into her own cognitive or physical shell while simultaneously neutralizing or aestheticizing the public spaces of the city. Urban retreat subsequently becomes the dominant metaphor in the dystopian image of urban life, whereby the urban citizen attempts to maintain a sense of "self" through the progressive creation of distancing mechanisms from the "other." Technology both comes to the aid of, and furthers, this management of urban space and cognition. Users increasingly choose to live in an increasingly privatized and "perpetual sound matrix" through which they "inhabit different sensory worlds" while sharing the same social space.[32]

The Limitations of Aesthetically Remaking the City

Epistemologically speaking—and following Herbert Marcuse—the audiovisual forms of aestheticization enacted by iPod users are largely transcendent.[33] To aestheticize is to simplify, to strip reality of its inessentials. The aesthetic principle is inherently one of transcendence. An essential component of this transcendence for the urban citizen is to replace the multirhythmic and hence unmanageable nature of urban life with her own manageable audiovisual monorhythms.

In enacting these practices, iPod use embodies the dialectic of utopian and dystopian impulses—aestheticization is an active mode of appropriating the urban, transforming that which exists by making it the user's own. The desire to engage in these processes derives both from the habitual predispositions of users located in wider media use—for are not television and film viewers equally in positions of imaginary omnipotence while they watch from the comforts of their own homes?—and as a response to the nature of urban space itself and the dislocation from it felt by the urban subject.[34] Yet in this denial of contingency lies a liberating moment wherein the city is re-enchanted through the individualizing of each journey; the city as "aura" is reclaimed through the sonic "tactics" of iPod users.[35] The price of this aesthetic enhancement, like Odysseus's communing with the Sirens, paradoxically is loss of the collective life of public space.

In the contemporary world of iPod desire, space is inhabited through the sounds of the culture industry entering directly into the ears of users. Like Odysseus, their sound-world is constructed through the transmission of sound from elsewhere. But in the present day, the Siren's voice is a domesticated and mechanically produced one. Unlike Odysseus, users suffer no penalties as a consequence of listening. Equally, their own

[32] David Howes, *Sensual Relations. Engaging the Senses in Culture and Social Theory* (Ann Arbor: University of Michigan Press, 2003), 14.

[33] Herbert Marcuse, *The Aesthetic Dimension* (Boston: Beacon Press, 1978).

[34] David Morley, *Home Territories; Media, Mobility and Identity* (London: Routledge, 2000).

[35] De Certeau, *Practice of Everyday Life.*

listening does not preclude others from listening—each in his or her own mediated and privatized sound-world. Contemporary users live in a more democratized consumer culture, in which many are like Odysseus and fewer of us are "oarsmen."

References

Auge, Marc. *Non-places: Introduction to Anthropology of Supermodernity*. London: Verso, 1995.

Adorno, Theodor. *The Culture Industry: Selected Essays on Mass Culture*. London: Routledge, 1991.

Benjamin, Walter. *Illuminations*. London: Penguin, 1973.

Bergson, Henri. *Introduction to Metaphysics*. London: Kessinger, 1998.

Bull, Michael. *Sounding Out the City: Personal Stereos and the Management of Everyday Life*. Oxford: Berg, 2000.

Bull, Michael. *Sound Moves: iPod Culture and Urban Experience*. London: Routledge, 2007.

Coyne, Richard. *The Tuning of Place: Sociable Spaces and Pervasive Digital Media*. Cambridge, Mass.: MIT Press, 2010.

De Certeau, Michel. *The Practice of Everyday Life*. Berkeley: University of California Press, 1988.

Debord, Guy. *Society of the Spectacle*. Detroit, MI: Black and Red, 1977.

Douglas, Susan. *Listening In: Radio and the American Imagination*. Minneapolis: University of Minnesota Press, 2004.

Dyson, Frances. *Sounding New Media: Immersion and Embodiment in the Arts and Culture*. Berkeley: University of California Press, 2009.

Geurts, Kathleen. *Culture and the Senses. Bodily Ways of Knowing in an African Community*. Berkeley: University of California Press, 2002.

Gibson, William, *Time Out* 6 (October 1993): 49.

Gleber, Ann. *The Art of Taking a Walk: Flanerie, Literature and Film in Weimar Culture*. Princeton, N.J.: Princeton University Press, 1999.

Horkheimer, Max, and Theodor Adorno. *The Dialectic of Enlightenment*. London: Penguin, 1973.

Howes, David. *Sensual Relations. Engaging the Senses in Culture and Social Theory*. Ann Arbor: University of Michigan Press, 2003.

Ito, Mizuko, Daisuke Okabe, and Misa Matsuda. *Personal, Portable, Pedestrian: Mobile Phones in Japanese Life*. Cambridge, Mass.: MIT Press, 2005.

Kracauer, Siegfried. *The Mass Ornament: Weimar Essays*. Cambridge, Mass.: Harvard University Press, 1995.

Korczynski, Marek. "Music at Work: Towards a Historical Overview." *Folk Music Journal* 8, no. 3 (2003): 314–334.

Layton, Deborah. *Seductive Poison: A Jonestown Survivor's Story of Life and Death in the People's Temple*. New York: Random House, 1998.

Lefebvre, Henri. *The Production of Space*. Oxford: Blackwell, 1991.

Lefebvre, Henri. *The Urban Revolution*. Minneapolis: University of Minnesota Press, 2003.

Lefebvre, Henri. *Rhythmanalysis. Space, Time and Everyday Life*. London: Continuum Press, 2004.

Marcuse, Herbert. *The Aesthetic Dimension*. Boston: Beacon Press, 1978.

Morley, David. *Home Territories: Media, Mobility and Identity*. London: Routledge, 2000.

Musil, Robert. *Man Without Qualities*. London: Picador, 1995.

Schafer, Murray. *The Tuning of the World*. New York: Knopf, 1977.

Sennett, Richard. *The Conscience of the Eye*. London: Faber, 1990.

Simmel, George. *Simmel on Culture: Selected Writings*. Ed. David Frisby and Mike Featherstone. London: Sage, 1997.
Sterne, Jonathan. *The Audible Past: Cultural Origins of Sound Reproduction*. Durham, N.C.: Duke University Press, 2003.
Todorov, Tzvetan. *On Human Diversity: Nationalism, Racism, and Exoticism in French Thought*. Cambridge, Mass.: Harvard University Press, 1993.
Turkle, Sherry. *Alone Together: Why We Expect More from Technology and Less from Each Other*. New York: Basic Books, 2011.

CHAPTER 37

ON SOUNDSCAPE METHODS AND AUDIOVISUAL SENSIBILITY

HELMI JÄRVILUOMA AND NOORA VIKMAN

THE concept of soundscape has been debated extensively in the research on audiovisuality. Among music scholars, those who have taken an interest in film music, such as Philip Tagg and Ola Stockfelt, were first to embrace concepts from soundscape studies in their writing.[1] More recently the media and film music scholar Anahid Kassabian has employed the concept of "ubiquitous music" to account for everyday soundscapes in which a multisensory, and therefore also audiovisual, aspect is unavoidably present.[2]

The term "soundscape" itself has been criticized for implying a visual metaphor in a field of study dedicated to shifting attention toward the previously neglected aspects of sonic experience. However, because of the recent shift in cultural theory toward the recognition of assemblages that occur between the senses and of the materialities and social collectives involved in everyday music making and usage, the idea of a multisensory notion of soundscapes is beginning to have greater appeal. This study adopts a feminist stance: it is not only possible but even desirable both to use a term and at the same time to trouble it. Soundscape can be regarded as shifting, processual, historical, and produced in specific contingent situations. Like the related concept of acoustic ecology, soundscape is a meta-discourse that should be understood not as a neutral field but as something ethically framed and intelligible only in relation to specific cultural and historical conditions.[3]

1 Philip Tagg, *Reading Sounds or an Essay on Sounds, Music, Knowledge, Rock & Society* (Gothenburg, Sweden: IASPM,, 1987); Ola Stockfelt, "Cars, Buildings, Soundscapes," in *Soundscapes: Essays on Vroom and Moo*, ed. Helmi Järviluoma (Tampere, Finland: Tampere University Department of Folk Tradition; Seinäjoki, Finland: Institute of Rhythm Music, 1994), 19–38.

2 Anahid Kassabian, "Ubiquitous Musics and Networked Subjectivity," *ECHO: A Music-centered Journal* 3, no. 2 (2001), at http://www.echo.ucla.edu/Volume3-issue2/kassabian/kassabian.pdf (accessed November 19, 2010).

3 Noora Vikman, *Akustisen ekologian ekologiset diskurssit*, AEC Working Papers 2 (Turku, Finland: University of Turku; Tampere, Finland: University of Tampere, 1999).

In the late 1980s the term "soundscape" was still not widely known, either by researchers or in society at large.[4] A few decades later, the term regularly appears in the media and at least in scholarly circles is widely known throughout Europe, Asia, and Latin America. Regarding the historicity of terms such as "soundscape" and "acoustic ecology," they are usefully considered in relation to ideational Darwinism, which draws attention to a tendency to favor the most politically acceptable and timely models and methods at any historical moment.[5] It might be claimed that the concepts of soundscape and acoustic ecology were especially timely in the late 1960s and 1970s, when they emerged from a growing environmental awareness as a result of R. Murray Schafer's exposure to environmental philosophies, among other factors.[6]

By the 1970s, those engaged in soundscape studies took an interest in all manner of sounds as materialities. Since the 1980s, in contrast, the linguistic focus of cultural studies and anthropology has placed the study of language, texts, symbols, and meanings at the center of scholarly interest. The early writings of acoustic ecologists and soundscape researchers, however, clearly predate this shift toward the linguistic.[7] In *Five Village Soundscapes*, for example, Schafer elevated such sound-producing materials as road surfaces and building materials to prominence as crucial components of soundscapes.[8]

Commensurate with the early sensory orientation of soundscape studies, one can detect a shift in the course of the past decade or so toward the *affective* and the *sensory* in the human and social sciences.[9] It is not surprising that proponents of the "sensory revolution," such as Michel Serres in *Five Senses*[10] and David Howes in *Empire of the Senses*,[11] are turning their backs on language and the linguistic turn, which implies the textualization of everything from dance to sound. An emerging trend in "new materialist musicology" attempts to bring its scholarly focus to bear squarely on the materiality of the body.[12]

4 Using the concept of soundscape emphasizes the ability of the subject and communities to listen to their acoustic environments. R. Murray Schafer, *Sound Education* (Indian River, Ontario: Arcana Editions, 1992); Barry Truax, *Acoustic Communication* (Westport, Conn.: Ablex, 2001).

5 See, for example, Risto Heiskala, *Toiminta, tapa, rakenne* (Helsinki: Gaudeamus, 2000), 11–12.

6 See, for example, Maria Anna Harley, "Canadian Identity, Deep Ecology and R. Murray Schafer's 'The Princess of the Stars,'" in *Yearbook of Soundscape Studies*, ed. R. Murray Schafer and Helmi Järviluoma (Tampere, Finland: Tampere University, 1998), 1:119–142.

7 Helmi Järviluoma, Meri Kytö, Barry Truax, Heikki Uimonen, and Noora Vikman, eds., *Acoustic Environments in Change*, TAMK Series A, Research Papers 13; Studies in Literature and Culture 14 (Joensuu, Finland: University of Joensuu, 2009); Noora Vikman, "Looking for a 'Right Method'—Approaching Beyond," in *Soundscape Studies and Methods*, ed. Helmi Järviluoma and Gregg Wagstaff, Finnish Society for Ethnomusicology Pub. 9; Department of Art, Literature and Music, A51, (Helsinki: Suomen etnomusikologinen seura, 2002), 143–170.

8 R. Murray Schafer, *Five Village Soundscapes* (Vancouver, B.C.: A.R.C. Publications, 1977).

9 See, for example, Anu Koivunen, "Affektin paluu," *Tiedotustutkimus* 31, no. 3 (2008): 5–24.

10 Michel Serres, *Five Senses: A Philosophy of Mingled Bodies*, Athlone Contemporary European Thinkers (London; New York: Continuum, 1998 [1985]).

11 David Howes, *Empire of the Senses: The Sensual Culture Reader* (New York; Oxford: Berg, 2005).

12 Milla Tiainen, "Becoming-Singer: Cartographies of Singing, Music-Making and Opera" (PhD diss., University of Turku, 2012).

Any convincing empirical study of sensory environments, however, requires openness on the part of the researcher to how the sensory and linguistic aspects of experience correlate. As the anthropologist Janne Rantala recently noted when discussing the anthropology of the senses, the textual turn, with its roots firmly in phenomenology, has paradoxically served as a foundation for the coming-of-age of the emerging paradigm of research into sensory formations.[13] This new area of interest is so strong that it is no longer accurate to talk about oculocentrism in scholarly work—so much new interest has developed in the topic of sound and culture. For example, the anthropology of the senses now has its own journal, and in 2011 several new journals were founded that are devoted to sound and music.[14]

This chapter focuses on a specific aspect of soundscape methodology that has proven useful when considering how research on the audiovisual might be advanced; namely, the idea of methods in motion. Soundscape studies have stressed from the very start that researchers sometimes need to leave the "laboratory" (the mediated reality offered by film or television screens, or equally, headphones or loudspeakers in the studio) and venture into "the field." Our aims in this chapter are threefold. We first direct attention to soundscape studies as the art and scholarly study of listening. We then illustrate the salience of this approach by introducing a particular form of method in motion: the *sensory memory walk*. This method was developed in the course of our work on the Acoustic Environments in Change research project, which charted local European soundscapes.[15] Finally, we introduce the *listening walk* as a method: what happens when researchers move, and listen, in their everyday audiovisual environment.

The Art and Scholarly Study of Listening

The earliest systematic explorations of acoustic environments originated in the experimental arts, as the Italian experimental composer and soundscape researcher Albert Mayr has pointed out.[16] Even while the concept of soundscape was becoming better known in the late 1960s,[17] "happenings" aimed at narrowing the gap between art and society.[18]

It is a peculiarity of the field of acoustic ecology that both artists and researchers work in the same field of inquiry. As an artistic practice, listening walks and soundwalks

[13] Janne Rantala, "Antropologi oom-ringissä—aistihavainto kenttätyössä," in *Vaeltavat metodit*, ed. Jyrki Pöysä, Helmi Järviluoma, and Sinikka Vakimo (Joensuu: Finnish Folklore Society, 2010), 258–284.

[14] See, for example, *SoundEffects—An Interdiciplinary Journal of Sound and Sound Experience* (Aarhus University), at http://www.soundeffects.dk/index (accessed December 6, 2011); and *Journal of Sonic Studies* (University of Leiden), at http://journal.sonicstudies.org (accessed December 6, 2011).

[15] Järviluoma et al., *Acoustic Environments in Change*.

[16] Albert Mayr, "Soundscape Studies, Experimental Music and Time Geography," in *Soundscape Studies and Methods*, ed. Järviluoma and Wagstaff, 27–38.

[17] R. Murray Schafer, *The New Soundscape* (Toronto: Berandol, 1968).

[18] Mayr, "Soundscape Studies, Experimental Music and Time Geography"; Allan Kaprow, *Essays on the Blurring of Life and Art*, ed. Jeff Kelley (Berkeley; Los Angeles: University of California, 1993).

may be regarded as a genre related to site-specific art. In reference to the audiovisual, it appears that soundscape research offers novel theoretical and methodological tools that can be used in studying and understanding experiences (*Erlebnis*), partly because such research borrows from both artistic methods and community art. The senses—and flirtation with them—are not regarded as the preserve of art alone.

Experimental engagement with creativity and experience requires the researcher to accept transience in the lives of the people being studied. Experimentalism, however, is not understood solely as a feature of art—or of research—but also as a potential dynamic force in all areas of daily life.[19] It is not only specialists, poets, and artists, therefore, who attempt to make their voices heard by aesthetic means; the aestheticization of everyone's lives is written into the assumptions of work in this field of inquiry.

Sensory Memory Walking as a Method: The Case of Lesconil

We now turn to the women of Lesconil, a fishing village in Brittany near Quimper, and their sensory memory walks, with a view to envisioning a shared understanding of past places. During the past 20 years ethnomusicologists in Finland have worked on a variety of soundscape projects, some extensive and others more modest in scale. Previously, in 1975, a group of Canadian soundscape researchers had visited five European villages, including Lesconil.[20] In 2000, in a follow-up project under the rubric Acoustic Environments in Change (AEC[21]), a different group of researchers, especially from Finland this time,[22] visited the same villages to study the changes that had occurred in their soundscapes.

The method employed to study people's sensory memories was first developed in cooperation with other AEC and CRESSON (The Centre for Research on Sonic Space and Urban Environment in Grenoble) researchers in Lesconil, then used again in Dollar, a small town in Scotland. In this approach listening walks employ a kind of *écoute resituée*, a term adapted from the parallel term *écoute située*, which was devised by Nicolas Tixier and the sound researchers at CRESSON.[23] Tixier and his colleagues developed their method on the basis of "commentaried" city walks made by the sociologist Jean-Paul Thibaud.

[19] See also Ben Highmore, *Everyday Life and Cultural Theory* (London: Routledge, 2002), 45–59.

[20] Schafer, *Five Village Soundscapes*.

[21] Järviluoma et al., *Acoustic Environments in Change*.

[22] Järviluoma, Vikman, Uimonen, and Hyvärinen, "Soundscapes in Change."

[23] Nicolas Tixier, "Street Listening: A Characterisation of the Sound Environment: The 'Qualified Listening in Motion' Method," in *Soundscape Studies and Methods*, ed. Järviluoma and Wagstaff, 83–90.

According to Doreen Massey,[24] different times cross-fertilize each other experientially and epistemologically in cultural and geographic spaces. During sensory memory walks, for example, various perceptions such as visual surroundings and smells awaken auditive memories. Given that sensory memory walks clearly involve multiple mediations among objects, houses, roads, and people moving, the result is the creation of situated collectives. As Seremetakis[25] has put it, the senses produce a corporate communication between the body and objects, the person and the world—they are firmly located in the social-material field.

In September 2004 one of the authors, Helmi Järviluoma, returned to Lesconil to develop further the idea of sonic memory walks.[26] Although not yet called "sonic memory walks," an early version of the method can be found in the project Five Village Soundscapes, in which researchers took the solicitor and town clerk David Graham to various places in Dollar in 1975. The method appeared to be a highly effective way of encouraging people to remember the sounds of various places. David Graham had no problem loosening the knots of his memories while visiting places familiar from his childhood and youth.

Järviluoma had noticed that as Lesconil had the identity of a fishing village, the researchers' interests naturally revolved around fishermen, and little attention was paid to women and children. She therefore decided to focus on the memories of middle-aged and elderly women, asking how the senses constructed an understanding of place for the women and children in Lesconil in the 1950s and early 1960s. She was further interested in the nature of their present situation and how the women created and shared understandings of past places, not only through verbal recollections, but also as they moved physically through the streets and fields that used to be so important to them.

Järviluoma recruited two groups of women who agreed to walk with her. On a piece of paper she wrote, in her imperfect French, the following request: "I would like you to choose a path that was important to you when you were children. Could you then please take me for a walk along that particular path? Can you tell me about the smells and sounds you sensed there when you were children?" After some reflection, Järviluoma concluded that it would be too difficult to try to separate specific "sonic memories" from the more fuzzy field of sensory memories. Hence she expressed herself in the request in such a way that the women would be encouraged to open up about the realm of sensory memories in general, but with an emphasis on the olfactory and sonic. If theorists of emplaced sensory memories, such as Casey,[27] were correct, bringing people back to

[24] Doreen Massey, *For Space* (London: Sage, 2005).

[25] Nadia Seremetakis, *The Senses Still: Perception and Memory as Material Culture in Modernity* (Boulder, Colo.; San Francisco; Oxford: Westview Press, 1994).

[26] See Helmi Järviluoma, "'Scythe-driven Nostalgia' and Soundscapes and Social Memory in Skruv," in *Acoustic Environments in Change*, 154–171.

[27] Edward S. Casey, *Remembering: A Phenomenological Study* (Bloomington: Indiana University Press, 1987); see also Steven Feld, "Waterfalls of Song: An Acoustemology of Place Resounding in Bosavi, Papua New Guinea," in *Senses of Place*, ed. Steven Feld and Keith Basso (Santa Fe, N.Mex.: SAR Press, 1996), 91–135.

the paths they had frequented 50 years earlier might act as a form of incitation. Thus, Järviluoma was acting as a kind of *provocateuse*, bringing people back to "the scene of the crime."

Sonic Memory Walks Through Lesconil

Two small groups of middle-aged and elderly women who were born in Lesconil walked with Järviluoma along the special path they had chosen. Together they ambled through a landscape that was heavily charged with meanings for the locals. In the course of the walk the women drew a map that stretched from the past to the present,[28] telling stories and recalling sights, sounds, and smells. For example, they were able to "paint" the sensory image of a complete farm while walking through an empty field that seemed and sounded more like a nonplace to the researcher—not even ruins were to be seen.

During the memory walk the group of Lesconil women talked about a sound that in the past used to echo down La Grande Rue: the strong clopping of the *sabots*—French wooden clogs—of the army of women who were on their way to work in the sardine factory. "That's a sound we will never forget," they said. Now why is that? The women stand with the researcher in a street and show her where the sound could once be heard. In the present they enter into a dialogue with the space, and it is duly activated. La Grande Rue is also brought into the present as a gendered place, where the dozens of pairs of *sabots*—their own and their mothers'—are still clacking in their memories. In their talk, this group of Lesconil women, with their working-class roots, have constructed the sound of *sabots* as a shared social memory. Thus a momentary collective is formed when the group stands on a particular Lesconil street corner. Two of the women had even worked at the fish factory in their youth. The factory had been an important means of livelihood for their families, but that was not something the mothers wished for as the only future for their daughters.

Feminist scholars of architecture emphasize that the sensate users of space need to be placed at the center of scholarly attention.[29] In the example presented here, the meanings of a lived space are created in the relationship between the user and the space; the women confirm these meanings when they move and stand on the street corner. They become the makers—or "authors of space"—and the researcher becomes involved so vividly in this creation that she almost feels as if the street corner were haunted by the sights and sounds of women walking the Grande Rue in their clacking *sabots*. Sounds, sights, and music are the elements in dialogue that should be examined when places—inhabited or

[28] Annette Kuhn, *An Everyday Magic: Cinema and Cultural Memory* (London: I. B. Tauris Publishers, 2002).

[29] Kirsi Saarikangas, *Asunnon muodonmuutoksia: Puhtauden estetiikka ja sukupuoli modernissa arkkitehtuurissa* (Helsinki: Finnish Literature Society, 2002).

haunted[30]—are the subject of study, while the researcher needs, in this case, to interpret the memory narration of these sights, sounds, and smells situationally.[31]

Listening Walks

Listening walks and sensory memory walks assist researchers in engaging with the everyday creative activities of the people studied. Listening while walking is a method that stimulates new experiential ideas about dealing with an acoustic environment, no matter whether we consider it pleasant, unpleasant, or merely insignificant. Listening and moving can provoke practical questions while also providing an opportunity for the participant to experience the connection between sounds and their sources in situ.

The difference between *soundwalking* and *listening walking* was generally defined in the early 1970s simply by referring to, for example, the level of preplanning and the amount of improvisation and freedom in choosing the routes taken.[32] Decisions made about the location, style, content, and montage of sound in both soundwalking and listening walking may have political, social, and ecological consequences.[33]

There are at least two kinds of listening walkers. The traditional listener *flâneur* and *flâneuse* enjoy the variety of details and report on their experiences through their subjective interpretations. They are passionate but detached observers of modern life, "who go botanizing on the asphalt"[34], and are trapped in the language of "atmospheres" and "feelings."[35] But in the same sound environment there is a mass of other individuals in their everyday sound environment whose listening habits the researcher still knows nothing about. This dilemma lies at the core of ethnographic studies of soundscapes. How could these different wanderers and their worlds meet? What are the potentially shared or aspects of their environment?[36]

30 See, for example, Ben Anderson and Paul Harrison, *Taking-Place: Non-Representational Theories and Geography* (Farnham, UK: Ashgate, 2010).

31 See also Helmi Järviluoma and Pirkko Moisala, "Not Only Vision—Analyzing Sound and Music From the Perspective of Gender," in *Gender and Qualitative Methods*, ed. Helmi Järviluoma, Pirkko Moisala and Anni Vilkko (London: Sage, 2003), 102–104.

32 Concerning these differences, see Olli-Taavetti Kankkunen, "Käy kuuntelemaan! Äänikävely ja ääniympäristön havainnointi," in *Järjen ja arjen ääniä*, ed. K. Ahonen and T. Juutilainen (Tampere, Finland: Tampere University Press, 2012), 119–153; Andra McCartney, "Soundwalking: Creating Moving Environmental Sound Narratives," in *The Oxford Handbook of Mobile Music Studies*, ed. Sumanth Gopinath and Jason Stanyek (Oxford: Oxford University Press, forthcoming 2013); R. Murray Schafer, "Listening," *Sound Heritage, III*: 4 (1974), 17; Schafer, *Five Village Soundscapes*, 212–213; Hildegard Westerkamp, "Sound Walking," *Sound Heritage* 3, no. 4 (2001 [orig. 1974]): 18–27.

33 McCartney, "Soundwalking."

34 Walter Benjamin, *Charles Baudelaire. A Lyric Poet in the Era of High Capitalism*. London: Verso (1983), 36.

35 See Lauri Mehtonen Lauri, "Rousseaun promenadi itseen," *Niin & näin* 69, no. 2 (2011): 30–33.

36 Tim Ingold and Jo Lee Vergunst, eds., *Ways of Walking. Ethnography and Practice of Foot*, Anthropological Studies of Creativity and Perception (Aldershot, UK: Ashgate, 2008).

The researcher as a colistener and advocate focuses on people's ways of feeling and thinking about their environment. But the method does not stop there. Researchers and participants involved in the situation feel, hear, and see the reality together, enriched with new imprints and interactions. The chosen instructions are formulated primarily to suit the means of communication and interaction between the participants in each particular case.

The researcher acting in the role of a facilitator first foregrounds the insights and inspirations of the various walkers. Another important goal is to catch the fresh moment by sharing the experiences immediately after the walk. After the group has collectively listened to a certain route, it is offered a forum in which it can reconstruct the experiences while giving expression to emotional responses. This forum transforms the immediate individual experiences from a collection of subjective soundscapes into a new collective sphere of shared observations and meanings that are not yet rationalized or fixed by rigid interpretations.

If groups of youngsters participate in listening walks, they easily become inspired to experiment with the physical objects they encounter. Especially when encouraged, they allow their visual observations to extend the experience in a multisensory manner, touching and playing with objects to make them sound. One young participant on Noora Vikman's listening walk, after receiving the usual instructions to listen and not to talk with others, started to listen to a statue. He indicated with his gestures that he could hear nothing from the statue, so he began to converse with and then to physically knock it. Soon most of the group was holding a concert, concentrating collectively on using the statue and other surrounding objects as their instruments. Much like these youngsters, other groups use their imaginations to read the acoustic signs of the environment by means of different "strategies."

At one open event organized by Pori Art Museum, Noora Vikman walked with a group of women. Before the walk all the women had pointed out that they wanted to experience something new. After the walk their experiences were discussed and the observations and feelings that mattered were listed in detail. The collective experience clearly knitted the group together.

Participatory research and reports offer support in the construction of collectively created soundscapes and forums so that they can be shared further. Various dynamics are involved in unwinding the experiences of the group. The auditive aspects reveal the details of people's relationships to their environment. Creativity is a matter of both knowing and doing, and the act of listening is always fruitful. For example, the children in Pori did not wait until the discussion after the walk, but found a way to interact with the statue and each other. The group of women used the moment of constructing the soundscape together to extend the pleasure of sharing an atmosphere. The research aim of such shared experiences is to shed light on the preconditions of living together and sharing a common space. Rather than summing up something about experiences, this method opens a route to a variety of further questions about this particular environment and the environment in general, leading to a recognition of commonalities and the discrepancies that it contains.

To deliberately attend to moving as a method is already a methodological choice. When the researcher steps out of the academy and into the field, she or he adopts a physical position alongside others who participate in experiencing the same environment. Everyday life is constructed on the basis of observations made by different eye and ear witnesses, not to mention the other modalities involved in everyday experience, such as touch and smell. The researcher creates and develops the research process involved in connecting those various subject positions. Communication evokes comparison between forms of information and the accumulation of experiential knowledge. The same cannot be achieved solely by the use of the imagination, non in situ. Furthermore, this type of methodological articulation, the dialogic attitude, means that the conceptual systems of researchers and those of the people and cases under study are always relational.

It is necessary to move physically toward the sound object to hear the physical environment from different angles and in all its variety. The living soundscape cannot be relocated or be heard in a different location without the aid of transphonic mediations.[37] Hence, a task when conducting research is to open up new opportunities to listen to and compare the ways in which the in situ experience of a soundscape differs, for example, from a recorded soundscape. Thus, the nature of listening walks and of sensory memory walks as methods includes both movement and intensive listening.

Another way out of the fuzziness and trap of cultural myopia is to contrast listening to visual perception. Our audiovisual culture is sometimes dramatized as being "deaf," which means that it is insensitive to acoustic phenomena. Without falling back on what Jonathan Sterne calls the "audiovisual litany,"[38] which in his view idealizes hearing as the manifestation of a pure interiority, it is safe to argue that the methods deployed in soundscape studies may be capable of articulating some intriguing differences and correspondences between seeing and hearing. The visual may be easier to grasp simply because there are more established models for its study. Paradoxically, it is easier to report listening experiences using metaphors borrowed from the visual sphere.[39] In addition, visual elements seem to be more permanent, or at least they carry more weight in the physical environment. They are not "born," and they do not "die out" as fast as sounds, which after all persist only as long as the sound waves themselves are in motion.

The world of sounds is above all one of events. Acoustic elements are related to action: when we listen to sounds, we are listening to echoes, hoofbeats, or door slams—in short, resonances to the audial results of action. In contrast, seeing represents

[37] A term coined by the Finnish soundscape researchers for use when the Schaferian term "schitzophony" sounds unnecessarily pejorative (see, e.g., Heikki Uimonen, *Ääntä kohti: Ääniympäristön kuuntelu, muutos ja merkitys* [Tampere, Finland: Tampere University Press, 2005]).

[38] Jonathan Sterne, *The Audible Past: Cultural Origins of Sound Reproduction* (Durham, N.C.; London: Duke University Press, 2003), 15.

[39] Noora Vikman, "Alussa oli askel: Katsaus kuuntelukävelyyn ympäristökulttuurin tutkimuksen metodina," in *Vaeltavat metodit*, ed. Jyrki Pöysä, Helmi Järviluoma, and Sinikka Vakimo (Joensuu: Finnish Folklore Society, 2010), 190–214.

something more stable, reflecting the world of physical objects.[40] The mechanisms involved when "closing our ears" frame spatial experiences differently from what is involved when "closing our eyes." During listening walks the possibility of being blindfolded provides space for auditively framed experiences and possibilities for ear witnessing. The immediate report of one young boy after listening while standing blindfolded at a city crossroad was a description of a rich acoustic event: "A breathless biker crossed the street against red lights."

The sociologist and soundscape researcher Jean-Paul Thibaud states about sensory responses:

> For example, when we enter a new place, we immediately feel its atmosphere and make sense of it. Our body responds to the place in some way or another. We tend to adopt its rhythm and its tonality. We are moved by the gentleness of the whispers, the brightness of a light, the coldness of the winter air or the spiciness of the smell. The ambience takes hold of us before we are able to clearly identify and represent the actual situation.[41]

Sensory experience can function informatively by imparting knowledge about a place. Contrary to color, which remains attached to the object, sound has the ability to separate itself from its source and liberate itself from directional movement. This idea led Jean-Paul Thibaud to follow the phenomenological psychiatrist Erwin Straus, who has associated acoustic space with the space of dance, because in both cases, "the body tends to move without direction and resonates with the its immediate surroundings."[42]

But what is the added value that movement brings to our method? Listening from a stable position makes the world sound as if it were flowing past. In the process of moving, it is possible to evaluate the borders of a territory acoustically: movement creates variation in listening points. The moving listener is also active in a different way, by making choices. The "freedom" to move provides space to turn toward what could be called the acoustic magnets of an environment. Changes in the various acoustics, acoustic horizons, and masking effects can be tested from different angles. Listeners may also become conscious of their own sound making and consider their own needs, adapting to the environment. It may be easier for the walking listener to cross or to become conscious of the hypothetical borders between seeing and hearing.

Acoustic variation along the course of the route may inspire the listener to form subjective soundscapes, entities in which the experienced elements imply meaningful relationships with each other. By taking heed of the variety of listening points, the listener does more than merely attend to the stable or precontrolled elements within an environment. In the process, the listener's presuppositions are tested experientially before the research setting is circumscribed too tightly.

[40] Paul Rodaway, *Sensuous Geographies: Body, Sense and Place.* (London: Routledge, 1994), 96–98, 101.

[41] Jean-Paul Thibaud, "A Sonic Paradigm of Urban Ambiances?" *Journal of Sonic Studies* 1, no. 1 (2011), at http://journal.sonicstudies.org/vol01/nr01/a02 (accessed December 11, 2012).

[42] Thibaud, "A Sonic Paradigm of Urban Ambiances??"

A Few Final Thoughts

> my academic safaris are conducted from the living room couch, whence I peer into the concrete and neon jungle of mass media entertainment on the tube: I don't even have to leave the apartment.[43]

Soundscape concepts have been employed for more than 20 years as a means of enriching studies of the audiovisual. Two decades ago, however, music scholars—such as Philip Tagg—who bridged the gap between soundscape studies and research on the audiovisual created anthropologies of TV music mostly from within the confines of their living rooms.

The present discussion has described some of the recent developments in the "marriage" of soundscape and audiovisual studies. We have taken soundings from various perspectives about what happens when researchers in the field actually move and listen in their everyday audiovisual environments. Theories and methods in this particular area of sound and music studies have developed a great deal over the past 20 years. We have experienced the affective and the new materialist turns and their effects on methodology. Sound studies are increasingly employed as a basis for the development of multisensory methodologies for studying times, spaces, and materialities to relocate sensate users of space at the center of the researcher's attention.

In 2010 Teemu Takatalo and Raila Knuuttila, two artists from our hometown of Joensuu, Finland, walked all the way from Brussels to Istanbul. When Takatalo was subsequently interviewed for a philosophical journal about the journey they had undertaken, he said that the most rewarding aspect was undoubtedly the extremely strong feeling of presence, a feeling of being in the moment. He suggested that in the process of walking, their perceptions were heightened, they sensed the smells they encountered, and there was a fresh clarity to the sounds that they heard: "Walking is a hugely holistic way of being."[44]

Both listening walks and sonic memory walks are above all about active presence in which the walker does not know where the experiment of surrendering will lead. The present discussion has focused on these two methods in motion, which do more than simply transform the border between the audio and the visual. Methodologically speaking, at their most fruitful these two approaches are movements within the labyrinth of categories, oppositions, and borders between presence and distance, thinking and not thinking, form and meaning, encouraging both fixed narrations as well as change, approaching and distancing, and the Kantian *Zweck ohne Zweck*.

[43] Philip Tagg, "An Anthropology of Stereotypes in TV Music," *Svensk tidskrift för musikforskning* 71 (1989): 19–42.

[44] Tere Vadén, "Kävely on matkustamista muodosta merkitykseen," *Niin & näin* 69, no. 2 (2011): 8.

Our focus throughout has been on listening to selected ways in which art and scholarly research together form a kind of force field that facilitates the study and understanding of experience. In this sense we remain engrossed in the same development that has, for example, persuaded the sound anthropologist Steven Feld to reorient his well-known concept "acoustemology" (acoustic ways of knowing) toward the notion of "relational ontology."[45] The force of this approach is acknowledged as especially relevant in recent discussions of the philosophies of art,[46] where an increasing focus is placed on how feeling and understanding, as well as being and knowing, may conjoin.

References

Anderson, Ben, and Paul Harrison. *Taking-Place: Non-Representational Theories and Geography.* Farnham, UK: Ashgate, 2010.

Benjamin, Walter. *Charles Baudelaire. A Lyric Poet in the Era of High Capitalism.* London: Verso, 1983.

Butler, Christopher. *Pleasure in the Arts.* Oxford: Oxford University Press, 2009.

Casey, Edward S. *Remembering: A Phenomenological Study.* Bloomington: Indiana University Press, 1987.

Feld, Steven. "Waterfalls of Song: An Acoustemology of Place Resounding in Bosavi, Papua New Guinea." In *Senses of Place*, edited by Steven Feld and Keith Basso, 91–135. Santa Fe, N.Mex.: SAR Press, 1996.

Feld, Steven. "Acoustemology as Relational Ontology." Speech presented at the Value, Agency, Soundspaces seminar, University of Liverpool, October 15, 2010.

Feld, Steven, and Virginia Ryan. "Contemporary Art in/as Anthropology." In *Between Art and Anthropology: Contemporary Ethnographic Practice*, edited by Arnd Schneider and Christopher Wright, 109–126. New York: Berg, 2010.

Harley, Maria Anna. "Canadian Identity, Deep Ecology and R. Murray Schafer's 'The Princess of the Stars.'" In *Yearbook of Soundscape Studies*, edited by R. Murray Schafer and Helmi Järviluoma, Vol. 1, 119–142. Tampere, Finland: Tampere University, 1998.

Heiskala, Risto. *Toiminta, tapa, rakenne* [Action, habit, structure]. Helsinki: Gaudeamus, 2000.

Highmore, Ben. *Everyday Life and Cultural Theory: An Introduction.* London: Routledge, 2002.

Howes, David. *Empire of the Senses: The Sensual Culture Reader.* New York; Oxford: Berg, 2005.

Ingold, Tim, and Jo Lee Vergunst, eds. *Ways of Walking: Ethnography and Practice of Foot.* Anthropological Studies of Creativity and Perception. Aldershot, UK: Ashgate, 2008.

Järviluoma, Helmi. "Soundscapes and Social Memory in Skruv." In *Acoustic Environments in Change*, edited by. Helmi Järviluoma, Meri Kytö, Barry Truax, Heikki Uimonen, and Noora Vikman, 138–153. Tampere, Finland: TAMK Series A, Research Papers 13; University of Joensuu, Studies in Literature and Culture 14. Joensuu, Finland: University of Joensuu, 2009.

[45] See also Steven Feld and Virginia Ryan, "Contemporary Art in/as Anthropology," in *Between Art and Anthropology. Contemporary Ethnographic Practice*, ed. Arnd Schneider and Christopher Wright (New York: Berg, 2010), 109–126; Steven Feld, "Acoustemology as Relational Ontology" (speech presented at the Value, Agency, Soundspaces seminar, University of Liverpool, October 15, 2010).

[46] Christopher Butler, *Pleasure in the Arts* (Oxford: Oxford University Press, 2009).

Järviluoma, Helmi, Meri Kytö, Barry Truax, Heikki Uimonen, and Noora Vikman, eds. *Acoustic Environments in Change*. Tampere, Finland: TAMK Series A, Research Papers 13; University of Joensuu, Studies in Literature and Culture 14. Joensuu, Finland: University of Joensuu, 2009.

Järviluoma, Helmi, Meri Kytö, Heikki Uimonen, and Noora Vikman. "Soundscapes in Change—From 1975 to 2000." In *Acoustic Environments in Change*, edited by Helmi Järviluoma, Meri Kytö, Barry Truax, Heikki Uimonen, and Noora Vikman, 224–281. Tampere, Finland: TAMK Series A, Research Papers 13; University of Joensuu, Studies in Literature and Culture 14. Joensuu, Finland: University of Joensuu, 2009.

Järviluoma, Helmi, and Pirkko Moisala. "Not Only Vision—Analyzing Sound and Music From the Perspective of Gender." In *Gender and Qualitative Methods*, edited by. Helmi Järviluoma, Pirkko Moisala, and Anni Vilkko, 84–106. London: Sage, 2003.

Kankkunen, Olli-Taavetti. "Käy kuuntelemaan! Äänikävely ja ääniympäristön havainnointi" [Listen! Soundwalk and the perception of the environment]. In *Järjen ja arjen ääniä: Tampereen normaalikoulu tutkii, kokeilee ja kehittää* [The Voices of everyday and sense], edited by. K. Ahonen and T. Juutilainen. Tampere, 119–153. Finland: Tampere University Press, 2012.

Kaprow, Allan. *Essays on the Blurring of Life and Art*. Edited by Jeff Kelley. Berkeley; Los Angeles: University of California, 1993.

Kassabian, Anahid. "Ubiquitous Musics and Networked Subjectivity." *ECHO: A Music-centered Journal* 3, no. 2 (2001), at http://www.echo.ucla.edu/Volume3-issue2/kassabian/kassabian.pdf (accessed December 11, 2012).

Koivunen, Anu. "Affektin paluu" [The return of the affective]. *Tiedotustutkimus* [Finnish journal of media and communication studies] 31, no. 3 (2008): 5–24.

Kuhn, Annette. *An Everyday Magic: Cinema and Cultural Memory*. London: I.B. Tauris Publishers, 2002.

Massey, Doreen. *For Space*. London: Sage, 2005.

McCartney, Andra. "Soundwalking: Creating Moving Environmental Sound Narratives." In *The Oxford Handbook of Mobile Music Studies*, edited by Sumanth Gopinath and Jason Stanyek. Oxford: Oxford University Press, forthcoming spring 2013..

Mayr, Albert. "Soundscape Studies, Experimental Music and Time Geography." In *Soundscape Studies and Methods*, edited by Helmi Järviluoma and Gregg Wagstaff, 27–38. Finnish Society for Ethnomusicology Pub. 9; Department of Art, Literature and Music, A51. Helsinki: Suomen etnomusikologinen seura, 2002.

Mehtonen, Lauri. "Rousseaun promenadi itseen" [Rousseau's promenade to oneself]. *Niin & näin: Filosofinen aikakauslehti* [Philosophical journal] 69, no. 2 (2011): 30–33.

Rantala, Janne. "Antropologi oom-ringissä—aistihavainto kenttätyössä" [On sensory perception in field work]. In *Vaeltavat metodit* [Traveling methods], edited by Jyrki Pöysä, Helmi Järviluoma, and Sinikka Vakimo, 258–284. Joensuu: Finnish Folklore Society, 2010.

Rodaway, Paul. *Sensuous Geographies: Body, Sense and Place*. London: Routledge, 1994.

Saarikangas, Kirsi. *Asunnon muodonmuutoksia: Puhtauden estetiikka ja sukupuoli modernissa arkkitehtuurissa* [Metamorphoses of dwelling: The aesthetics of purity and gender in modern architecture]. Helsinki: Finnish Literature Society, 2002.

Schafer, R. Murray. *The New Soundscape*. Toronto: Berandol, 1968.

Schafer, R. Murray. Listening. *Sound Heritage*. *III*, no. 4 (1974): 10–17.

Schafer, R. Murray. *Five Village Soundscapes*. Vancouver, B.C.: A.R.C. Publications, 1977.

Schafer, R. Murray. *Sound Education*. Indian River, Ontario: Arcana Editions, 1992.

Schafer, R. Murray, and Helmi Järviluoma, eds. *Yearbook of Soundscape Studies*, Vol. 1. Tampere, Finland: Tampere University, 1998.

Seremetakis, Nadia. *The Senses Still: Perception and Memory as Material Culture in Modernity*. Boulder, Colo.; San Francisco; Oxford: Westview Press, 1994.

Serres, Michel. *Five Senses: A Philosophy of Mingled Bodies*. [Translated by Margaret Sankey and Peter Cowley]. Athlone Contemporary European Thinkers. London; New York: Continuum, 1998 [1985].

Sterne, Jonathan. *The Audible Past: Cultural Origins of Sound Reproduction*. Durham, N.C.; London: Duke University Press, 2003.

Stockfelt, Ola. "Cars, Buildings, Soundscapes." In *Soundscapes: Essays on Vroom and Moo*, edited by Helmi Järviluoma, 19–38. Tampere, Finland: Tampere University Department of Folk Tradition; Seinäjoki, Finland: Institute of Rhythm Music, 1994.

Tagg, Philip. *Reading Sounds or an Essay on Sounds, Music, Knowledge, Rock & Society*. IASPM-Norden Working Papers. Gothenburg, Sweden: IASPM, 1987.

Tagg, Philip. "An Anthropology of Stereotypes in TV Music." *Svensk tidskrift för musikforskning* 71 (1989): 19–42.

Thibaud. Jean-Paul. "A Sonic Paradigm of Urban Ambiances?" *Journal of Sonic Studies* 1, no. 1 (2011), at http://journal.sonicstudies.org/vol01/nr01/a02 (accessed December 11, 2012).

Tiainen, Milla. "Becoming-Singer: Cartographies of Singing, Music-Making and Opera." PhD diss., University of Turku, 2012.

Tixier, Nicolas. "Street Listening: A Characterisation of the Sound Environment: The 'Qualified Listening in Motion' Method." In *Soundscape Studies and Methods*, edited by. Helmi Järviluoma and Gregg Wagstaff, 83–90. Finnish Society for Ethnomusicology Pub. 9; Department of Art, Literature and Music, A51. Helsinki: Suomen etnomusikologinen seura; 2002.

Truax, Barry. *Acoustic Communication*. Westport, Conn.: Ablex, 2001.

Uimonen, Heikki. *Ääntä kohti: Ääniympäristön kuuntelu, muutos ja merkitys* [Towards sound: Listening, change and meaning of the sonic environment]. Acta Universitatis Tamperensis 1110. Tampere, Finland: Tampere University Press, 2005.

Vadén, Tere. "Taiteilija Takatalo tramppaa: Kävely on matkustamista muodosta merkitykseen." Teemu Takatalon haastattelu [Walking is traveling from form to meaning. Teemu Takatalo interview]. *Niin & näin: Filosofinen aikakauslehti* [Philosophical Journal] 69, no. 2 (2011): 8–12.

Vikman, Noora. *Akustisen ekologian ekologiset diskurssi* [The ecological discourses of acoustic ecology]. Acoustic Environments in Change, Working Papers 2. Turku, Finland: University of Turku; Tampere, Finland: University of Tampere, 1999.

Vikman, Noora. "Looking for a 'Right Method'—Approaching Beyond." In *Soundscape Studies and Methods*, edited by Helmi Järviluoma and Gregg Wagstaff, 143–170. Finnish Society for Ethnomusicology Pub. 9; Department of Art, Literature and Music, A51. Helsinki: Suomen etnomusikologinen seura, 2002.

Vikman, Noora. "Alussa oli askel: katsaus kuuntelukävelyyn ympäristökulttuurin tutkimuksen metodina" [In the beginning there was a step: An overview of listening walks as a method of studying environmental culture]. In *Vaeltavat metodit* [Traveling methods], edited by Jyrki Pöysä, Helmi Järviluoma, and Sinikka Vakimo, 190–214. Joensuu: Finnish Folklore Society, 2010.

Westerkamp, Hildegard. "Sound Walking." *Sound Heritage* 3, no. 4 (2001 [orig. 1974]): 18–27, at http://www.sfu.ca/~westerka/writings%20page/articles%20pages/soundwalking.html (accessed December 6, 2012).

CHAPTER 38

LEAVING SOMETHING TO THE IMAGINATION: "SEEING" NEW PLACES THROUGH A MUSICAL LENS

MARIKO HARA AND TIA DENORA

SOMETIMES when one sense is impaired or deliberately hindered, another sense plays a "compensatory role." Disability research has focused increasingly on this form of sensory substitution in accounts of how visually impaired people are able to "see" and hearing impaired people to "hear." Within disability cultures, individuals with impairments may learn how to deploy a rich array of often tacit practices to engage in "sense switching." For example, people with impaired hearing may adopt specific practices of physical positioning so as to be able to lip-read and thus "hear."[1] In recent years technology has entered the picture to assist this process of adaptation. Interestingly, some technologies exploit the brain's capacity for synaesthesia, using one sense to enhance or augment another. A recent example, *VOICe,* uses a head-mounted camera that converts visual data into sonic data; after some learning, this device can enable the visually impaired to "see" features of the physical environment.[2]

Although most research associated with sensory substitution has been devoted to support for disability and rehabilitative medicine, it has more far-ranging implications. Insofar as these studies highlight the porous nature of the boundaries between the senses, they also show that the senses are normatively embedded in culture, technology, and social practice. The senses, in other words, have a history that builds on and enhances neurophysiological capacities. In addition, how they come to be distinguished

[1] Paul Higgins, "Encounters with the Hearing," in *The Production of Reality*, ed. Jodi O'Brien (Thousand Oaks, Calif.: Pine Forge Press, 2005), 223–234.

[2] Jamie Ward and Peter Meijer, "Visual Experiences in the Blind Induced by an Auditory Sensory Substitution Device," *Consciousness and Cognition* 19, no. 1 (2010): 492–500; Richard E. Cytowic, "Touching Tastes, Seeing Smells—and Shaking up Brain Science," *Cerebrum* 4 (2002): 7–26.

from each other is similarly configured in culture and place. Thinking about "seeing" and its relation to "hearing" leads us to consider anew the mutually referencing character of sensory apprehension, in audiovisual studies as well as the therapeutic disciplines that have generated this research. Now we come to our case in point: "seeing" through a musical as distinct from sonic lens.

The distinction between music and sound is important, even if the two categories overlap considerably.[3] Simultaneously, the music/sound distinction points to an associated distinction, between sound as a means of *sensing* the physical world (e.g., sound as a navigational tool) and as a means of *sensibly imagining* the world (physical, psychocultural, conceptual.) It is the latter topic—imaginatively seeing the world through music—that is of interest here.

Hearing Film and Seeing Sound

Often in film, sound either precedes or substitutes for visual data. Perhaps the most famous example in modern film is the shark motif in *Jaws*. This chapter, picking up on the theme of "hearing film," discusses "seeing sound," and more precisely, seeing through the medium of sound when it is not paired with visual imagery as it is in film.

In everyday life, people engage in imaginative visualization while listening to or thinking about music. Some forms of music therapy deploy imaginative visualization to music as a technique for working on trauma and other psychological troubles.[4] We suggest that an examination of "seeing through music" highlights the cross-sensory or synaesthetic dimension of perception and identification in naturally occurring settings. We then consider more specifically how musically led visualization may be part of how individuals imagine and then orient to phenomena that they have not yet encountered or "seen," which they may encounter in the future. We suggest that this process of virtual seeing highlights how music has been discussed as a "prosthetic technology" of the body/mind—in this case, a tool for visual enhancement in the sense described previously. This enhancement in turn may provide resources for future action, goals, and aspirations; in short, for "seeing" and acting in and acting upon future events. Finally, to the extent that music enables us to envision the future, we suggest how it can enable new learning.

Using examples drawn from an original study by Hara[5] of elders' musical lives in nursing homes, we focus in particular on an interview in which respondents described their initial exposure to Western classical music before and after World War II. Music

[3] Tia DeNora, "Two of More Forms of Music," in *International Handbook of Research in Arts Education*, ed. Liora Bresler (Dordrecht: Springer Verlag, 2007), 799–803.

[4] Lars Ole Bonde, "'Finding a New Place...': Metaphor and Narrative in One Cancer Survivor's BMGIM Therapy," *Nordic Journal of Music Therapy* 14, no. 2 (2005): 137–154; Helen L. Bonny, *Music and Consciousness: The Evolution of Guided Imagery and Music*, ed. Lisa Summer (Gilsum, N.H.: Barcelona Publishers, 2002).

[5] Mariko Hara, *Musical Orientation of Elderly People in Japan; Through Ethnographic Interview Research* (master's diss. Kobe University, Hyogo, Japan, 2007).

provided a prism through which subjects came to imagine foreign, "Western," "modern," "European" places. First we briefly consider guided imagery and music to illustrate how music, paired with self-generated imagery, can be understood to scaffold perception and thus the experience of events and places.

Guided Imagery and Music

Guided imagery and music (GIM) provides a clear example of music's role as a tool for thinking, and we can see its effects in real time as a subject articulates his or her consciousness of self and environment through ongoing narrative.[6] At the start of a GIM session, the subject is encouraged to focus on a particular experience. She is given a "relaxation technique." (The term, from Summer, involves a focus "upon the body; and a starting image... [that]...serves to hold the client in the internal experience and to begin the imaging process."[7]) In a state of relaxation, the subject listens to a 30-minute program of evocative Western classical music. During this time she is encouraged to respond with a variety of sensory imagery, feelings, and bodily sensations and to relate them to the therapist as they occur in real listening time.

As a therapeutic technique, GIM uses music as a scaffold[8] upon which to generate visual imagery. Using that scaffold, the subject can talk about difficult issues, problems, feelings, and concerns. Put differently, music provides sonic structures as templates for describing or constituting life experiences. As part of a "therapeutic triad" of client, therapist, and music, clients are encouraged to project their experiences outward into sound. That sound simultaneously pulls experience into its structures and forms; in this sense, music can lead consciousness in certain directions via clients' ongoing narratives. Music is thereby used in a therapeutic context to prompt narratives about extramusical or paramusical matters. In this sense, as Bonde puts it,[9] music provides a *source domain* in which to structure *target domains* such as emotions, conduct, consciousness, and health.

From GIM to Soundtrack in Everyday Life

In GIM, narratives are constructed through the triadic partnership of client, therapist, and music. The client composes the narrative, but as with all creative work, this

[6] Lisa Summer, "Group Music and Imagery Therapy: An Emergent Music Therapy," in *Guided Imagery and Music: The Bonny Method and Beyond*, ed. Kenneth E. Bruscia and Denice E. Grocke (Gilsum, N.H.: Barcelona Publishers, 2002), 297–306; Bonny, *Music and Consciousness*.

[7] Lisa Summer, "Group Music and Imagery Therapy," 298.

[8] Amaya Becvar Weddle and James D. Hollan, "Professional Perception and Expert Action: Scaffolding Embodied Practices in Professional Education," *Mind, Culture, and Activity* 17, no. 2 (2010): 119–148.

[9] Lars Ole Bonde, "Music as Metaphor and Analogy," *Nordic Journal of Music Therapy* 16, no. 1 (2007): 73–81.

composition taps resources outside his experience that affect the shape that narrative takes. For this reason, music's properties and structural parameters may serve as orientational devices for the composition of narrative accounts. Such structures as the sonata form (thematic statement, development, and recapitulation) or the harmonic principles of tension and resolution may impart some of their characteristics to extramusical structures; it is possible to see how music, one species of aesthetic material, "gets into" or offers structuring materials for action.[10]

Narrative accounts are not unmediated descriptions of experience. Rather, they construct and frame experience in a selective manner.[11] This framing can come to affect subsequent understandings of the narrated events and experiences. Narratives are orientation devices: they are performative and function as framing devices. In GIM practice, when clients engage in music-led narrative work to describe experience, they are producing audiovisual resources that can subsequently be used to redefine, transcend, or otherwise structure their experience of the past.

The explicitly therapeutic environment of GIM is by no means the only sphere of activity in which music can be seen as a template for the formation of narrative accounts of "what one is seeing." In daily life we often engage in a kind of GIM, just more informally. People use music as a technology of memory, a template with which to pair or map narratives, images, and even actions. A consideration of GIM helps to draw some of these everyday processes into relief, highlighting music as a source of *transferable* resources for engagement with the social world. By this we mean that music provides materials, extrinsic to individuals, with which to elaborate thought and imagining. We do this in daily life whenever we turn to music to "show" or "lead" us to understanding, conceptualizing, or describing something else. Moreover, drawing on music in this way connects music to other things; it is the means through which pathways between music and paramusical matters are forged.

However, there are some important differences between GIM and musical imagining in everyday life. First, in everyday life no one is cast fully in the role of therapist, and usually no one chooses (prescribes) the music or guides us on our musical journey (though we may turn to various experts for music that will soothe or energize, and we may use products such as CDs that are marketed for these purposes). Second, our exercise of musical imagining is voluntary; we do not have to engage in it, and we can stop the process, turn off the music player, whenever we wish. Finally, we might not engage in music imagining on our own. We might listen to and verbalize about music with others, in a music appreciation class or in a living room or bedroom, by sharing earbuds, or by otherwise musicking (doing, making, and talking about music) together.

How do some of the procedures associated with GIM enter into everyday music listening, and how is this listening at least sometimes associated with the envisioning of

[10] Giovanna Colombetti, "What Language Does to Feeling," *Journal of Consciousness Studies* 16, no. 9 (2009): 4–26.

[11] Paul Atkinson, "Narrative Turn or Blind Alley?" *Qualitative Health Research* 7, no. 3 (1997): 325–344.

places and events? We now pursue this theme by turning to the Japanese data and the topic of imagining place through music.

Case Study: Music in the Everyday Lives of Elderly Japanese

We draw on a study of music in the lives of thirty elderly Japanese people living in a care facility in Kobe, a city of approximately 1.5 million inhabitants in southern Japan. The data were collected through loosely structured, in-depth interviews.[12] They covered topics such as musical tastes and preferences, social connection to music, and reactions to the music provided in the nursing home. Each interview also sought to explore the subject's life soundtrack and his or her musical memories. These memories were in turn used to elicit autobiographical narratives. In what follows we draw only on those sections of interviews in which respondents described processes of envisioning place ("the West," "Europe") through music.

Each interview began by asking the subject about his or her views of music and its role in the place of residence.[13] The interviews were held in the common room of a residential care facility, home to the individuals interviewed. The location and collective music-making sessions in the nursing home provided the point of departure for each interview. For example, the following interview was with Kiku, who was over 90 years old at the time:

Q: How do you like the music session here?
A: I like to listen to the popular songs from the old times. Anything like "Kago-no-Tori" ("Bird in the Cage") or "Konjikiyasha" ("Golden Devil").
Q: You really like the old [popular love] songs, don't you?
A: Yes. You know, "Kago-no-tori" is one of the first popular songs that came to Kobe. When I was ten years old, I was very short, my height was like this [shows height with hands], and I sang this song. A woman sang next to the man who was playing the violin in the street. I learned the song standing next to them, and sang the tune at home. I was told off by my mum. She said, "Don't sing that kind of song!" It was at the station of Sannomiya.[14]

[12] Hara, "Musical Orientation of Elderly People in Japan."

[13] In the interviews, the concept of music was broad and followed the lead of how respondents defined that term, so "music" ranged from a fragment of a theme song from films viewed when young to whole works, associated with "good," "educational," "Western" music, the canon and the idea of the musical museum, in Lydia Goehr's sense (Goehr, *The Imaginary Museum of Musical Works: An Essay in the Philosophy of Music* [New York: Oxford University Press, 2007]). This chapter concentrates on how respondents described their experiences of "canonic" music.

[14] Sannomiya is the name of railway station in Kobe. It sometimes refers to the area around the station, which is a center of both entertainment and business.

I saw them with my own eyes, I still remember them. [She sings the tune.] I learned this song when I was ten years old! I felt happy when they sang next to me. [laughs] You know, everyone has been young some time. It makes me nostalgic when I remember the songs from my childhood. . . . It was the happiest period of my life, the time when my parents were still alive.

Q: Are there any songs that you used to sing with your family?

A: Oh, the record store was just across the road from my house. There were a lot of record stores. When the new records came out, the record store played them. At the same time, tearooms and department stores were also opened. We were so excited, and they caused a flutter! Since them, Sannomiya has changed a lot. It is no longer the Sannomiya of our dreams.

The first objective of the interviews was to explore music's role in evoking long-term memories, as illustrated in this excerpt. Kiku was describing the emotions she associated with the song heard in Sannomiya: excitement about the encounter, happiness, contentment with family, nostalgia for the place where she grew up, and a feeling of shame about the ways the city had changed over 80 years. This emotional reminiscence was linked, for virtually all the respondents, to visualizations of the past. Subjects recounted how hearing music in the past was also often linked to visualization. How, then, did the emotional experience and visualization associated with music come to be linked to, and act as a primer for, *new* experiences? We explore this question with data from one interview in which music was discussed as having primed or permitted the *previewing* of visual place. The example is from an interview with an elderly couple about their initial visualization and experience of Western places via music, as they "saw" Norway and Finland through the medium of music.

Encounters with Western Music before and after World War II

For many subjects, Western classical music was understood as belonging to the upper classes and therefore removed from the sphere of everyday life. At the same time, they conceived of it as edifying. For example, a former engineer, Keigo, in his eighties at the time of the interview, described Western classical music as "good music":

A: Speaking of music . . . well, I heard from my teacher that if we are exposed to good music when we are still infants, the sense of music develops inside you. I am from the countryside and tone-deaf. I was good at all the subjects [at school] except music. But I was an engineer, so I have a lot of mechanical knowledge. I made a radio for my sons. I let them listen to the good music through the radio while holding them. I was terrible at music, so I didn't want them to inherit my terrible sense of music. I remember what my teacher had told me about how important it is to be exposed to good music while we are still infants. After that, one of my sons played the organ and developed his musical sense. He wanted to study in a music conservatory, but I didn't allow him. I told him music is not in our blood. He became an engineer like me. Well, but I have proved the theory my teacher told me that if we listen to good music, we are able to develop [a good] musical sense.

Q: What kind of music was it?

A: I can't remember what it was, but it was very good, serious music, like unaccompanied piano music. I guess [Western] classical music. It wasn't the type of music sung by popular singers, nor the songs you find in a record store.

In the late nineteenth century and the first few decades of the twentieth, Western classical music in Japan was a symbol of modernization.[15] In the years shortly before and during World War II, however, Western music of all kinds was banned. At that time it became a symbol of otherness. As another respondent, Yoshi, over 90 years old, put it:

I thought western music only belonged to upper-class people. Even though we had an interest in western [classical] music, we couldn't be open about it while [the country was] under the influence of fascism. I had no choice but to enjoy Japanese folk songs.

For these respondents, the music of their youth mainly consisted of war songs. As one subject put it, "in those times, there were only songs to welcome back the soldiers."[16] Other respondents described how Western music came to be associated with longing for new ways, for modernization and detraditionalization in Japan.

Western Music as a Scaffold for Imagining the West

In the following extract Hana, an 83-year-old woman, described how she associated the Western world with her beloved father, with whom she listened to Western classical music:

A: You know, my father had an around-the-world trip to inspect the underground railway systems in Europe. I was two years old at that time. Later, my father sometimes showed me the pictures, and told me the stories of [these countries], which made me eager to go abroad.

Q: How old were you [when your father told you all the stories]?

A: That was when the war was still going on, so I guess when I was 17, 18 years old.

Q: Then, your father left for the trip when you were two...?

[15] Yasuhito Okunaka, *Nation and Music: Shuji Izawa's Effort to Modernize Japan* (Tokyo: Shunjyu-sha, 2008); Chiba Yuko, *Japanese Who Chose Do Re Mi* (Tokyo: Ongakunotomo-sha, 2007) (Bibliography translated from Japanese to English by Mariko Hara).

[16] At the time of the interview, more than 60 years after World War II, as many as six of the thirty respondents still exhibited a strong attachment to the war songs; in contrast, they expressed a sense of detachment from Western music—in some cases, aversion to it.

A: Yes. When I was two, he went to inspect the underground railway systems in Germany, and around the world, in order to establish the Osaka Underground Railway. Then, he told me many things he had seen there.
Q: Right.
A: He really treated me with love, so he told me how they were, and what he had seen. And these experiences became the foundation for my longing for foreign countries.
Q: How long was he traveling?
A: For a year. Back in that period, there were no airplanes, so he went by ship. I remember he left from Yokohama Harbor. He left Kobe in March. I was two, so I wasn't aware of anything, but it was in 1927. I was born in 1926. One year after I was born, my father was 31. He went alone and left my mother and his family, he went alone. After I became old enough to understand, he often told me stories about that trip. Yes, stories about foreign countries! That is how I started longing to go abroad so strongly.
Q: Was it "west" rather than "abroad"?
A: Yes, right. I mean Europe.
Q: And you longed even more after hearing your father's stories.
A: Yes, [I was] longing. Then, when I entered Jogakko (Girls' school), I came to like the western history class too. That [my father's stories] became the basis [for my longing for the west].
Q: He also showed you pictures, right?
A: Yes, the pictures had already turned brown, but we still have them at home.
Q: Wow.
A: Various places, Germany, England, France, Czechoslovakia.... Later, I did go to Prague, Budapest in Hungary, and the places my father has been.
Q: You traced his path?
A: Yes yes yes yes.
Q: So, how do you think it is connected, I mean your longing [for western countries] through the memory of your father and through music?
A: Well, let me see.... I always liked music from a long time ago. Yes, there are various classical music records at home, from small [45 rpm single] to big ones [33 rpm LP].
Q: So, your father let you listen to these with him?
A: The tenor singer, Yoshie Fujiwara[17].... You know what, my father was with Yoshie Fujiwara on the ship to Europe!
Q: Wow, on the way to go to Europe?
A: I wonder if it was on the way out or coming back. So, then, classic songs, like Tamaki Miura,[18] there were lots of records, all were burned during the war though...all of them. These [the records] made me like [the idea of being] abroad.[19]

[17] Fujiwara Yoshie was a Japanese male tenor singer who studied music in Milan in the 1920s and became a notable figure in Japanese opera.

[18] Miura Tamaki was a Japanese female soprano singer who studied in Germany in the 1910s and became famous for her performances in Puccini's *Madama Butterfly*.

[19] Hana often mentioned her father in the interview as well as outside of interviews and emphasized several times how much he loved her. She later said in the interview that memories of her father are the

Mutual Elaboration of Music and Image

For Hana and her husband, Taka, the scarcity of Western music during the war served to intensify their interest in the West. After they retired, and after a period during which they cared for elderly relatives, they began to travel to northern Europe. Their tours featured visits to the places where their favorite classical music pieces were composed. On these trips they encountered the "real" image of what had loomed large in their imaginations for years.

Hana's account of this experience (transcribed below) is both methodologically instructive and heuristic. It is of course an active narrative, which configures its subject matter in dialogue with the questions and the interviewer. That interviewer (Hara) is an active participant in framing the collaboratively produced account. At the same time, the narrative is heuristically interesting because it helps to highlight—as Hana tells us—how music presaged and helped to shape an encounter with the actual visual scenery. In the face of the real scenery, she then imagined the music that had previously served as the template for imagining the visual scenery. The music was imaginatively reheard (remembered, played over in memory) in the presence of the actual scenery, thus providing a medium for achieving imaginative and experiential continuity (the place was as she imagined it; her imagination of it was accurate). Imagined reality and reality were thus fitted together, in ways that allowed each to contextualize and mutually elaborate the other. When asked how it felt to be in the actual place after having so long imagined and longed for it, Hana replied:

> H: [Y]ou know Grieg, the piano concerto, right? Tatatatatata-nn (she sings).... I used to listen to it, and we visited Bergen in Norway. The music made me want to visit the place. Oh, we visited a fjord too, and a place a few hundred kilometers away from the north pole as well. We started from Oslo and went north. It was called Lapland, there were Sami [people there] and reindeer. We visited those places as well, the fjord was so beautiful. When we were there, Grieg's piano concerto came to my mind, and I could hear it in my head.
> Q: So, did this mean that you weren't surprised by the real image?
> H: No, it was exactly the image I had in my mind from the music.
> T: Oh, in Bergen, we visited Grieg's composer's hut.
> H: That is right, we did. We visited the hut where Grieg composed. The fjord was sweeping away in front of the hut. Yes, it was exactly like the image in my mind. [Hana, 83, and Taka, 83]

In this case, a phase of longing for the West and fondness for Western music (Grieg's piano concerto) "led" Hana and her husband to visit the place where the piece was

core of herself *and* her longing for the West. The stories her father told her, the pictures he brought home from his European trip, and various collections of Western classical music records, combined with the history she studied, increased her interest in the West.

composed. Once she was there, Hana's long-standing habit of imagining Norway through music structured the occasion of her actual perception (of Grieg's hut), such that when she came to see it for real, there were (according to her narrative) no surprises; the scene was "exactly" as she had imagined it would be. In other words, Hana "saw" what she had already seen via music, and on seeing the hut, she replayed in her imagination the music that had previously enabled this vision.

In some ways, music's ability to remediate visual experience, and equally important, to provide a template for seeing what is not readily or even ever available to the naked eye, can be understood as a variant on the notion that music is a prosthetic technology. Prosthetic technologies are instruments that extend bodily capacities, such as eyeglasses, telescopes, and microscopes. In earlier work that considers music in relation to physical exercise and physical therapy, DeNora[20] has described how music can be understood to extend bodily capacity, even to the point where it may be dangerous, distracting subjects from the perception of fatigue or pain. In the case of "seeing through music," it is possible to understand music as a prosthetic technology that extends the sense of sight by prestructuring seeing, cuing and framing the objects in view in ways that prescribe and focus perception. As Hana describes it, she heard the music (Grieg's piano concerto) in her mind when she encountered the real scenery. In this moment the hitherto imagined scenery came to be fulfilled as real, such that the "real" experience was in fact a creation. That creation was built from prior imaginative work and ways of seeing inculcated through music. In the creative process the "real" image refracted upon what had been imagined. Within this process, the music was incorrigible; its authority as an organizing device remained stable. The music did not mislead Hana, but rather served her as a kind of "magic mirror" in which she had been able to foresee what she was now seeing "for real." Hana described a similar process of going to visit Finland and Sibelius's house:

T: We also visited Finland.
H: Yes, we went to Sibelius' house, you know, Sibelius who composed Finlandia.
Q: How was it?
H: It was fantastic!!! We listened to pieces by Sibelius there. There was the piano Sibelius played, and also his chairs. When I listened to the pieces there, it was a totally different experience from listening to them at home. Finland was such a beautiful place, you know. Such a beautiful piece was composed because he was born there!
Q: So, you were convinced that the real scenery was exactly what you have imagined?
H: Yes, I was. In Finland, there was a forest. Deep in the woods, there was a lake, which turned back upon itself repeatedly. It was exactly like the stage for "Swan Lake." [laughs] We visited this too. I was impressed, you know, this was the place. I like music so I chose these tours to visit the places that my favorite music comes from.

[20] Tia DeNora, *Music in Everyday Life* (Cambridge: Cambridge University Press, 2000).

Q: So, music led you to these places?
H: Yes, yes, music led us, and I guess it was mixed with the stories that my father told me.

Hana was deeply impressed with the beautiful scenery of the place where *Finlandia* was composed and "convinced" that the greatness of music came from the beauty of the place. She also described how music broadened or helped to elaborate the image and stirred her emotions, in particular in relation to memories of her father.

After the stories about her longings and imaginings of the West in the interview, Hana returned to the subject of her father, noting that "my father's face came up," as if visiting the real place meant tracing her memory with her father and so entering yet another spiral of imaginative reality-generating work, binding imagery to memory, to feeling, and to music.

To speak about this spiral is to evoke how, after her visits to Norway and Finland, the connections between scenery and music were further strengthened as Hana encountered more images of these Western places back home. As she said, "When I watch music programs on television that show the same scenery I have seen with music, I am even more moved." Indeed, the connections she forged between the music of Grieg and Sibelius—images, memory, and emotion—were *so* enduring that they had the power to block out rival connections; for example, different soundtracks that might be paired with the imagery so dear to her. Hana complained, for example, about TV programs that put "noisy" songs alongside similar Western scenery: "I don't understand why they do that, with such beautiful western scenery." Of course places such as the Grieg hut and the Sibelius house have become more familiar with the advent of the Web and globalizing tendencies that proliferate visual imagery and thus make it more difficult to leave things to the imagination. Nonetheless, it is still possible to "see" even iconic objects for the first time through music, as described in the next section.

Excursis: One of the Authors at the Sibelius House

While preparing to write this chapter, one of us (DeNora) was also preparing for a visit to the Sibelius Academy in Helsinki, for the International Society for Philosophy of Music Education conference, including a visit to the Sibelius House, the place that Hana first came to know through Sibelius's music. ("There was a piano Sibelius played, and also chairs.") DeNora had never seen the house, but was familiar with Sibelius's work, in particular the violin concerto and the quartets. In an attempt to replicate the activity of seeing the Sibelius house through Sibelius's music, she listened to the music before she left (the opening movement of the violin concerto in particular, which she associated with a remote and wooded landscape; cool climate; possibly snow; and the colors green, grey, silver, and orange) and tried to "imagine" (envision) the appearance of the house, guided only by the quote from Hana.

The imagery she came up with consisted of a few key (and somewhat stereotypical) fragments: a wood-frame shingled house (painted dark red in her imagination, not, as it turned out to be, white) in the woods (it was), probably furnished with comfortable and arts-and-crafts type furnishings (also the case). She also pictured a pewter-colored lake (there was indeed a lake) and pine trees and a fire in some kind of stove (she did find a stove).

To be sure, DeNora's imagined images were guided by the music's conventions, the associations that have tended to saturate this music since it was composed, and her stereotypical assumptions about Finnish upper-middle-class country houses circa 1904. In addition, these images were fragmentary and incomplete. Because they were incomplete, they afforded subsequent and tacit modification as they came to be "matched" to the realities outside Helsinki.

Like Hana, DeNora was not "surprised," but rather found, on visiting the house, a confirmation of what she had come to expect from the musical primer. (On her visit to the Sibelius house no music was playing, though like Hana, she could hear in her head some fragments of the violin concerto, mainly the famous opening.) Because she was part of a group visiting outside normal hours, she was permitted to take photographs. In retrospect, she realizes that her (not terribly conscious, and somewhat hurried) choice of subject matter for these photos confirmed her preconceptions (musically imagined preview) of the house. Looking at the photos later on, she found that they confirmed her imagined vision of what the house would be like: the wooden walls and the furniture, the piano, a view of a pine tree from the window, and the green fireplace.

The whole set of audiovisual resources then at her disposal—the music, her initial imaginings, the experience of being in the house, looking back at the photos, and (at this point on this page) writing about that experience and its musical confirmation—all in their turn served to further specify the "reality" of what she saw. Like Hana, DeNora saw, at least in part, the Sibelius house through Sibelius's music, and the "guided imagery" of imagining that house against the scaffold of that music in turn structured her orientation to the actual house in ways that formed further alliances between it and the prior imagination of it.

Conclusion: Music as a Common Thread That Binds Fragments of a Life Together

"Seeing" is inevitably mediated, and music is one medium that can scaffold the processing of visual data. In other words, music can function as a prosthetic technology of seeing, leading us to see what we will later—in commonsense terms—speak about as having been there all along. As a form of audio experience, music enhances what is seen in the course of our lives, just as it does in film and musical theater. Indeed, music can help us to "see" what might otherwise go unnoticed (and in this respect, music has been hailed as an important, if too often unsung, resource in social change, activism, and utopian envisioning[21]). If this is so, then it is possible to speak of music as a material that organizes perception, our awareness and experience of our surroundings, and also holds otherwise disparate matters together through the ways it inflects them with its structural features. To the extent that music "gets into" our orientation to and consciousness of our environment, it can provide a thread or pathway that links features of experience and environment together, binding them into meaningful frameworks. Based on the examples we considered, where music scaffolds how we "see" new places, it plays an ambassadorial function. As a mediator, music leaves its imprint on the visual, or rather, on how we "see" or experience visual media, and thus renders things meaningful. In this way, the study of imaginative seeing through music highlights perception as perhaps inevitably cross-sensory and as mediated and constituted holistically and through reference to metaphor, analogy, and intersensory forms of awareness. In short, experience is constituted through a kind of multisensory integration, produced by actors themselves in real time as part of their tacit equipment of making sense of—and in—everyday life. This making sense in turn holds past and present (events, experiences, perceptions) together, allowing pathways to be created between them. As Hana put it:

> Everything is connected with everything else, memories of my father, my thoughts, imaginary scenes from the music my father bought. For me, seeking links with each other is to live life. Remembering old days doesn't mean clinging to the past. I don't look back. Rather, memories provide me with energy to continue to live in the present, my present life.

References

Atkinson, Paul. "Narrative Turn or Blind Alley?" *Qualitative Health Research* 7, no. 3 (1997): 325–344.

Bonde, Lars Ole. "'Finding a New Place...': Metaphor and Narrative in One Cancer Survivor's BMGIM Therapy." *Nordic Journal of Music Therapy* 14, no. 2 (2005): 137–154.

Bonde, Lars Ole. "Music as Metaphor and Analogy." *Nordic Journal of Music Therapy* 16, no. 1 (2007): 73–81.

Bonny, Helen L. *Music and Consciousness: The Evolution of Guided Imagery and Music*. Edited by Lisa Summer. Gilsum, N.H.: Barcelona Publishers, 2002.

Chiba, Yuko. *Japanese Who Chose Do Re Mi*. Tokyo: Ongakunotomo-sha, 2007. (Bibliography translated from Japanese to English by Mariko Hara.)

[21] Ron Eyerman and Andrew Jamison, *Music and Social Movements: Mobilizing Traditions in the Twentieth Century* (Cambridge: Cambridge University Press, 1998).

Colombetti, Giovanna. "What Language Does to Feeling." *Journal of Consciousness Studies* 16, no. 9 (2009): 4–26.

Cytowic, Richard E. "Touching Tastes, Seeing Smells—and Shaking up Brain Science." *Cerebrum* 4 (2002): 7–26.

DeNora, Tia. *Music in Everyday Life*. Cambridge: Cambridge University Press, 2000.

DeNora, Tia. "Two of More Forms of Music." In *International Handbook of Research in Arts Education*, edited by Liora Bresler, 799–803.Dordrecht: Springer Verlag, 2007.

Eyerman, Ron, and Andrew Jamison. *Music and Social Movements: Mobilizing Traditions in the Twentieth Century*. Cambridge: Cambridge University Press, 1998.

Goehr, Lydia. *The Imaginary Museum of Musical Works: An Essay in the Philosophy of Music*. New York: Oxford University Press, 2007.

Hara, Mariko. "Musical Orientation of Elderly People in Japan; Through Ethnographic Interview Research." Master's diss., Kobe University, Hyogo, Japan, 2007.

Higgins, Paul. "Encounters with the Hearing." In *The Production of Reality*, edited by Jodi O'Brien, 223–234. Thousand Oaks, Calif.: Pine Forge Press, 2005.

Okunaka, Yasuhito. *Nation and Music: Shuji Izawa's Effort to Modernize Japan*. Tokyo: Shunjyu-sha, 2008. (Bibliography translated from Japanese to English by Mariko Hara.)

Summer, Lisa. "Group Music and Imagery Therapy: An Emergent Music Therapy." In *Guided Imagery and Music: The Bonny Method and Beyond*, edited by Kenneth E. Bruscia and Denice E. Grocke, 297–306. Gilsum, N.H.: Barcelona Publishers, 2002.

Ward, Jamie, and Peter Meijer. "Visual Experiences in the Blind Induced by an Auditory Sensory Substitution Device." *Consciousness and Cognition* 19, no. 1 (2010): 492–500.

Weddle, Amaya Becvar, and James D. Hollan. "Professional Perception and Expert Action: Scaffolding Embodied Practices in Professional Education." *Mind, Culture, and Activity* 17, no. 2 (2010): 119–148.

INDEX

CPSIA information can be obtained at www.ICGtesting.com
Printed in the USA
BVOW09s1211120216

436509BV00007B/9/P

9 780190 24459